# THE MUSLI

# 100

*This book is dedicated to my late father*

**Muhammad Pathan Yawar Khan**
(b. 1932 – d. 1988)


*He worked very hard and sacrificed everything for us;*
*may the Most Merciful shower His mercy on him.*

# THE
# MUSLIM
# 100

## The Lives, Thoughts and Achievements of the Most Influential Muslims in History

## MUHAMMAD MOJLUM KHAN

**KUBE**
PUBLISHING

First published by Kube Publishing Ltd,
Markfield Conference Centre
Ratby Lane, Markfield,
Leicestershire LE67 9SY
United Kingdom
Tel: +44 (0) 1530 249230
Fax: +44 (0) 1530 249656
Website: www.kubepublishing.com
Email: info@kubepublishing.com

British Library Cataloguing-in-Publication Data

Khan, Muhammad Mojlum
    The Muslim 100 : the lives, thoughts and achievements of
    the most influential Muslims in history
    1.   Muslims - Biography 2. Civilization, Islamic 3. Islamic
        countries - Civilization
    I.   Title
    297'.0922

Typeset in Adobe Garamond
Printed in the United Kingdom by Anthony Rowe

ISBNs
978-1-84774-006-9 *paperback*
978-1-84774-007-6 *casebound*

Cover and Page Design: Nasir Cadir
Typesetting: Naiem Qaddoura
Calligraphy: M. Swallay Mungly
Indexing:  Abdassamad Clarke
            Uthman Ibrahim-Morrison

# Contents

# Introduction

EDMUND BURKE, the renowned Irish philosopher and statesman, once said, 'People will not look forward to posterity, who never look backward to their ancestors.' Likewise, Aldous Huxley, the acclaimed English novelist, wrote, 'That men do not learn very much from the lessons of history is the most important of all the lessons that history has to teach.' But what actually is history? Abd al-Rahman ibn Khaldun, the father of the philosophy of history, wrote in his famous *Muqaddimah fi'l Tarikh* (Introduction to History), 'History is a discipline that has a great number of approaches. Its useful aspects are very many. Its goal is distinguished. History makes us acquainted with the conditions of past nations as they are reflected in their national character. It makes us acquainted with the biographies of the prophets and with the dynasties and policies of rulers. Whoever so desires may thus achieve the useful result of being able to imitate historical examples in religious and worldly matters. The (writing of history) requires numerous sources and much varied knowledge.'

Few historians would disagree with Ibn Khaldun that writing history requires 'numerous sources and much varied knowledge.' I became fascinated by history, especially Islamic history, when I was in my early teens. To me the past is as important as the present, because without a proper understanding of the past we are unlikely to understand our present condition, and without a proper understanding of the present we will not be able to shape our future. Our past, present and future are therefore interconnected and interdependent. Indeed, I would go so far as to say our past is more important than our future, because we cannot control and shape our future if we are not aware of our past. Therefore knowing and understanding our history is not optional: it is a necessity. It is also true that the ancient Greek historians such as Herodotus of Halicarnassus and Thucydides of Athens wrote history as if history was no more than the unfolding of a sequence of events. Like them, the early Islamic historians such as Ahmad ibn Yahya al-Baladhuri, Ibn Jarir al-Tabari and Abul Faraj al-Isfahani also considered history to be a sequence of events. However, other Muslim historians like Abul Hasan al-Mas'udi, Abul Hasan Ali ibn al-Athir and Ibn Khaldun took a more logical and critical approach to history. The latter in particular sought to explore and identify the underlying causes or factors which triggered the sequence of events in the first place. That is why Ibn Khaldun considered history and philosophy to be two sides of the same coin. Therefore, in order to understand and fully appreciate history, he felt an understanding of philosophy was required and *vice versa*.

However, there is another group of historians who consider history to be no more than a playground for prominent peoples and personalities: as one famous historian said, 'There is properly no history: only biography.' This view was reinforced by the German philosopher Friedrich Nietzsche who stated that history was no more than 'His-story'. The proponents of this view are more concerned with the 'actors' (history-makers), rather than the actions (the sequence of events or historical process as such). However, from an Islamic perspective history is not merely a sequence of events, nor is it entirely a playground for influential people and personalities; it is both of these things and more. Indeed, the Qur'anic approach to history is integrative, holistic and comprehensive in the sense that it acknowledges the role played by 'creative personalities' (as Sir Arnold J. Toynbee put it), natural causes or phenomena and also direct Divine intervention in the process of history. Thus, according to the Qur'an, history is neither entirely pre-ordained nor wholly deterministic, like the Marxist and Hegelian notions of history and historical change. On the contrary it says, 'Surely, God will not change the condition of a people until they change their own condition.' (13:11). And, 'God is on the side of those who fear Him, and do good.' (16:128). Likewise, the Qur'an argues (see, for instance, *Surat Hud* verse 114) that the historical process is much more than a rigid chain of 'cause and effect' – unlike the views advanced by historians like Oswald Spengler. Instead, the notion of selectivity on the basis of moral imperative is central to the Qur'anic concept of historical change. 'God', says the Qur'an 'will not leave the believers in the condition in which they are until He separates the wrongdoers from those who are righteous.' (3:179). Thus, in addition to time-space factors and the moral imperative, direct Divine intervention (whether in the form of reward or punishment) is also an integral part of the Qur'anic understanding of history and historical change. 'Say: He has power to send calamities on you, from above and below, or to cover you with confusion in party strife, giving you a taste of mutual vengeance – each from the other.' (6:65). And, 'The reward of God is best for those who believe and work righteousness: but this none shall attain, save those who steadfastly persevere.' (28:80).

From the above discussion, it is clear that the Qur'anic concept of history, unlike the modern Western philosophies of history, is not only an integrative and multi-dimensional one, but is also based on a profound understanding of human nature and its possibilities. To his credit, Ibn Khaldun understood and appreciated this multi-layered approach to history, as is evident from his pioneering *Muqaddimah fi'l Tarikh*. Inspired by Ibn Khaldun and others, Arnold J. Toynbee also pursued a similar approach to history in his monumental *A Study of History*, but ultimately his notion of history was dominated by the Christian idea of a 'saviour' rather than the Qur'anic view of man and his role and purpose in the universe. 'And remember Abraham was tried by his Lord with certain commands, which he fulfilled: He said: "I will make you a leader to the nations." He pleaded: "And also (leaders) from my offspring!" He answered: "But My promise is not within the reach of the wrong-doers." ' (2:124). And '(remember) Noah, when he cried (to Us) aforetime: We listened to his (prayer) and delivered him and his family from great distress...And remember David and Solomon, when they gave judgement in the matter of the field into which the sheep of certain people had strayed by night: We did witness their judgement...And (remember) Job, when he cried to his Lord, "Truly distress has seized me, but You are the Most Merciful of those that are merciful."...And (remember) Ishmael, Enoch and Dhul-kifl, all (men) of constancy and patience... And remember Zun-nun (Jonah)...And (remember) Zachariah... And (remember) her (Mary) who guarded her chastity: We breathed into her of Our Spirit, and We made her and her son (Jesus) a sign for all peoples.' (21:76-91). In short, according to the Qur'an, the main purpose of history is to remind us of who we are, what our role and purpose is, and to learn lessons from the past.

If understanding human nature and our role and purpose within the Divine scheme of things is central to the Qur'anic view of history, then how should one explore and analyse Islamic history? And, indeed, what actually do we mean by Islamic history? Strictly speaking, Islamic history did not begin with the Prophet Muhammad or with Abraham or Ishmael. Rather, according to Islamic tradition, Adam was the first human being and also the first Muslim. Not surprisingly, the classical Islamic historians (such as al-Tabari and Ibn Kathir) began their works with Adam and covered the careers of all other prominent Prophets and Kings – including Noah (*Nuh*), Abraham (*Ibrahim*), Moses (*Musa*), David (*Dawud*), Solomon (*Sulaiman*), John the Baptist (*Yahya*) and Jesus (*Isa*) – all the way down to Prophet Muhammad, who is considered to be the Seal of Prophecy. Since these and all other Prophets are regarded as Muslims, the history of the whole of humanity was considered by the classical Muslim historians to be nothing other than the unfolding of Islamic history in its broadest sense. However, with regard to their methodology and approach, the vast majority of the classical and modern Muslim historians have explored Islamic history in a chronological way, without necessarily analysing their data and information in a rigorous and systematic manner.

This book, however, begins with the advent of the Prophet Muhammad and ends in our own time. Additionally, I have not adopted a chronological approach to the study of Islamic history. Instead, in this book an attempt has been made to explore Islamic history through the lives, thoughts and achievements of one hundred of the most influential Muslims. *Influence*, based on their contributions and achievements, was therefore my main criterion for selection and inclusion in this book. But this raises an interesting question, namely how the nature and extent of each person's *influence* was to be measured? I began by examining their lives and thoughts, and then proceeded to assess the nature of their contribution by evaluating what they actually did and what was so special or extraordinary about their deeds, actions and accomplish-

ments. In so doing, I was able to determine whether their contributions and achievements had made them national, regional or international figures. Against this I could evaluate the intellectual, social, political, economic or cultural importance, value and impact of their contributions and achievements over time. For example, by pursuing this approach I was able to include Muhammad Yunus (the great Bangladeshi economist, banker and the pioneer of the system of micro-credit) in this book, but exclude Sheikh Mujibur Rahman (the founding father of Bangladesh) since the latter's accomplishment has been largely 'national' or, at best, 'regional', while the former is today widely considered to be an important 'international' figure whose contribution and achievement has become 'global', thanks to the increasing popularity of micro-credit across the world.

Likewise, in the field of *hadith* literature, both Ibn Hajar al-Asqalani and Yahya al-Nawawi were two remarkable figures and it is not surprising that today they are highly regarded by the scholars of Islam, but it is also a fact that the works of the latter are much more widely-known throughout the Muslim world and in the West than those of the former. In fact, al-Nawawi's *Kitab al-Arba'in* (The Book of Forty *hadith*) and *Riyadh as-Saliheen* (The Garden of the Righteous) have not only been translated into all the world's prominent languages, but they are also very popular across the globe. Consequently, I had no choice but to include al-Nawawi in this book and exclude Ibn Hajar al-Asqalani – despite being a big fan of the latter. In short, the one hundred people who feature in this book have been chosen and ranked on the basis of their *all-round* influence, which in turn was determined mainly – though not entirely – by their contributions and achievements. And although I have tried to be logical, critical and also fair and objective in my approach to, and exploration of, the lives, thoughts and achievements of all the people included in this book, I am aware that my method of selection and ranking may nonetheless generate some discussion and debate among scholars and lay people, Muslims and non-Muslims alike. Since one of the aims of this book is to popularise Islamic culture and history, and encourage both Muslims and non-Muslims to directly engage with Islamic thought and culture, I will feel my efforts duly rewarded if this book manages to generate some discussion and debate about the role played by some of the Muslim world's most influential figures and personalities during more than fourteen centuries of Islamic history.

Issues of selection and ranking aside, exploring Islamic history through the lives of some of its most influential figures – whether that is ten people, fifty, or a hundred – does present a number of other challenges and difficulties. Not least of which was that I underestimated the amount of time, effort and energy that would be required to survey more than fourteen hundred years of Islamic history, beginning with the birth of the Prophet Muhammad and ending in our own time.

Additionally, given the multi-disciplinary nature of this book, I not only had to explore a large quantity of historical data and information; it was also necessary to acquire some understanding of *kalam* (Islamic theology), *tafsir* (Qur'anic exegesis), *hadith* literature, *falsafah* (philosophy), *fiqh* (jurisprudence), *usul al-fiqh* (science of Islamic jurisprudence), *tasawwuf* (mysticism), aspects of science, mathematics, Arabic literature, Persian poetry, heresiographical thought and architectural history among other subjects. What was even more difficult was selecting only a hundred people from the hundreds, if not thousands, of prominent and influential Muslims who have left their indelible marks in the annals of history. As one of the world's great religions, Islam created a dazzling culture and civilisation which today extends from Morocco in North Africa, all the way to Indonesia in the Far East; and from Yemen in the Arabian Peninsula, to as far as Uzbekistan in Central Asia.

Thus, consisting of more than fifty-five Muslim majority countries and over a billion people today, Muslims have left their fingerprints on every field of human endeavour. It is not surprising, therefore, that some of history's most influential men and women have been Muslims. In the words of George Sarton, the renowned historian of science

and author of *Introduction to the History of Science*, 'The main task of mankind was accomplished by Muslims. The greatest philosopher, al-Farabi, was a Muslim; the greatest mathematicians, Abu Kamil and Ibrahim ibn Sinan, were Muslims; the greatest geographer and encyclopaedist, al-Mas'udi, was a Muslim; the greatest historian, al-Tabari, was still a Muslim.' Chosen by the author, this book only briefly explores the lives, thoughts and achievements of one hundred such influential Muslim men and women. It should also be pointed out that Islamic scholars and historians have written extensively about most of the people covered in this book, so the readers should not take these biographies as the final word on the lives and thoughts of the people included here. Rather, I hope, this book will encourage and inspire the readers to pursue their own study and research into Islamic thought, history, culture and civilisation.

Due to geographical, cultural, intellectual and historical overlaps, it was not possible to avoid some repetition. Hopefully, the readers will understand and appreciate why this was unavoidable as they go through the book. I went to great lengths to avoid using unnecessary jargon and technical language, but in some places this was unavoidable (for instance, when discussing aspects of theology, philosophy or mysticism). In addition, all the chapters begin with an introductory statement which seeks to place the personality concerned within their socio-political or cultural context and I have ensured that all the entries are of roughly equal length. In order to simplify things, only the Gregorian dates have been provided within the main text of the book, but I have included their *hijri* (Islamic) equivalent in the chronology at the end of the book. Since the *hijri* year consists of twelve lunar months of 29 or 30 days each, the Islamic calendar is about 11 days shorter than its Gregorian equivalent; thus the converted dates – as they appear in the chronology – are approximate. Again, for the sake of simplicity, I have not used any diacritics except for such common words and names like the Qur'an, Mu'tazilah, al-Ash'ari and al-Ma'mun. Likewise, I have completely avoided footnotes because this book is aimed primarily at students and lay readers, but most of the books and articles I read and consulted are listed in the select bibliography. Nearly all the Arabic words and titles of books cited within the text have been translated into English for the benefit of the readers. Moreover, according to Islamic custom, when the name of the Prophet Muhammad is mentioned, the words *sallallahu alaihi wasallam* (peace and blessing of God be upon him) should be added. When the name of any other Prophet is mentioned, the words *alaihis salam* (peace be upon him) should be added. When the name of a male companion of the Prophet is mentioned, the words *radiAllahu anhu* (God be pleased with him) should be added. And, finally, when the name of a female companion of the Prophet is mentioned, the words *radiAllahu anha* (God be pleased with her) should be added. All Muslim readers are reminded to observe this Islamic custom, as I have not included these customary salutations within the main text of the book for the sake of brevity and simplicity.

My studies concerning Islamic thought, history, culture and civilisation have occupied me for nearly twenty years now, since I was about thirteen, and unquestionably this book could not have been written without the sources listed in the select bibliography. I am extremely grateful to the authors, editors, translators and publishers of these and other books and articles I have read, and should anything I say in this book appear in any way similar to their ideas and thoughts, it is because I have drawn my information from them. The first draft of this book was completed in November 2005, exactly a month before my thirty-second birthday, but due to a heavy workload it was not possible to thoroughly check and revise the manuscript at the time. However, during 2006 I revised the manuscript several times, and the final revision was completed in August 2007. And, given the nature and size of this book, it is possible that some errors have escaped my attention and scrutiny. Thus should anyone spot any factual inaccuracies or errors, I would be grateful if they could write to the publisher so that the errors can be rectified in any future edition of this book.

Finally, I need to thank a number of people. Firstly, I am grateful to Professor Dr. Muhammad Abdul Jabbar Beg, FRAS, who is a distinguished Islamic historian and a prolific writer, for thoroughly reading a draft version of this book and making numerous corrections and suggestions for improvement. I am indebted to Mawlana Mohammed Mushfiqur Rahman (who specialised in *hadith* literature at al-Azhar University) and Hafiz Abdullah Muhammad (a writer and Islamic researcher) for reading a draft version of this book and providing valuable feedback. Likewise, I am grateful to Ahmed J. Versi, the editor of *The Muslim News* (a leading British Muslim newspaper), for not only reading this book and making some useful and interesting comments, but also for encouraging me to write regularly for his esteemed newspaper. Rod Bushell agreed to thoroughly check the whole manuscript and, in the process, he raised numerous queries and questions which enabled me to clarify many issues and further improve and enhance the book.

My wife has been a source of blessing since our marriage nearly nine years ago. Without her support, encouragement and tolerance, this book could not have been written. At times I studied for more than twelve hours a day, but she accepted and tolerated my excesses and absent-mindedness; may the Almighty reward her most abundantly. As for my two young sons, Muhtadi aged six and Mustafa aged four, they kept-on asking when the book would be completed. To them, I say, it is now complete. Likewise, my sister Sabia helped produce the chronology, and Motin and Shelina assisted in so many other ways. My mother was keen for me to finish the book so I could take some rest. I am also grateful to Yahya Birt, Commissioning Editor, and all his colleagues at Kube Publishing for their constructive criticism, suggestions and contributions.

Ultimately, however, my success in my task can only come from Him; the One and Only (*al-Ahad*). Blessed is His Name and salutation (*salawat*) upon His most beloved, the light by whom others are guided to the Light (*al-Nur*), and to Him is our final return.

# I

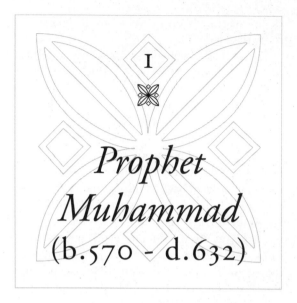

## Prophet Muhammad (b.570 - d.632)

HE WAS BORN an orphan and was brought up in the Arabian village of Ta'if. He was subsequently raised in the town of Makkah by his extended family. He worked as a shepherd and a merchant, and never set a foot inside a school or college and was known to have been *ummi*, or an unlettered man. He came to be known to his fellow countrymen for his absolute honesty, impeccable character and strong sense of justice and fair play – so much so that they fondly called him *al-amin* (the trustworthy) and *al-sadiq* (the truthful). He led a hitherto uneventful life without in any way showing the signs of the great man that he was to be. Arabia was not necessarily known for rearing men of universal appeal and renown. His birth put an end to that drought and, for the first time in their history, the Arab descendants of the great patriarch, Abraham (*Ibrahim*), had something they could truly celebrate: the birth of the most influential man ever to walk on the earth. His name means the 'praiseworthy one'.

To some Arabs, history actually began in 570, the year in which their greatest son was born into the noble Makkan tribe of Quraysh (in present-day Saudi Arabia). A direct descendant of Ishmael (*Ismail*), the father of the Semitic Arab race, he single-handedly dragged the Arab people from being a footnote of human history to be the founders of one of history's greatest civilisations. More importantly, he accomplished such an unprecedented feat without any wherewithal. Caesar had the pomp and power of Rome; Alexander had a mighty army; Heraclius had immense wealth and resources, while Napoleon was trained at a military academy; but he had none of these things. He started with nothing, but ended up with the whole world. That was the greatness of the man called Muhammad, history's most incomparable religious-cum-political genius.

Living in seventh century Arabia, Muhammad became increasingly detached from the superstitious beliefs and practices of his people. He began to explore, and take a closer interest in, spiritual matters by secluding himself on the Mount of Light (*jabal al-nur*), situated on the outskirts of the Arabian town of Makkah, for meditation and spiritual renewal. As political corruption, social inequality, economic disparity between the poor and rich, and religious superstition and tribal conflict increasingly became the order of the day in Makkah and across Arabia, Muhammad began to search for serious answers to his society's maladies. As he approached his fortieth birthday, his meditation and retreat on the Mount of Light intensified and reached its climax during one night in the month of Ramadan, which resulted in a direct visitation from archangel Gabriel (*jibrail*), conveying to him the first of a series of Divine revelations, which he continued to receive until his death in 632. The angel confirmed that he, Muhammad, was God's last and final Prophet (*nabi*) to humanity and the Qur'an, consisting of one hundred and fourteen chapters (*suwar*) of variable length, was God's last and final revelation (*wahy*) to mankind. This Divine intervention in history marked the beginning of Muhammad's Prophetic mission. The result was that Islam – meaning submission to the Will of One God (*Allah* in Arabic) – completely transformed Muhammad, and he went out to invite his fellow countrymen to the worship of One God. From that day on, the promulgation and propagation of Islam became his main preoccupation in life.

As soon as the Prophet publicly announced the message of Islam some, especially those who had suffered hardship under the oppressive rule of the Makkan oligarchy, responded positively to his call. However, the ruling Makkan elites became very hostile and abusive towards Muhammad as soon as the implication of his new message became clear to them. In a fiercely feudalistic, tribally entrenched and paternalistic Makkan society, the message of Islam advocated the need for a different approach to politics, social justice, economics and human spirituality. Indeed, in a grossly unjust and unfair Makkah (and Arabian society as a whole), the Prophet's message of freedom, equality, justice, fair play and brotherhood was nothing short of a breath of fresh air. Not surprisingly, the status quo maintained and perpetuated by a handful of tribal chieftains in order to protect their own politico-economic interests soon came under direct threat from Islam. Thus the Prophet and his message became the main target of their hostility and enmity. Undaunted by the severity of the hardship and hostility directed towards him and his small band of followers, Muhammad continued to proclaim

the message of Islam in and around Makkah for more than a decade.

In 622, the Prophet was invited by a delegation from the nearby oasis of Yathrib to move to their city. The Prophet accepted their offer and moved to Yathrib, which later became known as *madinat al-nabi* (or the 'city of the Prophet'). The Prophet's migration to Madinah (*hijrah*) thus became a momentous event in Islamic history. The Islamic calendar, known as the *hijri* calendar, is dated back to the day the Prophet left his native Makkah for Madinah. In this beautiful Arabian oasis, the Prophet received a hero's welcome, as its inhabitants came out in their droves and pledged allegiance to him by embracing Islam. From that day on, Madinah became a very special place for all Muslims; and it also became the hub of Islamic learning, culture and civilisation for all times to come.

When the Makkan chiefs were informed about the Prophet's success in Madinah, they became very shocked and alarmed. Having tried to undermine him and his mission in Makkah and failed most miserably, they now conspired to create unrest in Madinah by setting factions of hypocrites, rival tribes of pagans, Jews and the new immigrants (*muhajirun*) from Makkah against each other. But, thanks to the Prophet's polished diplomatic skills, their strategies came to nothing. Undeterred, the Makkan chieftains then marched to Madinah with a large contingent in order to obliterate the nascent Muslim community. The Prophet and his small band of followers met the advancing Makkan army at the plain of Badr, located on the outskirts of Madinah. More than one thousand strong, the well-equipped Makkah army fought just over three hundred ill-equipped and unprepared Muslims. Miraculously, the Prophet and his followers inflicted a crushing defeat on their Makkan foes. The Muslims returned to Madinah in elation, while the Makkan army returned home in total disarray. Determined to avenge their humiliation, the unrelenting Makkan chiefs attempted to obliterate the Muslims on a few other occasions, but they failed to breach the stiff defence put up by the Muslims. Demoralised by their failure to wipe out the Muslims, the Makkans were eventually forced to agree to a treaty with the Prophet and make peace. Even though the terms and conditions of the treaty were biased in favour of the Makkans, the Prophet agreed to sign it, despite protestations from some of his companions. This was a shrewd move on his part, because this period of peace gave the people of Makkah the opportunity to see Islam in action in Madinah for the first time. During their journeys to Madinah, the Makkans saw a society utterly transformed. The Prophet had turned a warring and bitterly divided oasis into a thriving civil society.

For the first time in its history, tribal factionalism, social injustice, economic inequality, political oppression, physical torture and abuse, maltreatment of women and cruelty towards slaves were no longer the order of the day in Madinah. On the contrary, brotherhood and fraternity between the believers; love, understanding and co-operation between kith and kin; respect for the rights of women; freeing of slaves and an unrivalled interest in learning and education became the key features of the new society created by the Prophet only a few hundred miles away from Makkah. This unparalleled transformation of a tribal society and its people's hearts, minds, thoughts, morals and customs was accomplished by the Prophet and done so within a matter of a decade. Muhammad led the people of Madinah by his personal example. He did not say one thing and do another. Whether it was in the intense heat of the battlefield or during prayers in the mosque; during the daylight or in the middle of the night; at times of hunger and hardship or in times of happiness and joy, he was at the forefront of everything. The people of Madinah became so fond of him that they meticulously moulded their actions, behaviour and even their style of dressing, eating, drinking and sleeping in accordance with the Prophet's norms and practices. To them, the Prophet Muhammad was simply *al-insan al-kamil* or 'the perfect human being'. Such unfailing love and devotion shown to their leader

by a people was not only unheard of, it was also unprecedented in the annals of history.

In the year 630, the Prophet and a large contingent of his devout followers marched into Makkah, the city of his birth, without a single drop of blood being shed. On seeing him enter Makkah, the people of the city came out in their droves and pledged allegiance to him by embracing Islam. The Prophet's most inveterate opponent, Abu Sufyan ibn Harb, was, however, offered protection by none other than the Prophet's uncle, Abbas ibn Abd al-Muttalib. Typical of the Prophet, on entering Makkah he announced that anyone who took shelter in the courtyard of the sacred Kabah, in the house of Abu Sufyan, or remained indoors would be safe. Even Abu Sufyan knew when Muhammad made a promise, he would stick to it come what might. The next morning, accompanied by Abbas, he went straight to the Prophet and most willingly pledged allegiance to him. The Prophet forgave him for his persistent past misdeeds and told him that he was free to go about his business as a free man. This was an extraordinary act of clemency and compassion. Hitherto, Abu Sufyan had been unrelenting in his pursuit of the Prophet and his followers, but Muhammad chose to forgive and forget rather than seek retribution. That was the quality and greatness of the man called 'a mercy to mankind' (*rahmatun lil alamin*).

With the conversion of Makkah and its neighbouring towns to the fold of Islam, the Prophet accomplished a feat never achieved by an Arab before him, namely to unite the constantly bickering and rival Arabian tribes under the banner of a common denominator. That common denominator was Islam, which transcended all tribal affiliations and internal factionalism, as it collectively channelled the Arabs' might and energy in one direction, namely the dissemination of Islam, and in so doing they transformed the course of human history forever. Muhammad, the Prophet *par excellence* and the Qur'an, the Divine revelation, thus combined to inspire the Muslims of Arabia to achieve the unprecedented success which they subsequently achieved. In just over two decades, Muhammad radically transformed a hitherto neglected, barren and primitive Arabian peninsula into a thriving centre of learning, culture, commerce and civilisation. By all accounts, this was a truly remarkable achievement, unprecedented not only in Arab history, but also global history. As he approached his sixtieth birthday, he knew his mission was drawing to an end. In the tenth year of the *hijrah*, the Prophet performed his farewell pilgrimage and delivered one of the most powerful, eloquent and inspiring sermons ever composed by a religious leader. Standing on the plain of Arafat in front of around one hundred and twenty thousand people, he began by praising and thanking God, and said:

'O people, lend me an attentive ear for I do not know whether, after this year, I would meet you again. Therefore, listen to what I am saying to you very carefully and take these words to those who could not be present here today. O people, just as you regard this month; this day; this city as sacred, so regard the life and property of every Muslim as a sacred trust. Return the goods entrusted to you to their rightful owners. Hurt no one so that no one may hurt you. Remember that you will indeed appear before God and answer for your actions. All dues of interest shall stand cancelled and you will have only your capital back; God has forbidden interest. You will neither inflict, nor suffer, inequity...'

'Beware of Shaytan (Satan) for the safety of your religion. He has lost all hope that he will ever be able to lead you astray in great things, so beware of following him in small things. O people, your wives have a certain right over you and you have certain rights over them. Treat them well and be kind to them, for they are your partners and committed helpers. And it is your right that they do not make friends with anyone who you do not like as well as never be unchaste.'

'O people, listen to me carefully! Worship God, perform your five daily prayers, fast the month of Ramadan, pay alms and make the pilgrimage if you can afford it. All humanity is from Adam and Eve. There is no superiority for an Arab over a non-Arab, nor for a non-Arab over an Arab; a white man over a black man, nor for a black man over a white man, except through piety. All the believers are brothers and the believers constitute one nation. You are not allowed to take the things belonging to another Muslim unless he gives it to you willingly. Do not, therefore, do injustice to yourselves.'

'O people, reflect on my words. Remember, one day you will appear before God and answer for your deeds. So beware, do not stray from the path of righteousness after I am gone. O people, be mindful of those who work under you. Feed and clothe them as you feed and clothe yourselves. O people, no prophet or messenger will come after me and no new faith will be born. Reason well, therefore, O people, and understand the words that I convey to you. I leave behind me two things: the Qur'an and my example (*sunnah*), and if you follow these you will not go stray. All those who listen to me shall pass on my words to others and those to others again; and may the last ones understand my words better than those who listen to me directly. Be my witness, O God, that I have conveyed Your message to Your people.'

The Prophet Muhammad was an outstanding orator and a master of succinctness. He spoke only when required, and did so in a brief but comprehensive manner. This sermon illustrates how beautiful and unsurpassed his oratory and communication skills were. Although he was unlettered, he could nevertheless communicate with both men and women, young and aged, lettered as well as the unlettered in a masterly fashion. Even his critics admired his sound logic, sharp intellect, organisational ability and his down-to-earth approach. He was neither extreme, nor too lax in his words or deeds; instead he preached and practiced moderation in everything. Whenever he was given an option between two things, he always chose the easy option and encouraged his companions to make religion easy for the people. According to his wife, Aishah, he was a 'walking Qur'an' who was very kind and generous to those around him, and personified angelic qualities and attributes.

With the successful completion of his mission, the Prophet returned to Madinah where he passed away at the age of sixty-three. The Prophet Muhammad's achievements are so varied and extensive that it would require a separate book to fully document them. He was an unusually gifted man who radically transformed the course of human history by the sheer dint of his unique character and powerful personality. Today, more than fourteen hundred years after his death, his powerful message and teachings continue to influence mankind's journey in tune with the march of time. No other single human being has been able to influence our minds, thoughts, ideas and destinies like him. That is why Prophet Muhammad is not only the greatest Muslim; he was also the most influential man ever to walk on the earth.

# 2

## Umar ibn al-Khattab (b.ca.581 - d.644)

AFTER THE PROPHET MUHAMMAD, Umar is undoubtedly the most influential and enduring figure in Islamic history. Strong, charismatic, firm but equally just; fair as well as a leader *par excellence*, gifted men like Umar are a very rare breed in human history. As an exceptional all-rounder, Umar was blessed with outstanding abilities in all spheres of human endeavour. Indeed, the Prophet Muhammad said if there was to be another prophet after him, it would surely have been Umar. The Prophet aside, Umar's achievements are second to none in Islamic history. That is why today Muslims in every corner of the earth are praying for a leader like Umar to emerge and guide the *ummah* (global Islamic community) through the turbulent waters of history.

Umar ibn al-Khattab ibn Nufail ibn Abd al-Uzza was born into the Adi branch of the Qurayshi tribe of Makkah. Of medium height and muscular build, he was an accomplished wrestler in his pre-Islamic days. He was also a forceful orator and one of only a handful of Qurayshis who knew how to read and write at that time. Umar grew up to be an honest and likeable young man who became a relatively successful merchant and trader during his early twenties. After Muhammad announced his

Prophethood, Umar became a persistent thorn in the Prophet's side. He actively discouraged people from embracing the new faith and never hesitated to attack those who ignored his advice. When it became transparent that the Prophet would not stop preaching Islam, the ruling elites of Quraysh decided to assassinate Muhammad. The indomitable Umar volunteered for the task. Everyone present at the meeting agreed that Umar was the best man for the job because he was brave, bold and well known for his fighting skills. Umar returned home to collect his sword and immediately set out in search of the Prophet.

On his way he bumped into Nu'aim ibn Abdullah who asked him where he was going. Umar told him he was out to exterminate the Prophet. But why would he want to commit such a heinous crime, reasoned Nu'aim. Umar explained how the Prophet and his message had set father against son, and brother against brother within Makkah. By doing away with the Prophet, he hoped to put an end to all the bitterness and hostility. As it happens, Nu'aim had already embraced Islam and was determined to dissuade Umar from his potentially disastrous mission, but Umar was equally determined to carry out his task. Nu'aim realised the gravity of the situation and told Umar to set his own house in order first. It transpired that Umar's own sister, Fatimah, and her husband had already secretly embraced Islam. This news shocked Umar and hurt his pride. He immediately turned around and headed for his sister's house. She was studying the Qur'an at the time with her husband. As soon as the door was opened, Umar landed an almighty blow on his brother-in-law. In the ensuing scuffle, he managed to land a blow on his sister and she began to bleed profusely. He was visibly shaken to see his sister's blood on his hand. He demanded to see the verses they were reciting. She bluntly told him that only the purified are permitted to touch the Divine revelation. When he returned after purifying himself, she gave him the parchment on which the Qur'anic verses were inscribed, and he began to read:

'Ta Ha. It was not to distress you that We sent down the Qur'an to you, but as a reminder for those who hold God in awe, a revelation from the One Who created the earth and the high heaven, the Lord of Mercy, established on the Throne. Everything in the heavens and earth, everything between them, everything beneath the soil, belongs to him. Whatever you may say aloud, He knows what you keep secret and what is even more hidden. God – there is no god but Him – the most excellent names belong to Him.' (*Surat Ta Ha*, verses 1-8)

As Umar continued to read, the expression on his face began to change. What he had just recited was neither poetry nor prose; it surpassed both. As a literate man, one of a handful in Makkah at the time, Umar knew in his heart of hearts that an illiterate man like Muhammad could not possibly have composed such beautiful and elegant words. He was convinced that it was Divine revelation. He demanded to be taken to Muhammad to pledge allegiance to the Prophet. From that day on, Umar became a powerful champion of Islam. Although he was still in his late twenties at the time of his conversion, Umar's coming to Islam delighted the Prophet and his small band of followers because he was a forceful

and indomitable character who was destined to play a legendary role in the annals of Islam. In the tribal Arab culture of the time, it was very common to strengthen friendships through marriage. Although the Prophet held Umar in high esteem for his devotion and dedication to Islam, he later consolidated his friendship with Umar by marrying his daughter, Hafsah. The Prophet thus became his son-in-law and Umar, in turn, became the Prophet's right-hand man for the rest of his life.

After the death of the Prophet in 632, Umar was the first person to pledge his loyalty to Abu Bakr al-Siddiq as the Prophet's successor, and the people of Madinah followed suit. Abu Bakr was duly elected *khalifat rasul Allah* (or 'successor to the Messenger of God') and he became the ruler of the Islamic State. Thanks to Umar's quick thinking, sharp intellect, powerful personality and standing within the early Muslim community, a potentially damaging succession battle was avoided and a smooth transition of leadership was achieved. The pivotal role played by Umar in this first major challenge faced by the early Muslims soon after the Prophet's death was a testament to his clear vision, organisational ability and greatness, even if the majority of Islamic historians have failed to appreciate the importance of the role played by Umar at this critical juncture in Islamic history. During the two years and three months of Caliph Abu Bakr's reign, Umar played the indispensable role of being an advisor, strategist and close confidant to the latter. After the Prophet, Abu Bakr was clearly the most insightful Muslim, and he knew Umar very well and trusted him more than anyone else. Lying on his deathbed, Abu Bakr called all the leading figures of the early Muslim community to a consultative (*shura*) meeting. He told them he wished to nominate Umar as his successor. No one present at the meeting raised any objection against Abu Bakr's proposal. Umar was a dominant figure among the companions of the Prophet. He was well known for his sacrifices for Islam, and everyone admired his sense of justice. In the circumstances, Abu Bakr felt he was the best person to lead the Muslim community. History bears testimony to the quality of Abu Bakr's wisdom and choice.

In 634, at the age of fifty-three, Umar assumed the leadership of the early Islamic State and ruled for just over a decade. During this period, Umar was able to achieve what others failed to achieve in a lifetime. With Umar in charge at Madinah, Muslims burst out of Arabia and overwhelmed the mighty Persian and Holy Roman Empires like a thunderbolt from heaven. In 638, the Muslim army conquered Jerusalem and the great Caliph himself went there to sign the peace treaty with the people of that historic city. As he approached Jerusalem, the people of the city could not believe what they were witnessing, for one of the great rulers of the time was proceeding into their city on foot, while his aide was riding the camel. When the aide offered to forgo his turn to ride the camel in favour of the Caliph, the latter refused the offer saying, "The honour of Islam is enough for us." When the time for prayer arrived, the Bishop of Jerusalem invited Caliph Umar to offer his prayer inside the Cathedral, but he politely refused. He did not want to give anyone an excuse for turning the Cathedral into a mosque in the future, he told an astounded Bishop. Clearly taken aback by Umar's grace, humility and tolerance, the Bishop offered him space outside the Cathedral where Umar led the faithful in prayers.

During the ten incredible years of his reign, he never forgot Caliph Abu Bakr's last words of advice to him: 'O Umar! Always fear God. An optional deed is not accepted unless the obligatory deed is done. The weight of your goodness would be heavy on the Day of Judgement if you follow the right path in this world. The deeds of people who followed the wrong path in this world will have no weight on the Day of Judgement. They will have a terrible time. Make the Holy Qur'an and Truth your guides for success. Umar, if you follow the path I propose for you, I will surely be by your side.'

Umar more than lived up to Caliph Abu Bakr's wise words; indeed, he thrived and excelled in so many ways that his reign has found its way into Muslim folklore. Muslim children across the globe grow up listening to their parents and grandparents relating tales about Caliph Umar and his glorious achievements. Some of Umar's salient contributions included the development of a functioning Islamic democracy, and the formation of a Council of Advisors to discuss and debate issues before final decisions were made. He established the rule of law across the rapidly expanding Islamic State and ensured that equality of treatment and freedom of expression were made the cornerstones of his reign. Ordinary people could stand up in the mosque and interrupt him in the middle of his sermon or announcement to challenge him on any policy issues including taxation, political administration, civil matters, military affairs or the allocation of marriage dowry. He was fully accountable to his people. If any complaint was raised, Umar made sure it was dealt with immediately and he never hesitated in correcting his own mistakes, or those of who served under him. If the complainants were found to be wrong, he reasoned with them on the basis of the Qur'an and Prophetic teachings (*sunnah*).

With the rapid expansion of the Islamic dominion, Umar devised a provincial system of administration and appointed governors to oversee the smooth running of each province, with all the governors reporting directly to him. Although he was based at his headquarters in Madinah, Umar always kept in close contact with all his governors, never failing to remind them about the importance of serving the people with honesty, fairness, justice and equality. A functioning judicial system was devised and implemented by Umar, so that legal disputes could be resolved in a fair and effective manner in accordance with Islamic principles and guidelines. He developed an equally efficient taxation and revenue department, which collected and distributed *zakat* (poor due), taxes and other revenues from all the regions of the Islamic State, under the supervision of the chief treasurer who reported directly to him. Looking after the welfare of the poor, needy, orphans and disabled people was vitally important to Umar, because he felt he was directly responsible for their well-being. In order to meet the needs of society's most vulnerable people, Umar established a social security system. Being one of the most learned companions of the Prophet, he promoted learning and education by constructing mosques and schools across the Islamic dominion. Indeed, during his reign, mosques and educational centres mushroomed throughout the Islamic State; he also helped to rebuild such prominent cities as Basrah, Kufah, al-Fustat and Mosul, and these subsequently became some of the most prominent centres of Islamic learning, culture and civilisation.

In addition, Umar kept a regular army that was well-disciplined, highly-skilled and dedicated, so that even the well-equipped, professional soldiers of the Persian and Byzantine Empires were not a match for them. It is to Umar's great credit that, for the first time in Islamic history, an Islamic calendar was introduced which Muslims could call their own. The *hijri* calendar was devised during Umar's reign, the first day being fixed as the one on which the Prophet left Makkah for Madinah in 622. Caliph Umar was a versatile genius, a great democratic ruler and, equally, a compassionate man who assumed leadership of the embryonic Islamic State and within a decade transformed it into a powerful empire, consisting of whole of Arabia and significant parts of the Persian and Byzantine Empires. That is why his reign is widely recognised as the Golden Age of Islam. Prior to his death, Caliph Umar appointed an illustrious six-man panel to nominate his successor. Being one of the most civilised and democratic rulers of his time, he deliberately chose not to nominate his successor.

Following in the footsteps of the Prophet and his immediate predecessor, Umar wanted the masses, or their representatives, to have a say in the matter. Umar – who was given the title of *al-faruq* (the differentiator between right and wrong) by the Prophet for his wisdom and sense of justice – passed away at the age of around sixty-three and was buried in Madinah next to the Prophet (his mentor and guide), and Caliph Abu Bakr, his best friend. It is not possible to exaggerate Umar's greatness, for as the Prophet once remarked, 'Among the nations before your time there have been inspired people (who were not prophets), and if there is one among my people he is Umar.' (Sahih al-Bukhari and Sahih Muslim)

# 3

## Ali ibn Abi Talib
### (b.ca.601 – d.661)

IN ANY BOOK of most influential Muslims, Ali ibn Abi Talib is bound to appear near the very top of the list. He is famous for his impeccable character, loving personality and unflinching devotion to Islam. As one of the foremost figures of early Islam, he is profoundly revered as one of the four 'rightly-guided caliphs' (*al-khulafa al-rashidun*) along with Abu Bakr al-Siddiq, Umar ibn al-Khattab and Uthman ibn Affan. However, within the Shi'a branch of Islam, Ali is a pivotal figure. So much so that without the charismatic and indomitable personality of Ali there would not be a Shi'a branch of Islam at all. As such, he occupies a prominent and unique position as the fourth Caliph of Islam, and the first Imam of the Shi'ias.

Born into the Hashimite family of the Quraysh tribe of Makkah, Ali ibn Abi Talib was a cousin of the Prophet Muhammad. He became a Muslim about a year after Muhammad announced his Prophethood. Ali was barely ten at the time and he became the first boy to embrace Islam. Brought up and educated by the Prophet, Ali became one of his foremost supporters from the outset. Once, the Prophet invited all the leaders of Quraysh to a meal in order to share the message of Islam with them but when none of them responded to his call, young Ali stood up and announced that he was ready to help and support the Prophet. His bravery and courage gave hope to the Prophet and shamed all the prominent leaders who had gathered at the Prophet's house. As it happens, Ali never failed to live up to his promise to stand by the Prophet. He remained at the Prophet's side both at times of hardship and joy; success and sorrow. When in the year 622, the Quraysh decided to assassinate Muhammad, Ali volunteered to stay in the Prophet's house so that the Prophet could slip out of Makkah without a trace, in the company of his friend Abu Bakr, and travel to Madinah. When the Makkans eventually entered the Prophet's house they were surprised to find young Ali sleeping in Muhammad's bed. After returning all the goods the people had entrusted to the Prophet for safekeeping, Ali set off for Madinah and joined him there.

Short in height, of muscular build, highly energetic and blessed with a well-proportioned body frame, Ali was also known to have been frighteningly quick. He is famous in the annals of Islam as an indomitable warrior who out-smarted his opponents on the battlefield with ease. In the year 627, when the Muslims of

Madinah were forced to dig trenches around the city to avert an imminent Makkan invasion, Abdwud, the famous warrior of Arabia, managed to cross the trench and challenged the Muslims to fight him one-to-one. No one dared to accept the challenge except Ali. He grabbed his favourite double-edged sword (*dhul fiqar*) and confronted the most accomplished fighter in the land. Within minutes, Abdwud realised that he had at last met his match. Soon the most famous fighter of Arabia found himself lying on the floor while the victorious Ali walked into the ranks of the Muslims in humility. Such fearless bravery and accomplishments on the battlefield soon established his reputation as one of the most successful warriors of Arabia, earning him the honorific title of *asadullah* or the 'lion of God' from none other than the Prophet himself.

Ali was not only a distinguished fighter and athlete, but also a man of profound wisdom and great learning. He was considered to be one of the most learned companions of the Prophet Muhammad. In addition to being an outstanding jurist-consult, a master of Arabic language and an accomplished orator, Ali knew the entire Qur'an by heart and was one of a few companions who had composed collections of *hadith* (Prophetic traditions) during the Prophet's own lifetime. Moreover, Ali is widely considered to be a pioneer of *tasawwuf*, or Islamic mysticism. As it happens, the majority of the prominent Sufi Orders (*tariqah*) trace their spiritual affiliation directly to the Prophet through Ali. Indeed, Ali became so famous for his prodigious learning and scholarship that the Prophet once remarked that he (the Prophet) was the city of knowledge, while Ali was its gate. Caliphs Abu Bakr and Umar both regularly consulted Ali on all important legal issues of the day before issuing religious edicts (*fatawa*). Ali's estimation in the sight of Caliph Umar was second-to-none when it came to juristic matters. He used to say, "Ali is the greatest jurist and judge among all of us". Ali and Caliph Abu Bakr were undoubtedly two of the most insightful Muslims after the Prophet himself.

When Caliph Uthman was brutally assassinated by a group of insurgents in 656 at the ripe old age of eighty, the unity of the Muslim world was shattered. Sheer commotion and hysteria soon spread across Madinah. It was at this critical period in Islamic history that Ali became the fourth Caliph of Islam. Like his predecessors, he assumed the office of Caliphate with some trepidation because he considered it to be a trust from God and a position of tremendous responsibility. After becoming Caliph he immediately encountered difficulties, facing stiff opposition from rival groups. He found himself caught between a rock and a hard place, as one group demanded that the murderers of Caliph Uthman be immediately apprehended and punished for their heinous crime, while the insurgents continued to wreak havoc within the Islamic State. Another group allied themselves with the Caliph and they became known as the *shi'at Ali* or the 'partisans of Ali'. This group not only supported him, they later developed their own theological views and political objectives. As a result, Shi'ism – as opposed to mainstream Sunnism – became a separate political and theological strand within Islam. At the same time, the *khawarij* (or the 'dissenters') emerged as a political splinter group; they considered all other groups except themselves to be heretical and misguided. Despite the brewing tribal rivalry and political factionalism, Caliph Ali tried to work with all the different groups in order to maintain Islamic unity and solidarity; he knew he could not afford to make a mistake at such a critical moment in Islamic history.

Being an acclaimed jurist, Caliph Ali understood more than anyone else the need to apprehend and punish the murderers of Caliph Uthman, but it was not possible to achieve this straight away given the prevailing chaos and disorder within the Islamic State. Caliph Ali's first and foremost priority was to re-establish a sense of civility and order across Madinah before he could focus his attention on other pressing issues. To make matters worse, the insurgents who were responsible for the murder of Caliph Uthman went underground, and it would have required a thorough investigation in order to identify and apprehend the culprits. A serious miscalculation by the Caliph at this stage would have allowed the insurgents to sow the seeds of further chaos and disorder within the Islamic State. Caliph Ali's polished diplomatic skills, coupled with his vast knowledge and understanding of Islam, enabled him to negotiate his way through all the political twists and turns. And, as always, his utmost priority was the welfare of his people and the unity of the Muslim *ummah* (global Islamic community).

No other person could have traversed such a complex and difficult path at such a critical period in Islamic history than the exemplary Caliph Ali. Using his polished negotiating skills and profound grasp of Islamic teachings, he was able to avert an all-out war in the Islamic State on more than one ocassion. When the situation inside Madinah eventually became intolerable, he moved his heartquarters to Kufah. He took this brave decision to prevent Madinah, the city of the Prophet, from becoming a battleground, thus frustrating the insurgents who were determined to turn this sacred city into a war zone. As a truly great champion of Islam, Ali fought tooth and nail to prevent the Muslims from fighting against each other; so much so that he even agreed to sign a truce with his most inveterate enemies in order to prevent war. He preferred to suffer personal humiliation rather than see innocent Muslims lose their lives and livelihood. His love, kindness and generosity turned him into a potent symbol of goodness and rectitude. Even those who disagreed with him never failed to admire his sincerity and wisdom. According to the historians, Muawiyah ibn Abi Sufyan – who was governor of Syria during the Caliphate of Ali and the leader of those who insisted that the Caliph should identify and apprehend the murderers of Uthman – once asked Dirar ibn Damrah al-Kinani, who was one of his close aides, to comment on Caliph Ali's character, morals and ability. Dirar responded:

'He was a man of strong will-power and determination. He always gave a just judgement, and he was a fountain of knowledge. His speech was full of wisdom. He hated the pleasure of this world and loved the darkness of night to cry before God. His dress was most simple and he liked simple meals. He lived like a common man and when anybody would put a question before him, he replied with utmost politeness. Whenever we asked him to wait for us he waited like common man. Although he was very near to us because of his high morals, we were afraid of him sometimes of his grandeur and eminence due to his nearness to God. He always respected a pious man and a scholar. He was nearest to the poor. He never allowed a powerful man to take advantage of his power. The weak were never disappointed of his justice. I bear witness that in many a battle he would wake up during the night and take hold of his beard and start to cry and weep before God as though he was in a state of commotion and exclaim: "O world! Do not try to betray me. I have left you long ago. Do not have any desire for me. I hate you. Your age is short and your end is long, and the way is full of danger…"'

On hearing this, Muawiyah apparently wept until his beard was wet and confirmed that Dirar's description of the qualities and attributes of Caliph Ali was true. During his turbulent reign as Caliph, Ali faced relentless opposition from various factions within the Islamic State. He not only reasoned with his opponents; he also pleaded with them to set their differences aside. He took military action only when all other options for resolving the conflicts were exhausted. By his very nature, Caliph Ali was a man of peace and harmony; indeed, he hated taking military action against fellow Muslims. But when his opponents were determined to fight him, he was not found wanting in that department either, as was the case during the Battles of Camel (*jamal*) and Siffin; he was courageous and brave enough to make a stand. This won him considerable plaudits from the other prominent companions of the Prophet who supported him during one of the most perilous times in the annals of Islam. There is no doubt that Caliph Ali was one of the most influential figures in Islamic history on account of his vast knowledge of Islam and tremendous contribution to the development of Islam as a religion, culture and way of life. Later, some of his sayings and exhortations were collected and compiled in the form of a book under the title of *Nahj al-Balaghah* (The Peak of Eloquence); this book is highly rated, especially by the Shi'a Muslims.

Ali was brutally murdered at the age of sixty by Abd al-Rahman ibn Muljam, a follower of the renegade *khawarij* sect. The *khawarij* initially supported Caliph Ali but they abandoned him after he agreed to resolve his differences with Muawiyah through arbitration (*tahkim*). The *khawarij* considered this to be a treacherous act and thus they became his most vociferous opponents. They planned to assassinate Muawiyah ibn Abi Sufyan, the governor of Syria, Amr ibn al-As, the famous Muslim military commander and conqueror of Egypt, along with Caliph Ali because they considered them to be the main sources of chaos and disorder (*fitna*) in the Islamic State. In their twisted understanding of the situation that prevailed in the Islamic State at the time, the *khawarij* thought that by murdering the three of them in one go they would put an end to the rivalry for the Caliphate. In the event, they only managed to assassinate Caliph Ali (both Muawiyah and Amr escaped similar attempts on their lives), and in so doing they brought the reign of the *al-khulafa al-rashidun* to an abrupt end. Some of Caliph Ali's most beautiful sayings and exhortations include:

'Fear God and you will have no cause to fear anyone else.'

'A believer always remembers God and is full of thoughts; he is thankful in prosperity and patient in adversity.'

'Lead such a life in this world that when you die, people may mourn you and while alive they may long for your company.'

'Knowledge is better than wealth, for you have to protect your wealth whereas knowledge protects you.'

'Wealth and greed are the roots of all evils and diseases.'

'Jealousy devours virtue as fire devours fuel.'

# 4

## Abu Bakr al-Siddiq
## (b.ca.573 - d.634)

IF PIETY, RIGHTEOUSNESS and love for Islam were the only criteria for selection, then after the Prophet Muhammad, Abu Bakr would certainly have led the way. No other person in the history of Islam can be compared to him when it comes to truthfulness, insight into Islamic teachings and devotion to God and his Prophet. He was so outstanding and unique in his commitment, sincerity and whole-hearted support and assistance to the Prophet from the outset that even the great Caliph Umar eventually confessed that he could not surpass Abu Bakr when it came to utter devotion and single-minded dedication to the cause of Islam. If outstanding leaders like Caliph Umar are rare in human history, then men of exceptional piety, profound wisdom and unusual insight into religious teachings, like Abu Bakr, are even rarer.

Abdullah ibn Abi Quhafah, better known by his patronymic Abu Bakr, was born into the clan of Taym of the noble Quraysh tribe; he was only two years younger than the Prophet himself. They not only became close friends during their early teens, they also had many things in common. This strengthened their friendship as they matured, undertook business expeditions together, and shared their dislike of idolatry and other unjust practices which prevailed in Makkan society at the time. Although a wealthy merchant, Abu Bakr was soft-spoken; kind-hearted and unusually generous in a society where materialism and greed was the order of the day. The situation in Makkah became so degenerate that the Arabs buried their baby girls alive because they were considered to be an economic burden on their families. Like young Muhammad, Abu Bakr despised such abhorrent practices and often helped the poor, needy and the destitute as much as he could. After Muhammad received his first revelation (*wahy*) from God, through the angel Gabriel, in the year 610 (while he was busy meditating on the Mount of Light (*jabal al-nur*), he shared the good news with his immediate family before approaching his best friend, Abu Bakr. Almost every other person the Prophet had invited to Islam asked questions or initially hesitated, but not so Abu Bakr. As soon as the Prophet informed him about his Prophetic mission, Abu Bakr accepted it without any hesitation whatsoever. At the time, if anyone could claim to have known Muhammad thoroughly, then that was Abu Bakr. His outright acceptance of Islam was an overwhelming vote of confidence in the Prophet, his character, personality and honesty. Conversely, Abu Bakr's acknowledgement of Islam delighted the Prophet, for Islam helped to strengthen their friendship which hereafter became a lifelong devotion and commitment for both of them.

For the next twenty-three years, Abu Bakr provided unflinching help and support to the Prophet. He involved himself in the thick of all the activities the Prophet undertook, and also accompanied him on his epoch-making journey from Makkah to Madinah (*hijrah*) for the sake of Islam. In the process, he suffered untold personal loss and hardship, yet he never hesistated to use his considerable wealth and properties for the cause of the Truth. As Islam became the *modus vivendi* of his life, the welfare of the Prophet and his small band of followers became Abu Bakr's main concern and preoccupation. In the tenth year of Muhammad's Prophethood, a momentous event took place. *Al-isra wa'l miraj* (or the Prophet's miraculous night journey from Makkah to Jerusalem, and ascension to heaven) occurred, and it was on this occasion that the five daily prayers were prescribed. On his return, the Prophet narrated the whole event to his friends and foes alike, but the Makkan chiefs joked and laughed at the Prophet. They then went to Abu Bakr and told him what the Prophet had related to them. Surely someone as down-to-earth as Abu Bakr could not believe such a fantastic tale, they thought to themselves. "Have you listened to your friend? He is claiming to have visited Jerusalem and the Sublime Throne in the heavens last night and talked with God Almighty. Would you believe it?" they asked Abu Bakr. "If he said so, then it is an absolute truth." retorted Abu Bakr without any hesitation. The Makkans were seriously taken aback by Abu Bakr's unflinching faith and confidence in the Prophet. From that day on, Abu Bakr became known as *al-siddiq* or 'the truthful' one.

Abu Bakr excelled in every possible way and had no match among the companions of the Prophet; he more than lived up to the Prophet's expectations and did so consistently. After the Prophet's migration to Madinah in 622, Abu Bakr

purchased a plot of land where the foundations of *masjid al-nabi* (or the 'Prophet's mosque') were laid in 623; he also led the first *hajj* (pilgrimage) to Makkah on behalf of the Prophet. Abu Bakr was more than a friend, supporter and close confidant of the Prophet; in fact, he was the only person to have been authorised by the Prophet to lead *salah* (daily prayers) while the Prophet was still alive. His estimation in the sight of the Prophet was second to none. Although the Prophet did not directly nominate a successor before he died, by nominating Abu Bakr to lead the daily prayers he had implicitly pointed the way forward. Nevertheless, the Prophet left the final decision on appointing his successor to the discretion of his companions, who numbered in their thousands at that time in Madinah. By choosing not to nominate his successor, he instituted and underlined the fundamental democratic principle of the people having a say in selecting their leader. Such a highly developed modern principle of governance was unheard of in the seventh century, but the Prophet was keen to give the people a say in the election or selection of their rulers.

After the Prophet passed away in 632, the news of his death spread across Arabia like a wildfire; this prompted many newly converted tribes of Arabia to revert back to their old ways. They thought that Islam would fizzle out after the Prophet's death. It was a critical period in Islamic history. The Muslim community could not possibly remain leaderless for long. Some leading companions of the Prophet, including Umar ibn al-Khattab and Abu Ubaida ibn al-Jarrah, saw the potential danger and played a pivotal role in electing a leader. After considerable discussion and debate, it was unanimously agreed by the companions of the Prophet to elect Abu Bakr *khalifat rasul Allah* ('successor to the Messenger of God'). He was elected on account of his leadership abilities, great insight into Islamic teachings and considerable experience of socio-political affairs. In other words, he was the most suitable person to lead the nascent Islamic State in the absence of the Prophet. After being elected the first Caliph of Islam, Abu Bakr went straight to the Prophet's mosque where he delivered his first address to the people. He declared:

'O people! I have been selected as your trustee although I am no better than anyone of you. If I am right, obey me. If I happen to be wrong, set me right. Of course truth is honesty and a lie is dishonesty. The weakest among you is powerful in my sight until I do not get him his due, God willing. The most powerful among you is the weakest in my sight until I do not make him pay his due rights to others, God willing. I ask you to obey me as long as I obey God and His messenger. If I disobey God and His messenger, you are free to disobey me.'

This speech was a milestone in Islamic political history because it not only skilfully articulated the fundamental Islamic constitutional principles, but also underlined the core precepts which should bind the Government of the day to their populace. Caliph Abu Bakr's reign, therefore, became the first fully-fledged democratic administration in Islamic history where the leader was not only elected by the people he was also fully accountable to them. Caliph Abu Bakr did not decide anything unilaterally. He formed an advisory council consisting of the leading companions of the Prophet and he regularly consulted them before authorising or undertaking any issues of importance. Immediately after assuming the office of the Caliphate, he instigated action against those tribes which had reverted back to their pre-Islamic practices in the belief that Islam would disintegrate following the death of the Prophet. Caliph Abu Bakr's uncompromising stance against political rebellion and social unrest helped put an end to all forms of political and social mischief in Arabia at the time.

After restoring peace and order across the land, Caliph Abu Bakr turned his attention to the external enemies of the Islamic State who were conspiring against the Muslims from the adjoining territories. In the year 633, he authorised Khalid ibn al-Walid, the great Muslim military commander, to take action against the subversive activities of the Persians. The Muslim army defeated the Persians and brought peace and order

to that area. In the following year, elements of the Byzantine army began to instigate military raids and other provocative actions against the Muslim territories. After consulting his advisory council, the Caliph took decisive action against the Byzantines. When Heraclius, the emperor of the Byzantine Empire, received news of the Muslim advance he sent a large army to crush the Muslims. Under Khalid's inspirational leadership, forty-five thousand Muslims inflicted a crushing defeat on the approximately one hundred and fifty thousand-strong Byzantine contingent.

This decisive and unprecedented victory, achieved at a critical phase in Muslim history, has today found its way into Muslim folklore. Of course, Caliph Abu Bakr's outstanding leadership played a pivotal role in this success. Indeed, he was an impressive leader who was both gentle and caring, but also tough and decisive when required. His unwavering commitment to Islam, political abilities and strategic brilliance enabled the Islamic State to become a strong and united entity, thus consolidating its position *vis-à-vis* the two leading powers of the time, namely the Persian and Holy Roman Empires. In just over two years, Caliph Abu Bakr helped transform the fortunes of Islam. More importantly, encouraged and supported by Umar, he brought together all the parchments (*suhuf*) on which the Qur'an was written during the Prophet's lifetime and compiled them in the form of one book (*mushaf*). He was therefore instrumental in preserving the Divine revelation in its original, pristine form for the benefit of posterity. Like the Prophet, Caliph Abu Bakr led his people by his example, and his main priority was the safety and welfare of the Muslim masses.

On a personal level, Abu Bakr led a very simple life; he ate most frugally and used to wake up in the middle of the night to cry before his Lord. Being very spiritually inclined, he had little time for the wealth and material possessions of this world. Once on seeing a bird in the garden, he remarked, "O bird! You are lucky indeed. You eat and drink as you like and fly, but do not have fear of reckoning on the Day of Judgement. I wish that I were just like you." Given Abu Bakr's mystical orientation, it is not surprising that a number of leading Sufi *tariqah* (or Islamic mystical Orders) such as the *naqsh-bandiyyah* trace their spiritual affiliation back to the Prophet through him. To Caliph Abu Bakr, the outstanding Muslim leader, great statesman and spiritual guide *par excellence*, the life of this world was no more than an illusion. It is here and will be gone soon. Only the love and pleasure of God, the Absolute Reality, mattered to him. This great servant of Islam breathed his last at the age of sixty-one and was buried in Madinah next to the Prophet, his mentor and guide. Such was the greatness of Caliph Abu Bakr that the Prophet once stated, 'Abu Bakr's name shall be called out from all the gates of Paradise, and he will be the first person of my community to enter it.'

# 5

## Uthman ibn Affan
### (b.576 - d.656)

BEFORE HIS DEATH, Caliph Umar appointed a six-man panel to nominate his successor. Just as the Prophet Muhammad did not nominate his sucessor, in the same way Umar decided not to nominate his own successor. Instead, he instructed the six-man panel (consisting of illustrious figures like Uthman, Ali, Sa'd ibn Abi Waqqas, Abd al-Rahman ibn Auf, Talha and Zubair), to select one person from among them as the next leader of the Islamic State. After careful consideration and intense discussion, it was eventually decided by the panel to appoint Uthman as the third Caliph of Islam. A son-in-law of the Prophet and a man of exceptional piety, Uthman was also one of the most generous and modest amongst the companions of the Prophet. He was loved and admired by everyone and is said to have personified angelic qualities. The Prophet had such respect and regard for Uthman that once, while he was sitting with a group of his companions, the robe covering the lower part of his leg fell. When he was told that Uthman was on his way, the Prophet quickly covered his leg saying, "Even the angels have regard for the modesty of Uthman."

Uthman ibn Affan ibn Abi al-As was born into the noble Umayyah family of the Quraysh tribe of Makkah. As a child, he had a privileged upbringing. Like his other family members, he became a hugely prosperous cloth merchant. In addition to being one of only a handful of literate people in Makkah, Uthman was known to have been very soft-hearted and a cultured person who was in the habit of helping the poor and the needy even in his pre-Islamic days. His charitable and philanthropic activities earned him considerable reputation and standing in Makkah at the time. Uthman was one of the first people to embrace Islam, after hearing Caliph Abu Bakr preach. Despite the intense political rivalry between the family of the Prophet (*banu hashim*) and that of Uthman (*banu umayyah*), he pledged allegiance to the Prophet. Unlike the rest of his tribesmen (who opposed the Prophet on the grounds that he was a Hashimate), Uthman overlooked the inter-tribal rivalry between the two tribes in order to acknowledge the truth of Islam as promulgated by the Prophet.

Uthman's decision to embrace Islam infuriated his tribesmen so much that they became hostile and antagonistic towards him. They accused him of treachery and hurled all sorts of verbal abuse and diatribes at him. When things eventually became unbearable, he approached the Prophet for his permission to seek refuge in Abyssinia (modern Ethiopia) along with a group of other persecuted Muslims. Uthman, therefore, became one of the first Muslim men to migrate to a foreign country with his family, for the sake of Islam. At the time, Uthman was married to the Prophet's daughter, Ruqayyah. After a few months' stay in Abyssinia, Uthman and his wife returned to Makkah where they stayed for another few years before joining the Prophet in Madinah, but his wife died soon after their return. The Prophet then married his third daughter, Umm Kulthum, to him. As a result, Uthman became known as *dhun-nurain* (or the 'man with two lights'). He also acted as a scribe to the Prophet from time to time, and generously spent his money and wealth for the cause of Islam. For instance, on his arrival in Madinah he purchased a large well for twenty thousand dirhams, so all Muslims could have free access to water. He then purchased a plot of land adjacent to the Prophet's mosque so that the mosque could be enlarged to accommodate more people for daily congregational prayers (*salah*). Uthman's generosity knew no bounds. Although there were other wealthy people around at the time, no one else was able to match Uthman when it came to spending for the cause of Islam.

During the Prophet's lifetime, Uthman actively helped and supported him in every possible way. After the Prophet's death, he rallied behind Caliph Abu Bakr and his successor, Caliph Umar, and acted in his capacity as a counsel and aide to both of them. Uthman became renowned for his invaluable services to Islam and was held in high estimation by all Muslims. Uthman's all-round services to Islam did not end there. His unique personal qualities and tremendous contribution to the cause of Islam were also widely recognised by the companions of the Prophet. That is why an ailing Caliph Umar included him in his distinguished six-man panel to nominate his successor. When the panel's decision went in favour of Uthman, he became the third Caliph in 644. Unlike Caliphs Abu Bakr and Ali, Uthman was very fortunate to have become Caliph at a time when the Islamic dominion was politically strong

and economically prosperous. Under Caliph Umar's outstanding leadership, the Islamic State became a great political, economic and military power of its time. The decision to nominate him as Umar's successor ensured that continuity, and another smooth transition of leadership, was achieved.

Immediately after becoming Caliph, Uthman strengthened the administrative base of the vast Islamic dominion. During Umar's Caliphate, the region comprising Syria, Palestine and Jordan was regarded as three separate provinces, but Caliph Uthman combined them to create one strong and united province, and confirmed Muawiyah ibn Abi Sufyan as governor of that large region. Likewise, Caliph Uthman abolished the two-tier administration developed by Caliph Umar in Egypt, and replaced it with one governor who was responsible for the governance of that strategically important province. Uthman took similar steps to improve and modernise the civil and administrative systems established by Caliph Umar in parts of Iraq and Iran. The administrative reforms carried out by Caliph Uthman sought to simplify and strengthen accountability, and remove unnecessary bureaucratic red tape. The measures taken by the Caliph helped clarify the roles and responsibilities of the provincial governors *vis-à-vis* the central Government. Such reforms would help to strengthen and consolidate Islamic rule as the Caliph's empire began to expand.

While Caliph Uthman was busy reforming the political structure of the expanding Islamic State, the Muslim army continued its march, both in the East and the West, and conquered many new territories. In addition to gaining control of Cyprus, the Muslim army raided parts of Persia and Armenia. With every success came more and more responsibility for Caliph Uthman. While the Caliph was busy contemplating the future direction of the rapidly expanding Islamic State, the news that the Byzantine Emperor Constantine had sent a fleet of five hundred ships to invade Alexandria reached him. In response, he dispatched a Muslim fleet to meet the advancing

Byzantines. One of Islamic history's first major naval battles thus took place in 651. The Muslims successfully fought back the Byzantines, who fled to the island of Sicily. The Caliph's political and military strategies worked exactly according to plan. However, Caliph Uthman's greatest single contribution to Islam was his codification and standardisation of the Qur'an, based on the original copy (mushaf) prepared during the reign of Caliph Abu Bakr al-Siddiq. Thus, the copy of the Qur'an we have today is same as that original Uthmanic text. In fact, according to some scholars, two copies of the original Uthmanic texts are still extant to this day. One copy is kept in the Topkapi Museum in Turkey, while the other is preserved in Tashkent in Uzbekistan.

There is no doubt that the first half of Uthman's Caliphate was immensely successful. This was partly because Caliph Umar had bequeathed to him a politically united and economically prosperous Islamic State, which Uthman strengthened further. But during the second half of his rule, the tide of history began to turn against him. As the Islamic dominion expanded rapidly, internal schism and social disorder started to rear their ugly heads in a number of provinces. A group of insurgents, led by Abdullah ibn Saba (a Yemenite Jewish convert to Islam), began to sow the seeds of political dissension and social disharmony among the Muslims by infiltrating Islamic groups. Ibn Saba and his followers initially targeted Kufah, Basrah, Syria and Egypt and turned those provinces into prominent centres of political insurgency. Under the pretense of being a pious Muslim, Ibn Saba enlisted the help of notable Muslim personalities, incited the locals to register complaints and also forged evidence against a number of prominent governors, accusing them of various alleged crimes, abuses, injustices and plundering of State resources. As a result, Ibn Saba and his co-conspirators managed to remove a number of leading provincial governors, such as Abu Musa al-Ash'ari and Walid ibn Uqbah from their posts. Since he and his followers' ultimate objective was to undo the vast Islamic State from within, targeting provincial

Muslim leaders (especially those who opposed their insurgency activities) became one of their favourite political strategies.

On one occasion, they accused Walid ibn Uqbah, the governor of Kufah, of drinking liquor and they forced witnesses to testify against him. This prompted Caliph Uthman to recall Walid to Madinah and punish him for his alleged misdemeanour. As soon as the Caliph carried out what Ibn Saba and his supporters demanded, they turned round and accused the Caliph of punishing innocent Muslims. In reality, Walid did not drink liquor and he was innocent of all the charges levelled against him. Likewise, when Abu Musa al-Ash'ari was replaced by Abdullah ibn Amir as governor of Basrah, Ibn Saba and his cohorts began to spread rumours that the Caliph had recalled Abu Musa and replaced him with Abdullah as governor because the latter was related to the Caliph. Seeking to pacify the hypocrites (munafiqun) was like fighting a losing battle. Indeed, they were bent on wreaking havoc within the Islamic State, but Caliph Uthman failed to understand the gravity of the situation and thus continued his dangerous policy of appeasement, which only served to encourage the enemies of the Islamic State. Being a gentle-natured and compassionate man, he devoted all his time, wealth and energy to the cause of Islam. But, unlike Caliph Umar, he was neither firm nor decisive in his dealings with the mischief-makers, who were bent on creating socio-political disorder within the Islamic State. Since Caliph Uthman had no intention of shedding Muslim blood, he hoped to win over the troublemakers through love and compassion. Although one cannot fail to admire his good intentions and sublime qualities, in the circumstances the strategy he pursued against a determined enemy, bent on destroying the Islamic State from within, was a wrong one.

As it transpired, the enemies of Islam took advantage of the Caliph's 'softly-softly' approach and intensified their designs against the Islamic State. It was not long before they began to falsify and fabricate evidence against the Caliph himself. Though he cogently refuted all their allegations publicly, his detractors were not satisfied with his explanations. As tension between the Caliph and the insurgents mounted, some of the leading companions of the Prophet urged Uthman to take action against the insurgents; but he refused to do so, saying he would rather die than shed Muslim blood. Caliph Uthman was a man of principles, and he decided to stick to his principles come what might. The insurgents were not willing to relent either. As it happens, they were not interested in peace at all; their foremost objective was to oust the Caliph from power. Thus one of the first major crises in Islamic history was now looming on the horizon. Ibn Saba, the ringleader of the hypocrites, eventually descended upon Madinah and openly laid siege to the frail Caliph's residence. They demanded that Uthman resign forthwith, otherwise they would kill him. Uthman replied, "I do not fear death,

but I do not want to shed Muslim blood." Again, a number of eminent companions of the Prophet urged him to take action against the insurgents. Yet again, he made it clear that he had no desire to shed Muslim blood. The insurgents then invaded his house and brutally murdered him while he was busy reciting the Qur'an. He was eighty years old.

Caliph Uthman's death was a watershed in Islamic history. His assassination sent an almighty shiver down the Islamic spine, signalling the end of Islam's political unity. The Muslim world became divided, never to unify again. Caliph Uthman chose to lay down his own life rather than spill Muslim blood. That is what he will be remembered for; he lived by his principles and he died for his faith. Refering to him, the Prophet Muhammad once said: 'Every Prophet has a friend and my friend is Uthman.'

# 6

## Aishah bint Abi Bakr
### (b.ca.610 - d.677)

WOMEN HAVE PLAYED a critical role in Islamic history. Some became famous for their courage and learning, while others contributed immensely to the development of Islam as a faith, culture and civilisation. Islamic history is replete with heroic deeds performed by Muslim women. In addition to being wives, mothers and sisters, they distinguished themselves as advisors to caliphs, sultans and military leaders, as well as teachers of some of the most renowned and acclaimed thinkers of the Muslim world. Of all the illustrious Muslim women who had played an instrumental role in the emergence and development of Islam as a religion, culture and civilisation, one stands out over all others. That outstanding woman was Aishah bint Abu Bakr. She was a truly gifted lady who, by the strength of her multi-dimensional personality, prodigious learning and unusual intellectual ability carved out a unique position for herself in the annals of Islam. Aishah was an all-rounder, and her achievements were so varied and startling that no other woman in Islamic history can be compared to her. She is, therefore, the most influential single Muslim woman in history.

Aishah bint Abi Bakr ibn Abi Quhafah was born into the Banu Taym clan of the Quraysh tribe of Makkah. Her father, Abu Bakr al-Siddiq, and her mother, Umm Ruman, became Muslims very early on. After Muhammad announced his Prophethood in 610, Abu Bakr was one of the first people to embrace Islam and, as such, Aishah grew up in a Muslim family. Even as a youngster, she became known for her remarkable ability to learn poetry and narrate genealogical information about her ancestors. She was so intelligent that one day while the Prophet was passing by Abu Bakr's house, he saw her playing with her dolls and a winged horse. When the Prophet asked her what it was that she was playing with, she replied that it was her favourite winged horse. When the Prophet told her that horses did not have wings, she responded saying that Prophet Solomon's horses had wings. Aishah's quick thinking, sharp intellect and apt reply brought a bright smile to the Prophet's face.

Furthermore, Aishah became well known for her sublime personal qualities and attributes even when she was in her early teens. She not only possessed a photographic memory; she was also a gentle and cultured lady. Her memory power was such that she could even recollect some of the most remote incidents which happened during her early years. For instance, she related that verse 46 of chapter 55 (*Surat al-Qamar*) of the Qur'an was revealed to the Prophet while she was playing with her toys. And, if the popular saying that all marriages are made in heaven is true, then one cannot blame Aishah for being proud of the fact that her marriage was literally decreed by God. According to a *hadith* (Prophetic tradition) recorded in the Mustadrak of al-Hakim, on one occasion the Prophet saw a vision in which an angel brought him a present wrapped up in silk. When he asked the angel what it was, he was informed that it was his wife. After opening the wrapping, the Prophet discovered that it was none other than Aishah.

Aishah was married to the Prophet when she was very young, although at the time she had matured both intellectually and physically way beyond her age. Later, she related that her marriage dowry (*mahr*) was around five hundred dirhams. Her marriage to the Prophet had profound socio-cultural ramifications within the Makkan society of the time. It directly led to the abolition of a number of Arab customs and taboos. For instance, according to the custom of the day, the Arabs refused to marry their daughters to those they considered to be their brothers for cultural reasons, even though they were not biological brothers. Since Abu Bakr used to call the Prophet a brother, this marriage clarified that a brother in faith was not same as a real blood-brother. The Arabs also considered the month of Shawwal (the tenth month of the Islamic calendar) to be an inappropriate time for the bride to move into her husband's house. Aishah's marriage to the Prophet also consigned this taboo to the dustbin of history. After her marriage, Aishah became the youngest wife of the Prophet; she was also much wiser than, and intellectually far superior to, the others. She was the only wife of the Prophet who was a maiden. Being literate and having also learned Arab history and genealogy from her father, she became a highly respected authority on those subjects. In short, she was the jewel in the Prophet's crown. Though the Prophet always treated his wives fairly and equitably, he could not hide his affection for Aishah because it was

a natural feeling. God, he said, has implanted such love and affection within all human beings and we all experience such feelings, and do so without being aware of them.

When Aishah went to live with the Prophet in the small apartment attached to his mosque in Madinah, she was perhaps around thirteen years old. However, according to another account, she was married to the Prophet when she was around sixteen and went to live with him at the age of nineteen. Either way, the Prophet's apartment was far from being a bed of roses. The Prophet led a very simple, scrupulously clean and spiritually enriched life without any trace of luxury, wealth or pomp. The roof of his tiny apartment frequently leaked rainwater, the walls were made of clay and the apartment only had one door, which was kept open most of the time with a blanket hung as a curtain. He had no possessions other than a straw mat, a thin mattress, a pillow made of dry tree barks and leaves, a leather water container, a small plate and a cup for drinking water. These were all the 'luxuries' Aishah found in the Prophet's apartment when she moved in. Even though the Prophet was the most powerful man in Madinah at the time and he could have chosen to live in an impressive mansion if he wished, he deliberately chose to live a very simple and Godly life.

The Prophet not only occupied himself in prayers and meditation, but also reminded his wives, children and followers not to become lured by the wealth, glitter and riches of this world. He often prayed to God to allow him to die in poverty and be resurrected in the company of the poor and needy. He therefore disliked all forms of pomp, pride and power associated with ostentatious display of wealth and profligate living. He made it very clear to all his family members (*ahl al-bayt*) and companions (*sahabah*) that this life was transient and that it would be foolish to become too preoccupied with the lures and attractions of this world. Aishah understood this better than anyone else, and was only too happy to live with the Prophet in his simple but clean apartment. She was not only an exceptionally intelligent and gifted lady; she was also very tender-hearted and frequently broke into tears. Once a poor woman appeared at her door with her two young children and asked for something to eat. Aishah only had three dates in the house, which she handed over to the lady to feed her children. The woman gave one date to each of her daughters and started to chew one herself. Meanwhile, one of her daughter had quickly eaten her share and began to stare at her mother. The mother immediately stopped chewing the date and broke it into two halves and gave them to her daughters. Moved by the mother's love and affection for her daughters, Aishah burst into tears.

If students are to be judged by the quality of their teachers, then Aishah could have claimed to be the best of all students because she was taught by the best of all teachers. Since the Prophet used to visit Abu Bakr frequently, Aishah knew the Prophet very well even before their marriage. During the subsequent decade or so that she spent with the Prophet until his death in 632, she became intimately acquainted with all aspects of his life, conduct and behaviour. No other person claimed to know the Prophet as well as Aishah. Her prodigious intellect and retentive memory enabled her to assimilate Islamic teachings with ease, becoming one of the most famous repositories of Islamic knowledge and wisdom, especially about the life and teachings of the Prophet. Aishah's enquiring mind and willingness to learn and disseminate knowledge endeared her to the Prophet. Indeed, whenever the Prophet prepared to deliver a sermon in the mosque, Aishah always made it a duty on herself to listen to him attentively and, if she was unsure about any issues, she never hesitated to ask for clarification. For instance, on one ocassion, the Prophet remarked, "Whosoever was subjected to accounting in the next life, punishment was his lot." If that was the case, reasoned Aishah, how is one to explain this Qur'anic verse, "Whoever is given his record in his right hand will have an easy reckoning."? (Holy Qur'an: *Surat al-Inshiqaq*, verses 7-8) The Prophet explained that this verse referred to individual accountability. That is to say, according to this verse, each individual will be presented with their own records in the hereafter and that should they be subjected to cross-examination and found wanting, then they would be in trouble. Thanks to Aishah, today we have a clear understanding of numerous Divine injunctions; in fact, some Qur'anic verses, including those relating to the performance of *tayammum* (dry ablution), were revealed directly because of her. The Prophet himself recognised Aishah's superiority over his other wives when he said: 'Among men there were many perfect persons but none among women except two: Mariam, daughter of Imran and Asiya, wife of Pharoah. And Aishah has superiority over other women as *tharid* (a dish) has over other dishes.'

As it happens, Aishah's contribution to the development of Islamic jurisprudence (*fiqh*), Qur'anic scholarship (*tafsir*) and exposition of Prophetic traditions (*hadith*) – especially in relation to the Prophet's personal and private life – was nothing short of unique and unprecedented. By virtue of her vast knowledge and understanding of the Qur'an and the teachings of the Prophet, she was able to clarify a host of conflicting views held by some companions of the Prophet about certain Islamic teachings and commandments. She was an equally unrivalled practitioner of analogical deduction (*qiyas*) in matters of Islamic jurisprudence. Her mastery of Islamic thought and its sources was so impressive that the companions of the Prophet considered her to be an eminent authority on Qur'anic exegesis, *hadith* and jurisprudence. In the words of Abu Musa al-Ash'ari, a prominent companion of the Prophet and an eminent jurist himself, 'We companions (of the Prophet) were never presented with a problem to which Aishah did not present a satisfactory solution.' (Sunan al-Tirmidhi) That is why Caliphs Abu Bakr al-Siddiq, Umar ibn al-Khattab and Uthman ibn Affan, who were three of the most prominent companions of the Prophet and outstanding jurists in their own right, regularly consulted her before deciding on complex and intractable legal issues during their reigns.

Aishah used to teach both male and female students. She was known to have been a very generous and approachable teacher. According to Urwa ibn Zubair, a distinguished student of Aishah, her knowledge and breadth of learning was not restricted to the religious sciences only; she was deeply proficient in Arab history, literature, rhetoric, poetry and genealogy, and was familiar with aspects of traditional medicine. She memorised and related more than two thousand *ahadith* of the Prophet, and was brave enough to lead an army into the battlefield and wage war. Aishah taught and mentored a number of great luminaries of Islam including Urwa ibn Zubair, Masruq and Amrah bint Abd al-Rahman. More importantly, she was a perfect wife to her husband and one of his greatest supporters. After the Prophet's death, she continued to champion the message her husband had promulgated and in so doing she contributed immensely to the development of Islamic thought and culture for the benefit of posterity. Aishah was a truly remarkable woman and a profoundly influential intellectual whose name and fame will no doubt continue to spread with the passage of time. Although born and brought up in a fiercely patriarchal society, she reached the highest summit of Islamic learning and scholarship by the sheer force of her powerful personality and incredible intellect. She was aware of her unique God-given qualities and attributes. On one occasion she said, 'I am not taking pride but I am mentioning it as a fact that God bestowed upon me nine things that He did not confer on anyone else in the world. Angels presented my figure before the Prophet in a dream; there was no other maiden amongst the wives of the Prophet; the Qur'an was revealed even when he occupied my bed; I was his favourite; some Qur'anic verses descended in relation to me; I saw Gabriel with my own eyes, and the Prophet died in my lap.' (*Mustadrak* of al-Hakim and *Kitab al-Tabaqat al-Kubra* of Ibn Sa'd).

Known reverentially as *ummul mu'minin* (the 'mother of the believers'), Aishah passed away at the age of sixty-seven. She was laid to rest in Madinah after Abu Hurairah, who was acting as governor of the city at the time, conducted her funeral prayers.

# 7

## Khadijah bint Khuwailid
## (b.555 - d.619)

AS A SYMBOL of honesty, faithfulness, integrity and unflinching steadfastness, Khadijah has no equals in Islamic history. Her devotion, dedication and wholehearted support for the Islamic cause proved invaluable to the Prophet from day one. Indeed, Khadijah's unshakeable faith in her husband and her commitment to the Divine message was such that it has earned her a pre-eminent position in the annals of Islam. Her remarkable contribution to the cause of Islam was acknowledged by the Prophet himself. That is why she came to symbolise the higher qualities and attributes which Muslim women aspired to acquire and personify although only a few, if any at all, managed to come anywhere near her in this respect. Khadijah was a truly inspirational figure, an outstanding role model for all Muslim women who has left her indelible mark in the history of Islam.

Khadijah bint Khuwailid ibn Asad was born and brought up in Makkah. Her father Khuwailid ibn Asad was an immensely wealthy merchant and an eminent leader of the Qurayshi tribe of Makkah. Surrounded by much wealth and luxury, Khadijah had a privileged upbringing. After the death of her father, she inherited the family business and became one of the wealthiest women in Makkah. After the untimely death of her first husband, Abu Halah ibn al-Nabbash (by whom she had two children), Khadijah married Atiq ibn Abid and they had one child. However, there is some disagreement among historians on this issue; some say Atiq was her first husband, while others say Abu Halah was her first husband. Either way, her second marriage, too, did not last long; it was terminated on the grounds of incompatibility. Khadijah then focused her full attention to raising her children and pursuing her business. Although Khadijah was a devoted mother to her children, she was not prepared to live on the wealth she had inherited from her father. She, therefore, developed a shrewd business strategy in order to expand her commercial stakes in and around Makkah. Being very intelligent, honest and upright, she soon became one of the most successful businesswomen of pre-Islamic Makkah, if not, Arabia.

In a patriarchal society, where women were treated like chattels, normally a widow like Khadijah would have found it impossible to establish herself in society, but Khadijah was an unusually gifted lady who defied the socio-cultural taboos of her society by becoming very successful. She traded in all types of goods and merchandise, and in so doing established a thriving import and export business. She recruited her own business managers, who regularly took her merchandise beyond the borders of Arabia and traded in neighbouring countries such as Syria. Her business expanded rapidly because she recruited some of the most honest, fair and trustworthy people to work for her and she also rewarded them handsomely. In a society where employees had no rights and were often treated harshly by their employers, Khadijah became renowned for treating her staff well and paying them on time. Her generosity was such that she often divided the profits in half, giving one half to her managers while retaining the other portion for herself. In a blatantly unfair and unjust pre-Islamic Arabia, Khadijah's profit-sharing arrangement was too good an offer to be refused by any man who wished to earn a good living in those days.

Khadijah's willingness to reward her staff handsomely meant she could pick and choose the most able candidates to undertake her business expeditions. Since she was an honest and trustworthy lady, she employed people who possessed similar qualities and attributes. When she was informed about the sublime qualities and attributes of the twenty-five year old Muhammad, the son of Abdullah, she went out of her way to recruit him into her expanding business. The offer of a rewarding job came at the right time for young Muhammad because Abu Talib, his uncle and guardian, was experiencing considerable financial difficulties at the time. Unbeknown to both Muhammad and Khadijah, this was to mark the beginning of a relationship which was destined to last a quarter of a century, and go down in the annals of Islam as a great partnership. Being scrupulously honest, morally upright, unusually intelligent and extremely trustworthy, young Muhammad was invited to assume responsibility for Khadijah's business affairs. Whenever Muhammad went out on a business expedition, he came back with more profits than Khadijah anticipated, thus proving his commercial acumen. Indeed, he was in a league of his own

among Khadijah's employees. As an intelligent lady, Khadijah always asked one of her aides to accompany Muhammad whenever he went on a business trip and assist him in his endeavours. Maisarah was one such aide who used to go on these business ventures with Muhammad, and on his return he regularly briefed Khadijah about the unique and unassailable qualities of her new business manager.

Impressed by Maisarah's tales about Muhammad's unique qualities and attributes, one day Khadijah went to consult her cousin Waraqa ibn Nawfal, a blind man who was well versed in ancient scriptures, about a dream where she saw the sun descending into her courtyard. Waraqa told Khadijah that Muhammad was special. On hearing this, she seriously thought about proposing marriage to him. However, since Khadijah was a very dignified lady, she could not persuade herself to propose directly to Muhammad. Instead, she approached her friend Nafisa who, in turn, spoke to Muhammad on her behalf. When Nafisa took the proposal to Muhammad he accepted the offer after consulting his uncle Abu Talib. By now Muhammad knew Khadijah well; she was an honest, truthful, generous and faithful lady who conducted her affairs in an impeccable manner. Everyone in Makkah respected her for the dignified way she lived her life. One could not find a better woman in all Arabia at the time. Lack of finance aside, there was no other reason for Muhammad to refuse the offer. At the time of their marriage, Muhammad was twenty-five while Khadijah was forty. Notwithstanding the fifteen year age gap, Muhammad and Khadijah were meant for each other. It proved to be an immensely blissful marriage and they were blessed with six beautiful children, fours girls and two boys. The sons died in their infancy, but the daughters survived and they became very loyal and loving children. Theirs was a peaceful and blessed family.

Although Khadijah was a very wealthy lady, she was not materialistic like most of the people in her society. Whenever Muhammad chose to seclude himself on the Mount of Light (*jabal* al-nur), situated on the outskirts of Makkah, for meditation and spiritual renewal, she would pack enough food and drink for him to last the whole period. One night, while Muhammad was meditating on the Mount of Light, he was visited by archangel *jibrail* (Gabriel) and the first verses of the Qur'an were revealed to him. Angel *jibrail* confirmed that he was God's last Prophet to mankind and that his mission in life was to propagate Islam, a religion and way of life chosen for all humanity by the Creator of the universe. After this terrifying encounter, the Prophet rushed home to Khadijah, completely shaken by the whole experience. He asked her to wrap him up with blankets. When the Prophet eventually regained his composure and related the whole experience to Khadijah, she did not doubt him at all. Khadijah's unshakeable faith in her husband reassured the Prophet. She not only became the first person to embrace Islam, she also threw all her weight behind her husband and his new mission. From that day on, Khadijah became Muhammad's greatest supporter and Islam's foremost benefactor, at a time when the Prophet had no one to turn to for help; but Khadijah stood by him like a pillar and encouraged him to carry out his Divine mission.

Khadijah was fifty-four when her husband became a Prophet and for the next ten years of her life she freely spent all her wealth, and devoted all her time and energy, for the cause of Islam. After the Prophet was commanded by God to proclaim Islam publicly, he became an open target for the Makkan elites who insulted, ridiculed and abused him but Khadijah encouraged, consoled and helped him at every step of the way. Indeed, the first ten years of the Prophet's mission were fraught with tremendous hardship, distress and suffering for his family and small band of followers, as his adversaries tried all the tricks in the book to dissuade him from propagating Islam. When this did not work, they offered him wealth and agreed to make him their ruler but he rejected all such offers. When every attempt to seduce the Prophet failed, the Makkan elite relentlessly pursued and persecuted him and his

followers, inflicting untold misery and hardship on them. It was a difficult and traumatic period for all the Muslims, especially the Prophet and his family.

At such a challenging time in Islamic history, Khadijah's unflinching help and support for her husband proved critical. Thanks to her reputation and standing in Makkah, coupled with her considerable wealth and commercial pulling-power, the Makkan oligarchy did not dare to compromise the personal safety and security of the Prophet. However, as more and more people continued to embrace Islam, in utter desperation the Prophet's opponents imposed a total boycott on *banu hashim*, the Prophet's tribe. This took place in the seventh year of his Prophethood. It was a particularly hard time for all Muslims, especially the sixty-one year old Khadijah. Having lived all her life surrounded by much wealth and luxury, now for the first time she was forced to endure hardship and starvation for the sake of her faith. Yet she came out of this ordeal stronger in her faith and the support for her husband never wavered for a moment. The Prophet himself acknowledged the pivotal role played by Khadijah in those early days of Islam when he said, '...She [Khadijah] had faith in me when everyone, even members of my own family and tribe did not believe me, and accepted that I was truly a Prophet and a Messenger of God. She converted to Islam, spent all her wealth and worldly goods to help me spread this faith, and this too at a time when the entire world seemed to have turned against me and persecuted me. And it is through her that God blessed me with children.'

After the Prophet, it is difficult to find another person who had more devotion, dedication, commitment and love for Islam than Khadijah. She was a symbol of hope in the face of adversity; a paragon of virtue and steadfastness, and an inspirational personality who continues to influence Muslims (especially Muslim women) to this day. Khadijah, the 'mother of the believers' (*ummul mu'minin*), passed away during the tenth year of Muhammad's Prophethood and was buried in Hajun, located on the outskirts of Makkah; she was sixty five at the time of her death. So great was her estimation in the sight of God that, according to Abu Hurairah: 'Jibrail (Gabriel) came to the Prophet and said, "O God's Messenger! This is Khadijah coming to you with a dish having some food (or drink). When she reaches you, greet her on behalf of her Lord (God) and on my behalf, and give her the glad tidings of having a palace made of Qasab in paradise, wherein there will be neither any noise, or toil.' (Sahih al-Bukhari)

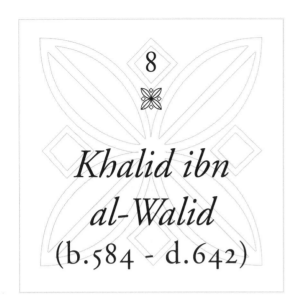

# 8

## Khalid ibn al-Walid
### (b.584 - d.642)

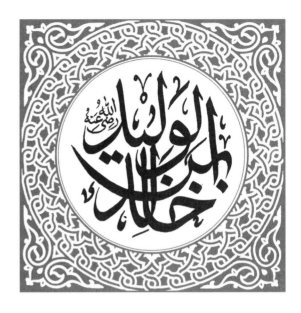

ALEXANDER WAS A great military commander; Genghis Khan was an immensely successful warrior, and Napoleon was a gifted strategist. However, only one military general possessed all of these qualities in the history of warfare. That was Khalid ibn al-Walid, 'the thunder from Arabia'. He was an incomparable military genius who single-handedly humbled two of the greatest empires of his time. A man of few words, Khalid allowed his unsurpassed achievements in the battlefield speak for themselves. As he burst out of Arabia, his name spread like a wildfire and Khalid's opponents feared no other man more than him. The son of al-Walid was a natural-born talent, a military genius who read his adversaries' weaknesses like the writing on the wall, and was able to inspire his men to victory even from the jaws of defeat. Khalid's astounding feats and unprecedented successes on the battlefield have found their way into Muslim folklore. Even today, children throughout the Muslim world grow up listening to his heroic feats.

Khalid ibn al-Walid ibn al-Mughirah was born into the respected Qurayshi tribe of Makkah. He was around twenty-four when Muhammad received his first revelation. Khalid's father, Walid ibn al-Mughirah, was a highly respected individual who was considered to be one of the wisest and most clever men of his generation. Like the father, the son grew up to be a highly accomplished young man. Imbued with natural talent and physical vitality, Khalid acquired a keen interest in the art of warfare from a young age. He became proficient in war strategies, tactics and planning even when he was in his teens. By the age of twenty, he acquired considerable reputation among his people for his expertise in archery, lancing and horse riding skills. In other words, he was a very quick, physically strong and agile young man. After the Prophet migrated (*hijrah*) from Makkah to Madinah in 622, his Makkan foes became alarmed when they heard that he and his followers had not only won over the people of Madinah to the new faith (*Islam*); but that they had also managed to unify the people of Madinah on the basis of equality, fraternity and brotherhood of man as envisaged by Islam. The Prophet's success frightened the Makkans more than anything else, so they resolved to take direct action against the nascent Muslim community. When a large Makkan army set out to obliterate the Muslims, the Prophet and his followers met the advancing Makkan army at Badr and inflicted a crushing defeat on them. This resounding victory was later dramatically reversed when the Makkans, determined to avenge their previous defeat, launched a fresh attack against the Muslims in 625. Thanks largely to the ingenious Khalid, the Muslims suffered heavy causulties in this battle. The forty-one year old Khalid's last-minute intervention totally reversed the outcome of the battle in favour of the Makkans. For the first time in his life, Khalid made a crucial intervention in a battle, and changed its oucome in favour of the Makkan army. This was to mark the beginning of an astonishing military career unparalleled in the history of warfare.

In 630, during the eighth year of the Prophet's migration to Madinah, the forty-six year old Khalid received a letter from his brother Al-Walid ibn Walid, who had already embraced Islam. The letter read: 'In the name of God, the Beneficent, the Merciful. I have not seen anything more surprising than you keeping away from Islam although you are a man of wisdom. No one (of your calibre) should remain ignorant of Islam. The Messenger of God also asked me: 'Where is Khalid?' He remarked, 'How is a man like Khalid ignorant of Islam? It would be good for him if he devoted his capabilities for the cause of the Muslims. We would have preferred him to the others.' My brother! Compensate now (for the mistake) that has been committed in the battles (against Islam).'

This letter shook Khalid to his core and suddenly the ray of Islam began to shine all over his being. Along with Amr ibn al-As, another brilliant Muslim general, Khalid left Makkah for Madinah and presented himself before the Prophet. 'O Messenger of God!' cried Khalid, 'I remember all the scenes of fighting with you, and my animosity with the Truth. Please pray to God to forgive me.' 'Islam wipes out all the wrongs that are committed before embracing it.' retorted the Prophet. On another occasion, the Prophet remarked, 'The better ones of you in the Days of Ignorance are the better ones of you in Islam when they understand (the faith).' The Prophet's words summed up Khalid's qualities as a new

Muslim; prior to his acceptance of Islam, he was a persistent thorn in the side of the Prophet and his companions but, after embracing Islam, he became an almighty hammer which helped crush Islam's opponents. The very mention of his name was enough to send shivers down his enemy's spine.

Given Khalid's abilities as a soldier and military tactician, the Prophet asked him to accompany the Muslim army and face the subversive Byzantines who had camped along the northern borders of Arabia. Led by three distinguished Muslim commanders, Khalid was only too happy to accompany the army onto the battlefield as an ordinary soldier. As it happens, only three thousand Muslims fought more than fifty thousand well-equipped and highly-trained Byzantine soldiers. In the ensuing battle, all three Muslim commanders fell one after another. As the tide of the battle began to turn against the Muslims, the indomitable Khalid assumed leadership of the Muslim army and saved the day. Hitherto the Muslims were fighting a losing battle but now, in the middle of the raging conflict, Khalid managed to re-vitalise the Muslim fortunes by launching a rear attack, which gave impression to the Byzantines that fresh reinforcements had arrived for the Muslims. In reality, Khalid had merely withdrawn some of his forces from the battlefield and instructed them to attack from the rear to divert the enemy's attention. This stroke of genius by Khalid enabled the Muslim army to create a buffer zone between them and their enemies. The Prophet received the news of the death of the three Muslim commanders by Divine inspiration (*wahy*) and remarked, 'Then a sword of God took hold of the banner and saved the day.' This was a reference to Khalid's heroic feat on the battlefield. From that day on, Khalid became known as *saifullah* or the 'Sword of God'.

After the death of the Prophet in 632, numerous dissident groups led by a number of opportunists and imposters (like Musailimah, Tulaiha and Sajah) emerged to create mischief across Arabia. Caliph Abu Bakr, the Prophet's successor, was determined to teach these miscreants a lesson or two. Khalid played a pivotal role in putting an end to all such subversive activities in the Arabian Peninsula, and in so doing he became a saviour of Islam in one of Islamic history's most critical periods. With great foresight and profound understanding of Khalid's unusual military abilities, Caliph Abu Bakr sent him to face the battle-hardened Persian army in 633. The Persians saw the rise of Islam in neighbouring Arabia as a threat to their interests and they began to instigate subversive activities against the new Islamic State. Not willing to tolerate Persian interference in the affairs of the Muslims, Caliph Abu Bakr summoned Khalid and told him to go and teach the Persians a good lesson in warfare. He marched out of Arabia and came in direct contact with the Persian army. He then wrote a letter to Hurmuz, the famous Persian military general, in which he spelled out his objective:

'Our aim is not to fight you. Accept Islam, the peaceful way, and you will be safe. If not then clear our way to the people so that we may explain this beautiful way of life to them...if you do not accept any of these conditions then the only alternative is the use of the sword. Before deciding on the third alternative you should keep in mind that I am bringing against you a people who love death more than you love your life.'

Hurmuz dismissed Khalid's letter and challenged him to fight one-to-one. Khalid accepted the challenge and put the most famous Persian general to the sword before he could even make a move. His frightening speed and awesome display of military skills left everyone spell-bound. A fierce battle then ensued. A poorly equipped and irregular Muslim army, led by a truly incomparable military genius, inflicted a crushing defeat on one of the greatest empires in history. Not surprisingly, the historians consider Khalid's victory over the Persians to be one of his greatest achievements. In total, Khalid fought fifteen battles against the Persians and on each and every occasion he brought them to their knees. The Persians feared Khalid more than anyone else.

After subduing the Persians, Khalid turned his attention to the infiltrative activities of the Byzantine army. They, too, feared the growing power of the Islamic State and indirectly encouraged the neighbouring states to rise up against the Muslims. Caliph Abu Bakr resolved to deal with the looming danger presented by the Byzantines. He created four different battalions, each led by a separate commander. Under the command of Abu Ubaida ibn al-Jarrah, Amr ibn al-As, Yazid ibn Abi Sufyan and Shurahbil ibn Hasanah, the four battalions set out in different directions to face the Byzantines. Since the Byzantines had dispatched a very large army to crush the Muslims, the Caliph ordered Khalid to leave his Persian garrison and join the army he had sent to face the Byzantines. In July 634, Khalid met up with the Muslim army at Ajnadayn. He held a council of all the Muslim commanders and suggested that one of them should take overall command of the army. The Muslim army consisted of forty-five thousand men, while the Byzantine army consisted of around one hundred and fifty thousand troops. The decisive battle of Yarmuk was now looming in the horizon.

Like the Persians, the Byzantines were also fascinated by the genius of Khalid; they were very keen to see the man Muslims fondly referred to as the 'Sword of God'. After due deliberation, the Muslim army (under the central command of Khalid) met the well-equipped, professionally-trained and highly-motivated soldiers of the Byzantine Empire and a fierce battle then ensued. During the battle, Khalid received a letter from Madinah informing him of the death of Caliph Abu Bakr. The letter, signed by Caliph Umar, instructed Khalid to hand over the central command of the Muslim army to Abu Ubaida ibn al-Jarrah. Khalid decided not to disclose the contents of the letter while the battle was raging, in order to avoid creating confusion among the Muslims. This was a very clever move by Khalid as it ensured the Muslim army did not lose heart at the news of the Caliph's death. Under Khalid's able leadership, forty-five thousand Muslims crushed the mighty Byzantine forces. After the battle, Khalid informed the Muslim army of the death of Caliph Abu Bakr and willingly placed himself under the command of Abu Ubaida ibn al-Jarrah as per Caliph Umar's instruction.

To Khalid, the great military genius, it did not matter who was in charge. What mattered to him, more than anything else, was that Islam gain victory over its adversaries. He lived a very simple, pious and austere life dedicated to the service of Islam and the Muslims. Refering to Khalid, Caliph Abu Bakr once remarked, 'O Quraysh! Verily your lion, the lion of Islam, had leapt upon the lion of Persia, and spoiled him of his prey. Women shall not bear a second Khalid.' As a military general, Khalid thrived in the lion's den. In the history of warfare, no other military general had achieved as much as Khalid did, in such a short period of time. Although Khalid became a Muslim only a few years before the conquest of Makkah in 630, he became one of the greatest champions of Islam immediately upon embracing the new faith. His firm commitment, selfless dedication and great sacrifices for the sake of Islam made him a symbol of pride and joy for all Muslims. Considered by the Muslim soldiers to be a great gift and a blessing from God, his unprecedented success on the battlefield convinced many Muslims that as along as Khalid was with them they would not lose a battle.

The perception of Khalid's invincibility among the Muslim soldiers clearly disturbed Caliph Umar, who immediately discharged him from his duties as commander of the Muslim army in order to remind the Muslims that it was God who granted victory. Moreover, Khalid would not have been able to defeat the Persians and the Byzantines, argued Umar, had it not been for Divine support and assistance. Caliph Umar did not demote Khalid out of jealousy or personal grudge, unlike suggestions by some historians. On the contrary, he was very fond of Khalid and considered him to be one of Islam's greatest sons. Khalid died of prolonged illness at the age of fifty-eight and was buried in Hims, in Syria; his desire to attain martyrdom was not realised. However, he understood why he could not die fighting in the battlefield, because that would have meant defeat for the 'Sword of God'. When the news of Khalid's death was relayed to Caliph Umar, he remarked, 'The death of Khalid has created a void in Islam that cannot be filled.' That was the greatness of the man who single-handedly humbled two of history's greatest empires.

# 9

## Hussain ibn Ali
## (b.625 - d.680)

ALL NATIONS HAVE their own heroes. Some attained fame and fortune by defending their nations against external aggression; others were glorified for their artistic achievements; yet others became symbols of hope in the face of great adversity. All great nations and civilisations, therefore, remember and commemorate, at one time or another, the heroic actions and deeds performed by their great historical figures. Islamic history, indeed human history, is replete with great feats performed by renowned personalities in different spheres of human endeavour; but very few people have been able to reach the sublime and exalted position attained by one man. He was braver than a lion, an angel among men and the prince of all martyrs. That was Hussain, the grandson of the Prophet Muhammad.

Hussain ibn Ali ibn Abi Talib was born in Madinah into the most noble and respected family of Arabia. His father was Ali ibn Abi Talib, the fourth Caliph of Islam, and his mother was Fatimah, the youngest daughter of Prophet Muhammad. Hussain's family lineage was, therefore, of the highest pedigree. Once Abdullah ibn Umar, the son of Caliph Umar, asked his father why he consistently treated Hussain and his brother Hasan more favourably than his own

sons. The great Caliph retorted, 'Abdullah, your remarks have hurt me. Don't you know that your grandfather stands no comparison with their grandfather! Do you think your grandmother can equal theirs? Has your maternal uncle the same standing as theirs? Can your maternal aunt compare with their aunt? Is your paternal uncle of the same rank as theirs? Can your paternal aunt be a match for theirs?' Abdullah, the son of Caliph Umar, understood what his father was trying to say. As far as family background and nobility of origin was concerned, no one was superior to Hussain; he was beyond comparison in this respect. As young Hussain grew up in Madinah under the watchful gaze of his beloved grandfather, the Prophet, and the loving care of his parents, Ali and Fatimah, he came to personify sublime qualities and attributes; indeed, honesty, integrity and piety became the hallmarks of his character and personality. Above all, Hussain grew up to be a man of sound beliefs and uncompromising principles. He inherited all the noble qualities and attributes of his parents, and received tuition in Islam from the Prophet himself. Being very fond of his two grandsons, the Prophet visited them daily and spent quality time with them. Often he would volunteer to feed Hussain and his older brother with his own hands, and became visibly distressed and anxious if he knew his grandsons were sick or upset.

One day when Hussain and his brother ran into the Prophet's mosque while he was delivering a sermon, the sight of his beautiful grandchildren – who were wearing new clothes and looked very handsome – touched the Prophet so much that he leaned forward and gently seated the boys next to him on the pulpit and said, 'How true is the word of God! Verily, children and worldly goods are the test of a man. When I saw these children coming in, I could not help but stop the sermon and run towards them.' Hussain spent his early years in the company of the Prophet, the greatest of all teachers, and he learned all his habits from his beloved grandfather. He enjoyed playing with the Prophet while the latter immersed himself in his daily prayers. He climbed onto his shoulders and played games like any other child of his age. Once, while the Prophet was holding Hussain in his lap, tears suddenly began to roll down his cheeks. When he was asked why he cried, he replied, 'Because angel *jibrail* (Gabriel) appeared just now. He has informed me that my followers are going to slay this grandson of mine. He has even shown me the dust of the spot where he is going to be butchered! The dust is red!'

Hussain was only seven when the Prophet passed away in 632. Six months later he suffered another shock when his beloved mother Fatimah also died, leaving him in the care of his father, Ali. It was a very difficult period for young Hussain, who suddenly found himself deprived of motherly love and affection. Being a very wise and learned man, Ali tried his best to fill the void left by his wife and took good care of Hussain, who also grew up to be a wise and handsome young man. When Uthman became Caliph, Hussain was about twenty years old and had become well known for his versatility, military skills and bravery. As an accomplished soldier, he participated in a number of battles against the adversaries of Islam, including the one that led to the conquest of Tabaristan. Hussain thus acquired a reputation in Madinah for his sacrifices for the sake of

Islam. However, during the latter part of Caliph Uthman's reign, internal frictions and schisms began to disrupt the unity of the Islamic State. Bent on wreaking havoc within the Islamic State, insurgents tried to blame the Caliph for the deteriorating situation in Madinah, but the aging Caliph refuted all their charges. Their failure to discredit the Caliph persuaded the insurgents to assassinate him. It was Hussain and his brother who stood at the front gate of the Caliph's house to protect him from his opponents.

Unfortunately, the insurgents managed to enter Caliph Uthman's house through the back door and brutally murdered him. Ali was then elected the fourth Caliph, in 656. During Ali's Caliphate, Hussain stood by his father like a rock and supported him as much as he could. Four and a half years into his Caliphate, Ali died of a stab wound inflicted by a member of the *khawarij* sect. Before his death, he called his sons Hasan and Hussain and told them: 'I want you to fear God always. Don't feel sorry for what you cannot get. Be good to the people. Help the weak against the oppressor.' Both Hasan and Hussain lived up to their father's advice. Hasan was naturally a gentle and peace-loving man who disliked conflict and bloodshed. Though immediately after his father's death he was elected Caliph, he abdicated in favour of his rival Muawiyah ibn Abi Sufyan to avoid yet another leadership contest. However, Hussain disagreed with his brother's decision and considered Muawiyah to be an opportunist and usurper. Known for his integrity and uncompromising principles, Hussain's stance on the issue of political leadership put him on a collision course with Yazid, the son of Muawiyah, who succeeded his father as the ruler of the Islamic State in 680.

Like his father, Yazid had a privileged upbringing but, unlike his father, he knew very little about Islam and was even less experienced in public affairs. Living in his father's imposing Caliphal Palace in Damascus, he became well known for his unscrupulousness and lack of diplomatic skills. Even those who knew him well considered him unsuitable for the highest office in the land, but Muawiyah ignored all friendly advice and insisted on nominating Yazid as his successor. To be fair to Muawiyah, before his death he advised Yazid to be kind and generous to his subjects, especially to those who lived in the sacred cities of Makkah and Madinah, but as soon as Yazid ascended the throne, he wasted no time in using force against those who refused to recognise him as the legitimate Caliph. Devoid of tact and intelligence, Yazid created chaos and disorder across the Islamic State. His choice of governors, civil servants and military commanders were equally appalling. He removed some of the most gifted and able governors and diplomats from their posts, and replaced them with some of the most corrupt and ruthless people. This helped to intensify the conflict between the ruling elites and the masses, who, as expected, opposed Yazid's choice of governors and administrators.

Against this backdrop, Hussain and Abdullah ibn Zubair emerged to challenge Yazid's right to rule the Islamic State. When Hussain refused to recognise Yazid as Caliph, the latter ordered his governor in Madinah to force both men to pledge loyalty to him. However, both Hussain and Abdullah slipped out of Madinah under the cover of darkness, and settled in Makkah. During his stay in Makkah, Hussain received countless letters from the people of Kufah, urging him to move to their city and spearhead the opposition against Yazid from there. Although a number of prominent companions of the Prophet advised Hussain against such a move, he did not listen to them and instead set out for Kufah. The governor of Kufah at the time was Numan ibn Bishr who was too lenient for the liking of Yazid and, therefore, he replaced him with a ruthless young man called Ubaidullah ibn Ziyad, who played a pivotal role in suppressing the *khawarij* sect. As soon as Ibn Ziyad was informed that Hussain was on his way to Kufah, he stationed guards on the outskirts of the city to capture him on his arrival. Oblivious of the tumultuous situation prevailing in Kufah at the time, Hussain walked straight into Ibn Ziyad's death-trap.

After entering Iraq, Hussain set up camp adjacent to a hill inside the border. Here, he reminded Ibn Ziyad's forces that he came to Iraq on the invitation of the people of Kufah but, as expected, the commander of the army denied having sent him an invitation and a quarrel broke out between the two parties. Ibn Ziyad then wrote to his commander to force Hussain to camp in a barren place where there was no water. That fateful place was Karbala. Here Hussain, his family and small band of followers camped, and it was here that one of Islamic history's most heinous crimes was to be perpetrated by Yazid's men – as prophesied by the Prophet decades earlier. After Hussain settled at Karbala, Ibn Ziyad sent Umar ibn Sa'd with a large contingent to confront Hussain and his men. However, Hussain and Umar tried to resolve the dispute through negotiation in order to avoid fighting and bloodshed. After much discussion, both parties agreed a peace plan. Umar then wrote to Ibn Ziyad with the proposed truce, but the ruthless governor rejected the truce; he was persuaded by his aide Shimar ibn Dhul Jawshan not to accept it. Instead, the governor urged Umar to fight Hussain and force him to pledge loyalty to Yazid.

Disaster was now looming on the horizon. Ibn Ziyad sent Shimar with the instruction to force Hussain to surrender. When Umar ibn Sa'd received Ibn Ziyad's letter, the former rebuked Shimar for wrecking his peace plan. Though Umar ibn Sa'd (who was the son of the distinguished companion Sa'd ibn Abi Waqqas) was keen to resolve the conflict without a fight, the bloodthirsty Shimar was keen to fight and shed innocent blood. When Hussain refused to surrender voluntarily, the hope of reaching a peaceful resolution vanished. That evening Hussain spoke to his family and friends and asked them to prepare for battle. This conflict was destined to become one of the most heartbreaking tragedies in the annals of Islam. The impact of this tragedy continues to upset Muslim feelings and consciousness to this day. On the tenth of Muharram, sixty one years after the *hijrah*, Hussain, his family and friends took a stand against political tyranny and oppression. Attacked by Ibn Ziyad's forces, Hussain and his followers fought like lions – and one by one they fell on the battlefield – except the indomitable Hussain who continued to fight. No one dared to touch the man who was the apple of the Prophet's eye. In desperation, as arrows pierced his body and neck, Hussain searched for water to drink but his heartless pursuers refused him relief. The cursed Malik then landed a blow on his head.

Lifting his eyes up to the heavens, Hussain cried, 'Lord, deprive these people of rain and the bounties of the earth…they invited us with the promise to support our cause. When we came, they turned against us and started butchering us.' Saying this, Hussain picked up his sword and marched towards the enemy and they fell upon him from all directions. His body was mutilated and the wretched Shimar cut off his head, and it was carried to the governor of Kufah who, in turn, sent it to Yazid in Damascus. According to the historians, Hussain's body was buried in Karbala but there is much disagreement concerning the burial site of his head. Some historians say it was taken to Madinah and buried in Jannat al-Baqi next to his mother's grave, while others say it was buried in Damascus. Either way, Hussain was brutally martyred at the age of fifty-five. He was a man of sound principles who lived by his principles and died fighting for justice and truth. Hussain's uncompromising stance against Yazid earned him the title of 'prince of martyrs', while Yazid became known to posterity as the 'king of hatred', the most despised man in Islamic history. More than half a century after Hussain's martyrdom, justice caught up with the wretched men who were responsible for the grisly murder of Hussain at Karbala. The House of Umayyah (the Umayyad dynasty) soon crumbled and the butchers of Karbala were caught and punished in an exemplary fashion by the Abbasids. Hussain did not die in vain; it was a battle of good against evil, right against wrong, and truth against false-hood. That is why today the name of Hussain has become totally synonymous with the fight against injustice, brutality and oppression throughout the Muslim world.

# IO

## Abu Hurairah
## (b.ca.601 - d.679)

ACCORDING TO THE Qur'an, the Prophet Muhammad was *uswatun hasana* (or the 'best role model') for all people for all times to come. The Qur'an provides the outlines of Islamic principles and teachings, while the normative practice (*sunnah*) of the Prophet is regarded as the most authoritative commentary on the Qur'anic revelation. For this reason, Muslims have always been keen to record the Prophet's words and deeds for a better understanding of the Qur'an, and for the benefit and guidance of future generations. It was by no means an easy task given the fact that in seventh century Arabia illiteracy was widespread and the vast majority of the people relied heavily on their memories for preserving information and passing important data from one generation to another by means of oral communication. The Arabs, however, were gifted oral communicators who had developed a fine tradition of promulgating genealogical information from one generation to another, spanning many centuries. Utilising the same methodology, the early Muslims recorded each and every word and deed of the Prophet for posterity. Amongst the companions of the Prophet, one man more than any other, stands out like a shining star for his utter devotion and dedication to preserving the *ahadith* (or sayings of the Prophet); he was Abu Hurairah.

His pre-Islamic name was Abd ash-Shams but after embracing Islam he changed it to Abd al-Rahman ibn Sakhr, although he became well known by his nickname, 'Abu Hurairah' (meaning the 'father of the kitten'), received due to his love and affection for his pet kitten. Born into the Daws tribe of southern Arabia, Abu Hurairah was about twelve when Muhammad became a Prophet and started preaching Islam in Makkah. Although little is known about his early life, like most of the Arabs of his time, he grew up in southern Arabia without any schooling and was known to have been illiterate. Young boys in those days often worked as shepherds, general labourers or, if they were lucky, they accompanied the merchants to neighbouring countries to conduct business. These long and often protracted journeys to and from leading trading centres, like Makkah, Damascus and Yemen, were considered to be highly lucrative, and only the wealthy traders engaged in such ventures. Abu Hurairah was still in his teens when the Prophet began to preach the message of Islam to his kith and kin. This was followed by an open call to all the people of Makkah. Young Abu Hurairah was, of course, unaware of Muhammad's Prophetic mission at the time.

After preaching in Makkah for more than a decade, the Prophet left his native city and moved to the nearby oasis of Madinah, where he received a warm welcome. At the time Abu Hurairah was in his early twenties. As an intelligent and contemplative young man, he led a very simple lifestyle even in his pre-Islamic days, and would have probably embraced Islam had he been living in Makkah when the Prophet first began his mission. As it happens, it was not until seven years after the Prophet's migration (*hijrah*) to Madinah that Abu Hurairah came to hear about the Prophet and his mission. Immediately he set out for Madinah in order to meet the Prophet. When he arrived (in 628), he was told that the Prophet was in Khaibar where he was seeking to put an end to the anti-Islamic activities which were being masterminded there at the time. Keen to meet the Prophet, he set out for Khaibar – which is located around one hundred and sixty kilometres from Madinah – and after a long and exhausting journey, he formally became a Muslim at the hands of the Prophet. He was about thirty at the time. Thereafter, Abu Hurairah became a very close associate of the Prophet, and regularly accompanied him wherever he went and, as a result, he learned and mastered all aspects of Islamic teachings and practices under the guidance of the Prophet.

Although Abu Hurairah came to Madinah empty-handed – without any wealth or material possessions – he received a warm welcome from all the close companions of the Prophet. On his return from Khaibar, he settled in Madinah and initially earned his living working as a general labourer; thus he divided his time between work and acquiring Islamic knowledge directly from the Prophet. His close friendship and interaction with the Prophet not only strengthened his faith; over time, he also became very fond of him. Eager to spend more time in the company of the Prophet, Abu Hurairah eventually gave up work and became a member of the *ashab as-suffah*. The *ashab as-suffah* consisted of a group of mainly

immigrant Muslims who, forced to flee from Makkah by their enemies, left all their wealth and possessions behind. On their arrival in Madinah, they had nowhere to go. The Prophet, therefore, built a simple thatched platform or lodge (*as-suffah*) in the corner of his mosque for these Muslims and most of them earned their living working as general labourers. Since the Prophet took direct responsibility for the welfare of the *ashab as-suffah*, he ensured they received regular supplies of food and clothing. However, the historians disagree as to how many people benefited from this lodge; some say it was around twenty people; others say it was about seventy, while according to others, the total number of people who benefited from this lodge was as high as four hundred and included such prominent companions as Abdullah ibn Umar, Abu Ubaida ibn al-Jarrah, Abdullah ibn Mas'ud, Salman al-Farisi and, of course, Abu Hurairah himself. This lodge, therefore, became the first residential college in Islamic history where the Prophet and his prominent companions taught *tajwid* (the art of reciting the Qur'an) and aspects of Islam to its residents.

As a leading member of the *ashab as-suffah*, Abu Hurairah became preoccupied with the pursuit of Islamic knowledge, especially that of *hadith*, or Prophetic traditions. As a perceptive individual who was blessed with a highly retentive memory, he became one of the most learned among the companions of the Prophet. This is evident from the fact that during the four years or so he spent with the Prophet, until the latter's death in 632, he not only became a very close friend of the Prophet; he also meticulously observed his behaviour, mannerisms and daily habits. Indeed he lived, ate, prayed, studied and travelled with the Prophet and, due to his superior memory power, memorised his every word and deed. Also, unlike the other companions of the Prophet, Abu Hurairah gave up work to become a full-time student in order to learn and commit the Prophet's sayings to his memory, while the other companions engaged in farming, business and other commercial activities. For this reason, he was able to learn more about the Prophet and his teachings in around four years than those who had embraced Islam much earlier and known the Prophet over a longer period.

It was Abu Hurairah's enquiring mind, coupled with his thirst for knowledge, which inspired him to learn and master so much within such a short period of time. He was never afraid to ask the Prophet questions on issues which he felt needed further clarification. On one ocassion, he asked the Prophet a question on something so minute and insignificant that the Prophet remarked, 'I was sure, O Abu Hurairah, that no one except you would ask such a question of me.' (Sahih al-Bukhari) His unwavering devotion and dedication to the Prophet and his teachings knew no bounds.

Since Abu Hurairah was determined to memorise and master as much as he could, and do so as quickly as possible, he was concerned that his memory was not up to the task; thus on one occasion he approached the Prophet to ask him to pray for him so he could retain information more easily. He related: 'People wonder how I narrate so many *hadith*. The fact is that my *muhajir* (immigrant) brothers remained busy trading and my *ansar* (helper) brothers did their farming, while I was among the people of *suffah*. I never cared to earn my living; I was contented with the little food that the Prophet (pbuh) could give me. I would be with the Prophet (pbuh) at times when no one else was there. I once complained to the Prophet (pbuh) about my poor memory. He said, 'Spread your shawl!' I did so. He made some signs on the shawl with his own hands and said, 'Now wrap this shawl around you.' I wrapped it around my breast. Since then, I never have forgotten anything that I have wished to remember.' (Sahih al-Bukhari)

Zaid ibn Thabit, who was a prominent companion and secretary of the Prophet, also said, 'Once while Abu Hurairah, a friend of ours, and I were praying and remembering God in the mosque, the Prophet came and joined us. He asked us to continue with our prayers. My friend and I prayed first, and then the Prophet said,

'Ameen.' Then Abu Hurairah prayed, 'O God, I ask of you what has been asked by my friend, and I, myself, for knowledge that I will never forget.' The Prophet said, 'Ameen.'

Abu Hurairah is a legend in Islamic history for not only narrating a vast quantity of Prophetic traditions, but also for his unique memory power. However, his claim to have learned such a vast quantity of *hadith* did not go unchallenged. Some of his contemporaries, such as Abdullah ibn Umar, questioned his reliability as a *hadith* narrator, but Abu Hurairah always proved his critics wrong. On one ocassion, Abu Hurairah related a *hadith* which referred to the degrees of benefits attainable from attending funeral prayers (*salat al-janazah*). But Abdullah ibn Umar, who was himself a formidable repository of *hadith* literature, questioned the authenticity of Abu Hurairah's narration. So he took Abdullah to the Prophet's wife, Aishah, who confirmed that Abu Hurairah's version of the *hadith* was sound. Abdullah duly apologised to him and acknowledged Abu Hurairah's superiority over others when it came to narrating *hadith*. In his old age, his memory was frequently put to the test by the people of Madinah in order to ascertain the veracity of his narrations. When Marwan ibn Hakam was the governor of Madinah, he once asked Abu Hurairah to narrate a number of *hadith*, which, unbeknown to Abu Hurairah, he had had transcribed by one of his secretaries, word for word, behind a screen. A year later, he recalled him and asked him to relate the same *hadith* again. To Marwan's astonishment, Abu Hurairah narrated the *ahadith* word for word, without a single mistake. This way Abu Hurairah was able to silence all his critics.

According to the scholars of *hadith* (*muhaddithun*), Abu Hurairah's authenticity as a narrator of *hadith* is beyond reproach. This does not mean to say, however, that other unscrupulous people did not later fabricate *hadith* and attribute them to him. Abu Hurairah's reputation as a narrator of a vast quantity of *hadith* made this a very attractive proposition for the fabricators of *hadith*. This is why all the great scholars of *hadith*, including Muhammad ibn Ismail al-Bukhari and Muslim ibn al-Hajjaj, pursued a thorough and rigorous methodology in order to ascertain the veracity of each and every *hadith* they incorporated in their famous anthologies. The fact that Abu Hurairah was an unsually learned, very pious and highly respected companion of the Prophet, who devoted all his life to the acquisition and dissemination of Islamic knowledge and wisdom, is today acknowledged by the majority of Muslims. But what is not known so widely is that he was also a hugely popular teacher, who personally taught and mentored more than eight hundred students and scholars of *hadith*. And like the Prophet, he used to divide his nights into three parts: he used to sleep during the first part, pray during the second and study during the third part.

According to the historian and traditionist Abd al-Rahman ibn Ali ibn al-Jawzi, Abu Hurairah narrated five thousand three hundred and seventy-four *hadith* in total, more than any other companion of the Prophet, including his wife, Aishah. During the reign of Caliph Umar, Abu Hurairah served as governor of Bahrain for a period, and also acted as governor of Madinah for a while during the early Umayyad period. Abu Hurairah's selfless devotion to Islamic learning and his efforts to disseminate *hadith* have today turned him into a household name throughout the Muslim world. Is it any wonder that *an Abu Hurairah radi Allahu anhu qala qala rasulullahi sallallahu alaihi wa sallam* (Abu Hurairah, may God be pleased with him, narrated that the Messenger of God, may the peace and blessings of God be on him, said...) has become the most famous introductory statement in the history of *hadith* literature? He breathed his last at the age of seventy-eight and was buried in Madinah, the city of the Prophet.

# II

## Fatimah bint Muhammad (b.607 - d.632)

PROPHET MUHAMMAD HAD six children (two sons and four daughters) by his first wife, Khadijah. The sons were al-Qasim and Abdullah, both of whom died in their infancy, and the four daughters were Zainab, Ruqayyah, Umm Kulthum and Fatimah. All four daughters of the Prophet lived, grew up, married and became shining examples of Islamic piety and goodness. Zainab was born when the Prophet was thirty-one and she married Abul As, who was a noble citizen of Makkah and they had three children. She died at the age of thirty-one – as a result of a wound she sustained during her migration from Makkah to Madinah. Ruqayyah, the Prophet's second daughter, was born when he was thirty-three and she was known to have been exceptionally beautiful and intelligent. When she reached maturity, all the prominent Makkan chiefs vied with one another to make her their daughter-in-law, but the Prophet married her to Utba, the son of Abu Lahab.

However, after Muhammad assumed Prophethood, Abu Lahab became his most inveterate opponent and ordered his son to divorce Ruqayyah. She was subsequently married to Uthman ibn Affan, a highly respected and wealthy businessman of the *banu umayyah* clan, who later became

the third Caliph of Islam. Ruqayyah bore him a son called Abdullah, who died at the tender age of six. Soon afterwards, she died at the age of twenty-three. The Prophet's third daughter, Umm Kulthum, was born when he was thirty-eight. She was married to Uthman after Ruqayyah's death. Umm Kulthum was twenty-five at the time of her marriage. After almost seven years of blissful marital life, she passed away at the age of thirty-two; she had no children. Of all the Prophet's children, it was his fourth daughter, Fatimah, who was destined to leave her mark in the annals of Islam, so much so that her name and fame continues to reverberate throughout the Muslim world to this day.

Fatimah was born in Makkah when her father was in his late thirties. The title of *az-zahra* (or 'radiantly beautiful') was conferred on her on account of her breath-taking beauty, personal piety and nobility of character. A year after her birth, her beloved father began his Prophetic mission and this immediately created rifts between him and some prominent members of his tribe. Although his wife Khadijah and his three older daughters embraced Islam immediately after he announced his mission, at the time Fatimah was too young to understand and appreciate the true nature of Islam and the impact it had on her family. The one time *al-amin* (the trustworthy) and *al-sadiq* (the truthful) of Makkah, overnight became public enemy number one. Why? Because he proclaimed that there was none worthy of worship except the One True God (*la ilaha illa Allah*). The Makkan chiefs (including the Prophet's uncle Abu Lahab) could not come to terms with the egalitarian and universal Islamic message which he preached, transcending as it did all political, social, economic and tribal categories, thereby connecting all people, irrespective of their racial and cultural backgrounds, to one common denominator, namely Islam. Fatimah grew up under the loving and tender care of her parents amidst the prevailing sociopolitical chaos and upheaval which the Prophet's message created in Makkah. Thus it was a very testing time for the Prophet and his family, but they bore the brunt of their opponent's cruelty and inhumanity with remarkable restraint and fortitude.

When all attempts to persuade the Prophet to stop propagating Islam failed, the Makkans instigated a three-year political and economic siege (*shi'ab abi talib*) on the Prophet's extended family. This inhumane boycott not only inflicted tremendous suffering and hardship on the Prophet and members of his extended family, but also became a collective punishment for all the believers. Such was the severity of this siege that the Prophet and his family were even deprived of basic necessities like food and water. Even by Makkan tribal standards, this was unusually harsh treatment and particularly affected the children and babies. As a consequence, young Fatimah suffered severe malnutrition which made her physically very weak and frail; she became so weak that she developed serious health problems, including suffering from severe exhaustion even after minimal physical activity (such as cooking, grinding wheat, and collecting water from the well). When three years of total boycott failed to dissuade the Prophet from his mission, the Makkans eventually relented and lifted it. However, for young Fatimah, the joy was

very short lived as her beloved mother, Khadijah, passed away soon afterwards. This was a terrible blow for the Prophet and his children. Khadijah was not only an exemplary wife to her husband, she was also respected throughout Makkah for her character, nobility and intelligence and, above all, she was a loving mother to her children. Thus her death deprived young Fatimah of much-needed motherly love, care and affection. To make matters worse, the Prophet also lost his uncle, Abu Talib, (who was his foremost supporter and benefactor) during this 'year of sorrow'. Despite the death of his wife and uncle, the Prophet remained very firm and steadfast. He tried his utmost to ensure that his beloved daughter received proper care and attention. Three years later, in 622, the Prophet migrated (*hijrah*) from Makkah to Madinah and Fatimah followed suit; she was only fourteen at the time.

She grew up in Madinah under the direct care and supervision of her father. During this period she learned the Qur'an from the Prophet, and began to practise Islam in the same way her father practised it. According to Aishah, her stepmother, no one was more devoted and dedicated to Islam than Fatimah. Her qualities of truthfulness, sincerity, piety and generosity made her very popular with her kith and kin. In the second year of the *hijrah*, she played an active part in the Battle of Badr, where she treated the sick and injured. Her exemplary actions enhanced her reputation further; thus she became well known in Madinah as a caring, intelligent and understanding young lady. Since she was also very attractive, and one of the Prophet's most beloved daughters, many distinguished companions asked for her hand in marriage, but the Prophet always remained silent on this matter.

But when Ali, the Prophet's cousin and the first boy to embrace Islam, approached him for Fatimah's hand in marriage, he first consulted her and then married her to him. After a simple marriage ceremony, Fatimah moved into her husband's house when she was about sixteen. Ali's apartment was far from being a bed of roses. Like the Prophet, Ali lived a very simple life; the contents of his house included a simple bed, a pillow filled with dried leaves of date palm, one plate, one glass, a leather water container and a stone for grinding flour. These were all the possessions Fatimah had in her house. Following in the footsteps of her father and husband Ali, Fatimah led a very simple life, far removed from the wealth, luxuries and material possessions of this world. She kept her house impeccably clean, cooked regular meals and did all her daily chores on her own. Throughout her married life she remained very conscious of her duties to her husband and always maintained a dignified lifestyle, focusing primarily on pleasing God and attaining His pleasure. Since the suffering and torment she endured during the three year siege in Makkah made her physically weak, she often struggled to complete her household chores due to excruciating physical pain and exhausation. Seeing his wife struggle with her daily chores prompted Ali to urge her to go to the Prophet and ask for a maid. When she spoke to her father, he taught her a special litany which he said would be more beneficial to her than a maid. Both Ali and Fatimah learned this litany and recited it daily before retiring to bed. It consisted of repeating *subhan Allah* (Glory be to God) thirty-three times, *al-hamdulillah* (All praise be to God) thirty-three times, and *Allahu akbar* (God is the Greatest) thirty-four times. This special invocation later came to be known as *tasbih al-Fatimah* (or 'Fatimah's litany').

The fact that Fatimah was the apple of her father's eye is not in doubt; he loved her more than any one else. So much so that whenever he came home from a journey it was his habit to visit Fatimah first. She, in turn, loved her father so much that whenever he visited her she always welcomed him with a huge smile and gave him a kiss on his forehead. Seeing her dear father filled her with joy and happiness; she also bore a striking resemblance to him, physically as well as in her etiquette and mannerisms. On one ocassion, when the Prophet was asked whom he loved the most, he replied that he loved his daughter Fatimah the most. He became unsettled and

unhappy whenever he heard that Fatimah was somehow in pain or distress, and the expression on his face used to change instantly. Fatimah – the Prophet used to say – was part of his heart and it pained him to see her sad and unhappy. When he was once asked whom he liked the most, Fatimah or Ali, he retorted that he loved Fatimah more than Ali but, he added, Ali was dearer to him than Fatimah. If this question was an extremely tricky one, then his answer could not have been any better.

Fatimah bore Ali five children, three sons and two daughters. Their eldest son was Hasan; their second son was Hussain and Muhsin was the third. The first two sons lived and became very famous Muslims, but their third son died in his infancy. The two daughters were Zainab and Umm Kulthum. The former was married to Abdullah ibn Ja'far, Ali's nephew, while the latter was married to Umar ibn al-Khattab, the second Caliph of Islam. Through her children, Fatimah's descendants multiplied and spread throughout the Islamic world. Her sons Hasan and Hussain not only became very famous Muslims, they also became great symbols of Islamic bravery and heroism. Thanks also to Fatimah, today there are hundreds and thousands, if not, millions of Muslims across the Islamic world who proudly claim to be the descendants of the Prophet. Even great political dynasties such as the Fatimids of Egypt and North Africa considered themselves to be the progeny and inheritors of the Prophet through Fatimah and Ali. To have a genealogical link to the Prophet through Fatimah often provided individuals, as well as various political and mystical groups, with much needed recognition and legitimacy throughout Islamic history.

More importantly, today Fatimah is very popular across the Muslim world due to her startling qualities as a perfect Muslim daughter, a devoted wife to her husband and an exemplary mother to all her children. Throughout Islamic history, Muslim women of all shades and colour have looked towards her life and thought for inspiration and guidance. Along with Aishah and Khadijah, she must be considered one of the most famous and influential women in Islamic history. That is why I have ranked her very highly in this book. She passed away six months after the death of her father, at the age of around twenty-seven. In accordance with her wishes, she was buried under the cover of darkness by her husband and two other Muslim ladies in Jannat al-Baqi, one of Madinah's most famous cemetries. Her greatness was such that the Prophet once said: 'One day, (the) angel came and told me the glad tidings that Fatimah will be the leader of women in heaven.'

# 12

## Bilal ibn Rabah
### (b.579 – d.641)

DURING THE EARLY days of Islam, several non-Arabs embraced Islam and became prominent companions of the Prophet Muhammad. Through their hard work and sheer devotion to the message of Islam, these hitherto unknown and obscure men suddenly became leading figures of the early Muslim community, firstly in Makkah and then in Madinah. They included Salman al-Farisi, Suhaib al-Rumi and Bilal ibn Rabah. The son of a notable Zoroastrian priest and *dihqan* (landlord), Salman was abducted in his childhood and brought to Syria in chains. Subsequently he embraced Christianity and was eventually sold as a slave to a Madinian Jew. He became a Muslim in Madinah and met the Prophet before the Battle of Khandaq. Thanks to his unflinching devotion to Islam, he later became one of the leading members of the early Muslim community. By contrast, Suhaib came from Byzantium although the historians disagree about his ancestry; some say he was a Roman, while others suggest he was of Arabian origin. Either way, he renounced all the joys and pleasures of this world to become a Muslim at a time when it was not fashionable to be a Muslim in Makkah. His love of, and devotion to, Islam won him much acclaim within the early Muslim community. Perhaps the most devoted and dedicated non-Arab to embrace Islam, however, was Bilal. Born into slavery, he rose to become one of Islamic history's most celebrated figures.

Bilal was born to an Abyssinian slave girl of Banu Jumah tribe of Makkah. He was brought up by his mother and worked as a slave labourer during his teenage years. When Bilal was in his early twenties, he was sold to Umayyah ibn Khalaf, a powerful Makkan chieftain, as a slave. Known to have been very dark, tall, slim and bushy-haired, Bilal lived with his master in Makkah and acquired something of a reputation for his scrupulousness and integrity even before he embraced Islam. When Prophet Muhammad started promulgating Islam in Makkah, Bilal was around thirty years old. The Prophet first invited members of his own family to the new faith including his beloved wife Khadijah, his daughters and his cousin Ali and adopted son Zaid, before approaching his best friend, Abu Bakr. None of them doubted his truthfulness and they responded positively to his call. It was not long before the Prophet gathered around him a sizable following in Makkan despite the opposition of its ruling elites. When the Prophet began to publicly invite all the people of Makkah to the truth of Islam, people like Abu Bakr, Ammar ibn Yasir, his mother Sumayyah, and Miqdad followed suit and publicly declared their new faith. This shocked and infuriated the Makkan elites so much that they began to persecute the new believers.

Only the Prophet and Abu Bakr were spared, as both of them were offered protection by their powerful relatives. Bilal was one of the first seven people to embrace Islam. As soon as he heard about Islam, he leaped at it like an arrow heading for its target. And since he was a slave labourer, he had no one to protect him from the wrath of his cruel master, Umayyah. When the latter discovered that Bilal had embraced Islam, he became so infuriated that he threw him out of the house and began to torture him severely. As one of Islam's bitter foes, Umayyah tried every trick in the book to force Bilal to renounce Islam, but the latter did not budge an inch. And although others, like Ammar and Miqdad, relented for a period after being severely punished, Bilal the Ethiopian continued to defy Umayyah in an heroic manner. When the persecution of Muslims became very harsh and unbearable, some Muslims pretended to have renounced Islam in order to avoid being tortured and persecuted, but Bilal refused to do this.

According to the historians, Umayyah used to make Bilal sleep on the scorching desert sand, tie him up, place a heavy stone on his chest and leave him in the desert to suffer. The burning sand melted his skin and caused him excruciating agony and pain. In desperation, he would cry out for help only for Umayyah to appear and ask him to renounce Islam. When he refused, Umayyah screamed abuse and insults at him. His master would not leave him in peace at night, either. He was regularly whipped at night which caused his skin to split open, but the iron-willed Bilal remained defiant as ever. He would not renounce Islam come what may; his faith was as solid as a rock. The more he was punished, the more vigorously Bilal chanted, 'Ahad' -The One (God), 'Ahad' -The One (God), 'Ahad' -The One (God) – thus reiterating the fundamental Islamic belief

that no one deserves to be worshipped and glorified other than Allah, the One and Only God, Who is the Creator, Cherisher and Sustainer of the entire universe. Since Bilal considered his battle against Umayyah to be a battle between the truth and falsehood, light and darkness, he was determined to win the contest for Islam. He may have been tall and slim but Bilal's temperament was solid steel, and his steadfastness in the face of torture and cruelty came to symbolise the true qualities and attributes of a Muslim. So much so that stories of his remarkable struggles and sacrifices continue to inspire Muslims to this day.

The severity of the punishment inflicted on Bilal by his master shocked and horrified everyone in Makkah. Moved by his suffering and plight, Abu Bakr, who was a wealthy businessman and an early convert to Islam, offered to buy Bilal his freedom. Being a cruel and repulsive man, Umayyah was only too happy to accept Abu Bakr's offer of money in exchange for Bilal's freedom. Now for the first time in his life, Bilal was a free man who bowed before none, other than the One True God. Bilal was very grateful to Abu Bakr for his kindness and the Prophet was also delighted when he was told that Bilal was at last a free man. Islam – as promulgated by the Prophet – was against slavery and bondage, and Muhammad never failed to remind his followers that it was a truly detestable practice which has no place in a civilised society. He, therefore, actively encouraged his companions to free people from slavery for, according to Islam, all human beings are born free, enjoying equal status and freedom before God, irrespective of their race, colour and gender. This revolutionary message spoke to Bilal in such a powerful way that even Umayyah's relentless persecution and punishment failed to undermine his love for Islam.

Though Bilal was now a free man, he knew living as a Muslim in Makkah would not be easy. Since even the Prophet and his prominent companions like Abu Bakr and Umar were not spared by the powerful Makkan chiefs, he decided to keep a low profile during this testing and tumultuous period in early Islamic history. He stayed with the Prophet as much as he could to study and learn about Islam in order to strengthen his faith and conviction. So, when the Prophet eventually left his native Makkah for Madinah in 622, Bilal followed suit. The Prophet and his companions received a warm welcome from the people of Madinah and Bilal helped to construct the *masjid al-nabi* (or 'the Prophet's mosque'), which subsequently became the main centre of activities for the early Muslim community. During this period he acted as an aide to the Prophet and kept a close eye on the income and expenditure of the first public treasury (*bait al-mal*) established by the Prophet. His role as an aide enabled him to work very closely with the Prophet and learn more about his personal habits and practices. Referring to the Prophet, Bilal once stated: 'He never kept anything for the future. I arranged money for him. When a needy person came to him, he would send him over to me and I would then arrange for his needs by borrowing money from someone. This is what usually happened.'

As a prominent aide and supporter of the Prophet, Bilal discharged his duties scrupulously; he was widely respected for his honesty, integrity and tremendous sacrifices for Islam during its early days and so was well qualified for this role. Being also very reliable and competent, Bilal fulfilled his responsibilities with both efficiency and effectiveness, so that whenever anyone came to the Prophet for anything, he would direct them to Bilal who ensured their needs were fully met. His devotion and dedication to the Prophet thus won him the support and admiration of everyone. Moreover, after the building of the Prophet's mosque was completed, he encouraged his companions to perform their five daily prayers (*salat*) in congregation (*jama'ah*) in the mosque, which the Prophet himself led. But when the Muslim community in Madinah began to expand rapidly, it was not always possible for everyone, especially those who worked in the farms and orchards, to know the precise time of each prayer. As the Muslims were aware that the Christians used bells to

call their people to the church and the Jews blew a horn to summon their people to religious service, a number of companions suggested that they, too, should devise a method for calling the faithful to the five daily prayers. The Prophet thought this was a good idea, but he was keen to devise a system which would differentiate the Muslims from the Jewish and Christian practices. Some companions suggested they should kindle a fire before every prayer, while others said they could clap two pieces of wood to signal the start of the prayer time. However, none of these suggestions appealed to the Prophet.

Then, one day, a companion called Abdullah ibn Zaid appeared before the Prophet and said he saw in a dream where a person was calling all the Muslims to prayer from the roof of the mosque. Subsequently, Umar appeared and confirmed that he had had a similar dream. The Prophet and his companions liked this idea. The *adhan* (or 'call to prayer') was thus instituted by the order of the Prophet. It consisted of repeating the following formulas:

*Allahu Akbar* (God is great),
*Ashadu Allah-ilaha illa Allah* (I bear wintness that there is no god but God)
*Ashadu anna Muhammadan Rasul Allah* (I bear witness that Muhammad is God's Messenger),
*Haiya alas salah* (Hasten to Prayer),
*Haiya alal falah* (Hasten to Success),
*Allahu Akbar* (God is great),
*La ilaha illa Allah* (There is no god but God).

Since Bilal had the most beautiful voice, the Prophet asked him to go into the *masjid al-nabi* and make the first historic call to prayer in his sweet and melodious voice. As soon as Bilal completed the first *adhan*, the Muslims of Madinah flocked to the Prophet's mosque and performed their prayers in a congregation led by the Prophet himself. Thus Bilal became the first, and the most famous, *mu'adhdhin* (or 'caller to prayer') in Islamic history. From that day on, the *adhan* became associated with the name of

Bilal. Indeed, following in his footsteps, Muslims have continued to implement the *adhan* in every corner of the earth in order to summon the faithful to five daily prayers. Today, every time an *adhan* is called out we are reminded of Bilal who first declared this beautiful announcement from the Prophet's mosque in Madinah. Thanks to the *adhan*, the name and fame of Bilal continues to spread across the world to this day. By contrast, Umayyah, his chief tormentor, is today remembered as a cruel and pathetic man who was put to the sword by Bilal at the Battle of Badr for his unspeakable cruelty and inhumanity towards him.

If Bilal was very fond of the Prophet, the Prophet in turn admired him for his devotion, dedication, hardwork and sincerity. Such was Bilal's greatness that the Prophet once asked him, 'What shoes were those you wore last night? Verily, as I journeyed in Heaven and was mounting the stairs of God I heard your footsteps before me though I could not see them.' Moved by these beautiful words, Bilal resolved to stay with the Prophet and serve him for the rest of his life. When the Prophet passed away in 632, Bilal was so devastated that he could no longer bear to live in Madinah, for his memories of happy times with the Prophet made him very sad and lonely. He eventually accompanied a Muslim army, led by Abu Ubaida ibn al-Jarrah, to Syria and settled in Damascus permanently. When he visited Madinah a few years later, the Prophet's grandsons, Hasan and Hussain, pleaded with him to make the *adhan*. As soon as he called the *adhan*, the people of Madinah came out of their houses and sobbed, for it reminded them of the happier times when the Prophet was alive. During the Caliphate of Umar, Bilal served as governor of Damascus for a short period and died around the age of sixty. Although he was born into slavery and, therefore, had no real status in society, he found lasting peace, great honour and true liberation in the fold of Islam. He attained such a lofty position within the early Muslim community that the great Caliph Umar used to call him 'our master' for his tremendous services to Islam. Today his name and fame have spread far and wide; he has also become an important symbol of honour and dignity for millions of African-American Muslims.

# 13

## Al-Bukhari
## (b.809 - d.870)

THE LIFE AND teachings of the Prophet Muhammad are an important source of inspiration, guidance and instruction for more than a billion Muslims across the globe today. From how to conduct a multi-billion pound business transaction in the international market-place, to the finer details of how to drink a glass of water, a Muslim can draw direct guidance for all spheres of his life from the vast corpus of *hadith* literature. The Arabic word *hadith* refers to a 'saying' or 'utterance' of the Prophet. No other human being is followed as meticulously as the Prophet is followed and imitated by the Muslims. He is seen as the epitome of virtue, goodness and humanity. That is why Muslims scrupulously emulate his deeds and actions (*sunnah*) in every sphere of their lives. In Islamic history, one man stands over and above all others when it comes to collecting, editing, analysing and verifying the sayings and utterances of the Prophet. He is none other than Imam al-Bukhari.

Abu Abdullah Muhammad ibn Ismail ibn Ibrahim ibn Mughirah ibn Bardizbah al-Bukhari was born in Bukhara, in Muslim Central Asia. Of Persian origin, al-Bukhari's ancestors were farmers who were taken captives during the Muslim conquest of that region in the early days of Islam.

Al-Bukhari's great grandfather, al-Mughirah, accepted Islam at the hands of Yaman al-Jufi, the then governor of Bukhara, and he had a son by the name of Ibrahim. Ibrahim's son, Ismail, was the father of al-Bukhari. Ismail was a relatively wealthy merchant and an accomplished scholar of *hadith* who became well known in his locality for his meticulous habits and strict adherence to the normative practice of the Prophet. He had two sons, Ahmad and Muhammad. Muhammad was the younger son, and became well known as al-Bukhari. Ismail died when al-Bukhari was still a child, and the family fell into povery and hardship. But young al-Bukhari's mother was a pious and determined lady who, in spite of her difficult economic circumstances, ensured her son received a good education.

Al-Bukhari was evidently a gifted student who possessed a photographic memory and great analytical skills. Of slim build and somewhat frail health, he nevertheless excelled in his studies. His ability to grasp complex arguments and reconcile often differing and contradictory views – thanks largely to his prodigious intellect and unusual memory power – elevated him to one of the highest positions ever to be attained by a scholar of *hadith*. Al-Bukhari's love for Islamic learning, especially his undiminished quest for Prophetic traditions, became very evident early in his life. It was his devoted mother who played a critical role in his early education, and it was her who inspired him to pursue the study of *hadith*. After successfully completing his initial education at the age of twelve, al-Bukhari pursued advanced training in Islamic sciences and specialised in *hadith* literature. His hard work and dedication to his studies paid off when he completed his study of *hadith* under the guidance of all the reputable scholars of Bukhara; he was only eighteen at the time. In fact, he was barely twenty when he came to be recognised as one of the foremost scholars of *hadith* in his locality. Thereafter, the study, collection and verification of Prophetic traditions became his lifelong preoccupation. It was this, combined with the compilation and codification of the Prophetic traditions, which established his reputation as one of Islam's greatest authorities on *hadith*, and represents his vast contribution and service to Islamic scholarship in general. The signs of his greatness were evident from the very outset. It is related that when al-Bukhari was only eleven he once corrected his own teacher's mistake. When the teacher refused to take him seriously, al-Bukhari reportedly challenged him to check his facts. After the teacher checked his manuscript, al-Bukhari was found to be correct.

After completing his higher education in Bukhara, al-Bukhari left his native city and went to Makkah, along with his mother and brother, to perform the sacred *hajj* (pilgrimage). He stayed in Makkah and Madinah for several years and pursued advanced training in *hadith* literature under the guidance of the leading scholars of the time. From Makkah he travelled to other great centres of Islamic learning in Egypt, Syria and Iraq before settling in Basrah where he conducted advanced research in *hadith*. Like many other great scholars of his era, al-Bukhari was a distinguished traveller who spent nearly four decades journeying from one place to another in pursuit of knowledge and wisdom. During his sojourns he came into contact with some of the

foremost *hadith* scholars of his time, including Ahmad ibn Hanbal, Abu Bakr ibn Abu Shaiba, Ishaq ibn Rahawaih, Ali ibn al-Madini and Yahya ibn Ma'in. These celebrated scholars of *hadith* played a pivotal role in the development and promulgation of *ulum al-hadith* (or 'the science of *hadith*'). Al-Bukhari learned and mastered the science of *hadith* – that is, the art of sifting, dissecting and distinguishing the authentic *hadith* from the fabricated, forged or manufactured ones – from these great pioneers of Islamic thought and scholarship. Sustained and systematic analysis of a *hadith* required a thorough familiarisation with, and mastery of, a number of research procedures and techniques. That is to say, the skills and ability to undertake rigorous scrutiny and cross-examination of each and every *hadith* from a multi-dimensional perspective was a *sine qua non* for ascertaining the veracity of the text (*matn*) of the *hadith*; its chains of narration (*isnad*), the background of the *hadith* narrator (*al-asma al-rijal*), as well as a sound knowledge and understanding of the Qur'an in order to determine whether the *hadith* was in compliance with the Divine revelation.

After rigorous and systematic investigation of the *ahadith*, the *muhaddithun* (or 'scholars of *hadith*') classified them into different categories such as sound (*sahih*), good (*hasan*), recurrent (*mutawatir*), solitary (*ahad*), weak (*daeef*), fabricated (*maudu*) and so on and so forth. However, given the fact that the quantity of *hadith* which were in circulation during al-Bukhari's time was mind-bogglingly vast, sifting the wheat from the chaff became a monumental task even for a gifted scholar like al-Bukhari. Nonetheless, his diligence, dedication and incredible retentive power enabled him not only to master the science of *hadith*, but also to commit around half a million *hadith* to memory. This established his reputation as a veritable master of *hadith* literature, and his fame soon began to spread across the Islamic East. After four decades of incessant quest for knowledge, especially that of the Prophetic traditions, al-Bukhari reached the summit of Islamic scholarship, a lofty position which no other scholar of *hadith* was able to rival after him.

For al-Bukhari, learning, collecting and disseminating *hadith* became a way of life, if not an obsession. He travelled distant lands, sacrificed all his time, energy and wealth in the pursuit of Prophetic *hadith*. He was also a man of impeccable character, piety and scrupulous manners and habits. He ate most frugally, and led a very simple and austere lifestyle. He literally followed in the steps of the Prophet whose sayings and utterances he was so eager to preserve for posterity. He became so proficient in *hadith* literature that on a number of occasions he allowed his knowledge of *hadith* to be tested by some of the most distinguished scholars of his time. During one such occasion, ten reputable scholars of Baghdad publicly put him to the test in order to ascertain his knowledge of Prophetic traditions. They deliberately changed and altered the chain of narration (*isnad*) of around one hundred different *ahadith*, and then recited them to him in front of the public. He was then asked to comment on them. Al-Bukhari confessed that he was not familiar with those *hadith*, and instead recited all the authentic versions of the same *hadith* with their correct chains of narration. He then commented that the scholars who had recited the hundred *ahadith* might have muddled and confused their chains of narration. Al-Bukhari's depth and breadth of learning left his interrogators, as well as the spectators, utterly spellbound. On another occasion, a number of acclaimed scholars of *hadith*, led by Abul Hussain Asakir al-Din Muslim ibn al-Hajjaj (better known as Imam Muslim), questioned him on several issues relating to the science of *hadith*, and they found him to be thoroughly proficient on the subject. In short, al-Bukhari emerged from these and many other similar tests he was subjected to during his lifetime, with his reputation enhanced.

If al-Bukhari was a great master and memoriser of *hadith*, then he was an equally prolific writer. After collecting more than half a million *hadith*, he systematically investigated and examined them in order to ascertain their veracity. There-

after, he classified all the *hadith* according to a grading scale, thus sifting the sound traditions from the fabricated and spurious ones. Such an advanced and scientific methodology, developed by al-Bukhari and his contemporaries, enabled him to collect and preserve only the authentic Prophetic traditions for the benefit of future generations. It is also worth highlighting that al-Bukhari began to write books from an early age. He composed his first book on *hadith* during his stay in Madinah, when he was only eighteen. This book contained a large collection of sayings and exhortations attributed to the Prophet's companions (*sahabah*) and their successors (*tabiun*). He also wrote a book on *hadith* narrators during his early years. In other words, his intellectual and literary accomplishments during his student days were nothing short of remarkable. All his teachers recognised and praised his intellectual abilities and vast learning, and some even predicted a bright future for him. As it transpired, he contributed more to Islamic thought and scholarship than any other scholar of his generation, while his anthology of *hadith* is today revered as one of the most authentic in the field of *hadith* literature. Of all his works, his most seminal contribution was *Jami al-Sahih*, better known as *Sahih al-Bukhari*. This collection of *hadith* was the product of an entire lifetime devoted solely to the study, research and verification of Prophetic *hadith*. Being his *magnum opus*, this anthology is today widely considered to be the most authentic book of Islamic teachings after the Holy Qur'an, the Divine revelation itself.

It is related that al-Bukhari was prompted to compose this book after the distinguished traditionist, Ishaq ibn Rahawaih, once publicly expressed his wish that a reputed scholar of *hadith* should prepare a large collection of authentic *hadith*. This remark apparently convinced al-Bukhari to muster all his might and energy for the compilation of his immortal *Jami al-Sahih*, a multi-volume work on *hadith* which has stood the test of time and remains an unrivalled work in the field of *hadith* to this day. Using strict criteria – to ascertain the genuineness of each and every *hadith* – he sifted through more than half a million *ahadith* and chose only the most authentic ones for inclusion in his *Jami al-Sahih*. He arranged the book subject-wise using different headings (including The Book of Knowledge (*Kitab al-Ilm*) and The Book of Ablution (*Kitab al-Wudu*), and finally completed his treasure trove of *hadith* after almost four decades of research. Consisting of a total of seven thousand, two hundred and twenty-two Prophetic narrations, this anthology of *hadith* has not only established al-Bukhari's reputation as one of the Muslim world's most famous and influential scholars, it has also immortalised his name. *Jami al-Sahih* thus represents the pinnacle of achievement in the field of *hadith* literature and it is very unlikely that another scholar of al-Bukhari's calibre will appear again.

After decades of travelling in the single-minded pursuit of Islamic knowledge and wisdom, al-Bukhari returned to Muslim Central Asia and settled in Nishapur; he was fifty-four at the time. The people of that city received him warmly, and he continued to study, research and teach Prophetic traditions until the local governor forced him to leave the city for refusing to deliver lectures on *hadith* at his official residence. Al-Bukhari then settled in a small town adjacent to his native Bukhara and passed away at the age of approximately sixty-one.

# 14

# Abu Hanifah
# (b.700 - d.767)

THE PRINCIPLES OF *shari'ah* (Islamic law) are derived from the Qur'an and the normative practice (*sunnah*) of the Prophet Muhammad. The early Muslims were fortunate enough to have lived during the lifetime of the Prophet, who guided them in their daily affairs. After the death of the Prophet, his leading companions, such as Abu Bakr al-Siddiq, Umar ibn al-Khattab, Uthman ibn Affan and Ali ibn Abi Talib, assumed the leadership of the Muslim community and ruled the expanding Islamic State in accordance with the teachings of the Qur'an and the Prophetic *sunnah*. Although Islamic principles and practices underpinned the affairs of the Islamic society established by the Prophet and his companions during the early days of Islam, the *shari'ah* was not codified in a systematic way at the time. After the period of the Prophet's companions, as the Islamic dominion continued to expand rapidly and Muslims came into contact with other cultures and traditions, and more and more non-Muslims embraced the faith of their conquerors, new and unexpected social, political, cultural, legal and economic challenges confronted both the rulers and the scholars of Islam. At such a critical time in Islamic history, Abu Hanifah emerged to

develop one of Islamic history's most influential legal synthesis.

Numan ibn Thabit ibn Zuta ibn Mah, better known by his patronymic Abu Hanifah, was born in Kufah (in modern Iraq) during the reign of the great Umayyad Caliph Abd al-Malik ibn Marwan. Of Persian origin, Abu Hanifah was brought up in a relatively wealthy Muslim family. His father, Thabit, was a noted business-man who had the honour of meeting Ali, the fourth Caliph of Islam, who reportedly prayed for Thabit and his family. Like his father, Abu Hanifah grew up to be a successful merchant. Since Kufah at the time was a major centre of Islamic learning and intellectual activity, some of the most famous companions of the Prophet (such as Abdullah ibn Mas'ud) settled in this city in order to disseminate Islamic learning and wisdom. Abu Hanifah was very fortunate to have met a number of prominent companions, includ-ing Anas ibn Malik, Sahl ibn Sa'd, Abu al-Tufail Amir ibn Watihilah and Jabir ibn Abdullah. That was why he considered himself to be a successor (*tabi*) of the Prophet's companions. However, some Muslim scholars have questioned whether Abu Hanifah did actually meet any companions of the Prophet, but according to luminaries such as Khatib al-Baghdadi, Yahya al-Nawawi, Shams al-Din al-Dhahabi, Ibn Hajar al-Asqalani and Zain al-Din al-Iraqi, he met between eight and ten companions of the Prophet.

Abu Hanifah spent his early years pursuing business and commercial interests. Since the tyrant Hajjaj ibn Yusuf ruled in at Kufah at the time, it appears that Abu Hanifah was only too happy to pursue his business affairs while Hajjaj was in charge. After the latter's death in 713, political turmoil and social unrest began to subside in and around Kufah. The death of Caliph al-Walid a year later also helped to restore peace and order across the Islamic world. Caliph Sulaiman, al-Walid's successor, was a relatively benevolent ruler who promoted learning and scholarship. The new, peaceful ambience created by Sulaiman's accession to power probably encouraged Abu Hanifah to devote more time to the pursuit of learning and education. It is related that one day while he was passing by the house of al-Sha'bi (an eminent scholar of the time), the latter – mistaking him for one of his students – asked him where he was going. Abu Hanifah replied that he was on his way to meet a certain merchant. Whereupon al-Sha'bi told Abu Hanifah that he showed signs of intelligence and he ought to devote more time to his studies. These words of advice apparently fired Abu Hanifah's imagination, and he began to dedicate all his time and energy to the pursuit of Islamic knowledge and wisdom.

By all accounts, Abu Hanifah was a late starter and most of his peers were way ahead of him when he began his studies. But, thanks to his indefatigable energy and intellectual brilliance, he soon became a prominent Islamic thinker and jurist. He may have embarked on the path of Islamic learning and education with some hesitation, but after he had started he was determined to reach the very summit of Islamic learning and scholarship. Hailed as *al-imam al-azam* (or 'the great scholar of Islam'), Abu Hanifah went on to become one of the Muslim world's greatest intellectuals and jurists. As a gifted and hardworking student, he rapidly made up for lost time by plunging himself deep into the ocean of Islamic learning and wisdom. He sat at the feet of great luminaries like al-Sha'bi, Salama ibn Kuhail, A'mash, Hammad and Amr ibn Murrah – all of whom were based in Kufah at the time – and received a thorough education and training in traditional Islamic sciences including Qur'anic exegesis (*tafsir*), Islamic theology (*kalam*) and jurisprudence (*fiqh*). In addition, Abu Hanifah gained proficiency in Arabic grammar, literature and aspects of history and genealogy before he proceeded to Basrah and attended the lectures of Qatada and Shu'ba, both of whom had learned *hadith* directly from the Prophet's companions. Abu Hanifah's sharp intellect, coupled with his unflinching dedication to his studies, enabled him to understand and assimilate Islamic knowledge very rapidly. So much so that his tutor Shu'ba once remarked, 'Just as I know that the sun is bright, I know for certain that learning and Abu Hanifah are doubles of each other.' Thus he not only became proficient in *hadith*, but Shu'ba also formally authorised him to impart knowledge of *hadith* to others.

Now increasingly recognised as an esteemed scholar in his own right, Abu Hanifah could have established his own school and begun to teach, but he decided to learn more. Thus he went to Makkah to perform the sacred *hajj* (pilgrimage) and during his stay there received advanced training in Islamic jurisprudence under the tutelage of the leading scholars of Makkah and Madinah. He enrolled at the school of Ata ibn Abu Rabah, who was considered to be one of the giants of Islamic learning and wisdom at the time. Referring to Ata, Abdullah ibn Umar, the distinguished companion of the Prophet, used to say, 'Why do people come to me when Ata ibn Abu Rabah is there for them to go to?' Such was his greatness as a scholar and repository of Islamic knowledge that Abu Hanifah attended his lectures regularly before refining his knowledge of *hadith* and jurisprudence under the guidance of Ikrima, who was an outstanding pupil of none other than Abdullah ibn Abbas, the cousin of the Prophet.

In the year 720, when Abu Hanifah was twenty-one, he left Makkah for Madinah where he learned *hadith* from Sulaiman and Salim ibn Abdullah. Sulaiman was an aide of *ummul mu'minin* (the 'mother of the believers') Maimuna, the wife of the Prophet, and Salim was a grandson of Umar, the second Caliph of Islam. They were considered to be two of the most learned scholars of Madinah at the time. Having travelled to some of the leading centres of Islamic learning and acquired thorough training in all the branches of Islamic knowledge under the guidance of some of the most eminent Islamic scholars of his time, Abu Hanifah became a great repository of Islamic knowledge. His mastery of Islamic thought elevated him to a new level within the firmament of Islamic learning and scholarship. Thanks to his vast knowledge, he became a very famous scholar, even during his own lifetime. As his reputation spread far and wide, certain unscrupulous people began to circulate misinformation and falsehoods about him; perhaps they were jealous of his personal standing and immense learning. Once, during his stay in Madinah, Abu Hanifah was introduced to Imam Muhammad al-Baqir by one of his colleagues. When the great Imam asked Abu Hanifah why he contradicted the *hadith* of the Prophet through *qiyas* (or analogical deduction), he retorted that he would never dare do such a thing. He then asked Imam al-Baqir to take a seat and he would explain his position. The following conversation ensured:

Abu Hanifah: *'Who is the weaker, man or woman?*
Imam al-Baqir: *'Woman.'*
Abu Hanifah: *'Which of them is entitled to larger share in inheritance?*
Imam al-Baqir: *'The man.'*
Abu Hanifah: *'If I had been making deductions by analogy, I should have said that the woman should get the larger share, since on the face of it the weaker one is entitled to more consideration. But I have not said so. To take up another subject, which do you think is the higher duty, prayer or fasting?*
Imam al-Baqir: *'Prayer.'*
Abu Hanifah: *'In that case, it should be permissible for a woman during menstruation to postpone her prayers and not her fasts. But the ruling I give is that she can postpone her fasting and not her prayers.'*

Hearing this Imam al-Baqir stood up, smiled and kissed Abu Hanifah on his forehead and acknowledged that he was no ordinary scholar; rather he was one of Islam's greatest legal minds.

As an Islamic thinker and pioneer of Islamic legal thought, Abu Hanifah was way ahead of his time. His grasp of Islam was as rigorous, comprehensive and authentic as it could ever be, but he knew more than anyone else that the law was meant to be followed and adhered to by the people, rather than kept in books. As such, he argued, law and legal principles had to be directly relevant to people's daily lives. Since people are mobile, society is constantly in flux. Thus a legal framework which remained static for too long could easily become irrelevant over time, unless it was constantly renewed in the light of new social, political, economic and technological developments. Abu Hanifah understood this process of socio-political change and historical evolution better than any other scholar of his generation, and he set about interpreting the Islamic scriptural sources [namely the Qur'an and the authentic *sunnah* (normative practice of the Prophet)] in direct response to the needs of his time. That is to say, he pioneered a new legal interpretative methodology based on the two fundamental sources of Islam and used this fresh, innovative and dynamic legal methodology to formulate Islamic answers to the problems and challenges which confronted the Muslims of his time.

Although the answers formulated by Abu Hanifah were based on a literalist understanding of the Qur'an and *sunnah* of the Prophet, he did not hesitate to use his intellectual discretion (*ijtihad*) where he felt this was appropriate. As an undisputed master of Islamic legal theory and jurisprudence, he was able to bridge gaps which others struggled even to see. Not surprisingly, even some of the most eminent Islamic scholars of his time initially misunderstood his ideas and thoughts. Thus, some people accused him of being a wilful innovator in religion, while others suggested he was misguided. Even a great scholar like Imam Abu Amr Abd al-Rahman ibn Amr al-Awza'i failed to understand his legal thought and methodology. Once Abdullah ibn Mubarak, who was a prominent student of Abu Hanifah, visited Imam al-Awza'i in Beirut to complete his study of *hadith* under the latter, but on his arrival there al-Awza'i asked him, 'Who is this man Abu Hanifah who has appeared at Kufah? I hear he makes all sorts of new points about religion.' Abdullah did not respond to his query and returned home to collect a manuscript authored by Abu Hanifah, and handed it over to al-Awza'i. After reading the entire text, al-Awza'i remarked, 'Who is this worthy, Numan?' Abdullah replied that he was a great scholar of Kufah under whom he had studied. 'A great man.' responded Awza'i. 'This is the same Abu Hanifah whom you called an innovator.' countered Abdullah. Al-Awza'i regretted his error.

All great pioneers have obstacles placed in their way by their detractors at one time or another, and Abu Hanifah was no different. He was an outstanding genius and a great visionary who not only acquired a thorough understanding of the Islamic sources, but also developed an unusual insight into human nature and its frailties. The vast corpus of juristic pronouncements (*fatawa*) developed by Abu Hanifah and his trusted disciples became so large that, over time, a school of Islamic legal thought emerged named after him. Known as the *hanafi madhhab*, this school of Islamic legal thought is today the Muslim world's most widely followed *madhhab*. Pioneered by Abu Hanifah and his distinguished pupils such as Zu'far ibn al-Hudhail, Abu Yusuf Yaqub ibn Ibrahim and Muhammad ibn al-Hasan al-Shaybani, this school of legal thought is most prevalent in India, Pakistan, Bangladesh, Afghanistan, Turkey, Syria, Iraq and Egypt. Towards the end of his life, Abu Hanifah was imprisoned by the Abbasid Caliph Abu Ja'far al-Mansur for refusing to take up the post of *qadi* (Judge) of the Abbasid Empire. But, according to another account, he was imprisoned for allegedly supporting the Zaydis (a Shi'a faction) who were bitterly opposed to the Abbasids. Either way, Abu Hanifah died in prison at the age of around sixty-seven and was buried in Baghdad, where a mausoleum was later built in his memory by Mimar Sinan, the famous Ottoman builder and architect.

# 15

## Abul Hasan al-Ash'ari
## (b.873 - d.941)

AFTER THE DEATH of Caliph Uthman, huge controversy ensued within the Islamic State regarding the question of leadership and political legitimacy. During this period, a number of political factions emerged including the *shi'at Ali*, *khawarij*, *murji'ah* and the *mu'tazilah*. Although these groups emerged due to differences of opinion over political matters, they subsequently went on to develop their own distinct philosophical and theological views. Of these factions, the most politically neutral were the *mu'tazilah* who later acquired a largely philosophical and theological contour under the influence of Wasil ibn Ata. A student of Hasan al-Basri, he parted company (*i'tizal*) with his tutor following an acrimonious dispute between the two men. Under Wasil's tutelage, Mu'tazilism became an influential philosophical-cum-theological edifice. Heavily influenced by political Mu'tazilism and Greek philosophical thought, Wasil and his associates formulated a distinct Mu'tazilite creed based on their rationalistic understanding and interpretation of the nature of God, His Essence and Attributes (*dhat wa sifat Allah*), the concept of Divine speech (*kalam Allah*) and the purpose of creation. The Mu'tazilite philosophical interpretation of these fundamental Islamic

beliefs and concepts was vehemently opposed by the traditionalists, but it received a favourable reception from the Abbasid elites. Thus famous Abbasid rulers like Harun al-Rashid and his son al-Ma'mun became ardent champions of Mu'tazilism; so much so that under al-Ma'mun's stewardship this creed was declared the dominant theology of the State. At a time when orthodoxy was shunned and heterodoxy became the order of the day, Abul Hasan al-Ash'ari, one of the Muslim world's most influential theologians (*mutakallimun*), emerged to turn the tables on Mu'tazilism.

Abul Hasan Ali ibn Ismail al-Ash'ari was born in Basrah (in modern Iraq) into a distinguished Muslim family which traced its lineage back to Abu Musa al-Ash'ari, who was a prominent companion of the Prophet. Ismail, the father of al-Ash'ari was a learned and highly respected citizen of Basrah. He died when al-Ash'ari was still a youngster, and this forced his family into poverty. Young al-Ash'ari thus suffered considerable personal hardship until his mother married Abu Ali Muhammad ibn Abd al-Wahhab al-Jubbai, who was one of the foremost students of Wasil ibn Ata. Based at the Mu'tazilite Basrah headquarters, al-Jubbai was widely revered as one of the great exponents of Mu'tazilism. Brought up and educated under the guidance and care of a leading figure of philosophical rationalism, al-Ash'ari mastered Arabic grammar, literature, Islamic sciences and the philosophical and theological doctrines of Mu'tazilism from an early age. As a teacher and writer, Abu Ali al-Jubbai was a powerful exponent of Mu'tazilism, but he was not noted for his debating or oratory skills. Raised and nurtured in the home of Mu'tazilism, al-Ash'ari became a committed and proficient exponent of Mu'tazilite beliefs and doctrines. Indeed, he mastered philosophical rationalism sufficiently enough to engage in debates and discussions concerning the finer points of Mu'tazilite philosophy and theology when he was barely twenty years old. His vast erudition and debating skills soon earned him much acclaim, even during Abu Ali al-Jubbai's own lifetime. Thus everyone expected al-Ash'ari to follow in the footsteps of his aged teacher, mentor and stepfather and become a champion of Mu'tazilism after the latter's death.

When al-Jubbai died in Basrah in 915, al-Ash'ari was forty-two and already widely recognised as one of the most learned and accomplished Mu'tazilite theologians of his generation. Although there were other respected Mu'tazilite scholars around at the time (including Abul Hashim, the son of al-Jubbai, who lived in Basrah and was considered to be a skilful interpreter of Mu'tazilism; Abul Hussain al-Khayyat and Abul Qasim al-Balkhi, both of whom were based in Baghdad), al-Ash'ari was considered to be far superior to all of them on account of his mastery of the finer points of Mu'tazilite philosophy and theology. Furthermore, in comparison with the other Mu'tazilite thinkers of the time, he was a better debater and orator especially when it came to defending Mu'tazilism against its traditionalist foes. In short, al-Ash'ari was in a league of his own and following Abu Ali al-Jubbai's death, he became the undisputed leader and champion of this philosophical creed.

Whilst everyone expected al-Ash'ari to succeed al-Jubbai as the pre-eminent leader of Mu'tazilism, events took an unexpected turn. According to al-Ash'ari, the Prophet Muhammad appeared to him in a dream and instructed him to champion the cause of Islamic orthodoxy, rather than that of Mu'tazilism. This Prophetic intervention proved decisive as far as al-Ash'ari was concerned. Although he considered himself to be a defender of the Mu'tazilite creed, the Prophet's repudiation of Mu'tazilite beliefs and practices shook al-Ash'ari to his core. He thus confined himself to his house for about two weeks, enduring a period of intense soul-searching and coming to terms with his new experience. After nearly forty years of learning, refining, mastering and hair-splitting debates and discussion on the finer points of Mu'tazilite philosophy and theology, it all now appeared to him to be false and spurious. Otherwise why would the Prophet of God appear to him in a dream and show him the way forward? Suddenly, it was as if al-Ash'ari woke up from a deep sleep, only to discover that he had already spent four decades of his life studying and championing the cause of an un-Islamic creed. According to al-Ash'ari, the unexpected visitation from the Prophet, coupled with the Divine light (*nur*) and blessing (*barakah*) which was bestowed on him, enabled him to come to terms with his predicament. After fifteen days of deep reflection, intense introspection and intellectual realignment, he emerged from his house on a Friday afternoon – prior to *salat al-jumu'ah* (or Friday congregational prayer) – and went straight to the central mosque in Basrah, which at the time was packed to its maximum capacity. He stepped onto the *minbar* (pulpit) and delivered an historic announcement. This announcement was to mark the beginning of the end for philosophical rationalism and the resurgence of Islamic traditionalism.

In his unique and inimitable style, al-Ash'ari proclaimed: 'He who knows me, knows who I am, and he who does not know me, let him know that I am Abul Hasan Ali al-Ash'ari; that I used to maintain that the Qur'an is created, that eyes of men shall not see God, and that the creatures create their actions. Lo! I repent that I have been a Mu'tazilite. I renounce these opinions and I take the opportunity to refute the Mu'tazilites and expose their inconsistencies and turpitude.'

His public repudiation of Mu'tazilism represented a milestone in Islamic intellectual history, for the battleline between Islamic orthodoxy and philosophical rationalism now became clear – especially as the Mu'tazilite rationalists lost one of their most formidable champions. Prior to his conversion to Islamic orthodoxy, the Mu'tazilites dealt with the traditionalists' attacks on their creed with ease, but following his conversion, he became their intellectual tormentor *par excellence*, as the Mu'tazilites found themselves caught between a rock and a hard place. As expected, a reinvigorated al-Ash'ari then launched a systematic and full-blown attack on the philosophical and theological foundations of their creed. Having studied Mu'tazilite ideas and thought under the guidance of its prominent thinkers (like Abu Ali al-Jubbai), and mastered the art of philosophical and theological discourse, he now became the Mu'tazilites most formidable intellectual adversary. Unable to answer his cogent and stinging philosophical and theological assaults on the very foundations of their school of thought, the Mu'tazilites suddenly found themselves stranded in an intellectual no-man's land.

Al-Ash'ari's repudiation of Mu'tazilism was both comprehensive and monumentally effective. He composed more than ninety books and treatises on all aspects of Islamic beliefs (*aqida*) and theology (*kalam*), in refutation of the Mu'tazilite creed, and aspects of Islamic epistemology and philosophy. And in so doing, he developed a powerful synthesis between reason (*aql*) and revelation (*wahy*), and philosophical rationalism and Islamic beliefs and religious dicta. His most famous books included *al-Ibana an-Usul al-Diniyya* (The Delineation of Religious Principles), *Kitab al-Luma* (The Luminous Book) and *Maqalat al-Islamiyyin* (Beliefs of Muslims). In these, and other books, he provided a systematic interpretation and exposition of core Islamic theological beliefs and concepts based

on his profound knowledge and understanding of the original Islamic scriptural sources on the one hand, and thorough acquaintance with the methods of the philosophers and the speculative theologians on the other. Like his *al-Ibana*, al-Ash'ari's *Maqalat* was rated very highly by the scholars of Islam, so much so that Ibn Taymiyyah wrote in his *Minhaj al-Sunnah al-Nabawiyyah* (Towards Prophetic Methodology) that he had not come across another book like it.

As philosophical rationalists, the Mu'tazilites believed in the pre-eminence of human intellect; that is to say, they considered Divine revelation (*wahy*) to be subservient to human reason (*aql*). Not surprisingly, they interpreted fundamental Islamic concepts – the Oneness of God (*tawhid*), Divine Names and Attributes (*al-asma wa'l sifat*), and the nature of the Qur'an – from a purely rationalistic perspective. The traditionalists not only considered such an interpretation of Islam to be unorthodox and blameworthy, they also considered the Mu'tazilites to be heretics and innovators in religious matters. Led by eminent Islamic scholars like Ahmad ibn Hanbal, the traditionalists vehemently opposed the philosophical interpretation of Islamic theological matters. They considered the 'external' (*zahiri*) meaning of the Divine revelation (the Qur'an) and the Prophetic traditions (*hadith*) to be sufficient for human guidance. By contrast, al-Ash'ari considered both of these views to be wrong and extreme. Instead, he took the middle path and argued that revelation and reason were equally indispensable for formulating a balanced interpretation and understanding of Islamic thought and worldview. He therefore devoted all his time and energy to reconciling these two extreme views, which at the time competed for the hearts and minds of the Muslims.

Refuting the Mu'tazilite belief that Divine Attributes were not real, and that human beings would not be able to see God in the hereafter without Him having to reincarnate Himself in a non-human form, al-Ash'ari stated that the Qur'an was the uncreated (*ghair makhluq*), eternal Word of God, and that only the ink, paper and individual letters were created. Unlike the Mu'tazilites, he further clarified that the Prophet Muhammad could intercede on behalf of Muslims in the next life, if he wished, by God's permission. This way, one by one, al-Ash'ari demolished the heretical creed of the rationalists, and reiterated traditional Islamic positions on all important theological matters.

Al-Ash'ari emerged at a time when Mu'tazilism was already on the wane following the death of Caliphs Mu'tasim Billah and Wathiq. Along with Abdullah al-Ma'mun, these two Abbasid rulers became very powerful benefactors of the Mu'tazilite creed, but this state of affairs changed immediately after Mutawakkil ala Allah ascended the Abbasid throne in 847. He demoted all the adherents and supporters of Mu'tazilism from the highest echelons of power and reinstated traditional Islam as the official religion of the Abbasid Empire. Despite this, the intellectual legacy of Wasil ibn Ata and his Mu'tazilite creed persisted within the intellectual and cultural circles of the Abbasid Empire. But thanks to al-Ash'ari's sustained and merciless critique of philosophical rationalism, the Mu'tazilite creed was eventually rooted out from the intellectual and cultural lives of Muslims.

Al-Ash'ari was not only an outstanding Islamic intellectual; he was also one of the greatest religious thinkers of all time. Not surprisingly, his religious thought and intellectual legacy continues to exert a profound influence on the way Muslims think, behave and lead their lives to this day. He died and was buried in a place close to *bab al-Basrah* (or 'the Gate of Basrah'); he was sixty-eight at the time. After his death, some of his prominent successors such as Abu Ja'far al-Tahawi of Egypt and Abu Mansur al-Maturidi of Muslim Central Asia endeavoured to formulate a unified theology (*kalam*), which they hoped would be acceptable to Muslims of all backgrounds. From that day on, Ash'arism became the most dominant religious theology in the Muslim world.

# 16

## Salah al-Din Ayyubi (b.1138 - d.1193)

THE TWELFTH CENTURY was one of the most difficult and chaotic periods in Muslim history. The unity of the Muslim *ummah* (global Muslim community) was shattered by incessant political rivalry and internal conflict. In the Islamic East, the once formidable Abbasid Caliphate and the Seljuk dynasty became politically very weak and were in power only in name. The same was true of the once-powerful Fatimid Kingdom of Egypt. In addition, the territories of the Islamic Fertile Crescent became divided and sub-divided into tiny fiefdoms, and their rulers frequently fought each other for political and military supremacy. To make matters worse, at the same time the Muslims also came under direct threat from a formidable foreign enemy, namely the Crusaders who had set out from Europe in order to subjugate the Islamic East. The Muslims were thus caught unprepared by the Crusaders, who captured a large stretch of Islamic territories on the coast of the Eastern Mediterranean. They then marched towards their biggest prize, *al-quds* or Jerusalem, the third sacred city of Islam. Of course, the bitterly divided Muslim rulers of the time had no answer to the might and firepower of the Crusaders who inflicted a crushing defeat on them by capturing Jerusalem and massacring

its citizens *en masse*. At a time when the Muslims found themselves hopelessly out-played and out-manoeuvred by the Crusaders, the legendary Sultan Salah al-Din emerged to restore the battered pride and prestige of the Muslim *ummah*.

Salah al-Din Yusuf ibn Ayyub, known in the Western world as Saladin, was born in Tikrit in modern Iraq. Of Kurdish origin, his family originally hailed from the Central Asian country of Armenia. After settling in the territory which now includes northern Iraq, parts of Turkey and Syria, the members of the Ayyub family became prominent citizens of their locality. Both Salah al-Din's father and uncle became distinguished members of Sultan Imad al-Din Zangi's political and civil administration. In the year Salah al-Din was born, his father Najm al-Din Ayyub was appointed governor of the ancient city of Heliopolis (later renamed Ba'alabek and today located in Lebanon). Thus young Salah al-Din spent his early years in this ancient city. Since his father was a learned individual of Sufi (or Islamic mystical) orientation, he erected a Sufi lodge (*zawiyyah*) for his spiritually-inclined friends and acquaintances. During his early years, Salah al-Din learned the Qur'an and received a thorough training in traditional Islamic sciences, as well as Arabic grammar, literature and poetry.

Ayyub's outstanding services to Imad al-Din, the reigning monarch, earned him considerable accolade but, following his patron's sudden death, Ayyub's family was forced to endure both political and economic hardship until he was persuaded by his brother, Asad al-Din Shirkuh (at the time in the service of Imad al-Din's son and successor Nur al-Din Zangi), to co-operate with the new master of the Zangid dynasty. Ayyub agreed to help Nur al-Din consolidate his grip on power and Nur al-Din, in turn, rewarded Ayyub for his co-operation with the governorship of Damascus. At the time Salah al-Din was a teenager and spent the next decade (that is, from 1154 to 1164) at his father's residence in Damascus. Being the son of the governor, he was held in high esteem by everyone; it is also related that during this period Salah al-Din became very fond of Nur al-Din on account of his personal piety and exemplary conduct and behaviour.

Impressed by Nur al-Din's unflinching devotion to Islamic principles and practices, Salah al-Din also moulded his own character and personality in accordance with Islamic teachings. Indeed, his regard for Islamic principles, coupled with his scrupulous habits and sublime qualities, later earned him great acclaim both in the East and the West. Even his critics could not help but admire him for his unusual acts of kindness, generosity and tolerance. As a matter of fact, Salah al-Din disliked pomp and pageantry, and instead devoted much of his time to daily prayers and other devotional acts (*ibadah*). Like Nur al-Din, he led a simple and austere lifestyle, far removed from the luxuries and material pleasures of this life. Until the age of twenty-five, he led a normal life without showing any signs of the great man that he was to be. Having led an uneventful and relatively tranquil childhood and early adult life, he expected to pass smoothly into a restful old age, he suddenly found himself forced into the murky and dangerous world of global politics.

Struck down by a malady, Sultan Nur al-Din was confined to his bed. That is when Shirkuh, the uncle of Salah al-Din and commander-in-chief of Nur al-Din's armed forces, approached the ailing Sultan for his permission to launch a military expedition against the subversive rulers of the Fatimid Kingdom of Egypt. After some hesitation, the Sultan authorised Shirkuh to lead an expedition against the Fatimids. During the ensuing campaign, Shirkuh – assisted by his nephew Salah al-Din – outmanoeuvred all his opponents, and assumed full control of Fatimid Egypt. Soon after capturing Egypt, Shirkuh died in 1169 without consolidating his grip on the country. Although Salah al-Din came with his uncle somewhat recluctantly – and was only too happy to let his battle-hardened and accomplished uncle make all the important decisions – now he had no choice but to take matters into his own hands and, in so doing, carve out a unique place for himself in the annals of history. Three days after Shirkuh's death, the reigning Fatimid Caliph al-Adid asked Salah al-Din to succeed his uncle, and he conferred on him the title of *al-malik an-nasir* (or 'the Supporting King'). He was only thirty at the time and his accession to power in Egypt made him a stronger, determined and wiser political operator, although he continued to lead a reclusive lifestyle far removed from the joys and pleasures of aristocratic life. According to his contemporaries, Salah al-Din's personal life remained as simple as ever and he continued to devote long periods to prayer and contemplation. Devout and sagacious, he also worked tirelessly to unify the Muslim world under the banner of Islam and, in so doing, established a powerful empire in the Islamic East with the aim of liberating the sacred city of Jerusalem from the grip of the Crusaders. 'When God Almighty granted me the land of Egypt', Salah al-Din later recalled, 'I was certain that Palestine would also fall to me.'

While Salah al-Din was busy planning to liberate Jerusalem from the Crusaders, the other Muslim rulers of the day were busy fighting each other in an attempt to increase their personal power and wealth. Then again, gifted men like Salah al-Din are not born every day; rather they emerge during critical times in human history and, by the sheer force of their character and personality, they change the course of world history. After becoming the ruler of Egypt, restoring the honour of Islam by driving out the Crusaders from Islamic Jerusalem became his main political objective. His unexpected success against the Crusaders firmly established his reputation as a great champion of Islam; he also became one of the most successful warrior-kings in the annals of history.

As *al-malik an-nasir*, Salah al-Din instigated wide-ranging reforms within the highest echelons of power in Egypt. By reshuffling the civil and administrative structures of his Government, he removed most of the corrupt, scheming and treacherous elements from his administration and replaced them with clean, honest and upright people. He then sent an invitation to his father, Ayyub, who at the time was living in Damascus, to come and join him in Egypt. Ayyub thus migrated to Egypt with his entire family, including his distant relatives and acquaintances. Surrounded for the first time by his close family members and friends, Salah al-Din at last became the undisputed ruler of Egypt. Needless to say, the consolidation of his grip on power in Egypt helped him to carry out further reforms, including the abolishment of the decadent Fatimid dynasty (accomplished after the death of the last Fatimid Caliph al-Adid) and the redistribution of all the wealth and properties the Fatimids had hoarded.

He divided this wealth into three portions, sending a share to the Abbasid Caliph in Baghdad, another portion to Damascus for Sultan Nur al-Din and deposited the remainder in the public treasury (*bait al-mal*) for the welfare of the Egyptian people. Salah al-Din refused to keep anything for himself or his family. His kindness and generosity soon endeared him to the masses as he lavished them with gifts and presents, while preferring to lead a very simple and austere lifestyle himself. Indeed, he refused to live in the pompous and extravagant Caliphal palaces built by the Fatimids, choosing instead to live in his rather old and dated residence in Cairo. When this residence eventually became too small for the smooth and effective operation of his Government, he built himself a simple but elegant building in Cairo so that he could perform his duties as the ruler of Egypt with efficiency and effectiveness. Soon after consolidating his power in Egypt, Salah al-Din received the news of Nur al-Din's death in 1174. He understood the gravity of the situation and moved swiftly to avert any internal conflict in Syria, and in so doing he assumed full control of that strategically important country. Following his annexation of Syria, he appointed his nephew, Farooq Shah, to be governor of that territory. Still only thirty-six, he now embarked on a series of military campaigns in order to strengthen and unify the warring neighbouring Muslim lands. In addition to Syria and Mesopotamia, he successfully captured a large part of North Africa including Tunisia, Libya and much of Arabia, as well as Yemen. Salah al-Din soon carved out a huge empire and as a result he became the undisputed leader of the Muslim world at the time.

As one of the most powerful Muslim rulers of his time, Salah al-Din could have chosen to spend the rest of his life in peace and comfort, if he wished, but instead he focused his attention on the subversive activities of the Crusaders who, at the time, maintained a tight grip on Palestine. After establishing themselves in that country, the Crusaders began to wreak havoc throughout the entire region. So much so, that on one occasion they marched very close to the precinct of Madinah, the city of the Prophet, and threatened to overwhelm the city. When Salah al-Din received news of the Crusaders' outrageous behaviour towards the people of Madinah, he vowed to punish the culprits with his own hands. As commander-in-chief of the armed forces, he left Egypt and marched with his army towards Palestine in order to confront the threat of the Crusaders. He came face to face with his opponents at a placed called Tiberias, near the Sea of Galilee, in 1187 and a fierce clash ensued. His troops launched such a vicious and co-ordinated attack on the Franks that soon the latter began to lose heart. In desperation, some Frankish generals abandoned their forces and came directly to Salah al-Din to plead with him to speed up his victory and ease their pain and agony. During this historic encounter, known as the Battle of Hittin (Hattin), Salah al-Din also taught the Frankish Crusaders a good lesson in kindness, generosity and compassion. From that day on, his name became a symbol of bravery and heroism both in the East and the West.

Victory at Tiberias opened the door to the rest of Palestine. He moved swiftly, before the Franks could regroup again, and Salah al-Din was able to offer his Friday congregational prayer inside the same mosque which had been converted into a church three generations earlier by the Crusaders. Salah al-Din single-handedly took on the combined might of Europe and cut it to pieces. It did not take him long to capture the rest of Palestine including, of course, Jerusalem – and he did so without shedding any innocent blood. By contrast, when the Crusaders first entered Je-rusalem they put all its inhabitants to the sword, so that the entire city ran red with blood. But Salah al-Din's acts of kindness, generosity and benevolence won the hearts and minds of all its population, and even the Christian chroniclers of the Crusades could not help but lavish much praise on him for his exemplary behaviour and attitude towards the people of Jerusalem.

Thanks to Salah al-Din, *al-quds* – the third sacred city of Islam – again came under Islamic rule. With his mission accomplished, Salah al-Din returned to Damascus where he built many schools, mosques and hospitals, and passed away around the age of fifty-five; he lies buried within the precinct of the city's historic Umayyad mosque. But his name and fame continue to reverberate throughout the Muslim world, as well as the West, to this day. A man of truly remarkable character and sublime qualities, it is not surprising that Salah al-Din is today considered to be one of history's most famous and influential Muslims.

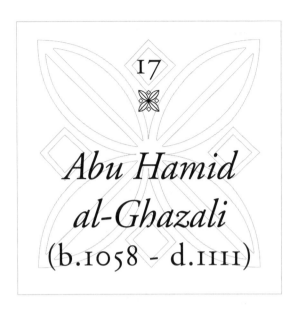

# 17

## Abu Hamid al-Ghazali (b.1058 ~ d.1111)

ALTHOUGH THE MAIN sources of early Islamic thought were the Qur'an and Prophetic *sunnah*, following the rapid expansion of Islam into Egypt, Persia and Syria the Muslims – for the first time – came directly in contact with foreign ideas and thoughts (such as ancient Greek philosophy) which subsequently exerted a profound influence on the Muslim intelligentsia. As a result, Islamic thought began to manifest itself in several different ways. For a start, although Mu'tazilism initially emerged as a political movement, it later assumed a wholly rationalistic contour under the influence of Wasil ibn Ata. Influenced by Hellenistic thought, the *falasifah* (or the Muslim philosophers) then emerged to pioneer a largely philosophical interpretation of Islam. Under Abul Hasan al-Ash'ari's guidance, speculative theology (*ilm al-kalam*) also became a powerful force within the Islamic intellectual firmament. Prior to that, under Hasan al-Basri's tutelage, Sufism (or Islamic mysticism) had become a potent force in the Muslim world. These rationalistic, philosophical, theological and mystical trends continued to compete for the hearts and minds of Muslims until the indomitable personality of al-Ghazali emerged in the eleventh century to champion and reassert

traditional Islamic thought and practices as never before.

Abu Hamid Muhammad ibn Muhammad ibn Muhammad al-Tusi al-Ghazali, known in the Latin West as Algazel, was born in the historic town of Tus in Khurasan (in present-day Mashhad in Iran). As the birthplace of the celebrated Sufi master Abul Hasan Ali al-Hujwiri, the outstanding epic poet Firdawsi and the renowned scholar and statesman Nizam al-Mulk, Tus was the hub of Islamic learning and scholarship at the time. Al-Ghazali's father was a devout Muslim, who died when his son was an infant. He and his brother Ahmad were, therefore, raised by their mother who ensured her two sons received a good education. Al-Ghazali attended the class of a local Sufi tutor and attained proficiency in Arabic language, grammar, Qur'an, *hadith*, jurisprudence (*fiqh*) and aspects of Sufi thought and poetry before he was fifteen. He then conducted a detailed study of *fiqh* under the guidance of Shaykh Ahmad ibn Muhammad al-Radhkani in Tus and Abul Qasim Ismail ibn Mas'ada al-Ismaili, who was a leading expert on the subject, at the seminary in Jurjan. He was seventeen when he successfully completed his study of *fiqh*, and returned home to Tus to continue his higher eduaction. Al-Ghazali was a gifted student who needed minimal guidance and supervision from his tutors. His unusual ability to grasp complex ideas and thoughts enabled him to absorb the principles and practices of Islam with ease.

He was barely twenty years old when he travelled to Nishapur to pursue advanced instruction in Islamic sciences. He was fortunate to study Islamic theology (*ilm al-kalam*) and *fiqh* under *imam al-haramayn* Abul Ma'ali Abd al-Malik al-Juwayni. Al-Juwayni was not only an outstanding exponent of Ash'arite theology, he was also one of the foremost Islamic scholars of his generation and lectured at the famous Nizamiyyah College in Nishapur. Al-Ghazali sat at the feet of this master, and became one of his favourite students. Like al-Juwayni, he became an Ash'arite theologian and a Shafi'i *faqih* (jurist). It was al-Juwayni who introduced him to the science of logic (*mantiq*) and the philosophical thought of the *falasifah* (Muslim philosophers). However, it was al-Ghazali's intellectual brilliance and analytical ability which impressed al-Juwayni the most; so much so that he nominated him to become his teaching assistant. This established al-Ghazali's credentials and enhanced his newfound reputation as a young Islamic scholar. It was during this period that he composed his *al-Mankhul min Ta'liqat al-Usul* (The Sifted Notes on the Methods of Fundamentals), wherein he elucidated the fundamental principles of Islamic law and legal methodology.

As a leading centre of Islamic learning, Nishapur also attracted eminent Sufi personalities who lived there and imparted knowledge of Islamic esoteric (*batin*) sciences to their followers and sympathisers. Al-Ghazali also attended these Sufi lodges (*zawiyyah*) and received training in the theoretical and practical dimensions of Sufism under the able guidance of Abu Ali Fadl ibn Muhammad ibn Ali al-Farmadhi, who was a widely respected Sufi personality of Nishapur and a pupil of the renowned al-Qushairi. In 1085 al-Juwayni died and al-Ghazali was asked to become professor of Islamic thought at the Nizamiyyah College in Baghdad by none other than Nizam al-Mulk himself, the great Seljuk Prime Minister and founder

of the Nizamiyyah College. At the age of around thirty-four, he became the youngest professor at Nizamiyyah. This was an extraordinary honour for young al-Ghazali since the Nizamiyyah College of Baghdad was the Oxford or Harvard of its time. As soon as al-Ghazali started teaching *fiqh*, *kalam* and *hadith* at Nizamiyyah, his name and fame began to spread across the Islamic dominion and Nizam al-Mulk became his patron, regularly consulting him on all the important religious and political issues of the day. Al-Ghazali's daily lectures at Nizamiyyah became so popular that up to three hundred students came to listen to him at a time. However, just when he thought he had achieved all that was possible for someone so young to achieve, he suddenly found himself stranded in the middle of an intellectual crisis.

This crisis made al-Ghazali restless. Being inherently inquisitive, and sceptical of received wisdom, he thrived in the lion's den. He questioned everything and, in the process, left no stone unturned. He was profoundly disturbed by the apparent conflict between the views of the rationalists, who argued that human reason (*aql*) was superior to revelation (*wahy*), and the traditionalists who considered Divine revelation to be infallible and, therefore, more authoritative in comparison with fallible human reason. Although al-Ghazali was not a philosopher *per se*, he had studied philosophical thought during his period with al-Juwayni. This enabled him to understand and evaluate the various strands of philosophical and theological thought which prevailed in the Muslim world at the time. His observations disturbed him profoundly and made him very restless. He discovered that a huge array of religious sects and groups had emerged which also espoused their own sets of doctrines, beliefs and concepts which, he felt, were not only heretical in nature, but also directly contradicted traditional Islamic teachings and practices. How was he to determine which group was right and which one was wrong in the face of these diverse claims and counter-claims?

This prompted al-Ghazali to resign from Nizamiyyah College and study all the prominent religious sects and groups. In the course of his studies, he became aware of the limitations of existentialism and rationalism. He found them to be unreliable categories for reaching the Truth. The more al-Ghazali questioned the more he doubted the very foundation of knowledge. Thus, for a period, he became a fully-fledged sceptic, living in a state of doubt and depression. However, it should be noted here that the Ghazzalian doubt was not the opposite of faith; rather it was an integral part of faith because his scepticism did not lead him to doubt the existence of God. Yet, it is true that he found himself stranded in an intellectual no-man's land and that he found no comfort in rational arguments or in logical proofs as a means of solving his predicament. That was when he claimed to have been saved by the ray of Divine light (*nur*) which entered his heart and delivered him from his intellectual dilemma. Al-Ghazali considered this to be a gift from God Who had chosen to guide him to the straight path (*sirat al-mustaqim*). This brought much needed peace and solace to his tortured mind and body as he affirmed the superiority of prophetic revelation and intellectual intuition over human rationality. At peace with himself, and reassured of the authenticity of his approach to Islam, he now continued his study of all the religious sects and groups in order to discover the truth for himself.

He began by studying and analysing the works of the philosophers and theologians. He divided seekers-after-knowledge into four different categories, namely the scholastic theologians (*mutakallimun*), the philosophers (*falasifah*), the doctrinaires (*ta'limiyya* or Ta'limites), and the Sufis (Islamic mystics). During this period he delved deep into theology, natural philosophy, religious heresy and the supra-rational world of mysticism, until he attained a thorough understanding of these subjects. Al-Ghazali set himself a formidable task but he was determined to complete his mission. Having already studied scholastic theology under al-Juwayni's tutelage at Nizamiyyah College, he was thoroughly familiar with this subject. Nevertheless, he undertook a fresh analysis of its

basic principles and logical parameters, only to discover that it had major shortcomings. The theologians' prodigious ability to theorise, debate and argue their case aside, al-Ghazali found no common ground on which all theologians could agree. He argued, therefore, that scholastic theology would be of no value to anyone unless they believed in the indispensability of human reason. During this period he authored a number of books on theology, before pursuing research in philosophy.

For the next three years (that is, from 1091 to 1094), he conducted a thorough study of *falsafah* (or Islamic philosophy). Through extensive study and research he became fully acquainted with the works of the philosophers including those of great Muslim philosophers like al-Farabi and Ibn Sina. He considered their ideas and thoughts to be confused and misguided. The outcome of his study of philosophy was *Maqasid al-Falasifah* (The Intentions of the Philosophers) which al-Ghazali intended to serve as an introduction to his famous *Tahafut al-Falasifah* (The Refutation of the Philosophers). In this book, he systematically analysed and repudiated Peripatetic (*mashsha'iyyah*) philosophy as propounded by al-Farabi and Ibn Sina. In the preface to this book, he explained that his intention was to free Islamic thought from the stranglehold of Greek philosophy. By refuting the 'errors and heresies' of the philosophers, he hoped to safeguard the masses from doubt and confusion. Al-Ghazali's attack on Peripatetic philosophy proved so successful that Greek philosophical thought never managed to re-emerge in the Muslim world in a significant way after that. He single-handedly accomplished a feat which even a group of gifted intellectuals would have struggled to achieve. By all accounts, this was a truly remarkable achievement. Astonishingly, al-Ghazali was only thirty-six when he authored his hugely influential *Tahafut*.

After philosophy, al-Ghazali turned his attention to a doctrinare sect called the Ta'limites. This group believed that an 'infallible teacher' would one day appear and restore peace and order throughout the land. Al-Ghazali studied the beliefs and doctrines of this sect, and refuted their claims in his books. *Fada'ih al-Batiniyya wa Fada'il al-Mustazhiriyya* (The Infamies of the Batinites and the Virtue of the Mustazhrites) was one such work, and it sparked off a huge debate between al-Ghazali and the supporters of this sect. After this, he immersed himself in the ocean of Sufi thought and practices. Following a thorough study of the works of prominent Sufis like Abu Talib al-Makki, Harith al-Muhasibi, Abul Qasim al-Junayd al-Baghdadi, Abu Bakr al-Shibli and Abu Yazid al-Bistami, al-Ghazali realised that 'empirical' – as opposed to 'theoretical' – knowledge was the foundation of Sufism. This prompted him to renounce all worldly pleasures and plunge himself whole-heartedly into the vast ocean of Sufism, only to experience yet another crisis. This time he suffered a serious nervous breakdown which badly affected his physical health, and he also developed speech problems. According to al-Ghazali, his situation did not improve until God again delivered him from his predicament by illuminating his heart with the spirit of truth. Now he was able to differentiate between 'theoretical' knowledge and 'experiential' knowledge. Hereafter, he devoted all his time and energy to seeking experiential knowledge in order to move closer to Divine proximity like the Sufis. He felt that endless theological debates, philosophical hair-splitting and heretical interpretations of Islamic beliefs and principles were

unlikely to bring about peace and happiness in this life, or success in the hereafter; rather he found peace of mind and intellectual reassurance in the message of Sufism.

Although al-Ghazali left Baghdad in 1095 (at the age of thirty-seven) in order to perform the sacred pilgrimage, he returned to his native Tus in around 1100 only to be recalled to Nishapur by Fakhr al-Mulk to teach at the Nizamiyyah College. He wrote a number of influential books during this period, including his famous autobiography *Munqidh min al-Dalal* (Deliverance from Error) and completed his voluminous *magnum opus*, *Ihya Ulum al-Din* (The Revivification of the Religious Sciences.). In the latter, he presented a detailed and thought-provoking ethical overview of Islamic teachings covering all aspects of life. This book established al-Ghazali's reputation as one of the Muslim world's most gifted scholars and thinkers. Moreover, his religious ideas and thoughts have not only influenced some of the most renowned Muslim scholars, intellectuals, Sufis and religious reformers; his philosophical and theological views also exerted considerable influence on renowned Jewish and Christian thinkers like St Thomas Aquinas, Ramon Lull, Blaise Pascal and Musa bin Maimon (Moses Maimonides) among others. Al-Ghazali eventually returned to his native Tus in 1110 and, a year later, he died at the age of fifty-three. He was buried in the cemetery close to Sanabad.

# 18

## Al-Shafi'i
## (b.767 - d.820)

IF *SHARI'AH* (Islamic law) is a vast and complex subject, then the 'science of Islamic jurisprudence' (or *usul al-fiqh*) is even more complex and sophisticated. And although the Qur'an and *sunnah* (the normative practice of Prophet Muhammad) are two of the most important sources of Islamic jurisprudence, how these two sources should be analysed, interpreted and implemented in a constantly changing and expanding Islamic society soon occupied the minds of the early Islamic scholars (*ulama*) and jurists (*fuqaha*). Following the death of the Prophet, the Islamic State continued to expand rapidly, and new challenges began to confront the early Muslim community. This prompted scores of prominent Islamic scholars to carry out a systematic study of the Qur'an and the Prophetic *sunnah,* and in so doing they developed *usul al-fiqh* (or the 'science of Islamic jurisprudence') in order to meet the challenges of their time. And although it is true that Abu Hanifah – assisted by his talented students like Zu'far, Abu Yusuf and Muhammad ibn al-Hasan – pioneered Islamic legal methodology, after his death his disciples focused their attention more on the substantive aspects of Islamic law, rather than continue to refine and systematically codify the overarching principles and methodology of

*usul al-fiqh.* This important and challenging task was undertaken by al-Shafi'i, who is today widely considered to be the 'father of the science of Islamic jurisprudence'.

Abu Abdullah Muhammad ibn Idris al-Shafi'i was born in the city of Gaza in southern Palestine, and his family claimed to be direct descendants of the Prophet Muhammad. He grew up there and received elementary education in Arabic language and grammar, and committed the entire Qur'an to memory before he was seven. When Shafi'i was still young, his father died and this prompted his mother to migrate to their ancestral home in Makkah, where members of her family and close relatives (who were of Yemeni origin) lived at the time. He then received further training in Arabic grammar, literature and history, and also became proficient at archery. Here Shafi'i and his mother were forced to endure considerable personal and financial hardship but, despite their abject economic situation, his devout mother was keen to give her son a good start in life by continuing with his education.

From the outset, Shafi'i's prodigious memory and sharp intellect endeared him to his teachers. According to his biographers, he could commit large collections of *hadith* (sayings of the Prophet) to memory with ease. Since Malik ibn Anas's *al-Muwatta* (The Beaten Path) was a popular religious text at the time, all the brightest students of Islamic sciences were expected to learn it by heart. He consequently memorised this anthology of Prophetic traditions in its entirety before he was fifteen years old. He mastered this book so well that he was considered to be a great authority on the religious thought of Malik as recorded in his *al-Muwatta*. Shafi'i then studied Islamic jurisprudence (*fiqh*) under the guidance of Sufyan ibn Uyayana and Muslim ibn Khalid al-Zanji, both of whom were respected jurists of their time. Impressed with Shafi'i's intellectual abilities, the governor of Makkah then personally wrote a letter to his counterpart in Madinah to request that Malik, the compiler of *al-Muwatta*, should teach Shafi'i, who was only twenty at the time. In Madinah, he devoted all his time and energy to the pursuit of *hadith* and *fiqh*, and studied the *al-Muwatta* under Malik's personal supervision. Some of Malik's eminent students at the time included scholars like Muhammad ibn al-Hasan al-Shaybani, who came all the way from Iraq to attend Malik's lectures. Although he was happy to be in the company of such an illustrious group of Islamic legal minds, on a more personal level, he began to experience considerable financial hardship at the time. Unlike the other students, he had no one to support him financially but, given his intellectual brilliance, Malik offered him a regular stipend which enabled him to complete his advanced education. His stay in Madinah proved so productive that Malik subsequently asked him to become his teaching assistant. By the time Malik died in 795, Shafi'i had already become recognised throughout Madinah as an eminent Islamic scholar and jurist.

Deeply saddened by Malik's death, he soon left Madinah and returned to his native Makkah. Here his reputation spread across the Hijaz on account of his vast knowledge of Islamic sciences. On one occasion, when the governor of Yemen happened to be in Makkah, he was informed about Shafi'i's intellectual abilities and legal expertise. This prompted the governor to approach him and invite him to accompany him to Yemen, where he promised to make him the Chief Justice of the city of Najran. The tall, slim and always immaculately dressed Shafi'i accepted the offer and moved to Yemen at the age of thirty-one. However, his transition from the world of academia to the murky and uncertain world of politics and diplomacy did not go according to plan. As a gifted jurist and Islamic scholar, he was not only scrupulously clean, honest and trustworthy, he was also determined to uphold the truth and administer justice as fairly and equitably as he could, but his strict and uncompromising application of Islamic law did not go down too well with certain factions in the corridors of power in Najran. Oblivious of the unease and discontent he was creating within the local Governmental circles, Shafi'i continued to apply Islamic law without any fear or favouritism. This eventually brought him into direct conflict with members of the ruling political and religious elites. Keen to have him dismissed, they falsely accused Shafi'i of sympathising with a rebellious Shi'a faction which was bitterly opposed to the Abbasids at the time.

Though the charge of treason levelled against Shafi'i was both false and unsubstantiated, he was found guilty of harbouring the rebellious Shi'as. Chained from head to toe by the authorities in Najran, he was deported to the highest Abbasid court in Baghdad in 803. The thirty-six year old Shafi'i was summoned by Harun al-Rashid, the famous Abbasid Caliph, to appear before him, along with the other alleged conspirators to answer the charges. The following day, Shafi'i went to the Caliph's court and, one by one, he refuted all the charges levelled against him. Harun al-Rashid was so impressed with his vast erudition and logical arguments that he engaged him in debate and discussion for a long period. They discussed the finer points of Islamic theology, jurisprudence, logic and even aspects of Greek thought. As a great patron of learning and scholarship, the Caliph deeply admired Shafi'i's intellectual brilliance. By coincidence, Muhammad ibn al-Hasan al-Shaybani (Shafi'i's old classmate at Madinah), happened to be the Chief Justice of Baghdad at the time and he vouched for Shafi'i to the Caliph and requested that the Caliph to free Shafi'i, who he said was one of the most famous scholars of his generation. The Caliph not only spared Shafi'i's life, he also requested that he stay in Baghdad and help him promote learning and scholarship throughout the land.

Relieved to have been spared, Shafi'i settled in Baghdad and vowed never to become a Government official again. Instead, he resumed his career as an academic and researcher in Islamic sciences, for that was his real passion. In Baghdad he conducted advanced research in *fiqh* and *hadith* under the guidance of its leading scholars, and regularly attended the lectures of Muhammad ibn al-Hasan al-Shaybani. Being one of the foremost students of Abu Hanifah, al-Shaybani was considered to be one of the great scholars of Islam and an eminent authority on Islamic law at the time. Shafi'i learned *hanafi* jurisprudence under al-Shaybani's guidance and became highly proficient in the legal thought of this school. In the course of his heated discussion and debates with the leading *hanafi* scholars, Shafi'i deliberately emphasised the significance of *hadith* in the formulation of Islamic legal principles and practices. He felt *qiyas* (analogical deduction) played a far greater role within the *hanafi* legal methodology than was necessary, and thus he highlighted the importance of relying on Prophetic *hadith* where it was possible to do so. Not surprisingly, he emerged from his discussions with the *hanafis* as a great champion of Prophetic *hadith*. That is not to say, however, that the *hanafi* scholars did not uphold the *hadith*. On the contrary, the *hanafis* zealously adhered to authentic *hadith* but, unlike the *malikis* and Shafi'i himself, they placed greater emphasis on the need for human individuality and freedom.

Nevertheless, it is very true that *hanafi* legal thought is characterised by its considerable reliance on the construction and deduction of principles from the scriptural sources of Islam, namely the Qur'an and authentic *sunnah* of the Prophet. Shafi'i was acutely aware of this and he deliberately engaged the *hanafis* in debates and discussion on the finer points of their legal thought, and in so doing he successfully mastered the legal thought of both Abu Hanifah and Malik. This was a remarkable achievement for Shafi'i who was now able to analyse, refine and even critique the legal thought of two of the Muslim world's most influential jurists. And although Shafi'i rightly considered Abu Hanifah to be the father of Islamic legal thought – and considered Malik to be a great authority on *hadith* – he knew that the science of Islamic jurisprudence had to be systematically developed and codified for the benefit of posterity. Of course, he knew this would not be an easy task, but he was more than qualified to undertake this challenging but important work. His success in this earned him a unique place in the intellectual history of Islam, as the first systematic formulator of the science of Islamic jurisprudence.

In 804 Shafi'i left Baghdad and moved to Syria, and from there he went to Makkah where he began to deliver regular lectures on *fiqh* and *hadith* at the *haram al-sharif* (the Sacred Mosque). Hundreds of students, including the famous Ahmad ibn Hanbal, travelled from across the Muslim world to attend his inspiring talks on all aspects of Islam. Perhaps influenced by the *hanafi* scholars of Baghdad, Shafi'i changed his views on certain aspects of *maliki* legal thought during this period, even though he continued to hold Malik (and especially his famous *al-Muwatta*) in very high regard. After six years of teaching and travelling across Syria and Arabia, Shafi'i returned to Baghdad in 810 only to find al-Ma'mun, the son and successor of Caliph Harun al-Rashid, on the Abbasid throne. Al-Ma'mun immediately asked Shafi'i to become the Chief Justice (*qadi al-qudat*) of Baghdad but, given his previous bad experience in Najran, the latter politely turned down the offer. Moreover, since al-Ma'mun was a champion of the heretical Mu'tazilite creed, Shafi'i – like the other traditionalist scholars of the time – considered him to be a mischief-maker; but al-Ma'mun took exception to Shafi'i's snub. Realising the gravity of the situation, he quietly left Baghdad in 814 and proceeded to Egypt.

At the time, Egypt was a very peaceful and intellectually conducive place. Here he came into contact with scores of renowned Islamic scholars and jurists, including Rabi ibn Sulaiman al-Marali and Abu Ibrahim ibn Yahya al-Muzani. He frequently engaged in discussion and debate with these scholars on different aspects of *fiqh* and *hadith*, which further polished and refined his own ideas and thoughts on these subjects. Convinced that he had fully grasped the complexities and intricacies of Islamic jurisprudence, he then sat down to formulate a systematic and coherent theory of Islamic legal thought. He took into consideration the views of the *hanafis* as well as the *malikis* and in so doing he presented a comprehensive but, equally refreshing, exposition of Islamic legal principles in order to address the new challenges of his time. He recorded his ideas and thoughts in his celebrated *Kitab al-Umm* (The Book of Essence) and *al-Risalah* (The Treatise). In these two books, he – for the very first time in Islamic history – systematically formulated the fundamental principles of the science of Islamic jurisprudence. He studied under the guidance of both the *hanafi* and *maliki* scholars, but he did not follow them blindly; instead, he developed his own methodology and approach to the scriptural sources of Islam and in the process became the pioneer of *usul al-fiqh*.

The balanced approach adopted by Shafi'i *vis-à-vis* the revealed sources of Islam enabled him to emphasise the pre-eminence of *hadith* while he was in the company of the *hanafis*, and also highlight the role of human nature and its frailties (in the context of legal theory and practice) when he was with the *malikis*. In short, by harmonising the legal methodologies of Abu Hanifah and Malik, Shafi'i created a new, comprehensive and original legal synthesis. He was so successful in his task that a Shafi'i *madhhab* (or school of legal thought) subsequently emerged and spread across the Muslim world. Today, this *madhhab* is widely followed in Egypt, Yemen, Indonesia, Malaysia, and parts of South America and East Africa. Blessed with a prodigious memory and remarkably sharp intellect, Shafi'i left his indelible mark on the intellectual history of Islam as one of its greatest legal theorists and synthesisers. He died and was buried in al-Fustat, Egypt at the age of fifty-three. Later, in 1211, the Ayyubid ruler Afdal built an impressive mausoleum, which still stands to this day, as a tribute to his memory.

# 19

# Al-Khwarizmi
# (b.780 - d.847)

THE ORIGIN OF all the physical sciences can, one way or another, be traced back to mathematics. That is why mathematics is generally considered to be the mother of all these disciplines. In its early days, mathematics manifested itself in mainly three different forms, namely arithmetic (counting with numbers), geometry (measurement of areas), and algebra (calculating by means of symbols and their relationships). These mathematical techniques enabled ancient people to think; to reason and express themselves in a relatively exact and precise way in their daily affairs. Although arithmetic is considered to be the first, and perhaps the most ancient, form of mathematics, very little is known about its origin. According to the historians, archaeological excavations carried out in the Nile Valley and Mesopotamia have shown that counting was familiar to both ancient Egyptians and the Babylonians. The Chinese and Indians also devised their own distinctive ways of counting, just as the Arabs used the position of their fingers to help them count during the time of the Prophet Muhammad. Like the Greeks and the Romans before them, the Arabs also used their alphabets for counting purposes; that is, until the advent of Arabic numerals. Though the zero-based number

system was known to the ancient Indians, it was the Muslims who invented the word 'zero'. Derived from the Arabic *sifr*, meaning 'nothing' or 'nil', the Muslim mathematicians developed a rigorous decimal system which subsequently became known as the Arabic numerals. When the Muslim mathematicians were busy conducting complex and sophisticated mathematical equations in their research laboratories in Baghdad, Damascus, Cairo and Merv, the Europeans were struggling to perform simple mathematical calculations using Roman numerals. Trying to conduct a simple mathematical equation using Roman numerals was an uphill job; frankly, it was a hopeless task. By contrast, the introduction of Arabic numerals represented nothing short of a major revolution in mathematical study and research. It helped the early Muslim mathematicians to develop and refine the entire discipline of mathematics for the benefit of humanity. No other mathematician played a more pivotal role in the development of algebra and Arabic numerals than al-Khwarizmi. That is why he is today considered to be one of the greatest mathematical geniuses of all time.

Abu Abdullah Muhammad ibn Musa al-Khwarizmi was born in Khwarizm, in the Central

Asian province of Khurasan. Khurasan at the time was a thriving centre of commerce and literary activities. Under the patronage of its ruling elites, schools and colleges mushroomed across the province; both the religious and scientific subjects were taught and studied by some of the leading Muslim scholars and thinkers of the day. Born into a family where the pursuit of knowledge was valued more than anything else, al-Khwarizmi's family migrated to the district of Qurtrubulli, located on the outskirts of Baghdad, when he was still a child. Though very little is known about al-Khwarizmi's early life, it was the custom of the day for young children to attend their local schools and receive basic instruction in Arabic and traditional Islamic sciences, followed by more intensive training in Arabic grammar, literature, poetry and aspects of Islamic theology and philosophy. The students who were considered to be most capable and gifted by their tutors were then encouraged to pursue research in medicine, astronomy, alchemy and mathematics, thereby widening their intellectual horizons. As an unusually talented student, al-Khwarizmi pursued the standard curriculum of the day and soon impressed everyone with his mastery of the religious, philosophical and scientific knowledge of the time.

When al-Khwarizmi's reputation as an accomplished religious scholar, scientist and mathematician reached the corridors of power in Baghdad, the reigning Abbasid Caliph, Abdullah al-Ma'mun, invited him to join his celebrated *bait al-hikmah* (The House of Wisdom) in Baghdad around 820; he was around forty at the time. Like his illustrious father, al-Ma'mun became a generous patron and benefactor of philosophical and scientific research; indeed, he promoted learning, research and inquiry into all branches of learning and education. Originally founded by Harun during his reign as Caliph, the *bait al-hikmah* became one of the Muslim world's most famous and influential libraries and centres of research under Caliph al-Ma'mun's patronage. He went out of his way to recruit some of the most talented philosophers, scien-

tists, geographers and mathematicians of his time to this institute in order to teach and conduct advanced research in science, mathematics and philosophy. As expected, al-Khwarizmi occupied a prominent position in *bait al-hikmah*, where he studied and conducted research in a host of disciplines including astronomy, geography, history, music and mathematics, which was his most favourite subject. Deeply impressed by al-Khwarizmi's mathematical abilities, the Caliph personally asked him to head the department of astronomical research at *bait al-hikmah*. He not only excelled in astronomy, he also went on to make seminal contributions in a number of other scientific subjects, and authored an influential book on history entitled *Kitab al-Tarikh* (The Book of History), which later inspired celebrated Muslim historians like Abul Hasan al-Mas'udi and al-Tabari to produce their own works on the subject.

It was under Caliph Harun al-Rashid's patronage that pioneering Muslim scholars and translators like Hajjaj ibn Yusuf ibn Matar al-Hasib and Abu Yahya al-Batriq first began to translate the philosophical and scientific contributions of the ancient Greeks into Arabic. The Muslim scientists and mathematicians not only translated and preserved ancient Greek intellectual heritage (such as Euclid's *Elements*, Ptolemy's *Almagest* and the vast corpus of Aristotelian logic for the benefit of posterity), they also explored and analysed the intellectual and cultural contribution of other ancient civilisations, including those of Persia, India and China. Their thirst for knowledge and wisdom inspired them to learn, assimilate and refine the works of the ancients and make their own original contributions in all the branches of knowledge. According to some historians, al-Khwarizmi's quest for knowledge took him all the way to India, where he mastered traditional Indian science and mathematics. It was also during his stay in India that he became familiar with the zero-based decimal system for the first time. Although it is not clear how long he stayed in India, he lived there for long enough to have gained proficiency in Sanskrit, the *lingua franca* of ancient India, as he was thoroughly familiar with this language. During this period al-Khwarizmi discovered that the ancient Indians used a blank space to denote 'nothing' or 'nil' (*sunya*), which inspired him to coin the Arabic word *sifr* meaning 'nothing', just as its Latin equivalent, *ciphrium,* later came to denote 'zero'. However, according to other historians, there is no credible evidence to suggest that al-Khwarizmi visited India. On the contrary, they argue that he became familiar with Indian arithmetic and astronomy from translated manuscripts which were available in Baghdad at the time. Either way, his discovery of the concept of 'zero' enabled him to lay the foundations of a new decimal system, which is today widely known as Arabic numerals, and in so doing he revolutionised the study of mathematics forever.

By all accounts, al-Khwarizmi's contribution to mathematics was both unique and unprecedented. In addition to systematically analysing the geometric algebra of the Greeks and the arithmeticised algebra of the Indians, he also conducted research into Babylonian algebra. His complete mastery of Greek, Indian and Babylonian mathematics enabled him to critically evaluate the contribution of the ancients before he went onto develop his own fresh ideas and thoughts on the subject. The originality of his mathematical contribution is most evident from the fact that the word 'algebra' was derived directly from the title of his famous book on the subject, entitled *Kitab al-Mukhtasar fi Hisab al-Jabr wa'l Muqabalah* (The Summarised Treatise on the Process of Calculation for Integration and Equation). This book was one of the first of its kind written by a Muslim. In this book, he systematically defined and developed algebra for the first time in the history of mathematics (it was later translated into Latin by Robert of Chester, under the title of *Liber Algebras et al-Mucabala*). Known popularly as *Hisab al-Jabr wa'l Muqabalah*, this seminal mathematical treatise was divided into five chapters, in each of which the author rigorously and systematically examined and analysed different dimensions of algebra.

In the first chapter, al-Khwarizmi discussed the nature of linear and quadratic equations, and showed how they could be explained and resolved without providing any demonstrative proof. He also divided quadratic equations into six categories in order to highlight their separate geometrical configurations. During his investigations, he discovered that quadratic equations had two different roots, one being positive which he accepted, and the other being negative which he rejected. In so doing, he developed a fresh approach to the study and exploration of such equations. In the next chapter, al-Khwarizmi showed how quadratic equations could be resolved in a demonstrative way by utilising geometric methods. In the third and fourth chapters, he analysed and explored problems posed by multiplication and explained how differences between sums, squares and methods of locating square roots of hidden or unknown quantities in equations could be resolved. In the fifth and final chapter of the book, he developed solutions for a host of mathematical problems using different algebraic formulae. As expected, these mathematical problems were complex and multi-layered, and they required original and imaginative solutions, but al-Khwarizmi was able to define and resolve them, one by one, in a masterly fashion. Indeed, he used around eight hundred different demonstrative equations to show how calculations of integration and equation could be performed.

Al-Khwarizmi's work in the field of arithmetic and algebra was of such a high standard that it would not be an exaggeration to say that he was the pioneer, or father, of these important branches of mathematics. His book on arithmetic entitled *Kitab al- Jam' wa'l Tafriq bi'l Hisab al-Hindi* (The Book of Aggregation and Division in Indian Mathematics) was not only a pioneering mathematical contribution, it also became a hugely influential book. After Bon Compagni translated it into Latin in 1157, it became a popular textbook on arithmetic throughout medieval Europe. A copy of this translation is still extant to this day in Rome. The book also introduced Arabic numerals and the concept of 'zero' or 'cipher' into the Western world for the very first time, and in so doing it helped to popularise the application of basic arithmetic into every area of modern life. Al-Khwarizmi's scholarship had such a pervasive influence on Western science and technology that he became known as 'Algorithm' across Europe, and throughout the centuries his Latinised name became synonymous with the word 'arithmetic' in the West. Today 'algorithm' refers to a technique which is used in the field of computer science for carrying out analysis using recurring methods. Without al-Khwarizimi's seminal contributions in arithmetic, algebra, trigonometry and other branches of mathematics, it would not have been possible for Copernicus, Kepler, Galileo, Newton and others to achieve as much as they did in the field of astronomy, physics, mathematics and chemistry. Thanks also to al-Khwarizmi, today man can travel to space; fly aeroplanes; watch satellite television, and also count up to a zillion without any problems or difficulties. By revolutionising the study of mathematics, he completely revolutionised our vision of ourselves and, indeed, our vision of the future for the benefit of whole humanity.

If scientists like Sir Issac Newton were a rare breed, then geniuses like al-Khwarizmi were even rarer. His contribution to mathematics aside, al-Khwarizmi was also a brilliant astronomer and geographer. Once, when Caliph al-Ma'mun commissioned him to measure the meridian from a location close to the Euphrates, he accomplished the task by inventing an astronomical device which was far superior to anything the Greeks had produced. In fact, he not only accurately measured and determined the sphericity of the earth, he also suggested ways in which the process could be made easier in the future, by improving the device he had invented. Towards the end of his life he authored a book on geography entitled *Kitab Surat al-Ard* (The Book on the Shape of the Earth). In this book, he went to great lengths to correct Ptolemy's misconceptions about different aspects of geography, geology and other related sciences. The publication of this book also marked the beginning of the science of geography in the Muslim world. All subsequent Muslim scientists and geographers (such as Abu Kamil, Sind ibn Ali, Sinan ibn Fath and Abul Wafa al-Bujazani) were one way or another influenced by this pioneering book. In total, al-Khwarizmi authored more than a dozen books on all the sciences of his time. He died at the age of sixty-seven and was laid to rest in Baghdad.

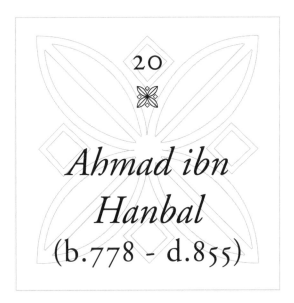

# 20

## Ahmad ibn Hanbal
## (b.778 - d.855)

ISLAMIC HISTORY IS replete with scholars who distinguished themselves by the breadth of their learning and courage. These scholars were both pious and profoundly knowledgeable in Islamic principles and practices, and they cared little about the wealth and material possessions of this world. They humbled themselves before their Creator during the darkness of the night, and continued their quest for knowledge and wisdom during the day. They also endured considerable personal and financial hardship, and were often made to suffer for their faith and conviction, but they never bowed before a King or Queen. To them, the life of this world was like an illusion; without a reality of its own. The pursuit of truth, justice, equality and the welfare of the poor and needy became their main mission in life. They were men of remarkable character, enduring personality and profound courage and determination. Such exemplary scholars appeared at various times in Islamic history and they fulfilled their vocation with patience, perseverance and great success. Ahmad ibn Hanbal was one such towering scholar and reformer who emerged to defend traditional Islam at a critical time in Islamic history, and thereby left his indelible mark in the annals of Islam.

Abu Abdullah Ahmad ibn Muhammad ibn Hanbal al-Shaybani was born into the noble Arab tribe of al-Shayban. Ahmad's grandfather, Hanbal ibn Hilal, occupied a prominent position as governor of the province of Sarakhs under the Umayyads, while his father, Muhammad, was a valiant warrior who participated in a *jihad* (military expedition) led by the Umayyads and died on the battlefield while he was in his thirties. Ahmad was about two years old when his father died, and he was brought up in very difficult economic circumstances by his devout mother, Safiyya. He attended his local schools and successfully committed the entire Qur'an to memory before he was ten. Influenced by his mother, Ahmad began to study *hadith* (Prophetic traditions) at the age of sixteen and fell in love with the subject. He was not only a bright student, but also deeply religious during his early years. His scrupulous character and friendly personality endeared him to his teachers. During this period he worked as a clerk at his local post office to supplement his family's meagre income, and regularly drafted letters for the illiterate villagers free of charge. He thus combined his education in *fiqh* (Islamic jurisprudence) and *hadith* under the guidance of Abu Yusuf Yaqub ibn Ibrahim with his extra-curricula activities. Abu Yusuf was one of the foremost students of Abu Hanifah and an outstanding Islamic scholar and jurist in his own right. Although Abu Hanifah died about fourteen years before Ahmad was born, he was very fortunate to study *hadith* and *fiqh* under Abu Yusuf who was considered to be one of the most gifted jurists of his generation. Like Abu Hanifah, Abu Yusuf emphasised the importance of scholarly discretion (*ijtihad*) through analogical deduction (*qiyas*), and this became a key feature of *hanafi* legal thought and methodology. Ahmad attended Abu Yusuf's lectures regularly and became thoroughly familiar with *hanafi fiqh*.

He then studied *hadith* and *fiqh* for another four years under the guidance of Haitham ibn Bishr, who was one of the foremost scholars of *hadith* in Baghdad. As the political capital of the Muslim world and a thriving city, Baghdad attracted some of the Muslim world's most prominent scholars to live and teach there. Eager to complete his education, Ahmad then attended the classes of luminaries like Abd al-Rahman ibn Mahdi and Abu Bakr ibn Ayyash, and rapidly assimilated Islamic knowledge and wisdom. His devotion, dedication and commitment to his studies, especially of Prophetic *hadith,* was such that he often left his home well before the dawn prayer (*fajr*) and waited for his teachers to arrive to begin the first class of the day. After completing his studies under the renowned scholars of Baghdad, he travelled to other major centres of Islamic learning (including Basrah, Kufah, Makkah, Madinah, Yemen and Syria) in pursuit of *hadith*. During his *wanderjahre*, he came into contact with Muhammad ibn Idris al-Shafi'i, who was living in Makkah at the time. Although Ahmad was much younger than Shafi'i, the latter was deeply impressed by his vast knowledge of Islam. Many years later, these two luminaries of Islam met again; this time in Baghdad. By then Shafi'i had already developed his theories of Islamic jurisprudence in a rigorous and systematic way. Likewise, Ahmad became widely recognised as an eminent scholar of *hadith*, having mastered all the nuances and intricacies of this subject

under the tutelage of the Yemeni scholar Abd al-Razzaq ibn Hammam, the author of the highly rated *Musannaf*. Here in Baghdad, the two men regularly engaged in debate and discussion on the finer points of *fiqh* and *hadith*. Shafi'i soon acknowledged Ahmad's superiority in *hadith*, and regularly consulted him on difficult issues relating to *hadith*.

Since Ahmad's main preoccupation in life was the pursuit of knowledge, he happily travelled long distances in search of Islamic knowledge and wisdom. He was not one of those who expected his teachers to come to him; rather he went out of his way to visit his teachers to learn from them. So much so that when he first met his tutor Abd al-Razzaq in Makkah during the *hajj* (pilgrimage) season, his colleague Yahya ibn Ma'in, the tutor of the celebrated al-Bukhari, suggested they should start learning from him there and then. Ahmad disagreed with him and instead he travelled all the way to Sana, the capital of Yemen, to study *hadith* under Abd al-Razzaq. As an honest and passionate seeker of knowledge, he was happy to spend his money and endure hardship in his quest for knowledge, but he never liked to compromise his beliefs and principles in the process. Ahmad's collaboration with Shafi'i proved extremely beneficial for him for a number of reasons. Hitherto he had been busy writing and memorising *hadith* and *fiqh*, but Shafi'i helped him to develop a critical approach to these subjects. An outstanding analyst and synthesiser, Shafi'i explained to him his theories of Islamic jurisprudence, including all the intricacies involved in the construction and deduction of the principles of *usul al-fiqh*, which enabled Ahmad to revisit the large quantity of *hadith* he had learned. His critical examination of *hadith* literature enabled him to ascertain their relevance to Islamic law and legal theory. This represented a major turning point in Ahmad's intellectual journey. He was now in a position to develop his own approach to *fiqh*, thanks to his colossal knowledge of *hadith*, the sayings of the *sahabah* (the Prophet's companions) and those of the *tabiun* (or successors of the companions).

Ahmad's mastery of both *hadith* and *fiqh* was then publicly acknowledged by Shafi'i himself when he said: 'I am leaving Baghdad when there is none more pious, nor a greater jurist than Ahmad ibn Hanbal'. He was about forty at the time.

Normally a scholar of Ahmad's calibre and accomplishment would have started his own religious seminary long before he reached forty, but he refrained from doing so. Why wait so long? Some historians say he followed the Prophet's example; that is to say, since the latter did not attain his Prophethood and begin to propagate Islam until he was forty, so Ahmad waited till he reached his fortieth birthday. Others say he decided not to teach while his own teachers were still alive, out of respect for them. Interestingly, Shafi'i died in the year Ahmad turned forty. It is not clear whether his death played a part in his decision to start teaching. Perhaps it was a combination of all these factors which encouraged him to set up his own class. Either way, Ahmad started teaching *hadith* and *fiqh* at the age of forty, and soon gathered around him a large following. Having suffered considerable financial hardship during his student days, he gave preference to the poor students, especially those who were not in a position to pay for additional tuition. When he delivered lectures on *hadith* and *fiqh*, his students listened to him in absolute silence, and often the locals came along to hear him analyse and dissect *hadith* and aspects of *fiqh* in his unique and inimitable style. It was not long before his reputation spread in and around Baghdad. According to some historians, his lectures were attended by hundreds of students at a time. Unflustered by the mass attention he now received, Ahmad continued to lead a simple and ascetic lifestyle, far removed from the wealth and luxuries of this world.

If any of his well-wishers sent him any money or gifts, he gave them away to the poor and needy. On a number of occasions, the Caliph sent him parcels of gifts, but he refused to accept them. When his sons asked him why he refused to accept such gifts, he explained that giving and taking gifts was not unlawful *per se*; rather, it was perfectly acceptable – and even encouraged – to give and accept gifts, and he also stated that one could even perform *hajj* with money given as gift. However, he refused to accept the Caliph's gifts, he explained, due to prudence and personal abstinence. Like so many other great Islamic scholars (such as al-Shafi'i and al-Bukhari), he refused to accept money or gifts from the rulers of his time just in case they happened to come from an unlawful source. Instead he lived on income from a small rented apartment he owned. When he ran out of money, which he did regularly, he used to skip meals. On one occasion he became so desperate that he could not afford to replace his old and worn out clothes but, when the locals offered to buy him new ones, he politely refused. Since his poverty and deprivation was self-imposed, Ahmad maintained his self-respect and dignity by not accepting anything without paying for it. Only when his situation became very desperate, did he accept small amounts of money, but always on the condition that he repaid it later. His sincerity, simplicity and profound insight into Islamic teachings made him very popular with the masses in Baghdad.

He lived at a time when Mu'tazilism (or philosophical rationalism) became the dominant creed of the Abbasid Empire under the stewardship of Caliph al-Ma'mun. As a champion of rationalism, the Caliph and his immediate successors (Caliphs Mu'tasim Billah and Wathiq) not only turned Mu'tazilism into an official creed of the State, they also imposed it on the people by force. After a Caliphal decree was issued which stipulated that all the scholars in Baghdad had to subscribe to the Mu'tazilite creed and anyone who refused to do so would be severly chastised, Ahmad's life was suddenly turned upside down. Since the Mu'tazilites believed that the Qur'an was created (contrary to the traditional Islamic view, which stated that the Qur'an was the uncreated Word of God), many traditional Islamic scholars flatly refused to accept the Caliphal decree. But when these scholars were threatened with severe chastisement by the ruling Abbasid elites, most of them pretended to subscribe to the Mu'tazilite creed in order to save their skins. Only a handful of scholars continued to defy the Caliphal decree – and Ahmad was one of them. When the Caliph eventually ordered all the defiant scholars to be brought to his palace in chains, they all relented save one. That indomitable scholar was Ahmad ibn Hanbal.

Chained from head to toe, he was brought before Caliph Mu'tasim Billah who questioned him about his beliefs and convictions for more than four days and urged him to change his views, but Ahmad remained firm. The battle between Islamic traditionalism and philosophical rationalism was now truly engaged. When it became abundantly clear that Ahmad would not recant, his tormentors threatened him with severe chastisement but he remained defiant. Ahmad was then beaten until the whip broke into two pieces, before being dragged before the Caliph for more questioning; but again he refused to budge an inch. The Caliph then ordered more punishment. This time he was tortured so severely that eye-witnesses said even an elephant would not have been able to endure such treatment. Yet Ahmad remained as firm as ever, refusing to bow before the scourge of rationalism, which at the time was threatening to undermine the very foundation of Islam.

His courage and bravery in the face of such barbarism even won over his erstwhile opponents.

As expected, soon his name and fame spread across the Islamic world like a wildfire, and his peers lavished much praise on him for keeping the flame of Islamic traditionalism alive. So much so that one renowned scholar of the time remarked, 'When you find someone setting his affections on Ahmad ibn Hanbal, then know that he is a follower of the Prophet's tradition.' Ahmad continued his struggle against the Mu'tazilites until, in 847, Mutawakkil ala Allah ascended the Abbasid throne and reversed his predecessor's harsh policies. The new Caliph also freed Ahmad from captivity so he could resume his normal activities. During this period he wrote numerous books on *hadith* and *fiqh* including his famous *al-Musnad,* which contains more than thirty thousand *ahadith* and a large selection of views and opinions of the Prophet's companions about different aspects of Islam.

Ahmad ibn Hanbal died and was buried in Baghdad at the age of around seventy- seven. After his death, a new school of Islamic legal thought emerged named after him. The *hanbali madhhab* is today followed mainly in Palestine and Saudi Arabia, but his religious ideas and thoughts have influenced generations of influential Islamic scholars and reformers like Ibn Taymiyyah, Ibn Qayyim al-Jawziyyah, Ibn Kathir, Muhammad ibn Abd al-Wahhab, Sayyid Ahmad Barelvi and Haji Shari'atullah of Bengal among others.

# 21

## Ibn Khaldun
## (b. 1332 – d. 1406)

THE QUR'AN CONSTANTLY exhorts Muslims to study history and explore the past; indeed, a large portion of the Divine revelation consists of information and data about the past. The stories of Adam, Noah, Abraham, Moses, Joseph, David, Mary and Jesus are all related in considerable detail to encourage people to ponder over, and learn lessons from the past. The Qur'anic exhortations inspired the early Muslims to record historical information in a meticulous way. Like people of other ancient civilisations, Muslims not only wrote history, they also played a pivotal role in the progress and development of historiography as a subject. As ancient Greek historians like Herodotus of Halicarnassus considered history to be a mere sequence of events, they did not conduct a rigorous scrutiny of their data to sift the wheat from the chaff in order to ascertain the authenticity of their source material. Nor did they seek to decipher the underlying causes of historical events or identify the factors which lead to the progress or decline of human society. The root causes of historical progress eluded the ancient historians until the Muslims pioneered historicism (or the science of historical inquiry). The father of the philosophy of history, and one

of the most influential historians of all time, was Ibn Khaldun.

Abd al-Rahman ibn Muhammad ibn Muhammad ibn Khaldun was born in Tunis (in present-day Tunisia) into a family of distinguished politicians and civil servants. Of Yemeni origin, Ibn Khaldun's family members settled in Tunis in 1248 and became prominent figures in Andalusian and North African politics and public affairs. However, his father chose to pursue academic research rather than become a politician. As a noted scholar of Arabic language, literature, Islamic jurisprudence, *hadith*, Sufism and poetry, he supervised his son's early education at home and ensured that young Ibn Khaldun learned the whole Qur'an by heart while he was still in his early teens. He then studied Arabic grammar and literature, before pursuing traditional Islamic sciences. Ibn Khaldun excelled in his studies and completed intensive training in Arabic grammar, theology, aspects of Islamic mysticism and specialised in the *fiqh* of the *maliki madhhab* (or Islamic jurisprudence as interpreted by Malik ibn Anas of Madinah) under the guidance of leading *maliki* scholars of the time. He combined his studies in Islamic sciences (*ulum al-din*) with a thorough training in the philosophical sciences (*ulum al-aqliyyah*) including metaphysics, logic, mathematics, philosophy and aspects of medicine. Ibn Khaldun's extensive training in both the Islamic and philosophical sciences not only expanded his intellectual horizon, it also sharpened his mind in a powerful way. Raised in a politically active family and having also received a thorough education in the religious and philosophical sciences of his day, he was able to transcend the superficial and observe things as they were in reality. Since he was a talented student, he liked to question and analyse received wisdom; indeed, his intellectual questioning and curiosity enabled him to understand and grasp things which others failed to see. Not surprisingly, he became one of the most profound and insightful observers of human behaviour and society in the annals of history.

Although Ibn Khaldun continued his formal education until he was about eighteen, his education was frequently interrupted by a combination of natural and man-made disasters and calamities. On one such occasion a significant part of the Muslim world was ravaged by a deadly plague; this epidemic wreaked havoc across the Islamic world and virtually decimated the population of Tunis. Ibn Khaldun lost his parents, close relatives and teachers during this harrowing period in the history of North Africa. This left the twenty-year-old Ibn Khaldun rather lonely and isolated. Devastated by his loss, he turned down the offer of a civil service job and went to Fez, which at the time was one of North Africa's most prosperous and thriving cities. Here he joined the civil service of Sultan Abu Inan, the ruling Marinid monarch, and pursued advanced training in Islamic and philosophical sciences under the tutelage of the city's leading scholars. By combining his studies with Government employment, he gained direct access to high-ranking politicians, civil administrators and also gained first-hand knowledge and experience of political life. His theoretical knowledge of science, coupled with his practical experience of working within the civil service, sharpened his

understanding of politics, public affairs and the social dynamics of his society.

The faint-hearted rarely succeed in the murky and uncertain world of politics, but Ibn Khaldun was not one of them. He thrived in his new role as a political administrator, and Sultan Abu Inan was so impressed with his performance that he promoted him to a position of considerable political eminence. He thus became a high-ranking politician who wielded considerable political power and influence in North African public life whilst he was still in his early twenties. He continued to serve Sultan Abu Inan conscientiously until he was accused of disloyalty and subsequently incarcerated. After Abu Inan's death in 1358, Ibn Khaldun was released by his successor and again he returned to political life. He was barely twenty-eight when he was appointed a judge (*qadi*) on account of his expertise in *maliki* jurisprudence. However, he found his new job very tedious, cumbersome and repetitive. This prompted him to leave North Africa and move to Granada. Not keen on leading a quiet and lonely life, he thrived in the prevailing culture of political uncertainty and social upheaval. Not surprisingly, his biography reads more like an action packed James Bond story than the life of one of history's most influential Muslim thinkers. After he moved to Granada in 1362, he received a warm reception from its ruling elites including Lisan al-Din ibn al-Khatib, the learned Chief Minister of the State, who subsequently became one of his closest allies. Both being intellectuals and politicians they had many things in common, especially their passion for learning and scholarship which strengthened and fortified their friendship, although later on mutual jealousy and rivalry was to drive them apart in an acrimonious way.

Prior to their falling-out, Ibn al-Khatib had nominated Ibn Khaldun – who had become a scholar of repute and a politician in his own right – to lead a mission to Pedro, the King of Castile. The purpose of this mission was to sign a peace treaty between the King and the Muslims of Granada. During this period he visited Seville, the city of his ancestors, and acquired considerable skills and expertise in international politics and diplomacy. On his return to Granada, his reputation as an electrifying orator, politician and public figure made many of his erstwhile friends, including the Chief Minister Ibn al-Khatib, very jealous of him. Thus they began to make life difficult for him. In the end, he had no choice but to leave Granada and return to North Africa. At the time North Africa was passing through one of the most volatile periods in its history, and Ibn Khaldun found himself caught in the middle of prevailing political uncertainty and social upheaval. For the next decade or so he led a politically active life, which was often interrupted by periods of personal difficulties and incarceration. As a result, he suffered, struggled and faced considerable personal challenges but, on each and every occasion, he came through unscathed. It would not be an exaggeration to say that Ibn Khaldun was the ultimate survivor, in the sense that one day he would be sitting next to the Sultan, while on another day he would find himself locked in a prison. In fact, his political life was neither static nor dull; rather he was a risk-taker whose whole life was full of drama, uncertainty and suspense. Every where he went, he found himself caught in the middle of political plots, coups and intrigues.

Tired of political uncertainty, he eventually withdrew from public life for good and began to pursue his intellectual and literary interests. He was around forty-five when he settled with his family in a quiet location in the district of Bani Arif, and spent the next four years living like a hermit. It was during this period that he authored his voluminous and universally acclaimed *Kitab al-Ibar wa Diwan al-Mubtada wa'l Khabar fi Ayyam al-Arab wa'l Ajam wa'l Barbar* (The Book of Instructive Examples and Register of Subjects and Predicates Dealing with the History of the Arabs, Persians and Berbers), which was destined to immortalise him. Ibn Khaldun's early training in traditional Islamic sciences, coupled with his expertise in philosophy, law and politics, enabled him to undertake a systematic study and analysis of North African culture and society. Being a brilliant intellectual, he understood the nature of social trends and the factors which influenced historical change better than anyone else; thus he was not only able to formulate a fresh and innovative methodology for analysing human culture, but also explained the factors which led to the rise and decline of societies. Ibn Khaldun's thinking on this issue was both refreshing and profound because he was not interested in merely explaining the external factors which contributed to social and historical change; rather he was eager to identify and explain the underlying causes of such phenomena. In other words, he was determined to investigate, decipher and demonstrate the relationship between the external (*zahiri*) and internal or invisible (*batini*) factors which contributed to the rise and decline of cultures and civilisations. Applying his unique scientific approach to understanding human culture and society, he systematically analysed the external data *vis-à-vis* the internal currents of change, in order to demonstrate the true nature of social phenomena and historical changes.

According to Ibn Khaldun, a scientific analysis and interpretation of external data showed that there was an underlying rational structure behind all social and historical events. By exploring the nature of social organisation, identifying the nature and characteristics of leadership, and exploring the impact of the environment on human character, personality and social ethos, he was able to demonstrate that a combination of factors – some of which were external, while others were internal – contributed to the rise and decline of human culture, society and civilisation. He also compared primitive societies with the urbanised cities of his time to prove his theory. Indeed, he analysed the North African Berber society and discovered that the group with the most robust *asabiyah* (or 'sense of social solidarity') tended to dominate those that lacked a similar sense of social unity and cohesion, until there eventually emerged a unified political structure (for example, a monarchy) which expressed their social solidarity. Following further socio-cultural expansion and political consolidation, a new civilisation emerged. This, in turn, led to the formation of urbanised towns and cities where cultural, artistic and scientific pursuits flourished, until the people began to succumb to the lures of luxuries and pleasure, which precipitated the age of decline and disintegration. Though Ibn Khaldun's analysis of the rise and decline of civilisation was restricted to the North African Berber society, the quality and originality of his social analyses, cultural insights and historical observations were both profound and pioneering. No other historian or social philosopher, before or after him, had been able to analyse human culture and history in such a thoroughly modern, scientific and innovative manner. In fact, he was the first historian and philosopher to develop an integrated approach to the study and interpretation of human history and culture. And in so doing he effectively inaugurated what is today known as 'social science', even though he referred to it as the 'science of culture'. Not surprisingly, he is today widely considered to be the founding father of both the sociology and philosophy of history.

Ibn Khaldun completed his *Kitab al-Ibar* in 1382 at the age of fifty. Known as the *Muqqadimah fi'l Tarikh* (Introduction to History), in the first part of this voluminous book, he systematically developed his new theoretical approach to socio-historical analysis of culture, society and civilisation. Sir Arnold J. Toynbee, the acclaimed British historian and author of *A Study of History*, rated this book so highly that he described it as 'undoubtedly the greatest work of its kind that has ever yet been created by any mind in any time or place.' In the second part of the book, Ibn Khaldun analysed the history of the Arabs, up to to his own time. In the third, and last part, he provided an historical account of Western Islam, including the history of the Berbers of North Africa. His autobiography, entitled *al-Ta'rif,* also appears at the end of the third book. This autobiography contains valuable information about his background, childhood, early education and career as a politician and judge. Experts in Arabic

literature have rated this autobiography very highly for its literary merit and eloquence. After completing his monumental *Kitab al-Ibar*, Ibn Khaldun travelled to Egypt in 1382 with a view to performing the sacred *hajj* (pilgrimage). But on this occasion he was unable to go to Makkah, and instead he went to Cairo where he began to deliver regular lectures on political thought, Islamic history and *maliki* jurisprudence at the world famous al-Azhar University (it is interesting to note that the great scholar of *hadith* Ibn Hajar al-Asqalani and the renowned historian Ahmad ibn Ali al-Maqrizi attended his lectures during this period.). His vast knowledge of Islamic law and jurisprudence subsequently prompted the Mamluk Sultan al-Zahir Barquq, the reigning monarch of Egypt, to make him a judge but soon he became embroiled in yet another political coup and more intrigue.

During this period he suffered a great shock when his wife and seven children perished in a shipwreck en route to Cairo. This prompted him to go to Makkah and perform the *hajj* in 1387. At the same time he also visited Damascus and Palestine, including the historic city of Jerusalem. He then volunteered to go and meet Amir Timur, who is better known in the West as Tamerlane, in order to dissuade the fearsome Mongol conqueror from attacking Damascus. After his return to Cairo in 1401, he spent the next five years of his life in peace and tranquility. He died at the age of seventy-four and was buried in the Sufi Cemetry on the outskirts of Cairo. Ibn Khaldun's inspiring personality and vast learning, together with his remarkable contribution to the development of modern social science and philosophy of history, represents an important milestone in the annals of human thought. It is very doubtful whether great Western scholars and thinkers (such as Arnold Toynbee) would have achieved as much as they did without Ibn Khaldun's seminal contributions in the field of social science and history. That is why humanity will forever remain indebted to this most profound and original Muslim thinker.

# 22

# *Malik ibn Anas (b.711 - d.795)*

AS ISLAM IS not only a religion but also a complete way of life, the Holy Qur'an and the normative practice (*sunnah*) of the Prophet provide detailed and comprehensive guidance for Muslims, covering every sphere of their life. After preaching and propagating Islam in Makkah for more than a decade, the Prophet migrated to Madinah in 622 and devoted the next decade of his life to transforming that Arabian oasis into a fully-fledged Islamic society. The Prophet not only imparted Islamic knowledge to the people of Madinah, he also developed the social, political, economic and legal apparatus of that society in the light of the Divine revelation, and in so doing he established the first Islamic State in history. From that day on, Madinah became the model Islamic society, a shining example of what a Muslim State ought to be like. Ever since then, Muslims have continued to admire, study and analyse the key features and characteristics of that early Madinian society as established by the Prophet. Probably more than anyone else, one man played a pivotal role in recording the norms and culture of that early Madinian society; he was Malik ibn Anas.

Abu Abdullah Malik ibn Anas ibn Malik ibn Abi Amir al-Asbahi, known as Imam Malik,

was born in Madinah during the reign of the Umayyad Caliph al-Walid ibn Abd al-Malik. Hailing from the Yemeni province of Himyar, Malik's grandfather came to Madinah and settled there with his family during the reign of Caliph Umar. Living during the early days of Islam, his grandfather and father acquired a thorough education in Islam under the supervision of the Prophet's companions (*sahabah*). Young Malik was thus brought up in a deeply religious environment, where everyone lived their lives in accordance with the Prophetic norms and practices. After memorising the whole Qur'an, he received instruction in Arabic grammar and traditional Islamic teachings at home. He then acquired a thorough familiarisation with the fundamentals of Islam under the supervision of his learned father, Anas, and uncle, Rabi. Being very studious, he preferred to occupy himself with his studies rather than pursue a career in trade or commerce. Such was his thirst for knowledge and education that he chose to stay at home and study, rather than go out and play games with other children. His love for learning remained with him for the rest of his life, as he went onto become one of the Muslim world's most celebrated scholars and jurists. As a gifted student, he excelled in his studies and outshone not only his peers but also his older brother, Nadhr ibn Malik. Though Damascus was the political capital of the Islamic world at the time, Madinah remained the hub of Islamic learning and scholarship by virtue of the fact that it was the city of the Prophet (*madinat al-nabi*), and the first civic capital of the Islamic State. Brought up and educated in this blessed city, Malik developed instant affinity with the normative practice of the Prophet. Not surprisingly, the study of Prophetic *hadith* (or tradition) became his favourite preoccupation in life.

Since his uncle Abu Suhail al-Nafi was an eminent authority on *hadith* literature, Malik began to study this and other related subjects under his guidance. Al-Nafi was fortunate to have studied Islamic sciences, especially *hadith*, directly under the supervision of Aishah, the Prophet's beloved wife, and famous companions like Abu Hurairah and Abdullah ibn Umar. Malik sat at the feet of al-Nafi, and began to absorb Islamic knowledge in a systematic way. Other outstanding students of al-Nafi included al-Zuhri, al-Awza'i and Ibn Jarir, but it was the precocious Malik who was destined to outshine all of them on account of his unrivalled mastery of the Prophetic *hadith*. Malik may have been gifted, but he was equally selfless and hardworking. He made it a rule for himself to visit his teachers in their homes and wait as long as it was necessary for them to come out of their houses and teach him. Adverse weather and difficult terrain notwithstanding, he always insisted on visiting all the luminaries of Madinah including Muhammad ibn Yahya al-Ansari, Abu Hazim Salmah ibn Dinar and Yahya ibn Sa'id in order to learn *hadith* from them. Thus he spent considerable sums of money, endured physical hardship and even experienced personal difficulties in his quest for Prophetic *hadith*.

After completing his formal study of *tafsir* (Qur'anic exegesis), *fiqh* (jurisprudence) and *hadith*, Malik began to attend the class of Rabi'ah ibn Abd al-Rahman and Sa'id ibn Musayyib, two of the greatest Islamic scholars of their generation. As a passionate exponent of independent reasoning in juristic matters (*ijtihad*), the former argued that the ability to exercise scholarly discretion was a *sine qua non* for a correct understanding and application of Islamic principles at a practical level. Thus he did not hesitate to push the boundaries of scholarly discretion beyond their limits where he felt it was appropriate to do so, although most of his peers tried to curtail the use of intellectual discretion in interpreting the revealed scriptural sources of Islam. Keen to master the art of independent reasoning in juristic matters, Malik attended Rabi'ah's lectures and became highly proficient in exercising intellectual discretion. The need for such an interpretive approach *vis-à-vis* the revealed sources of Islam was recognised as soon as the Muslims began to encounter new challenges during the rapid expansion of the Islamic world following the death of the Prophet in 632. Faced with new challenges and difficulties, the early scholars of Islam approached the Divine revelation and Prophetic *hadith* with critical minds in order to derive guidance from them in providing Islamic answers to the problems of their time.

Although the justification for formulating such an interpretative methodology already existed in the Qur'an, the majority of the scholars were reluctant to go down this road until Abu Hanifah emerged to develop the methodology in a rigorous and systematic manner, thus making it a key feature of *hanafi* legal thought. Not content with what he had learned so far, Malik then mastered *hadith* under Hisham ibn Urwa, Abd al-Rahman ibn Hurmuz and Sa'id ibn Musayyib. Despite being a prominent follower (*tabi*) of the Prophet's companions and an eminent authority on *hadith*, Sa'id was so impressed with Malik's knowledge of *hadith* that he formally authorised him to teach. Malik then attended Ja'far al-Sadiq's lectures on the Qur'an, *hadith* and *fiqh* at the *masjid al-nabi*. As well as being a direct descendant of the Prophet, Ja'far was a great Islamic scholar and sage of his time; Malik studied under Ja'far's tutelage and the latter was also deeply impressed with his vast knowledge of Prophetic traditions. But after the emergence of various religious groups like the *shi'at Ali*, *khawarij*, *mu'tazilah* and the *murijah*, political rivalries and religious schisms began to spread across the Islamic dominion. The rise of both political and theological differences within the early Muslim community prompted Malik to familiarise himself with the views of all these sects and groups, and become a champion of traditional Islam.

By the time Malik reached his fortieth birthday, he was already widely recognised as an eminent Islamic scholar and jurist throughout Madinah, not least because more than seventy distinguished scholars of *tafsir* and *hadith* had authorised him to teach the Islamic sciences. Since he was also a strict adherent of the Prophetic *sunnah* and the practice (*amal*) of the people of Madinah, he cared little about the wealth and luxuries of this world; indeed, he chose to live in virtual poverty, far removed from the wealth and pleasures of this life. As expected, his piety, simplicity and asceticism (*zuhd*) boosted his standing in Madinah and the locals became very fond him. After the death of his beloved teacher Rabi'ah in 755, he came to be regarded as one of Madinah's most learned scholars. And since there was no better place to start teaching than in the Prophet's own mosque, Malik began to deliver daily lectures on *hadith* and *fiqh* in the *masjid al-nabi*. Being a polite and friendly teacher, he always encouraged his students to ask questions and he, in turn, also provided simple and straightforward answers. And although he was an undisputed master of Prophetic traditions and the norms and ethos of the people of Madinah, people often tested his knowledge of Islam by posing difficult political and theological questions *vis-à-vis* the behaviour of the city's ruling elites. But he always responded to such questions in a measured, relevant and succinct way. His honesty, sincerity and unusual grasp of Islamic teachings and practices, coupled with his photographic memory and intellectual brillance, made him a popular figure not only in Madinah but also across the Islamic dominion. So much so that, on one ocassion, al-Zuhri, who

was also a great scholar of *hadith* and a contemporary of Malik, referred to him as a 'great vessel of knowledge'.

Malik's lectures at the *masjid al-nabi* became so popular that thousands of students came from all over Arabia and other parts of the Muslim world to hear him speak. Some of his famous students included al-Shafi'i, Abu Yusuf, Muhammad ibn al-Hasan al-Shaybani and Abdullah ibn Mubarak. According to some scholars, Abu Hanifah, Abbasid Caliphs Abu Ja'far al-Mansur, al-Mahdi and Harun al-Rashid and his young sons (who later became Caliphs al-Amin and al-Ma'mun) had also attended Malik's lectures. However, other scholars have questioned this claim; they argue that Abu Hanifah, Abu Yusuf, al-Amin and al-Ma'mun probably had not even heard of Malik, not to mention attending his lectures. Either way, as a gifted scholar, he developed his own style of textual exposition and delivery. He used to sit on the pulpit (*minbar*) in the Prophet's mosque with a copy of the Qur'an on one hand and his collections of *hadith* on the other, and delineate the fundamental principles and practices of Islam; firstly in the light of the Qur'an, and then further illuminating the issues concerned by examining them in accordance with the Prophetic *sunnah*. His methodical approach to the textual sources of Islam, coupled with his slow but measured delivery, enabled his students to understand his explanations and also take copious notes at the same time. When the number of people attending his lectures became very large, Malik appointed several teaching assistants who repeated his words aloud so that eveyone could hear him. This style of teaching proved so successful that later it became institutionalised in the form of *madrasah* (Islamic seminaries) across the Islamic world.

Central to Malik's religious thought and world-view were the Qur'an and Prophetic *sunnah*; indeed, even his personal views, opinions and lifestyle were moulded by these two fundamental sources of Islam. Whenever people sought his advice and guidance, he counselled them in accordance with the teachings of the Qur'an and *sunnah*. If he found a *hadith* which contradicted the Qur'an, he rejected it immediately. Since the Qur'an was the foremost source of authority in Islam, he felt the authentic *sunnah* had to be subordinate to it. Like Abu Hanifah, he was thoroughly acquainted with the methods of independent scholarly discretion, and also considered Islamic teachings to be completely in harmony with human reason and logic. However, unlike Abu Hanifah, he regarded the norms and ethos of Madinian society to be a fundamental source for the interpretation of Islamic principles and practices. Shaped by the Prophet in the light of Divine guidance, the customs (*urf*) and practices (*amal*) of the people of Madinah, therefore, became an important component of Malik's legal theory and methodology. In addition to this, his famous *Kitab al-Muwatta* (The Book of the Beaten Path), composed at the behest of Abbasid Caliph Abu Ja'far al-Mansur, became one of the first and most important anthologies of *hadith* ever produced. After carefully examining and scrutinising a large quantity of Prophetic traditions, he collected around one thousand legally-orientated *ahadith* into one book. He supplemented the *hadith* with the views and opinions of the Prophet's companions, followed by the customs and practices of the people of Madinah, along with his own views and opinions on the issues concerned.

Upon completion, this book became an instant success. It became so popular across the Muslim world that, on one occasion, Caliph Harun al-Rashid asked Malik for his permission to make his book the law of the land. But, being a wise scholar, he told the Caliph that it would not be appropriate to make his book the law of the land because it was based primarily on the norms and ethos of the people of Madinah. He felt it would be inappropriate to limit Islam and Muslims to one particular interpretation of Islamic law only. Nevertheless, this pioneering work later inspired generations of Islamic scholars like al-Bukhari, Muslim ibn al-Hajjaj, Abu Dawud, al-Tirmidhi and others to compose their own voluminous collections of *hadith*. Widely considered to be one of the great anthologies of Prophetic traditions, some scholars of *hadith* (such as Shah Waliullah of Delhi) even rated *al-Muwatta* higher than *Sahih al-Bukhari* and *Sahih Muslim* on account of its authenticity as a book of Islamic teachings and practices. Malik was not only a great scholar of *hadith*, *fiqh* and theology; he was also a fearless defender of traditional Islam. Repeatedly flogged and chastised by the Madinian authorities for speaking the truth and defending Islamic principles, his firm and uncompromising stance against the corrupt rulers of his time won him the love and affection of the locals. Malik died in Madinah at the advanced age of around eighty-five and was buried in the city's famous cemetery, Jannat al-Baqi. Named after Malik, the *maliki madhhab* (school of legal thought) later emerged and spread across the Muslim world. Today the adherents of this school are to be found mainly in Egypt, North and West Africa, and the Gulf States of Kuwait, Qatar and Bahrain.

# 23

# Umar ibn Abd al-Aziz (b.682 - d.719)

THE ERA OF the first four Caliphs of Islam is widely considered to be the Golden Age of Islam. Caliphs Abu Bakr, Umar, Uthman and Ali were not only close companions of the Prophet, they were also exceptionally loyal and gifted Muslims. During their reigns, the four Caliphs conducted their affairs strictly in accordance with the teachings of Islam; that is to say, they tried to discharge their duties and obligations to all the citizens of the Islamic State with equity, justice and fairness. Following in the footsteps of the Prophet, they served their people in an exemplary way. Wealth, luxuries and the possessions of this world failed to distract them from their main purpose and mission in life, namely to see Islam gain ascendancy in all spheres of human life. However, after the period of the first four Caliphs, the Muslim world entered a long phase of dynastic rule. Founded by Muawiyah ibn Abi Sufyan, the Umayyads became the first dynasty in Islamic history and went onto rule the Muslim world for nearly a century. During the rule of this dynasty, a hugely inspirational Muslim leader emerged who became known as the 'fifth rightly-guided' Caliph. The Prophet and his first four successors aside, Muslims have revered this ruler probably more than any other

in the annals of Islam. His name was Umar ibn Abd al-Aziz.

Abu Hafs Umar ibn Abd al-Aziz ibn Marwan ibn Hakam was born in Madinah into an aristocratic family of the Umayyad dynasty. A direct descendant of Caliph Umar, through his son Asim, Umar ibn Abd al-Aziz was brought up and educated in Madinah. He completed his early education in Arabic and also memorised the Qur'an and *hadith* (Prophetic traditions) under the supervision of Salih ibn Kaisan and several other companions (*sahabah*) of the Prophet, and their successors (*tabiun*), such as Abdullah ibn Utbah ibn Mas'ud. He then received advanced training in Arabic grammar, literature, poetry and *hadith*. Young Umar became so proficient in Arabic literature and Islamic sciences that some of the leading scholars of the time tested his knowledge of the intricacies of Islamic jurisprudence (*fiqh*) and Prophetic traditions, but he passed their tests with flying colours. Not surprisingly, prominent Islamic scholars and writers like Shams al-Din al-Dhahabi considered Umar to be a competent scholar of *tafsir* (Qur'anic exegesis), *hadith* and *fiqh*. By virtue of his scholarly achievements, he became known throughout Madinah as one of the most learned of the Umayyad princes.

After completing his formal education, he moved to Egypt where his father, Abd al-Aziz ibn Marwan, served as governor. As a prominent member of the ruling Umayyad clan, his father was a close confidant of the Caliph and this no doubt enabled Umar to become a member of the Umayyad family's inner circle. Being an Umayyad prince and a prominent member of the royal family, he had a privileged upbringing, surrounded by much wealth, luxury and material extravagance. Like the other Umayyad princes of the time, he was offered a high-ranking post within the Umayyad administration which enabled him to lead a life of comfort and indulgence. And although all the other Umayyad princes wore expensive clothes, applied the best perfume and walked through the streets of Damascus with their heads held high, young Umar always went out of his way to impress everyone around him. Of fair complexion, refined manners and always immaculately dressed, he was constantly surrounded by servants who were happy to comply with his every whim and desire. Not surprisingly, he came to symbolise the pomp, pride and material extravagance of the ruling Umayyad family. After the death of his father Abd al-Aziz, the reigning Caliph Abd al-Malik offered the hand of his daughter, Fatimah bint Abd al-Malik, to him; Umar not only accepted the marriage proposal, he also thanked the Caliph for his kindness and generosity.

As an intelligent and gifted scholar, he could have occupied one of the Muslim world's highest seats of learning at the time but, thanks to his strong family connection with the Umayyads, he decided to pursue a political career instead. Appointed governor of the province of Khanasarah by Caliph Abd al-Malik, his father-in-law, Umar took charge of this region and became very popular with the locals for his sense of justice, fairness and equality. After the death of Caliph Abd al-Malik, his son al-Walid ascended the Umayyad throne and he promoted Umar to the governorship of Madinah. Although this was a tremendous honour for him, he made it clear to the new Caliph that he had no desire to follow in the footsteps of his predecessors and behave ruthlessly towards the people of Madinah. Al-Walid agreed with him and he set out for Madinah, the city of the Prophet, where he had spent his early years studying under the great scholars of the city. Though only twenty-five years old, he discharged his duties as governor with loyalty, dedication and understanding. Soon after becoming governor, he invited all the leading scholars and citizens of Madinah to dinner and established a consultative (*shura*) council. Consisting of religious scholars, civil servants and prominent local people, the remit of this council was to discuss and debate important policy issues of the day and offer advice to the governor. Since Umar's jurisdiction also encompassed Makkah and Taif, his willingness to listen to the people and address their concerns quickly won him the support of the locals, who pledged to co-operate with him fully.

Then, to his dismay, Umar noticed how the *masjid al-nabi* (the 'Prophet's mosque') had been neglected by his predecessors. The mosque was so small that it overflowed with worshippers; it had not been renovated since Marwan ibn Hakam carried out some repairs during his tenure as governor. He therefore wrote to Caliph al-Walid for his permission to expand the mosque. The last time the mosque had been expanded significantly was during the Caliphate of Uthman, and it required urgent attention. When Caliph al-Walid gave the go-ahead, Umar summoned all the prominent scholars of Madinah (including al-Qasim, Salim and Abu Bakr ibn Abd al-Rahman) to seek their advice on the matter. Following the consultation, the old mosque was demolished and a new one was built, thus creating a mosque which could accommodate more worshippers. According to the historians, Caliph al-Walid even wrote to the Byzantine Emperor requesting him to make a contribution towards the cost of building the mosque. The Emperor obliged by sending a large quantity of gold and precious mosaic tiles, along with one hundred craftsmen to assist with the construction. This mammoth project took nearly two years to complete, and Caliph al-Walid came to inspect it during the *hajj* (pilgrimage) season in 709. The Caliph was so impressed with the new mosque that he publicly praised Umar for his remarkable achievement. When it was pointed out to the Caliph that Umar had also constructed a fountain near the Prophet's mosque to supply free, fresh water to the worshippers, he acknowledged Umar's superior qualities and attributes.

Umar remained governor of Madinah for six years before he was removed from his post in 711. The historians have provided conflicting accounts for his removal from the governorship. According to al-Tabari, the Caliph removed him from his post on the advice of Hajjaj ibn Yusuf, who was an iron-fisted military general, because he considered him to be too lenient towards their adversaries. However, according to Abd al-Rahman ibn Ali ibn al-Jawzi, he was not removed from his post; rather he resigned after discovering that he had punished an innocent man on the orders of the Caliph and as a result the victim had died. When Umar was informed of the man's death, he apparently jumped up from his seat and exclaimed, 'From Allah we come and to Him we will return.' and fainted. This incident stung his conscience and he resigned his post as governor. However, after al-Walid's death in 715, his brother Sulaiman became the Caliph and the latter, being very fond of Umar on account of his loyalty, principles and honesty, appointed him special advisor and thus he became a key figure within the Umayyad administration again. And although Caliph Sulaiman's reign lasted barely two years, before his death he had anonymously nominated Umar as his successor and this proved to be one of the best decisions he made during his short reign.

With his accession to the Umayyad throne in 717, Umar became one of the most powerful rulers of his time. If 'power tends to corrupt and absolute power corrupts absolutely' as Lord Acton put it, then Umar ibn Abd al-Aziz was an exception to this rule. As a strict adherent of the Prophetic *sunnah* and the way of the *al-khulafa al-rashidun* (the first four 'rightly-guided Caliphs'), he refused to let power go to his head; rather his assumption of political responsibilities made him more humble and sagacious. So much so that he insisted on conducting his official inauguration ceremony riding his own horse, flatly refusing to mount the royal ceremonial horses which were prepared for him with great care and attention. The pomp and pageantry, pride and prestige associated with Umayyad power failed to impress Umar. Indeed, he developed a profound dislike of such lavish and extravagant displays of wealth and power. Being once a hugely wealthy and pampered Umayyad prince himself, his accession to power transformed him for good. Thus, despite being one of the most powerful rulers of his time, he preferred to live like a hermit rather than a King. The Prophet and the first four Caliphs of Islam aside, Umar ibn Abd al-Aziz is the closest one can get to a saintly King.

According to Umayyad custom, the new Caliph was expected to collect all his predecessor's belongings and distribute them among their children. Umar deliberately broke this custom by emptying his predecessor's wardrobe and dispatching all its contents to the public treasury (*bait al-mal*), notwithstanding fierce opposition from the entire royal family. He then refused to move into the plush Caliphal Palace; instead he erected a tent for himself. As he sat inside the tent agonising about the huge political responsibility which had been placed on his shoulders, a servant appeared in front of him and remarked, 'You look very worried, Sir.' He replied, 'It is a great worry that in the East and the West there is no follower of Prophet Muhammad's *ummah* (global community) who does not have a right upon me which it is my duty to fulfil without demand or notice.' The thought of being responsible for all the citizens of the vast Islamic State concerned Umar so much that he went straight to the local mosque – and following in the footsteps of the first four Caliphs of Islam – announced: 'O people, the burden of Caliphate has been put on me without obtaining my opinion, without me desiring it, and without consulting the Muslims at large. I remove the collar of allegiance to me that has been put round your necks. You are now free to choose whoever you like as your Caliph.' The people in the mosque responded, 'We choose you as our Caliph and agree to your Caliphate.' After pausing for a moment, Umar then proclaimed, 'O people, it is incumbent upon you to obey one who obeys God. It is not incumbent upon you to obey one who disobeys God. As long as I obey God, obey me. As soon as I disobey Him, you cease to owe me any obedience.' With this historic announcement, Caliph Umar ibn Abd al-Aziz restored the democratic right of the people to choose and elect their ruler, a precedent originally set by the Prophet himself, within the Islamic polity, almost a century earlier.

With the full backing of the people, Umar focused his full attention on the affairs of the vast Umayyad Empire. Aware of the oppressive and dictatorial policies and practices of his predecessors, he began to redress the injustices and wrongs perpetrated by the Umayyads in the past. Known for their political notoriety and wilful misappropriation of public wealth and property for the royal family's benefit, none of the Umayyad rulers were popular with the masses except Umar, who dramatically reversed the policies of his predecessors and returned to the people their stolen goods, properties and lands. He pursued this policy so ruthlessly that every member of the Umayyad family, including his own wife Fatimah, was asked to return to the public all the goods that had been taken from them unlawfully. His wife complied with his order and returned to the public treasury all the precious jewellery given to her by her father, Caliph Abd al-Malik. Although Umar's policy angered all the members of the royal family, he did not relent or back down until all the confiscated goods, properties and lands were returned to their rightful owners. So much so, that soon all the members of the Umayyad family found themselves on the verge of poverty and destitution. Even though this remarkable and unprecedented act of restorative justice made him very unpopular with the

leading members of the ruling Umayyad clan, no one dared to oppose him directly. In desperation, Hisham ibn Abd al-Malik, who was a leading member of the royal family, pleaded with Umar not to return anymore of the Umayyad wealth to the public. Characteristic of Umar, he retorted that he would continue to render justice until all known injustice had been corrected, 'For fear of punishment on the Day of Judgement prevents me from disobeying God.' During his short reign of two years, Caliph Umar ibn Abd al-Aziz succeeded in restoring justice, fairness and equality across the vast Umayyad Empire. Unlike his predecessors, he was not keen on pursuing military expeditions abroad when social injustice, economic inequality and political oppression reigned supreme at home.

Thus it was his habit to send regular communications to all his governors to remind them to fear God, to observe justice and treat all their subjects well, whether they happened to be Muslims or non-Muslims. He also reminded all his provincial governors that it was incumbent upon them to restore to the people all the lands, properties and goods which had been wrongfully confiscated from them in the past. If any of his governors failed to comply with his instructions, he immediately removed them from their post. As expected, Umar's sound principles and impeccable sense of justice and fair play soon made him very popular with the masses. Conversely, his refusal to give up his policy of restorative justice began to create much resentment within the Umayyad family; indeed, some of them even began to secretly conspire against the Caliph. But unable to topple him, they reportedly poisoned him instead. According to some of his biographers, after twenty day's illness, Caliph Umar ibn Abd al-Aziz passed away at the age of around thirty-seven. He died reciting, 'We make this last home for those who neither seek superiority on earth nor make trouble, and peace is only for the God-fearing.'

His death shocked and horrified everyone within the Islamic world and all the people, young and old, men and women, Muslims and non-Muslims, shed tears for him. Influential Islamic scholars and sages like Hasan al-Basri not only prayed for him, they also fondly remembered him as an exemplary ruler. When the news of Umar's death was relayed to the Byzantine Emperor, he also paid him one of the most glowing tributes, saying, 'If there was any man after Jesus who could have brought the dead back to life, it was Umar ibn Abd al-Aziz. I do not marvel at the monk who renounces the world, shuts himself up and devotes himself entirely to prayer. I marvel at the man who had the world at his feet and who, trampling upon it, took to a monk's life.'

That was the greatness of the man who came to symbolise true Islamic qualities and attributes, both as a citizen and ruler of one of the Muslim world's greatest empires. That is why Umar ibn Abd al-Aziz, the great Saint-King of Islam, continues to inspire Muslims to this day. His love for Islam and Muslims, coupled with his desire to promote peace, justice and fair play throughout his vast dominion, turned him into a powerful symbol of justice, goodness and rectitude. Today, across the Muslim world, people are crying out for a leader like Umar ibn Abd al-Aziz to emerge and guide them through the unpredictable and tumultuous waves of history.

# 24

## Abd al-Qadir al-Jilani
### (b.1077 - d.1166)

IT WOULD NOT be an exaggeration to say that the Muslim world has produced some of the world's great spiritual teachers who devoted their entire lives to acquiring a better understanding of the meaning and purpose of creation, and man's role in this vast universe. Unlike the philosophers, theologians and scientists, their *modus vivendi* was to 'experience' knowledge as such. According to them, the universe and the human soul are not mere abstract concepts which are independent of each other, for at a certain level all things are inter-connected and inter-dependent, being ultimately connected to a common denominator. These great spiritual teachers were eager to understand the true nature of reality, that is to say, they sought to transcend the 'exterior', and plunge into the ocean of 'inner' meanings of things in order to attain 'experiential' knowledge which, they believed, would enable them to move closer to Divine proximity – the origin of all that exists. One of the Muslim world's most influential, and arguably the most revered, Sufi (or spiritual teacher and guide) was Abd al-Qadir al-Jilani.

Sayyid Muhyi al-Din Abu Muhammad Abd al-Qadir Hasani al-Jilani was born in Nif, a district town of Jilan in the province of Tabaristan, located on the coast of the Caspian Sea. His family traced their lineage back to Hasan, the eldest son of Caliph Ali and a grandson of the Prophet, through Sayyid Hasan Muthanna. Abu Salih, his mystically inclined father died when he was a child, but his unusually pious mother, Umm al-Khair Fatimah, raised him with the support of her scholarly and saintly father, Abdullah al-Suma'i, who claimed to be a descendant of Hussain ibn Ali through his son Ali Zain al-Abideen. Abd al-Qadir received his early education in Arabic, committed the whole Qur'an to memory and studied aspects of *hadith* (Prophetic traditions) at home under the supervision of his mother and maternal grandfather. He then began his formal education at a local school when he was about ten. Thereafter, he pursued his intermediate studies at his local religious seminaries and acquired a sound knowledge of traditional Islamic sciences and Sufism (Islamic mysticism) before he reached his eighteenth birthday.

In 1095, Abd al-Qadir left his native Jilan and journeyed to Baghdad, which was the capital of the Muslim world at the time. However, on his way to Baghdad his caravan was surrounded by a group of robbers who confiscated the travellers' belongings by force. When one of the robbers asked young Abd al-Qadir if he had any valuables on him, to the surprise of the robber, he said his mother had stitched forty gold coins up his sleeves. At first the robber did not take him seriously, presumably because he thought the youngster was pulling his leg. But when the leader of the gang questioned Abd al-Qadir and demanded to see the hidden gold coins, he opened up his sleeves and showed him the money. The robbers found his actions both puzzling and very unusual, to say the least. When they asked him why he admitted to having the gold coins, to their amazement, he replied that his mother's parting words to him were that he must always speak the truth. Since denying that he had any money on him would have been to utter a falsehood, he decided to tell the truth, he said. Abd al-Qadir's truthfulness and honesty clearly stirred the robbers' consciences and they reportedly fell to the ground and begged for his forgiveness and clemency. After thanking him for teaching them a lesson in good behaviour, ethics and morality, the robbers returned all the goods they had seized from the people, and promised to change their ways.

After a long and eventful journey, he finally reached Baghdad. At the time Baghdad was a thriving centre of Islamic learning and commercial activity. He also found the people of Baghdad very friendly and hospitable. Although joining the Baghdad branch of the famous Nizamiyyah College (founded in 1065 by the celebrated Seljuk Prime Minister Nizam al-Mulk) would have been an attractive option, he decided not to join this college. Instead he studied Arabic grammar, literature, *tafsir* (Qur'anic exegesis), *hadith* and *fiqh* (Islamic jurisprudence), especially *hanbali fiqh*, under the guidance of Baghdad's leading scholars and teachers. He paid for his educational and maintenance costs out of the forty gold coins his mother had given him, but when the money ran out he began to experience considerable financial and personal hardship. His financial situation became so dire that he was not always able to afford to eat. Despite these hardships, he remained upbeat and was determined to

complete his advanced education. Known for his love of Prophetic traditions, Abd al-Qadir began to study *hadith* literature under the supervision of a number of prominent traditionists (*muhaddithun*) including Shaykh Abu Ghalib Ahmad and Shaykh Abul Qasim Ali. During this period he also studied Arabic literature under the guidance of Abu Zakariyya Yahya al-Tabrizi, who was an authority on Arabic literature and the principal of Baghdad's renowned Nizamiyyah College. In addition to this, Abd al-Qadir received thorough training in *hanbali* legal thought and methodology under the tutelage of Baghdad's leading *hanbali fuqaha* (jurists), including Abu Sa'id Mubarak ibn al-Mukharrimi.

After completing his formal education, he sat at the feet of Shaykh Abul Khair Hammad ibn Muslim al-Dabbas who was an illiterate, but prominent, authority on Islamic spirituality and gnosis, and from him received training in Sufism. Under Shaykh al-Dabbas's instruction he not only learned the theories and methods of Sufism, but also became exposed to a new universe of meaning, purpose and spiritual fulfilment – one where the 'inner' meaning and implication of religious teachings became clear to him for the first time. The move from the 'text' to the 'spirit of the text' enabled him to purify his soul and continue his quest for spiritual development and fulfilment. Being a Sufi himself, the *hanbali* jurist Abu Sa'id also played a decisive role in Abd al-Qadir's early quest for spirituality and fulfilment. He personally guided him in the methods and practices of Sufism, until the latter had attained complete mastery of Islamic spirituality and gnosis, whereupon he conferred on him the robe of an initiate of Sufism. During this period Abd al-Qadir earned his livelihood by cultivating crops and vegetables, and he only spoke when it was required. After living amidst the ruins of Mada'in (Ctesiphon) like a hermit for eleven years, in 1117, at the age of forty, he finally returned to Baghdad where he soon established his reputation as a gifted scholar of the Qur'an, Prophetic traditions, *hanbali* jurisprudence and practitioner of Sufism. This prompted the locals to appoint him head of the same *madrasah* (Islamic seminary) where his former mentor Abu Sa'id once served as principal.

According to Abd al-Qadir, it was during this period that the Prophet Muhammad visited him in a dream and advised him to preach Islam and admonish the locals. At the time he was busy lecturing on the religious sciences at the local seminary, without showing any desire or inclination to become a social activist and popular disseminator of Islam. However, his encounter with the Prophet, coupled with the encouragement he received from Khwajah Yusuf Hamdani (a notable savant of Baghdad), prompted him to begin delivering public lectures on all aspects of Islamic thought and practice, in order to encourage and inspire the locals to lead a more Islamic life based on the teachings of the Qur'an and *sunnah* (normative practice of the Prophet). As a prominent scholar of traditional Islamic sciences and master of Islamic spirituality, Abd al-Qadir was able to interpret Islamic teachings in a traditional, yet spiritually enhancing, way so that both the traditionalist scholars and the Sufis used to sit side by side to listen to his inspiring lectures on all aspects of Islam, without raising any objections. His remarkable and unique ability to combine Islamic traditionalism with Islamic spirituality made him a hugely popular figure during his lifetime. If al-Ghazali played a pivotal role in intellectually harmonising traditional Islam with Sufism, then the credit for fully explaining this synthesis – to the religious scholars, Sufis and the masses – must go to Abd al-Qadir.

According to his biographers, he became such a popular lecturer that the college grounds where he used to deliver his talks regularly overflowed, as thousands of people flocked from in and around Baghdad to hear him speak. Thanks to his intellectual brilliance and unique style of delivery, hundreds of non-Muslims (including Jews and Christians) embraced Islam and thousands of ordinary Muslims began to take their faith seriously. To accommodate the large crowds attending his lectures, the houses adjacent to his college were later purchased and demolished to create more space for the people. Indeed, he became one of the first Sufi scholars in the annals of Islam to acquire such a mass following. His ability to transcend theological differences and sectarian barriers encouraged the leading religious scholars, jurists, mystics, preachers and even the politicians of his day to set their differences aside, and unite under the banner of Islam. He used to deliver lectures three times a week: on Friday morning before the weekly Friday congregational (*salat al-jumu'ah*) prayer; on Tuesday evening, and also on Sunday mornings. More than seventy thousand people used to attend his lectures at any one time and around four hundred scribes used to write down his talks for the benefit of posterity.

Abd al-Qadir enjoyed such success and popularity because he was able to combine practical Islam with its spiritual dimension. Not surprisingly, he did not consider himself to be an esoteric or an exoteric; he did not believe in one without the other. Though he was a strict adherent of the Prophetic norms and practices, he also found time to engage in spiritual retreat. He emphasised the importance of leading a balanced and moderate lifestyle, focusing on the need to purify one's heart, mind and thought. Like Maruf al-Karkhi and Abul Qasim al-Junayd al-Baghdadi before him, Abd al-Qadir was a 'sober' Sufi, who strictly avoided the path of 'intoxication' pursued by other Sufis like Abu Yazid al-Bistami, Abul Hussain al-Nuri and Hussain ibn Mansur al-Hallaj, and in so doing he tried to revive the authentic norms and practices of the Prophet. As it happens, Abd al-Qadir was one of the most meticulous followers of the Prophetic *sunnah*. Unlike many other Sufis, he married, even if it was late in life – at the age of fifty-one – and he ensured his personal and family life were regulated strictly in accordance with the teachings of the Prophet; indeed, he refused to eat a meal if it was not prepared in accordance with the Prophetic *sunnah*. His contribution to the revival of Prophetic *sunnah*, as well as Islamic spirituality, thus earned him the coveted title of *muhyi al-din* (or the 'reviver of Islam') during his own lifetime.

Thanks to his band of dedicated scribes, Abd al-Qadir's lectures were preserved in the form of books and manuscripts for the benefit of posterity. They include *Al-Fath al-Rabbani* (The Opening Discourse), which contains sixty-two sermons delivered between 1150 and 1152; *Al-Ghunyah li-Talibi Tariq al-Haqq* (That Which is Sufficient to the Seekers of True Path), wherein he explained the traditional Islamic principles and practices in considerable detail, and *Futuh al-Ghaib* (Disclosure of the Unseen), which consists of seventy-eight sermons on the mystical dimensions of Islam, and was compiled by his son, Abd al-Razzaq. In total, more than twenty-four books and manuscripts have been attributed to Abd al-Qadir but, according to his biographers, some of these books are not his own works; they have been wrongly attributed to him by other people. Inspired by the Qur'an and Prophetic wisdom, Abd al-Qadir argued that man was a creature of God Who created him only to serve Him. Abd al-Qadir did not consider God to be a theological construct or a logical abstract; rather, he believed, He is One Who resides in our hearts and continues to influence us in every sphere of our life – both individually as well as collectively – so that man can experience Divine grace, mercy and compassion in this life and the hereafter, guided as ever by the supreme example and personality of the Prophet.

Abd al-Qadir's unique and hugely influential interpretation of Islamic spirituality led to the emergence of one of the most powerful spiritual movements in the annals of Islam. Named after him, the *qadiriyyah* Sufi Order is today followed by millions of people throughout the Muslim world. The majority of the Sufi theoreticians and practitioners who came after him were one way or another influenced by his religious ideas and spiritual practices, and includes Khwajah Mu'in al-Din Chishti, Shihab al-Din Umar al-Suhrawardi and Muhyi al-Din ibn al-Arabi. Aware of his immense influence and standing, Abd al-Qadir himself once remarked, 'My foot is on the head of every saint.' He died at the venerable age of around eighty-nine and was buried in Abbasid Baghdad.

# 25

## Ibn Sina
## (b.980 - d.1037)

MODERN WESTERN SCIENTIFIC thought and culture owes a tremendous debt to the early Muslim philosophers, scientists and thinkers who, by the sheer strength of their characters, intellectual brilliance and powers of imagination lit up the firmament of human thought, culture and civilisation like never before. The Muslim contribution to the study of philosophy and medicine was such that it paved the way for the emergence of modern philosophical and scientific thought. Indeed, mankind's achievements in these domains were primitive and severly limited when compared to the dazzling contributions the early Muslims made in these fields of human thought and endeavour. But our failure to show our appreciation and acknowledge our profound debt to those remarkable early Muslim philosophers and scientists only reflects negatively on us. One man who dominated the field of philosophy and medicine more than probably anyone else in the history of human thought was Ibn Sina, known in the West as Avicenna. This great and hugely influential Muslim philosopher and physician blazed an intellectual trail which continues to burn to this day.

Abu Ali Hussain ibn Abdullah ibn Hasan ibn Ali ibn Sina was born in Afshanah, a small town located close to Bukhara (in present-day Uzbekistan). As the capital of the reigning Samanid dynasty, Bukhara was a bustling centre of learning and commerce. Originally from Balkh, Ibn Sina's father, Abdullah, moved to Afshanah where he met his Persian wife, Sitara, and became a prominent member of the Samanid civil service. His second son, Hussain (better known as Ibn Sina), was born a few years later. When Ibn Sina was around five, his family left Afshanah for Kharmayathnath, a town located on the outskirts of Bukhara, where his father became governor. Abdullah, Ibn Sina's father, was a very learned and cultured man who ensured his son received a thorough education in both the religious and philosophical sciences. According to the custom of the day, young Ibn Sina committed the whole Qur'an to memory before he was ten, and became thoroughly familiar with the traditional Islamic sciences. Blessed with a prodigious memory and precocious intellect, he devoured all the religious, philosophical and scientific literature available to him in his locality. His ability to read rapidly and absorb complex ideas and thoughts with ease enabled him to acquire a comprehensive knowledge of Islamic jurisprudence (*fiqh*), logic (*mantiq*), mathematics, philosophy (*falsafah*), medicine and astronomy. Indeed, he was able to engage in heated discussion and debate with some of the most learned scholars of his time even, before he reached his eighteenth birthday.

Some of Ibn Sina's early teachers included Shaykh Ismail al-Zahid, who taught him Islamic theology (*kalam*) and jurisprudence; the eminent mathematician Abu Abdullah al-Natili taught him Ptolemy's *Almagest* and Euclid of Alexandria's *Elements*, and aspects of logic; Abu Sahl al-Jurjani and Abu Mansur al-Qamari guided him in physics, medicine and philosophy. Such was his thirst for knowledge that he read, and became thoroughly familiar with, al-Farabi's voluminous commentary on Aristotle's metaphysics, before he was eighteen. His vast knowledge of all the sciences of his day soon made him a popular figure in his locality. It was also during this period that the reigning Samanid monarch, Nuh ibn Mansur al-Samani, was taken seriously ill and none of his court doctors were able to cure him. But after Ibn Sina's fame as a skilled medical practitioner reached the corridors of power, he was asked to treat the ailing monarch. He not only diagnosed the illness, he also successfully treated it and restored the monarch to full health. Profoundly impressed with the young doctor, the Samanid ruler gave him the keys to his private library where Ibn Sina found enough religious, philosophical and scientific literature to keep him occupied for a long time. Being an omnivorous reader, he studied everything he found in the library and became a master of medicine, philosophy, logic, theology and literature. Convinced of his superior intellectual ability and maturity of thought, he then began to write profusely. In addition to a treatise on mathematics, he authored a book on ethics and also compiled an encyclopaedia of all the sciences of his time. Astonishingly, he was only twenty-one when he composed these books. Revered by politicians and lay-people alike for his erudition, scholarly achievements and medical skills, it was not long before he became a celebrity in his locality.

Living as he did in a volatile period in the history of Muslim Central Asia, Ibn Sina also became a victim of the mindless political rivalry and military hostility which the various Muslim rulers of that region pursued against each other. Following the death of his father in 1002, he left his home town and moved to Jurjaniyyah, the cosmopolitan capital of the Khwarizmi dynasty, where he received a warm welcome from its ruling elites, including the reigning Khwarizm-shah Ali ibn al-Ma'mun. Although Ibn Sina did not stay here for long, his time in Jurjaniyyah proved very productive from a literary point of view. During this period he composed two more books on mathematics and astronomy, before he was forced to leave the city due to the growing power of the great Ghaznavid ruler Sultan Mahmud. For the next nine years – that is from 1012 to 1021 – Ibn Sina was compelled by the unfavourable political circumstances of the time to travel from one place to another. During this period of travel and political uncertainty, Ibn Sina found time to write his philosophical masterpiece *Kitab al-Shifa* (The Book of Healing) in eighteen volumes, and his famous medical encyclopedia *Kitab al-Qanun fi al-Tibb* (The Canon of Medicine) in another fourteen volumes. He also began work on a summarised version of his *Kitab al-Shifa* under the title of *Kitab al-Najah* (The Book of Deliverance) and wrote a collection of essays. On one occasion, he even served as a Minister in the court of the Buwayhid (or Buyid) monarch Shams al-Dawlah, until he fell out with his son and successor, Sama al-Dawlah, who imprisoned him for four months. After escaping from captivity by disguising himself as a Sufi dervish, he fled to Isfahan.

The peace and tranquility of this city was a breath of fresh air for him; he spent the next fifteen years of his life here writing and pursuing academic research. He completed his *Kitab al-Najah* and wrote a number of other highly rated books and treatises, including *Al-Isharat wa'l Tanbihat* (The Remarks and Admonitions) and *Danishnama-yi alai* (The Book of Science Dedicated to Ala al-Dawlah). Under Ala al-Dawlah's stewardship, Isfahan became a renowned centre of learning and scholarship. In appreciation of the monarch's kindness and generosity to him, he dedicated his *Danishnama-yi alai* – written in Persian – to Ala al-Dawlah. It is not known exactly how many books Ibn Sina wrote in total since a large number of his works have perished, including his ten-volume *Kitab Lisan al-Arab* and twenty-volume *Kitab al-Insaf*. However, a substantial number of his books and treatises (that is, around two hundred and fifty) have survived, including his world famous *Kitab al-Qanun fi al-Tibb*, *al-Shifa*, *Kitab al-Najah*, *al-Isharat wa'l Tanbihat* and his incomplete autobiography, which was later completed by his talented student Abu Ubaid al-Jurjani, before al-Bayhaqi and Ibn Khallikan popularised it.

By all accounts, Ibn Sina was a versatile genius whose scholarly interests covered all the major branches of learning known during his lifetime. But it was his seminal contribution in the fields of medicine and philosophy which earned him universal fame and recognition. His accomplishments in medicine were such that it is not possible to speak about them except in superlatives. His *Kitab al-Qanun fi al-Tibb*, which became known throughout the Western world as the *Canon*, is considered by medical historians to be one of the greatest medical encyclopaedias of all time. As the Bible of medieval medicine, it was a compulsory textbook for all medical students at the leading European universities until as late as the eighteenth century. In the East, however, it continues to be used as a standard work of reference by the practitioners of traditional medicine to this day. As it happens, Ibn Sina's popularity as a medical writer and thinker was such that he became known as the 'Prince of Physicians' (*rais al-atibba*) throughout medieval Europe and his *Canon* became one of the most famous textbooks in medical history. Divided into five main chapters, in turn sub-divided into smaller sections, the *Canon* consisted of around a million words in total. The first chapter dealt with human physiology, symptomatology and the main principles of diagnostic therapy. In chapter two, he provided an in-depth analysis of animal, vegetable and mineral types, highlighting the

meaning, value and purpose of various minerals and herbs as cures for different ailments. Chapter three focused on pathology, where Ibn Sina showed how to diagnose, treat and cure illnesses of different parts of the human body. In chapter four he explained aspects of cosmetics, diseases related to hair, nails and obesity, and he showed how these ailments could be treated successfully. The fifth and last chapter of the book consisted of a large number of prescriptions in the form of tablets, pills, powders, syrup, herbs and various plant extracts. Ibn Sina's approach to medicine was rational as well as holistic, because he explored the human body in its totality; that is to say, he believed it was important to take both physiological and psychological factors into consideration for an effective treatment of illnesses. Uniquely, he even emphasised the importance of psychotheraphy in combating certain types of illnesses, and did so around nine hundred years before Sigmund Freud wrote on the subject.

Ibn Sina's *Canon* became so popular in the West that it was repeatedly translated into Greek, Latin and Hebrew between 1079 and 1608. Also used as a standard textbook at the universities of Paris, Montpellier and Louvain, the *Canon* was published in Europe more than thirty-five times during the sixteenth and seventeenth centuries. Interestingly, a recently discovered manuscript authored by Ibn Sina – entitled *Kitab al-Adawiyyah al-Qalbi* (Treatise on Cardiac Drugs) and kept at Jamia Millia library in New Delhi – shows that he was not only an undisputed master and synthesiser of Greco-Islamic medicine, but also proves that he made remarkable and original contributions in the field of medicine in his own right. He was rated so highly by the celebrated Italian poet Dante Alighieri that he placed Ibn Sina on par with Galen and Hippocrates in medicine, and considered him to be far superior to both of them in philosophy. If Ibn Sina was a great physician, then he must be considered one of the most eminent philosophers of all time; indeed, his voluminous *Kitab al-Shifa* is widely considered to be a philosophical masterpiece.

Focusing on four main topics, namely logic, physics, mathematics and metaphysics, in this encyclopaedic work he provided a detailed exposition of his entire philosophy. Nevertheless, his *al-Isharat wa'l Tanbihat*, which focuses mainly on logic, physics and metaphysics, is generally considered to be his most complex and sophisticated philosophical work.

As a Neoplatonist, Ibn Sina's philosophical views proved to be highly controversial, to say the least. Influenced by the *ikhwan al-safa* (The Brethren of Purity), al-Farabi and others, he argued that the purpose of philosophy was to determine the true nature and reality of things to the best of one's ability. Thus, he was of the opinion that theoretical philosophy seeks the knowledge of truth by perfecting the soul through the pursuit of knowledge alone, while practical philosophy seeks goodness through assimilation of knowledge of things that must be done. As a philosopher, he was fiercely independently-minded and developed his own views and thoughts on the subject, and also wrote prolifically on it. Though some of his ideas and thoughts concerning the nature of God, His Attributes and the concept of the eternity of the cosmos were considered heretical by his critics (such as al-Ghazali, al-Shahrastani and Ibn Rushd), he was far from being an unbeliever. Like his medical theories, Ibn Sina's philosophy became hugely influential both in the East and the West. Not surprisingly, his philosophical ideas and thoughts influenced some of the greatest thinkers of the Muslim world, including Ibn al-Nafis, al-Ghazali, Nasir al-Din al-Tusi, Ibn Rushd, Shihab al-Din Suhrawardi and Mulla Sadra. Likewise, influential Western thinkers like Albertus Magnus (also known as Albert the Great), William of Auvergne, St Thomas Aquinas, Roger Bacon and Immanuel Kant were influenced by his philosophy and metaphysics.

Ibn Sina was not only intimately acquainted with the theological, philosophical and scientific ideas of his day, he was also familiar with the diversity of religious thought and interpretation which existed within the Muslim world at the time. Born into an Ismaili family, his teacher Shaykh Ismail al-Zahid was a Sunni jurist and theologian, and he was also familiar with the Twelver (*ithna 'ashari*) Shi'a theology. His awareness of these different Islamic groups and sects enabled him to engage in religious and philosophical discourse with scholars of all persuasions. Though it is not possible to say unequivocally whether he was a Sunni or Shi'a, there is no doubt that he considered himself to be a sincere Muslim, and he respected both points of view. Ibn Sina fell ill and died on his way to Hamadan at the age of fifty-seven. Known in the Muslim world as *shaykh al-rais* (or the 'Chief of the Wise'), his imposing portrait continues to grace the Great Hall of Paris University School of Medicine to this day, in recognition of his outstanding services to medicine and philosophy.

# 26

# Ibn Taymiyyah
(b.1263 - d.1328)

'BACK TO THE Qur'an and *sunnah*' is a famous slogan which has been used by Muslim scholars and reformers throughout Islamic history to summon wayward Muslim rulers and the masses back to the original, pristine Islam as promulgated by the Prophet Muhammad. The call, more often than not, worked due to the Muslim belief that the Qur'an is God's final communication to mankind, while the normative practice (*sunnah*) of the Prophet provides a powerful and pertinent commentary on the Divine revelation. In other words, these two sources combined to provide a potent methodology for living a truly Islamic life. For this reason, Muslim scholars and reformers have been able to repeatedly utilise this slogan with much success throughout Islamic history. *Shaykh al-Islam* Ibn Taymiyyah was one such extraordinary scholar and reformer whose religious ideas and thoughts have continued to exert a powerful influence on Muslim scholars and reformers up to the present day.

Taqi al-Din Abul Abbas Ahmad ibn Abd al-Halim ibn Taymiyyah was born in Harran, a city located on the outskirts of Damascus, into a distinguished family of writers, scholars and theologians. His father, Abd al-Halim, and grandfather, Majd al-Din, were acclaimed *hanbali fuqaha*

(jurists) who had authored numerous books on Islamic jurisprudence (*fiqh*) and *hadith* (Prophetic traditions). Brought up in an intellectually friendly environment, Ibn Taymiyyah memorised the entire Qur'an and received training in Arabic language, grammar, *hadith* and aspects of *fiqh* (Islamic jurisprudence) under the guidance of his learned father. When he was barely seven, his entire family was forced to flee from Harran in the face of an imminent threat of a Mongol onslaught on the city. The Mongol hordes stormed out of Asia like a thunderbolt from the heavens, and inflicted a crushing blow on the Muslim world by invading Baghdad, the seat of the Abbasid Caliphate, and destroying everything before them with unspeakable brutality; at the time the entire Muslim world was gripped by fear and trepidation. Although the Mongol invasion of Baghdad represented one of the most destructive periods in Islamic history, it was the valiant Egyptian Mamluk soldiers who finally stopped them in 1260 at the Battle of *ayn jalut* (or the 'Spring of Goliath'). The Mamluk victory at *ayn jalut* saved Egypt, Arabia and the neighbouring Islamic lands from Mongol invasion and pillage. Despite suffering a crushing defeat at *ayn jalut*, the Mongols remained a serious threat.

Not prepared to take the risk, Ibn Taymiyyah's family moved to the safety of Damascus, which was then controlled by the victorious Mamluks. In Damascus, Ibn Taymiyyah's family received a warm welcome from the locals as well as the city's governor. On account of his scholarly and literary accomplishments, his father was appointed principal of a local Islamic seminary (*dar al-uloom*), where he delivered regular lectures on traditional Islamic sciences. When his name and fame began to spread across Damascus, he was invited to deliver regular sermons (*kutbah*) at the city's historic Umayyad mosque. Like his father and grandfather, young Ibn Taymiyyah was an exceptionally bright student who was blessed with a sharp intellect and retentive memory. Not surprisingly, he committed vast quantities of information (including the whole Qur'an, large collections of *hadith*, juristic rulings (*fatawa*), poetry and books on philosophy and logic) to memory with ease. His remarkable retentive power aside, Ibn Taymiyyah was a wide-ranging reader who studied books on Qur'anic exegesis (*tafsir*), theology (*kalam*), Islamic jurisprudence and philosophy quicker than an average person could eat their dinner. His thirst for knowledge was such that he claimed to have studied under no fewer than two hundred eminent Islamic scholars of his day, including Shaykh Ahmad ibn Abu al-Khair, Yahya ibn al-Sairafi, Ibn Abu al-Yusr and Shams al-Din al-Maqdisi, who was the Chief Justice of Damascus. Along with his father, Abd al-Halim, and uncle, Fakhr al-Din, these were some of the most reputed scholars of *tafsir*, *hadith* and *fiqh* in Damascus at the time. He sat at the feet of these luminaries and thoroughly mastered traditional Islamic sciences. So much so that Shams al-Din, the Chief Justice, considered Ibn Taymiyyah to be competent enough to issue juristic rulings (*fatawa*) when he was barely seventeen years old.

Though Ibn Taymiyyah's formal education was that of a *hanbali* theologian and jurist, he was very fond of the Qur'an from the outset. He spent hours on end studying and meditating on the meaning of the Qur'anic chapters (*suwar*)

and verses (*ayat*); he even claimed to have read more than two hundred different commentaries (*tafasir*) of the Qur'an in order to familiarise himself with the diversity of views on Qur'anic thought and scholarship. Indeed, Ibn Taymiyyah's reading was nothing short of astonishing in its breadth and scope, covering as it did all aspects of theology, Sufi thought, Islamic history, heresiographical literature, comparative religion and Greek philosophy and logic as interpreted and championed by Muslim philosophers like al-Farabi and Ibn Sina. After conducting extensive research in almost all the branches of learning prevalent during his time, he became recognised as a versatile Islamic scholar and thinker. Following the death of his father, he was appointed professor of Islamic Thought at the same institution where his father once taught; he was only twenty at the time. According to the historian Shams al-Din al-Dhahabi, Ibn Taymiyyah ate very little; he had no more than a few clothes and was totally devoid of sexual passion, thus he remained a confirmed bachelor all his life.

Whilst still in his twenties, Ibn Taymiyyah's fame began to spread far and wide. Then, in 1292, he went to Makkah to perform the sacred *hajj* (pilgrimage). After completing the *hajj*, he returned to Damascus where he began to lecture at the city's famed Umayyad mosque. Being an inspirational and thought-provoking speaker, his lectures attracted people from all around. His ability to recall Qur'anic verses and Prophetic traditions with ease made him very popular with the people of Damascus, who used to flock to the mosque in their thousands to hear him speak. However, his growing fame and popularity made certain elements of the local theological and political elites very angry and jealous. Since Ibn Taymiyyah was very outspoken, these people hated him and they wanted him thrown out of Damascus. In 1298, when he was thirty-five, the first of a series of unfortunate incidents took place which became a source of misery and hardship for him. Not keen on only preaching, he went out of his way to issue legal edicts (*fatawa*) on several controversial theological issues, this infuriated the established scholars of Damascus who called on the local authorities to punish him for alleged heresy. Eager to quell the uproar, the authorities complied with the scholars' demands and imprisoned Ibn Taymiyyah.

As a gifted scholar, Ibn Taymiyyah defied intellectual categorisation. Though brought up and educated as a *hanbali* theologian and jurist, he pushed the boundaries of established theological and legal thought to their very limits. Theologically speaking, neither Ash'arism nor Mu'tazilism appealed to him. On the contrary, he vehemently refuted both theologies, preferring to interpret Islamic beliefs and concepts in accordance with the methodology of the pious predecessors (*salaf al-salih*) – based as it was on a literalist understanding of the Qur'an, *hadith*, sayings of the Prophet's companions (*sahabah*) and their successors (*tabiun*). Despite being a *hanbali* jurist, he refused to adhere exclusively to any one of the four prominent schools of Islamic legal thought (*madhahib*), thus leaving himself wide open to accusations of heresy and religious innovation (*bida*). Instead of imitating (*taqlid*) one of the existing *madhahib*, he used his own intellectual discretion (*ijtihad*) and, in so doing, he attempted to develop a fresh understanding of the Islamic scriptural sources, especially if he felt the views of the existing schools contradicted the original Islamic sources. However, unlike what some of his so-called followers say today, he did not reject the existing *madhahib* per se. As a *mujtahid* (one who was competent to exercise *ijtihad*), he felt he was not duty-bound to follow any one of the existing schools of law; that is why he developed his own interpretation and understanding of Islamic theology and jurisprudence. Not surprisingly, his attempts to analyse and interpret the Qur'an, Prophetic *hadith* and the views of the early Muslims in the light of his own existential condition met with stiff opposition from the established *ulama* (religious scholars) of Damascus.

Being uncompromising and at times very stubborn, Ibn Taymiyyah rarely backed down in a confrontation with his opponents. On one occasion, when he was asked to explain the Divine Names and Attributes (*al-asma wa'l sifat*) in the light of the Qur'an and Prophetic traditions, he provided a detailed answer to the question, but his detractors accused him of anthropomorphism. During this period, he engaged in regular polemical debates with his opponents until, in 1300, the Mongol hordes unexpectedly breached the heavily fortified defences erected by the Mamluks and occupied Syria. In response, Ibn Taymiyyah urged the people of Damascus to engage in *jihad* (military struggle) and liberate their country from Mongol occupation. His declaration of *jihad* so inspired the Syrian people that they took up arms to repel the invaders. Impressed by Ibn Taymiyyah's ability to rally the masses as well as the troops, the governor of Damascus requested that he to go to Cairo and ask Sultan Nasir to assist the Syrians in their battle against the Mongols. Moved by Ibn Taymiyyah's appeal for help, Sultan Nasir agreed to support the Syrian people. Thanks to Ibn Taymiyyah, a combined Egyptian-Syrian army confronted the Mongols in 1302 and in the ensuing battle he fought like a lion until the enemy was driven out of Mamluk territories. While Ibn Taymiyyah was busy fighting valiantly on the battlefield, his detractors were nowhere to be seen; indeed, some of them even fled the battlefield as soon as they saw the advancing enemy.

His role in the war against the Mongols won him national recognition in Syria. Incensed by the heroic reception granted to him by the Syrian people, his detractors again began to conspire against him. Their hatred of Ibn Taymiyyah's radical theological and legal thinking, coupled with his newfound fame and popularity with the Syrian people and the reigning Sultan (who regularly consulted him on both the political and religious issues of the day), prompted them to engage in religious debate and political intrigue in order to undermine his politico-religious standing. Ibn Taymiyyah was not only an open adversary of those who practiced *taqlid* in matters of law, he went out of his way to expose what he considered to be the unorthodox beliefs and practices of the Sufis, especially the metaphysical thought of Ibn al-Arabi. He also attacked the philosophical and speculative discourse of al-Farabi, Ibn Sina, Fakhr al-Din al-Razi, al-Shahrastani and even called into question aspects of al-Ghazali's theological views. Moreover, he comprehensively repudiated Christian views about Jesus, and also systematically refuted the beliefs and practices of scores of other religious groups and sects. His intellectual brilliance, coupled with his extensive study of Islamic thought, philosophy, logic and comparative religion, enabled him to analyse and evaluate the beliefs and practices of all of these groups in the light of the Qur'an and Prophetic *sunnah*, before he openly pronounced his verdicts on them, something which earned him the wrath of the ruling elites.

Since his main mission in life was to purify Islamic beliefs, teachings and practices from the stranglehold of *bida* (blameworthy innovation) and *shirk* (associationism), he remained very resolute and uncompromising in his efforts to revive the Prophetic norms and practices. His stance on various religious issues led to his imprisonment on more than one ocassion including once in 1306, again in 1309, yet again in 1318 and finally in 1326. However, he endured these trials and ordeals with patience and perseverance. His spells in prison proved intellectually very productive, because it was during these periods that he wrote most of his books. As an undisputed master of traditional Islamic sciences and a prolific writer, according to al-Dhahabi, he authored around one hundred books and treatises on Islamic sciences, comparative religion and aspects of philosophy, and logic and mysticism. According to his other biographers, he authored as many as five hundred books, treatises and essays on a wide range of subjects. His most famous books include *Minhaj al-Sunnah al-Nabawiyyah* (Towards Prophetic Methodology), *Majmu al-Fatawa* (Collection of Legal Edicts), *Al-Radd ala al-Mantiqi'in* (The Refutation of Logic), *Al-Siyasah al-Shari'ah* (Policy of Islamic Law), *Al-Hisba fi'l Islam* (Public Duties in Islam) and *Jawab al-Sahih* (The Authentic Response). He also authored a forty-volume commentary on the Qur'an under the title of *Bahr al-Muhit,* but this has not survived.

Ibn Taymiyyah died in prison at the age of sixty-five. When the news of his death was relayed across Damascus, the people of the city came out in great numbers to mourn his death. It is not possible to exaggerate Ibn Taymiyyah's influence and greatness. Widely considered to be one of the Muslim world's greatest thinkers, ideologues and warriors, his religious ideas and thoughts have inspired generations of outstanding Islamic scholars, thinkers and reformers such as Ibn Qayyim al-Jawziyyah, Ibn Kathir, Sham al-Din al-Dhahabi, Muhammad ibn Abd al-Wahhab, Shah Waliullah, Sayyid Ahmad Barelvi, Shah Ismail Shahid, Muhammad Abduh, Haji Shari'atullah of Bengal, Hasan al-Banna and Abul A'la Mawdudi among others.

# 27

## Nizam al-Mulk
## (b.1020 – d.1092)

THERE IS NO shortage of influential statesmen, philanthropists and educationalists in Islamic history. These remarkable people played a key role in the promotion of religious, philosophical and scientific learning in the Muslim world. Without their invaluable contributions, the Muslim world would certainly have been much poorer in comparison with other great world civilisations. In fact, it is largely due to the vision and dedication of these great statesmen and philanthropists that the Islamic civilisation attained such dazzling heights in educational, cultural and artistic pursuits. One Muslim statesman and educationalist played a far greater role in the rise and development of a world-class educational system in the Muslim world than probably any other. His love of knowledge and desire to eliminate illiteracy throughout his dominion led to the emergence of a new and vibrant culture of learning across the Muslim world. As the founder and patron of the famous Nizamiyyah Colleges, Nizam al-Mulk is today considered to be one of Islamic history's most celebrated philanthropic statesmen and educators.

Abu Ali Hasan ibn Ali ibn Ishaq, better known as Nizam al-Mulk, was born in Radhkan, a small village located in Tus in the Persian province of Khurasan. The son of a Ghaznavid revenue collector, Nizam al-Mulk was brought up in a family where religious practices were rigorously observed; his family members also valued educational and artistic pursuits most highly. During his early years, he studied Arabic language, grammar and aspects of Islamic jurisprudence (*fiqh*) in his native Radhkan. After completing his elementary education, he travelled to Nishapur where he received advanced training in Arabic and Persian literature, mathematics and traditional Islamic sciences under the guidance of eminent scholars such as Shaykh Hibatullah al-Muwaffaq, who was a noted authority on Islamic jurisprudence. In Nishapur, his classmates included Umar Khayyam, the famous poet, scientist and mathematician, and Hasan-i-Sabbah, the infamous founder of the neo-Ismaili Assassin sect. According to the Persian historian Rashid al-Din al-Tabib, the three of them became good friends during their student days and on one occasion they made a solemn pledge that which ever of them attained success first would help the others. Although some historians like Sayyid Sulaiman Nadwi have questioned the authenticity of this story, they do not dispute the fact that Nizam al-Mulk, Umar Khayyam and Hasan-i-Sabbah were contemporaries, and that they had studied together in Nishapur.

By the time Nizam al-Mulk had completed his advanced education, the political landscape in the Muslim world had shifted radically. Named after their ancestral leader Seljuk (Saljuq), the Turkish Oghuz (also known as Ghuzz or Dokuz) clans converted to Islam during the early part of the eleventh century. Based in a region close to the north of the Caspian and Aral Sea, they mobilised their political power and military might against their main rivals, the Ghaznavid and the Buwayhid (or Buyid) dynasties. As a result, they inflicted crushing defeats on the former in 1040 and on the latter in 1060, and in so doing they became one of the Muslim world's most powerful political dynasties of the time. After restoring the traditional Caliphate in Baghdad, the Seljuks successfully thwarted Fatimid attempts to gain full control of the Muslim world. Grateful to the Seljuks for defending the Abbasid Caliphate from Fatimid encroachment, the reigning Abbasid Caliph Malik al-Rahim officially crowned the first Seljuk ruler, Tughrul Beg, as the 'King of the East and West'. Only twenty-eight at the time, Nizam al-Mulk began his career as a civil servant in the provincial administration of Adud al-Dawlah Abu al-Shuja, better known as Alp Arsalan (or the 'valiant lion'), a nephew of Tughrul Beg.

As a civic and political administrator, Nizam al-Mulk proved remarkably efficient and effective. His sharp intellect, coupled with his superior education and diplomatic skills, set him apart from his peers. Being honest, loyal and cultured, Prince Alp Arsalan was also impressed with Nizam al-Mulk's polished administrative and organisational skills. After being swiftly promoted to one of the highest posts within the prince's provincial Government, Nizam al-Mulk also proved to be a gifted political operator. Following the death of Tughrul Beg in 1063, a protracted power struggle broke out within the Seljuk royal family, but eventually Alp Arsalan emerged victorious and became the Sultan of the Seljuk dynasty. Immediately after ascending the throne, he promoted Nizam al-Mulk to the post

of *wazir* (or Prime Minister) of his vast kingdom. As Prime Minister, and one of the Muslim world's most powerful men at the time, he instigated a thorough reform of Seljuk political, economic, social and educational policies. Being Turks, the Seljuks preferred to employ and promote fellow Turks to the highest posts within the Seljuk civil, administrative and military services. But, keen to promote peace and prosperity at home and maintain a powerful army to defend his kingdom from his external enemies, Alp Arsalan broke away from his family tradition and appointed Nizam al-Mulk, who was of Persian origin, to the highest post in the land. As committed Sunni Muslims, both Alp Arsalan and Nizam al-Mulk became champions of Islamic orthodoxy; they were also keen to protect and preserve the Baghdad-based Abbasid Caliphate from the Fatimids of Egypt, who were at the time busy planning its downfall. Motivated by their common interests, the Sultan and his Prime Minister worked closely to maintain Seljuk power and continue their domination of the Muslim world.

After becoming Prime Minister of the Seljuk kingdom, Nizam al-Mulk decided to fulfil the pledge he made to Umar Khayyam and Hasan-i-Sabbah back in Nishapur during his student days. Accordingly, he summoned Umar Khayyam to his office in Isfahan and offered him the post of Chief Government astronomer; Khayyam afterwards played a pivotal role in the development of a refined calendar (known as the *jalali* calendar), later presented to Sultan Jalal al-Din Malik Shah as a gift. Next, he contacted Hasan-i-Sabbah and offered him a high-ranking post within the Seljuk civil service, but he had become embroiled in a political conspiracy and was forced to flee to Fatimid Egypt, where he transformed a disgruntled group of Nizari Shi'as into a dangerous politico-religious faction. Known as the Assassins, this group instigated subversive activities against the Seljuks but, being the Prime Minister of the Seljuk kingdom, Nizam al-Mulk was able to counter their activities very successfully. Indeed, during Alp Arsalan's reign of nine years, he was the sole playmaker in the Seljuk kingdom, while the Sultan played only a ceremonial role. This gave Nizam al-Mulk all the freedom he needed to reform the civil and administrative structures of the kingdom. By reorganising and unifying the civil and administrative systems of the Government – whose remit extended from Syria at the one end, to Iran at the other – he was able to stamp out corruption and malpractice, and improve accountability and efficiency. Under Nizam al-Mulk's stewardship, the Seljuk dynasty became one of the most powerful, prosperous and culturally advanced dynasties of its time. Being also a wise and enlightened politican, he promoted learning and education across the vast empire; so much so that he turned it into a thriving centre of commercial activity and Islamic learning, scholarship, culture and arts.

He despised illiteracy so much that he promoted free education throughout the dominion and encouraged the people to pursue higher education, and undertake research and expand their intellectual horizons. To facilitate this task, he embarked on one of the most ambitious educational programmes ever undertaken by a Muslim leader; namely, he authorised the construction of a series of large educational institutions throughout the land. Begun in 1066, when he was only forty-six, these educational institutions were established in all the major cities of the Seljuk kingdom including Nishapur, Baghdad and Damascus. They not only became some of the first colleges of their time, but also became some of Islamic history's finest institutions of higher education. After constructing the colleges, Nizam al-Mulk went out of his way to recruit some of the brightest minds of the Muslim world to come and teach at them. After the college in Nishapur was completed, he hired *imam al-haramayn* Abul Ma'ali Abd al-Malik al-Juwayni to come and teach there. Al-Ghazali, who later became one of the Muslim world's most celebrated scholars, also served as Professor of Islamic Thought at the same institution. Known as *madrasah al-nizamiyyah* (or 'the Nizamiyyah College'), these institutions of higher education were the Harvard and Oxford of their time. Not surprisingly, they produced some of the most famous and renowned thinkers of the Muslim world including Shaykh Sa'di of Shiraz who studied at Nizamiyyah College's Baghdad campus. Nizam al-Mulk's spending on education was more than generous; indeed, he allocated the lion's share of his annual budget to the promotion of learning and education. Known for his prudent management of Seljuk finances, he was nonetheless exceedingly generous when it came to spending on education.

If Nizam al-Mulk was a great educationalist, then he was an equally successful politician. Being caring, sensitive and a benevolent administrator, he took measures to address his people's daily needs and requirements. He not only increased annual food production, he also introduced a fair tax system and reformed the *bait al-mal* (public treasury) to improve its efficiency. He closely supervised the collection and distribution of *zakat* (obligatory alms), modernised the roads and reorganised the Seljuk judicial system. In addition, he constructed medical clinics and hospitals which offered free health care and medication to the people. Moreover, he built sufficient mosques to meet the people's spiritual needs, and also stepped-up security throughout the Seljuk kingdom in order to counter crime and banditry. Following in the footsteps of the Abbasid Caliph Harun al-Rashid, he built resting places along the main trade routes to encourage and faciliate trade and commerce, and instructed the locals to dig wells to provide free, fresh water to the travellers and merchants alike. In addition to this, Nizam al-Mulk maintained a well-equipped and disciplined army to defend the Seljuk kingdom from its external enemies. He made it an obligation on himself to go out and personally survey the condition of the people, their towns and cities on a regular basis; he liked to speak to them about their problems, difficulties and hardships. His exemplary conduct not only won him tremendous respect and affection throughout the vast empire; he also became one of the most influential and revered Muslim statesmen of all time – along with Umar ibn Abd al-Aziz, Abd al-Rahman III, Sultan Nur al-Din Zangi, Salah al-Din Ayyubi and Sulaiman the Magnificient.

Nizam al-Mulk was fifty-two when Sultan Alp Arsalan was brutally murdered in 1072, but Malik Shah, his son and successor, asked him to stay on as Prime Minister. As it happens, Malik Shah rated him so highly that he crowned him *atabeg* (or the 'father-figure'). As a wise and skilled political operator, Nizam al-Mulk continued to strengthen the State's security services, which enabled him to counter the insurgency activities of his enemies with tremendous success. And as an adherent of *shafi'i madhhab* (school of law), he was always in the habit of consulting the eminent religious scholars of his time (including al-Ghazali) to secure their support for his political and educational programmes.

During his long tenure as Prime Minister, Nizam al-Mulk worked tirelessly to protect and perserve the life, property and dignity of the people. His honesty, integrity and transparency in his dealings with his officials helped to create a just and equitable system of Government; one where corruption and malpractice were not toler-ated. After his retirement from politics, he wrote a book on political administration for the benefit of young Sultan Malik Shah. Entitled *Siyasat Namah* (A Treatise on Politics), this book covered all aspects of Islamic political administration, including the role of the Prime Minister and the responsibilities of other Government Ministers. It also explained the purpose of the judiciary; the qualities and qualifications required of judges and civil administrators; it covered aspects of taxation policy, State security and espionage, and even how to tackle corruption and rebellion. It is worth pointing out that Nizam al-Mulk wrote on political thought and administration around three hundred years before Machievalli was born. Not surprisingly, according to some researchers, it was Nizam al-Mulk's *Siyasat Namah* which inspired Niccolo Machiavelli to pen his famous book *The Prince*. This may or may not be true, but what is beyond doubt is that Nizam al-Mulk was one of the Muslim world's most influential educationalists, political thinkers and statesmen. Attacked by an agent of Hasan-i-Sabbah while he was on his way to Baghdad, he died at the age of seventy-two.

# 28

## Al-Kindi
## (b.801 - d.873)

SOME DISCIPLINES, such as mathematics and biology, are more precise and better defined than other subjects like philosophy. Both the mathematicians and biologists on the whole are agreed on what it is that they seek to study and explore, but that is far from being the case with the philosophers. The very definition of philosophy is controversial, and the diversity of views and controversies which once existed within philosophical circles persists to this day. Generally defined as the love of wisdom (being derived from the Greek word *philos*, a friend, and *sophos*, wise), philosophy was therefore considered to be the pre-occupation of wise friends. The ancient Greek philosophers such as Socrates, Plato and Aristotle became great champions of philosophical thinking, but they did not pursue philosophy in a unified way. Their seminal contribution to philosophical thought remained in the doldrums for hundreds of years until the sun finally shone on Arabia in the seventh century. Rescued from being a footnote of history by the Prophet Muhammad, the Arabs embraced learning, culture and civilisation like never before. The early Muslim scholars and philosophers not only translated original Greek philosophical works into Arabic, they also wrote extensive commentaries on them,

thus refining the ideas and thoughts of the ancient Greek philosophers, and in so doing they paved the way for the emergence of *falsafah* (or Islamic philosophy). It was al-Kindi, that hugely influential Islamic philosopher - known in the West as the 'philosopher of the Arabs' (*faylasuf al-Arab*) - who played a central role in the development of philosophical thought in the Muslim world.

Abu Yusuf Yaqub ibn Ishaq al-Kindi, known in the Latin West as Alkindus, was born in the Iraqi city of Kufah. Hailing from the south Arabian tribe of Kindah, his grandfather, al-Ash'ath ibn Qais, claimed to be a companion of the Prophet Muhammad. His father, Ishaq ibn al-Sabbah, was a respected member of the Abbasid political administration and served as governor of Kufah during the reign of Abbasid Caliphs al-Mahdi, al-Hadi and Harun al-Rashid. Along with Basrah, Baghdad, Damascus, Makkah and Madinah, Kufah was one of the foremost centres of Islamic learning at the time. Brought up in a prosperous, wealthy and learned family, al-Kindi attended his local schools. He studied Arabic language, grammar, literature and traditional Islamic sciences during his early years before specialising in Islamic theology, mathematics, astronomy and philosophy. As a gifted student, he excelled in his studies and was able to assimilate both the religious and philosophical sciences of his day with ease.

After completing his formal education in Kufah, al-Kindi moved to Baghdad, the political capital of the Islamic world, to pursue advanced training in the religious and philosophical sciences. After the death of Harun al-Rashid in 809, his son al-Ma'mun – having defeated al-Amin – became the Caliph and vigorously promoted the study of the rational sciences, including Greek philosophy and science, across the Muslim world. This created an intellectually friendly ambience for Muslim scientists and philosophers to conduct their research and inquiry into scientific, philosophical and religious subjects. In Baghdad, al-Kindi enjoyed the patronage of Caliph al-Ma'mun who encouraged him to pursue his studies at the *bait al-hikmah* (House of Wisdom), the celebrated library and research centre originally founded by Harun al-Rashid, where some of the leading Muslim philosophers and scientists of the day pursued their research into their chosen areas of specialisation. At the *bait al-hikmah*, al-Kindi devoted all his time and energy to the study of mathematics, astronomy, chemistry, musical theory and philosophy. During this period he earned his livelihood working as a calligrapher at the Caliphal court in Baghdad.

Along with other luminaries of the time, including al-Khwarizmi the great mathematician and scientist, and al-Farghani the renowned astronomer, al-Kindi became a prominent member of the *bait al-hikmah*. Together they transformed this institute into one of the most famous centres of academic study and research in the Muslim world at the time. Though some of the theological and philosophical views of these intellectuals were considered to be controversial by the traditionalist scholars such as Ahmad ibn Hanbal, Caliph al-Ma'mun gave them his full support and encouraged them to continue their intellectual activities. Given al-Kindi's intellectual brilliance and great linguistic abilities, Caliph al-Ma'mun became very fond of him and asked him to spearhead the pioneering task of translating Greek, Persian and Indian philosophical, mathematical and scientific works into Arabic for the benefit of the Muslim scholars and researchers. Being an accomplished linguist and an expert in ancient Indian, Greek and Persian philosophy and thought, al-Kindi was appointed head of a team of dedicated scholars who conducted extensive research into comparative thought. They also translated and edited a large quantity of ancient philosophical and scientific literature into Arabic for the very first time. Thanks to al-Kindi and his colleagues, the study of comparative thought became one of the foremost intellectual preoccupations of the early Muslim philosophers and scientists.

As one of Caliph al-Ma'mun's favourite intellectuals, he not only translated philosophical and scientific works from ancient languages and undertook research in almost all the branches of learning known during his time, but was also later chosen by Caliph Mu'tasim Billah to teach and guide his son. Held in very high esteem by the new Caliph for his invaluable contribution to learning and research, al-Kindi was appointed chief astrologer at the Caliphal court in Baghdad when he was only thirty-two years old. Blessed with a powerful memory and an encyclopaedic mind, he excelled in a wide range of subjects including mathematics, astronomy, physics, chemistry, astrology, music, optics, geography, religious sciences, comparative thought and literature. However, it was in the fields of optics, music and philosophy that he made some of his most original contributions.

For the first time in the history of optics, al-Kindi fully explained the principle of rectilinear progress of light emerging from a luminous object. As one of the most fundamental principles of optics, this is common knowledge today, but back in the ninth century it was considered to be one of the most remarkable discoveries ever made in this field, especially because he was able to prove his theory by conducting experiments. Using a lit candle, hence becoming known as the 'candle experiment', al-Kindi was able to demonstrate that light progressed in a straight line. Furthermore, his books on geometrical and physiological optics were so accurate and advanced for the time that they subsequently became standard works of reference in optical science both in the East and the West. His contribution in the field of musical theory was equally remarkable. Widely considered to be one of the greatest musical theorists in history, he penned seven books and treatises on the subject. According to the historians, he was one of the first to write on music and musical theory and as such should be considered the father of this branch of learning. In his writings, al-Kindi explained in considerable detail the meaning and significance of rhythm, especially focusing on its role in classical Arab music. Since musical songs formed an important part of Arab culture, he was keen to develop a theoretical understanding of music – a branch of learning which the Muslims later exported to the West. Without al-Kindi's original contribution in this field, the world of music would certainly have been much poorer in its understanding and appreciation of the aesthetic dimension of music.

Though al-Kindi's contributions in optics and musical theory were nothing short of remarkable, today he is most famous for his philosophical originality and writings. The author of twenty-two books on philosophy, he became a towering figure in this subject both in the Muslim world and in the West, where he became widely known as the 'philosopher of the Arabs' as a result of his considerable influence on Western philosophers and thinkers. In his famous *Fil Falsafah al-Ula* (On First Philosophy), he defined philosophy as 'the knowledge of the nature of things in so far as this is possible for man. The aim of the philosopher is, as regards his knowledge, to attain to the truth, and as regards his action, to act truthfully.' To al-Kindi, philosophy consisted of three parts, ranked in order of importance: theology, mathematics and physics. By elevating theology to the highest point in philosophical discourse he incurred the wrath of the traditional religious scholars, who argued that rational thinking on matters of religious beliefs was nothing short

of heresy. Al-Kindi, however, disagreed with the traditionalists. But he was far from being a heretic, as some claimed; indeed, he remained a sincere and committed Muslim who practised traditional Islamic teachings both in public and in private. However, unlike the traditionalists, his adherence to Islam did not prevent him from learning and championing ancient Greek philosophical thought and he frequently expressed his profound admiration for Plato and Aristotle – being the first and only great Arab philosopher to do so – but he did not compromise his Islamic faith and beliefs in the process. He remained a devout Muslim all his life.

The traditional religious scholars of his time considered religion and philosophy to be incompatible, but al-Kindi profoundly disagreed with this view. He considered religion and philosophy to be compatible in the same way that reason and revelation are harmonious. In his philosophical works, he thoroughly analysed and dissected Greek philosophical thought from an Islamic perspective in order to reconcile classical Greek philosophy, especially Neoplatonism and Aristotelian thought, with the Qur'anic worldview. His attempts to harmonise the two perspectives proved so successful that it paved the way for the emergence of a separate Islamic philosophical tradition. As a philosopher, al-Kindi did not discover or introduce a new principle in philosophical thinking; rather his originality lay in the fact that he was able to survey the Greek philosophical tradition through the philosophical lens of Islam. In his definition of philosophy, al-Kindi identified two components which formed the foundation of his philosophical discourse; 'true knowledge' and 'true action'. The correlation between knowledge and action was highly significant for al-Kindi because philosophy and the practical ethics of Islam were, in his opinion, inter-connected both at a theoretical level and in the daily affairs of the Muslims.

According to al-Kindi, philosophy relates to the nature of God, Divine Attributes, creation and time. Since the classical Greek philosophers, particularly the Aristotelian conception of God as the unmoved mover of all, was so similar to the Islamic conception of Divinity – the Qur'an says God is One Who created everything *ex-ni-hilo* – al-Kindi had no problems in accepting the Greek view on this matter. Unlike many other great Muslim philosophers, such as Ibn Sina, he believed that creation was not eternal; rather he considered time, space and the chain of causality to be finite. Only God was infinite, he argued, because He was the first cause which was not an effect. He also insisted that the human body would be resurrected in accordance with Islamic teachings, and he was a firm believer in universal Divine Providence. He was quick to point out that perfect order and harmony in creation was a further indication of the existence of God, although al-Ghazali later thoroughly discredited the teleological argument for the existence of God. Nevertheless, al-Kindi's translations, extensive commentaries and his synthesis of Islamic thought with the Greek worldview opened the way for eminent Muslim philosophers and thinkers like al-Farabi, Abu Bakr al-Razi, Ibn Sina, al-Ghazali, Ibn Bajjah, Ibn Tufayl and Ibn Rushd to emerge and formulate a more comprehensive Islamic philosophical discourse.

According to the renowned bibliographer Ibn al-Nadim, al-Kindi authored exactly two hundred and forty-two books and treatises on all the sciences of his day. But, according to other researchers, he wrote as many as two hundred and eighty works. Either way, the vast majority of al-Kindi's books are no longer extant. Nevertheless, the historians are agreed that he was a truly great philosopher, encyclopaedist and a prolific writer. His achievements were so wide-ranging that influential European thinkers like Roger Bacon considered him to be one of the world's greatest minds. After a number of his books were translated into Latin by Gerard of Cremona, al-Kindi became popular in the West as a philosopher and optician, while in the Muslim world he became known as the 'father of Islamic philosophy'. As an ardent champion of philosophy and scientific thought, al-Kindi suffered persecution at the hands of the traditionally-minded Caliph Mutawakkil ala Allah who, after ascending the Abbasid throne, drove out the philosophical rationalists from the Caliphal court in Baghdad. Ironically, al-Kindi survived his tormentor by more than a decade and died at the age of seventy-two.

# 29

## Muawiyah ibn Abi Sufyan (b.ca.605 - d.680)

THE REIGN OF the first four Caliphs of Islam became known as the period of the 'rightly-guided Caliphs' (*al-khulafa al-rashidun*) because they ruled in accordance with the teachings of the Qur'an and the Prophetic *sunnah* (norms and practices). After the death of Uthman, the third rightly-guided Caliph in 656, the Muslim world was plunged into serious political and social turmoil. The death of Caliph Uthman shattered the political unity of Islam and, as a result, internal political and religious rifts began to appear within the early Islamic State. Although Ali, the cousin and son-in-law of the Prophet, succeeded Uthman as the fourth Caliph, he was not able to put an end to the political rivalry and tribal infighting. As political dissension and social disorder broke out within the Muslim community, rival sectarian groups emerged to exacerbate the socio-political situation by spreading further confusion and disaffection among the people; all of this posed a serious challenge to the authority of the early Muslim leaders. Amidst the prevailing chaos and disorder, Muawiyah ibn Abi Sufyan emerged to establish the Umayyad dynasty, which subsequently became one of the most powerful dynasties to rule the Muslim world.

Muawiyah ibn Abi Sufyan ibn Harb was born into the powerful Makkan clan of Banu Umayyah. His father, Abu Sufyan, was a wealthy and powerful Makkan chieftain who was known for his intelligence and leadership skills. As a distinguished merchant, Abu Sufyan regularly led business expeditions to Syria, Yemen and other commercial centres in and around Arabia. Brought up in a wealthy and prosperous family, Muawiyah grew up to be an intelligent, wise and pleasant young man. As a wealthy and powerful Makkan leader, his father became one of the most inveterate opponents of the Prophet as soon as the latter announced his Prophethood in 610. The Prophet's message of unity, brotherhood, justice and equality clearly threatened Abu Sufyan and his like. Not willing to relinquish their grip on politico-economic power in Makkah, they began to oppose the Prophet and his message tooth and nail. Their opposition against Islam, however, was motivated more by their desire to maintain the status quo rather than out of personal enmity against the Prophet. Muawiyah would have been too young to understand and appreciate the tensions generated by the Prophet's message in Makkah at the time.

During the next thirteen years, Abu Sufyan – actively encouraged by his wife Hind bint Utba – opposed the Prophet and his small band of followers with great determination. After the Prophet migrated (*hijrah*) to the nearby oasis of Madinah, Abu Sufyan spearheaded a series of military expeditions against the nascent Muslim community but on each and every ocassion he failed to breach the strong defence put up by the Muslims. During these years of great danger and insecurity, the Prophet never failed to reassure his companions that Islam would not be defeated by its enemies. Muawiyah was in his early twenties at the time, and actively supported his father in his campaigns against Islam. Eventually, in 630, the Prophet, accompanied by his companions, returned to Makkah unopposed and it was then that Abu Sufyan embraced Islam but Muawiyah had already become a Muslim a year earlier. The Prophet treated Abu Sufyan with due respect, for after all, he was his father-in-law. Umm Habibah, the daughter of Abu Sufyan, had embraced Islam much earlier, and she was married to the Prophet. Muawiyah was around twenty-five when he embraced Islam. Like his father, he was an educated, intelligent and capable person. For this reason he volunteered to be one of the Prophet's secretaries (*kuttab al-wahy*); he also read and responded to letters on his behalf and supervised his administrative affairs.

After the Prophet's death in 632, Muawiyah played an active part in the affairs of the early Islamic State. The premature death of his brother, Yazid, during the expedition to Syria opened the way for Muawiyah to assume the leadership of his family and become a prominent member of the early Muslim community. His wise and disciplined approach, coupled with his services to the Prophet and the early Muslim community, prompted Umar, the second Caliph, to appoint him governor of Syria in 639, following the death of Abu Ubaida ibn al-Jarrah. He excelled in his role as governor, overseeing the political and civic affairs of Syria with much efficiency and effectiveness. After establishing a sound political base in Syria, he appointed some of his most

trusted and loyal lieutenants to key positions in Government, and in so doing he devised and delivered a first class service to the Syrian people. Under his governorship, Syria became one of the most politically stable and economically prosperous provinces of the Islamic State. Following Umar's assassination in 644, Uthman became Caliph and he ruled for twelve years before he, too, was assassinated by a group of insurgents in 656. During the reign of Caliph Uthman, Muawiyah continued to serve as governor of Syria. His long tenure in the post enabled him to consolidate his position in that province so that, when political rivalry and religious schism began to spread during the second half of Uthman's Caliphate, Muawiyah remained politically aloof and undisturbed by the events which unfolded in Madinah. Instead, he continued to strengthen and consolidate his position in Syria, making new alliances and forging a good working relationship with the Syrian people. By the time Ali became Caliph, Muawiyah was already considered the undisputed ruler of Syria in all but name.

Although the brutal murder of Caliph Uthman shook the foundations of the Islamic State and created much disunity and schism within the early Muslim community, Caliph Ali, his successor, was far from being prepared for the challenges which lay ahead. Different political-religious groups emerged, some with genuine grievances which needed to be addressed swiftly, while others were no more than opportunists bent on wreaking havoc within the Islamic polity. The new Caliph found himself in an extremely difficult position. Unable, in the circumstances, to hunt down Uthman's assassins or restore peace and security across the Islamic State, the new Caliph was now fighting a losing battle. To be fair to Ali, he was in a no-win situation; all the groups expected him to fulfil their demands and address their grievances, but to do so without their help, support or co-operation. To make matters worse, a group of Uthman's close relatives, led by his widow Nailah bint Farafisah, then proceeded to Syria and provocatively paraded the bloodstained robes of Uthman before Muawiyah and the people of Syria. As expected, this only added more fuel to the fire. Since Muawiyah and Uthman belonged to the same Umayyah clan, Caliph Ali now found himself in conflict with yet another group of Uthman's supporters in Syria who openly refused to pledge allegiance (*bay'ah*) to him.

To add to the prevailing confusion, Muawiyah then sent a letter to Caliph Ali with simply the words *bismillah al-rahman al-rahim* (In the name of God, Most Gracious, Most Merciful) inscribed on it. To Ali, this represented an open refusal to acknowledge his Caliphate. But, according to Muawiyah, this was a demand for the Caliph to apprehend and punish Uthman's murderers before he was prepared to pledge allegiance to him. The Caliph, on the other hand, demanded an unconditional pledge of loyalty, but Muawiyah refused this. Thus the Caliph and the rebellious governor were set on a collision course. Not willing to tolerate open rebellion, Ali marched to Syria with a fifty thousand strong force and camped at Siffin. Muawiyah came out with his forces to meet the Caliph's army. When the two Muslim armies were about to clash, the Caliph decided to give peace another chance. He sent a three-man deputation to Muawiyah in order to find a peaceful resolution, but the governor reiterated his demand, saying he would not pledge allegiance to the Caliph unless the latter first apprehended and punished Uthman's assassins. In response, the Caliph also reiterated his demand of an unconditional pledge of loyalty. When the deadlock could not be broken, the two armies clashed on the field of battle at Siffin. It was a surreal affair – and the combatants were at first hesitant to attack each other – for Muslims were now fighting Muslims. As the Caliph's army was about to inflict a crushing defeat on Muawiyah's forces, the latter called for arbitration (*tahkim*). Ali stopped the fight and agreed to resolve their differences through arbitration. This was a shrewd move on the part of the governor because his forces were facing imminent defeat on the battlefield. Politically speaking, the decision to engage in arbitration proved fatal for Ali because

it led to considerable political tension and dissension within his camp, while Muawiyah went onto become politically stronger by the day. Ali's reign came to an abrupt end in 661, when he was fatally stabbed by a member of the extremist *khawarij* sect.

Following Ali's assassination his eldest son, Hasan, was elected Caliph but he subsequently abdicated. Being a gentle and peace-loving person – and also politically inexperienced – he decided not to compete with the determined and hugely experienced Muawiyah for the highest post in the land. But after the latter became the ruler of the Muslim world in 661, he rewarded Hasan with a generous State pension for stepping out of his way. After being crowned Caliph, Muawiyah swiftly restored Islamic political unity and actively promoted peace and prosperity across the Islamic dominion after many years of political infighting and religious discord. Although he was in his mid-fifties at the time, he was widely considered to be a veteran politician and shrewd strategist; indeed, according to some historians, he was one of the most gifted political and civil administrators of his generation. Having lived and worked under the supervision of the Prophet and the first three "rightly-guided Caliphs" of Islam, he developed a thorough understanding of Islamic principles and practices. Also, as the brother of Umm Habibah, the Prophet's widow, he not only became a regular member of the Prophet's household, but also learned about Islam from his sister and the Prophet, and in so doing became an important member of the early Muslim community. For this reason, most of the prominent Islamic historians say Ali was indeed the rightful claimant to the Caliphate but, at the same time, they have refused to condemn Muawiyah because, according to them, Muawiyah simply made a mistake in his exercise of juristic discretion (*ijtihad*) in his dispute with Caliph Ali. As such, they argue, taking sides between Ali and Muawiyah serves no purpose or benefit to the Muslim *ummah* (global Islamic community), as both of them thought they were fighting for the best interests of the Muslims.

Moreover, according to the classical Islamic historians, Muawiyah was gifted with the quality of *hilm*, that is shrewdness, moderation, balance and self-control. He preferred to consolidate his rule through persuasion, reason, signing agreements, forging ties and developing friendship and understanding, rather than through force and warfare. His well-known motto was, 'I do not use my sword where my stick is sufficient, and I do not use my stick where my words are sufficient; and if there is only a hair (of understanding) between me and the people, I will not allow it to be cut.' After transferring the capital of the Islamic world from Kufah to Damascus, he transformed the city into a prominent centre of Islamic learning, culture and civilisation. Although he expected all his governors to be loyal and supportive, he exercised considerable flexibility in his dealings with them, and often allowed them to retain significant sums of money to spend on their own provinces. Unlike Caliph Ali, he was not known for dismissing governors; rather he encouraged mutual understanding and co-operation between the central Government and the regional authorities. The balanced approach adopted by Muawiyah enabled him to win over his erstwhile opponents and critics to his side, and enabled him to galvanise the Muslim world under his wise and able leadership. During his reign, the Islamic dominion also expanded rapidly both in the East and the West. Under the command of Uqba ibn Nafi, the

Muslim forces not only reasserted their authority in North Africa, but also mounted naval expeditions to Sicily and laid unsuccessful siege to Constantinople. Likewise, in the East, Muslims successfully captured Kabul, Khurasan, Bukhara and Samarqand, thanks to Muawiyah's outstanding and inspirational leadership.

Muawiyah served as a governor for twenty years, and as a Caliph for almost another two decades. After nearly four decades of continous service to his people, he surprised everyone with his nomination of Yazid as his successor, even though the latter was not fit for the post of Caliphate. As a playboy who thrived on material comforts and luxuries, Yazid was devoid of both intelligence and political ability. Even Muawiyah's personal advisors considered Yazid to be hopeless, but the aged Caliph insisted that his son should succeed him on the throne. Muawiyah died at the age of about seventy-five and was buried in Damascus. But, by nominating his son as his successor, he had in effect inaugurated the first monarchy in Islamic history. This was an unprecedented move which directly contradicted the practice of the first four "rightly-guided Caliphs" who were all elected, so to speak, by the prominent figures of the Islamic State. However, by installing Yazid in his place, Muawiyah became the founder of the first, and one of the Muslim world's most powerful, political dynasties. The Umayyads ruled the Muslim world for nearly a century before the Abbasids overthrew them in 750.

# 30

## Jalal al-Din Rumi
### (b.1207 - d.1273)

THE THIRTEENTH CENTURY of the Common Era and the seventh century of Islam was a difficult and challenging period in Muslim history. Having assumed control of North Africa, the Muslims successfully crossed into Sicily, Gibraltar and southern Spain, before they began to knock on the door of mainland Europe. At the same time, in the subcontinent, Muhammad Ghuri became the first native Muslim monarch to rule India. As the Muslims made rapid political progress both in the East and the West, the Mongol hordes unexpectedly emerged from Asia and ransacked Baghdad, the capital of the Islamic world, leaving behind nothing but death and destruction. Political set-backs, cultural decline and moral degeneration, coupled with petty rivalries between the protagonists of different religious sects and groups, led to intolerance, mutual hatred and animosity across the Muslim world; the core values and principles of Islam were ignored and openly violated in many parts of the Islamic world. From the chaos, the towering figure of Rumi emerged to champion the higher values and principles of Islam like never before.

Jalal al-Din Rumi was born in the city of Balkh (in present-day Afghanistan), which at the time was a part of the Persian province of Khurasan.

His family claimed descent from Abu Bakr, the first Caliph of Islam; his grandfather Hussain ibn Ahmad and father Baha al-Din Walad ibn Hussain were renowned Islamic scholars of their time. In fact, Baha al-Din was such an outstanding Islamic scholar and spiritual figure that he was known as the *sultan al-ulama* (or supreme religious authority) of his age. Brought up in a family of scholars and spiritual guides, Rumi's education began at home under the watchful gaze of his learned father who taught him Arabic, Persian, traditional Islamic sciences and poetry during his early years. Since his father was widely revered by the people of Balkh for his profound learning and spiritual attainments, young Rumi accompanied his father on his travels and in the process he met the leading Islamic scholars of the time.

Rumi was influenced by his father's religious ideas and thoughts and he, in turn, was heavily influenced by the teachings of the celebrated al-Ghazali. As a vociferous opponent of Neoplatonic thought, al-Ghazali launched a vicious intellectual attack on the thoughts of the leading *falasifah* (Islamic philosophers) including al-Kindi, al-Farabi and Ibn Sina, and championed the cause of Islamic traditionalism and Sufi thought and practices. Inspired by al-Ghazali, Baha al-Din not only became a vociferous critic of Islamic philosophy, he also became a champion of Islamic spirituality, ethics and moral values and practices. His stance against philosophy pitched him against another great luminary of Islam, namely Fakhr al-Din al-Razi, who vigorously opposed Baha al-Din's attitude towards Islamic philosophy, culminating in a huge controversy between the two men. But their rivalry came to an end in 1209 with al-Razi's death. Three years later, Baha al-Din left Balkh for Nishapur with his whole family in the wake of an imminent Mongol invasion. In Nishapur, young Rumi encountered the celebrated poet Farid al-Din Attar, the author of the famous *Mantiq al-Tair* (The Conference of the Birds), who gave him copies of his books and prayed for his family's wellbeing. From Nishapur, Rumi's family continued their journeying and travelled to Baghdad and Syria, before arriving in Makkah in time for the annual *hajj* (pilgrimage).

Rumi's family finally settled in Larinda, a small town in the province of Arzinjan, when he was around eighteen years old. Here he married, and a son was born a year later. His family stayed in Larinda for a while before moving to Konya, the capital of the Turkish Seljuk dynasty, in 1229. Two years later, Baha al-Din died and Rumi, who was only twenty-four at the time, was suddenly expected to shoulder all his family responsibilities. As a gifted young scholar who was blessed with a powerful imagination and sharp intellect, he soon became one of the prominent scholars of his locality, thanks to his vast knowledge and understanding of Islam. Having already studied traditional Islamic sciences under the guidance of his father and his personal tutor, Shaykh Burhan al-Din Muhaqqiq al-Tirmidhi, he was very keen to pursue advanced training in the Islamic sciences. Accordingly, he travelled to Halab and Damascus, where he devoted the next seven years of his life to the pursuit of advanced Islamic knowledge. After completing his advanced education, he returned to Konya where he lived with Shaykh Burhan al-Din, his former tutor

and mentor, who encouraged him to engage in ascetic practices in order to attain spiritual purification. He was barely thirty-four when he became widely recognised as a prominent scholar, a worthy successor to his pre-eminent father, and it was not long before he established his own religious school, delivering regular lectures on Qur'anic exegesis (*tafsir*), Islamic jurisprudence (*fiqh*), *hadith*, and aspects of Islamic spirituality, morals and ethics. His lectures became so popular that students came from across Konya to listen to him.

Through his sermons on aspects of Islamic theology, jurisprudence and Prophetic *hadith*, Rumi sought to encourage the locals (whether they were literate or not) to take their faith more seriously and bring about personal, as well as collective, reformation; thereby attaining success in this life and salvation in the hereafter. While he was busy lecturing on traditional Islamic sciences, suddenly there appeared a sixty-year-old man who turned his life completely upside down. Clad in tatty and coarse clothes, this old man was both aggressive and possessed of a very domineering personality. He was Shams al-Din al-Tabriz, an ascetic Sufi, who had renounced all material comforts and pleasures of this life in favour of Sufi devotional practices. Hailing as he did from the family of Hasan-i-Sabbah, the founder of the infamous neo-Ismaili Assassin sect, Shams was a remarkable ascetic whose piety and spirituality completely swept Rumi off his feet.

Although his lectures on the religious sciences made him very popular throughout Konya, after his encounter with Shams, Rumi resigned his professorship at the local college and became Shams's full-time student and devotee. As an Islamic theologian, he had previously condemned music as being a blameworthy activity, but now he became obsessed with music, singing and dancing to the utter shock and surprise of the locals. The people could not understand why an outstanding theologian and religious scholar like Rumi would behave in such a flagrant and loutish manner. More importantly, the locals could not understand how an aged mystic like Shams could influence such a learned, sober and gentle scholar like Rumi into following his ascetic ways. No doubt Shams was a charismatic figure who, having devoted his entire life to the pursuit of Islamic spirituality and gnosis, had acquired a powerful moral and spiritual aura which clearly deeply affected Rumi. In other words, in the person of Shams, he saw what he did not perceive in others: the luminous light of Divine love, compassion and mercy exemplified at its best. Shams became a mirror in which Rumi could see his own spiritual weaknesses, moral failings and physical frailties like never before. What he saw truly shocked and horrified him: in his obsession with Islamic law he had overlooked the very substance of Islam. Thus in the life and spiritual teachings of Shams, he discovered the true meaning and significance of Islam. However, the more his devotion to Shams increased, the more his behaviour became erratic and unpredictable, which led to a huge row between Shams and Rumi's relatives, friends and students; indeed, they eventually forced the former out of Konya.

Rumi's separation from Shams made him so depressed and miserable that his son volunteered to go out in search of Shams and bring him back to Konya. He found him in Damascus and returned home with the aged mystic only for the locals to once again show him their profound hostility. Why? Because they felt he had misled and deceived one of their brightest scholars; but Rumi did not see things in that way. To him, Shams was the embodiment of purity, peace, spirituality and Divine gnosis and, like him, he too longed to attain the summit of Islamic spirituality. But the people of Konya did not share Rumi's profound love and enthusiasm for Shams, and he was either forced to leave the city or he may have been murdered, probably by someone close to Rumi. Either way, Shams suddenly disappeared – never to return again. His disappearance affected the forty-one year old Rumi profoundly; indeed, many people thought he had gone 'mad' because he refused to believe that Shams had disappeared. During this period he became completely obsessed with singing and dancing, which

the traditional Islamic scholars considered to be an abhorrent practice. But he found peace, solace and reassurance in Sufi music and dance which, he argued, represented an expression of Divine love and grace in its highest form.

After many years of self-imposed suffering and emotional agony, Rumi eventually came to terms with his separation from Shams, thanks to a local goldsmith. One day while he was dancing about in the street, he suddenly stopped upon hearing the rhythmic sound of the goldsmith's hammer, and he suddenly regained his balance and composure. The beat of the goldsmith's hammer restored Rumi's physical and intellectual composure; he also began to refocus his spiritual energy in the pursuit of Divine gnosis. After thanking the illiterate goldsmith for his timely intervention, he gave up his quest for Shams, for it became clear to him that he was in reality looking for none other than his own innermost self. So, at the age of fifty-four, he finally attained the inner peace and certainty which he had been seeking for so long. It was during this period that Rumi composed his immortal *Mathnavi*, which the renowned Persian poet and writer Abd al-Rahman Jami once referred to as the 'Persian Qur'an' due to its sublime teachings and wisdom. It took Rumi nearly twelve years to dictate the twenty-five thousand and seven hundred verses to his loyal friend and confidant Husam al-Din. Originally entitled *Husam Namah* (or 'The Book of Husam'), this monumental work later became known as the *Mathnavi*. Prior to the *Mathnavi*, Rumi composed another book of around thirty-five thousand verses and odes in memory of Shams al-Din al-Tabriz. In this book, entitled *Divan-i-Shams-i-Tabriz*, he explored different aspects of mystical love, questing and longing. But it was his *Mathnavi* which was destined to leave a permanent mark in the annals of Islamic literature.

As a compilation of mystical teachings, spiritual exhortations and religious parables in the form of poetry, the central message of the *Mathnavi* was one of a universal Divine love which transcended all artificial boundaries, sectarian denominations and crude cultural constraints. Rumi appealed directly to the very source of mystical love, God Almighty, with an overwhelming sense of grace and humility, and in so doing he conveyed his universal message of love, compassion and mercy to all people. His mysticism was a unifying force, one where Divinity and humanity met rather than drifted apart. Through this, he hoped to promote mutual understanding and tolerance and establish peace and harmony between people of all faiths, cultures and traditions. Since Rumi, like us, lived in an age when greed, anger, hatred and hostility led to considerable chaos, disorder, bloodshed and instability around the world, his message of universal love is as relevant today as it was during his own lifetime. Also, as a champion of human freedom and individuality, he constantly stressed the need for the attainment of true peace and liberation by moving closer to Divine proximity. This coming together did not entail absolute union between the Creator and His creatures; rather, according to Rumi, it represented the meeting of the lover with the object of his love. Love, argued Rumi, was an innate, cosmic feeling which cannot be experienced except by connecting oneself with the Spirit of the universe. Nor can it be experienced by mere performance of external deeds and actions, devoid of inner meaning and content. This universal message of love, compassion and mercy was, therefore, central to Rumi's mysticial philosophy which he expounded in a masterly fashion in his vast collection of poetry and odes.

Though Rumi was thoroughly familiar with Islamic theology and philosophy, he did not consider himself to be a theologian or philosopher *per se*. He was essentially a mystical poet, arguably one of the most influential in history, and his *Mathnavi* is today widely considered to be one of the most powerful and imaginative poems of all time. In total he composed more than seventy thousand verses of poetry in Persian, but as the founder of the *mawlawiyyah* Order of Sufism, he must also be considered as one of the most influential practitioners of Sufism, along with Abd al-Qadir al-Jilani, Baha al-Din Naqshband, Mu'in al-Din Chishti and Abul Hasan al-Shadhili. Known as the 'whirling dervishes' for their love of Sufi music, singing and whirling dance, the adherents of this *tariqah* have been living in Turkey since the early Ottoman period. Revered both in the East and the West for his remarkable poetic output, Rumi's ideas and thoughts have influenced scores of prominent Islamic scholars, thinkers and poets like Abd al-Rahman Jami and Sir Muhammad Iqbal. Today, he has also become one of the most popular and widely read Muslim poets in the West, especially in the United States. Rumi died at the age of sixty-six and was buried in Konya (in present-day Turkey).

# 31

## Harun al-Rashid
### (b.766 - d.809)

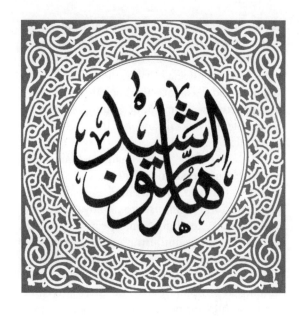

THE ABBASID EMPIRE was one of the foremost political dynasties to have ruled the Islamic world. The Umayyad era came to an abrupt end following the Abbasid revolution of 750 when Marwan II, the last Umayyad ruler, was resoundingly defeated by the supporters of Abul Abbas Abdullah ibn Muhammad ibn Ali ibn Abdullah ibn Abbas (otherwise known as Abul Abbas al-Saffah), after which the Abbasids went on to rule the Muslim world until the Mongol hordes emerged from Asia in the thirteenth century. Though al-Saffah is generally considered to be the founder of the Abbasid Empire, it was his brother Abdullah ibn Muhammad ibn Ali ibn Abdullah ibn Abbas (better known as Abu Ja'far al-Mansur) who played a pivotal role in consolidating Abbasid rule across the Islamic world. Al-Mansur was a shrewd and gifted ruler who was equally famous for his personal piety and unusual political and diplomatic skills. After the death of al-Saffah, he not only swiftly established his authority as Caliph, but also founded the city of Baghdad in 762 and ensured that a smooth political transition would take place after his reign. Abu Abdullah Muhammad ibn al-Mansur (better known as al-Mahdi) succeeded his father, al-Mansur, and ruled for a decade. He had seven sons including Musa and Harun. After al-Mahdi's death, his son Musa ascended the Abbasid throne, but his rule only lasted a year. He was succeeded by Prince Harun al-Rashid who went onto become one of the Muslim world's most famous and influential rulers.

Born in the central Iranian city of Rayy, Harun was the favourite son of his parents. At the time of his birth, his father al-Mahdi was the governor of the Eastern region of the Abbasid Empire and his beautiful Yemeni mother, Khayzuran bint Ata, was his father's favourite wife. Like his mother, Harun was an attractive child who grew up under the watchful gaze of his parents within the governor's palatial residence surrounded by much wealth and luxury. Educated in Arabic and aspects of Islamic sciences during his early years, Harun soon became well-known for his bravery, intelligence and loyalty to the Abbasid clan. Like his grandfather al-Mansur, his father al-Mahdi was very fond of the people of Makkah and Madinah. When he visited the sacred cities in 777 he showered the locals with money and gifts, and took a keen interest in carrying out restoration works on the sacred mosque (*haram al-sharif*) in Makkah. As a youngster, Harun accompanied his father to Makkah and Madinah during the *hajj* season, and instantly fell in love with the people of the two sacred cities. Al-Mahdi's generosity won over the people of Arabia and this helped to consolidate his Caliphal authority across the Islamic world. Also, at this time, al-Mahdi took the opportunity to introduce young Harun to the people of Makkah and Madinah as his potential successor.

On their return to Baghdad, al-Mahdi entrusted Harun's educational needs to Yahya ibn Khalid al-Barmaki, his talented Persian political advisor and administrator. Yahya groomed him with care, teaching him aspects of political strategy and civil administration, and preparing him for political leadership in the near future. Yahya influenced Harun's education and political thinking so profoundly that the latter also came to rely on him for both psychological and emotional support. As expected, Harun grew up to be a very able and competent young man. Indeed, he was barely fifteen when his knowledge of military strategy and tactics was put to a severe test. Appointed commander of the Abbasid army in 780, his orders were to go and neutralise the Byzantine forces which had become a persistant thorn in the side of the Abbasid army. By nominating Harun to lead the Abbasid forces against the Byzantines, al-Mahdi effectively nominated his favourite son to succeed him as Abbasid Caliph. Harun's military campaign against the Byzantines proved very successful, and he acquired first-hand experience of leading an army on the battlefield. During his time with the army he established a good rapport with the generals who became very fond of the young prince. Two years later, Harun was commissioned to lead another large scale military campaign against the Byzantines and again he returned home triumphant, having besieged the Greeks inside Constantinople, before Empress Irene came out and pleaded for peace. This was a remarkable achievement for the sixteen-year-old Harun whose efforts earned him the title of *al-rashid*, meaning 'the rightly-guided one'.

Due to over-indulgence, the Muslim rulers of the time often tended to die unexpectedly whilst still in their prime, and this prompted al-Mahdi to officially nominate his successor in order to avoid a bitter political struggle after his death. Having groomed his sons Musa and Harun for political leadership, he ensured everyone pledged their loyalty to Musa as his heir-apparent, while young Harun was confirmed as Musa's successor. When al-Mahdi died in 785, Harun was the governor of the Western region of Abbasid Empire which extended all the way from Tunisia at one end, to Anbar on the outskirts of Baghdad at the other. Likewise, Yahya ibn Khalid, his mentor and guide, was put in charge of the political and civil administration of this vast province, with Harun as the governor being mainly a figurehead. Musa, who took the title of al-Hadi, succeeded his father as Caliph but his reign did not last long. Like his father, he died in mysterious circumstances barely a year after ascending the Abbasid throne. Historians have provided conflicting accounts about the circumstances which led to al-Mahdi and al-Hadi's deaths. When rumour, speculation and gossip began to spread throughout Baghdad like wildfire (especially after the death of al-Hadi), Khayzuran, the mother of Harun, stepped to the fore and took matters into her own hands. She summoned her favourite son, who was next in line to ascend the Abbasid throne, and installed him as the new Caliph.

Only twenty-one at the time, the young Caliph appointed the aged Yahya ibn Khalid as his personal advisor and guide, the highest-ranking Government post in the land. With Yahya to guide him through the massive task of administering both the internal and external affairs of the vast Abbasid Empire, Harun soon established himself as the undisputed ruler of the Muslim world. As a loyal, committed and extremely experienced bureaucrat, Yahya enjoyed Harun's full support and confidence, so much so that the young Caliph used to fondly refer to him as his 'father'. However, it was Yahya's younger son, Ja'far, who forged a close friendship with the young Caliph. Like Harun, he was in his early twenties and was well-known for his love of glamour, fun and adventure. They had so much in common that Ja'far subsequently became famous as Harun's loyal companion in the world-famous adventure tale *The Thousand and One Nights* (*alf layla wa layla* – also known as *The Arabian Nights*). As prominent members of Harun's inner circle, Yahya and his sons Fadl and Ja'far wielded considerable power within the Abbasid political hierarchy. The Barmakids (as Ja'far's family were called) also had open access to the Caliph, thanks to their continued political support and loyalty to him as advisors and guides.

If Harun became famous as a glamorous and fun-loving Caliph, then he was equally well-known for his personal piety and benevolence. As a devout Muslim, he became the first and only Caliph to have had performed the *hajj* no fewer than eight times together with his beloved wife Zubaida. Following in the footsteps of his father al-Mahdi and grandfather al-Mansur, every time Harun visited Makkah and Madinah he lavished the locals with gifts of clothing and money. Prior to each *hajj* season, he took it on himself to personally prepare for the journey. He also encouraged his officials as well as the masses to accompany him, leaving the affairs of the State in the safe hands of his Barmakid viziers and other high-ranking Government officials. During his reign as Caliph, he also radically reformed the civil and administrative systems of the State in order to increase efficiency and effectiveness across all levels of his Government. To put an end to all Byzantine incursions, he instigated military campaigns against them and, in so doing, became the first ruler in Islamic history to have had led the *hajj* delegation, and also an army onto the battlefield in the same year. Harun's greatness lay in the fact that he not only preached, but also led his people by his personal example. This naturally made him very popular with his officials, as well as the masses.

In fact, during his reign as Caliph, Harun sent military expeditions against the Byzantines every year. Determined to undermine their stratagems, he utilised his profound knowledge and under-

standing of military strategy and tactics against the Byzantines with remarkable success. He often left the political and civil affairs of his Government in the hands of the Barmakids so that he could focus his full attention on the external foes of his empire. His reign thus represented the zenith of Abbasid glory and achievement. After establishing political stability, increasing economic prosperity, raising educational standards and promoting social peace and solidarity across the Islamic world, he founded the first fully-operational hospital in Baghdad. He also established a library and research centre, which became known as *bait al-hikmah* (or the 'House of Wisdom'), where Muslim scientists, astronomers and philosophers pursued pioneering studies and research in all the sciences of the day. Moreover, he was instrumental in the development of an effective postal system across the Abbasid Empire; he constructed new roads and highways in order to facilitate trade and commerce, as well as long-distance travel and communication between the different regions of his empire.

Under Harun's wise and inspirational leadership, a thriving and tolerant society emerged in the Muslim world, where scholars, writers and thinkers were able to engage in debate and discussion on religious, philosophical, scientific and literary themes without any fear of political, religious or social sanctions. For this reason, his reign became known as the Golden Age of Abbasid rule, and echoes of this period naturally found their way into the stories of the famous *Thousand and One Nights*. Being the main hero of this epic tale, he is depicted roaming around Baghdad, the magnificent city of palaces, populated by wealthy civil servants and middle-class merchants, engaging in hilarious adventures (often in the middle of the night) accompanied by his colleagues Ja'far the Barmakid and Abu Nuwas, the well-known poet. Although the *Thousand and One Nights* is a fictional account of Caliph Harun al-Rashid's supposed exploits, it does bear a striking resemblance to the real Caliph because he never failed to appreciate and admire the lighter and humorous side of life. As an intelligent and cultured man, he enjoyed life to its full and did so without in any way making a mockery of his faith and beliefs.

Though Caliph Harun transformed Baghdad into one of the world's most advanced and dazzling cities, he did not like its intense heat and hot climate. Throughout his reign, he went back and forth from one city to another in search of his ideal location and environment. He preferred a cool, lively and refreshing breeze which, of course, was conspicuous by its absence in Baghdad. After a long quest for his ideal location, he finally settled in the ancient Roman city of Callinicum, which had been transformed by his grandfather al-Mansur into a thriving metropolis. Later renamed al-Rafiqa, it is today located in Syria. In 802, Harun went to perform yet another *hajj* and this time he took his sons Muhammad (who later became known as Caliph al-Amin) and Abdullah (who took the title of Caliph al-Ma'mun) with him. They visited the cities of Makkah and Madinah, where he distributed huge sums of money to the locals and also introduced his sons, and future successors, to the people of Makkah and Madinah; the Caliph was only thirty-six at the time.

On his return from *hajj*, he sensed something was not right at the Court and his response took everyone around him by complete surprise. He removed the Barmakids, namely the vizier Yahya and his two sons Ja'far and Fadl, from their high-ranking Government posts and placed them under house arrest. Ja'far was eventually murdered. Harun's drastic and heavy-handed action against his erstwhile supporters continues to baffle and bemuse historians to this day. As expected, without the support and guidance of his loyal and somewhat flamboyant Barmakid viziers, he struggled to maintain peace and stability throughout the Abbasid Empire. This prompted him to appoint Fadl ibn Rabi, the son of the distinguished vizier Rabi, who had served his grandfather al-Mansur and his father al-Mahdi very loyally, to the post of Chief Minister but he, too, struggled to maintain the peace and security of the Abbasid Empire. During the final years of his reign, Harun became preoccupied with military campaigns against the Byzantines and his political opponents at home. He died of illness at the age of forty-three, during a military expedition to Persia, and was buried in the ancient city of Tus. Before his death, he stipulated that his son al-Amin should succeed him as Caliph and he, in turn, was to be succeeded by al-Ma'mun; by this he hoped to avoid a protracted succession battle after his death but his plans did not work out as he hoped. All in all, with the death of Caliph Harun al-Rashid, a glorious chapter in Islamic history came to an abrupt end. As one of the Muslim world's most influential rulers, he is today famous both in the East and the West for his wide-ranging contributions to the rise and development of Islamic culture and civilisation.

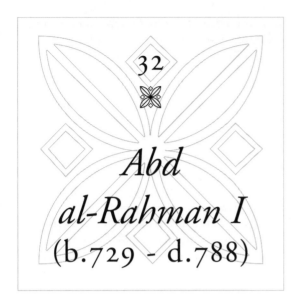

# 32

# Abd al-Rahman I
# (b.729 - d.788)

FOUNDED BY MUAWIYAH ibn Abi Sufyan in 661, the Umayyad dynasty was one of the most powerful empires to have ruled the Muslim world. Of the fourteen Umayyad sovereigns who ruled between 661 and 750, the reigns of Muawiyah, Abd al-Malik ibn Marwan, Umar ibn Abd al-Aziz, al-Walid I and Hisham were the most successful. Others such as Yazid I, al-Walid III and Marwan II proved to be both incompetent and tyrannical rulers who struggled to maintain peace and stability within the Islamic dominion. After taking full advantage of Umayyad failings, the Abbasids emerged to challenge Umayyad power and authority, and in so doing they eventually ousted their rivals from power in 750. The demise of the Umayyad dynasty, and the rise of the Abbasids during the middle of the eighth century, represented a momentous change in Islamic history; one influential political dynasty gave way to another, which went on to rule the Muslim world for more than five hundred years. But, thanks to Abd al-Rahman, a young Umayyad prince, the flag of the Umayyads continued to fly high in the Islamic West for almost another three hundred years. The King is dead, long live the King!

Abd al-Rahman ibn Muawiyah ibn Hisham, also known as *sahib al-andalus* (or 'the Lord of

Muslim Spain'), was born in Damascus during the reign of his illustrious grandfather, Caliph Hisham, who ruled the Muslim world for nearly two decades and thereby consolidated Umayyad power and authority across the length and breadth of the Islamic world. Brought up and educated within the confines of the royal palace in Damascus, Abd al-Rahman had a privileged upbringing, surrounded by great riches and luxury. As one of the favourite grandsons of the Caliph he was considered to be an unusally intelligent youngster, whom the Caliph predicted would one day revive Umayyad fortunes after their decline. Thus the Caliph encouraged his son, Muawiyah, to take good care of his grandson. When Prince Abd al-Rahman was around fourteen, his grandfather Caliph Hisham died in 743. The death of Hisham marked the beginning of the end for the Umayyads as a protracted succession battle ensued, which severely undermined the Umayyad grip on power. The political situation within the Umayyad family spiralled completely out of control between 743 and 744 when no fewer than three Umayyad princes, Walid II, Yazid III and Ibrahim, simultaneously laid claim to the Umayyad throne; all three of them failed to assert their political authority and this inevitably led to considerable political unrest and social upheaval across the Muslim world. Seeing the Umayyads in utter disarray, the Abbasids swiftly galvanised their forces in Khurasan and launched a series of daring raids against the incumbent Umayyad governors in Rayy and Isfahan. As the Abbasids marched towards Damascus, the last Umayyad ruler fled to Eygpt, thus clearing the way for Abbasid victory.

Abul Abbas, who was also known as 'al-Saffah' (or 'the blood-shedder'), was the leader of the Abbasids at the time and went on to become the first Abbasid ruler. Immediately after being sworn in as Abbasid Caliph, he organised a lavish feast in Damascus for all the Umayyad princes and had nearly all of them systematically butchered so that there could never be an Umayyad uprising against the Abbasids. As fate would have it, only Prince Abd al-Rahman, who was twenty at the time, and his younger brother, escaped the ensuing massacre. The two of them fled the scene and hid in a village close to the Euphrates. When their pursuers traced their whereabouts, they tried to flee once more. But, unable to outrun his pursuers, his thirteen-year-old brother was captured and beheaded as young Abd al-Rahman watched in the distance. Although he was shocked and horrified by the inhumanity of their pursuers, he was determined to avoid the fate which had befallen the rest of his family – and to live to tell the tale. From the banks of the Euphrates, he went to Palestine and Egypt, travelling by day and night to avoid being captured and put to the sword by the Abbasid henchmen. On one occasion, his pursuers came very close to capturing him but he evaded them by hiding under the dress of his host's wife. After living in hiding for several years, Abd al-Rahman set out for North Africa. It was a harrowing journey, fraught with dangers; he travelled by foot, caravan and by boat, and often did so under the cover of darkness to avoid his enemies, before finally arriving in Morocco where he was offered refuge by the North African tribe of Banu Nafisa. It had taken the tall, slim, strong and determined Abd al-Rahman around five years travelling from place to place before he

finally reached Morocco, the land of his maternal ancestors. Here he soon established himself as an inspirational leader and military strategist. As the only surviving Umayyad prince, he received much needed help and support from the locals, and they in turn respected him for his intelligence and boundless energy. With the Abbasids now firmly in control of the Islamic East, Abd al-Rahman knew that a return to Damascus was no longer a viable option; instead, he decided to carve out a bright future for himself in the Islamic West.

Abd al-Rahman arrived in North Africa at a critical time in the history of the Islamic West. It was a time when the Muslims of *al-andalus* (or Islamic Spain) became bitterly divided along ethnic lines. Thus rival Arab and Berber groups became locked in a battle to gain political and military ascendancy. When the news of the chaotic political situation which prevailed across the sea in Spain reached Abd al-Rahman, he skilfully exploited the situation to his advantage in order to install himself as the ruler of Islamic Spain. Accordingly, he sent Badr, his supporter and aide, to the chief of the Arabs in Spain (many of whom were loyal supporters of the Umayyad family) to ascertain whether they would support him if he came over to Spain to unify the country under his leadership. Since the Spanish Arabs were very sympathetic towards the Umayyads, they assured Badr that should Abd al-Rahman decide to come, they would help him to reunite the country under his leadership. During his visit, Badr also obtained the support and co-operation of the Yemenite tribes of Spain, and returned to North Africa to inform Abd al-Rahman of the good news. Excited, he reportedly exclaimed, 'We shall attain our objective and conquer the land!' before boarding a vessel destined for Muslim Spain. He reached the shores of *al-andalus* in 755 at the age of twenty-five. Thus a new chapter began in the history of Islamic Spain, under the wise and able stewardship of Prince Abd al-Rahman.

As soon as the news of his arrival reached the Muslim masses in Spain, they flocked to pledge allegiance to the young Umayyad prince, leaving the incumbent governor of the country isolated. After recruiting a sizeable military force, he annexed Archidona and Seville and marched towards Cordova, the capital of Islamic Spain, and challenged the authority of the reigning Abbasid governor, Yusuf al-Fihri. Abd al-Rahman's twenty thousand troops met the forces of the governor in 756 at Masara, east of Cordova, and inflicted a crushing defeat on them, forcing al-Fihri to flee to Toledo. This represented a decisive victory for Abd al-Rahman who now became the undisputed ruler of Islamic Spain. This did not mark an end to all troubles for the new ruler, however; he faced several other rebellions in Loxa, Toledo and the Yemenite tribes also turned against him a few years later, but Abd al-Rahman managed to suppress these revolts and rebellions with ease. His biggest test, though, came in 763 when the great Abbasid Caliph Abu Ja'far al-Mansur dispatched a powerful army under the command of Ala ibn Mughis, in order to drive him out of Spain. Abd al-Rahman, however, organised his armed forces with such skill and efficiency that his forces repelled the advancing Abbasid army with great success. Indeed, in the battle, Abd al-Rahman killed Ala ibn Mughis with his own hands and sent his remains – wrapped in an Abbasid flag – to Caliph al-Mansur in Baghdad.

His resounding victory over the Abbasids established his authority across Islamic Spain for good. This was also the last time the Abbasids attempted to oust Abd al-Rahman, whom the historian Ibn al-Athir fondly refers to as *sahib al-andalus* (or the 'Lord of Islamic Spain'). It was not until almost a decade later that the Abbasid Caliph al-Mahdi sent an envoy to Emperor Charlemagne of France to urge him to attack Muslim Spain in order to overthrow Abd al-Rahman. The combined Abbasid-French forces attacked Islamic Spain simultanously, but they failed to break down the resolute defence put up by Abd al-Rahman's army and eventually Charlemagne was forced to retreat, in 778, having suffered heavy losses. Later, Charlemagne signed a peace treaty with Abd al-Rahman and promised not to attack Islamic Spain again; indeed, he even of-

fered to marry his daughter to Abd al-Rahman, but the latter politely declined the offer.

Now, at last, he became recognised as the undisputed master of *al-andalus*. This was a far cry from his humble beginnings as a lonely young man who had arrived in Spain without an army of his own and without support from any other ruler of his time, yet within a matter of few years he managed to reunite the people of Islamic Spain under his leadership. Indeed, the various warring factions came in their droves to pledge their allegiance to him and help restore political stability, increase economic prosperity and establish peace and security across the land. Only a few years earlier, these same people were at each other's throats, indeed they were on the verge of civil war but, following the arrival of the Umayyad prince, the fortunes of Islamic Spain changed for the better. He worked closely with all the different ethnic groups and treated them all fairly and squarely, and in so doing won the respect, support and admiration of all his people. They not only trusted his judgement and obeyed his commands, but after many years of internal dissension and tribal rivalry, they were only too happy to unite under his wise and inspirational leadership. After restoring peace and stability across the land, Abd al-Rahman began to construct schools, colleges, hospitals, mosques, fountains and public baths across Spain, and he encouraged the locals to use these state-funded facilities and to do so free of charge. Since many years of political in-fighting and insurgency had resulted in extensive damage and destruction to many of Cordova's old buildings, he refurbished all the damaged buildings and constructed new ones to meet the needs of his people. During this period he also initiated the building of massive city walls around Cordova in order to protect it from foreign invaders; in so doing he restricted access to the city except through seven narrow gates which were manned by armed guards round-the-clock.

Having spent his early years in the beautiful gardens of the royal palace in Damascus, Abd al-Rahman was keen to re-create the same ambience in and around his beloved Cordova. Accordingly, he sponsored the construction of a beautiful garden on the outskirts of Cordova for the people of Spain to view and admire. As an educated and cultured sovereign, and also a gifted poet, he became one of Europe's most generous patrons of learning and education of the time. Moreover, he overhauled both the political and administrative systems of his Government, and appointed regional governors who were responsible for their own areas, but reported directly to the central Government based at Cordova. His Ministers, or viziers, were assigned the task of day-to-day administration of different departments of the Government, and they were supervised by the Chief Minister who reported directly to Abd al-Rahman. Also, as the commander-in-chief of his armed forces, he remained directly in charge of his army. He paid his armed forces good salaries and in return he expected them to be very loyal, supportive and hardworking. At a time when the rest of Europe was emerging from the Dark Ages, Abd al-Rahman transformed Islamic Spain into one of medieval Europe's most prosperous and advanced centres of culture and civilisation. In his spare time he wrote beautiful poetry, and regularly engaged in intellectual debate and discussion with the leading scholars, writers and poets of his time who found him to be a generous patron and an erudite interlocutor. The great mosque of Cordova, which Abd al-Rahman built during his long reign of thirty-two years still stands to this day, as an enduring tribute to one of the Muslim world's (and also Europe's) most successful rulers.

Abd al-Rahman died at the age of fifty-nine and was buried in the great Palace of Cordova. The Umayyad rule of Islamic Spain, initiated by Abd al-Rahman, persisted for nearly three hundred years. During this period Islamic Spain produced some of the Muslim world's most influential rulers, scholars, thinkers, philosophers and scientists, thanks to Abd al-Rahman 'the Immigrant' (*al-dhakil*).

# 33

## Tariq ibn Ziyad
## (b.ca.650 - d.ca.728)

WITHIN A FEW decades following the death of the Prophet, Muslims burst out of Arabia and overwhelmed the Persian and Byzantine Empires, two great superpowers of the time. This opened the floodgates for Islam both in the East and the West. After assuming full control of the region known today as the Middle East, Muslim forces marched into Africa. Although it was during the reign of Caliph Umar that Muslims first made in-roads into North Africa, it was Muawiyah ibn Abi Sufyan, the first Umayyad ruler, who commissioned large-scale campaigns into that part of the world. This led to the conquest of Tunis and the establishment of the historic North African city of Qayrawan in 670 under the leadership of Uqba ibn Nafi. Following in the footsteps of Muawiyah, the Umayyad ruler Abd al-Malik ibn Marwan initiated a series of campaigns across *ifriqiyah* (or North Africa) which eventually led to the triumph of Islam in that region. Thanks to Caliph Abd al-Malik's efforts, Islamic rule became firmly established in North Africa. After Caliph Abd al-Malik's death, he was succeeded, one after another, by his four sons who followed in their father's footsteps and commissioned further daring military campaigns in the West, which eventu-

ally brought Muslims directly into contact with mainland Europe.

In 708, the Umayyad ruler al-Walid appointed the great Muslim general Musa ibn Nusayr as governor of North Africa. After taking up his post, he successfully established Umayyad political authority across that region. He then promoted Islamic missionary activities which led to the mass conversion of the Berbers into the fold of Islam, thus consolidating his position further. Within a very short period, Musa became the undisputed master of all North Africa. His remarkable achievement has rightly earned him an enviable place in the history of Muslim North Africa. It was also during Musa's reign as governor of North Africa that Muslims first sailed across the sea and marched into Spain under the command of the legendary Muslim general Tariq ibn Ziyad.

Tariq hailed from the North African Berber tribe of Nafzawah and was born into a poor Muslim family. His father, Ziyad, embraced Islam when Uqba ibn Nafi conquered North Africa and established his headquarters at Qayrawan. During this period of war and political uncertainty, Ziyad became a staunch supporter of the Muslim army and Uqba rewarded him handsomely for his loyalty and support. After Ziyad's death, his young son Tariq followed in his footsteps and joined the Muslim army. At the time the Muslims were busy fighting the insurgency activities of their enemies who were determined to drive them out of North Africa. Trained in military strategy and warfare by the illustrious Musa ibn Nusayr, Tariq soon began to shine and out-smart his peers. Impressed with his highly refined and effective military skills, Musa selected him for promotion as his lieutenant-general. He served Musa with loyalty and dedication, and in so doing won the latter's full support and confidence, and was rewarded when soon afterwards Musa appointed him governor of Tangier (in present-day Morocco). When Tariq proved himself to be both gifted and competent in warfare as well as in political and civil administration, Musa ibn Nusayr, his mentor and guide, became one of his good friends and supporters. They worked together to protect the interests of Islam across North Africa; they treated their subjects with fairness, justice and equality, and encouraged the freeing of slaves. Thus peace and prosperity began to spread throughout that region.

In contrast, the situation across the sea in the Iberian Peninsula could not have been more desperate. King Roderick (or Rodrigo), the reigning Visigoth ruler of Spain, presided over a people who still lived in the Dark Ages. The ruling elites of Iberia surrounded themselves with much wealth and luxury and enjoyed a sumptuous lifestyle, while the majority of their people were forced to beg for charity. To add insult to injury, the King mercilessly pursued and punished the Jewish population of Iberia with the support and approval of the Catholic Church. Indeed, the Church was only too happy to see the decadent feudal system which then prevailed in the Iberian Peninsula remain in place, because it served the interest of the Catholic bishops and priests. Being profoundly unhappy and dissatisfied with the status quo, the masses began to call for a fair and equitable distribution of land and wealth across the country. As the masses intensified their

campaign for freedom and liberation from the despotic rule of King Roderick, Musa ibn Nusayr felt the situation was ripe for external intervention. But after some deliberation, he decided not to launch a hasty invasion and risk suffering significant loss of property and personnel.

While Musa was still in two minds about whether to launch a military campaign against King Roderick or not, Ilyan (or Julian), the governor of Ceuta, went to Qayrawan to see Musa and urge him to attack Iberia because he considered Roderick to be a corrupt and unprincipled ruler. His hatred of Roderick intensified after the latter violated his daughter during her stay in Toledo, the capital of the Visigoth kingdom. Eager to exact revenge, Ilyan came to Musa to seek his assistance in order to overthrow the despotic ruler. Although Musa sympathised with Ilyan's plight, he was not prepared to risk Muslim lives in order to exact personal revenge. Furthermore, the Muslims were not familiar with Iberia as it was separated from the Muslim territories by the sea, which could pose a serious danger to the Muslim army. As such, Musa told Ilyan he could not justify launching a military campaign against Roderick simply on the basis of what he had told him. Since Musa was not sure whether Ilyan was as sincere as he claimed to be – or an opportunist who intended to betray the Muslims – he told him to return home and organise his own army to fight Roderick. If he was willing to do that, argued Musa, then he would consider authorising a military incursion into the Iberian Peninsula. Ilyan returned home and did exactly as he was told, namely he instigated a military strike against Roderick's forces, took some captives and booty, and returned home unharmed. This convinced Musa of Ilyan's sincerity and he decided to instigate an incursion into Iberia. But to do so, he needed the Caliph's approval, so he sent an urgent message to Caliph al-Walid in Damascus for his permission to invade Iberia. Al-Walid sent a positive response, with the proviso that Musa should first carry out a thorough reconnaissance in order to ascertain Roderick's military strengths and capabilities.

The reconnaissance expedition, led by Tarif ibn Malik, returned home with positive feedback. Ilyan then visited Musa for the second time and pleaded with him to authorise military action against Roderick. Accordingly, Musa summoned his favourite general, Tariq ibn Ziyad, and instructed him to lead a sortie into Iberia. The indomitable Tariq set off in 711 with seven thousand Muslim soldiers of different backgrounds including Berbers, Arabs and Persians. They were all united by the unifying strength and power of Islam. Ilyan promised to supply the Muslim army with boats so that they could cross the sea which separated Iberia from North Africa. During this short boat journey, Tariq fell asleep and the Prophet Muhammad reportedly appeared to him in a dream, and urged him to proceed bravely, for victory was assured. Immediately upon reaching the shores, he ordered the Muslim army to disembark as discreetly as possible, and all the boats to be destroyed. His bemused soldiers could not understand how they would return home if all the boats were destroyed. Tariq told them: they must either conquer *al-andalus* or die fighting for Islam. Hereafter this place became known as Gibraltar, derived from the Arabic *jabal al-tariq* (the Mount of Tariq), and thus the name of Tariq ibn Ziyad became immortalised. To this day, all travellers who pass through the Strait of Gibraltar are reminded of Tariq, the legendary North African Muslim general, who liberated this land from the grip of Roderick, the despotic Visigoth ruler.

When Tariq landed at Gibraltar, he discovered that King Roderick was engaged in military action against the Basque people in northern Iberia. The Basques had revolted against Roderick and tried to oust him from power but he suppressed them ruthlessly, thanks to his superior military power. However, when the news of Muslim incursion into Iberia was relayed to Roderick, he set off for the south with a large contingent to meet the Muslim army of around twelve thousand soldiers, led by the inspirational Tariq. After reaching Cordova, he prepared to attack Tariq's forces, but before doing so he decided to spy on the Muslims in order to ascertain their military strength. He sent one of his trusted lieutenants to infiltrate the Muslim camp and gather as much information as possible. Dressed in Arabic attire, his spy entered the Muslim camp but as soon as Tariq was informed of the presence of an intruder, he ordered a dead body to be brought and boiled as if it was being prepared for their meal. When the body was cut into pieces and the flesh was cooked as per Tariq's instructions, the spy began to tremble with fear and awe. He thought the Muslims were cannibals, and hurried back to Roderick to inform him that his kingdom had been invaded by a people who fed on human flesh. On hearing this, Roderick and his men trembled with fear and consternation.

But backing off and fleeing was not an option as far as Roderick was concerned. He therefore mustered all his forces and decided to attack the Muslim army. The two armies met at Guadalete. Standing before his men, Tariq delivered one of the most inspirational speeches ever composed by a Muslim military commander. He concluded his lengthy speech with these words, 'Bear in mind that Allah the Almighty will select according to this promise those who distinguish themselves most among you, and grant them due reward, both in this world and in the world after this; and know likewise that I shall be the first to set upon you the example, and to put into practice what I recommend you to do; for it is my intention, on the meeting of the two hosts, to attack the Christian tyrant Roderick and kill him with my own hands, if Allah be pleased. When you see me bearing against him, charge along with me; if I kill him, the victory is ours; if I am killed before I reach him, do not trouble yourselves about me, but fight as if I were still alive and among you, and follow up my purpose; for the moment they see their King fall, these unbelievers are sure to disperse. If, however, I should be killed, after inflicting death upon their King, appoint a man from among you who unites both courage and experience, and may command you in this emergency, and follow up the success. If you attend to my instructions, we are sure of the victory.'

Tariq had no doubt that the Muslims would win the Battle of Rio Barbate. And so it proved. Under his inspirational leadership, the Muslim forces completely routed Roderick and his much larger, superior army. By all accounts this was a truly remarkable achievement, especially considering the fact that the Muslim army was made up of old and part-time soldiers who were poorly equipped and thoroughly unfamiliar with the Iberian terrain. Nevertheless, they managed to inflict a crushing defeat on a large and professional force, and did so in their own land. Victory over Roderick opened the door to the rest of Iberia: Tariq moved swiftly to other parts of the peninsula and conquered a large part of the country before proceeding to Toledo. When Musa received the news of Tariq's success, he also crossed into Iberia, in 712, with a large army and successfully conquered such prominent Iberian cities as Sidonia, Carmona and Seville before joining Tariq in Toledo. Both Tariq and Musa remained in Muslim Spain for three years, and during their stay there they treated the locals with justice, fairness and equality, unlike their former ruler. Their exemplary behaviour impressed the locals so much that they began to embrace Islam in their droves. Those who chose to remain Christian were tolerated and allowed to live in peace, along with a significant number of Jews who continued to live and thrive in Islamic Spain. Under Muslim patronage, Judaism flourished throughout Spain and this period became known as the Golden Age of Judaism in Europe, where great Jewish scholars and thinkers like Musa bin Maimon (better known as Maimonides), Ibn Gabirol and Ibn Daud later lived and produced some of their most influential works. The arrival of the Muslims not only marked a fresh beginning for Spain, it also marked a new beginning for Europe as a whole. Through Islamic Spain, Muslims introduced the concept of freedom, tolerance, civil society, arts, science, mathematics and philosophy into Europe for the first time in its history. Had it not been for Tariq's military excursion into Spain, this may not have happened at all. For this reason alone, Tariq deserves to be recognised as one of the most influential and pioneering military geniuses of all time.

As Tariq and Musa prepared to advance towards the south of France, the news of Muslim success in Iberia reached Caliph al-Walid in Damascus and he ordered both Tariq and Musa to report to him immediately. Caliph al-Walid's unexpected intervention not only saved France, it also saved the rest of Europe from Muslim domination. After returning to Qayrawan where he stayed for a while, Tariq eventually set out for Damascus. According to some historians, Caliph al-Walid was still alive when Tariq reached Damascus. But, according to others, he had already died by the time Tariq arrived. Either way, on his arrival in Damascus, he received a lukewarm reception from the Umayyad ruling elites and he slipped into obscurity, dying in his late seventies. Tariq was not only the first Muslim to set foot on mainland Europe, he was also responsible – along with Abd al-Rahman I – for initiating more than seven centuries of Islamic rule in Spain. There is no doubt that Tariq was a truly inspirational military commander who, on account of his remarkable achievements on the battlefield, carved out a unique place for himself in the annals of history.

# 34

## Sultan Muhammad II (b.1429 - d.1481)

THE OTTOMAN EMPIRE (known in Arabic as *al-khilafah al-uthmaniyyah*) was one of the most powerful and enduring dynasties to have emerged in Islamic history. Founded in 1300 by the Turkish chieftain Uthman Bey (who was also known as Osman or Ottoman), this dynasty rapidly expanded under the stewardship of Uthman's successors. In all, thirty-six Sultans ruled the Ottoman Empire from 1300 to 1922. At its zenith, the Ottoman dynasty stretched from Yemen in the Middle East, as far as as Greece, Bulgaria, Rumania, Hungary, Albania and the former Yugoslav States of Serbia, Croatia, Bosnia, Macedonia and Kosovo in the West. The rise of the Ottoman Empire, therefore, represented a truly fascinating event not only in the history of Islam, but also of Europe not least because Ottoman contributions in the field of arts, science and architecture were unusually advanced for their time. Not surprisingly, more than five centuries of Ottoman achievements and legacy is today admired by Muslims and Europeans alike. By contrast, modern Turkey only comprises a fraction of its former extent. Also, caught between its glorious Islamic past and its future aspirations to be an integral part of the European Union, today Turkey finds itself at the

crossroads. If modern Turkey is confused about its future direction, then the reign of one of its greatest sons, Sultan Muhammad II, represents the complete opposite, namely the Ottoman's greatest triumph over its European adversaries.

When Sultan Murad II, the father of Muhammad II, ascended the Ottoman throne in 1421, he inherited a strong and united empire which he further consolidated during his reign of three decades, and in so doing established Ottoman dominance across a significant part of Europe, Asia and the Middle East. Born eight years after his father's accession to power, Muhammad II was considered far too weak and feeble to follow in his father's footsteps and take on the enormous responsibility of ruling a vast empire. Brought up and educated within the royal palace, he received a privileged upbringing and was surrounded by much wealth and luxury. As part of his royal education, he received tutorials in Arabic, the Qur'an and aspects of traditional Islamic sciences from some of the best teachers of the time. Since he was confined to his father's imposing royal palace, he had very limited contact with the outside world during his early days, but later he acquired a considerable interest in hunting, aspects of military strategy and tactics, and became fluent in five different languages.

When Sultan Murad's health began to deteriorate, he encouraged his young son to assume both the political and civil responsibilities of the Ottoman Empire. While he was still in his teens, Muhammad was appointed governor of the province of Amasya by his father to prepare him to ascend the Ottoman throne after his death. In 1451, Sultan Murad II died of apoplexy and, as expected, he was succeeded by his son, who became known as Sultan Muhammad II. Although he was barely twenty at the time, the young ruler soon rose to the challenge of political leadership and instigated much-needed reforms within the Ottoman political system. His personal courage, sound judgement and ability to carry out necessary reforms at a difficult time in the history of the Ottoman Empire reassured everyone that the affairs of the dynasty were indeed in safe hands. For the next thirty years, the Sultan not only sat securely on the Ottoman throne, he also carved out a unique place for himself in the annals of history by becoming one of the Muslim world's most successful military commanders, strategists and statesmen. As a ruler, he pursued his political and military objectives ruthlessly and this made him one of the most successful rulers of the Ottoman Empire. He also championed the cause of toleration, co-existence and mutual understanding between all his subjects. Indeed, Sultan Muhammad was fiercely independent-minded and he rarely asked others for advice or counsel. Unlike his predecessors, he preferred to lead a solitary life and even refused to share meals with his Ministers and viziers. And more often than not, he made decisions unilaterally without even consulting his personal secretaries or military advisors. If anyone dared to cross his path, he taught them a lesson they never forgot. As for his avowed opponents, he relentlessly pursued them without any mercy or forgiveness. However, it was his rare combination of foresight, great strategic ability, single-minded dedication to his task and this measure of ruthlessness which enabled the

Sultan to pursue his objectives with such efficiency and success.

Not surprisingly, soon after ascending the Ottoman throne, he initiated fresh diplomatic missions both in the East and the West and, in due course, he signed peace treaties with all the rival powers of his time. This move enabled him to focus his full attention on things closer to home. Although his predecessors did attempt to capture the ancient city of Constantinople from its Christian rulers, they failed to breach the city's heavily fortified walls. After the Prophet of Islam prophesied the Muslim conquest of the city back in the seventh century, Muslim armies had been knocking on its doors repeatedly, but without much success. Caliph Muawiyah ibn Abi Sufyan, the founder of the Umayyad dynasty, was one of the first Muslim rulers to send an expedition to capture Constantinople. Abu Ayyub al-Ansari, a distinguished companion of the Prophet, accompanied this expedition and died fighting valiantly against the Byzantines; he was buried on the outskirts of Constantinople. Many other attempts were later made by other Muslim rulers to annex Constantinople, but they also failed to capture this historic capital. As destiny would have it, the onus of taking this last bastion of the Holy Roman Empire fell on the shoulders of Sultan Muhammad II. Keen to expand his rule into mainland Europe, and thereby become the most powerful ruler of his time, the Sultan was determined to liberate Constantinople. The liberation of this city, he felt, would consolidate his position as the undisputed master of the Muslim world and earn him a unique place in the annals of history. Known to antiquity as Byzantium, Constantinople was named after the Roman Emperor Constantine, who moved the capital of his empire from Rome to this ancient and strategically situated city on the Bosporous, bridging the continents of Asia and Europe.

But the Sultan was not in a hurry to take the city. He decided against launching a hasty attack and, like his illustrious predecessors, be forced to retreat without taking the prize. As a gifted military strategist and inspirational leader,

Sultan Muhammad II was convinced that he could capture the city even though he knew it would not be an easy task, especially if the past was anything to go by. To achieve his objective, he knew he had to devise a meticulous plan and execute it with great care and determination. He began by recruiting military experts and engineers from Hungary and paid them handsomely to design a large quantity of cannonballs and several delivery systems. The engineers worked round the clock to develop cannons capable of firing stone balls of up to two-and-a-half feet in diameter, and weighing up to one hundred and fifty pounds each. The idea was to fire the stone balls at the city's heavily fortified walls in order to breach them and allow the Ottoman army to enter the city. As the weapons were being prepared, the Sultan gathered his one hundred and fifty thousand strong army, which included his twelve thousand elite infantrymen known as the Janissaries (derived from the Turkish *yen cheri*, meaning 'new troops'). They were also joined by a large number of religious leaders, scholars and Sufi saints who actively encouraged the Ottoman soldiers to fight valiantly. In 1453, the Sultan marched towards Constantinople with his contingent and camped close to the city's walls. Although he was only twenty-two at the time, the news of his arrival sent shock waves through Constantinople. In response, the reigning Byzantine Emperor Constantine ordered the city walls to be strengthened further to withstand the Ottoman assault on the city. But the Sultan was in no rush to take the city, so he patiently waited outside the city walls, biding his time and planning the siege. This prompted the Byzantine forces to order more supplies to sustain them during the siege, as they feared the Islamic army would not depart in the near future. It was not long before one of the Sultan's Ministers came to him with the news that a saintly Shaykh had informed him that the fall of Constantinople was now imminent. This prompted the Sultan to lay siege to the city in April 1453.

For the next month, the Ottoman army pounded the walls of Constantinople both from the land and sea. The bombardment caused serious damage to the triple-lined and heavily fortified walls of Constantinople, so that large gaps began to appear in the city's walls, although they were not large enough to enable the Ottoman army to enter the city. With limited supplies and only around eight thousand soldiers, the Byzantine Emperor managed to put up a good fight; but without any external assistance from other European nations he knew he was fighting a losing battle. Despite his repeated appeals to his fellow Christians across Europe, he received no help or support from any European nations. If they had responded, it is doubtful whether Sultan Muhammad would have been able to take the city. As it transpired, after weeks of heavy bombardment, the Ottoman army failed to make much progress. The defence put up by the Byzantines proved highly effective both on land and on sea. The problem required a swift and ingenious solution; the Ottoman ships had been unable to break through the boom laid across the mouth of the Golden Horn (the marine inlet protecting the northern side of the city). It was at this point, with the siege of Constantinople reaching its climax, that the Sultan showed his true colours as a military genius. He ordered his fleet of vessels to be transferred from the Bosphrous into the Golden Horn by land. All his generals assured him this was a mission impossible. Typical of the Sultan, he brushed their objections aside and ordered his army to construct a road, made from wooden planks, from one end of the Bosphorus and leading to the Golden Horn; animal fat was then applied to grease the planks so that the Ottoman fleet, which consisted of more than eighty large vessels, could "sail" overland and into the Golden Horn under the cover of darkness. Arriving within a few hundred yards of the northern walls of Constantinople, the Ottoman army took the enemy by complete surprise. From the sea, the vessels opened fire from the north, while the troops on the ground simultaneously launched cannonballs from the west, and in so doing they smashed the walls of Constantinople to rubble. The Sultan then performed his second miracle and called on his twelve thousand elite infantrymen, the Janissaries, and they attacked and routed the remaining enemy forces. The Ottoman army, led by the Sultan, then marched into the historic city of Constantinople. As for the Byzantine Emperor and his troops they died fighting bravely, but the victorious Ottomans entered the city greeted by shouts of *Allahu akbar* (or 'God is Most Great').

By conquering the historic city of Constantinople, the Sultan became known to posterity as *al-fatih*, meaning 'the Conqueror'. After entering the city, he changed its name to *Istanbul* (or the 'city of Islam'), and the more than eight-hundred-year-old prophecy of the Prophet Muhammad, which predicted the fall of Constantinople, became a reality on 29th May 1453. As expected, the Sultan went straight to the splendid surroundings of the Hagia Sophia (Aya Sofia) and offered his prayers there, and thanked the Almighty for the monumental victory granted to Islam. When a large city like Istanbul is captured after a long and protracted battle, normally looting and plundering ensues, but the Sultan acted swiftly to ensure no such disorder and lawlessness broke out. He treated the inhabitants of the city with respect and courtesy, allowing the Christians and Jews to continue to live there with their wealth and properties, if they so wished. In order to reassure his non-Muslim subjects, he even crowned the Greek patriarch with his own hands. Thereafter, he began to rebuild the city's political, civil and educational infrastructure. Unlike the city's previous Byzantine ruler, the Sultan's sense of fairness, justice, equality and tolerance surprised the city's non-Muslim populace. In addition to retaining all the city's historic buildings and institutions, he also refurbished all the buildings which were damaged during the siege. He also

ordered two minarets to be added to the exquisite Hagia Sophia, which came to symbolise Islam's great victory over its Byzantine rival. He then transferred the capital of the Ottoman Empire from Adrianople (Edirne) to Constantinople (Istanbul). Most astonishingly, the Sultan was only twenty-two years old when he achieved the unprecedented feat of conquering Constantinople.

During the next twenty-eight years of his reign, he helped to rebuild and repopulate the entire city, and in so doing transformed Istanbul into one of the world's most beautiful and attractive cities, thus reflecting its former glory again. As a generous patron of culture and the arts, the Sultan also commissioned the construction of mosques, schools, colleges, hospitals and promoted art, architecture and education throughout the Ottoman Empire. At the height of his power, the Sultan was considered to be the undisputed leader of the Islamic world, and the Ottoman Empire became one of the great superpowers of its time. His large army, consisting of well-paid and professional troops, was feared more than any other military force of the time. And his fleet of vessels, which roamed the seas without any opposition, was also considered to be the world's most advanced naval power of the time. After annexing Greece and venturing as far as Italy, the Sultan effectively became the Muslim world's (and also Europe's) most powerful political and military leader. There is no doubt that his thirty year reign represented a glorious period in the history of Islam. But it was as the conqueror of Constantinople that he became famous both in the East and the West. The venerable Sultan died at the age of forty-nine and he was the first Muslim ruler to be buried in Istanbul. Thanks also to him, today we still hear people talk about 'the day the ships came sailing overland'.

# 35

# Al-Biruni
# (b.973 – d.1051)

THE PROPHET OF Islam always encouraged his followers to seek knowledge from the cradle to grave, to which end he made the pursuit of knowledge and wisdom a compulsory obligation upon all Muslims, both male and female. The Qur'anic verses as well as the Prophet's sayings and exhortations, therefore, generated tremendous interest, enthusiasm and love for learning and education within the early Muslim community and this, in turn, prompted the early Muslim scholars, thinkers and writers to devote their entire lives to the pursuit, acquisition and dissemination of knowledge. 'Knowledge', said the blessed Prophet, 'is the lost property of the believer, so let him pick it up wherever he finds it.' Very few Muslim scholars and thinkers followed this Prophetic advice more rigorously and resolutely than the industrious and unusually gifted al-Biruni.

Abu Raihan Muhammad ibn Ahmad al-Biruni was born near the city of Khwarizm in the Central Asian province of Khurasan. As the birthplace of some of Islam's greatest scholars, thinkers and scientists (including the great Muhammad ibn Musa al-Khwarizmi), Khurasan at the time was a very large and thriving province. Though his real name was Muhammad, he became famous

by his surname, al-Biruni. Born and brought up in an intellectually friendly environment, young al-Biruni pursued his early education in Arabic and Persian languages, before receiving training in traditional Islamic sciences, literature and the physical sciences. From an early age, he became interested in mathematics and the physical sciences. Besides acquiring knowledge of the religious sciences under the guidance of prominent local scholars, for many years al-Biruni studied the physical sciences under the tutelage of notable authorities like Abu Nasr al-Mansur, who was not only a distinguished astronomer and mathematician of his time, but also a prominent student of the renowned Muslim astronomer and scientist Abul Wafa al-Bujazani. Based at the celebrated *bait al-hikmah* (or the 'House of Wisdom') in Baghdad, Abul Wafa became an astronomer *par excellence* and authored more than a dozen books and treatises on the sciences of his time. According to some historians, al-Biruni also studied under Abul Wafa's guidance, but this view has been dismissed by the majority of historians because he had died in 993, when al-Biruni was around twenty. Since al-Biruni was still living in Central Asia at the time, most of historians say it was very unlikely for him to have met, much less studied under the guidance of, that great astronomer.

Indeed, it was not until 995 that al-Biruni began to travel in pursuit of knowledge. During this period he visited some of the most prominent centres of learning in Central Asia, before finally settling down in the Persian city of Jurjan in 998 and working for its incumbent ruler, Shams al-Ma'ali Qabus ibn Washmgir. He lived and worked here for more than a decade and pursued advanced study and research in all branches of science and mathematics. At the age of twenty-seven, al-Biruni wrote his acclaimed book *Kitab al-Athar al-Baqiyah an al-Qur'an al-Khaliyah* (A Treatise on the Chronology of Ancient Nations). In this treatise, he explored the nature and concept of time in the light of historical evolution and change, focusing on the lives and times of the ancients and their fate. By developing an interesting and illuminating analysis of historical progression and geological changes, he was able to evaluate how such changes impacted on the lives of ancient peoples. In this book, he also analysed, and refuted, the views of those philosophers who considered time and creation to be eternal. Rather, he argued, historical evidence and changes in the earth's geological formation proved, if proof was required, that time and creation were finite. This argument, formulated by al-Biruni, reiterated the Qur'anic view on this matter, namely that only God is infinite and eternal, while His creation is finite and temporal. Since he was a keen student of the Qur'an, it is not surprising that al-Biruni's intellectual world-view was heavily influenced and underpinned by the Qur'anic concept of God, creation and time.

In 1012, al-Biruni returned to his native Khwarizm where he resumed his studies into different branches of learning under the guidance of Abd al-Samad al-Awwal, who was a prominent scholar of his time. While he was busy pursuing his studies, the political situation in Central Asia began to suddenly change for the worse, as the rulers of the different Central Asian fiefdoms fought each other for political and military supremacy. This state of affairs persisted until the Ghaznavids appeared on the political scene, under the able leadership of Sultan Mahmud, and assumed overall control of the region. In 1017, the Sultan marched into Khwarizm and occupied it and the surrounding region, taking al-Biruni and his tutor Abd al-Samad al-Awwal back to Ghazna as captives. Charged and found guilty of heresy, the latter was sentenced to death by the ruling elites, but al-Biruni's life was saved by the timely intervention of the Sultan's chief advisor. Already widely recognised as a distinguished scholar and scientist, Sultan Mahmud did not want to lose a scholar of al-Biruni's calibre, so he appointed him as his senior astronomer and scientific advisor. Hereafter, he regularly accompanied the Sultan on his journeys and military expeditions. Although al-Biruni personally disliked warfare – and often expressed his profound reservations about launching military expeditions to foreign countries (especially the Sultan's repeated incursions into India) – he persuaded Sultan Mahmud to preserve some of India's most ancient cultural and religious heritage. In other words, al-Biruni was not only a great scientist and intellectual, he was also a cultured individual who loved and admired different languages, traditions and cultures; thus he was very keen to preserve ancient Indian cultural heritage for the benefit of posterity.

He stayed in India from 1021 to 1031 and during this period he devoted all his spare time and energy to the pursuit of knowledge and wisdom. Despite being recognised as a versatile polymath who knew more about mathematics, astronomy, physics, medicine, chemistry, biology, history, philosophy, geography, geology, literature, poetry and religion than probably any other scholar of his time, he was eager to study and learn Indian sciences. Indeed, it would not be an exaggeration to say that al-Biruni was one of the most learned and gifted Muslim intellectuals of all time. His ability to learn and retain information on such a wide range of subjects and assimilate them to create a powerful intellectual synthesis was almost unrivalled. Just as a sponge sucks up water from a surface leaving it clean and dry, so al-Biruni's brain absorbed knowledge. And although during the early part of his life he specialised in mathematics, physics and astronomy, he later developed a considerable interest in other scientific disciplines such as chemistry, optics, pharmacology and medicine. His enthusiasm for religious, cultural and linguistic studies, as well as the social sciences, continued to increase as he matured, so that upon his arrival in India, he quickly mastered Sanskrit, the *lingua franca* of ancient India, which exposed him to the treasures and wisdom of the Indian civilisation. He studied anything and everything he could lay his hands on and became thoroughly familiar with Hindu religion, culture and traditions.

As one of the first Muslim scholars to travel to India and study there, al-Biruni was in a unique position to learn Sanskrit and undertake a decade-long wide-ranging study of, and research into, ancient Indian languages, culture, history, geography, religion and philosophy. The outcome of this research was his monumental *Kitab Tarikh al-Hind* (The History of India) which is today not only considered to be a unique source of information about ancient India, but is also considered to be a pioneering contribution to the study of human culture and civilisation. Written by one of the Muslim world's brightest minds, *Kitab Tarikh al-Hind* was one of the first books to be composed on the subject of inter-civilisational studies and dialogue. A quick browse through this book is sufficient to prove that al-Biruni acquired an intimate knowledge and understanding of Indian thought, culture and history; indeed, his knowledge of India's geography and demographic makeup was both extensive and authoritative. After surveying India's different climatic conditions and demographic configurations, he measured the size and distance of its major towns, cities and rivers with remarkable accuracy. He was also the first scholar to point out that the region known as the Indus valley consisted of largely delta land during the prehistoric period, which modern scientific research has confirmed as an accurate

assessment. Moreover, al-Biruni played a pivotal role in the translation of ancient Indian texts into Arabic and *vice versa*. For instance, he was one of the first to translate Euclid's *Elements* and Ptolemy's *Almagest* into Sanskrit, while his translation of the *Yoga-sutras* of Patanjali from the original Sanskrit into Arabic has remained extant to this day. In addition to this a number of his other works, including *Kitab al-Saidanah* (The Book of Civilisation), are littered with facts, figures and quotations from some of the most revered religious texts of Hinduism, including the *Bhagavad-Gita*, which proves that al-Biruni was thoroughly familiar with the religious beliefs, customs and practices of the Hindus.

As an outstanding polymath and prolific writer, al-Biruni wrote a large number of books and treatises; the exact number of his works is not known because most of them are no longer extant. However, according to some historians, he wrote one hundred and eighty books, while others suggest the number may be closer to two hundred books and treatises in total. Either way, some of his most famous books include *al-Qanun al-Mas'udi* (The Canon of Mas'ud), *Kitab Tarikh al-Hind* (The History of India), *Kitab al-Shamil* (The Book of General Knowledge), *Kitab al-Tafhim* (The Book of Understanding), *Kitab Tahdid Nihayat al-Amakin* (The Determination of the Co-ordinates of the Cities) and *Kitab al-Athar al-Baqiyah* (A Treatise on Choronolgy of the Ancient Nations). In these books, he provided a systematic analysis of a wide range of subjects including astronomy, cultural history, comparative religion, geology, philosophy and aspects of geography. His sharp intellect, coupled with his prodigious learning and remarkable linguistic skills, enabled al-Biruni to learn, assimilate and master knowledge from many different sources and write prolifically and authoritatively on almost all the sciences of his day. So much so that it is not possible to put al-Biruni into any one particular category of learners or seekers of knowledge. His learning and erudition encompassed such a wide range of subjects that he defies classification. It is remarkable how one person could have acquired so much knowledge within such a short lifespan, yet that is precisely what al-Biruni achieved. Most interestingly, despite being fluent in Persian and Sanskrit, he chose to write mainly in Arabic, perhaps because that was the *lingua franca* of the Islamic world at the time.

As a devout Muslim, al-Biruni never compromised his Islamic beliefs and practices in the pursuit of his scholarly aims and objectives. Unlike many other great Muslim scholars and thinkers (including Ibn Hazm al-Andalusi, Abul Fath Muhammad al-Shahrastani and Ibn Taymiyyah), his approach to the study of comparative religion was neither sectarian nor eclectic; rather, he had a profound respect and regard for all the world's great religions, cultures and traditions. And being a wise and tolerant writer and intellectual, he had no interest in the intra-Islamic sectarian conflicts which prevailed between the Sunnis and Shi'as at the time; although, according to some historians he was a Sunni Muslim who had a profound knowledge and understanding of the *shari'ah* (Islamic law) from the Sunni perspective. In other words, al-Biruni preferred to focus more on the universal dimension of Islam than engage in petty and often fruitless theological/doctrinal hair-splitting. To him, Islam was a universal faith and message which sought to unify people of different racial and cultural backgrounds, rather than divide them; thus he was in the habit of constantly emphasising the oneness of our common humanity. The incessant pursuit of knowledge was more important to him than anything else because it enabled a Muslim to acquire an in-depth understanding of his own faith, and also promote the need for greater awareness and understanding of religious and cultural diversity. In so doing, he hoped to foster inter-religious and cross-cultural understanding and tolerance between people of all backgrounds. In short, al-Biruni was not simply an outstanding visionary; he was also one of the great pioneers of inter-civilisational dialogue and understanding.

In 1031, when he was around fifty-eight, he left India and returned to Ghazna where he received a warm reception from Mas'ud, Sultan Mahmud's son and successor. Under the patronage of the new Ghaznavid Sultan, he composed most of his books and treatises, including his famous *al-Qanun al-Mas'udi* on the subject of astronomy, which – as the title of the book suggests – he dedicated to Sultan Mas'ud. Profoundly impressed, the Sultan sent him an elephant loaded with silver coins but he politely returned the gift, saying he served knowledge out of love rather than for material benefit. Al-Biruni spent the rest of his life in Ghazna and passed away at the age of seventy-eight. Unlike al-Kindi, Abu Bakr al-Razi, al-Farabi, Ibn Sina and al-Ghazali, the works of al-Biruni were not translated into European languages until relatively recently. As a result, his ideas and thoughts did not receive much circulation in medieval Europe. By contrast, in the East he is revered as one of the Muslim world's most influential thinkers and polymaths, so much so that in the intellectual history of Islam the period from 973 to 1051 is known as the 'Age of al-Biruni'.

# 36

## Sulaiman the Magnificent (b.1494 - d.1566)

HISTORIANS OFTEN CLASSIFY Islamic history into what is known as the 'classical' and 'modern' periods. Two of the greatest empires of the classical period were the Umayyad and the Abbasid dynasties which collectively ruled the Muslim world for around six centuries without serious opposition. But this was far from being the case during the modern period, when the political situation shifted radically within the Muslim world following the emergence of a number of regional powers. Three of the most influential political powers of this period were the Ottomans, the Safavids and the Mughals. Like the Safavid and Mughal dynasties, the Ottomans left a remarkable and enduring historical and cultural legacy. At the height of its power, the Ottoman Empire extended across three continents, namely Europe, Africa and Asia. Founded in 1300 by Uthman Bey, a Turkish chieftain, the Ottoman Empire became a formidable political and military superpower during the sixteenth century under the wise and able stewardship of Sulaiman the Magnificent, the tenth ruler of the Ottoman Empire.

Born in the Asiatic province of Trabzon, Sulaiman's great-grandfather was Sultan Muhammad II, the conqueror of Constantinople; his father,

Sultan Salim I, ascended the throne relatively late in life in 1512, and ruled for eight years with some success. His mother, Aishah, was a noble lady who became his first tutor and guide. Known to have been very wise and handsome, Sulaiman grew up under the watchful gaze of his loving parents. As the Sultan's only son, he was groomed for political and military leadership from the very outset, and thus he was expected to lead the vast Ottoman Empire into the new century. Although his early education consisted of tutorials in Arabic, the Qur'an and aspects of Islamic legal, ethical and moral principles and practices, he later gained first-hand knowledge of political and civil administration as governor of Crimea and other provinces, which provided him with much-needed experience of political administration and diplomacy before he ascended the Ottoman throne.

In 1520, Sultan Salim died at the age of fifty-four, having successfully spearheaded a series of military expeditions and thereby consolidated Ottoman rule across much of Europe, Asia and Africa. As expected, Sulaiman succeeded his father without facing any political or military opposition. Only twenty-six at the time of his accession, he instantly became one of the most powerful rulers of his time. The age of Sulaiman was a unique period in history because a number of other famous rulers such as Emperor Charles V of Germany, Henry VIII and Queen Elizabeth of England, Francis I of France, Emperor Akbar of India and Shah Ismail of Safavid Persia became witnesses to each others' greatness. However, Sulaiman outshone all his contemporaries by the force of his sublime character and personality. As the ruler of the vast Ottoman Empire, which extended all the way from Europe as far as the Middle East and Asia, he filled the length and breadth of his dominion with peace, justice, fairness, tolerance and prosperity. With Islam being the official religion of the State, Sulaiman made Turkish the main language of his empire and promoted it throughout his dominion.

As a gesture of goodwill, immediately after ascending the Ottoman throne, he abolished all the harsh policies which were enacted and implemented by his father during his reign. He also freed all the slave labourers his father had brought from Egypt and took measures to restore all the money, goods and properties confiscated by his father from the Ottoman traders for engaging in commerce with the Safavids, who were their main rivals. Sulaiman's wise and decisive actions instantly won over the people to his side. He made it clear that he would not tolerate injustice and oppression, no matter who happened to be the perpetrator. He then took action to root out bribery and corruption from within Ottoman central Government, as well as provincial political and administrative circles. His wide ranging reforms, coupled with his determination to eradicate political corruption from within the Ottoman Government, made him very popular with his people who soon became very fond of him for his wisdom, generosity and fair play. Since the main purpose of his reforms was to eradicate injustice and corruption from all levels of his administration, he established an imperial council (*divan*) which consisted of Government Ministers, senior civil servants, military generals, provincial governors, senior judges and some of the most prominent *ulama* (religious scholars)

of the time. The members of this council were required to oversee the affairs of the State and regularly discuss and debate all the significant issues of the day. They were also required to monitor existing Governmental policies and where appropriate produce new policy proposals, although the final decision always rested with the Sultan himself. By restructuring and reorganising the Ottoman Government, Sulaiman hoped to communicate and engage directly with his subjects; this also enabled his people to voice their concerns and provide regular feedback on the performance of his Government.

After setting up the imperial council, Sulaiman reformed the archaic Ottoman legal system. He was not interested in tinkering with the system; rather he completely overhauled the entire legal system in order to ensure that justice, fairness and equality prevailed across his empire. The legal system implemented by Sulaiman enabled both Muslims and non-Muslims to seek redress for their grievances through the Ottoman courts; these courts applied a combination of *shari'ah* (Islamic law) and imperial Ottoman law (*qanun*). Like the other Ottoman rulers, Sulaiman's political thinking was influenced by his desire to see peace, justice and prosperity prevail across his dominion; indeed, their desire to render justice and win the hearts and minds of their people often provided the Ottoman rulers with much needed political legitimacy. For this reason, Sulaiman was determined, if not ruthless, in his pursuit of political, legal and administrative reforms. And it was not long before he succeeded in restoring peace, security and prosperity across the Ottoman Empire, thus further consolidating his position as the supreme ruler of the Muslim world. Impressed by his political, social, economic and legal reforms, his subjects conferred on him the coveted title of the 'law-giver' or *qanuni*.

With peace and prosperity restored throughout the Ottoman Empire, Sulaiman turned his attention to international politics and diplomacy. At the time, the rebellious activities of the governor of Syria became a pressing issue for him. He may have been a gentle, peace loving and generous sovereign, but he was far from being a pacifist. Faced with open rebellion in Syria, he mustered a large army and sent an expedition to Syria to bring its treacherous governor to heel. In the ensuing battle, the governor and his supporters were routed by Sulaiman's forces. After dispatching a new governor to Syria to oversee the administrative affairs of the country, Sulaiman was also forced to take action against the King of Hungary for humiliating his emissary, who had gone there to collect the annual levy from the King. So it was that in 1521, at the age of twenty-seven, Sulaiman organised a large expedition and marched towards the city of Belgrade, which he captured after seven days of heavy fighting. The conquest of Belgrade was a major achievement considering that the city had resisted the Ottomans on more than one occasion, including during the reign of his great grandfather Sultan Muhammad (Fatih) II. After establishing a garrison in Belgrade, he began to devise his next military plan.

A year later, Sulaiman moved towards the strategically important Mediterranean island of Rhodes, which at the time was firmly in the grip of the fanatical Knights of St John. When the Knights began to intensify their subversive activities against the Ottomans, Sulaiman resolved to deal with them once and for all. Accompanied by a one hundred thousand strong force and three hundred formidable vessels, he spearheaded a massive military assault on the island. The Knights fought back with great determination and resisted the Ottoman army for nearly nine months before they were forced to surrender. But the Sultan treated the people of the island with kindness, sympathy and respect. He also agreed to let those Knights who did not wish to live there anymore to leave with their personal belongings. Then, in 1526, Sulaiman authorised one of the most important campaigns of his reign, namely the Ottoman invasion of Hungary. Equipped with superior weaponry, the Ottoman forces left their military base in Belgrade and marched towards Budapest, the capital of Hungary. In the ensuing battle Louis II, the King of Hungary, and

his senior officials died fighting as the Ottoman forces, led by Sulaiman, crushed the Hungarians. After building a large military base in Budapest, he returned to Istanbul, having subdued most of his enemies. But a few years later, in 1529, Sulaiman was again forced to return to Budapest to put an end to a civil war which had broken out there between his governor, Zapolye, and a rival militia led by Ferdinand, the brother of King Charles V of Germany. Following a fierce battle, he entered Budapest and restored peace and security throughout the city. He then proceeded to Vienna and laid siege to that historic city. This siege lasted nearly three months before a combination of limited provisions, dwindling military supplies and adverse weather forced him to lift the siege and return to Istanbul. The Ottoman failure to take Vienna represented a major turning-point in both Islamic and European history, because this brought an end to the Ottoman advance into the rest of Europe.

As soon as Sulaiman lifted his siege on the city, the people of Vienna, and the rest of Europe, rejoiced and celebrated. This day became known throughout Europe as 'the Day of Deliverance'. Subsequently, Sulaiman spearheaded many other minor military campaigns across Europe, Persia and Egypt during his reign. History shows he was a veteran military commander who personally led no fewer than thirteen major military expeditions during his rule, ten of which were in Europe, and the other three in Asia. He developed and strengthened Ottoman military power and supremacy like never before. His fleet of warships became one of the world's largest naval powers under the stewardship of his gifted Admiral Khair al-Din Barbarossa, so that the Ottoman navy had complete supremacy of the seas. His vast army was also one of the most disciplined and professional combat forces of the time. In short, under Sulaiman's able leadership, the Ottoman Empire became one of the world's great military superpowers.

Away from the battlefield, Sulaiman distinguished himself as a generous patron of learning, culture, art, architecture and science. During his reign he built scores of beautiful and breathtaking mosques, schools, colleges, palaces and other similar buildings. His most famous architectural works include the magnificent Sulaimaniyyah Complex built in Istanbul by Mimar Sinan between 1550 and 1557; Sinan was his personal builder and one of the world's greatest architects. This huge, but equally superb, mosque was meant to symbolise the glory of Ottoman power and might in the form of architecture. Since this period represented the height of Ottoman political, military and architectural achievement, Sulaiman also became recognised as the undisputed ruler and champion of the Muslim world at the time. In addition to the Sulaimaniyyah Complex, he constructed many other impressive buildings including the elegant Salimiyyah Complex, the impressive Bayazid Jami mosque and the awe-inspiring Sehzade Complex. These magnificent buildings completely transformed the skyline of the historic city of Istanbul. As a profoundly cultured and enlightened sovereign, and an accomplished poet and devout Muslim, Sulaiman showered his subjects with money, wealth and gifts at a time when his European counterparts were busy oppressing, looting and humiliating their people. According to the historians of the time, the European visitors to Istanbul returned to their native countries to relate stories about Sulaiman's sense of justice, fair play, tolerance and civility. Indeed, the Europeans not only considered him to be an exemplary ruler, they also rated his achievements very highly and wished their own rulers were as just, civilised and enlightened as he was. That is why Sulaiman became known throughout Europe as *el magnifico* (or 'the Magnificent'). Moreover, he was the first Muslim ruler to develop formal diplomatic relations with several prominent European powers including France, Venice and England, and in so doing he actively promoted trade and commerce with the rest of Europe.

On a personal level, Sulaiman was an educated, gentle and determined individual. Being deeply religious, in his spare time he used to commit the Qur'an to paper, and copies of the Qur'an written by his own hand are still extant to this day. More importantly, he was a humble sovereign who ruled his people with understanding, a sense of justice and tolerance. He was not only 'the magnificent'; he was also the greatest of all Ottoman Sultans and arguably one of the Muslim world's most successful rulers. He died at the age of seventy-two and was buried in his beloved Istanbul. After his death, the Ottoman Empire began to decline irreversibly.

# 37

## Ja'far al-Sadiq
## (b.700 - d.765)

IF THE ACQUISITION and dissemination of knowledge are noble and praiseworthy deeds, then the ability to acquire profound insight into religious teachings and mould one's life according to that teaching is yet more superior. Though a perceptive and penetrating mind is a heavenly gift which is bestowed on only a chosen few, the ability to move from the exterior to the interior – and from the form to the substance – and develop an intimate knowledge and understanding of the essence of Islamic spirituality, moral and ethical teachings and values, and remain completely focused on that path throughout one's life is, by all accounts, a truly great achievement. One man who attained this exalted ability through his single-minded devotion and dedication to Islamic principles and practices, notwithstanding all the obstacles that were placed in his path by his enemies and detractors, was the celebrated Ja'far al-Sadiq.

Ja'far ibn Muhammad ibn Ali Zain al-Abideen ibn Hussain ibn Ali was born in the sacred city of Madinah (in present-day Saudi Arabia) into the most illustrious and noble family of Arabia. His father, Muhammad al-Baqir, was the son of Ali Zain al-Abideen, the son of Hussain ibn Ali, the hero of Karbala and son of the fourth Caliph of Islam. Ja'far was, therefore, a direct descendant of the Prophet Muhammad through his youngest and most beloved daughter, Fatimah. On his mother's side, his ancestral pedigree was also a noble one. His mother, Umm Farwa, was the great-granddaughter of Caliph Abu Bakr, through his son Muhammad. Born and raised in a family where Islam first planted its seeds, young Ja'far absorbed Islamic knowledge and wisdom directly from the descendants of its first followers and disseminators. By rubbing shoulders with those who exuded Islamic wisdom and spirituality as taught and exemplified by the Prophet and his close companions, Ja'far developed an instant affinity with Islam as a religion and a way of life. Since his father Muhammad al-Baqir was one of Madinah's leading scholars of the time, he taught him Arabic language, grammar, Qur'an, *hadith* (Prophetic traditions) and *fiqh* (Islamic jurisprudence).

When Ja'far was a youngster his paternal grandfather, Ali Zain al-Abideen, was still alive, although it is not certain whether he studied Islam under his guidance. However, the historians are agreed that he pursued his advanced Islamic education under the tutelage of his maternal grandfather, al-Qasim ibn Muhammad, who was one of the greatest Islamic scholars of his generation and a pre-eminent *tabi* (successor of the Prophet's companions). Being the city of the Prophet, Madinah was at the time one of the foremost centres of Islamic learning and education. This was because during the early part of the eighth century, some of the Muslim world's most illustrious Islamic scholars, such as al-Qasim ibn Muhammad, happened to live and teach there. As great authorities on the Qur'an, *hadith* and *fiqh*, these eminent scholars of Islam not only became the fountainhead of true Islamic knowledge, wisdom and spirituality, but also attracted students from across the Muslim world who came to study under their guidance. No doubt their presence in Madinah also spurred young Ja'far to attend their classes and expand his knowledge and understanding of the Islamic sciences.

As a bright and gifted student, he mastered Islamic sciences while he was still in his early twenties and his fame soon began to spread throughout Madinah on account of his profound intellectual ability and deep insight into Islamic moral, ethical and spiritual teachings. Being also polite, gentle and spiritually-orientated, he never engaged in any form of political dispute or intellectual debate; he even refrained from attacking or criticising others. Likewise, he shunned frivolous and time-consuming activities, and instead devoted all his spare time to prayers, recitation of the Qur'an and other devotional activities. It was not long before his breadth of learning and spirituality attracted students from Madinah and across the Muslim world. From his base in Madinah, he began to deliver regular lectures on all aspects of Islam. His lectures were attended by some of the Muslim world's greatest scholars, thinkers and historians, including Abu Hanifah, Malik ibn Anas, Muhammad ibn Ishaq, Yahya ibn Sa'id, Sufyan al-Thawri, Shuba ibn al-Hajjaj, Sufyan ibn Uyayna, Abd al-Malik ibn Juraij and Jabir ibn Hayyan among others. Indeed, according to the historians, he taught Qur'an, *hadith*, *fiqh* and aspects of medicine, alchemy and Islamic spirituality to more than four thousand students from across the entire Islamic world. Revered by

his contemporaries for his unrivalled mastery of the Islamic sciences, Ja'far was also considered to be one of the most meticulous narrators of Prophetic traditions – so much so that his peers conferred the title of *al-sadiq* (or 'the truthful') on him due to his scrupulousness as an *hadith* narrator . Indeed, according to some historians, even Wasil ibn Ata, the founder of Mu'tazilism (philosophical rationalism), had attended his lectures for a short period, although there is no conclusive historical evidence to prove this claim.

Thus, as a scholar and teacher, Ja'far was a powerful intellectual trail-blazer who personally taught and mentored some of the Muslim world's most influential Islamic scholars and thinkers. No single other Muslim scholar could claim to have trained and nurtured so many outstanding Islamic scholars and thinkers at any one time in the intellectual history of Islam. Most interestingly, many of his students were his contemporaries. For instance, Abu Hanifah, the famous Islamic jurist (*faqih*) and founder of *hanafi madhhab* (which is today by far the most widely-followed school of Islamic legal thought), was the same age as Ja'far, while Muhammad ibn Ishaq, the celebrated author of the first comprehensive biography of the Prophet, was only four years younger than him. Ja'far, it should also be pointed out, lived at a time when learning and pursuit of knowledge was an integral part of Islamic culture and way of life. In those days, one's racial origin, social class or age was not considered to be an important factor, especially when it came to learning and education. Also, since most, if not all, of the teachers in those days taught and imparted knowledge free of charge, students of all ages and backgrounds flocked to Madinah to study Islamic principles and practices under the guidance of the city's leading tutors. Ja'far was one such scholar whose lectures attracted students of all ages and backgrounds, thanks to his unrivalled mastery of Islamic sciences and spirituality.

Indeed, his interpretation of the Qur'an and *hadith* was so refreshing and wide-ranging that a new school of Islamic legal thought, the *ja'fari madhhab*, later emerged and spread to different parts of the Muslim world. Like the *hanafi, shafi'i, maliki, hanbali* and *zaydi madhahib*, it also originated and evolved during this formative period of Islamic legal thought. Living in a tumultuous period in Islamic history, when political tyranny and corruption became widespread within the Umayyad hierarchy, Ja'far deliberately stayed away from the limelight. Although he was born during the reign of the Umayyad Caliph Abd al-Malik ibn Marwan, and lived through the reigns of nine other Umayyad rulers, as well as two Abbasid Caliphs, he did not join or support any particular political party or group. Despite the tyranny of some Umayyad rulers, Ja'far remained politically neutral, even though those close to the ruling political elites often accused him of siding with their opponents. They even fabricated evidence in order to implicate him in political disputes and intrigues, but Ja'far always stood his ground and proved his innocence. Since political rivalry between the ruling Umayyads and their Abbasid counterparts became very intense then, Ja'far chose to tread the path of political neutrality – a path which was fraught with many obstacles and dangers – especially considering that he was very popular with the masses. However, he stuck to his principles and remained very firm and politically impartial throughout his life.

Notwithstanding his political neutrality, Ja'far was summoned to Baghdad on several occasions by the Abbasid ruler Abu Ja'far al-Mansur, who accused him of taking part in political intrigues and fanning the flames of civil unrest and social disturbance. A tall, slim and always neatly dressed Ja'far attended the charismatic Caliph's court on more than one occasion and refuted the charges levelled against him with great wit and eloquence. When al-Mansur called him to his Caliphal court in Baghdad for the very last time, everyone at the court expected the Caliph to lose his patience and treat Ja'far harshly, but as soon as the great scholar walked into the packed Caliphal court, al-Mansur rose to his feet, paid his respects to him and invited Ja'far to sit next

to him. The Caliph's attitude and behaviour towards Ja'far surprised everyone at the Caliphal court. Suddenly, out of the blue, there appeared a fly which began to distract the Caliph while he was busy talking to Ja'far. Soon the Caliph lost his patience and asked the learned scholar if he could explain why God had created flies. A sharp, witty, but equally fearless, Ja'far replied that God had created flies in order to humble the pride of tyrannical and despotic rulers. Everyone inside the court was taken aback by his answer, except al-Mansur; he understood the full meaning and import of Ja'far's answer and treated the great scholar with courtesy and respect during his stay in Baghdad.

Moreover, whenever Ja'far visited Baghdad, the people of that city always gave him a warm reception. The scholars and students of Baghdad also came in their droves to learn from him and ask him questions on different aspects of Islam. From time to time, he delivered lectures on the Qur'an, *hadith*, aspects of *fiqh* and Islamic spirituality, all of which attracted large audiences. As one of the most influential Islamic scholars of his generation, Ja'far was respected and revered by both kings and paupers, rulers and the ruled, and scholars and students throughout the Islamic world. According to Ja'far, the most learned person is the one who is most acquainted with the differences of opinion (*ikhtilaf*) among the scholars. Not surprisingly, he was considered to be the most learned when it came to understanding, analysing and explaining the differences of opinion which existed among the Islamic scholars concerning the interpretation of the Qur'an, *hadith* and aspects of *fiqh*. After closely studying and analysing the different strands of opinions which prevailed in Madinah, Makkah, Kufah, Basrah, Baghdad and Damascus at the time, he became an unrivalled master and exponent of comparative *fiqh*.

Keen to put his knowledge of Islamic jurisprudence to the test, Caliph al-Mansur once asked Abu Hanifah, who was himself an outstanding jurist, to prepare a list of forty of the most difficult and complex legal questions he could think of, and put them to Ja'far in front of a packed audience in his Caliphal court; the ingenious Ja'far answered all the questions and did so without falling into the trap set by al-Mansur. He answered the questions like this: the people of Madinah say "so and so" on this issue, while the jurists in Baghdad say "this or that". The scholars of Kufah disagree with them but the experts in Makkah agree, while the specialists in Damascus hold a completely different view altogether. He concluded his answers by saying that one was free to choose any of these views because they were all valid and acceptable in their own right. This way, he was able to dumbfound al-Mansur and his cohorts, who tried to pick holes in his beliefs and practices. As a gifted scholar and intellectual, Ja'far was blessed with a perceptive and penetrating mind which enabled him to delve deep and acquire profound insight into the moral, ethical and spiritual dimensions of Islam. On a personal level, he led a simple and austere lifestyle, devoted solely to the service of Islam. This earned him much fame across the Muslim world, so that even his critics could not help but admire him for his piety, honesty and profound learning.

Today Ja'far is widely revered for his incalculable service to traditional Islamic learning and scholarship. However, within the *ithna 'ashari* (Twelver) Shi'a branch, he occupies the position of the sixth Imam. The other five Shi'a Imams include Caliph Ali, his sons Hasan, Hussain, Ali Zain al-Abideen and Muhammad al-Baqir,

the father of Ja'far al-Sadiq. According to the Shi'a, the Prophet Muhammad communicated some special knowledge (including that of the unseen) to Ali, and this knowledge passes from one generation to another through a chain of twelve hereditary Imams, of which Ja'far was the sixth. Since the Shi'a branch of Islam is divided into a number of sects and sub-sects their understanding of the doctrine of Imamate, and who is entitled to occupy that position, varies from one group to another. By contrast, the Sunnis, who form the vast majority of the world's Muslim population, do not subscribe to the doctrine of Imamate; they consider Ja'far to be one of the Muslim world's most gifted scholars and sages. And since it is not possible to ascertain whether the various spiritual teachings and moral aphorisms which are today attributed to Ja'far were his own work, or attributed to him by others, it is not surprising that the publishers of *The Lantern of the Path* pointed out that there was no conclusive evidence to prove whether Ja'far was the real author of this book.

Ja'far al-Sadiq died at the age of around sixty-five and was buried in the famous cemetery of Jannat al-Baqi in Madinah. When the news of his death was relayed across the Muslim world, great luminaries like Abu Hanifah, Malik ibn Anas and Jabir ibn Hayyan paid glowing tributes to him. Even Abu Ja'far al-Mansur, the incumbent Abbasid Caliph, was forced to concede that Ja'far al-Sadiq had been the real sovereign of the Muslims.

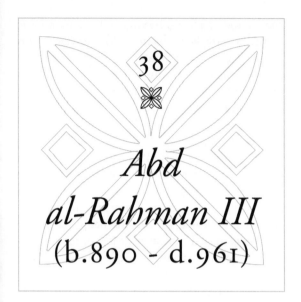

# 38

# Abd al-Rahman III (b.890 - d.961)

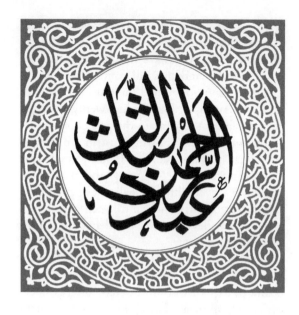

THE UMAYYADS RULED the Muslim world from 661 to 750, but when the Abbasids came to power they put most of the Umayyad princes to the sword. Only a handful of Umayyad princes escaped the ensuing massacre. Abd al-Rahman, the grandson of Umayyad ruler Hisham ibn Abd al-Malik, was one of them. He fled Damascus and travelled on foot and by ship for many years before he finally reached North Africa, where he received a warm welcome from the Berber tribe of Banu Nafisa (in present-day Morocco). During his stay there he received news of the political chaos and disorder which prevailed across the sea in *al-andalus* (Islamic Spain) at the time. When he was informed that the Muslims in Spain had become bitterly divided into two factions – one faction supported the reigning governor, Yusuf ibn Abd al-Rahman al-Fihri, while the other group opposed him – Prince Abd al-Rahman immediately contacted the governor's opponents and enlisted their help in order to overthrow him. In 756, he led an army into battle and defeated the governor's forces before proceeding to Cordova, the capital of *al-andalus*, and in so doing inaugurated Umayyad rule in Spain. Known also as *al-dhakil* (or 'the Immigrant') and *sahib al-andalus* (or 'the Lord of

Islamic Spain') on account of his outstanding political leadership and organisational ability, Abd al-Rahman and his descendants went on to rule Muslim Spain for nearly three centuries. During this period Muslim Spain produced a number of influential rulers, but the most outstanding of them all was Caliph Abd al-Rahman III.

Abd al-Rahman ibn Muhammad, better known as Abd al-Rahman III, was born in Cordova during the reign of his grandfather, Amir Abdullah. When he was still a boy, his father was poisoned by one of his uncles due to political in-fighting. Young Abd al-Rahman therefore grew up under the care of his Frankish mother, Muzna, and his grandfather, Amir Abdullah. As a youngster, he received a varied education including tutorials on the Qur'an, Islamic moral and ethical teachings, as well as Arabic literature, poetry and history. He was short in height, of muscular build, had dark blue eyes and somewhat reddish hair, making his appearance more European than Arab – perhaps because his mother, Muzna, and grandmother, Iniga, were of European origin. And although his grandfather Abdullah ruled Islamic Spain from 888 to 912, he proved to be both incompetent and cruel; not surprisingly, political instability and civil disorder soon broke out across the land. His decision to use force rather than engage in dialogue with his opponents not only created political strife and mass discontent against his rule, but also undermined the staus quo and alienated his people. During his twenty-two year reign he failed to maintain the peace, prosperity and progress achieved by his illustrious predecessors (such as Abd al-Rahman II and Muhammad I between 822 and 886). Young Abd al-Rahman was aware of the difficult challenges which confronted his country and contributed as much as he could to alleviating the problems until Amir Abdullah died in 912.

He succeeded his grandfather at the age of twenty-two and became the new ruler of Islamic Spain. By then he was already recognised as an experienced politician, having played a prominent role in the country's political and civil administration under his grandfather. However, unlike his grandfather, he became an able, wise and gifted ruler and politician. Widely respected and admired by his people, his accession to the throne brought much joy and happiness throughout the country. Being also a just, kind and benevolent ruler, his reign marked a fresh start for Islamic Spain. Since Abd al-Rahman considered the post of Caliphate to be an enormous trust and responsibility which his people had placed on his young shoulders, he was determined not to let them down. Immediately after becoming Caliph, his main priority was to restore political stability and civil order across *al-andalus*. He thus appealed to his people for their help, for without their support and co-operation, he told them, he would not be able to pull Islamic Spain back from the brink of civil war. He spelled out the choice facing his people in no uncertain terms; the choice, he stated, was one of life or death, survival or extinction. Without political unity, social solidarity and religious harmony, the Muslims of Spain faced the serious danger of being obliterated by their Christian adversaries who were closely monitoring the socio-political situation in Islamic Spain at the time. The Abbasid Caliph in Baghdad, he reminded his people, would not come to their aid should the neighbouring Christian powers decide to attack *al-andalus*. His message to his people was very loud and clear: unite or you will be consigned to the dustbin of history. Moved by Abd al-Rahman's message of hope, reconciliation and unity, the antagonistic and bitterly divided Muslims of Spain finally laid down their arms and united under his wise and able leadership. Unlike his grandfather, Abd al-Rahman was a gifted communicator who preferred to talk and engage in dialogue with his opponents rather than use force. His honesty and friendly approach endeared him to his people so much that he managed to restore peace, order and stability across the country within the first three months of his reign.

After establishing political and civil order across Cordova and its immediate surroundings, Abd al-Rahman turned his attention to other major cities like Seville and Toledo, which at the time were ruled by various dissident groups who had taken control of those cities in open defiance of the central Government. Determined not to allow this state of affairs to persist for much longer, he sent delegations to the rulers of those cities with a view to reasserting his political authority over them. But when these self-appointed rulers rejected his conciliatory measures, he launched military actions against them. His forces routed their enemies and marched into Seville in 913 without encountering much resistance. However, Muhammad, the governor of Seville, allied himself with Abd al-Rahman and continued to serve as governor of that city. By contrast, Toledo presented a different proposition altogether. When the ruler and people of the city resisted Abd al-Rahman's forces, he laid siege to it, and it was nearly two years before the people of Toledo relented and unconditionally surrendered to him.

During this period Abd al-Rahman found himself fighting a battle on two fronts. On the one hand, he was busy fighting the rebellious Muslim rulers inside Islamic Spain itself; on the other hand he was forced to take action against the encroaching Christians of the north who, encouraged by the chaos which prevailed within the Muslim territories at the time, decided to launch fresh raids against them. Since Ordono II, the Christian ruler of Leon, was the chief instigator of these raids, Abd al-Rahman sent an expedition and inflicted a crushing defeat on his forces in 923. The subjugation of the Christians in the north brought much-needed peace and tranquility in *al-andalus*. He then instigated military action against the perennial mischief-maker, Ibn Hafsun the ruler of Bobastro, and brought that principality under his suzerainty in 928. After successfully subduing these cities, Abd al-Rahman finally restored peace, order and security across much of *al-andalus*. Thanks to his vision, courage and bravery, Abd al-Rahman won over the hearts and minds of his people. Thus, in 929, at the age of thirty-nine, he became the undisputed master of Islamic Spain and adopted the title of *al-khalifah al-nasir li-din Allah* ('the Caliph, the Defender of the Religion of God'). This was to mark the beginning of a new era of political stability, economic prosperity and great scientific and cultural achievements across Muslim Spain under the outstanding leadership and patronage of Caliph Abd al-Rahman III.

Indeed, under his stewardship, Spain became a beacon of light for the rest of Europe. He built beautiful mosques, schools, colleges and promoted learning and education throughout *al-andalus*. When there was hardly a college or library worth its name in Europe, *al-andalus* boasted some of the finest, and also largest, libraries and educational institutions in the Western world. Subsequently, students flocked from the rest of Europe to Cordova, the magnificent capital of Islamic Spain, in order to study under the tutelage of some of Europe's most influential Muslim philosophers, scientists and intellectuals like Ibn Hazm, Ibn Bajjah (Avempace), Ibn Tufayl (Abubacer) and Ibn Rushd (Averroes) who transformed the Academy in Cordova into one of the world's most dazzling centres of higher education and research. Also during Abd al-Rahman's glorious reign, Cordova reached its cultural height, boasting more than six hundred

elegant mosques, fifty hospitals, nine hundred public baths and countless markets; the town centre was in turn surrounded by two hundred thousand beautiful houses, connected by well-planned roads and streets which were illuminated during the night by roadside lamps – and at a time when the rest of Europe was still lingering in the Dark Ages. The thriving and tolerant civil society, known as the *convivencia*, fostered by Caliph Abd al-Rahman enabled everyone including Muslims, Jews and Christians to live and work together in peace and tranquility. The Jews were granted full freedom to lead their lives according to the dictates of their faith and culture. Indeed, under Islamic rule, the Jews and Judaism flourished in Spain to the extent that this period of Jewish history is widely considered to be the Golden Age of Judaism by the European Jews. Renowned Jewish thinkers such as Ibn Gabirol and Judah Halevi also lived and thrived in Islamic Spain.

Then, in 936, Caliph Abd al-Rahman ordered the construction of a new palace city which became known as *madinat al-zahra* (or 'the dazzling city'). This mammoth project took more than forty years to complete and became known later as the 'tenth century Versailles'. The splendour and magnificence of *madinat al-zahra* was simply breathtaking. Considered to have been an architectural masterpiece, it remained an unrivalled architectural edifice throughout Europe for a long time. And although it is true that Abd al-Rahman started this project, unfortunately he could not complete it; it was in fact Caliph al-Hakam, his son and successor, who finally achieved this in 976. As a passionate builder, Abd al-Rahman also constructed a large number of magnificent palaces, but nothing was to compare with his immortal *madinat al-zahra* in both size and beauty. It was not only a landmark in European cultural history; it was also a lasting tribute to the memory of one of Islamic Spain's most influential rulers.

In his book, *The Muslims of Spain*, the distinguished historian Stanley Lane-Poole summed up Islamic achievements in Spain in these words:

'For nearly eight centuries, under her Moham-medan rulers, Spain set to all Europe a shining example of a civilized and enlightened State. Her fertile provinces, rendered doubely prolific by the industry and engineering skill of her conquerors, bore fruit a hundredfold. Cities innumerable sprang up in the rich valleys of the Guadelqui-vir and the Guadiana, whose names, and names only, still commemorate the vanished glories of their past. Art, literature, and science prospered, as they then prospered nowhere else in Europe. Students flocked from France and Germany and England to drink from the fountain of learning, which flowed only in the cities of the Moors. The surgeons and doctors of Andalusia were in the van of science: women were encouraged to devote themselves to serious study, and lady doctors were not unknown among the people of Cordova. Mathematics, astronomy and botany, history, philosophy and jurisprudence were to be mastered in Spain, and Spain alone. The practi-cal work of the field, the scientific methods of irrigation, the arts of fortification and shipbuild-ing, the highest and most elaborate products of the loom, the graver and the hammer, the potter's wheel and the mason's trowel, were brought to perfection by the Spanish Moors. In the practice of war no less than in the arts of peace they long stood supreme. Their fleets disputed the command of the Mediterranean with the Fa-timites, while their armies carried fire and sword through the Christian marches. The Cid himself, the national hero, long fought on the Moorish side, and in all save education was more than half a Moor. Whatsoever makes a kingdom great and prosperous, whatsoever tends to refinement and civilisation, was found in Moslem Spain.'

Although other Spanish Muslim rulers like Abd al-Rahman II, Muhammad I and al-Hakam II had also achieved a tremendous amount and contributed greatly to the prosperity and progress of *al-andalus*, it was during the glorious reign of Abd al-Rahman III that Islamic Spain reached its political, social, cultural and intel-lectual zenith. His reign of forty-nine years was therefore a truly remarkable period in the history of Islamic Spain and Europe as a whole. In less than half a century, he transformed a political-ly disunited and economically ruined country into one of medieval Europe's most dazzling and prosperous nations. As an enlightened, tolerant and generous ruler, he showered his subjects with wealth and gifts and they, in turn, revered him more than anyone else. Caliph Abd al-Rahman III died in Cordova at the age of seventy-one. *Al-andalus* began to decline after his death and the Umayyads of Spain were eventually ousted from power in 1031.

# 39

## Ibn Ishaq
## (b.704 - d.767)

KEEN TO PRESERVE and protect the Qur'anic revelation and the Prophetic traditions (*hadith*), the close companions of the Prophet Muhammad began to memorise and meticulously record the Divine revelation and his sermons and exhortations for their own guidance, and for the benefit of future generations. Some of the most prominent companions who recorded the Prophet's sayings and sermons during his own lifetime included Abdullah ibn Amr ibn al-As, Abdullah ibn Umar, Abdullah ibn Abbas, Anas ibn Malik and Ali ibn Abi Talib. Following the death of the Prophet in 632, written information about his life and Prophetic career began to proliferate. Renowned scholars like Muhammad ibn Muslim ibn Shihab al-Zuhri took it on themselves to collect, edit and compile detailed accounts of the Prophet's life and times, and in so doing they meticulously preserved a large quantity of data about his life, Prophetic career and military campaigns. As one of the foremost authorities on *fiqh* (jurisprudence), *hadith* (Prophetic traditions), *maghazi* (Prophetic military campaigns) and *sirah* (Prophet's life), al-Zuhri and his prominent disciples such as Musa ibn Uqba, Yaqub ibn Ibrahim, Muhammad ibn Salih and Abd al-Rahman ibn Abd al-Aziz played a pivotal role in

compiling and preserving information about the life and times of the Prophet. One of al-Zuhri's favourite students, and arguably the most influential biographer of the Prophet, was Ibn Ishaq.

Abu Abdullah Muhammad ibn Ishaq ibn Yasar ibn Khiyar was born in Madinah during the Caliphate of Abu Bakr. His grandfather, Yasar ibn Khiyar, was captured by the great Muslim general Khalid ibn al-Walid during his military campaign in the Iraqi province of Ayn al-Tamr and sent to Madinah. On his arrival, the Caliph handed him over to the Madinian tribe of Abdullah ibn Qais where he earned his living as a slave labourer. After he embraced Islam Yasar was freed from bondage, but he continued to live and work with the people of Ibn Qais, having married the daughter of another former captive. Yasar's sons, Muhammad and Musa, thus grew up in Madinah and became highly distinguished scholars of *hadith* and *fiqh*. Ibn Ishaq's early education began at home under the supervision of his learned father who taught him the basics of Islam. Since Madinah at the time was one of the foremost centres of Islamic learning and education, and where some of the Prophet's close companions continued to live, it was not necessary for young Ibn Ishaq to travel to other prominent centres like Makkah or Kufah to acquire higher education. After learning the Arabic language, grammar, the Qur'an and aspects of *hadith*, he pursued advanced Islamic education and was fortunate to have met and acquired *hadith* from the famous companion, Anas ibn Malik.

Ibn Ishaq was not only a *tabi* (successor of the Prophet's companions); he also became a renowned scholar by virtue of his vast knowledge of *hadith* and the Prophet's military campaigns. A contemporary of distinguished traditionists and scholars like Asim ibn Umar ibn Qatada, Musa ibn Uqba, Hisham ibn Urwa and Abdullah ibn Abu Bakr, Ibn Ishaq's thirst for knowledge of the Prophet's life and career earned him huge respect throughout Madinah; his contribution in this field made him famous throughout the Muslim world. His devotion and dedication to his studies enabled him to learn a large quantity of Prophetic traditions from the leading scholars of Madinah while he was still in his early twenties. After completing his higher education, Ibn Ishaq left Madinah for Egypt where he studied *hadith* under the guidance of a number of leading scholars of *hadith,* including Yazid ibn Abu Habib. However, his mastery of *hadith* was such that even Yazid was surprised by his expertise in this subject, and it is related that after he returned to Madinah, Yazid began to narrate *hadith* on his authority.

Some of the prominent teachers of Ibn Ishaq included Asim ibn Umar ibn Qatada and Ibn Shihab al-Zuhri, both of whom were great scholars of their generation. In fact, al-Zuhri was considered to be one of the greatest scholars of *hadith* and *sirah* of his generation. Not surprisingly, his contribution in the field of *hadith* and *sirah* has profoundly influenced all the subsequent great scholars of these subjects. And since Ibn Ishaq's love for the Prophetic traditions endeared him to al-Zuhri, the latter instructed his guard to allow Ibn Ishaq to come and see him whenever he wished. His gesture of goodwill did not, however, apply to any other scholar of the time. If any of those scholars wanted to see him, they were required to make an appoint-

ment in advance – and often they were made to wait outside al-Zuhri's house for the great man to come out and see them. By contrast, Ibn Ishaq had free access to him, thanks to his love for, and complete mastery of, *hadith* and *sirah* which earned him the respect of his teachers and contemporaries alike. Al-Zuhri rated him so highly that he once remarked that Madinah would never become deprived of knowledge so long as Ibn Ishaq remained there. While still in his mid-thirties, his reputation spread beyond the borders of Madinah. It was also during this period that a number of leading scholars of Madinah, such as Malik ibn Anas and Hisham ibn Urwa, began to criticise Ibn Ishaq's ideas and thoughts on the life of the Prophet; and some even began to question his credibility as a narrator of Prophetic *hadith*.

Like Ibn Ishaq, Malik was a great scholar of Prophetic traditions, but rivalry and misunderstanding between the two men erupted due to differences in their approach to Prophetic traditions, rather than out of personal enmity. The methodology pursued by Ibn Ishaq was, first and foremost, that of an historian and biographer, while Malik was steeped in Islamic jurisprudence as interpreted from the perspective of Madinian social ethos (*urf*) and cultural practices (*amal*). The intellectual differences between the two men revolved around the question of what actually constituted an authentic Prophetic tradition. According to Malik, Ibn Ishaq's methodology for ascertaining certain aspects of *hadith* literature was not as rigorous as it ought to be, but the latter fiercely disagreed with him and this led to considerable intellectual rivalry and accusations of bad faith on both sides. The main reason why Malik and others questioned Ibn Ishaq's reliability as a *hadith* narrator was due largely to the fact that he had obtained information about the Prophetic military campaigns (including that of the Battle of Khaibar) from both Jewish and Christian converts to Islam, rather than for any other reasons. Malik was of the opinion that these converts were not reliable narrators and, as such, he refused to accept Ibn Ishaq's information about the Prophet's military campaigns.

That aside, Malik had no problems in accepting Ibn Ishaq as an authentic and credible narrator of *hadith*.

But, unlike Malik, Ibn Ishaq considered these converts to be reliable sources of information about the Prophet's military campaigns. He claimed to have examined their narrations with great care and found their information reliable in so far as Khaibar and other battles were concerned. Unable to reconcile his differences with Malik, Ibn Ishaq was eventually forced to leave Madinah and move to Egypt. Notwithstanding Malik's reservations about Ibn Ishaq's reliability as a narrator of the Prophetic military campaigns, other great scholars of *hadith* and *maghazi* including Ibn Shihab al-Zuhri, al-Shu'ba, Sufyan ibn Uyayna, al-Shafi'i, Yahya ibn Ma'in, Ahmad ibn Hanbal, Muhammad ibn Ismail al-Bukhari and Ibn Hisham considered him to be a very trustworthy and reliable scholar. Ibn Ishaq's scrupulousness as a narrator of Prophetic traditions is most evident from the fact that his entire biography of the Prophet is punctuated with phrases such as 'God knows best' and 'May God protect me from attributing to the Prophet words he did not utter', especially when describing events which appear to be contradictory and where he was unable to ascertain their veracity. Rightly considered to be one of the greatest scholars of *hadith*, *maghazi* and *sirah* by the leading scholars of his day, Ibn Ishaq became an indefatigable collector of Prophetic traditions. Indeed, he conducted a systematic study of this subject and constantly refined his methodology for analysing and ascertaining relevant information and data, before passing them on to his students and contemporaries, who lavished much praise on him for his vast contribution to the development of *sirah* literature.

Ibn Ishaq stayed in Egypt for a short period before moving to Kufah, where he settled down and began to teach *hadith*, *maghazi* and *sirah*. His lectures were attended by a large number of students including some of the leading scholars of Kufah. Some of his prominent students included distinguished Islamic scholars like Ali ibn Mujahid, Yunus ibn Bukhair, Salama ibn al-Fadl and Ziyad ibn Abdullah ibn Tufayl al-Bakha'i. These eminent scholars learned *hadith*, *maghazi* and *sirah* directly from Ibn Ishaq and became reliable, trustworthy and renowned scholars in their own right. Ibn Ishaq lived at a very exciting period in Islamic intellectual history; there was so much interest in the *sirah* of the Prophet that virtually all the renowned scholars of the time authored a book or treatise on the subject. Thus highly respected scholars like al-Zuhri, Muhammad ibn Abd al-Rahman ibn Nawfal, Musa ibn Uqba and Wahb ibn Munabbih had written books on the life and military campaigns of the Prophet. However, it was Ibn Ishaq's voluminous biography of the Prophet which represented the very first systematic and substantial study of the life and career of the Prophet. As such, his book was a pioneering work on the subject of *sirah* and continues to exert a powerful influence to this day.

Based on his lectures on the Prophet's *sirah*, Ibn Ishaq's *Kitab Sirat Rasul Allah* (The Biography of God's Messenger) provides a detailed exposition of the Prophet's life and times, focusing especially on his military campaigns. Divided into three sections, the first part of the book began with the story of creation, tracing the genealogy of the Prophet from Adam to Abraham (*Ibrahim*), and then from Abraham to the Prophet himself through Ishmael (*Ismail*). The second part of the book narrates the Prophet's birth, early life and Prophetic mission. He devoted the third part of the book to the Prophet's military campaigns. Ibn Ishaq completed his monumental biography of the Prophet during his stay in Kufah and Rayy, before he eventually settled in Baghdad at the behest of the Abbasid Caliph Abu Ja'far al-Mansur. After he completed his biography of the Prophet, his prominent students (such as Yunus ibn Bukhair, Salama ibn al-Fadl and Ziyad ibn Abdullah ibn Tufayl al-Bakha'i) made copies for themselves. It is claimed by the historians that Ibn al-Athir's main source of information on the life and career of the Prophet came from Yunus ibn Bukhair's copy of Ibn Ishaq's original manuscript. It is also true that al-Tabari, the celebrated Qur'anic commentator and historian, obtained his information on the life and times of the Prophet from the copy made by Salama ibn al-Fadl during Ibn Ishaq's stay in Rayy. In the same way, the distinguished traditionist and historian Abu Muhammad Abd al-Malik ibn Hisham al-Himyari obtained his copy of Ibn Ishaq's biography of the Prophet through the latter's student, al-Bakha'i, who made two copies of the biography for himself.

Ibn Hisham was an extremely reliable historian, an expert in Arabic literature and prominent scholar of *hadith* who not only studied and analysed Ibn Ishaq's voluminous biography of the Prophet, but also completely reviewed and re-edited the entire book and published it under the title of *al-Sirat al-Nabawiyah* (although it became popular as *Sirat ibn Hisham* or 'Ibn Hisham's Biography of the Prophet.'). This book was destined to become the most famous and influential biography of the Prophet ever written and virtually all the other biographers of the Prophet used it as a standard reference on the subject. Ibn Ishaq's contribution to the field of *sirah* was, therefore, unique and unprecedented. His monumental biography of the Prophet rightly earned him universal acclaim and all the great historians of Islam, commentators of the Qur'an, scholars of *hadith* and *sirah* (including Ibn al-Qutaiba, al-Baladhuri, al-Tabari, Ibn Sa'd, Ahmad ibn Hanbal, Ibn al-Athir, Abd al-Rahman al-Suhayli, Ibn Kathir, al-Suyuti, Ibn Hajar al-Asqalani and Ibn Sayyid al-Nas) drew information about the life and career of the Prophet from his *magnum opus*. Without Ibn Ishaq's monumental biography, our knowledge and understanding of the *sirah* of the Prophet would certainly have been much poorer than it is today. After completing his biography of the Prophet, Ibn Ishaq presented a copy to the Abbasid Caliph Abu Ja'far al-Mansur who reportedly rewarded him handsomely for his efforts. Muhammad ibn Ishaq died and was buried in the cemetery of Khayzuran in Baghdad, the capital of the Abbasid dynasty, at the age of sixty-three.

# 40

# Abdullah al-Ma'mun (b.786 - d.833)

THE QUESTION OF political succession has often been a major stumbling block in Islamic political history. In the absence of any clear religious guidelines or rules, political succession often came to be decided through protracted political struggle or infighting between rival claimants to the Caliphate. Keen to avoid a similar conflict after his death, the celebrated Abbasid Caliph Harun al-Rashid took the unusual step of nominating his successor during his own lifetime. According to the agreement formulated by Harun, he was to be succeeded by his son, Muhammad, who became known as Caliph al-Amin. It also stated that al-Amin, in turn, was to be succeeded by his brother, Abdullah, who later became known as Caliph al-Ma'mun. Thus, as per Harun's instructions, al-Amin succeeded his illustrious father after the latter's death and ruled for four years during which he fought tooth and nail to prevent his brother from becoming Caliph after him. Instead, he nominated his own son, Musa, as his heir, and thus openly violated the oath of allegiance he had signed with his father. Not unexpectedly, al-Ma'mun denounced his brother as a traitor and this set the two brothers against each other, leading to considerable political infighting and loss of life. The scene of carnage

and devastation wrought upon the House of Harun al-Rashid would have been enough to make him turn in his grave. However, al-Amin's dishonourable actions earned him nothing but condemnation and disgrace, while his brother, al-Ma'mun, not only went onto become one of the Muslim world's most prominent rulers, but also carved out an important place for himself in the intellectual history of Islam.

Abdullah al-Ma'mun ibn Harun al-Rashid was born in Baghdad after his father's accession to the Abbasid throne at the age of twenty-two. Hailing from an Arabian family, al-Ma'mun's mother was a beautiful lady who was deeply adored by her husband, Caliph Harun al-Rashid. Unfortunately, she died while al-Ma'mun was still in his infancy. The young boy was therefore brought up by his father. Being a wise and kind father, Harun showered his children with much wealth and luxury, whilst also ensuring that they received a thorough education. Despite the obvious tension and jealousy which existed within Harun's family between the supporters of his son al-Amin by his Arab wife Zubaida (who was an Abbasid princess), and the supporters of al-Ma'mun (whose mother came from a lower-class Arab family), he treated all his children fairly and equitably without showing any bias or favouritism. Keen to educate his children in both the religious and scientific subjects of the day, the Caliph invited the leading scholars to come and teach al-Ma'mun. He thus received a thorough education in Arabic language, literature and aspects of Islamic sciences. Since Malik ibn Anas of Madinah was one of the most prominent Islamic scholars of his generation, Harun sent a letter to the venerable scholar requesting him to come to Baghdad to teach his children. Malik turned down the offer, saying that true seekers of knowledge do not expect knowledge to come and knock on their doors; instead they go out in search of knowledge. The Caliph understood exactly what the wise scholar meant and immediately set out for Madinah, with his children, to attend Malik's lectures. However, according to some historians, there is no evidence to suggest that al-Amin and al-Ma'mun did actually attend Malik's lectures. Either way, young al-Ma'mun acquired considerable knowledge of Islamic sciences and became thoroughly familar with the Qur'an. The Caliph then placed him under the care of his Chief Minister, Ja'far al-Barmaki, who trained him in both political and civil administration.

Like his father, al-Ma'mun was a handsome young man who was blessed with a sharp intellect and polished diplomatic skills. In 798, when al-Ma'mun was only twelve, Harun asked all members of his family to pledge their allegiance to al-Ma'mun as a future Caliph. The deed of political succession – prepared by Harun and preserved in its entirety by the historian al-Tabari – stipulated that al-Ma'mun would become Caliph after the death of his brother al-Amin, thus ensuring a smooth transition of power from one to the other. Although the hierarchy within Harun's armed forces preferred al-Amin over al-Ma'mun, the Caliph was determined that the latter should not in any way be disadvantaged or sidelined after his death. He, therefore, personally inscribed al-Ma'mun's name on the deed of succession and thus ensured that he was in line to ascend the Abbasid throne after al-Amin. Al-Ma'mun became an able and experienced

political and civil administrator, eventually being appointed governor of the large province of Khurasan, which extended all the way from Hamadan to the eastern frontiers of the Abbasid Empire. As expected, his successful reign as governor of Khurasan enhanced his political power and personal standing within the royal family. Thus, by the time his father fell out with Ja'far the Barmakid and sentenced him to death, al-Ma'mun was already recognised as an able and experienced provincial administrator.

In 809, Caliph Harun al-Rashid died at the age of forty-three. During his reign of twenty-two years he completely transformed the fortunes of the Abbasid Empire. He restored peace, order and security throughout his vast empire; Baghdad, the capital of the Abbasid Empire, also became a cosmopolitan city, boasting hundreds of renowned schools, colleges, libraries, hospitals and markets. In other words, under Harun's patronage, Baghdad became one of the Muslim world's most famous educational, cultural and architectural centres. Unfortunately his son and successor, Caliph al-Amin, failed to live up to his father's high standards. Although Harun had twelve sons, only al-Amin, al-Ma'mun and Mu'tasim were groomed for leadership by their father, and all three of them occupied prominent political positions during their father's reign. After Harun's death, the three brothers remained faithful to the deed of succession prepared by their father and regularly exchanged messages of peace, support and goodwill. This state of affairs persisted until Caliph al-Amin, urged by his chief political advisor Fadl ibn Rabi, openly violated the deed of succession. Since Fadl hated al-Ma'mun and thought Caliph Harun had granted him too much power and autonomy, he convinced Caliph al-Amin to remove his name from the deed of succession, and instead nominate his own son as his successor. This was not only an insensitive move; it also proved to be fatal for Caliph al-Amin who now found himself at odds with his brothers al-Ma'mun and Mu'tasim.

Based at his headquarters at Merv (in present-day Turkmenistan), at the time the provincial capital of Khurasan, al-Ma'mun was urged by his advisor Fadl ibn Sahl not to give up his claim to the Caliphate. Beneath the surface, the two Fadls were in reality engaged in a bitter power struggle of their own, each determined to preserve their own personal interests, wealth and position. Being an Arab, Fadl ibn Rabi supported Caliph al-Amin, who was the son of an Arab princess, and was determined to keep power in the hands of the Arabs. By contrast, Fadl ibn Sahl was of Persian origin and was also determined to ensure that al-Ma'mun, the son of a lower-class lady, ascended the Abbasid throne. If al-Ma'mun became the Abbasid Caliph, he obviously expected to be rewarded handsomely for his loyalty and support. Indeed, had it not been for Fadl ibn Sahl's loyalty, support and encouragement, al-Ma'mun might have relinquished his claim to the throne but, thanks to Fadl's persistence, he decided to fight for his right to ascend the Abbasid throne. By openly violating the deed of succession, Caliph al-Amin thus instigated a protracted internal feud within the House of Harun al-Rashid.

As a result, al-Amin's reign became dominated by a war of attrition with his brother. Though Harun had placed the deed of succession in the *haram al-sharif* ('the sacred mosque' in Makkah) as a trust, al-Amin had it brought to him whereupon he tore it into pieces with his own hands. He then tried to remove al-Ma'mun from his post as governor of Khurasan, but Fadl ibn Sahl went out of his way to muster sufficient popular support for him so that he could openly defy the Caliph's order and refuse to relinquish his governorship. In response, Caliph al-Amin sent a large contingent under the command of Ali ibn Isa in order to forcibly remove al-Ma'mun from power. However, the latter fought back and inflicted a crushing defeat on the Caliph's forces, firstly at Rayy and then at Hamadan in 811. Al-Ma'mun then went on to capture the cities of Basrah and Kufah, and in 812, he also took the northern Iraqi city of Mosul. It was not long before he was declared Caliph, while al-Amin – betrayed by his bodyguard – was captured and brutally murdered by the supporters of the new Caliph. His greed

and jealousy led to his premature death at the age of only twenty-seven. So it was that the twenty-two-year-old al-Ma'mun ascended the Abbasid throne and went onto exert tremendous influence on the Muslim world.

Al-Ma'mun initially ruled from his headquarters in Merv, but when political rebellion and social disorder broke out in different parts of the empire, and rebel groups and bandits began to wreak havoc across his dominion, he decided to return to Baghdad and reassert his political and military authority. From having been once economically very prosperous and culturally advanced, Baghdad now lay in ruins. The war of attrition fought by the two brothers had brought this great city to its knees, turning most of Baghdad into rubble. This sorry state of affairs moved and deeply saddened al-Ma'mun on his arrival in Baghdad in 819. Thus he went out of his way to mend broken fences by reconciling himself with his erstwhile opponents within the royal family. Keen to win the support of Zubaida, Caliph al-Amin's mother, he restored all her wealth and properties to her. After reuniting the royal family under his able leadership, he turned his attention to events outside the capital and instigated military actions to put an end to all the subversive activities which were taking place within the Abbasid dominion at the time. The political situation had deteriorated so badly that many Abbasid territories, such as Tunisia, proclaimed their independence from Abbasid rule. But, thanks to al-Ma'mun's wise, timely and decisive actions, peace and security was soon restored across the Muslim world; he became the undisputed ruler of the Abbasid Empire.

As an educated and cultured ruler, al-Ma'mun was very fond of intellectual debates and discussions. He also established a Council of the State, comprising representatives from different regions of the empire. These regional representatives had a permanent seat at the Council and provided feedback on central Government performance, its policies and programmes. Since al-Ma'mun was very keen to engage directly with his subjects, he took the views of the regional representatives into consideration before deciding on the vital issues of day. Being a great organiser and motivator of people, he also encouraged his generals to instil discipline and moral values within the ranks of his armed forces. Determined to stamp out corruption and dishonest practices from his Government and armed services, he paid his senior civil servants and army generals handsomely and also supplied them with all the necessary equipment, weaponry and training needed to perform their duties. He was especially generous towards his Ministers and Chief Advisor, Fadl ibn Sahl; indeed, he authorised the latter to draw an annual salary of three million dirhams from the State coffers. Although this was an enormous sum, al-Ma'mun was keen to reward his staff handsomely so as to prevent corruption, bribery and malpractice from rearing their ugly heads within his Government, and in this respect he was very successful.

Like his father, al-Ma'mun transformed Baghdad into a thriving city. Under his stewardship, it became the world's most dazzling capital city, being renowned for its schools, colleges, hospitals, markets, bookshops and libraries. As a generous patron of learning and education, he transformed the *bait al-hikmah* ('the House of Wisdom'), which was originally founded by his father Caliph Harun al-Rashid, into one of the Muslim world's most famous libraries and research centres. He not only expanded its activities and renamed it as *dar al-hikmah* ('the Abode of Wisdom'), he also went out of his way to recruit some of the Muslim world's brightest minds, including al-Kindi, al-Farghani and Muhammad ibn Musa al-Khwarizmi to this centre of learning so they could pursue advanced research in science, philosophy, mathematics and literature. Caliph al-Ma'mun ruled at a time when the Islamic world became polarised into two major philosophical and theological camps. Prominent religious scholars, like Ahmad ibn Hanbal, became the champions of Islamic traditionalism, while the philosophers and rationalists became the supporters of the Mu'tazilite creed. Though al-Ma'mun was well-versed in traditional Islamic sciences (having, according to some scholars, attended Malik

ibn Anas's lectures in Madinah), he chose to champion the views of the Mu'tazilites with the result that, during his reign, Mu'tazilism became the official creed of the State.

As a ruler, al-Ma'mun was neither despotic nor tyrannical but, as a champion of Mu'tazilism, he was both stubborn and uncompromising. When a controversy concerning the nature of the Qur'an flared up during his reign, he ruthlessly imposed his theological views on his opponents. Unlike the Islamic traditionalists, who argued that the Qur'an was the uncreated Word of God, al-Ma'mun – like the Mu'tazilites –considered it to be a created Word of God; and anyone who dared to preach otherwise was treated harshly by him. When Ahmad ibn Hanbal, who was a leading Islamic theologian and scholar, began to oppose al-Ma'mun's religious views, he and his successors severely chastised him. Al-Ma'mun's attitude and behaviour towards Ahmad ibn Hanbal was both strange and inexplicable, because his reign as Caliph otherwise represented a great period of political stability, economic prosperity and intellectual progress and advancement across the Muslim world. Keen to teach the Islamic traditionalists a good lesson, however, the leading Mu'tazilite scholars encouraged al-Ma'mun to take a firm and uncompromising stance against their traditionalist opponents. Needless to say, al-Ma'mun's action against the traditionalists was both foolish and unwise, not least because it has tarnished and undermined his reputation as a wise and tolerant sovereign.

Caliph al-Ma'mun's reign of two and a half decades came to an end when he was forty-seven. He died in the village of Budandun (in present-day Pozanti) during a military expedition he led against the Byzantines. Before his death, he reportedly confessed his theological errors and prayed for forgiveness. His body was transferred to Tarsus where he was laid to rest following a simple funeral. Unlike his father, al-Ma'mun left no instructions or guidelines with regard to political sucession; but, as expected, his half-brother Abu Ishaq Muhammad Mu'tasim Billah succeeded him as Caliph.

# 41

# Ibn Rushd
# (b.1126 – d.1198)

WHEN TARIQ IBN ZIYAD crossed the sea and landed in Gibraltar in 711, he found Europeans were still living in the Dark Ages. His excursion into Spain thus represented a new dawn for Europe as a whole. For nearly eight centuries, the Muslims of *al-andalus* (or Islamic Spain) became the pioneers of a new European civilisation, and captured the imagination of all Europe with their dazzling contributions in all spheres of human endeavour. And so the light of civility and civilisation – lit by the Muslims of Spain – continued to burn fiercely across Europe, right up until the modern period. Through Islamic Spain, Muslims not only introduced Plato, Aristotle, Algebra and paper-making to Europe, they also built magnificent works of art and architecture, and established some of Europe's first schools, colleges, libraries and hospitals. Moreover, it was during this period that the Spanish roads and streets became some of Europe's first to be lit by lamps, thanks once again to the Muslims. It should also be pointed out that it was the Spanish Muslims who played a pivotal role in the development and cultivation of the European mind. Thus great European Muslim philosophers and thinkers like Ibn Hazm, Ibn Massarrah, Ibn Bajjah, Ibn Tufayl and Ibn al-Arabi blazed a trail

which captured the European imagination like never before. These remarkable philosophers and thinkers were not only Muslims; they were also some of medieval Europe's most influential intellectuals and writers. However, one man exerted more influence on medieval European philosophy and thought than probably any other; he was none other than Ibn Rushd.

Abul Walid Muhammad ibn Ahmad ibn Muhammad ibn Rushd, known in the Western world as Averroes, was born in Cordova, the capital of Muslim Spain, which at the time was one of the most famous centres of learning and higher education in Europe. Born into a distinguished Muslim family of educationalists, judges and intellectuals which occupied senior Governmental positions in Spain, Ibn Rushd's grandfather, Abul Walid Muhammad, was a respected authority on Islamic jurisprudence (*fiqh*) and served as an *imam* of the Grand Mosque in Cordova; his father, Abul Qasim Ahmad, was the leading Islamic scholar of his generation, who served as *qadi* (judge) of Cordova and acquired a considerable reputation for his profound knowledge of traditional Islamic sciences. During his early years Ibn Rushd studied Arabic, the Qur'an and aspects of *fiqh* under his father's tutelage, as well as *hadith* (Prophetic traditions) and *usul al-hadith* (science of *hadith*). Ibn Rushd then received advanced training in Islamic jurisprudence and mastered *maliki* legal thought. As a gifted student, he excelled in *maliki fiqh*, and pursued higher education in scientific and philosophical sciences including astronomy, mathematics, philosophy, logic, medicine and history. Being the only great Muslim philosopher to have been an expert on comparative *fiqh*, he later became renowned for his grasp of juristic differences (*ikhtilaf*) and served in the capacity of judge and jurisconsult for many years. Known to have been very hardworking and industrious, he used to read for up to sixteen hours a day and did so even when he was in his late sixties; he was also familiar with both Greek and Hebrew.

Ibn Rushd lived in a politically volatile period in the history of Islamic Spain. After the Umayyad rule of Spain came to an end in 1031, political in-fighting and ethnic rivalry broke out until the Moroccan-based al-Moravids (*al-murabitun*) marched into Spain under the able leadership of Yusuf ibn Tashfin and reunited the warring factions. In 1146, when Ibn Rushd was only twenty, the al-Moravids were overthrown by the al-Mohads (*al-muwahhidun*), another powerful politico-religious movement, founded by Abu Abdullah Muhammad ibn Abdullah ibn Tumart in Morocco, which went on to rule Islamic Spain for nearly a century. Despite the unpredictable socio-political circumstances of the time, Ibn Rushd continued to serve the interests of the Muslims by remaining loyal to the al-Mohads, although he also had close family ties with the al-Moravids. This was indeed a trickly balancing act for him, especially because the al-Mohads had received only a lukewarm reception from the people of *al-andalus*. In the circumstances, his decision to serve the new rulers was a courageous act rather than an opportunistic one because he could have chosen to move to Morocco if he wished. Indeed, his old friend Ibn Tufayl, whom he had met at Abu Yaqub Yusuf's court in Seville around 1160, did just that. As the governor's personal physician, Ibn Tufayl wielded considerable political power and it was on his recommendation that Ibn Rushd came to enjoy the governor's patronage after he became the Caliph of Muslim Spain.

Soon after becoming Caliph, Abu Yaqub Yusuf transferred the capital of Islamic Spain to Seville and appointed Ibn Rushd a *qadi* (judge) in 1169. Deeply impressed by his profound knowledge of Islamic jurisprudence, medicine and philosophy, the Caliph promoted him to the highest position within his judiciary. As a devout Muslim and competent judge, he was a firm believer in the principles of justice, fairness and equality, and sought to uphold the Divine law (*shari'ah*) and render justice irrespective of one's race, colour, creed or position. His profound knowledge of Islamic law, coupled with his qualities of honesty, fair play and impartiality in legal matters, soon won him much acclaim and endeared him to Caliph Abu Yaqub Yusuf. As a *qadi*, Ibn Rushd not only discharged his legal duties with honesty, efficiency and effectiveness, but also engaged in advanced research in aspects of law, philosophy and science during his spare time. Although he wrote numerous books and treatises on Islamic jurisprudence, his *Bidayat al-Mujtahid wa Nihayat al-Muqtasid* (An Opening for Those Who Exert and an End for the Contented) is widely considered to be an invaluable contribution in the field of Islamic jurisprudence. Focusing primarily on the differences of opinion between the different schools of Islamic legal thought, in this book he argued that diversity in the interpretation of the law (*ikhtilaf*) did not entail distortion of the truth; rather it is another way of reaching the truth in its broadest sense. *Ikhtilaf* therefore represented a methodology and a process rather than an obstruction or impediment to the attainment of a better understanding of the spirit of the Divine law. Needless to say, his approach to Islamic law was both philosophical and theoretical, not least because he sought to transcend the artificial differences which existed within Islamic legal thinking at the time; in so doing he developed a dynamic and evolving legal methodology to address some of the over-arching, yet fundamentally important, legal problems of his time. Ibn Rushd's *Bidayat* is therefore an extremely important work on Islamic legal thought which continues to be read and widely consulted by Islamic jurists to this day.

If Ibn Rushd's achievements in Islamic jurisprudence were considerable, then his contributions in the fields of science and philosophy were nothing short of remarkable. In addition to studying astronomy and mathematics, he excelled in medicine and, after Ibn Tufayl's retirement in 1182, Caliph Abu Yaqub Yusuf called him to Marrakesh and appointed him to be his personal physician. Ibn Tufayl was a renowned physician of his time who had served the Caliph with great distinction but Abu Yaqub Yusuf's decision to appoint Ibn Rushd as his personal physician said more about Ibn Rushd's skills and abilities as a medical practitioner than it did about the Caliph himself. As it happens, his decades of research in medical science, coupled with many years of professional experience as a phyiscian, earned him widespread recognition across Cordova as an eminent authority on medicine. Being thoroughly familiar with the medical thought of both Galen and Ibn Sina (who were arguably two of the most famous physicians of all time), he attempted to combine ancient Greek medical thought with Islamic medical practices, and in so doing hoped to develop an original synthesis of the two schools. He wrote more than twenty books and treatises on all aspects of medicine, including his famous *Kitab al-Kulliyyat fi al-Tibb* (The Book of Universal Rules of Medicine), which was a medical encyclopaedia written at the request of Caliph Abu Yaqub Yusuf. In this book, he expounded the fundamental principles and practices of medicine from a rationalistic point of view. According to Ibn Rushd, the finer points of medicine actually reside beyond the realm of empirical observation; that is to say he believed an exploration of the link between a phenomenon and its cause was indispensable for a better understanding and appreciation of medical theory and practice. By adopting such a rationalistic approach to medicine he sought to move from the physical realm to the rational

dimension in order to develop a new synthesis between Galenic thought and Islamic medicine – as previously expounded by Ibn Sina in his monumental *al-Qanun fi al-Tibb* (The Canon of Medicine). Ibn Rushd's approach to medicine was not only sophisticated, it was also holistic and very refreshing. He continued to serve Caliph Abu Yaqub Yusuf – and then his son and successor Abu Yusuf al-Mansur – as personal physician until in 1194, when at the age of around sixty-eight, he was ordered by the Caliph to leave Marrakesh in order to appease the conservative *ulama* (religious scholars) who considered Ibn Rushd's philosophical and theological ideas to be unorthodox and heretical. During this period his books were publicly burnt by the conservative *ulama* and a huge public outcry broke out across the city, which forced the Caliph to restrict the teaching of philosophy and other rational sciences for a while. Later, the Caliph recalled Ibn Rushd to Marrakesh where he continued to write and pursue research in philosophy, theology and medicine.

As an encyclopaedic genius of the highest order, Ibn Rushd did not believe in the compartmentalisation of knowledge and, therefore, he refused to confine himself to one subject alone. In addition to being an eminent jurist, a distinguished physician and an outstanding theologian, he was also one of the greatest Muslim philosophers of all time. Since his breadth of learning was colossal and his approach to theology (*kalam*) and philosophy (*falsafah*) both sophisticated and analytical, the conservative *ulama* – despite their repeated attempts to read and understand his philosophical and theological works – failed to grasp the subtlety of his ideas, thoughts and arguments. Not surprisingly, the vast majority of them either misunderstood or deliberately misinterpreted his philosophical and theological views, leading to considerable public outcry against him. Wrongly accused of heresy, the beleaguered Caliph ordered him to flee to Lucena, a town located towards the south east of Cordova. Although Ibn Rushd's writings on theology and philosophy were of the highest order, unfortunately his critics failed to understand and appreciate the sheer scope and intensity of his religious thought and scholarship. Blessed with an unusually sharp and penetrating mind, he acquired an unrivalled mastery of Islamic thought and worldview. His ability to delve deep into the finer points of Islamic theology, philosophy and jurisprudence – whether to vindicate, offer fresh interpretation or refute a specific idea or thought – was nothing short of breathtaking. If an Islamic intellectual of Ibn Taymiyyah's calibre struggled to understand the complexity of Ibn Rushd's ideas and thought, it is not surprising that the ordinary mortals on the streets of Cordova failed to grasp the subtleties of his interpretations.

Some of Ibn Rushd's major theological and philosophical works included *Fasl al-Maqal* (The Decisive Chapter), *Kashf an-Manahij al-Adilla fi Aqa'id al-Milla* (Revelation of Methods of Proofs concerning the Beliefs of the Nation) and *Tahafut al-Tahafut* (Refutation of the Refutation). These three books were written in Seville on his return from Morocco in 1178. As a devout student of the Qur'an, in these works, he argued that the Qur'an not only encouraged Muslims to think, ponder and contemplate but also to utilise their rational faculties in order to acquire a better understanding of creation and physical phenomena in general. According to Ibn Rushd, there was no conflict between reason and revelation, and therefore religion and philosophy were not incompatible in Islam, despite al-Ghazali's stinging critique of philosophy in his *Tahafut al-Falasifah* (The Refutation of Philosophy). In this acclaimed treatise, al-Ghazali accused the philosophers of heresy, but Ibn Rushd repudiated his views and defended the ideas and thoughts of the philosophers with great wit and eloquence. In his *Tahafut al-Tahafut* he analysed al-Ghazali's arguments point by point and refuted them in a cogent manner. Although he accepted that religion based on revelation was far superior to a purely rational approach to religion, he vehemently disagreed with those who argued that reason had no role to play in religion. Ibn Rushd championed a form of religious rationalism which

sought to reconcile religion with philosophy, and faith with reason.

Furthermore, he argued that the study of philosophy was far from being a blameworthy activity; rather it was an important and admirable pursuit. Indeed, according to Ibn Rushd, from an Islamic legal perspective, the study of philosophy could be classified as a noble and recommended preoccupation. However, his critics refused to accept his philosophical interpretation of Islam because he was heavily influenced by Aristotle. His religious rationalism, they argued, represented nothing more than the Aristotelianization of Islam. Though Ibn Rushd was undoubtedly influenced by Aristotle's philosophy and thought, his critics were wrong to accuse him of espousing a form of Islamic Aristotelianism. The truth was, he was too good an intellectual to engage in such an intellectually anarchistic enterprise. He also repeatedly pointed out how his critics had failed to understand his rationalistic approach to religion, and thus their charge of heresy levelled against him was both unfair and unjustified.

In addition to numerous works on philosophy, law and medicine, Ibn Rushd published scores of books and treatises on logic, astronomy, physics and cosmology. Although it is not known how many books and treatises he produced in total, according to some historians he composed as many as seventy major works. Also, his mastery of Greek philosophy and extensive commentaries on the major works of Aristotle later earned him the coveted title of 'The Commentator'. Considered to be Europe's greatest authority on Aristotle, his commentaries were read and studied widely; he was also revered throughout medieval Europe as a philosopher *par excellence*. The famous Italian poet Dante Alighieri rated him so highly that he mentioned him by name in his acclaimed book, *The Divine Comedy*. He wrote, 'And Linus, Tully and moral Seneca, Euclid and Ptolemy, Hippocrates, Galenus, Avicen, and him who made that commentary vast, Averroes'. (Inferno, IV) Here he mentioned two great Muslim philosophers by name, Ibn Sina (Avicenna) and Ibn Rushd (Averroes), both of whom had exerted tremendous influence on all the great medieval and modern European scholars and thinkers, including St Thomas Aquinas, Albertus Magnus (also known as Albert the Great), Micheal Scot, Musa bin Maimon (better known as Maimonides), Roger Bacon, Ramon Lull, John Locke, Blaise Pascal and Immanuel Kant. Indeed, Ibn Rushd acquired such a large following in Europe that his followers later became known as the 'Latin Averroists' and his works were avidly studied at universities across Europe including Avignon, Paris, Padua, Bologna and Naples among others.

Accused and vilified in the Islamic East for his supposed heresy, Ibn Rushd became an intellectual trail-blazer in medieval Europe, thus paving the way for the Renaissance. After a lifetime devoted to the pursuit of knowledge and wisdom, Ibn Rushd, the great European Muslim philosopher, died in Marrakesh (in present-day Morocco) at the age of seventy-two, although later his remains were transferred to his native Cordova.

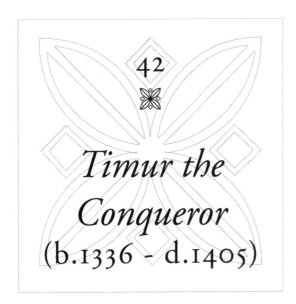

# 42

## Timur the Conqueror
## (b.1336 - d.1405)

THERE IS NO doubt that Alexander the Great, Genghis Khan, Hannibal and Napoleon were great conquerors. Alexander burst out of Macedonia in 334BC and overwhelmed the mighty Persian Empire, although unfavourable circumstances forced him to return home without conquering India. After instigating a series of remarkable conquests within a short period, he died at the age of thirty-two. The Mongols, led by Genghis Khan, suddenly emerged from North-east Asia in the twelfth century and rapidly conquered China, India, Persia and southern Russia. The Mongols' reputation for carrying out wholesale massacres and brutality made their opponents shake in their boots. Genghis Khan died in 1227 after falling off his horse. Hannibal, on the other hand, was appointed commander of the Carthaginian army when he was only twenty-six. With a contingent of forty thousand men, thirty-eight elephants and some horses, he fought a vicious battle against the Romans and successfully conquered northern Italy. Fearing betrayal, he poisoned himself in 183BC. By contrast, Napoleon Bonaparte received training at the military academy in Paris and fought numerous battles before becoming the Emperor of continental Europe. Following crushing defeats at Leipzig (1814) and Waterloo (1815), he died in 1821. By all accounts, these conquerors were very brave and gifted military leaders who performed wonders in the battlefield, but they all pale into insignificance when compared with Timur, who was undoubtedly history's most successful conqueror.

Amir Timur, known as Tamerlane in the West, was born into a noble Muslim family in the village of Khoja Ilgar close to Shakhrisabz, the Green City, in modern-day Uzbekistan. His father, Taraghay, was the chief of the Barlas tribe whose members originally hailed from the north-eastern region of Mongolia and settled in Central Asia during the time of Genghis Khan. Historically, the Central Asian region had been a melting-pot for people of different racial, cultural and linguistic backgrounds, including nomads from Mongolia, Persians, Turks, Arabs and Europeans. People of all backgrounds converged on the region, where they mingled and interacted with the natives and created a vibrant and distinctive socio-cultural ambience there. Since the cold, harsh and treacherous terrain of the steppes made their surroundings very bleak and dangerous, the locals adapted themselves to the unfriendly terrain by establishing their own versions of close-knit, nomadic havens. The name Timur, meaning lion, says much about the character, attitude and aspirations of the Turkicised descendants of Genghis Khan who became known as the Tartars. The Tartars were tough, resilient and ruthless warrior-like people, who became famous for their bravery, sense of purpose and military prowess. Then again, such qualities and attributes were indispensable for leading a successful nomadic existence.

Brought up under the watchful gaze of his parents, Timur preferred to play games than pursue education during his early years. After receiving training in combat, archery and horse-riding, he became a skilled hunter. During this period he suffered a serious injury which earned him the nickname 'Timur the Lame' (derived from the Persian *timur-i lang*). For this reason, he later became widely-known in the West as Ta-merlane. Despite his crippling injury, he became an accomplished polo and chess player. His deter-mination to overcome his deformity earned him much respect from his fellow tribesmen. Unlike his devout father, who used to spend much of his time in the company of the religious scholars and Sufis, Timur became fascinated by combat and warfare. As expected, he followed in the tradi-tions of his people and become a skilled archer, huntsman, soldier and military tactician. The art of combat and warfare which he learned during his early years later stood him in good stead as he unleashed his tribal warriors against his enemies across Central Asia, the Middle East and parts of Africa.

Timur was born during a chaotic period in the history of Central Asia. After the death of Genghis Khan in 1227, the Mongol Empire began to dis-integrate rapidly as his descendants engaged in a protracted succession battle. During the ensuing upheaval, the Mongol chiefs carved out their own principalities, thus dividing the Mongol Empire among themselves. Young Timur witnessed the bitter political rivalry which prevailed at the time between Amir Qazaghan of Mawarahnahr and Moghul Khan of Moghulistan. The two men fought tooth and nail for power, until Amir

Qazaghan was assassinated in 1358. This prompted Moghul Khan to instigate military action against Mawarahnahr in order to reunify the two princi-palities under his political leadership. When the news of Moghul Khan's advance towards Mawa-rahnahr was relayed to Haji Beg, the chief of the Barlas clan, he chose to flee rather than fight and defend his homeland. Timur followed Haji Beg and went as far as the Oxus river before he had a sudden change of heart; he returned to Barlas with a group of young fighters and decided to defend his homeland against the encroaching Moghul Khan. On his return home, however, he decided not to resist the Khan because he felt it would be a futile task given the size of his army. Instead he offered his services to Moghul Khan, who rewarded him handsomely and made him the leader of the Barlas clan; he was only twenty-five at the time.

Although Timur loathed Khan and was eager to force him out of Mawarahnahr, adverse politi-cal circumstances forced him to co-operate with him. Then again, given his meagre resources, he could not dare to challenge Moghul Khan. So he decided to forge an alliance with Amir Hussain, the grandson of Qazaghan, who at the time was the ruler of Balkh (located in northern Afghanistan). Timur strengthened his relationship with Amir Hussain by marrying his sister, Aljai Turkhan-Agha, and also agreed to collaborate with him in order to oust Moghul Khan. Things did not work out as they planned and in due course both of them were forced to go underground. After conducting several years of guerrilla warfare, Hussain fled leaving Timur to fight on his own. His guerrilla activities eventually culminated in the subjugation of the small Sarbadar Kingdom of Samarqand. After the overthrow of the Sarba-dars, he installed himself as the new ruler of that kingdom. He then removed Amir Hussain, the ruler of Balkh, from his path in 1370 and in so doing he became the supreme ruler of Chaghatay at the age of thirty-four.

With Chaghatay firmly under his control, Timur focused his attention on the neighbour-ing States of Qungirat and Moghulistan. Before embarking on a large-scale military campaign against them, he decided to strengthen his forces with sufficient weaponry and food supplies. He achieved this by transferring Amir Hussain's assets from Balkh and distributing everything amongst his fighters. As a strong, fearless and intelligent warrior, Timur trained and rewarded his fighters better than any of his rivals; likewise, he became well known for his generosity to his family, friends and guests alike. Unfortunately, his fierce and ruthless behaviour on the battlefield often overshadowed his frequent acts of kindness and generosity. In truth, Timur was his own man and was motivated more by combat and warfare than anything else, and if anyone dared to cross his path or challenge his authority, he ruthlessly suppressed them. His desire to gain victory over his enemies kept him on his toes – even when the odds were firmly stacked against him. As a natural-born fighter, he thrived in the lion's den so much so that on one ocassion when he was locked in a vermin-infested shed by his enemies, he managed to escape completely unscathed. Being a ruthless and ambitious warrior, he was not interested in ruling a small kingdom; he was determined to conquer and rule the whole world.

After mobilising his forces in 1370, he led an expedition against the Moghul ruler Qamar al-Din but, on this occasion, he only managed to partially best his rival. He then launched several other military campaigns against the Moghuls before finally defeating them in 1383. During this period he also fought on a northern front, launching expeditions against Khowrizm. As a beautiful and fertile territory, Khowrizm was renowned for its fruits and agricultural produce and had previously captured the imagination of Ibn Battutah, the famous Muslim globetrotter, when he visited that region during the fourteenth century. After annexing this territory, Timur arranged a regular supply of fresh fruit and vegetables for his forces. He then returned to Samarqand in 1372, only to discover his son, Jahangir, had died of flu. Stricken with grief, he was inconsolable; he struggled to come to terms with his loss because Jahangir was

his oldest and most beloved son. After a period of mourning, he regained his composure and again plunged himself into the grand theatre of warfare and conquest.

With Mawarahnahr and Khowrizm now firmly under his control, in 1379 he turned his attention towards the Kart dynasty which, at the time, ruled a large territory including most of modern Afghanistan. After consolidating his armed forces, Timur marched into the historic city of Herat without any opposition. He then pushed on towards Mazandaran and captured this territory in 1382. The Persian city of Sultani-yya was a strategically important centre and it succumbed soon afterwards. This was followed by the annexation of Tabriz, the capital of Azerbaijan. Almost unstoppable, he was now on a rampage. Thus, in 1387 he reached Tbilisi, the capital of Georgia, and ransacked the entire city. After subduing Azerbaijan, Georgia and Armenia, his forces marched towards Asia Minor at a lightning speed and captured the historic cities of Isfahan and Shiraz. By 1385, Timur had carved out a huge empire which extended from Samarqand at one end, to Georgia at the other. Keen to expand his empire further, he then turned his eyes towards the Islamic East and soon captured Baghdad. Although the brave people of Baghdad put up a determined resistance, Timur's forces entered the city and created much havoc there. From Baghdad, his forces then proceeded towards the Caucasus.

Later, in 1398, Timur marched into India and subjugated Delhi, leaving behind only a pile of dust and rubble. He then captured Aleppo and Damascus in 1400 and 1401, respectively, but his greatest victory was yet to come. In 1402, he took on the might of the Ottoman Empire and inflicted a humiliating defeat on the forces of Sultan Bayazid at the Battle of Ankara. The Ottomans were considered to be one of the great superpowers of the time, and Timur's victory over them sent shock waves around the world. Indeed, when the news of the Ottoman defeat was relayed across Europe, the people of that continent openly celebrated and expressed their thanks and gratitude to Timur, because a significant part of Europe at that time was firmly under Ottoman control. Ironically, it took one emerging Muslim power to inflict defeat on another great Islamic superpower. Although this was certainly not the first time that Muslims had ended up fighting fellow-Muslims, there is no doubt that Timur's resounding victory over his Ottoman rivals severely undermined their military power and strength, much to the delight of the Europeans. Thereafter, Timur set out for his final military campaign, in 1405, against the Ming Emperor of China, but on his arrival in Otrar (in modern Kazakhstan) he died of fever at the age of sixty-nine (although according to some historians, Timur actually died at the age of seventy-one). Nonetheless, he had already carved out one of the largest empires in history, extending all the way from Siberia to Smyrna, and from Damascus to Delhi and in so doing he became one of the most powerful men who ever lived.

Timur was not only a remarkable conqueror, he was also a gifted political administrator. He organised his army with care and great tactical ability, and also devised and implemented a workable politico-civil administration across his territories which encouraged travellers and traders to engage in commercial activities, thereby generating much social and economic development across his vast empire. Having said that, Timur was not an average politician, and nor did he pretend to be one; rather he was a gifted warrior, military commander and an exceptionally successful conqueror who became one of history's greatest imperial rulers. As a military genius, he carefully identified his military targets and pursued them most ruthlessly; he had no time for love, emotion or tears, except only for those who were very close and dear to him. He decorated Samarqand, his imperial capital, with beautiful buildings, elegant gardens, impressive mosques, schools and colleges and also recruited religious scholars to teach and impart knowledge to the locals. Towards the end of his life, he liked to sit in the company of the religious scholars and Sufis, although it is not clear how he managed to reconcile his Islam with his personal thirst for combat and warfare. Since he was a product of many conflicting forces, including his nomadic background, Mongol ancestry, Central Asian heritage and Islamic culture, Timur's character and personality also reflected much tension, confusion and contradiction. He lies buried in the Gur Amir mausoleum in Samarqand (also known as Samarkand).

# 43

# *Akbar the Great*
# *(b.1542 - d.1605)*

AFTER THE DEATH of Amir Timur in 1405, the vast empire he had created began to rapidly disintegrate, thanks to his immediate descendants who fought each other for overall political supremacy: in the process they only succeeded in dividing the Timurid Empire into several principalities. The ensuing fighting forced many of his descendants to flee from Samarqand and seek refuge elsewhere. Zahir al-Din Muhammad, better known as Babar (Babur), was one of them. Descended from two great Asian conquerors, Timur on his father's side and Genghis Khan on his mother's side, Babar marched into Kabul in 1504 at the age of twenty-two and established his political base there. From Kabul, he launched raids into India and routed his opponents with great skill and determination before establishing Mughal supremacy in 1526. Babar, the founder of Mughal Empire, died soon afterwards without fully consolidating his new kingdom. Humayun, his son and successor, was too romantic, fun-loving and indecisive to make much of an impact. He also died in his forties without securing Mughal rule. It was left to the genius of Akbar, the greatest of Mughal Emperors and one of the most influential rulers of Muslim India, to fully consolidate Mughal rule throughout the subcontinent.

Abul Fath Jalal al-Din Muhammad was born in Umarkot in the northern Indian province of Sind (in present-day Pakistan). His father, Humayun, married Hamida Banu Begum, the daughter of a noble Persian scholar who served his youngest uncle, Hindal, as a civil servant. Akbar was born at a time when his father had lost much of his power to his opponents – including his own brothers – before he took military action in order to regain his lost territories. Since he had few supporters in Sind, he proceeded to Persia to ask the reigning Safavid monarch, Shah Tahmasp, for his political and military support. Backed by the Safavids, Humayun spearheaded military action against his rebellious brothers Kamran, Askari and Hindal. After subduing them, he took action against the rebellious governors of Lahore, Punjab, Delhi and Agra, and in so doing reasserted his political authority across that region. During this period of military campaigns, Humayun and his family were forced to move from one place to another, which deprived young Akbar of much in the way of formal education and training. For this reason, he failed to gain proficiency in literacy.

Although adverse political circumstances prevented Akbar from learning to read and write during his early years, later in life he surrounded himself with people who were highly educated; if he wished, he could have acquired literacy skills but it appears he was not interested, perhaps because he preferred to learn through the spoken word rather than rely on pen and paper. Blessed with a prodigious memory and sharp intellect, he learned and mastered a wide range of subjects including history, philosophy, religion, art and poetry with ease. During his early years, Akbar's mentor and guide was Bairam Khan, a loyal, trusted and experienced Mughal civil servant, who trained him in all aspects of political, civil and military affairs, and prepared him to succeed his father as the ruler of the Mughal dynasty. During this period, young Akbar lived with his mother in Punjab and he was considered to be a bright, cultured and sensible young man who understood the special position he occupied. He may not have fully understood and appreciated the tremendous responsibility he was expected to shoulder after the death of his father, but Bairam Khan ensured he was prepared for such an eventuality should it arrive. Akbar was only thirteen when his father suddenly died in 1556 and, as expected, he succeeded him as the ruler of the Mughal Empire. His accession to power was to mark the beginning of a glorious era in the history of Muslim India.

Akbar may have been illiterate but he was certainly not short-sighted or unintelligent. He knew that his father had tried his best to reassert his authority across the Mughal territories, but had failed to achieve all his objectives. After ascending the Mughal throne, he instigated military action in order to regain the lost territories, and thereby restore political stability, social peace and security across the Mughal dominion. Operating under the guidance and stewardship of Bairam Khan, he took action against all the remaining rebellious governors and Sultans, before winning a decisive victory at Panipat in 1556, where he inflicted a crushing defeat on Hemu, his most powerful Hindu rival, who at the time ruled both Delhi and Agra. Although Hemu had mustered a large army, Akbar did not feel in-

timidated; instead, he bravely marched onto the battlefield with his army and routed his opponent's forces. This decisive victory strengthened Akbar's position both politically and militarily, thus enabing him to focus his attention on the north. Bairam Khan, his chief political advisor and military commander, had played a pivotal role in consolidating Mughal power and authority throughout northern India. However, as Akbar began to tighten his grip on India, the aged Bairam Khan increasingly became a liability rather than an asset to the Mughals, due to his political authoritarianism and heavy-handed military tactics. In 1560, Akbar lost patience with his erstwhile mentor and guide, dismissed him from his post as chief advisor, and assumed full political and military responsibility himself. A year later, Bairam Khan was attacked and killed by a disgruntled Afghan warlord while he was on his way to Makkah to perform the sacred pilgrimage.

Akbar was only eighteen when he became a fully-fledged Mughal ruler and military commander. His bold and decisive action against his political opponents enabled him to consolidate Mughal rule across a large part of India and thereby completely transformed the fortunes of his dynasty. Keen to expand Mughal rule further, he then took the fight to the rulers of the neighbouring territories. Thus, from 1568 to 1569, he conducted military expeditions against the Rajputs of Rajasthan as they began to threaten Mughal interests. He headed a large expeditionary force and went to attack the Rajputs who were eventually defeated, despite stiff resistance, due to his superior military power. After annexing Rajasthan, he proceeded towards the State of Gujarat. With its thriving ports and coastal resorts, Gujarat was a strategically important province and major commercial centre at the time. For this reason, Akbar was very keen to capture this province. Indeed, as soon as he received news of riots in Ahmedabad, the provincial capital of Gujarat, he immediately set off with his forces – travelling as he did at lightning speed and covering around six hundred miles in just over a week – and took the rebels inside the city completely by surprise. He took the capital of Gujarat without encountering much resistance and thus connected his empire to the Arabian Sea, thereby opening up a naval route to the rest of the world.

Akbar then marched into Surat in 1573; Bengal, the wealthy northern Indian province also fell to the Mughals in 1576, as did Kabul in 1585. A year later, he annexed the beautiful valley of Kashmir; this was followed by Orissa in 1592; Sind and Baluchistan also became integral parts of the Mughal Empire between 1590 and 1595. Following this astonishing series of conquests, Akbar managed to establish Mughal power and authority throughout northern India. This period therefore represented the height of Mughal political power and military might. Despite his lack of formal education and training, Akbar was an accomplished ruler and gifted military strategist. Known to have been physically very strong, unusually brave and intelligent, he proved a success both on and off the battlefield. According to his son Salim (who later became Emperor Jahangir), 'Although he was illiterate, so much became clear to him through constant intercourse with the learned and the wise in his conversations with them that no-one knew him to be illiterate, and he was so well acquainted with the niceties of verse and prose composition that his deficiency was not mentioned. He passed his nights in wakefulness and slept little in the day…He counted his wakefulness at night as so much added to his life. His courage and boldness were such that he could mount raging, rutting elephants, and subdue to obedience murderous elephants.'

As an intelligent ruler, Akbar knew that brute force only breaks; it does not mend and fix. Having expanded Mughal rule across such a large area through military force, he knew it would not be possible to unify and strengthen these territories without developing and implementing an effective political and civil administrative system to govern them. Since all the previous Indian Muslim dynasties had disintegrated within a few decades of their inception, Akbar was determined not to allow the same to happen to the Mughals. But to achieve his objectives, he knew he had to make plans for the long-term and establish proper political governance and increase economic growth. However, he could not achieve this without the support and co-operation of the masses, so Akbar decided to win the hearts and minds of his people – that is, particularly the Muslims and Hindus – by promoting dialogue and mutual understanding between two of India's most prominent religions, namely Islam and Hinduism. By championing religious dialogue and cultural understanding between the Muslims and Hindus he hoped to establish lasting political stability, social solidarity and cultural understanding and tolerance throughout Mughal India. In order to achieve this objective, Akbar reformed the existing Mughal political and administrative structure which depended heavily on the goodwill and support of the wealthy, independent feudal chiefs to function effectively. So long as these chiefs remained loyal to the Mughals, they were – in the past – left to their own devices, although this had often led to political mismanagement, economic corruption and social discontent in many parts of India. Akbar changed this system and instead appointed provincial governors who were responsible for overseeing the affairs of their own provinces and regularly reported directly to him. He then went out of his way to forge alliances with several influential Hindu groups, including the Rajputs, who subsequently joined the Mughal political, civil and military services; in so doing he ensured that both Muslims and Hindus played an active part within his administration. This strategy proved very effective, not least because Muslims and Hindus came together and helped to consolidate Mughal political power and authority across India. Thus, politically speaking, Akbar's efforts to unite Muslims and Hindus proved a success, but the same cannot be said of his attempts to harmonise Islam and Hinduism.

As a fiercely monotheistic religion, Islam preaches the absolute Oneness of God (*tawhid*), thus negating all forms of associationism (*shirk*).

By contrast, the Hindus believe in multiple gods and goddesses, and also worship statues, idols and various animals. As such, these two religions are more diametrically opposed to each other than probably any of the other major world faiths. Yet, inspired by his Timurid ancestry, early contact with Sufism and subsequent encounter with Hinduism, Akbar decided to engage in highly questionable religious and cultural experimentation. Although his motive (namely to develop cultural understanding and religious tolerance between his Muslim and Hindu subjects), was indeed a praiseworthy one, his approach to inter-faith dialogue proved both inept and foolish. Exasperated by incessant Hindu-Muslim communal rivalry and conflict, Akbar and his advisors began to explore ways in which they could end these bitter conflicts by emphasising the common elements between the two faiths, rather than focus on the differences; this eventually inspired them to create a new religious synthesis by combining aspects of Islamic mysticism and Hindu philosophy. But, far from uniting the two rival religious factions, this only served to make matters worse, because both orthodox Muslims and Hindus considered Akbar's religious eclecticism very offensive.

Although he was a Muslim, he was now branded a heretic by orthodox Muslims and Hindus alike. The charge of heresy levelled against Akbar was justified, but he was not an unbeliever as such. Indeed, one of his favourite sayings was, 'If I have knowingly taken a step which is displeasing to God or have knowingly made an aspiration which was not according to His pleasure, may that elephant finish us, for we cannot support the burden of life under God's displeasure.' As a religious freethinker, he was fascinated by religion and philosophy and regularly engaged in religious discussion and debate with the leading Muslim, Hindu and Christian scholars of his time, for he was very keen to discover the truth about religion. He accepted the authority of the Qur'an, but also believed in the spiritual unity of religions (that is to say, he believed that all religions were true and authentic in their essence, only their forms differed.). This became the basis of his new religious synthesis, namely *din-i-ilahi* (or 'the Divine Religion'), which, as expected, was vigorously opposed by both orthodox Muslims and Hindus. Akbar's controversial and highly questionable religious and cultural reforms aside, his long reign of forty-nine years represented one of the most important periods in the history of Mughal India. He not only established political stability, reformed the Mughal civil administration and promoted economic prosperity across the land, he also built some of India's most magnificent buildings including the breathtaking Fatehpur Sikri, which is today considered to be one of the most beautiful sites in India along with the immortal Taj Mahal.

As a ruler, Akbar was determined and ruthless, but also benevolent; his most famous motto was 'Servant of all and master of none.' Despite being illiterate, he was very fond of books and loved classical Persian poetry, which he regularly had read out to him by his close friends and advisors, Faidi and Abul Fadl. Under his able stewardship, the Mughal Empire became one of the most influential political and military powers of the time. And having once fallen out with his only surviving son, Salim (Emperor Jahangir), Akbar became reconciled with him just before his death; he died at the age of sixty-three and was buried inside the mausoleum he had prepared for himself at Sikandra, located about five miles west of Agra, India.

# 44

## Al-Farabi
## (b.870 - d.950)

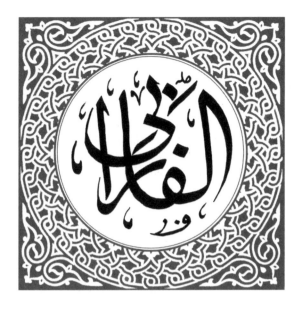

WHILST ANCIENT GREEK philosophy and science (as championed by prominent thinkers and scientists like Socrates, Plato, Aristotle, Galen and Hippocrates) was completely neglected in the West, the Muslims – in the Islamic East – embraced their ideas and thoughts with open arms. The Muslim philosophers, scientists and translators not only preserved these philosophical and scientific contributions, but also carried out a systematic analysis and evaluation of ancient Greek thought, and in so doing they made significant original contributions of their own. Thanks largely to the strenuous efforts of the early Muslim scientists and philosophers, today the ideas and thoughts of Plato, Aristotle, Galen and Hippocrates have become widely known both in the East and the West. As a matter of fact, the Western world came to discover and embrace ancient Greek philosophy and science as late as the fourteenth and fifteen centuries, facilitated by the Muslims of *al-andalus* (or Islamic Spain). More than any other Islamic philosopher, al-Farabi acquired a thorough mastery of ancient Greek philosophy and thought before he went on to develop a systematic interpretation of *falsafah* (or 'Islamic philosophy') for the very first time.

Abu Nasr Muhammad ibn Muhammad ibn Tarkhan ibn Uzalagh al-Farabi, better known in the Latin West as Alpharabius, was born in Wasij, a small village located close to Farab in the province of Transoxiana in Turkistan. Of Turkish origin, his father initially served as an army captain, and later he became a prominent member of the Persian military service. And although his father wanted his son to follow in his footsteps and join the elite Persian army, destiny had other plans for the young al-Farabi. During his early years he attended his local schools and followed the standard curriculum of the day which included Arabic, Persian, poetry, literature and aspects of Islamic sciences, focusing primarily on the Qur'an and Prophetic traditions (*hadith*). Since Farab and its surrounding areas came under Muslim rule only a few decades prior to al-Farabi's birth, his family may have embraced Islam during this period and become adherents of the *shafi'i madhhab* (school of legal thought), which subsequently spread throughout that region. This prompted young al-Farabi to specialise in *shafi'i* jurisprudence. As a bright student, he excelled in his studies beyond his family's expectations and was encouraged to pursue higher education rather than follow his father's military career.

From an early age, he showed an interest in all the sciences of his day and acquired proficiency in several languages and dialects. Blessed with an unrivalled linguistic ability, he continued to develop this ability throughout his life and probably knew more languages and dialects than any other Muslim thinker of his generation. Arabic and Persian aside, he mastered Turkish, Greek, Syriac and Hebrew, not to mention many other local languages and dialects. Though short in stature, al-Farabi always dressed immaculately and was very fond of beautiful Turkish attire, even though he became most famous for his unquenchable thirst for knowledge and wisdom. Brought up and educated at a time when the Samanid ruler Nasr ibn Ahmad actively promoted learning and higher education, al-Farabi, went on to receive advanced training in linguistics and Islamic sciences. He became so proficient in *fiqh* (Islamic jurisprudence) that he was appointed *qadi* (judge) while he was still in his twenties, although he later became bored with legal and administrative work. As a natural-born thinker and philosopher, he found the monotonous nature of legal routine suffocating, and abandoned his legal career in favour of higher education in the philosophical sciences.

After studying philosophy under the tutelage of prominent local scholars, he began to travel in search of further knowledge. From Farab, he moved to Merv (or Mary, located in present-day Turkmenistan), which at the time was a prominent centre of religious and philosophical learning and where some of the leading scholars of the day lived and taught. Here he studied logic and philosophy under the guidance of Yuhanna ibn Haylan, who was not only a master of philosophy, but also one of the leading exponents of Greek thought. It was in Merv that he encountered Greek philosophy for the first time and began to study the major works of Aristotle in Greek, as well as in Syriac translation. So it was that, he became one of the first Muslim philosophers to study Aristotelian logic and philosophy

directly from original Greek under the tutelage of some of its leading authorities and, as a result, he rapidly assimilated ancient Greek philosophical thought. From Merv he went to Baghdad, which was the capital of the Abbasid Caliphate and one of the Muslim world's foremost centres of learning at the time. Al-Farabi arrived in Baghdad when he was around thirty and pursued advanced training in Arabic grammar and syntax under the guidance of Abu Bakr ibn al-Sarraj, who was one of the most distinguished linguists and grammarians of his generation. Impressed with al-Farabi's profound knowledge of logic, al-Sarraj asked the former to teach him logic. After several years in Baghdad, he travelled to the northern Iraqi city of Harran and from there he went to Constantinople (modern Istanbul) before finally returning to Baghdad in around 910. Thus, at the age of forty, al-Farabi became widely recognised as a prominent jurist, logician, philosopher, linguist and theologian. Given his remarkable academic achievements, he could have started teaching on his arrival in Baghdad, but instead joined the class of Abu Bishr Matta ibn Yunus, who was one of the most respected Arabic translators of Aristotle's works. After completing his advanced training in Aristotelian logic under Abu Bishr's guidance, he became an unrivalled master of Greek philosophical sciences, so that subsequently he became one of the foremost authorities on the thought of Aristotle, and also the first systematic Muslim philosopher.

Al-Farabi lived in Baghdad for another three decades, during which he taught and pursued research on all the sciences of his day. Given his prodigious learning and scholarship, he could have acquired much fame and wealth if he wished, but instead he shunned public life, wealth and glamour in favour of a life devoted entirely to the pursuit and dissemination of knowledge and wisdom. As a bookworm and an eclectic reader, he reportedly read Aristotle's *Physics* more than forty times and his *De Anima* around two hundred times. In addition to this, he produced nearly seventy volumes of notes and writings on all aspects of philosophy. And although this figure may be somewhat exaggerated, the fact that al-Farabi was a gifted scholar and an industrious writer is not in doubt. As an outstanding polymath, he was thoroughly familiar with all the branches of learning known during his time, but he became most famous for his contributions in three disciplines: logic, political science, and philosophy and metaphysics. His works in these subjects are considered to be nothing short of great monuments in the annals of human thought.

Devoid of philosophical and technical jargon, al-Farabi's writings are unusually simple and easy to understand. Thus, even those who are not philosophically-minded can read and make sense of his ideas and thoughts without much difficulty. And despite being familiar with more than twenty languages and dialects, he deliberately chose to write all his works in Arabic. This was perhaps due to the fact that Arabic was the language of the Qur'an – the official language of Islamic learning and scholarship – and also the *lingua franca* of the Muslim world at the time. Another reason could be that he wanted to reach a large audience, in which case Arabic again would have been his obvious choice. Al-Farabi authored most of his books during his long stay in Baghdad, although some were composed during the final years of his life in Syria. In total, he wrote more than one hundred books on all the sciences of his time including seventeen commentaries, fifteen treatises and around sixty books and manuscripts. Unhappily, the vast majority of his works have perished; only a small number – no more than twenty – have survived, primarily in Hebrew and Latin translations.

Of his major writings, the most important were *Kitab Ihsa al-Ulum* (The Book of Enumeration of Sciences); commentaries on Aristotle's *Organon* (which comprised the *Categories*, *Hermeneutics*, *Prior Analytics*, *Posterior Analytics*, *Topics*, *Sophistics*, *Rhetoric* and *Poetics*), as well as *Sharh Kitab al-Sama al-Tabi'i Li-Aristutalis* (The Commentary on Aristotle's *Physics*). In addition to this, he wrote several treatises rebutting the ideas and thoughts of other prominent Muslim phi-

losophers like Abu Bakr al-Razi. In his *Kitab Ihsa al-Ulum*, al-Farabi – for the first time in Islamic intellectual history – developed a coherent and comprehensive classification of the sciences of his day. In doing so, he – again for the very first time – analysed, interpreted and introduced Greek philosophical sciences into the Muslim world in a systematic way. His commentaries on the works of Aristotle were some of the most erudite and wide-ranging books to have been produced on Aristotelian logic and philosophy. This rightly earned him the coveted title of *al-mu'allim al-thani* (The Second Teacher) with Aristotle being *al-mu'allim al-awwal* (The First Teacher). If al-Farabi was a great philosopher, then he was an equally peerless exponent of logic. His contribution in this field was so vast and original that he became widely known as 'the father of logic'. So much so that the great Jewish philosopher and theologian Musa bin Maimon (better known as Maimonides) once told one of his friends that al-Farabi's works on logic were 'finer than flour' and urged him not to bother consulting the works of other logicians.

Unlike al-Ghazali and many other prominent Islamic thinkers, al-Farabi considered philosophy to be entirely unified. Also, he was of the opinion that in essence there was only one true philosophy; thus he argued that both Plato and Aristotle expounded the same truth. He articulated these views in several books including his *Kitab al-Jam baina Ra'yai al-Hakimain Aftalun al-Ilahi wa Aristutalis* (The Book of Reconciliation of the Opinions of the Two Divines, Plato and Aristotle). After harmonising the philosophical ideas and thoughts of Plato and Aristotle, he argued that similar harmony existed between Islam and Greek philosophy. As a insatiable reader of Islamic scriptural sources and Greek thought, he devoted a considerable part of his intellectual life to seeking to reconcile these two supposedly conflicting worldviews. Although al-Ghazali questioned and attacked certain aspects of al-Farabi's cosmology, and even accused him of blindly following Aristotle and other prominent Greek philosophers on issues such as the nature of creation and the theory of the intellect, it should be pointed out that al-Farabi's philosophical thinking also profoundly influenced al-Ghazali himself, not to mention other renowned Islamic philosophers like Ibn Sina, Suhrawardi, Mulla Sadra and Shah Waliullah of Delhi.

As a devout Muslim and also a practising Sufi, al-Farabi focused more on the spiritual, than on the practical, dimension of things. Nevertheless, he found time to think about and write profusely on both political philosophy and ethics. Indeed he was one of the first to write on these subjects in the Muslim world. In summary, his political philosophy and science of society (*ilm al-madani*) was underpinned by an integrated spiritualist view of human life and society; one where the achievement of existential happiness and eternal salvation went hand in hand – as opposed to emphasising the importance of one without the other. In other words, his approach to political philosophy and ethics was thisworldly and at the same time other-worldly; that is to say, he combined the practical and spiritual dimensions of Islam to create a solid foundation for a balanced social, political and ethical framework. He developed his political and ethical ideas in scores of treatises including *Kitab al-Siyasat al-Madaniyyah* (The Book of Political Governance), *Kitab al-Millat al-Fadilah* (The Book of the Noble Nation), *Kitab Tahsil al-Sa'adah* (The Book of Attainment of Happiness) and *Kitab ara Ahl al-Madinat al-Fadilah* (The Book of Views of the Inhabitants of the Noble City). Inspired by Islamic scriptural sources, as well as ancient Greek thinkers like Plato, Plotinus and Aristotle, in these books he formulated a refreshingly unified political synthesis which took into consideration the practical and spiritual dimensions of human life and society. Also, the fact that he was an expert in traditional Islamic sciences (who specialised in *shafi'i* jurisprudence during his early years) comes across more clearly in his political and ethical works than it does in his philosophical and cosmological output.

Al-Farabi was in his early seventies when political instability began to spread across Baghdad, and this prompted him to move to Damascus in 942. Here he worked as a gardener for a period before moving to Egypt, only to return to Damascus again in 949. This time he received a warm welcome from the reigning Hamanid ruler, Sayf al-Dawlah, who invited him to join his royal court, but a spiritually-inclined al-Farabi politely refused the monarch's offer. The latter then offered him a large sum of money but he refused that, too, saying he only needed an allowance of four dirhams to cover his daily expenses so that he could continue his study and research. A year later, al-Farabi died at the age of eighty and was buried in Damascus following a simple funeral led by Sayf al-Dawlah himself. Like al-Kindi, al-Khwarizmi and Abu Bakr al-Razi, he was a versatile genius and one of the most influential Muslim philosophers of all time. It is not surprising, therefore, that his ideas and thoughts influenced some of the most famous thinkers of the Muslim world including Ibn Sina, al-Ghazali, Ibn Tufayl, Ibn Rushd, Ibn Khaldun and Shah Waliullah. Likewise, his works influenced prominent Jewish and Christian thinkers like St Thomas Aquinas, John Duns Scotus, Musa bin Maimon (Maimonides) and Leo Strauss among others.

THE PRE-ISLAMIC ARABS became renowned for preserving and transmitting historical and genealogical information from one generation to another through oral communication. After the emergence of Islam in Arabia in the seventh century, the Arabs – for the first time in their history – embraced learning and education with much interest and enthusiasm. And one subject in which the early Muslims excelled more than any other was history. But that was not too surprising given the fact that a large portion of the Qur'an consisted of historical information and data about the ancient people and their activities. The study of history thus became one of the foremost preoccupations of the early Muslim scholars, thinkers and writers. Although Ibn Khaldun is today widely considered to be the most influential Muslim historian of all time (on account of his profound originality and subsequent influence on the development of modern social sciences and historicism), the coveted title of 'father of Islamic history' has rightly been conferred on al-Tabari for his monumental contribution to Islamic historiography. Indeed, he is today considered to be one of the Muslim world's most influential historians and Qur'anic exegetes.

Abu Ja'far Muhammad ibn Jarir ibn Yazid al-Tabari was born in Amul in the Persian province of Tabaristan, now in eastern Azerbaijan. His father was a wealthy Persian businessman who ensured his son received the best education that money could buy. After learning Arabic and Persian, young al-Tabari successfully committed the entire Qur'an to memory when he was only seven. He then studied Arabic literature and traditional Islamic sciences. As a precocious child, he completed his early education while he was still in his teens. Encouraged and financed by his wealthy family, he then moved to the historic Persian city of Rayy to pursue further education. Unlike Amul, Rayy was a flourishing centre of Islamic learning and commercial activity. Here he attended the lectures of the city's leading scholars and became thoroughly familiar with Arabic, Persian, *tafsir* (Qur'anic exegesis), *hadith* (Prophetic traditions), *fiqh* (jurisprudence) and aspects of history (*tarikh*). As a true seeker of knowledge and wisdom, he preferred to read and study, rather than play games or engage in other worldly activities during his early years. Impressed with his son's unusual intellectual ability and scholarly outlook, his father encouraged him to pursue higher education rather than join the family business.

Supported financially by his wealthy father, al-Tabari devoted himself to his studies and devoured books and treatises on all aspects of traditional Islamic sciences. He read voraciously during the night and attended the lectures of the local scholars during the day, until he completed his formal education. Blessed with a highly retentive memory and a keen intellect, he was able to assimilate vast quantities of information with ease and out-performed many of his contemporaries. From Rayy he went to Baghdad, the capital of the Abbasid Empire, to study under the guidance of the famous Ahmad ibn Hanbal. But when he arrived in Baghdad, at the age of twenty, he discovered that Ahmad ibn Hanbal had already passed away. After touring the city and having also attended the lectures of some of its leading scholars, he moved to Basrah and eventually settled in Kufah. Shocked and dismayed by the political chaos and confusion which ensued following the murder of Abbasid Caliph Mutawakkil ala Allah by his Turkish bodyguard in 861, the quiet, peaceful and studious al-Tabari left Kufah and moved to Syria.

During this period he lost contact with his family and began to experience considerable financial hardship and personal suffering. Although his father had left behind considerable wealth and estates back in his native Tabaristan, al-Tabari was unable to obtain any financial support. However, as a firm believer in the traditional Islamic saying that "a luxurious lifestyle and learning do not go hand in hand", he endured all the financial difficulties and personal hardships with great resilience and fortitude. Indeed, during this period he was forced to go without any proper meals, surviving on biscuits and water only. In desperation, he once sold the sleeves of his shirt so he could buy breadcrumbs for a meal. Despite suffering much pain and hardship, his stay in Syria proved very fruitful as he devoted all his time to the study of *hadith*. In fact, during this period he memorised a large number of Prophetic traditions, collected information about the life and times of the Prophet, and became thoroughly familiar with the views and opinions of the Prophet's companions on all aspects of Islam. He lived at a time when travelling in pursuit of knowledge was considered to be a *sine qua non* for all true seekers of wisdom; that was the only way a student could attend the lectures of all the leading scholars of the day where they lived and taught in prominent centres of Islamic learning and scholarship like Makkah, Madinah, Baghdad, Basrah, Kufah and Damascus. As expected, al-Tabari travelled extensively in pursuit of knowledge and studied in Damascus, Makkah and Egypt, before finally returning to Baghdad.

After completing his advanced education, he began to teach and soon his name began to spread across Baghdad, thanks to his profound knowledge and understanding of Islam. Despite being a strict adherent of the Prophetic *sunnah* (norms and ethos), he never married and remained a confirmed bachelor all his life. Instead he devoted his entire life to the pursuit and dissemination of Islamic knowledge and later became one of the most influential Islamic scholars of all time. When al-Tabari's reputation as a prominent Islamic scholar reached the corridors of power, the ruling Abbasid elites offered him lucrative Government posts but he politely declined their offers, preferring to live frugally, and continue his study and research into all the branches of Islamic learning. He led a simple, pious and austere lifestyle, and deliberately shunned the wealth and luxuries of this world, remaining totally focused on his intellectual pursuits. This in itself was a remarkable achievement considering the fact that, at the time, the forces of materialism and hedonism had not only entered the Governmental circles in Baghdad, but had also infiltrated the ranks of the religious scholars. But al-Tabari, who was now widely considered to be a master of *hadith*, *fiqh*, *tafsir* and Islamic history, remained totally aloof. More importantly, his achievements in these Islamic subjects were nothing short of breathtaking.

As a jurist, he initially followed the school of Abu Hanifah but, after carrying out a thorough and systematic study of *maliki*, *shafi'i* and *hanbali fiqh*, he became an adherent of *shafi'i* jurisprudence. He followed the *shafi'i madhhab* for nearly a decade before he developed his own interpretation of Islamic jurisprudence. Al-Tabari's understanding of *fiqh* was both sophisticated and remarkably fluid and, as such, he continued to develop his ideas and thoughts on juristic matters right to the end of his life. Based on his interpretation of Islamic jurisprudence, a different school of Islamic legal thought known as the *jariri madhhab* later emerged in the Muslim world. This *madhhab* initially claimed a sizeable following, but it subsequently died away. Although in principle, al-Tabari's approach to Islamic jurisprudence was very similar to that of Shafi'i, in practice it was considerably different. Since al-Tabari was thoroughly acquainted with all the prominent schools of Islamic jurisprudence, his ideas and thoughts were variously influenced by all of them. Not surprisingly, his *madhhab* reflected the views of the *hanafi*, *shafi'i* and *hanbali* jurists as much as it reflected his own views. Having said that, al-Tabari was an outstanding jurist in his own right and his contribution to the field of Islamic jurisprudence was both considerable and noteworthy.

Yet it is true that al-Tabari is today most famous for his contribution in the field of *tafsir*. After travelling far and wide, he collected a large quantity of information about the Qur'an, its history and methods of interpretation, and thus he became thoroughly familiar with all aspects of Qur'anic sciences and exegesis. He was in his sixties when he vowed to write two large books; one on the Qur'an and the other on history. As a scholar and writer of truly astonishing industry, he used to study round the clock and wrote more than twenty pages daily for around forty years. Although these figures may be somewhat exaggerated, the fact that al-Tabari was an unusually prolific writer is not in doubt. Entitled *Jami al-Bayan fi Tafsir al-Qur'an* (The Exhaustive Commentary on the Qur'an), this Qur'anic commentary consisted of more than three thousand pages and was published in thirty bulky volumes.

Also known as *Tafsir-i-Tabari* (al-Tabari's Commentary), this book is not only a treasure trove of information about the Qur'an, its history, meaning and interpretation, it is also one of the largest commentaries ever written on the Qur'an. Not surprisingly, the Islamic scholars (*ulama*) and Qur'anic commentators (*mufassirun*) have continued to use it as a standard work of reference on *tafsir* to this day. All the great Qur'anic commentators such as al-Qurtubi, Ibn Kathir, al-Zamakhshari, Fakhr al-Din al-Razi, al-Suyuti, al-Baydawi and al-Alusi among others were profoundly influenced by al-Tabari's monumental *tafsir*.

As a commentator on the Qur'an, al-Tabari was a strict traditionalist who relied entirely on the Prophetic traditions, the views and opinions of the Prophet's companions (*sahabah*) and those of their successors (*tabiun*) to explain the message of the Qur'an, rather than use his own rational discretion. For this reason, his exegesis of the Qur'an is considered to be a *tafsir bi'l riwayah* or a commentary by way of transmission and evaluation of Prophetic traditions through the mechanism of *isnad* (chain of narration). Nevertheless, he has been criticised by some Qur'anic commentators for incorporating information into his commentary without sifting the wheat from the chaff. For example, he has included the corpus of *isra'iliyat* (or questionable data of Jewish origin) into his commentary. Then again, it is not surprising that some questionable data or information had crept into his commentary, given the voluminous nature of the work. But, overall, al-Tabari's commentary is nothing short of a remarkable contribution in the field of *tafsir*. In fact, had it not been for his splendid efforts, the world of Qur'anic scholarship would have been deprived of a great treasure trove of information and data.

If al-Tabari's *tafsir* was an invaluable contribution, then his *Kitab Tarikh al-Rusul wa'l Muluk* (The Book of the History of Prophets and Kings) must be considered one of the greatest works of history ever written. When he decided to write this voluminous work, he reportedly asked his friends whether they would be interested in reading a book on history. When his friends asked him how big it would be, he said it would be around sixty thousand pages long. The sheer size of the book prompted his friends to reply that they could not hope to finish such a large book. Al-Tabari was dismayed by his friends' remark, and felt the people of Baghdad no longer had any aspirations or ambitions. Undeterred by his friends' apparent reluctance to read, he went onto compose his monumental *Kitab Tarikh al-Rusul wa'l Muluk*. Beginning with an account of creation, the book traced the journey of humanity through the lives and careers of all the prominent Prophets including the final Messenger of God, Muhammad, his four rightly-guided Caliphs and the reign of the Umayyads before concluding with an entry in 915. Although the original copy of this book was about sixty thousand pages long, the edition that has survived is much shorter. Even so, its English edition consists of thirty-eight bulky volumes, ten thousand pages in total.

Unlike Abul Faraj al-Isfahani, Abul Hasan al-Mas'udi or Ibn Khaldun, al-Tabari was primarily a compiler of historical information. History, according to him, was no more than a sequence of events which he recorded and transmitted, and did so without seeking to analyse or identify the underlying factors which triggered the sequence of events in the first place. That is why he meticulously recorded as much information as he could about the early Muslim community, without subjecting his data to rigorous examination or scrutiny. In that sense, he was very much like Herodotus, the ancient Greek historian, who also recorded his data without critically examining them. For this reason, all prominent Islamic scholars, Qur'anic commentators and historians have continued to approach al-Tabari's history of the world with care and due diligence. But, given the size of the work, he probably thought it would be a hopeless task seeking to ascertain the authencity of all the information he had collected, and thus left the task of sifting the wheat from the chaff to his successors such as al-Baladhuri, al-Isfahani, al-Miskawayh, Thabit ibn Sinan and Ibn al-Athir.

After a lifetime devoted to the pursuit of Islamic sciences and history, al-Tabari, the 'father of Islamic history' and the 'Livy of the Arabs', passed away at the ripe old age of around eighty. But his remarkable contribution, especially in the field of *tafsir* and Islamic history, has remained unrivalled to this day.

## 46

## *Ibn Battutah*
## (b.1304 - d.1378)

MUHAMMAD IBN AHMAD ibn Jubayr was not only one of the Muslim world's most prominent globetrotters, he was also one of the great travellers of medieval Europe. He left Islamic Spain and travelled across the Islamic East (including Egypt, Arabia and Syria) before finally returning home to record his views and experiences of those lands in the form of memoirs which later became famous both in the East and the West. It was a century later that Marco Polo, the celebrated Venetian merchant and adventurer, travelled extensively across Europe and Asia. In addition to Baghdad, he visited China where he reportedly served Kublai Khan, the famous Mongol ruler, for a period before he returned home to Venice in 1295. He later wrote a detailed account of his travels and adventures which continues to be read widely to this day. Both Ibn Jubayr and Marco Polo were great travellers who undertook their journeys at a time when long distance travelling was far from being the norm. A year after Marco Polo's death, a young North African Muslim set out to discover the world, travelling a significant part of the then-known world on foot, riding on mules and sailing on boats, and in so doing he became arguably the greatest traveller in human history. This fearless,

indomitable and inspirational globetrotter was none other than the influential Ibn Battutah.

Abu Abdullah Muhammad ibn Abdullah ibn Muhammad ibn Ibrahim al-Luwati, better known as Ibn Battutah, was born in Tangier (in present-day Morocco) into a distinguished family of Islamic scholars and judges. Although his ancestors originally hailed from the outskirts of Egypt, his family members later became prominent figures of the Berber tribe of Luwata. Brought up and educated in a learned and wealthy family, Ibn Battutah studied Arabic language, literature and traditional Islamic sciences during his early years. Since his father and uncles were notable Islamic scholars and prominent members of the local judiciary, he also received advanced training in Islamic jurisprudence (*fiqh*). Encouraged by his father to follow in his footsteps and become a lawyer, Ibn Battutah completed his formal education in the religious sciences, focusing on Islamic jurisprudence, before he decided to go to Makkah to perform the pilgrimage. Only twenty-one at the time, he was nonetheless very keen to undertake the long and arduous journey to Makkah in order to accomplish the fifth pillar of Islam and also pursue higher education in Islamic jurisprudence, presumably to enhance his chances of obtaining a prominent judicial post on his return to Tangier.

In 1325, he bade farewell to his family and set out for Makkah. In those days, journeys from North Africa to Arabia were undertaken by caravan, and often took several months (if not longer) and were always fraught with danger, hardship and difficulties; but the brave and indomitable Ibn Battutah set out on his own. From Tangier, he travelled to Tilimsan and from there he went to Algiers in the company of a group of merchants. Passing by Constantine, he reached Tunis just in time for the Islamic festival of *eid al-fitr* (or the feast which marks the end of the sacred month of Ramadan). On his arrival, he fell ill but, luckily, he soon recovered. He then discovered that the people of Tunis were busy preparing their own pilgrim caravans. When he approached them to request passage with them, they nominated him to lead the caravans to Makkah, presumably because he had superior knowledge of Islamic principles and practices. After reaching Tripoli (in present-day Libya), he married for the first time but the marriage soon ended in divorce, owing to an acrimonious dispute between Ibn Battutah and his father-in-law. Undeterred by this bad experience, he then married for a second time and celebrated the occasion with a lavish banquet. In April 1326, he arrived in Alexandria with the pilgrim caravans and met a Sufi dervish (Islamic mystic) who apparently prophesied that he would one day travel across the world.

Prior to Ibn Battutah's encounter with the Sufi, he had no intention or desire to travel anywhere other than Makkah and Madinah, but now the idea and possibility of travelling and exploring the world really fascinated him. Keen to complete the pilgrimage, he left Alexandria by boat and arrived in Cairo in July 1326. He not only toured Cairo, he also provided a detailed survey and description of this historic city. He liked what he saw and decided to continue travelling. From Cairo, he travelled across the barren desert and visited Gaza, Hebron, Bethlehem and Jerusalem. During his stay in Jerusalem, Ibn Battutah

visited *masjid al-aqsa* and the Dome of the Rock (*qubbat al-sakhra*), which is the Muslim world's third holiest site, and he was overwhelmed by the mosque's great beauty and grandeur. After touring Palestine, he proceeded to Syria, visiting Aleppo and Antioch, before finally arriving in Damascus in August 1326. Like his illustrious predecessor Ibn Jubayr, he found Damascus to be an extremely beautiful city. Here he claimed to have encountered one of the city's most distinguished citizens, namely *shaykh al-Islam* Ibn Taymiyyah, the great Islamic thinker and reformer. But, according to the historians, Ibn Battutah could not have encountered Ibn Taymiyyah because the latter had been incarcerated a month before his arrival in Damascus; this therefore appears to be a chronological, if not a factual, error on his part. Nevertheless, he stayed in Damascus for a period and attended the lectures of its leading scholars. As a keen student of Islam, he soon obtained certification (*ijaza*) in the traditional Islamic sciences. Here he also married for the third time. But a month later, he left Damascus and set out for Madinah, the city of the Prophet, via Tabuk. As soon as he reached Madinah, he went straight to the Prophet's mosque to pay homage to the blessed Prophet and his close companions, Abu Bakr al-Siddiq and Umar ibn al-Khattab. After four days of prayer and devotion, he went to Makkah to perform another pilgrimage. With great joy and happiness, he completed all the rites of the pilgrimage. Then, in November 1326, he left Makkah by caravan and soon reached Iraq. After touring all the prominent Iraqi cities, including Najaf, Basrah, Baghdad, Kufah, Mosul and parts of southern Persia, he again returned to Makkah accompanied by a caravan of pilgrims. During his stay in Makkah, he devoted much of his time to prayer and devotional activities, and completed his third successive pilgrimage.

A year later, he performed his fourth pilgrimage and obtained certification in advanced Islamic studies. Having chosen not to return home to Tangier, Ibn Battutah decided to travel around the world. Still only twenty-six years old at the time, he left Makkah and sailed to Yemen where he visited both Sana and Aden, before proceeding to Oman. He found this country very fertile and full of trees, plants and all kinds of fruits and vegetables. From Oman, he moved to Hormuz and Bahrain, and eventually returned again to Makkah in time for his fifth pilgrimage in 1332. After completing the pilgrimage, he decided to go to India and see the land of Sultan Muhammad ibn Tughluq for the very first time. From Makkah, he went to Yemen, hoping to get on a ship bound for India. During his previous trip to Yemen, the locals had told him how thoroughbred horses were regularly shipped to India from Yemen and this, no doubt, encouraged him to go there to board a ship to India. However, his plans did not work out as he hoped and instead he was forced to take the difficult route to Ladhiqiya via Cairo, Syria and the Palestinian cities of Gaza, Hebron and Jerusalem. Here he was fortunate to board a Genoese vessel destined for the ancient Turkish region of Anatolia. After ten days and ten nights at sea, an exhausted Ibn Battutah eventually arrived in Anatolia, where he received a warm welcome from the locals, despite not being able to speak a word of Turkish.

From Anatolia, he proceeded to Konya, where the mausoleum of Mawlana Jalal al-Din Rumi the great Sufi thinker and poet, had become an important centre of Sufi activities. From Konya, he continued his journey towards Amasya where he celebrated the annual Islamic festival of *eid al-adha* (the feast of sacrifice) in the distinguished company of its governor. Then he headed in the direction of the Caucasus, the land of Sultan Muhammad Uzbeg Khan of the Golden Horde. But the bitterly cold and harsh environment of the Caucasus prompted him to proceed to the capital of Greater Bulgaria, and from there he went to the ancient city of Constantinople (present-day Instanbul) in the company of Sultan Muhammad Uzbeg Khan's third wife. Unlike his stay in the Caucasus, his time in Constantinople proved very fruitful, not least because he was able to tour the whole city and provide an elaborate survey and description of what he saw. However, according to some historians, he may not have

visited all the places he mentioned in his *Rihla* (Travels), although no serious reader of, for example, his description of Sarai, the capital of the Tatar dynasty, can help but feel that they are reading anything but an eye-witness account of that place. Furthermore, Ibn Battutah's accounts of his travels in Asia Minor have been proven and corroborated by other historical sources. So, from Sarai he travelled through Khwarizm, Khiva, Bukhara, Samarqand and Balkh before he reached the historic province of Khurasan. From here, he went to Kabul, the capital of modern Afghanistan, and in September 1333, at the age of twenty-nine, he finally reached the borders of India. After crossing the Indus River, he went to Multan where he received a warm welcome from its governor. From there, he set out for Delhi, the magnificent capital of Muslim India, where he joined the reigning Sultan's civil service. However, given his superior education and extensive knowledge of Islamic law, the ruling elites within the Sultan's administration not only became very jealous of him, but also began to conspire against him.

He stayed in India for a long time and travelled extensively across the country. He closely observed the local people, their culture, customs and habits. Other than Abu Raihan al-Biruni, the celebrated Muslim astronomer and scientist (who composed his famous *Kitab Tarikh al-Hind* (History of India) during his long stay in India from 1021 to 1031), no other medieval traveller or writer had provided such a detailed description of India as did Ibn Battutah. According to Ibn Khaldun, the great historian of Islam, his accounts of India were so detailed, bewildering and adventurous that, on his return to Morocco, he received a mixed reaction at the court of Sultan Abu Inan. And although he may have slightly overstated or embellished his adventures in India, even a discerning historian like Ibn Khaldun did not question the soundness or authenticity of his travel accounts, which have also been substantiated by other reliable historical Indian sources. After almost a decade in India, just as Ibn Battutah finally decided to return to

Makkah, the reigning Sultan summoned him to his court and requested him to head a diplomatic mission to the Mongol ruler of China. Keen to undertake yet another adventure, he accepted the Sultan's offer and set out for the Far East.

The journey through mainland India was fraught with many dangers and difficulties. On one occasion he was taken prisoner by local tribesmen, but fortunately managed to escape unscathed. After reaching Calicut, he embarked on a Chinese vessel but as soon as he boarded the vessel it sank, leaving him stranded on the shore. Eventually he reached the Maldive Islands, where he stayed for eighteen months and married for the fourth time, and also worked as a *qadi* (Islamic judge), before proceeding to Ceylon (modern Sri Lanka). Ibn Battutah's description of the Maldive Islands is today considered to be one of the most detailed and illuminating travel accounts of all time. No other writer or traveller has been able to surpass his description and account of these stunning islands and their people. In Ceylon, he toured the country and even scaled its highest mountain, commonly known as 'Adam's Footprint', before he sailed to Chittagong in East Bengal (in present-day Bangladesh). From East Bengal, he travelled to the Indonesian island of Sumatra and there boarded a vessel which took him on to China. According to Ibn Battutah, China was a beautiful country and he found the Chinese people very kind and courteous. But, as a practising Muslim, he found their eating habits repulsive; he noted, to his disgust, how the Chinese were very fond of pork.

Although Ibn Battutah stayed in China for only a short period, he observed Chinese culture, customs and habits at first hand. From China, he returned to Sumatra and from there he went on to Malabar. Now in his mid-forties, he finally decided to head westwards. Travelling along the Persian Gulf, he soon reached Baghdad and from there he went to Syria where, for the first time, he witnessed the havoc wreaked by the deadly plague known as 'the Black Death'. From Syria,

he went via Egypt to Makkah, to perform yet another pilgrimage. After completing the pilgrimage, he again returned to Egypt to sail from Alexandria to Tunis, and from there he took a ship to Algiers and reached his native Morocco in November 1349. After travelling around the world, in 1352, at the age of forty-eight, he embarked on yet another adventure. He crossed the Strait of Gibraltar and arrived in Granada. From there, he returned to Morocco and crossed the Saharan desert to spend some time with the Muslim Mandingos in Niger. There he was surprised to discover that the locals constructed their houses with rock salt. Today, his travel accounts of Niger and Timbuktu are considered to be an invaluable source of medieval African history and culture. Ibn Battutah eventually returned to Fez at the age of fifty and by royal order he dictated his *Rihla* (Accounts of Travel) to Sultan Abu Inan's personal secretary, Muhammad ibn Juzayy, under the title of *Tuhfat al-Nuzzar fi Ghara'ib al-Amsar wa Aja'ib al-Asfar* (A Gift to Observers, Dealing with the Curiosities of Cities and the Wonder of Travels).

Ibn Battutah spent the next twenty-four years of his life in Fez. During this period he also served as a judge and eventually died at the age of seventy-four. Known widely as the 'Traveller of Islam', he travelled more than seventy-five thousand miles and did so all on his own. He achieved this unprecedented feat at a time when long distance travel was far from being straightforward or free from peril. As such, it would not be an exaggeration to say that he was one of the great pioneers of international travel and cultural reporting. Indeed, his record of seventy-five thousand miles remained unbeaten until steam engines were invented in the eighteenth century. Thanks to Sir Hamilton A.R. Gibb, the renowned British Arabist, his entire *Rihla* is now available in English. In fact, as early as 1929, he published an abridged edition of the *Rihla* under the title of *The Travels of Ibn Battutah*, which continues to be read widely to this day.

# 47
## Jabir ibn Hayyan
## (b.738 - d.813)

CHEMISTRY IS CONCERNED with the composition of matter (gas, liquid or solid), and of the changes that take place therein under certain conditions. Along with physics and biology, it is one of the three major physical sciences. And as in physics and biology, the Muslim contribution to the development of chemistry was both profound and unprecedented; indeed, the origin of the word 'chemistry' can be traced back to its Arabic root *al-kimiya,* which was also translated as alchemy. Perhaps the word *al-kimiya* originated from the Egyptian *khem,* meaning 'black'; both the ancient Egyptians and Greeks considered chemistry to be the 'art of *khem'.* As such, they sought to discover the mysteries which surrounded the practice of this 'black art', especially the transformation of base metal into solid gold or silver, presumably for economic reasons. Among the early Muslim practitioners of alchemy were Khalid ibn Yazid, the grandson of Caliph Muawiyah, and Ja'far al-Sadiq, the prominent Islamic scholar of Madinah who acquired knowledge of this subject from a combination of religious and Syriac sources. However, their understanding of chemistry was only confined to aspects of fusion, distillation and fabrication of certain chemical substances to produce desirable products, without undermining their spiritual dimension. Rather, the early Muslim alchemists or chemists considered alchemy – in its highest form – to be a spiritual science, thus capable of purifying and liberating the human spirit without undermining the physical dimension of those chemical substances. This state of affairs prevailed until Jabir ibn Hayyan, known in the Latin West as Geber, emerged to pave the way for the emergence of alchemy as an independent branch of science.

Jabir ibn Hayyan ibn Abdullah al-Kufi al-Sufi was born in Tus in the Persian province of Khurasan. Hailing from the southern Arabian tribe of Azd, his ancestors moved to Kufah during the early years of Islamic expansion. His father was a noted medical druggist who supported the Abbasids in their political campaign against their Umayyad rivals. Perhaps it was his political links with the Abbasids which prompted him to leave Kufah for Khurasan, where he continued to support the Abbasid insurgency against the Umayyads. While Jabir was a child his father was captured and sentenced to death by the Umayyad judiciary for supporting politically subversive activities. After his father's execution, Jabir and his family rapidly fell into poverty, leaving his mother with no alternative except to send her son to Arabia to continue his education there. He studied Arabic language, literature and traditional Islamic sciences before receiving advanced training in Islamic sciences, spirituality and aspects of alchemy under the guidance of Ja'far al-Sadiq, who was at the time one of the Muslim world's most renowned authorities on Islamic sciences and spirituality. Thereafter, he studied astrology, cosmology and further aspects of medicine and alchemy.

Blessed with a sharp intellect and an inquisitive mind, Jabir was admired by all his tutors for his utter devotion and dedication to his studies. As a practising Sufi, he was also in the habit of going into spiritual retreats but his Sufism was far from being other-worldly, for he found time to learn and master the experimental sciences too. An adherent of the Sufi *tariqah* (or Order) founded by Abul Hashim of Kufah, Jabir successfully combined spiritualism with physical and intellectual activism, which in itself was a very rare achievement considering that the pursuit of both spirituality and worldly knowledge was not considered to be tenable at the time. Nevertheless, after completing his formal education in the empirical sciences, he became a successful medical practitioner and his reputation soon began to spread far and wide. When Harun al-Rashid, the celebrated Abbasid Caliph, came to hear about Jabir, he went out of his way to recruit him to his research centre in Baghdad. Renowned for promoting learning and higher education, the ruling Abbasid elites encouraged Muslim scholars, philosophers and scientists to come to Baghdad and pursue their research in all branches of science. Jabir thus became associated with the Abbasids, especially the Barmakids who at the time served as chief advisors to the Caliph. Thanks to the Abbasids' generosity, his dire economic situation improved, enabling him to pursue research in the experimental sciences, especially in alchemy.

Although Jabir continued to live in Kufah, he travelled regularly to Baghdad to collaborate with the leading Muslim scholars and scientists of the day. As a scientist, he was interested in both theoretical as well as experimental science; indeed, such was his love of learning and scholarship that he became thoroughly familiar with a wide range of subjects including theology (*kalam*), Sufism, astrology, cosmology, medicine and music. However, it was in the field of alchemy, or chemistry, that he made his lasting contribution. In addition to studying ancient Egyptian and Greek alchemy (as expounded by Hermes, Pythagoras, Socrates, Zosimus and Bolos Democritus), Jabir acquired a profound knowledge and understanding of traditional Islamic sciences, and this enabled him to develop a fresh approach to the study of alchemy. Before his own time, alchemy was widely considered to be a spiritual rather than an experimental science, but post-Jabir it became an experimental science, detached from its spiritual roots. Although Jabir was the pioneer of experimental alchemy, he did not fail to highlight the spiritual or esoteric dimension of alchemy, and in so doing he tried to maintain the continuity between a purely spiritual, as opposed to a thoroughly experimental, alchemy. Nonetheless, his advocacy of experimental alchemy did represent a significant break with the past; a positive step forward in the advancement of chemistry as we know it today. Had it not been for Jabir's bold and innovative experimental scientific methodology, the development of chemistry as a separate scientific discipline would no doubt have been delayed by at least a few centuries, if not longer.

Jabir may not have been the first Muslim to study achemy, but he was certainly one of the first to engage in experimental alchemy. For this reason today he is widely considered to be the 'father of Islamic alchemy' and one of the pioneers of chemistry. For the first time in the history of chemistry, he founded a fully operational chemical laboratory, in his native Kufah, where he devised and conducted a large number of chemical experiments to prove or refute his theoretical views on many chemical matters. By personally devising and carrying out live chemical experimentation in his private laboratory, he banished the ghosts of secrecy and superstition which had overshadowed alchemy, and elevated this important branch of learning to a level equivalent with that of astronomy, medicine and mathematics. This also prompted other Muslim and non-Muslim scientists to pursue further studies and research in chemical science. Jabir's experimental approach to alchemy, coupled with the discovery of his private chemical laboratory in Kufah two centuries after his death, proved, if proof was required, that he was a great alchemist and pioneering chemist.

Using his experimental approach to alchemy, Jabir named and classified chemicals and minerals into three broad categories. The first category consisted of spirits (such as sulphur, mercury, camphor and arsenic compounds) which, he argued, could be refined through the application of heat. The second category included metals like gold, silver, lead, tin, copper, iron and zinc. The final category consisted of pulverised substances, even though he pointed out that some pulverised elements, such as living creatures, were made of both spirit and matter. In his attempt to provide a scientific explanation of the composition of the body-spirit, he also highlighted the role and relationship between these two elements in the formation of a balanced living creature. And, in the process, he formulated an original scientific theory which came to be known as the 'Sulphur-Mercury Theory'. He not only conducted scores of chemical experiments to prove this theory, but also explained how chemists could propose theories about the nature of various chemicals or substances before carrying out practical experimentation to ascertain the veracity of their theoretical propositions. Thus Jabir did much more than develop an experimental methodology in his study of alchemy; he went further, by suggesting new techniques and procedures which could be utilised in chemical study and research.

Not surprisingly, he is today considered to be the pioneer of the chemical processes of distillation, filtration, crystallisation, sublimation, reaction and fixation which all students of chemistry take for granted as standard procedures in experimental chemistry. For the first time, he explained the chemical process which facilitated the preparation and purification of various mineral acids such as sulphuric, hydrochloric and nitric acids. By conducting extensive chemical experimentation in his laboratory, Jabir made a number of remarkable discoveries. For instance, by developing a special acidic powder he was able to dissolve solid gold, and also produced a chemical substance which enabled him to separate gold from silver. In addition to this, he discovered a number of other important chemicals including white lead, sulphur, silver and mercury compounds which are today used by commercial industries all over the world to produce household products like paint and washing powder. Likewise, he coined scores of technical terms such as *alkali*, *antimony*, *alembic* and *cinnabar* which have today become commonplace around the world. In short, his contribution to the development of science, especially experimental alchemy or chemistry, was nothing short of remarkable.

Like many other great medieval Muslim scholars and scientists, Jabir's motivation for pursuing scientific research was to develop a better understanding of man and his environment, rather than seek personal glory or acquire material benefits. On the contrary, he led a very simple, pious and productive life, devoted entirely to the pursuit of knowledge. And given his close friendship with the Barmakids during the early years of Caliph Harun al-Rashid's reign, he had free access to all the royal libraries in Baghdad, but after the Barmakids fell from Abbasid grace, Jabir also lost his personal patronage. This prompted him to return home to Kufah where he continued his research in alchemy. Jabir died at the age of seventy-one and was buried in Kufah. He was not only an outstanding chemist, he was also a prolific writer who authored more than one hundred books and treatises on aspects of alchemy, chemistry, cosmology, astrology, medicine, music and spirituality. Although Ibn al-Nadim, the celebrated bibliographer and author of *al-Fihrist*, did record the names of some of his books and treatises, unfortunately his list is not complete.

According to other historians, most of Jabir's books perished in 1258 during the Mongol sack of Baghdad.

Given that the number of writings attributed to him was so large, some historians consider most of the books attributed to him were not solely written by him, but rather were written by a group of scholars who used his name to gain wider circulation and acceptance. However, the majority of historians have dismissed this view. As a versatile thinker, scientist and creative writer, they argue, it would not have been impossible for Jabir to write as prolifically as he did because al-Kindi and Ibn Sina, both of whom were also great scientists, managed to author more than two hundred books and treatises each. Nevertheless, it is an exaggeration to say that Jabir authored three thousand books, as some scholars have suggested. Inspired by Jabir's remarkable contribution in the field of alchemy and chemistry, other great Muslim thinkers and scientists, like al-Kindi and Abu Bakr al-Razi, pursued their own research in these subjects. Likewise, after his works were translated into Latin and other European languages during the thirteenth and fourteenth centuries, Jabir's ideas and thoughts had a profound impact on medieval European thinkers and scientists – so much so that great Western thinkers like Richard Russell, Albertus Magnus (also known as Albert the Great) and Roger Bacon used to fondly refer to him as that 'famous Arabian Prince and Philosopher'.

# 48

# Mimar Sinan
# (b.1489 – d.1588)

MUSLIMS NOT ONLY dominated science, mathematics and philosophy during the medieval period, they also contributed considerably to the development of the arts and architecture. Indeed, some of the world's most beautiful and historic buildings were constructed by the Muslims under the patronage of influential rulers like Abd al-Malik ibn Marwan, Abd al-Rahman III, Sulaiman the Magnificent and Emperor Shah Jahan. Whether it was the magnificent Alhambra in Granada or the exquisite Sulaimaniyyah Complex in Istanbul; the immortal Taj Mahal in Agra or the incredible Badshahi (Royal) Mosque in Lahore; the revoluntionary Sears Tower in Chicago or the breathtaking Dome of the Rock in Jerusalem; the impressive Umayyad Mosque in Damascus or the historic al-Azhar University in Cairo; the elegant Friday Mosque in Isfahan or the remarkable Salimiyyah Complex in Edirne, Muslims built these and numerous other impressive buildings and historical monuments throughout the ages, symbolising the beauty and artistic dimension of Islam like never before. More often than not, great works of architecture are produced by great architectural minds and the Muslim world has produced some of the world's great architectural geniuses includ-

ing Muhammad Tahir Agha and Mahmud Agha, the two brothers who built the magnificent Blue Mosque in Istanbul, and Fazlur Rahman Khan, the brains behind the Sears Tower in Chicago, which was once the world's tallest building. But the greatest Muslim architect, and arguably the most prolific builder of all time, was Sinan.

Mimar Sinan was born in the central Anatolian province of Qaisariyyah (in present-day Turkey). Of Greek origin, his father, Abd al-Mannan, embraced Islam and became a notable member of the Ottoman civil and administrative service. Sinan was therefore born and brought up in a family noted for its services to the Ottomans. Like his father, young Sinan became a loyal supporter of the Ottomans, although during his early years he showed no signs of the great imperial architect that he was to become. After completing his early education, he followed in his father's footsteps and joined the Janissaries – derived from the Turkish *yeni cheri* (meaning 'new troops') – in order to serve the powerful Ottoman army. Founded by the Ottomans in the fourteenth century to strengthen their army, the Janissaries were an elite military force, a fact which no doubt prompted Sinan to join this fearsome, but equally revered, brigade. He must have been physically very strong and well-disciplined, for only the very brave and chivalrous were allowed to join this elite force. The Janissaries were professionally trained soldiers, recruited from across the Ottoman Empire, but especially from the Balkans. The recruits were given Turkish names, offered tutorials in Islam and trained in all aspects of warfare before they graduated with military honours. As the Sultan's elite soldiers, they were also rewarded handsomely for their personal bravery, unfliching support and superior military skills.

Thanks to his physical prowess, sharp intellect and organisational ability, Sinan won instant recognition within the Ottoman army. But it was his contribution as a tactical operator, military strategist and designer of military equipment and devices which earned him an enviable position in the Ottoman army. During the reign of Sultan Salim I he helped build more than one hundred and fifty warships to give the Ottomans navy superiority over their rivals. After Sulaiman the Magnificent succeeded Salim I in 1520, the Ottomans launched a large-scale military operation against the Hungarians and subdued Belgrade after seven days of intensive bombardment. Sinan and the Janissaries played a pivotal role in the fall of Belgrade. Then, in 1522, Sultan Sulaiman led a campaign against the island of Rhodes and again Sinan played an important role in the fight against the fanatical Knights of St. John. During this battle he devised and developed a formidable artillery system which enabled the Janissaries to outflank their opponents and capture the island. Impressed with Sinan's clever thinking and innovative military tactics, the Sultan swiftly promoted him to the position of Chief of Staff within the Cannon Operations Department of the Ottoman army. Able to think and act quickly, and do so often in the middle of the battle, he built bridges, fixed damaged roads and constructed war vessels at short notice. This enabled the Janissaries to prepare and launch surprise attacks against their opponents and win battle after battle with ease.

After he polished his design and architectural skills in the Ottoman army, in 1538 at the age of around forty-nine, Sinan was promoted by Sultan Sulaiman to one of the highest posts within the Ottoman imperial court; that is to say, he became the Sultan's chief architect and builder. Although the Sultan already had more than a dozen accomplished architects in his service at the time, he became determined to recruit Sinan to design and supervise his major building projects. This period not only marked the beginning of a new phase in Sinan's life, but also proved to be one of the most productive periods in the history of Islamic art and architecture. Under Sultan Sulaiman's patronage, he constructed some of the Muslim world's most dazzling and inspirational works of architecture. Following the Ottoman conquest of the ancient city of Constantinople under the leadership of Sultan Muhammad II (which at the time represented the Ottoman's most resounding victory over their Byzantine foes), this historic city was renamed Istanbul (or the 'city of Islam') by its new conqueror. Thereafter, the Ottomans began to transform the skyline of this ancient city by constructing some of the Muslim world's most breathtaking works of architecture. As one of the oldest buildings in Istanbul, the Hagia Sophia (Aya Sofia) had been neglected by the Byzantines. Originally built by Greek architects for Emperor Justinian, this historic building was thoroughly repaired and restored to its former glory by the Ottomans. This mammoth task was entrusted to none other than Sinan, who refurbished the entire building and added beautiful new minarets to it to symbolise the Ottoman's victory over their old Byzantine rival. As an unusually industrious architect and builder, Sinan pursued his passion for planning and constructing large architectural projects with great vigour and enthusiasm, and did so well into his later years.

For more than half a century, he worked full-time for three different Ottoman rulers, Sulaiman I, Salim II and Murad III, and during this period he built scores of magnificent mosques, palaces, mausoleums, libraries, schools and bridges throughout the Ottoman Empire (which at the time extended all the way from the Balkans in Europe, to Sana in Yemen). In addition to designing and constructing the mausoleums of Abu Hanifah (located in Baghdad) and Jalal al-Din Rumi (in Konya, in present-day Turkey), he designed and built the seven-hilled city close to the Bosphorus. But his first major architectural project was the Sehzade Mosque Complex in Istanbul. This building was begun in 1544 at the behest of Sultan Sulaiman; he wished to pay a lasting tribute to his son, Prince Muhammad, who died of smallpox at Manisa at the age of twenty-two. Sinan designed and executed this project along the lines of the old Byzantine cross-dome churches, consisting of a mausoleum, religious school, lodging house and kitchen for the poor. It took four years to complete this building but reportedly he was not happy with the finished product. He considered it to be the work of an apprentice, although it was a highly decorative and impressive edifice. But Sinan set himself very high standards and always tried to surpass the Sultan's expectations.

His second major project was the magnificient Sulaimaniyyah Mosque Complex in Istanbul. He started work on this memorable edifice only two years after completing the Sehzade Mosque Complex. This building was supposed to represent an architectural statement of Ottoman power, might and glory, thus surpassing all previous works of Ottoman architecture. Sultan Sulaiman personally chose the site of the new building; he wanted this building to grace the skyline of Istanbul in the same way the Dome of the Rock (*qubbat al-sakhra*) has been gracing the city of Jerusalem for so many centuries. In 1550, after meticulously preparing for this colossal task, Sinan laid the foundation-stone of this building in the presence of the Sultan himself. He was very keen not to let this golden opportunity to build an architectural masterpiece pass by, not least because the Sultan took such a great interest in the project.

According to Mustafa Ali, the noted Ottoman historian, Sultan Sulaiman was not only an out-standing ruler, he was an equally prolific builder who was determined to leave his mark in the annals of Islam by constructing some of the Muslim world's most breathtaking works of architecture. The Sultan therefore wanted the Sulaimaniyyah Mosque Complex to be one of the world's most impressive and elegant buildings. Sinan worked on this massive project round-the-clock for seven years. He planned and supervised the work from start to finish with great care and precision. Like the Sultan, he was determined to produce an architectural masterpiece which would rise over the great city and reflect the glory of Islam, the Sultan and his empire. In 1557, the Sulaimaniyyah Mosque Complex was formally opened by the Sultan and in so doing helped to completely transform the skyline of Istanbul for good. After completing this project, Sinan was so pleased with the finished product that he considered it to be one of his best works. But, being a perfectionist, he felt he could do even better in the future.

That opportunity came after Sultan Sulaiman died in 1566. Like his father, Sultan Salim II (who was Sulaiman's only surviving son) requested the aged Sinan (who was in his mid-seventies at the time) to plan and execute yet another architectural masterpiece; this one was to be built in Edirne. After meticulously working on the Salimiyyah Mosque Complex for nearly a decade, Sinan finally unveiled the building in 1574. After completing this project, he reportedly exclaimed that with God's help he had at last surpassed the Greek architects who had built the ancient Hagia Sophia. The Salimiyyah Mosque was the largest of all the Ottoman buildings and is today considered to be one of the world's most beautiful works of architecture. Sinan's creativity, coupled with his organisational ability and powerful imagination, enabled him to plan and build some of the most sophisticated and beautiful works of architecture ever executed by a single individual. His buildings are famous for their elegance, clarity of interior space and simplicity of external design; indeed, they represented a new and innovative approach to art and architecture. In that sense, Sinan was a unique architect and builder, who understood the need for space, but not at the expense of beauty, elegance and grandeur. All of these elements blended quite remarkably in all his major works. Although the Sulaimaniyyah and Salimiyyah Mosque Complexes are today considered to be two of his most impressive works, he actually planned, supervised and built more than three hundred and fifty construction projects in total, including eighty-one mosques, fifty-five schools, thirty-four palaces, eight bridges and nineteen mausoleums.

Sinan was not only an industrious builder and gifted architect, he was also a loyal Muslim who served the Ottomans with unsurpassed distinction. Although he died at the advanced age of ninety-nine and was buried in a mausoleum he had built close to the Sulaimaniyyah Mosque Complex in Istanbul, the beauty and elegance of his architectural contribution and legacy will no doubt continue to grace the Muslim world for a long time to come. Indeed, his achievements are second-to-none in the annals of Islamic art and architecture.

# 49

# Abu Bakr
# al-Razi
# (b.841 - d.ca.925)

A VISITOR TO the Chapel of Princeton University in the United States cannot fail to notice the picture of a bearded, turban-wearing, Eastern-looking person represented on its window. According to George Sarton, the renowned historian of science, the person depicted on the window of the Chapel is none other than 'the greatest clinician of Islam and of the whole Middle Ages. He was the most celebrated and probably the most original of the Arabic writers.' This great Muslim physician and philosopher had such a profound impact on medieval Christendom that the Christians considered it appropriate to embed his image inside a Chapel, their most sacred place of worship. Although during the medieval period the Islamic world produced some of history's most influential philosophers, mathematicians and physicians, including Jabir ibn Hayyan (Geber), al-Kindi (Alkindus), al-Khwarizmi (Algorithm), Ibn Sina (Avicenna) and Ibn Rushd (Averroes), the Western world had not paid such a unique and glowing tribute to any other great Muslim thinker and scientist. Some historians have compared him with Hippocrates, the famous Greek physician, while according to others he was one of history's most pioneering medical practitioners. This remarkable Muslim

physician and philosopher was none other than Abu Bakr al-Razi.

Abu Bakr Muhammad ibn Zakariyya ibn Yahya al-Razi, known in the West as Rhazes, was born in the Persian city of Rayy (located close to modern Tehran), at the time a thriving centre of educational and commercial activity. Al-Razi was brought up and educated in Arabic, Persian and Islamic sciences before pursuing advanced training in physical sciences under the guidance of prominent local scholars like Abul Hasan Ali ibn Sahl al-Rabbani. As a noted student of Hunayn ibn Ishaq (who was a leading figure at the famous *bait al-hikmah* (The House of Wisdom) in Baghdad and translator of a large corpus of Greek philosophical and scientific works into Arabic), al-Rabbani was widely recognised as a pre-eminent authority on the physical sciences. Al-Razi thus studied physical sciences and aspects of philosophy under his tutelage. Thereafter, he became fascinated by music and musical theory, and during this period learnt to play the flute with considerable proficiency. Then, while he was still in his late twenties, he became interested in alchemy and went on to rapidly master this subject, too. Inspired by the works of Jabir ibn Hayyan, the father of Islamic alchemy and chemistry, al-Razi became a widely respected authority on experimental alchemy. Unlike Jabir, however, he was more interested in the external or experimental dimension of alchemy, rather than the inner, esoteric or symbolic meaning of phenomena, as such.

When the focus and intensity of his chemical experimentation began to strain his eyesight, he was forced to scale down his chemical research and exploration. Despite this his eyesight continued to deteriorate, eventually forcing him to turn his back on alchemy and chemistry for good, and instead he began to study medicine under Abul Hasan Ali ibn Sahl al-Rabbani's guidance. As an eminent authority on Greek, Syriac and Indian philosophy and medicine, al-Rabbani taught him all aspects of medicine until he acquired proficiency in this subject, and also became thoroughly familiar with Greek philosophy and metaphysics. Being a gifted student and a wide-ranging reader, al-Razi soon became a respected intellectual and skilled medical practitioner. Although he did not begin to study medicine until he was in his late twenties, his single-minded devotion and dedication to his studies enabled him to master this subject within a relatively short period. Indeed, he attained such proficiency in medicine that his reputation as a medical practitioner soon spread in and around Rayy. This prompted al-Mansur ibn Ishaq, the city's governor, to appoint him director of the local hospital.

As a physician and medical administrator, al-Razi was not only required to treat the sick and injured, but he also had to manage and co-ordinate the activities of the entire hospital. But in his spare time he continued to read extensively and write prolifically on the philosophical and scientific thoughts of the day. In addition to mastering alchemy, medicine and philosophy, he acquired considerable proficiency in logic, cosmology, theology and aspects of mathematics. Indeed, al-Razi became an outstanding encyclopaedist who was familiar with all the major branches of learning known during his time. However, his contribution in the field of philosophy was quite considerable both in terms of scope and quantity.

Even if the majority of his philosophical works are no longer extant, the small numbers which have survived provide ample evidence of his mastery of Greek and Islamic philosophical thought. As a radical thinker who not only helped to transform alchemy into a purely physical science by stripping it of its spiritual content (thus paving the way for the emergence of modern chemistry), he adopted an equally radical approach to the study of philosophy. Unlike al-Ash'ari and al-Kindi, he espoused and championed a purely rationalistic philosophy. Thus, reason and revelation, he argued, were incompatible and any attempts to reconcile the two were bound to fail.

According to al-Razi, philosophy and religion cannot be reconciled because most religions, if not all, are opposed to philosophical rationalism and unfettered scientific inquiry and research. Despite being thoroughly familiar with the philosophical ideas and thoughts of all the great ancient Greek thinkers (including Pythagoras, Socrates, Plato, Aristotle, Democritus, Plotinus, Porphyry, Alexander of Aphrodisias, Proclus and Plutarch), he became a champion of Platonic philosophy. Not surprisingly, his philosophical worldview revolved around the five eternal principles of Creator, Universal Soul, Primeval Matter, Time and Space. But his critics (such as Fakhr al-Din al-Razi and al-Shahrastani) accused him of being heavily influenced by non-Islamic ideas and thoughts, especially Manichaeism. As such, they dismissed his philosophical (or rationalistic) interpretation of fundamental Islamic beliefs and practices as being heretical and reprehensible. There is no doubt that al-Razi's philosophical thought was influenced by a combination of Platonic and Manichaeistic ideas, which prompted him to champion a purely rationalistic approach to religion and thus reject the necessity of prophecy. Human reason, in his opinion, was far superior to revelation and, as such, he was one of the most rationalistic of all Muslim philosophers. Like the Mughal Emperor Akbar, he was a freethinker and, not unlike Akbar's eclectic philosophy of *din-i-ilahi* (or 'the Divine Religion'), his philosophical thought never took off in the

Muslim world. While certain aspects of al-Razi's philosophy were indeed misguided and heretical, it would be equally wrong to dismiss his entire philosophical corpus as being heretical *per se*, for that was far from being the case.

His philosophical hedonism aside, al-Razi otherwise led a thoroughly Islamic lifestyle. In his *Kitab al-Sirat al-Falsafiyyah* (The Book of the Philosophical Way of Life), he explained how he had tried to lead a balanced and active life as a medical doctor, treating both the rich and poor in order to restore their health – and did so with God's help and support. Although accused of heresy, al-Razi's unflinching faith in God prevented his most vociferous critics from branding him an unbeliever or atheist. And despite being financially very well-off, he shunned luxurious living and material extravagance. He rarely argued or quarrelled with anyone, and was known to have been very fair and just in his dealings with others. Indeed, he was in the habit of helping others, often at the expense of his own comfort and convenience. He led a simple, austere and disciplined lifestyle, thus avoiding excess in all matters except in the pursuit of knowledge and wisdom. He read extensively and wrote copiously; on one occasion he wrote more than twenty thousand pages in a single year. And whenever he was informed that a learned scholar was visiting his locality, he used to go and sit in his company in order to learn something new. In old age, when he could no longer read or write due to failing eyesight, he paid people to read books to him so that he could continue to learn. In short, al-Razi's devotion and dedication to learning and scholarship was nothing short of remarkable.

If his philosophical thought was radical, then his contribution to medicine was truly remarkable. Along with Ibn Sina and al-Zahrawi, he must be considered one of the most influential Muslim physicians of all time. Indeed, as a medical clinician, he was far superior to Ibn Sina in that his diagnostic and observational skills were second-to-none. In addition to this, he was a supremely successful medical administrator who managed two of the leading hospitals of his day; one

was based in Rayy and the other was located in Baghdad. When he was not in the hospitals, he taught and wrote prolifically on all aspects of medicine. Thanks to his vast learning, advanced scientific methodology and clinical approach to medicine, students flocked to his house to learn from him. This forced him to turn one of his rooms into a study-cum-classroom, where he delivered regular lectures on all aspects of medicine, including how to recognise different ailments, their symptoms and ways to treat them. Being a cultured and dignified teacher, he used to treat all his students well and regularly provided free food to them. Later in life, he wrote a powerful critique of Greek medicine, especially Galen's cosmological and medical thought, under the title of *Shukuk ala Jalinus* (Doubts about Galen); in this book, he highlighted all the major errors contained in Galen's medical works.

Al-Razi's other major medical contributions included *Kitab al-Mansuri* (The Book of Mansur), *Kitab al-Jami al-Kabir* (The Great Medical Book) and *Kitab al-Hawi fi al-Tibb* (The Comprehensive Book of Medicine), which was later translated into Latin under the title of *Continens*. Dedicated to his patron and benefactor al-Mansur ibn Ishaq the Samanid governor of Rayy, *Kitab al-Mansuri* was an enormous encyclopaedia which provided a detailed exposition of all the major medical topics, accompanied by a brief commentary. This book was translated into Latin in the twelfth century by Gerard of Cremona under the title of *Liber Medicinalis ad Almansorem* and was used as a standard textbook on medicine across Europe until the sixteenth century. Likewise, his *Kitab al-Jami al-Kabir* was a voluminous encyclopadia on medicine which not only covered all aspects of medicine in detail, but also provided fresh clinical insights into the causes of different diseases and illnesses, as well as ways to treat them.

However, al-Razi's *Kitab al-Hawi* was arguably the most comprehensive medical work ever produced in Arabic. Consisting of twenty-five hefty volumes, this monumental work was much larger than Ibn Sina's famous *al-Qanun fi al-Tibb* (The Canon of Medicine). Being his private medical notebook, he arranged it anatomically into thirty-seven different chapters. In this book, he provided a detailed explanation of all important medical topics including pathology, dermatology, personal hygiene, therapuetic techniques and other remedies he had learned from Greek, Indian, Babylonian and Syriac medicine. The Latin translation of this book was begun in 1280 and completed in 1542. This book established his reputation as one of the most influential Muslim physicians and clinicians of all time. His other famous works included *Kitab al-Jadari wa'l Hasbah* (The Treatise on Smallpox and Measles). As one of the oldest and most original treatises on smallpox and measles ever written, in this book, al-Razi accurately described these two deadly infections for the very first time. Originally translated into Latin in 1493, it was later published in French in 1762 and in English in 1848. Considered to be one of the masterpieces of medical writing, it was used as a standard textbook on smallpox and measles until the modern period. In addition to this, al-Razi wrote extensively on gallstones, kidney, bladder and urinary diseases (his most notable contribution in this field was *Kitab al-Hasa fi'l Kula wa'l Mathana* or The Treatise on Stones in the Kidney and Bladder).

According to Abu Raihan al-Biruni, the famous Muslim scientist and historian, al-Razi authored one hundred and eighty-four books and treatises on all branches of learning, including eighty books on philosophical and theological topics alone. But, according to other historians, he wrote more than two hundred and forty books, most of which have, unfortunately, perished. More of his medical works have survived than his philosophical ones, perhaps due to the fact that his approach to philosophy and theology was considered to be controversial, to say the least. By contrast, his medical works remained very influential both in the East and the West up to the modern day. Hailed as the 'Arab Galen' across medieval Europe, al-Razi became blind towards the end of his life, due to excessive reading and writing. He died at the age of about eighty-four and was buried in his native Rayy.

50

# Hasan al-Basri
# (b.642 - d.728)

FOLLOWING THE ASSASSINATION of Caliph Uthman in 656, the early Muslim community became bitterly divided, which led to considerable political infighting and rivalry during the Caliphate of Ali. And after the latter was brutally murdered in 661, Muawiyah ibn Abi Sufyan not only became the ruler of the Islamic world, but also established the first political dynasty in Islamic history. Although this created considerable unease within the early Muslim community, Muawiyah proved to be a highly skilful political operator who ruled the Islamic world with wisdom, understanding and great tactical ability and awareness. Indeed, his balanced and sensible approach to politics and diplomacy enabled him to win over many of his erstwhile adversaries, thus restoring Islamic unity and solidarity after nearly a decade of political infighting. Nevertheless, the formation of the Umayyad dynasty shattered the balance struck by the *al-khulafa al-rashidun* (the four 'rightly-guided Caliphs') between the religious and political dimensions of Islam. After Muawiyah's death, the gulf between the Umayyad rulers and the masses continued to widen as the ruling elite indulged themselves in excessive pleasure-seeking and hedonism, while the masses drifted away from the original pristine

Islam as taught and practised by the Prophet and his close companions. This prompted a number of prominent Islamic scholars to warn both the Umayyad rulers and the people of the dangers of excessive materialism and hedonism. One such influential Islamic scholar and sage was Hasan al-Basri whose profound knowledge and understanding of Islamic principles and practices, coupled with his bold and fearless articulation of Islamic morality, ethics and spirituality, earned him widespread acclaim throughout the Muslim world.

Abu Sa'id Hasan ibn Abi'l Hasan Yasar al-Basri, better known as Hasan al-Basri, was born in Madinah during the reign of Caliph Umar. Of Persian origin, his father, Yasar, was captured in the Iraqi province of Maisan by the Muslim army and sent to Madinah in 635 where he became a close associate of Zaid ibn Thabit, the famous companion and scribe of the Prophet. After embracing Islam, he gained his freedom and married Khaira, a freedwoman of Umm Salama, the widow of the Prophet and settled in Wadi al-Qura. It was here that Hasan al-Basri was born and brought up, before migrating to Basrah when he was a young man. Along with Makkah, Madinah and Kufah, Basrah was one of the foremost centres of Islamic learning and scholarship. Being very fond of learning and education, on his arrival in Basrah he fell in love with the city and settled there for good. Born and brought up in the early days of Islam, Hasan reportedly met and studied Islam under the tutelage of several prominent companions of the Prophet, including Anas ibn Malik. But it was Imran ibn Hussain, a noted companion, *qadi* (judge) and prolific narrator of *hadith* (Prophetic tradition), who influenced Hasan the most. Known for his ability to endure extreme personal hardship and suffering, Imran led an ascetic lifestyle, committed entirely to worship and other devotional activities in order to attain personal purification and spiritual elevation. Needless to say, his simplicity and detached attitude to life left an indelible mark on young Hasan, who emulated his teacher and spiritual mentor by rejecting the comfort, luxuries and material possessions of this world.

After studying the Qur'an, *hadith*, *fiqh* (jurisprudence) and aspects of Islamic spirituality under the guidance of several prominent companions of the Prophet and their students, Hasan became very knowledgeable regarding Islam and Islamic spirituality. However, he refused to become an intellectual recluse or a hermit. On the contrary, from 663 to 665, he volunteered for military service and actively participated in expeditions led by the Muslims in many distant lands, including as far away as modern Afghanistan. For a period he also served as secretary to the governor of the Persian province of Khurasan. He was admired and respected by his friends and foe alike for his profound knowledge and understanding of Islam. He disliked material extravagance and self-indulgence, and led an honest and austere lifestyle from an early age, which won him considerable plaudits from his contemporaries. Having also served as a soldier in the army and worked as a civil servant in Khurasan, he acquired first-hand knowledge and experience of politics, leadership and power. This enabled him to understand and appreciate how easily politicians and rulers can succumb to the lures of luxury and worldly pleasures. The

fact that political power had the potential to corrupt even a pious and righteous ruler, and the far-reaching consequences this example could set to the masses, alarmed Hasan. Profoundly disturbed by this insight into the true nature of power and politics, he resigned from his job as political secretary to the governor of Khurasan and became a champion of Islamic morality, ethics and spirituality, at a time when both the rulers and the masses were openly embracing a hedonistic lifestyle.

Although the exact date of his move from Khurasan to Basrah is not known, it probably took place during the final years of Muawiyah's reign, because Hasan was in Basrah when Muawiyah decided to nominate his son, Yazid, as his successor. To bolster support for his chosen successor, Muawiyah then approached all the leading Islamic scholars and personalities of the time including Hussain ibn Ali, Abdullah ibn Umar, Abdullah ibn Zubair and Abdullah ibn Abbas and urged them to pledge their loyalty to Yazid, but they all flatly refused to do so. As a distinguished Islamic scholar and sage of Basrah, Hasan also refused to pledge loyalty to Yazid. He considered the latter to be a spoilt and over-indulged playboy, who led a hedonistic lifestyle and was devoid of intelligence, tact and humility. As far as Hasan was considered Yazid represented a throwback to the Dark Ages of pre-Islamic Arabia and he openly protested against Muawiyah's choice of Yazid as his successor. Although Hasan was only in his late thirties, he had already acquired a considerable following in Basrah on account of his profound knowledge and understanding of Islam. And despite his protests against Muawiyah's choice of successor, he did not directly participate in any political rebellion or military uprisings against Yazid. Nor did he condone any form of subversive activity against the State. His stance against Yazid was a principled one; he argued that Yazid was unfit to lead the Islamic State on account of his moral laxity, political inexperience and lack of popular support. Thanks to his bold and uncompromising stance on this issue, Hasan not only earned the respect of his peers, but also received widespread support from the people of Basrah. This was typical of Hasan, who became renowned for his outspoken defence of Islamic morality and ethics.

A contemporary of such Islamic luminaries as Ata ibn Rabah, Ibn Sirin and al-Sha'bi, Hasan stood over and above them by virtue of his great character, courage, learning and uncompromising defence of Islam. According to al-Ghazali, the celebrated Islamic thinker of the eleventh century, his religious teachings and spirituality bore a striking resemblance to the message of Islam as originally promulgated by the Prophet and his companions. Likewise, other eminent scholars like Thabit ibn Qurrah praised Hasan for his piety, forbearance, rectitude, asceticism and unusual insight into Islamic teachings and practices. His regular lectures on Islam became so popular that students and scholars flocked to Basrah from across the Muslim world to listen to his inspirational talks on the Qur'an, *hadith*, *fiqh* and aspects of Islamic spirituality. In addition to being an undisputed authority on traditional Islamic sciences, Hasan became one of the Muslim world's most famous practitioners of asceticism (*zuhd*) and spirituality (*tasawwuf*). At a time when the forces of materialism and hedonism threatened to overwhelm the Muslim world, his religious teachings and spirituality were considered to be a breath of fresh air by his peers and the masses alike. Indeed, his blistering attacks against the forces of materialism and hedonism won him such popularity in Basrah that even the military strongman Hajjaj ibn Yusuf never dared to cross his path. Hajjaj was not only a ruthless governor, he was also one of the great orators of his generation yet, according to Abu Amr ibn al-Ala, the renowned Qur'anic reciter (*qari*), Arabic linguist and grammarian, Hasan was a better orator than Hajjaj ibn Yusuf.

Although Hasan was a fierce critic of all the cruel politicians of his time (including Yazid ibn Muawiyah, Hajjaj ibn Yusuf and Yazid ibn Abd al-Malik), he was of the opinion that they should nevertheless be obeyed. He vehemently opposed any form of armed rebellion against the rulers of his time – even the tyrannical ones – especially if he felt such action could lead to a greater *fitna* (chaos and bloodshed). If the repressive actions of tyrants like Hajjaj were a collective punishment upon the people from God, argued Hasan, then taking up arms against them would not reprieve the people from God's punishment. But if it was a trial from God, then he felt they should patiently wait for the Divine plan to take its course. His views on this issue remained unchanged all his life. By contrast, his views on eschatological matters were dominated by his ascetic view of life, even though his asceticism did not entail a total renunciation of the material world. He may have been an ascetic, but he was also an optimist for he believed in the human capacity to do what is good and champion what is right. Furthermore, he argued that all human actions and behaviour must be motivated by a concern for the hereafter. That is to say, an individual's personal as well as collective duties and obligations must be underpinned by faith and morality, even if his actions occasionally fall short of God's standards.

As a gifted exponent of traditional Islam, Hasan endeavoured to rejuvenate Islamic moral, ethical and spiritual principles and practices without completely renouncing the material world. He sought to bridge the gap which had appeared within the Muslim mind between matter and spirit, the body and the soul, and this life and the hereafter. Almost single-handedly, he managed to restore the equilibrium which was so characteristic of traditional Islamic thought, worldview and practices. He remained apolitical all his life and refused to side with either the supporters, or opponents, of the Umayyads, but he was never afraid to criticise those who attempted to dilute or undermine Islamic principles and practices. If he thought a ruler, political group or even a scholar had deviated from the pristine and unadulterated teachings of Islam, he first admonished them, failing which he rebuked them for their un-Islamic behaviour. Thanks to his profound learning and piety, he was reportedly appointed *qadi* of Basrah during the reign of Caliph Umar ibn Abd al-Aziz; he was in his late seventies at the time.

His religious ideas and thoughts exerted a tremendous influence on mainstream Islamic thought and his spiritual teachings inspired all the prominent Islamic mystical Orders, including the *qadiriyyah, chishtiyyah* and *naqsh-bandiyyah*. Thus prominent Sufis like Habib al-Ajami, Rabi'a al-Adawiyyah, Dawud al-Ta'i and Abul Qasim al-Junayd al-Baghdadi among others were directly influenced by Hasan's spirituality. Even the *mu'tazilah* (or the philosophical rationalists) considered him to be one of their forerunners because Wasil ibn Ata, the founder of Mu'tazilism, attended his lectures for a period. He died at the advanced age of eighty-six and was buried in Basrah. His funeral prayers could not be held in a mosque because most of the people of Basrah turned up to pay tribute to one of the Muslim world's most influential scholars and reformers.

51

*Ibn al-Haytham*
*(b.965 – d.1039)*

AS ONE OF the oldest of scientific disciplines, astronomy is concerned with the study and observation of the celestial bodies such as the sun, the moon, the stars, the planets, the galaxies and, in fact, every other object that exists in the universe. And although according to the historians of science, it was the ancient Babylonian, Egyptian, Chinese, Indian and Mexican people who first pursued astronomical study and observation, it was the ancient Greeks who made a serious contribution to the development of science in general and astronomy in particular. The Greeks produced scores of eminent astronomers including Thales, Pythagoras, Eratosthenes of Cyrene, Hipparchus and Ptolemy of Alexandria. As the *Almagest* of Ptolemy was one of the most popular works of Greek astronomy, this treatise was translated into Arabic by the early Muslim scholars and translators which enabled them to become thoroughly familiar with Greek scientific works. However, following Ptolemy's death in 180BC, Greek science began to decline rapidly; but, thanks to the strenuous efforts of the early Muslim scholars and scientists, ancient Greek science in general, and astronomy in particular, was revived and preserved; the Muslims also went onto create a fully-fledged Islamic scientific

culture so that from the beginning of the eighth to the sixteenth centuries, Muslims led the rest of the world in scientific study and research. One of the most outstanding and influential Muslim scientists and polymaths of this period was Ibn al-Haytham.

Abu Ali Hasan ibn al-Haytham, known as Alhazen in the West, was born in the Iraqi city of Basrah during one of the most politically tumultuous periods in the history of the Muslim world. The once invincible Abbasid Empire was no longer a united and powerful entity and had become divided into numerous autonomous kingdoms. Thus, for instance, the Tulunids ruled Egypt and Syria, the Fatimids reigned supreme in North Africa and the Buwayhids (or Buyids) controlled Persia. Though al-Muti' continued to exercise his religious authority as Abbasid Caliph, he was no longer in charge, politically or militarily. Raised and educated in Basrah amidst the prevailing political uncertainty and social upheaval, Ibn al-Haytham studied Arabic language, literature and aspects of traditional Islamic sciences during his early years. He then received advanced education in literature, mathematics and astronomy, initially in Basrah and subsequently in Baghdad. As the political capital of the Muslim world, Baghdad was considered at the time to be one of the world's most prominent centres of scientific study and research. Under the generous patronage of successive Abbasid Caliphs, Muslim scholars, thinkers and scientists conducted research in all branches of the sciences, thus paving the way for the emergence of science and technology as we know them today. Following in the footsteps of the pioneering early Muslim mathematicians and scientists, Ibn al-Haytham studied science under the guidance of some of the leading scholars and scientists of his day, and became thoroughly familiar with mathematics, astronomy, physics and optics.

He attained such a mastery of science that his fame soon began to spread beyond the borders of Iraq. When the Fatimid rulers of Egypt came to hear about his scientific expertise, they invited him to move to Cairo and pursue his studies and research under their patronage. Given the political tension and uncertainty that gripped the Buwayhid territories at the time, Ibn al-Haytham was only too happy to move to Egypt, not least because the Fatimids were renowned for their generous patronage of learning and higher education. After his move to Cairo, he was approached by the Fatimid ruler, al-Hakam, to devise a plan to control the excessive flooding of the Nile. Although he knew this would be an incredibly difficult task, Ibn al-Haytham was not one to back down from a challenge. Thus he made all the necessary preparations and began work on a flood-prevention plan, but soon realised the task was a multi-faceted problem which he could not solve on his own. He therefore returned to the Fatimid ruler and explained the situation to him, but the latter was not satisfied with his explanation. His failure to devise an effective flood-prevention plan cost him dearly as royal patronage was withdrawn from him, which forced him to sell copies of his books and manuscripts to pay for his daily expenses.

Along with medicine, mathematics and philosophy, astronomy was one of the favourite subjects of the early Muslim scholars and scientists. Before Ibn al-Haytham's time, prominent

Muslim scientists like al-Farghani, al-Khwarizmi, the Banu Musa Brothers (Muhammad, Ahmad and Hasan), al-Battani and Abul Wafa, among others had carried out extensive research in astronomy. In doing so, they contributed immensely to the development of astronomical knowledge across the Muslim world. The Muslim scientists dominated the study of astronomy during the medieval times, and composed some of the most invaluable and authoritative works on the subject which were rated highly both in the East and the West right up until the modern period. Unlike Ptolemy and other Greek astronomers, the Muslims adopted an empirical approach to the study of astronomy, emphasising the importance of undertaking practical observations (using astronomical devices and instruments) to facilitate a better understanding of the celestial bodies. Not surprisingly, Ibn al-Haytham's work in astronomy was both practical as well as theoretical; indeed, he questioned, and critically evaluated, existing astronomical knowledge and refused to accept the ideas and thoughts of his predecessors at face value.

By adopting an experimental approach to the study of astronomy, he discovered how his predecessors had accepted aspects of Greek astronomical thought without subjecting them to critical scrutiny. In the process he made a number of invaluable contributions, including carrying out a critical appraisal of Ptolemaic astronomy in *The Summary of Astronomy*. In this book he argued that the scientific methodology employed by Ptolemy in his famous *Almagest* to explain the planetary motions was inconsistent and false; instead he proposed a fresh approach to the study of science and astronomy. And it was his cogent critique of Ptolemaic planetary theory which later inspired other prominent Muslim astronomers, like Abu Ishaq al-Bitruji of Islamic Spain and Abul Hasan Ali ibn al-Shatir of Damascus, to make fresh attempts to develop non-Ptolemaic planetary models which, in turn, influenced the works of great Western scientists like Copernicus and Kepler. The move from Greek notions of abstract heavens to one of a solid and observable physical reality (consisting of celestial bodies) was not only a radical shift in the study of astronomy, but was also one of Ibn al-Haytham's major contributions to the study of science. This paved the way for his successors, especially those based at the famous Maraghah Observatory in Persia, to flourish and inspire famous Western thinkers and scientists like Galileo, Tycho Brahe, Copernicus and Kepler to achieve as much as they did. Thus it was not a coincidence that the planetary models developed by Ibn al-Shatir and Copernicus were later found to be virtually identical, differing only in minor details. Author of more than twenty-eight books and treatises on all aspects of astronomy, there is no doubt that Ibn al-Haytham's astronomical ideas and thoughts profoundly influenced both Ibn al-Shatir and Copernicus, thus contributing to the emergence of modern science.

If Ibn al-Haytham's contribution in astronomy was remarkable, then his works in the field of physics and optics were nothing short of astounding. Until relatively recently, physics was widely considered to be a natural philosophy, so that even Sir Issac Newton considered himself to be a natural philosopher, rather than a physicist. In the same way, the early Muslim physicists like Abu Raihan al-Biruni and Ibn al-Haytham studied this subject as if it was a branch of natural philosophy (*tai'yyat*), rather than physics as we know it today. Nevertheless, Ibn al-Haytham's contributions in physics, and especially in optics, were both original and hugely influential. As a scientific iconoclast, he formulated a new and unique 'experimental' approach to the study of science which was probably his most important and lasting contribution. That is to say, he developed and single-handedly championed an 'empirical' scientific methodology which emphasised the need for practical demonstrations of theoretical propositions and assumptions. This empirical scientific research methodology – pioneered by Ibn al-Haytham in the course of his study of physics and optics – established his reputation as a great scientist and arguably one of the most influential Muslim physicists of

all time. Not surprisingly, his *Kitab al-Manazir* (The Book of Optics) – written over a period of ten years from 1028 to 1038 – became the most sought-after book on the subject soon after its publication in 1038. First translated into Latin in around 1250 and later reprinted many times throughout Europe, including once in Basle in 1572, this book went on to exert a huge influence on prominent Western thinkers like Robert Grosseteste, Roger Bacon, Witelo, Theodoric of Freiburg, Kepler and Newton among others.

In his *Optics*, Ibn al-Haytham moved away from the ideas and thoughts of his predecessors and developed a new approach to optics based on his personal study and research. Breaking new ground in both optics and physiology, in this book, he dismissed the ancient Greek theory of vision. Light, according to the Greeks, emerged from one's eyes and then fell on an object to make it visible. Being the first scientist to formulate a correct theory of vision, Ibn al-Haytham explained how light emerged from a luminous object and then entered the eye to form an image, thus making the object visible. As a pioneer of scientific 'experimentation', he proved his theory by carrying out several practical experiments and in the process also explored the anatomy and physiology of the human eye. He not only accurately explained the function of its various parts (including the conjunctive, iris, cornea and the lens) he also diagnosed several diseases of the eye and suggested possible remedies.

Thereafter, he discovered and explained the laws of reflection and refraction in Book 4 of his *Optics*, in addition to providing an accurate explanation of the nature of atmospheric refraction. Ibn al-Haytham then discussed the purpose of numerous experiments he had conducted in order to acquire a better understanding of starlight, rainbow and different colours, and in so doing discovered the principle of the *camera obscura* while observing the sun's image during an eclipse. Thanks to his scientific discoveries, the way was cleared for developments of perspective in images and, ultimately, the ability to take photographs using a camera. Indeed, he studied and explained the principle of the *camera obscura* centuries before Kepler, Leonardo de Vinci and Newton wrote on the subject. After studying Ibn al-Haytham's *Kitab al-Manazir*, another renowned Muslim scientist, Kamal al-Din al-Farisi, wrote an extensive commentary on it under the title of *Tanqih al-Manazir* (The Review of Optics). He wrote this book after repeating and improving many of Ibn al-Haytham's original experiments, in order to clarify aspects of his scientific ideas and thoughts for the benefit of posterity.

Ibn al-Haytham was not only a pioneering astronomer and scientist, he was also an outstanding philosopher, mathematician and physicist who contributed immensely to the development of an experimental scientific methodology. As a prolific writer and outstanding encyclopaedist, Ibn al-Haytham authored more than two hundred books and treatises on astronomy, physics, medicine and mathematics, in addition to several commentaries on the works of Galen and Aristotle. Indeed, his expertise in astronomy, physics and optics was such that he was considered to be one of the Muslim world's leading authorities on these subjects. After devoting his entire life to the pursuit of scientific knowledge and wisdom, he died at the age of seventy-four and was buried in Cairo. But, thanks to his remarkable scientific discoveries, humanity will forever remain indebted to this outstanding Muslim genius.

# 52

## Muslim ibn al-Hajjaj
## (b.817 - d.875)

ISLAMIC HISTORY IS replete with great *mu-haddithun* (scholars of *hadith*) who received widespread acclaim for their seminal contributions in the field of *hadith*. Thus scholars like Malik ibn Anas, al-Zuhri, al-Awza'i, Abdullah ibn Mubarak, Yahya ibn Ma'in and Ahmad ibn Hanbal have left their indelible marks in the annals of *hadith* literature. Thanks to them, the preservation and dissemination of *hadith* and *usul al-hadith* (science of *hadith*) not only became possible, but also enabled them to become some of the most popular branches of the traditional Islamic sciences (*ulum al-din*). However, the names of two remarkable scholars, al-Bukhari and Muslim, have today become household names across the Muslim world on account their selfless devotion, assiduous scholarship and seminal contributions to the collection and dissemination of the Prophetic traditions. Although al-Bukhari is widely considered to be the most famous scholar in the history of *hadith* literature, the popularity of Muslim ibn al-Hajjaj must not be underestimated. Indeed, according to some scholars of *hadith*, Muslim's anthology of *hadith* is superior to that of al-Bukhari. Nevertheless, the collections of both al-Bukhari and Muslim are today regarded as two of the most authentic and authoritative antholo-

gies of Prophetic traditions ever produced. For this reason, both al-Bukhari and Muslim have been rated very highly in this book.

Abul Hussain Asakir al-Din Muslim ibn al-Hajjaj ibn Muslim ibn Ward was born in Nishapur (located in the Persian province of Khurasan) into a respected Arab family of the tribe of Qushair. His ancestors included people such as Haida, Qurra ibn Hubairah and Ziyad ibn Abd al-Rahman who had all played prominent roles within the Islamic State during the time of the Prophet and the *al-khulafa al-rashidun* (the four 'rightly-guided Caliphs'). Following the rapid expansion of Islam during the reign of Caliphs Umar and Uthman, Muslims began to move from Arabia and settle in the newly-conquered territories in Syria, Egypt and Persia to pursue commerce and also engage in missionary activities. It was during this period that Muslim's ancestors left Arabia and settled in Nishapur. As a prominent scholar of Islam and noted authority on *hadith* literature, his father taught him Arabic, the Qur'an, *hadith* and aspects of *fiqh*. Raised in a family where the Prophetic traditions were not only revered but also rigorously followed, young Muslim became fond of *hadith* literature from an early age. Blessed with a keen intellect and highly retentive memory, it did not take him long to acquire proficiency in Arabic language, grammar and aspects of traditional Islamic sciences. Given that a thorough study of Arabic language and grammar was a *sine qua non* for undertaking advanced training in the Qur'an and *hadith*, Muslim's father ensured his son acquired all the linguistic skills necessary to carry out such a task. Indeed, it was his father's profound reverence and admiration for the Prophetic traditions which inspired Muslim to specialise in *hadith* literature.

He began his advanced training in *hadith* at the age of fifteen, and after completing a thorough study of *hadith* sciences under the tutelage of some of Nishapur's leading scholars (including the respected traditionist Muhammad ibn Yahya al-Dhuhali), he went to Makkah to perform the sacred pilgrimage (*hajj*). During his stay in Makkah he attended the lectures of some of the city's prominent scholars before he eventually returned home to Nishapur. Here he soon encountered the celebrated al-Bukhari whom he was delighted to meet. Although he was only a few years younger than al-Bukhari, by then he had also become widely respected in and around Nishapur for his vast knowledge of Prophetic traditions. According to the historians, when al-Bukhari met Muslim, the latter stood up and kissed the former on his forehead, saying, 'Let me kiss your feet, O master of *hadith* scholars and specialist in Prophetic traditions.' Thereafter Muslim studied *hadith* under al-Bukhari's tutelage for a period and polished his knowledge and understanding of *hadith* and *usul al-hadith*. Still eager to learn more, at the age of thirty-three, he travelled to some of the leading centres of Islamic learning in Persia, Iraq, Arabia, Syria and Egypt, and devoted yet more time to the study of *hadith*. This enabled him to learn more Prophetic traditions and master the art of investigating and sifting the sound *hadith* from the weak and spurious ones. In those days, *rihla* (travel) from one place of learning to another was a necessity, indeed a fundamental requirement, for all true seekers of knowledge – especially if

they wished to receive advanced training in any branch of Islamic learning – because most of the renowned scholars of the time lived in different parts of the Muslim world. Thus students like al-Bukhari and Muslim had no choice but to travel extensively in search of knowledge and in the process they met with, and studied *hadith* under the guidance of, hundreds of eminent scholars and traditionalists of their time.

Some of Muslim's prominent teachers included Ishaq ibn Rahawaih, Ahmad ibn Hanbal, Qutaibah ibn Sa'id, Yahya ibn Ma'in, Uthman ibn Abu Shaiba, Ubaidullah al-Qawariri, Zuhair ibn Harb, Sa'id ibn Mansur, Abdullah ibn Maslama, al-Bukhari and Muhammad ibn Yasar among many others. These scholars were not only great authorities on *hadith* literature, they were all pioneers of the science of *hadith*. Muslim sat at the feet of these luminaries and learned Prophetic traditions until he also became an eminent authority in *hadith* literature. When he was convinced that he had acquired an unrivalled mastery of Prophetic traditions, he returned home to Nishapur where his fame began to spread far and wide on account of his profound knowledge and expertise in *hadith* literature. Indeed, he became such a popular tutor that, during his own lifetime, he was hailed as a great authority on Prophetic traditions along with al-Bukhari of Bukhara, Abu Zur'ah of Rayy and al-Darimi of Samarqand. But in Nishapur he had no rivals; here he was revered more than any other scholar of his generation.

If Muslim was an Islamic scholar and traditionist of the highest calibre, then he was also a man of great character and personality. He loved simplicity and openness, and followed these principles very rigorously. Thus when, on one occasion, al-Dhuhali, who was one of his teachers, disagreed with al-Bukhari on a certain scholarly matter, he barred all his students from attending al-Bukhari's lectures, but Muslim continued to visit him. When al-Dhuhali was informed about this he accused Muslim of disloyalty, although the latter did not consider this to be the case. Indeed, he felt offended by al-Dhuhali's insensitivity and over-reaction in his dispute with al-Bukhari; so much so that he took all his lecture notes and returned them to al-Dhuhali. As a true seeker of knowledge and wisdom, Muslim did not believe in intellectual rivalry or personal enmity. He followed the Prophetic traditions to the letter and even refused to criticise or speak unfavourably of others. He earned his livelihood from his small family business, and in his spare time he delivered lectures on *hadith*. His lectures became so popular that hundreds of students came from far afield to listen to him. Prominent scholars like al-Tirmidhi, Ibn Khuzaimah, Ibrahim ibn Muhammad ibn Sufyan and Ibn Abu Hatim al-Razi also attended his lectures. Considered to have been one of the most pious and upright Islamic scholars of his generation, Muslim was an equally great admirer of the Prophet, and authored scores of books on *hadith*, *usul al-hadith*, *asma al-rijal* (biographies of *hadith* narrators) and aspects of Islamic history.

Although he composed more than twenty books on different aspects of *hadith*, only six of his books have survived, including *al-Jami al-Sahih* (better known as *Sahih Muslim*). This anthology of *hadith* is not only his most famous work, but, along with *Sahih al-Bukhari,* it is today considered to be one of the most authentic books of Islamic teachings after the Qur'an itself. Revered as one of the great works of traditional Islamic learning and scholarship, the importance and relevance of this vast collection of Prophetic traditions cannot be emphasised enough. After fifteen years of meticulous research and investigation in the field of *hadith* (which involved sifting through hundreds of thousands of Prophetic traditions in order to separate the authentic narrations from the weak or fabricated ones), Muslim incorporated around seven thousand *ahadith* in his anthology.

A pioneer of Islamic scholarship, Muslim helped to develop and disseminate a rigorous research methodology in the field of *hadith* literature. He classified *hadith* narrators into three broad categories. The first category consisted of narrators who possessed a highly retentive

memory, because they maintained consistency in their narrations. This enabled Muslim to compare their narrations with those of other respected and reliable narrators in order to ascertain their veracity. The vast majority of *hadith* contained in *Sahih Muslim* falls into this category. By contrast, the second category consisted of those narrators who had weak memories; thus their narrations were ocassionally found to be inconsistent. Muslim accepted their narrations only if their versions of *hadith* agreed with, or corroborated, the narrations of the first category. On the other hand, the third category consisted of those narrators who were considered to be unreliable and untrustworthy; Muslim completely rejected their narrations. Using such a rigorous system of checks and counter-checks, he successfully sifted the *sahih* (authentic) traditions from *hasan* (good) and the *daeef* (weak) from the *maudu* (fabricated). In doing so he produced an anthology of Prophetic *hadith* which today enjoys the full support and confidence of the Muslim community. Also, a reader of *Sahih Muslim* cannot help but notice how different versions of the same *hadith* repeat themselves; this is because Muslim deliberately included a second version of the first *hadith* in order to corroborate and reinforce the message of the first narration.

The rigorous research methodology formulated by Muslim and his contemporaries not only enabled them to check and re-check the authenticity of all the *hadith* they collected, but it also served another important purpose: for a *hadith* to be considered beyond reproach, it had to have a sound *matn* (text) as well as a sound *isnad* (chain of narration), among other things. Thus, for instance, if the *isnad* of a narration was considered to be reliable but its *matn* was found to be illogical or contradictory, then that narration was classified as "unreliable". Conversely, if the *matn* of a narration was considered to be sound but its *isnad* was found to be defective, then that narration was also considered to be "unreliable". However, if a particular *hadith* reached Muslim through more than one chain of narration (*sanad*), he incorporated the narration with a weaker *isnad* (which contained a narrator with a weak memory) as confirmation of the first narration, because the latter had met all his stringent tests.

Of the seven thousand Prophetic traditions he incorporated in his *Jami al-Sahih*, four thousand belonged to the first category, while the remaining three thousand fell into the second category. This two-fold strategy employed by Muslim ensured his anthology contained only the most authentic narrations. After completing this voluminous work, he presented copies to some of his great contemporaries, including Abu Zur'ah of Rayy. After thoroughly checking the book, they all confirmed that it contained nothing other than authentic Prophetic traditions. Indeed, according to Hussain ibn Ali al-Nishapuri, who was himself an eminent scholar of *hadith*, *Sahih Muslim* is one of the most authoritative anthologies of *hadith* ever produced. This is because, unlike many other prominent compilers of *hadith* (including al-Bukhari), Muslim appears not to have made any mistakes in the *isnad* or the *matn* of the traditions he incorporated in his *Sahih*.

Not surprisingly, his anthology is today considered to be one of the two most important collections of *hadith,* along with that of al-Bukhari. That is why so many famous scholars have written commentaries on *Sahih Muslim,* including the influential Syrian scholar and traditionist Abu Zakariyya Yahya ibn Sharaf al-Nawawi. In his voluminous *Al-Minhaj fi Sharh Sahih Muslim ibn al-Hajjaj,* al-Nawawi also incorporated separate chapter headings to facilitate quick referencing. As the *Sahih Muslim* is rated very highly as a source of Islamic teachings, it would not be an exaggeration to say that the world of traditional Islamic learning and scholarship would have been much poorer without this great anthology. Muslim ibn al-Hajjaj died at the age of about fifty-nine and was buried in his native Nishapur. But his name and fame will no doubt continue to endure for a long time to come.

# 53

## Mahmud of Ghazna
## (b.967 - d.1030)

AFTER THE OVERTHROW of the Umayyads in 750, the Abbasids assumed political leadership of the Muslim world. At that time the Muslim world extended from Spain in the West, to the banks of the Indus in the East. And although prominent Abbasid Caliphs like Abu Ja'far al-Mansur and Harun al-Rashid consolidated and substantially expanded Abbasid rule, their successors failed to maintain their grip on power and, as a result, the vast Abbasid Empire broke up into a series of regional political entities during the tenth century. One of the most prominent regional powers of the time was the Ghaznavids. Inaugurated in 961 by Alptigin, a charismatic Turkish military commander (who once served the Samanids of Khurasan and Transoxiana), the first independent Ghaznavid principality was formally established in 977 by Sebuktekin (also spelt as Sabuktagin), a son-in-law of Alptigin. By all accounts, Sebuktekin was a fearless military commander and a wise political administrator who, during his reign of two decades, not only consolidated Ghaznavid rule, but also established peace, order and security across his kingdom. Following his death in 997, his young son Ismail ascended the throne but he proved to be inexperienced and incompetent, and was therefore succeeded by his

older brother, Mahmud. It was under Mahmud's stewardship that the Ghaznavids became one of Asia's most prominent political powers, as well as generous patrons of learning and education.

Mahmud ibn Sebuktekin al-Ghaznavi was born into a prominent Turkish family of soldiers and military leaders. Hailing from the steppes of Central Asia, his ancestors were originally recruited by the Abbasids in order to bolster their military might and power. Bold, fearless and loyal, these fresh recruits were offered military training and rewarded handsomely by the Abbasid elites to maintain the status quo. Their bravery, courage and loyalty soon won them the favour of their Abbasid rulers, who promoted them to the highest echelons of their armed forces. Mahmud's ancestors belonged to this privileged group who later came to exercise considerable political and military power within their localities. Although Mahmud's father, Sebuktekin, initially worked for the Samanids' leader, Alptigin, the two went on to become friends, with Sebuktekin marrying Alptigin's daughter, who bore him a son; this son was Mahmud. Educated by his mother at home, Mahmud committed the entire Qur'an to memory during his early years. Known to have been a talented student, he swiftly acquired proficiency in Arabic language, literature, poetry and aspects of traditional Islamic sciences. Impressed by his son's intellectual ability and literary interests, his father (who at the time served as governor of Khurasan under Nuh II of Bukhara), then trained him in the arts of political governance and military strategy. During this period Mahmud served his father as his deputy, and acquired first-hand experience of political and civil administration.

After his father's death, he overthrew his younger brother from power, and ascended the Ghaznavid throne at the age of around twenty-eight. Like his father, he was a wise and energetic ruler, and soon after becoming Sultan prepared his armed forces in order to execute his first military expedition. In fact, within the first year of his reign he overthrew the Samanids and conquered all their territories up to the Oxus. Hitherto restricted to the province of Ghazna in eastern Afghanistan (including parts of North-eastern Iran), the Ghaznavid dynasty now received an unprecedented political and military boost under Mahmud's able leadership. By inflicting a crushing defeat on the Samanids, he proved his credentials as a military commander and gifted strategist. A year later, he marched into Kohistan and added this territory to his rapidly expanding empire. He then turned his attention towards India, and in 1001 launched his first military campaign against the Hindu ruler Jaipal I of Punjab. The two armies clashed near Peshawar (in present-day Pakistan) and after a fierce battle, Sultan Mahmud's forces inflicted a crushing defeat on their enemies; Jaipal I was also captured during the battle.

Later released on condition that he should not instigate any further attacks against the Ghaznavids and also pay an annual tribute to the Sultan, Jaipal I violated the agreement soon after his release by launching two further attacks against the Sultan's forces. However, on each occasion he suffered a heavy defeat. Distressed and devastated by his defeats, Jaipal I abdicated and committed suicide; the victorious Sultan Mahmud, however, went on to extend his territorial control all the way to the banks of the Indus. Only thirty at the time, he became the ruler of an empire which now extended all the way from Central Asia to the Indus valley – and did so from his political base in the eastern Afghan province of Ghazna. Then, in 1002, the Sultan captured the province of Sistan before making preparations to cross the Indus. Two years later, he crossed the river with his large army and swiftly annexed the region which is today known as Bhera. In the following year he captured Ghur and Multan, and ousted its ruler, Dawud, (an adherent of the heretical Carmathian creed) from power. As expected, the Sultan's instant and overwhelming success against his enemies caused intense consternation to all the reigning Hindu rulers. Worried that the Sultan was getting too close to their territories for their comfort, the Hindu rulers came together to create a confederation of Hindu principalities in order to confront the advancing Ghaznavid conqueror.

The combined might of the Hindu forces clashed with the Sultan's army in 1008, close to modern Hazro. Led by Anand Pal, the son and successor of Jaipal I, the Hindu contingent consisted of troops from across India, including Gwalior, Kalanjar, Delhi and Ajmer. Likewise, Sultan Mahmud's forces were an organised and disciplined fighting force and, as expected, they fought with great skill and determination. In the ensuing battle, the Sultan's forces gained the upper hand and forced their adversaries to flee in disorder. This was one of the major military victories of Sultan Mahmud's career and enabled him to further extend Ghaznavid suzerainty. Keen to press home his advantage, he quickly reorganised his forces and marched into Punjab in 1009 in order to teach the treacherous Anand Pal a lesson for violating his agreement to pay an annual tribute to the Ghazanvids. Over the next decade or so, the Sultan faced stiff opposition and repeated attacks from various Hindu factions – both from the land and sea – but he vanquished his opponents on each and every occasion. And in so doing he extended Ghaznavid rule into mainland India. After establishing a permanent political and military base in Lahore, which became the capital of Ghaznavid Punjab, Sultan Mahmud went on to consolidate his rule across the north-west of India, including the province of Sind.

Subsequently, in 1018, the Sultan turned his attention towards the West and swiftly over-threw the Khwarizmshahs of Central Asia. He then launched an expedition against the Buway-hids (or Buyids) and in the process captured the historic Persian city of Rayy. Indeed, he dominat-ed Central Asia to such an extent that he became the undisputed ruler of that whole region. In the East, the Sultan fought a total of seventeen dif-ferent battles against various Indian rulers and thereby established Ghaznavid supremacy across a large part of India. As a result, he became one of the most powerful and influential Muslim rulers of the eleventh century. And although some Hindu and Muslim historians have accused him of being a brutal, bloodthirsty and uncivilised military conqueror, a balanced and impartial as-sessment of his life and career provides a rather different picture of the man who went onto es-tablish an empire which would dominate Asian history for more than two hundred years.

The Sultan's Hindu critics misrepresented him because he detested idolatry, and repeatedly crushed his Hindu opponents on the battlefield. As a practising Muslim, he considered the Hindu practice of worshipping and adoring idols an abomination, but he did not force the Hindus to renounce their faith and convert to Islam. As a *hafiz* (one who had committed the entire Qur'an to memory), he was aware of the explicit Qur'anic injunction concerning the freedom to choose and practice one's faith. Thus, far from being anti-Hindu, he went out of his way to employ Hindus within his military and civil services; indeed, he even promoted them to positions of considerable power and authority. For instance, Tilak Roy and Soni were two of his most prominent Hindu military generals and served him with great loyalty and distinction. Furthermore, a third of his army consisted of Hindus, while five out of his twelve senior generals were of Hindu background. As a

devout Muslim, the Sultan understandably had little sympathy for those who, having pledged loyalty to him, subsequently tried to betray him. For such people he had no mercy or compas-sion; rather he punished them in an exemplary manner in order to deter others from doing the same. It is also true that on various occasions he attacked and destroyed several Hindu temples (such as the Somnath Temple) but, to be fair to him, he did this out of political necessity rather than any other consideration. As it happens, his Hindu opponents regularly stored gold as well as arms and ammunition inside their temples, from which they also often attacked his forces so that he had no option but to retaliate and in the process he damaged and destroyed several Hindu temples. Unlike many other influential Asian rulers, the Sultan was not a racist or a religious zealot; on the contrary, he tried to follow Islamic principles and practices to the best of his ability, and did so both in times of war and peace.

That does not mean to say that he was totally innocent; no doubt he had his share of faults and made mistakes, and he would have been the first person to accept this. Thanks to his early training in Islamic theological and legal sciences, he genu-inely tried to make things easier for his Muslim and non-Muslim subjects alike. In that sense, he was much wiser and tolerant than many other great Asian rulers and conquerors. Indeed, Sultan Mahmud was not only a great conqueror; he was also one of Asia's most educated and articulate rulers. He transformed Ghazna, the capital of his vast empire, into one of Asia's most prominent centres of learning and culture of the time. As a generous patron of science, literary activities, arts and architecture, he constructed scores of beau-tiful mosques, colleges, libraries, fountains and reservoirs throughout his empire, especially in Ghazna.

Thanks to his love of learning and education, he also recruited some of the Muslim world's great scholars, thinkers and literary figures to his court in Ghazna including Abu Raihan al-Biruni, the famous scientist and historian; al-Farabi, a great philosopher and logician; Unsuri, a distinguished linguist and grammarian, and Abul Qasim Firdawsi, the celebrated poet laureate. Under the generous patronage of Sultan Mahmud, these and other great Muslim scholars and thinkers not only pursued their study and research in science, mathematics, philosophy, history, linguistics and comparative religion, but also produced some of their most influential works. As if this was not enough, the poets who lived in his court regularly competed with each other to compose verses in praise of the Sultan in order to win his favour. Firdawsi was one such poet and composed his monumental *Shahnama* (The Book of Kings) during Sultan Mahmud's reign, and dedicated it to him. In appreciation of his efforts, the Sultan sent him a sack containing sixty thousand gold coins, but unfortunately Firdawsi died before the caravan carrying the money reached his native Tus. Today, the *Shahnama* is widely considered to be one of the greatest epic poems of all time.

Keen to maintain Islamic unity and solidarity, Sultan Mahmud also became a friend and ally of the orthodox Abbasid Caliph in Baghdad. After recognising Caliph al-Qadir as the Caliph of all Muslims, he restored the practice of mentioning the Caliph's name in the Friday prayer sermon (*kutbah*) across the Ghaznavid territories. In response, the Caliph bestowed the grand title of 'Friend of the Commander of the Faithful and Right Hand of the State, the Faithful, and the Community' on Sultan Mahmud. During his thirty-one year reign the Sultan completely rewrote the history of not only Asia, but also the Muslim world as a whole. He died at the age of sixty-three and was buried in Ghazna (located in present-day Afghanistan).

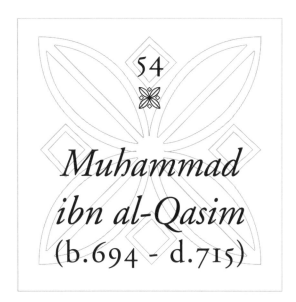

# 54

## Muhammad ibn al-Qasim (b.694 - d.715)

PRIOR TO HIS death in 705, the great Umayyad Caliph Abd al-Malik ibn Marwan nominated his eldest son, al-Walid, as his successor and he went on to rule the vast Islamic dominion for a decade, during which he spearheaded some of Islamic history's most astonishing military conquests. Under Caliph al-Walid's leadership, Muslims launched simultaneous military expeditions in Africa, Europe and Asia, and successfully out-manoeuvered their opponents on all three continents. In Central Asia, Qutaiba ibn Muslim embarked on a military campaign which led to the capture of Balkh, Bukhara, Khiva, Samarqand and Chinese Turkistan. While Qutaiba was making rapid progress in Central Asia, the legendary Tariq ibn Ziyad left North Africa and landed in Gibraltar (the name Gibraltar is derived from the Arabic *jabal al-tariq* or the 'Mount of Tariq'), and from there moved into Spain; thus for the first Islam came into direct contact with mainland Europe. During this momentous period in Islamic history Muslims also spearheaded military campaigns in the subcontinent. Under the inspirational leadership of young Muhammad ibn al-Qasim, Muslims marched as far as the Indus valley and brought a large part of India under Islamic rule for the first time.

Muhammad ibn al-Qasim ibn Abu Aqil was born during the successful reign of Caliph Abd al-Malik. Originally from the Arab tribe of Thaqif, his ancestors moved to the town of Taif (located close to Makkah) before the birth of the Prophet, and they became prominent members of their locality. Surrounded by orchards and the fertile valley, the people of Taif cultivated fresh fruit and vegetables, which formed the basis of the wealth and prosperity of the town. Thus the Thaqifites were not only wealthy and prosperous people; they later became renowned for their political and diplomatic skills. Indeed, some of the most prominent political and military leaders of the early Muslim community hailed from this tribe including Mughirah ibn Shuba, Ziyad ibn Abihi and Hajjaj ibn Yusuf. Young Muhammad ibn al-Qasim grew up at a time when his uncle, Hajjaj ibn Yusuf, served as a prominent member of the Umayyad political administration. Appointed governor of Arabia by Caliph Abd al-Malik and subsequently transferred to the troublesome Eastern province, Hajjaj became a dominant military figure and an unrelenting political operator; indeed, his ruthlessness as a military commander shocked and surprised his friends and foes alike. However, thanks to his fierce political loyalty and outstanding military services to the royal family, successive Umayyad rulers promoted and rewarded him handsomely for his unflinching support.

When Muhammad ibn al-Qasim reached maturity, he married governor Hajjaj's daughter and settled in Kufah, perhaps hoping to follow in the footsteps of his uncle and father-in-law and become a powerful political player within the Umayyad administration. But, unlike his father-in-law, Muhammad ibn al-Qasim was a gentle, tolerant and mild-mannered young man, who probably resented Hajjaj's political heavy-handedness and military ruthlessness. At the same time, he must have admired Hajjaj for his unflinching support and loyalty to the royal family. After establishing Umayyad suzerainty throughout the Eastern province, Hajjaj hoped to send a military expedition to India. Although Muslims had conquered most of Persia during the Caliphate of Umar and thus established Islamic rule as far as Makran on the border of India, the Muslim army had not gone into India at the time. It was at the behest of Umayyad Caliph al-Walid that Hajjaj finally got the chance to send an expedition to India. The opportunity to launch a military expedition came when Hajjaj received news that Raja Dahir, the Hindu ruler of Sind, had become a thorn in the side of the Muslims of Makran by instigating politically subversive activities against them. Simultaneously, he received news about the plight of a group of Muslims who, while travelling from Ceylon (present-day Sri Lanka) to Arabia to perform the sacred *hajj* (pilgrimage to Makkah), were forced by unfavourable conditions at sea to dock at the port of Debul, only for them to be taken captive by a group of pirates.

Renowned for their sailing and navigational skills, the early Muslim traders and merchants travelled regularly to distant lands in pursuit of commerce. Some even settled on remote Indian Ocean islands, like Ceylon, where they established businesses and befriended the locals and their rulers. As sea-pirates were a real menace in those days, travelling by boat was considered to be a risky affair; however, a group of Ceylonese Muslims boarded a vessel and set out for Makkah to perform the sacred pilgrimage. However, they were caught, robbed and taken captive by the pirates at Debul. Only a handful managed to escape the ordeal and arrived in Basrah to beg Hajjaj to free their colleagues from captivity. The tale of a woman who faced a harrowing ordeal at the hands of the pirates reportedly moved Hajjaj, and he instructed his secretary to write to Raja Dahir to demand the immediate release of all the captives and the return of their belongings. But an arrogant Raja Dahir responded saying he knew nothing about the incident and that he was not in a position to resolve the matter; instead he urged Hajjaj to take military action if he wished. Raja Dahir's audacity infuriated Hajjaj who vowed to teach him a lesson. Thus, according to one historical account, an army was sent to Sind to oust Raja Dahir from power, but the latter defeated the Muslim army. Hajjaj then sent a second force against the Hindu ruler who again crushed the Muslim army with the assistance of his traditional war elephants. However, according to other historians (such as al-Baladhuri), Hajjaj had in fact sent only one expedition against Raja Dahir.

Either way, the governor turned to Muhammad ibn al-Qasim (his seventeen year old nephew and son-in-law) to take matters into his hands and bring the arrogant Hindu ruler to heel. Raja Dahir not only refused to apprehend the pirates and release the Muslim captives, he also openly defied Hajjaj by granting sanctuary to Muhammad ibn Muaqiyyah, one of Hajjaj's avowed political opponents. Raja Dahir's actions enraged Hajjaj so much that he called on one of his best battalions (comprising the *crème de la crème* of his armed forces) and he instructed the young and inexperienced Muhammad ibn al-Qasim to take the battle to the Hindu ruler. Despite his youth and inexperience, Muhammad ibn al-Qasim was rated very highly by Hajjaj on account of his superior personal qualities; that is, he was known to have been a brave, honest and intelligent young man. After putting his trust in his nephew and son-in-law, Hajjaj sent the battalion on its way to Makran, accompanied by three thousand camels carrying their baggage and supplies. A young but inspirational Muhammad ibn al-Qasim led the Muslim army to Makran – unaware of the fact that he was about to walk straight into the history books as one of the Muslim world's great military generals.

From Iraq, he travelled swiftly through the province of Fars to the Makran desert and on the way he was joined by another Muslim battalion, thus reinforcing his contingent. After making the necessary preparations, he sent all his artillery on to their destination by sea. This was a clever move considering the fact that the artillery included, among other things, a catapult capable of propelling huge stones at the enemy. As this catapult needed a large number of soldiers to operate it at any one time, moving such a large piece of equipment by land would have been an exhausting task, not least because the soldiers would have had to cross barren deserts and pass through foreign territory before they came in direct contact with the enemy – an enemy which, according to one account, had already inflicted crushing defeats on the Muslims on two previous occasions. After travelling for many days and nights, Muhammad ibn al-Qasim eventually arrived at the outskirts of the heavily fortified Hindu fortress of Debul, and set up camp outside it. In response, the Hindus shut the gate of the fortress and prepared to defend it to the last man. Keen to subdue the town quickly, Muhammad ibn al-Qasim immediately brought his catapult into action after receiving information from a disgruntled local Hindu priest.

The superstitious Hindus believed that no enemy would be able to subdue them so long as the red flag continued to fly on the roof of the town's highest temple. Muhammad ibn al-Qasim therefore instructed his catapult operators to deliberately target the temple and bring down the red flag in order to frighten the people inside the fortress. On the third attempt, the catapult hit the target and this caused widespread panic and commotion inside the fortress; it was not long before the Muslims captured the town. Though the Hindus of Debul expected Muhammad ibn al-Qasim to be a harsh and ruthless leader like their previous rulers, to their surprise he turned out to be a wise and tolerant conqueror. After releasing all the Muslims from captivity in Debul – and having also secured a part of the Indian Ocean for the Arab navy – Muhammad ibn al-Qasim vowed to bring the treacherous Raja Dahir to justice. From Debul, he proceeded to Nirun (located near the modern Pakistani city of Hyderabad), which at the time was an important fortress. In 712, when he was barely eighteen, he took control of this fortress without shedding a drop of blood. Again the locals were taken aback by his kind, tolerant and progressive behaviour and attitude. As he moved in, Jai Singh, the ruler of Nirun and son of Raja Dahir, slipped out of the fortress and joined his father in the heavily fortified city of Brahmanabad.

From Nirun, Muhammad ibn al-Qasim set out in pursuit for Brahmanabad. On his way he conquered Sehwan and from there the news of his sense of justice, tolerance and fair play soon spread across the Indian province of Sind, which prompted many local Hindu priests and tribal leaders to come and pledge their support to him. They agreed to help him oust the tyrannical Raja Dahir from Brahmanabad. As a great leader and motivator of men, Muhammad ibn al-Qasim preferred to win the hearts and minds of the locals through justice, kindness and fair play, rather than use the sword; indeed, he only used the sword as a last resort. His regard for Islamic principles and practices, coupled with his sense of justice and impartiality, irrespective of one's race, class, colour or creed soon won him widespread acclaim. Even the local Hindu priests and tribal leaders admired him for his wisdom, organisational ability and leadership skills. Thanks to his liberal and humane behaviour towards the local Hindus, the city of Sisam (situated towards the west of Sind) also succumbed to the Muslims without a fight. Thereafter, he ordered boats to be prepared in order to build a floating bridge to enable his forces to cross the Indus.

Anticipating the arrival of Muhammad ibn al-Qasim, Raja Dahir organised a large army of fifty thousand horsemen and war elephants, and camped on the plains of Rawar, not far from the banks of the Indus. In June 712, Muhammad ibn al-Qasim led the Muslim army into one of the most decisive battles of his military career. Despite being heavily outnumbered, he inspired his men to fight like lions and after a fierce contest they eventually cut the enemy defences to pieces. Led by Jai Singh, the defeated Hindus fled to Brahmanabad but Rawar soon fell into the hands of the Muslims. During his stay there Muhammad ibn al-Qasim devised and implemented a new political and civil administrative system; he also sent governors to Rawar, Sehwan and Nirun to ensure these towns and cities were properly governed. He issued strict guidelines to all his governors with regard to their duties and obligations to their people; he also reminded them to observe Islamic principles and practices, and urged them to promote justice, tolerance and understanding throughout their territories.

From Brahmanabad, Muhammad ibn al-Qasim proceeded to Aror and annexed the city after a siege of several weeks. He then captured Bhatia, Iskalandah, al-Sikka and Multan. Thanks to young Muhammad ibn al-Qasim, the large Indian province of Sind eventually became an integral part of the vast Umayyad Empire. The territorial foundations laid by Muhammad ibn al-Qasim back in the eighth century endure to this day, in the form of the Islamic Republic of Pakistan. Unfortunately, due to a family dispute back in Damascus, Caliph Sulaiman later recalled Muhammad ibn al-Qasim from the subcontinent and reportedly had him tortured to death at the age of twenty-one. If he had not been recalled from Sind, who knows where his story might have ended. Muhammad ibn al-Qasim's tragic and premature death not only deprived the Muslim world of one of its most celebrated military generals, it also delayed Islamic expansion into the rest of the subcontinent by another three hundred years.

# 55

## Musa ibn Nusayr (b.ca.639 - d.716)

THOUGH MUSLIMS FIRST made inroads into North Africa during the reign of Caliph Umar, the Byzantines re-conquered their lost territories during the conflict which ensued between Caliph Ali and Muawiyah; thus the Muslims were not able to consolidate their presence in North Africa at the time. After Muawiyah ascended the Umayyad throne in 661, he not only reunited the Muslim world under his leadership but also launched expeditions to North Africa and thereby brought a large part of that region back under Umayyad authority. Under the able leadership of Uqba ibn Nafi, the Umayyad forces drove out the Byzantines and in 670 the Muslims founded the historic city of Qayrawan (in present-day Tunisia), thus consolidating Islamic power in that region for the first time. Following Uqba's ousting from power in 672, Abu Muhajir Dinar was appointed governor, but he proved to be both incompetent and ineffective. To make matters worse, Yazid then ascended the Umayyad throne in 680 and, having taken his eyes off events in North Africa, he engaged in a war of attrition with fellow Muslims at home. This enabled the Byzantines to recover and inflict a crushing defeat on the North African Muslims. In desperation, Yazid recalled Uqba ibn Nafi

from retirement and sent him to the Maghreb to prevent the impending military disaster. On his arrival, Uqba swiftly reorganised the Muslim army under his leadership and drove back the Byzantines, extending Umayyad rule all the way to the Atlantic coast. However, soon afterwards Uqba and his forces were soundly defeated by the North African Berber tribes and, again, the Umayyad grip on that region became precarious until the heroic Muslim general Musa ibn Nusayr emerged to permanently establish an Islamic presence in that part of the world.

Musa ibn Nusayr was born during the reign of Caliph Umar. His family hailed from the noble Arab tribe of Lakhm, whose members once occupied prominent positions in the Lakhmid dynasty of Hira (in present-day Iraq). His father, Nusayr, was rescued from a Christian monastery in Ayn al-Tamr (in western Iraq) by the Muslim army led by Khalid ibn al-Walid (during the reign of Caliph Abu Bakr), and he later worked as a bodyguard for a number of prominent Umayyad leaders, including Caliph Muawiyah and Abd al-Aziz ibn Marwan, the governor of Egypt. Raised in a relatively wealthy family, young Musa aspired to follow in the footsteps of his father and join the Umayyad military service. Tall, slim and of solid build, he was – like his father – very brave and ambitious, and a young man who also had a taste for the good things in life. Thanks to his father's support for, and fierce loyalty to, the Umayyad royal family, Musa had unlimited career options available to him but, in the end, he chose to enter the Umayyad armed forces and become a soldier. Known for his bravery, courage and tactical ability, he made his mark as a soldier on the battlefield, and played an active part in the Umayyad conquest of Cyprus during the reign of Caliph Muawiyah. His loyalty and devotion to the Umayyads endeared him to the ruling elites, who swiftly promoted him to one of the highest posts within the Umayyad army.

When Abd al-Malik ibn Marwan ascended the Umayyad throne in 685, he appointed his brother, Abd al-Aziz, to the post of governor of Egypt. At the time Musa was in his mid-forties and had already acquired something of a reputation as a military general, thus he became an advisor and aide to both Caliph Abd al-Malik and his brother. He served the Caliph and his brother in various capacities until 692, when he was sent to Basrah to take over the vacant post of chief revenue collector. During his stay there he served the Caliph's brother, Bishr ibn Marwan, for a period and thereafter worked under Hajjaj ibn Yusuf. As a result, he became a proficient civil servant whose knowledge and understanding of political governance and civil administration was widely admired. However, he later became embroiled in a dispute over financial impropriety. Although Hajjaj accused him of misappropriating State revenue, Musa vehemently rejected the charge. But since Hajjaj was a ruthless and uncompromising governor (who regularly executed his opponents without giving them a fair hearing), Musa did not pursue the matter further and instead fled to Egypt to save his skin. There he sought refuge with Abd al-Aziz, his close friend and governor of Egypt, but when the news of his arrival in Egypt was relayed to the Caliph, the latter summoned him to Damascus. He arrived in Damascus accompanied by Abd al-Aziz, who defended his friend's reputation with such vigour

and eloquence that the Caliph cleared him of all charges of corruption. Musa then went to Egypt with the governor and helped Abd al-Aziz restructure his civil service with great skill and determination.

Given Musa's considerable experience as a military general and civil administrator, Abd al-Aziz considered him to be a great asset to the Umayyads. Thus he helped the governor consolidate his political authority across Egypt, until in 699 Abd al-Aziz appointed him commander of a large military expedition. The purpose of this expedition was to sweep through North Africa and crush the growing unrest, whipped up by the Berbers, against Umayyad rule. This military foray was Musa's first encounter with the North African Berbers. Musa carried out this task with such success that the Berbers refrained from instigating any further political uprising. His achievement also pleased Abd al-Aziz who handsomely rewarded him for his efforts. Subsequently, Abd al-Aziz recalled Hassan ibn al-Nu'man, the incumbent governor of North Africa, and replaced him with Musa. Normally, he would have had to consult Abd al-Malik, his brother and Caliph, before appointing Musa to the governership, but on this ocassion he deliberately did not consult the Caliph because, he felt the latter might overrule him on account of Musa's alleged financial impropriety. But Abd al-Aziz had no doubts about his integrity and suitability for this post, especially given his extensive experience as a military commander and civil administrator, so he appointed him governor. And although the Caliph was not happy with Abd al-Aziz's decision to promote Musa, he nevertheless reluctantly accepted his brother's decision.

Musa was about sixty when he moved to North Africa with his extended family and took up his new post. His arrival was to mark the beginning of a new era in the history of that entire region. He may have been a good governor, but he was also a firm disciplinarian who did not tolerate any form of subversive activity against the State. Upon his arrival in Qayrawan, he launched military expeditions against the rebellious Berber tribes who were bent on wreaking havoc in the Umayyad territories. In so doing he undermined the authority of all the Berber chiefs guilty of instigating political and military uprisings against the Umayyads. He continued his battle against all subversive forces until they submitted to his authority. It is true that all the previous Muslim rulers of North Africa also faced determined opposition from the Berbers – many struggled to control these cunning, stubborn and unruly tribes – but Musa pursued them with such skill and determination that they had no option but to lay down their arms and submit to his authority. He took responsibility for restoring law and order in the urban areas, while his sons Abdullah and Marwan crushed all resistance to his rule in the rural areas. Most astonishingly, within a few months of his arrival in Qayrawan, Musa managed to restore peace and security across North Africa. By all accounts, this was a truly remarkable achievement. He had done what no other Muslim ruler had been able to achieve and, in the process, collected a large quantity of booty, one fifth of which he sent to the Caliph in Damascus; a portion was distributed to his troops, while the remainder was sent to the provincial treasury (*bait al-mal*). When Abd al-Aziz received news of Musa's success, he felt his decision to promote the latter to governorship was vindicated, and even the Caliph was elated by the news of Umayyad progress in North Africa. However, after Abd al-Aziz's sudden death in 704, the Caliph appointed his brother, Abdullah, governor of Egypt. Although he supported Musa in his efforts to strengthen Umayyad rule in North Africa, a year later Caliph Abd al-Malik also died. He was succeeded by his son, al-Walid, who changed the existing political arrangements and restricted the power of the governor of Egypt. Hereafter, Musa was required to report directly to Caliph al-Walid in Damascus.

After consolidating his rule across much of North Africa, Musa decided to bring the whole of the Maghreb fully under his control. After the Caliph's confirmation of him as governor of the Maghreb in 707, he organised a large army and left Qayrawan for Tangier in order to bring that region under Umayyad political control. Despite the Berber's stiff resistance, Musa triumphantly marched into Tangier where Ilyan (or Julian), the Christian ruler, submitted to Umayyad authority without a fight – as he had done previously to Uqba ibn Nafi. The rapid capture of Tangier without a fight encouraged Musa to continue his march towards the province of Sus. Led by Musa and Tariq ibn Ziyad, the Umayyad army advanced very rapidly and soon brought the entire Maghreb under Umayyad control. He then established a permanent garrison in Tangiers while Ilyan, the Christian ruler, moved to Ceuta where he lived with his people under Umayyad protection. A few years later, Ilyan played a pivotal role in the Islamic conquest of both Gibraltar and Spain under the leadership of the legendary Muslim general Tariq ibn Ziyad.

After annexing the entire Maghreb, Musa appointed Tariq as his deputy governor of Morocco, and also instigated a large scale reconstruction programme. Soon scores of mosques, schools and colleges were built across the Maghreb and in so doing he encouraged the Berbers to embrace Islam. His efforts bore fruit as the Berbers began to enter the fold of Islam in their droves. As such, Musa's role in the conquest of North Africa and the Maghreb, not to mention his role in the conversion of the North African Berbers to Islam, was nothing short of phenomenal. Indeed, the credit for establishing a permanent Islamic presence in North Africa and the Maghreb must go mainly to Musa. He stayed in Tangier long enough to devise and implement a functioning political and civil administrative system there and also established several military bases across the Maghreb in order to maintain socio-political peace, order and security throughout that region. During those early days of Muslim rule in North Africa, Musa's extensive experience as a political operator and military commander stood him in good stead, as the Umayyad Empire expanded rapidly both in the East and the West. After securing Tangier, he returned to Qayrawan as North Africa's most effective and powerful governor. Thanks to his personal bravery, polished political and diplomatic skills, and great organisational ability, Islam became a permanent part of the North African cultural landscape. It was also Musa who nominated Tariq ibn Ziyad to spearhead the campaign to conquer Gibraltar and Spain. When Tariq's expedition proved a success, he joined forces with him and brought a significant part of Spain under Umayyad rule. If Musa and Tariq had not been recalled by Caliph al-Walid to Damascus, they probably would have gone further into mainland Europe. However, with the departure of Musa and Tariq from North Africa, Islamic conquests of the rest of Europe ground to a halt, even though Spain remained a Muslim country for more than another seven hundred years.

Given Musa's remarkable achievements as a ruler and military commander, one would have thought the Umayyad Caliph would have granted him a warm reception on his arrival in Damascus, but unfortunately Caliph Sulaiman, al-Walid's successor, completely ignored the great Muslim conqueror. He died in poverty at the age of around seventy-seven and was buried in Wadi al-Qura, located in Syria.

# 56

## Shah Jahan (b.1592 – d.1666)

FOUNDED BY ZAHIR AL-DIN BABAR (Babur) in 1526, the Mughal dynasty ruled the Indian subcontinent for more than three centuries with great splendour and munificence. Expanded and consolidated by Akbar the Great during his long reign of forty-nine years, the Mughal dynasty subsequently became one of the Muslim world's foremost political and military powers, along with the Ottomans and the Safavids. After the death of Akbar in 1605, his son Salim (also known as Emperor Jahangir) ascended the throne and attempted to further consolidate Mughal power and authority, but he encountered many political obstacles and internal challenges. Jahangir may have been a successful ruler but he was also a pleasure-seeker who surrounded himself with much wealth and luxury. After securing Mughal rule in Bengal, he built some of the most beautiful fountains and gardens ever constructed by a Mughal ruler. And unlike his father, Jahangir was highly educated and wrote his autobiography, *Tuzuk-i-Jahangir* (Memoirs of Jahangir), which is today considered to be a work of considerable historical significance and literary merit. The fact that Jahangir was more a conqueror of hearts than of land is most evident from the fact that peace and prosperity reigned supreme during his rule.

But towards the end of his reign of twenty-two years, he became embroiled in a serious internal family dispute, sparked off by the question of political succession. The ensuing discord divided the royal family and severely undermined his political power and authority. Jahangir was eventually succeeded by his son, Shah Jahan, who went onto become one of the Muslim world's most famous and romantic rulers.

Abu Muzaffar Shihab al-Din Muhammad Sahib-i-Qiran II, better known as Shah Jahan ('King of the World'), was born during the long and successful reign of his grandfather, Akbar the Great. His birth was considered to be a good omen for the Mughals because, in that same year, Akbar went on to extend Mughal rule in the north of India. Overjoyed at the birth of his third grandson, Akbar named him Khurram, meaning 'joy and happiness'. The Mughal astrologers apparently observed the constellations of the stars at the time of Shah Jahan's birth and, according to them, they were similar to the constellations observed at the birth of Amir Timur, the great ancestor of the Mughals, and this was considered to be a good omen for the boy. Brought up by his father, young Shah Jahan received a thorough education in the languages, arts and religious sciences. Though his father, Jahangir, led a lavish lifestyle and was very fond of wine, Shah Jahan grew up to be a sensible young man who despised alcohol. Such was his aversion to uninhibited materialism and pleasure-seeking that he even reproached his father for his addiction to alcohol. Perhaps it was his early Islamic education which safeguarded him from the wayward and un-Islamic practices which prevailed within the royal family at the time.

In 1611, when Shah Jahan was only nineteen, his father married Mihr al-Nisa, popluarly known as Nur Jahan ('Light of the World'), who was the daughter of a Persian immigrant. Being very intelligent, exceptionally beautiful and highly ambitious, she began to exert undue influence on her husband shortly after their marriage. She convinced her husband to appoint her father, Itimad al-Dawlah, and her brother Asaf Khan to two of the highest political posts in the land. She then married her daughter by her first husband to Jahangir's youngest son, Prince Shahryar, thus further strengthening her position in the Mughal hierarchy. As Jahangir increasingly became reliant on his domineering wife to carry out his duties and obligations as emperor, Shah Jahan, who at the time lived with the royal family, co-operated closely with Nur Jahan and her brother Asaf Khan (who was the Prime Minister at the time) to discharge the affairs of State. But he co-operated with them on the understanding that he was his father's heir-apparent. Not surprisingly, during this period Shah Jahan served his father with much loyalty and distinction including leading several military expeditions against their rivals. Indeed, when he captured the kingdom of Ahmadnagar in 1616, Jahangir was so delighted with his son's achievement that he conferred on him the royal title of 'Shah Jahan'.

However, Nur Jahan was not very fond of Shah Jahan; she became very jealous of him to the extent that she began to secretly plot against him. Soon after marrying her daughter to Prince Shahryar, she began to exert her political authority and push for her son-in-law to be crowned emperor after her husband's death, even though

everyone within the royal family knew that Shah Jahan was Jahangir's nominated heir. This was a dangerous and unprecedented move on the part of Nur Jahan. As an intelligent young man, it did not take Shah Jahan too long to realise what was happening, but he was determined not to be sidelined or pushed aside. Predictably, this sparked off a serious and damaging succession battle within the royal family. Exasperated by Nur Jahan's political intrigues and by his father's apparent inability to restrain her, Shah Jahan eventually revolted against the emperor. The timing of his rebellion could not have come at a worse time for Emperor Jahangir because at the same time the Mughals had also lost the northern province of Qandahar to Shah Abbas, then the Safavid ruler of Persia. Faced with foreign invasion in the Northwest and open rebellion from his son at home, Jahangir found himself caught between a rock and a hard place. When the news of Shah Jahan's annexation of Bihar and Bengal was relayed to Jahangir, he sent Prince Parvez and Mahabat Khan to go and crush his rebellious son and his supporters. After suffering defeat on the battlefield, Shah Jahan went on the run, only to be reconciled with his ailing father in 1625. By then, however, considerable loss and damage had already been inflicted on Mughal power and authority. As for Nur Jahan, the instigator of this whole sorry tale, her hopes of seeing her son-in-law succeed her husband were also dashed.

Indeed, as soon as the news of Jahangir's death was announced, Prince Shahryar took control of the public treasury in Lahore and installed himself as the new Mughal emperor, but Shah Jahan had other ideas. Hitherto confined to the Deccan region on his father's orders, he swiftly moved to Agra, the capital of the Mughal dynasty, and found a powerful supporter and ally in the person of Asaf Khan, his father-in-law and the incumbent Prime Minister. In the ensuing battle, Shah Jahan's forces, led by Asaf Khan, routed Shahryar's army, thereby paving the way for Shah Jahan to formally ascend the Mughal throne at the age of thirty-six. After being crowned emperor, Shah Jahan transferred more political power to Asaf Khan, the Prime Minister, while Nur Jahan was dispatched to Lahore where she eventually died in 1645. Unlike his father, Shah Jahan was a bold and decisive ruler. He swiftly removed all rivals from his path and consolidated his power and authority throughout the Mughal Empire. Although he inherited from his father a beleaguered administration which suffered from much corruption and lack of accountability, he reformed the organisation and this helped him to face the new challenges which confronted the Mughals at the time. Everything went according to plan at the beginning, and the emperor was delighted by the progress he was making.

However, his success and optimism were soon dampened by two early rebellions against his rule. In the first year of his reign, Jujhar Singh, the Bundela chief, instigated an uprising against Shah Jahan, but he was soundly defeated and driven into the mountains by the Mughals. A year later, another powerful uprising was led by Khan Jahan Lodi, who was an Afghan ruler, but the Mughals hunted him from one place to another before inflicting a final defeat on him. During the next two years Shah Jahan remained busy dealing with the appalling impact of famine in both Deccan and Gujarat. According to Abd al-Hamid Lahori, the noted Mughal historian, this famine was so devastating that the people were forced to devour human remains. During this period he also had to come to terms with the death of his beloved wife and consort, Mumtaz Mahal (meaning 'Chosen One of the Palace'), the daughter of Prime Minister Asaf Khan. Mumtaz was the real love and passion of his life, and her premature death in 1631 was a major blow to Shah Jahan. She not only bore him fourteen children, her death completely changed his outlook on life. Overwhelmed by grief and sadness, his hair turned white and he began to wear dark spectacles to hide the marks of tears.

As a prolific builder, during his thirty year reign Shah Jahan constructed some of the subcontinent's most dazzling works of architecture including the Shalimar Gardens near Lahore, the historic Jami Masjid (Central mosque) in Delhi and the elegant Moti (pearl) mosque in Agra. He also built two impressive mausoleums, one in memory of his father, Jahangir, and another in remembrance of Asaf Khan, his loyal Prime Minister and father-in-law, both of which are located in Lahore. In addition to this he built numerous hunting lodges and gardens in Sirhind, Lahore and Srinagar, and authorised the construction of a new city called Shahjahanabad in 1639. This city was completed in 1648 and is today known as Old Delhi. Undoubtedly the most dazzling work of architecture ever produced by a Muslim is the world famous Taj Mahal (Crown Palace), which is the mausoleum constructed in memory of his beloved wife, Mumtaz Mahal. The Taj was designed to symbolise the greatness and enduring nature of his love for Mumtaz. He personally chose the site, located on the banks of the river Yamuna in Agra, and authorised the construction of this immortal building in 1632. Thousands of labourers worked round-the-clock under the supervision of such eminent Mughal architects as Ustadh Makramat Khan and Ustadh Ahmad Lahori in order to complete the huge project on time. After many years of careful planning and hard work, the Taj Mahal was eventually completed in 1648. Made entirely from white marble from the quarries of Rajasthan, the edifice was exquisitely decorated with Arabic calligraphy and floral designs. More than three and a half centuries after its completion, the Taj Mahal continues to inspire and overwhelm its visitors to this day. It is not only a symbol of eternal and everlasting love, today it is also considered to be one of the seven architectural wonders of the world.

As Shah Jahan was a prolific builder, so was he also a just and competent ruler who took decisive action against his opponents as and when required (including the Hindu Rajputs who were bent on wreaking havoc within the Mughal territories). After abolishing his father and grandfather's unfair political, economic, legal and religious policies (which they enacted in order to win the support and favour of the Hindus at the expense of the Muslims), he restored the faith and confidence of the *ulama* (traditional Islamic scholars) and the Muslim masses in the Mughal authorities. Unlike his predecessors he proudly wore a beard, respected and observed Islamic principles and teachings, and outlawed the practice of bowing before the emperor. Shah Jahan's early Islamic education influenced his thinking and behaviour on these and other similar matters. Although some Indian historians have accused him of pursuing anti-Hindu policies, he was far from being a racist or religious bigot. He offered full protection and support to all his Hindu subjects. Indeed, he allowed the Hindus to observe their religious rites and cultural practices without any hindrance whatsoever. Thus Shah Jahan was a wise, tolerant and just sovereign who ruled his subjects with more understanding and sensitivity than probably any other Mughal ruler.

Unlike his grandfather, Akbar, he was not a military conqueror. Keen to avoid unnecessary military confrontation, he took action only against those who encouraged or supported subversive activities against the Mughals. To that effect, in 1636, he sent his son, Awrangzeb, to confront the Sultan of Bijapur for his persistent opposition to the Mughals. Being more radical and enthusiastic than his father, Awrangzeb was on the verge of crushing the Sultan and his militia when Shah Jahan intervened to prevent unnecessary bloodshed – on the condition that the Sultan paid an annual tribute to the Mughals. Perhaps the only unprovoked military campaign he undertook was the attempt to annex Samarqand the land of his legendary ancestor, Amir Timur. In 1646, while the Uzbeks were busy fighting amongst themselves, Shah Jahan organised a large military expedition against the ruler of Balkh, with a view to proceeding to Samarqand. Led by Prince Murad, the expedition returned home having failed to capture Balkh. Shah Jahan then sent a second expedition, led by Awrangzeb, which forced the Uzbeks to retreat and seek assistance from neighbouring Persia. This time, faced by the might of these combined forces, the Mughals suffered a crushing defeat and were forced to return home without having conquered Samarqand. The campaign to conquer the 'Blue Pearl of the Orient' thus proved to be disastrous for the Mughals both financially and militarily. Their only consolation was that they recaptured Qandahar from the Persians.

His Central Asian debacle aside, Shah Jahan's reign of thirty years was otherwise supremely successful. He strengthened and consolidated Mughal power and authority across the subcontinent, built some of the Muslim world's most beautiful mosques and mausoleums, and spread social harmony and economic prosperity throughout the Mughal Empire. In addition, he promoted understanding, tolerance and dialogue between all his subjects, including Muslims, Hindus, Buddhists, Christians, Jains and others. For this reason, Shah Jahan's reign is today considered to be the 'Golden Age' of Muslim rule in India. In 1657, he fell seriously ill, which sparked off a civil war between his four sons as they each simultaneously laid claim to the Mughal throne. Shah Jahan's last years were therefore the most tragic period of his life. He died at the age of seventy-four and was buried next to his beloved wife, Mumtaz Mahal, inside the immortal Taj Mahal in Agra.

# 57
## Abul Hasan al-Mas'udi (b.ca.895 - d.957)

AFTER THE EMERGENCE of Islam in seventh century Arabia, the once illiterate and uncivilised bedouins of the desert burst onto the global stage under the banner of their new faith and transformed the course of human history. The Arabs crushed the mighty Roman and Persian Empires and carved out for themselves one of the greatest empires in history; they also learned and assimilated the intellectual heritage of ancient Greece, Babylon, China and India, and thereby dominated human thought, culture and civilisation for more than a thousand years. As the Muslim world became a beacon of light for the rest of the world, people flocked to the foremost centres of learning and higher education in Baghdad, Damascus, Cordova and Cairo to study science, philosophy, mathematics, arts and architecture under the guidance of some of the Muslim world's greatest minds. In doing so, Muslims prepared the way for the emergence of modern science, culture and civilisation. The tenth century was one of the most intellectually productive periods in the history of Islam, for it was during this period that great Muslim thinkers like Ibn Sina, al-Farabi, al-Razi, al-Biruni and Ibn al-Haytham lived and thrived; they collectively helped to push the boundaries of human thought and raise the pursuit of knowledge to a new and higher level. Al-Mas'udi, the famous Muslim scholar and polymath, also lived during this period and contributed immensely to the development of science, philosophy, Islamic history, geology, geography and natural history.

Abul Hasan Ali ibn Hussain ibn Ali al-Mas'udi was born in Baghdad during the reign of the Abbasid Caliph Mu'tadid. His family traced their ancestry back to Abdullah ibn Mas'ud, the famous companion of the Prophet, and thus were known to have been a noble and respected Arab family. Al-Mas'udi grew up at a time when the influence of Mu'tazilism was still very strong within the intellectual and cultural circles of Baghdad, which at the time was one of the Muslim world's foremost centres of philosophical and scientific learning. During his early days he came under the influence of philosophical Mu'tazilism to the extent that he became a prominent exponent of Islam from a Mu'tazilite perspective. Heavily influenced by the ideas and thoughts of Mu'tazilite thinkers like Abu Ali al-Jubbai, Abul Hashim and *qadi* Abd al-Jabbar, he also became interested in history and the natural sciences. After completing his formal education, he left his native Baghdad and travelled extensively in pursuit of knowledge. He started his journeys relatively young; he was in his early twenties when he first began to travel in pursuit of knowledge. Despite visiting and studying at all the prominent centres of learning in Iraq and the neighbouring Arab countries, his thirst for knowledge remained unquenched. Like Ibn Sina, al-Razi and al-Biruni, the incessant pursuit of knowledge and wisdom became his main pre-occupation in life.

Although al-Mas'udi travelled the length and breadth of the Arab world, he did not travel for the sake of travelling; in fact, his journeys were motivated by a higher goal. Everywhere he went he carefully observed both the geographical and demographical make-up of the place, and took copious notes about the locals, their culture, traditions and social habits. At a time when even travelling from one town to another was considered to be a hazardous task, he became one of the most prolific travellers in history. Three centuries before Marco Polo and Ibn Batuttah were born, he travelled across a significant part of the then-known world on his own. From his native Baghdad, he journeyed across Persia and reached India while he was still in his twenties. In India, he visited the provinces of Sind, Punjab, Konkan and Malabar. His detailed description of the principality of Mansura, which was the commercial heart of Muslim Sind at the time, was as vivid as it was enlightening. Named after Mansur ibn Jumhur, the Umayyad governor of Sind, the city was situated on the banks of the Indus and al-Mas'udi considered it to be one of the most prosperous places he had visited in India. From India, al-Mas'udi retreated to Kirman in Persia, where he stayed for a period before returning again to India. This time he travelled further into India and, as he did so, he was surprised to encounter Muslim traders and merchants who had sailed from as far away as Yemen and settled among the Hindus in some of India's most remote and secluded regions.

From India, he proceeded to Ceylon (present-day Sri Lanka) and from there he sailed down the Indian Ocean and reached Zanzibar and Madagascar. After a short stay in Madagascar, he set out for what is now the Gulf State of Oman, via Basrah. Then he sailed along the shores of the Caspian Sea and visited parts of Central Asia, Syria and Palestine before finally returning home to Baghdad. Eager to learn more, al-Mas'udi then travelled across the Middle East and Asia in pursuit of knowledge, and in the process he became a pioneering cultural explorer as well as a great geographer. He not only carefully observed all the places he visited but, most crucially, recorded his views and opinions about all these places in the form of a book which has remained extant to this day. As an eminent scholar and scientist, al-Mas'udi was not interested in gossip or hearsay; rather he surveyed most of the geographical literature of his time – some of which he mentioned in his book by name – and did so in order to improve the historical, geological and geographical ideas and thoughts of his predecessors. Prior to his time, some of the Muslim world's great thinkers and scientists (like al-Khwarizmi, al-Kindi and al-Sarakhsi) had researched and written extensively on these subjects. Indeed, al-Khwarizmi's celebrated book *Kitab Surat al-Ard* (Book on the Shape of Earth) was a pioneering work in the field of geography which later inspired other Muslim scientists and geographers to pursue advanced research in this subject. Although al-Khwarizmi's book laid the foundations for the study of geography among the Muslims, it was al-Mas'udi who pushed the frontiers of geological and geographical knowledge, thanks to the fresh information and data he had obtained from across the world during his *wanderjahren*.

It was during his stay in Basrah that al-Mas'udi recorded his ideas and thoughts on a wide range of subjects (including history, geology and geography) in the form of a book. Entitled *Muruj al-Dhahab wa Ma'adin al-Jawhar* (The Meadows of Gold and Mines of Gems) he provided, in this voluminous book, a detailed account of his travels in Persia, India, Ceylon and Central Asia; he also recorded new information about these places and highlighted their histories, geological variations and demographic structures. In addition to providing an illuminating description of all the places he visited, he compared and contrasted the traditions, cultures and habits of, for example, the Persians with those of the Indians. In doing so, he paved the way for other Muslim thinkers, such as Ibn Khaldun, to pursue their sociological analysis of culture and society. He then analysed the nature of earthquakes, geological formations and even explained how a windmill he had seen in the city of Sijistan (located in the Persian province of Khurasan) actually worked. The accounts of his journeys were accurate, vivid and comprehensive. A reader of this book cannot help but admire al-Mas'udi for his rigorous methodology, insights into different cultures, varied interests, and of course his remarkable ability to sift through such a large quantity of historical, geological, geographical and anecdotal information about so many different cultures and countries, before compiling them in the form of a book.

Considered to be one of the most comprehensive works ever written on the subject of history, geology and geography, al-Mas'udi completed the first draft of his book in 947. He later revised it in 956 and a French translation was published in Paris between 1861 and 1877 in nine bulky volumes. Al-Mas'udi's contributions in the fields of geology, geography and navigation were such that his pioneering works influenced prominent Muslim scientists and geographers like al-Biruni, al-Maqdisi and al-Idrisi. Many years later, most of the medieval Muslim geographers, like al-Idrisi, travelled across the Muslim world and parts of Europe, knowing only too well that pioneering scholars and explorers like al-Mas'udi had already preceeded them many centuries earlier. And although it is true that eminent scholars and geographers like al-Idrisi broke new ground in the study of geography by developing cartography, which enabled them to produce the first accurate map of the world (depicting its sphere in the form of a disc), a careful study of their work – especially al-Idrisi's famous *Nuzhat al-Mushtaq fi Ikhtiraq al-Afaq* (Entertainment for Those Who

Wish to Travel Around the World), also known as *Kitab al-Rujar* (The Book of Roger) – shows that their works were profoundly influenced by the geographical ideas and thoughts of al-Mas'udi.

In addition to being a pioneering explorer, a gifted geologist and an outstanding geographer, al-Mas'udi was also an historian of the highest calibre. Along with al-Baladhuri, al-Tabari, al-Isfahani, Ibn al-Athir and Ibn Khaldun, he is today considered to be one of the Muslim world's greatest historians. Inspired by the Prophet of Islam, the early Muslims preserved as much information as possible about the life and times of the Prophet (*sirah*), his companions (*sahabah*), and those of their successors (*tabiun*) for the benefit of future generations. Al-Mas'udi followed in their footsteps and became a prolific writer and historian. Indeed, along with his illustrious contemporaries al-Tabari and al-Isfahani, he produced some of the most celebrated works of history ever written in Arabic. A work of universal history on a colossal scale, al-Tabari's *Kitab Tarikh al-Rusul wa'l Muluk* (The Book of the History of Prophets and Kings) begins with creation and traces the lives and careers of all the prominent Prophets, including an extensive account of the life and times of Prophet Muhammad and his companions. It concludes with some of the major events which took place during the author's own lifetime. Hailed as a masterpiece, this work has recently been published in English in thirty-eight volumes.

Like al-Tabari, Abul Faraj al-Isfahani was an outstanding historian who wrote his *Kitab al-Aghani* (The Book of Songs) in more than twenty volumes. As a work of cultural history, this book is rated very highly by the Islamic historians. Like al-Tabari and al-Isfahani, Ahmad ibn Yahya al-Baladhuri was another outstanding early Muslim historian who wrote two famous books, namely *Futuh al-Buldan* (The Conquest of Countries) and the voluminous *Ansab al-Ashraf* (The Lineage of the Nobles). In these two books, he provided a wealth of information about the early Islamic conquests, as well as detailed accounts of the life and times of the first four Caliphs of

Islam and the Umayyad period. However, unlike these historians, al-Mas'udi did not collect a large quantity of information and compile it in chronological order; instead he adopted a critical approach to writing and interpreting history. This is evident from the fact that his magisterial *Muruj al-Dhahab* surveys the same historical period as that of al-Tabari's *Tarikh*, yet his work is much superior to the latter in terms of quality of scholarship and literary production. Indeed, inspired by the critical and engaging historical methodology of the early Islamic historians such as al-Mas'udi, four hundred years later Ibn Khaldun, the celebrated North African Muslim historian, authored his world famous *Muqaddimah fi'l Tarikh* (Introduction to History).

Towards the end of his life, al-Mas'udi left Basrah and moved to Syria for a period. He then went to Cairo where he composed another voluminous work on history. Entitled *Akhbar al-Zaman* (An Account of Times), this work on history and culture consisted of around thirty volumes. In the final year of his life, he completed yet another important book *Kitab al-Tanbih wa'l Ishraf* (Book of Indication and Revision). In this treatise, he explored aspects of human geography, climatology, oceanography, ecology, natural history and the philosophy of nature. Widely considered to be one of the greatest Muslim polymaths of all time, across medieval Europe al-Mas'udi became known as the 'Herodotus and Pliny of the Arabs'. He died at the age of sixty-two and was buried in al-Fustat, Egypt.

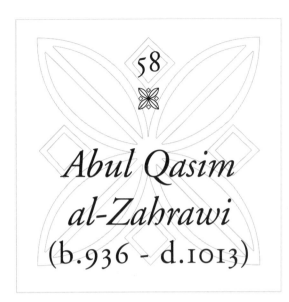

## 58

# Abul Qasim al-Zahrawi (b.936 - d.1013)

AFTER THE UMAYYADS were ousted from power by the Abbasids in 750, Prince Abd al-Rahman ibn Muawiyah fled Damascus and arrived in North Africa. From there he reached Cordova, the capital of *al-andalus* (Muslim Spain) in 756, and swiftly assumed control of that country. Abd al-Rahman's unexpected rise to power in Islamic Spain assured the continuation of Umayyad rule in the Islamic West for almost another three hundred years. By unifying Spain under his able leadership, he also inaugurated one of the most memorable periods in European history. Under the guidance of his descendants such as Abd al-Rahman II and Muhammad I, Spain became one of the most advanced European nations of the time. During the reign of Abd al-Rahman III and Hakam II the fortunes of Islamic Spain increased so rapidly that Cordova became one of Europe's most impressive capitals. Thanks to their generous patronage of learning and higher education, Caliph Abd al-Rahman III and his successors turned Cordova into a thriving centre of intellectual, cultural and literary activities. As a result, scholars, scientists, mathematicians, philosophers and theologians flocked from across Europe to the leading Spanish cities in order to learn, study and master the finer points of their chosen pursuits under the tutelage of Europe's great minds. At the time, some of Europe's leading scientists, intellectuals and writers happened to be Muslims who flourished in Spain under the generous patronage of the Umayyad rulers. Al-Zahrawi was one such outstanding scholar and scientist whose contribution and achievement in the field of medicine and surgery was unique and unprecedented.

Abul Qasim Khalaf ibn Abbas al-Zahrawi, known in medieval Europe as Abulcasis, was born in the royal suburb of al-Zahra in Cordova during the glorious reign of Caliph Abd al-Rahman III. Born and raised at a time when Islamic Spain was at its intellectual zenith, al-Zahrawi grew up to be a prodigiously talented child who excelled in his studies. Thanks to Caliph Abd al-Rahman III's long and wise reign, political stability was restored across Muslim Spain and material prosperity spread throughout the country like never before. This encouraged both Muslim and non-Muslim scholars and scientists to collaborate and make some of medieval Europe's finest scientific and literary contributions, complementing the great cultural and architectural achievements of the time. After completing his early education in Arabic and aspects of Islamic and physical sciences, al-Zahrawi developed a keen interest in the medical sciences. Thus he received advanced training in medicine at Cordova under the guidance of its leading Muslim physicians, and rapidly acquired something of a reputation for his skills as a medical practitioner. It was during this period that Caliph Abd al-Rahman III came to hear about the young physician and, accordingly, he invited al-Zahrawi to the Caliphal court. Although he was barely in his mid-twenties at the time, the Caliph was deeply impressed by al-Zahrawi's profound knowledge and understanding of medicine and asked him to become his personal physician. He went on to serve the Caliph in the capacity of personal physician until the latter died in 961 at the age of seventy-one, having ruled Islamic Spain for no less than half a century.

As a physician, al-Zahrawi was a proud inheritor of traditional Islamic medicine. If ancient Greek physicians like Hippocrates, Galen, Dioscorides and Paul of Aegina were highly-skilled medical practitioners who contributed immensely to the development of medicine, then gifted Muslim physicians like al-Kindi, Ali ibn Rabban al-Tabari and Abu Bakr al-Razi were the first to study and integrate ancient Greek medical thought into the Islamic worldview, and thereby produce a powerful and authoritative medical synthesis which influenced the study and practice of medicine up to the modern period. And although it is true that the Greeks considered medicine to be yet another scientific discipline like astronomy and cosmology, the early Muslim scientists and physicians refused to compartmentalise science; instead they developed an integrated and holistic approach based on the fundamental principles and practices of Islam. That is to say, influenced by the principles of *tibb al-nabi* ('the Prophetic medicine'), the early Muslim physicians formulated an essentially Islamic approach to medical science which sought to remedy the physical ailments, but to do so without overlooking the emotional and spiritual dimension of man. This explains why they went out of their way to organise their

healthcare programme in accordance with the all-encompassing Islamic approach to life, health and well-being. Following in their footsteps, al-Zahrawi also studied and practiced medicine from an holistic perspective and, like his illustrious predecessors, he believed that diseases and ailments were best treated in their wider context rather than in isolation.

Al-Zahrawi was barely twenty-five when al-Hakam ascended the throne in Cordova and asked him to serve as his personal physician. Like his father, al-Hakam was a wise, peaceful and benevolent ruler who became renowned for his love of learning and scholarship. To this end he promoted learning and education across Muslim Spain, and transformed the Academy in Cordova into one of the largest institutions of higher education in Europe at the time. Likewise, the libraries of Cordova were packed with books and manuscripts on all the sciences of the day. The Caliph also recruited some of the brightest minds of the time to his institutions of higher education, and thereby blazed a trail which continued to burn across Europe for centuries. Such was al-Hakam's enthusiasm for learning and scholarship that the historians have compared him with the Abbasid Caliph Abdullah al-Ma'mun who was also a formidable champion of higher education and learning. As the Caliph's personal physician, al-Zahrawi had full access to his private library which contained some of the best medical textbooks of the day, and this enabled him to devote all his spare time and energy to advanced study and research into all aspects of medicine. Although there were many other outstanding Muslim scientists (most notably Abul Qasim Maslamah al-Majriti, Abu Yusuf ibn Ishaq ibn Shabrut and Areeb ibn Sa'd al-Katib al-Qurtubi) who lived and practiced medicine in Cordova at the time, it was al-Zahrawi who was destined to carry out ground-breaking research in medicine and develop scores of new surgical tools and techniques for the benefit of future generations.

During the course of his medical career, al-Zahrawi pursued theoretical research, but also carried out practical experiments in order to demonstrate or verify his theories at a practical level. As a pioneer of surgical anatomy, he performed a large number of operations, ranging from simple Caesarean sections, to more complex and delicate eye operations. He performed such complex and often critical surgical operations at a time when there were no suitable medical tools or equipment to assist him. This prompted him to devise and develop the surgical equipment which would enable him to perform medical operations with success, and in so doing he laid the foundations for the modern science of surgery. No doubt the reluctance of the early Muslim physicians to carry out surgical operations hindered the development of clinical anatomy in the Muslim world until the pioneering al-Zahrawi took the initiative and invented the surgical tools necessary for performing operations. He not only invented a large number of surgical tools, but also performed numerous operations using the same tools and equipment, thus paving the way for the emergence of surgical procedures and techniques as we know them today. Moreover, as an accomplished practitioner of cauterisation (the practice of searing a wound by burning it with a hot iron to destroy the infection), al-Zahrawi was able to utilise this technique to treat other medical conditions such as haemorrhoids, malignant tumours and excessive bleeding. The medieval Muslim physicians preferred this method because traditional Islamic teachings justified it as a legitimate practice. Not surprisingly, al-Zahrawi recommended it for the treatment of apoplexy, epilepsy, bone fractures and dislocations, as well as various other surgical disorders.

As a practising Muslim, he understood and appreciated why women preferred to be operated on by women rather than men, so he used to train midwives to carry out emergency Caesarean operations and other clinical procedures on women. If an operation turned out to be more difficult than anticipated, he provided guidance and instructions to the midwives from behind a screen. In short, had it not been for al-Zahrawi

the Muslim contribution to the development of the science of surgery would not have been worth mentioning. After a lifetime devoted to medical research and surgery, al-Zahrawi eventually decided to write a book on the subject. At the same time as al-Zahrawi was busy writing his book, Ibn Sina (the renowned Muslim physician and philosopher) was also in the process of writing his famous *al-Qanun fi al-Tibb* (The Canon of Medicine) which subsequently became one of the most popular medical encyclopaedias of all time. Like Ibn Sina's *Canon*, al-Zahrawi's monumental *Kitab al-Tasrif Liman Ajaz An-il Ta'alif* (An Aid to Him Who Lacks the Capacity to Read Large Books) played a pivotal role in the development of modern medicine and surgical procedures and techniques. Consisting of thirty chapters, this book was in fact a massive encyclopaedia on medicine and surgery and soon after its publication it became one of the most sought-after surgical textbooks of its time. After providing a detailed and systematic explanation of cauterisation and how this medical procedure is to be carried out, al-Zahrawi explained how surgical operations, including ocular and dental surgery, should be performed using a scalpel. In addition to this, he covered aspects of obstetrics and explained how gallstones should be removed, among many other topics. He was of the opinion that a decaying tooth should be removed and, in certain circumstances, how it could be replaced with artificial tooth or one extracted from animals. As an accomplished dentist, he was thoroughly familiar with all aspects of oral hygiene and dentistry.

In the last part of his *Tasrif*, he provided a detailed explanation of bone fractures and dislocations; he argued that fractures and dislocations could be treated successfully without having to operate on them. For the first time in medical history, he correctly diagnosed that paralysis resulted from the fracture of the spine. He then explained all aspects of gynaecology (including childbirth) and also identified what is today widely known as 'Kalcher's Position'. Most significantly, al-Zahrawi's book contained illustrations of around two hundred different surgical tools and equipment, most of which he had invented himself, and all the illustrations were accompanied by a brief but precise explanation of each tool, its meaning and purpose. The surgical part of his book became so popular in Europe that it was first translated into Latin by Gerard of Cremona and published in Venice in 1497. Thereafter, it was published in Strasbourg in 1532, Basle in 1541 and Oxford in 1778. This book was rated so highly by the Europeans that it was prescribed to all medical students at Europe's leading universities until as late as the eighteenth century. The famous French surgeon Guy de Chauliac considered it to be such an important textbook on surgery that he included it in one of his own works.

Though al-Zahrawi became famous in the West as the 'father of surgery', his works did not receive similar recognition in the Islamic East, perhaps because surgery was never a popular branch of medicine in the Muslim world. Nevertheless, al-Zahrawi was an unusually gifted physician who contributed more to the development of surgery and surgical tools and procedures than any other single individual in the history of medicine. He died at the age of seventy-seven and was buried in his native Cordova.

# 59

## Ibn al-Arabi
## (b.1165 - d.1240)

FOLLOWING THE ESTABLISHMENT of Umayyad rule in Spain in the beginning of the eighth century, towering Umayyad rulers like Abd al-Rahman III and al-Hakam transformed the fortunes of *al-andalus*. Though their rule represented one of the most glorious periods in the history of Western Islam, the Umayyads were eventually ousted from power in 1031. This led to the chaotic period of 'the petty States' (or *muluk al-tawa'if*) which endured for more than half a century before the North African al-Moravid (*al-murabitun*) ruler Yusuf ibn Tashfin marched into Spain and reunited the country under his leadership. Peace and security was restored across Spain until the al-Moravids lost their grip on power in 1145. As anarchy and disorder spread throughout the land, another North African power, the al-Mohads (*al-muwahhidun*) led by Abd al-Mu'min, defeated the rebels and again restored peace and order across Spain. The al-Mohads ruled Spain for just over a century before disorder returned yet again. This was a topsy-turvy period in the history of Islamic Spain, when successive political dynasties emerged and assumed control of the country but failed to maintain their grip on power. Amidst the prevailing political chaos and disorder, one of the Muslim world's most influ-

ential mystical philosophers emerged to develop a powerful and, equally, controversial metaphysical theory. This remarkable thinker and writer was none other than Ibn al-Arabi.

Muhyi al-Din Abu Abdullah Muhammad ibn Ali ibn Muhammad ibn al-Arabi al-Hatimi al-Ta'i, known as *shaykh al-akbar* ('the Great Master'), was born in Murcia (*mursiyah*) in Islamic Spain. He was also known as Ibn Arabi – without the definite article *al* – to distinguish him from the renowned Muslim jurist (*qadi*) Abu Bakr ibn al-Arabi. His father, Ali, worked as a civil servant in the administration of Muhammad ibn Sa'id, who was an independent ruler of Murcia, until the al-Mohad ruler Abu Yaqub Yusuf marched into Murcia, Valencia and Lorca in around 1172 and annexed those territories. This forced the family to move to Seville, where his father joined the local civil service and they began to rebuild their lives. As the son of a respected civil servant and Sufi sage, Ibn al-Arabi grew up to be a sensible, intelligent and disciplined young man. During his early years he received training in Arabic language, literature and aspects of the traditional Islamic sciences. Fascinated by Sufism (Islamic mysticism), he studied and acquired profound insights into aspects of Islamic spirituality while he was still in his teens. According to Ibn al-Arabi, he was fifteen when he met Ibn Rushd (Averroes), the famous Muslim philosopher and jurist of Spain, and the latter was apparently impressed by his grasp of Islamic teachings and spirituality. After marrying at a young age, he worked as a clerical assistant to the governor of Seville. During the next decade he pursued advanced education in Islamic sciences, including *tafsir* (Qur'anic exegesis), *hadith* (Prophetic traditions) and *fiqh* (Islamic jurisprudence). He specialised in *zahiri* legal thought (as championed by Ibn Hazm al-Andalusi) and studied under the guidance of some of Seville and Ceuta's leading Islamic scholars. Then, at the age of thirty, he left Spain and moved to North Africa. His stay in Tunis must have kindled his desire to explore the eastern heartlands of Islam, although he claimed to have been instructed in the form of a vision to proceed to the East. Either way, in 1200 he journeyed to the Islamic East where he remained for the rest of his life. Two years later, Ibn al-Arabi went to Makkah to perform the sacred *hajj* (pilgrimage) and, during his stay there, he befriended a Persian mystic whose pious but attractive daughter inspired him to compose his *Tarjuman al-Ashwaq* (The Interpreter of Desires), which is a small collection of mystical-cum-romantic odes.

For the next two decades he travelled extensively in pursuit of knowledge, and received advanced training in all aspects of Islamic spirituality and gnosis. After visiting Baghdad, Makkah, Madinah, Aleppo, Mosul, parts of Central Asia and Turkey, he eventually settled in Damascus in 1223 with his small band of disciples. By then, he was considered to be a veritable master of traditional Islamic sciences including *tafsir*, *hadith*, *fiqh* and *ilm al-kalam* (speculative theology), in addition to being recognised as an authority on Sufism. Like many other Muslim scholars of the past, he acquired such a mastery of Islamic sciences that his close disciples considered him to be an exceptionally gifted exponent of Islamic principles and practices. However, what set Ibn al-Arabi apart from his peers were his inner qualities,

spiritual attainments and powerful imagination. In other words, his profound knowledge and understanding of Islamic mysticism, coupled with his unusual ability to communicate his spiritual teachings and insights to his disciples, both verbally and in writing, established his reputation as one of the Muslim world's most gifted metaphysicians and writers. Despite being a master of traditional Islamic sciences, he was keen to distinguish the 'outer' (*zahiri*) reality of Islamic rites and rituals, from the 'inner' (*batini*) dimension of Islamic principles and practices.

The 'men of reason', according to Ibn al-Arabi, focus all their attention on the 'form' of religious practices while the 'men of vision' seek to transcend the 'form' to reach the 'substance' of religious experience. Thus, the formal religious teachers (like the theologians and jurists) practice and adhere to the 'outer' dimension of religion, but the Sufis (or mystics) long for the 'unveiling' (*kashf*) of the Ultimate Reality before the eye of the heart in order to attain spiritual illumination. Ibn al-Arabi claimed to have attained spiritual 'unveiling' relatively easily. During one of his spiritual retreats, he claimed, he was blessed with a series of mystical inspirations and insights which he recorded in the form of books, manuscripts and letters. He and his disciples believed this to be an inner light (*nur*) bestowed on him by God; he also claimed to have been blessed with numerous supernatural experiences and visions (including encounters with the Prophet Muhammad, Jesus and some of his spiritual masters like Abul Abbas al-Uryabi). Although he was a strict adherent of Islam in its exoteric form, Ibn al-Arabi nevertheless felt it was necessary for him to plunge deep into the ocean of Islamic esotericism (*tasawwuf*) in order to explore its limits and possibilities, even if it meant incurring the wrath of the religious orthodoxy.

In addition to the Qur'an and *hadith*, he surveyed Platonic, Neoplatonic, Hermetic, Gnostic and Ismaili literature and oral traditions, and thereby assimilated their esoteric ideas and thoughts, before developing his own metaphysical theory. It is true that Ibn al-Arabi possessed a fertile and powerful mind which enabled him to draw information from many different – and often conflicting – sources, and in so doing he formulated a comprehensive and coherent metaphysical system which continues to exert a powerful influence on Islamic philosophical and mystical thinkers to this day. Unlike Abd al-Qadir al-Jilani, Jalal al-Din Rumi, Baha al-Din Naqshband, Mu'in al-Din Chishti or Najm al-Din al-Kubra, he did not initiate a Sufi *tariqah* (Order), nor did he establish a specific *madhhab* (school of thought); instead he devoted all his spare time and intellectual energy to formulating his mystical ideas and thoughts in the form of books and manuscripts for the benefit of posterity. Apart from a few close disciples whom he taught and initiated into his mystical ways, he was not in the habit of surrounding himself with a large band of followers, unlike the other great Sufi masters of the past. Indeed his main objective, it seems, was to formulate a comprehensive mystical philosophy so that the masses could draw on it as and when they needed, in order to quench their intellectual and spiritual needs.

To achieve this objective, he wrote and wrote at a phenomenal rate. As a mystical thinker and one of the Muslim world's most prolific writers, he – not unexpectedly – provided a supernatural explanation for his phenomenal literary output. According to Ibn al-Arabi, as soon as he engaged in spiritual retreat, mystical ideas and thoughts flooded into his mind like a torrent. Thus, writing was an effortless process for him. According to some of his biographers, he authored as many as eight hundred books and treatises on all aspects of Islamic mystical thought, but other scholars claim he wrote no more than a few hundred books. However, all his biographers agree that a large number of his works have remained in manuscript form, still waiting to be edited and published for the first time. Of his published works, the most famous are *Al-Futuhat al-Makkiyyah* (The Makkan Revelations), which as the title suggests was written during his stay in Makkah; the *Fusus al-Hikam* (The Bezels of Wisdom) was written in Damascus, while the

*Tarjuman al-Ashwaq* (The Interpreter of Desires) was also written in Makkah. Published in four bulky volumes, the *Futuhat* consists of more than five hundred chapters and is considered to be an encyclopaedia of religious and spiritual sciences. In this book, Ibn al-Arabi provided a comprehensive mystical interpretation of fundamental Islamic religious practices, including the five daily prayers (*salat*), fasting (*siyam*), pilgrimage (*hajj*) and poor due (*zakat*). He also explained the nature of the various mystical stages which the Sufis pass through during their spiritual enlightenment and, in the process, he developed a mystical interpretation of various Qur'anic verses and Prophetic traditions. Moreover, he explored the meaning of the ninety-nine Divine Names and Attributes (*al-asma wa'l sifat*) as mentioned in the Qur'an.

Ibn al-Arabi may have been a prolific writer, but he was far from being an organised and systematic thinker. The mystical ideas and thoughts he formulated in his *Futuhat* are not presented in a logical or coherent manner; rather he wrote as and when ideas appeared to him and did so without giving much thought to their context or format. However, the same cannot be said about his *Fusus al-Hikam*, which is probably his most popular book. In it he claimed to have presented a systematic interpretation of Islamic mystical philosophy as revealed to twenty-seven Prophets, beginning with Adam and concluding with Muhammad, the Seal of the Prophets (*khatm al-anbiya*). The popularity of this book is most evident from the fact that more than one hundred commentaries have been written on it. Ibn al-Arabi himself wrote a short treatise entitled *Naqsh al-Fusus* (The Imprint of the Bezels) in which he summarised the central message of the book. Also his close disciples, like Sadr al-Din Qunawi and Afif al-Din al-Tilimsani, wrote voluminous commentaries on this treatise. In these and numerous other books, Ibn al-Arabi formulated a mystical philosophy which not only proved to be influential, but also controversial. Indeed, his entire metaphysical theory revolved around the notion that, at a certain level, all Being is fundamentally

One (*wahdat al-wujud*), while, at another level, everything is only a manifestation of the Divine Substance. Although, metaphysically speaking, he made a fine distinction between God's *wujud* and that of His creatures (in the sense that God's *wujud* was a Necessity (*wajib*) and His creatures' was a contingent (*mumkin*)), his critics argued that his demarcation between the two was not sufficiently clear; thus they accused him of espousing pantheistic beliefs and ideas. However, according to Ibn al-Arabi's disciples, such misunderstandings arose because his critics took passages from his *Futuhat* out of context – and in so doing they failed to understand his metaphysical theory in its entirety.

In fact, Ibn al-Arabi's concept of Oneness of Being, or monism (*wahdat al-wujud*), coupled with his mystical interpretation of Divine Names and Attributes (*al-asma wa'l sifat*) along with his notion of Perfect Man (*al-insan al-kamil*), not to mention his claim to have been the Seal of Muhammadan Sanctity, proved hugely controversial. Thus some of his most vociferous critics (including prominent Islamic scholars like Ibn Taymiyyah, al-Taftazani, Ibn Umar al-Bika'i and Shaykh Ahmad Sirhindi) not only accused him of misinterpreting traditional Islamic sources, but also censured him for 'twisting' the meaning of Divine Oneness (*tawhid*) and for deifying the Prophet. They also accused him of making all religions equal, and of idolising women, among many other things. However, his views were robustly defended by other equally renowned Islamic scholars and thinkers like Abd al-Razzaq al-Kashani, al-Firuzabadi, al-Suyuti and Shah Waliullah. To be fair to Ibn al-Arabi, even his most fervent critics raised objections only against certain aspects of his thought: they did not consider his entire metaphysical theory to be heretical or reprehensible as such. Even Ibn Taymiyyah, who along with Shaykh Ahmad Sirhindi was one of Ibn al-Arabi's most fierce critics, accepted this fact (it is interesting to note that Ibn Taymiyyah himself was linked to the mystical tradition of Abd al-Qadir al-Jilani.). As for Shaykh Ahmad Sirhindi, he proposed *wahdat al-shuhud* (Oneness of Being in perception, or unity of witnesses) as a corrective to Ibn al-Arabi's *wahdat al-wujud* (Oneness of Being, or monism). Nevertheless, it would not be an exaggeration to say that Ibn al-Arabi's mystical philosophy has been hugely influential in the Muslim world.

This is most evident from the fact that leading Islamic scholars, reformers and mystics like Amir Abd al-Qadir, Abd al-Karim al-Jili, Abd al-Rahman Jami, Mahmud Shabistari, Abd al-Ghani al-Nabulusi, Abd al-Wahhab al-Sha'rani, Hamzah Fansuri, Mulla Sadra, Shah Waliullah, Shaykh Ahmad Sirhindi and even Sultan Muhammad (Fatih) II were influenced by Ibn al-Arabi's mystical philosophy and thought. Likewise, the religious ideas and thoughts of many modern Muslim scholars and mystics, such as Rene Guenon (Abd al-Wahid Yahya), Frithjof Schuon (Isa Nur al-Din Ahmad al-Shadhili al-Darqawi al-Alawi al-Maryami), Martin Lings (Abu Bakr Siraj al-Din), Seyyed Hossein Nasr and Charles (Hasan) Le Gai Eaton have been heavily influenced by Ibn al-Arabi's writings. Indeed, according to Miguel Asin Palacios, an eminent Spanish writer and expert on Ibn al-Arabi, famous Western thinkers like Dante Alighieri and Ramon Lull were also inspired by the *shaykh al-akbar*. Ibn al-Arabi died at the age of seventy-five and was buried in Damascus. Later, in the sixteenth century, a mausoleum was built there in his memory by the Ottoman Sultan Salim I and it stands to this day.

# 60

## Umar Khayyam
## (b.ca.1048 - d.ca.1129)

THE PERIOD FROM the eighth to the six-teenth century is generally considered to be the age of Islamic supremacy. During this period Muslims dominated a significant part of Asia, Africa and Europe. Under the patronage of prom-inent Muslim rulers and statesmen like Harun al-Rashid, Abdullah al-Ma'mun, Nizam al-Mulk, Sultan Mahmud of Ghazna, Akbar the Great and Sulaiman the Magnificent, the Muslim world led the rest of the world in educational, artistic and cultural pursuits. Not surprisingly, some of the greatest scientists, philosophers, writers and poets of the time were Muslims who, in turn, ushered in an era of intellectual creativity and socio-cultural progress across the Islamic world. Their contribution to the progress of human thought and culture later inspired the Europeans to throw off the yoke of feudalism and backward-ness which reigned supreme across Europe at the time, and emulate the greatness and splendour of Islamic civilisation at its height. The tenth and eleventh centuries were, arguably, the most intel-lectually and culturally progressive period in the annals of Islam, for it was during this period that some of the Muslim world's most influential sci-entists, philosophers, theologians and education-alists, like Ibn Sina, al-Biruni, Ibn al-Haytham,

al-Ghazali, Abul Majd Majdud Sana'i and Nizam al-Mulk, lived and flourished. Umar Khayyam, who was a renowned astronomer and mathema-tician and one of the most famous Muslim poets in the Western world, also lived during this unu-sually creative period in the intellectual history of Islam.

'Ghiyath al-Din' Abul Fath Umar ibn Ibrahim Khayyam, better known as Umar (or Omar) Khayyam, was born in the Persian provincial city of Nishapur. His forefathers belonged to an Arab tribe whose members apparently excelled in tent making. But, following the Muslim conquest of Persia, his family moved to Nishapur where they also became successful tent merchants; hence the surname *al-khayyam* (or 'the tent merchants or sellers'). Unfortunately historians like Ibn Khal-likan and Ibn Shakir do not say much about him in their works; thus very little is known about Umar Khayyam's childhood and early education. Al-Bayhaqi, on the other hand, knew him well and recorded some information about his life, work and activities. As one of the foremost centres of Islamic learning and commerce, Nishapur at-tracted some of the leading scholars and theolo-gians of the time (including *imam al-haramayn* Abul Ma'ali Abd al-Malik al-Juwayni) who lived and taught there. Students thus flocked there from across Khurasan and the neighbouring provinces to study under the guidance of these eminent scholars. Brought up in a lower-middle class family, Umar Khayyam received his early education in Arabic, Persian and Qur'anic sciences under the guidance of his local teachers, people such as Qadi Muhammad and Abul Hasan al-Anbari. As a gifted student, he excelled in his studies and his teachers encouraged him to enrol at the renowned Nishapur College, where he mastered Arabic and Persian before developing a keen interest in mathematics, astronomy and the other physical sciences of his day. Impressed by his son's intellectual abilities, his father encouraged him to pursue higher education in mathematics and science.

As a prominent educational institution, Nishapur College only attracted the brightest students. Thus, according to historians like al-Bayhaqi, some of Umar Khayyam's classmates at Nishapur College included Nizam al-Mulk, who later became a celebrated educationalist and statesman within the Seljuk administration, and Hasan-i-Sabbah, the future founder of the notorious neo-Ismaili Assassin sect. Although some historians have questioned the authenticity of this story, they do not dispute the fact that the three of them had studied together. In fact, at Nishapur College they became good friends and on one occasion reportedly promised to help each other should any one of them attain a position of prominence. Like his friends, Umar Khayyam was a bright student but, unlike them, he was reserved and studious, and remained preoccupied with his studies. By contrast, Nizam al-Mulk was a natural born politician who soon rose to prominence within the Seljuk administration and appointed his former classmate, Hasan-i-Sabbah, to a high-ranking Government post. But, being a crafty individual, he fell out with Nizam al-Mulk and moved out of Seljuk territories and established the Assassin sect. From his base in the fortress of Alamut (situated towards the northeast of Qazwin), he and his followers masterminded assassination attempts on their enemies. Nizam al-Mulk and his Seljuk benefactors were thus placed on the top of their target list. Unlike Nizam al-Mulk and Hasan-i-Sabbah, who were very ambitious individuals, Umar Khayyam deliberately remained detached from politics and public life. Instead, he travelled in pursuit of knowledge and visited some of the most prominent centres of learning in Samarqand, Bukhara, Isfahan and Balkh. In so doing, he completed his advanced training in philosophy and science under the guidance of some of the leading scholars of his time. He then returned to Nishapur, where he began to teach mathematics and the physical sciences at his old college. In addition to mastering mathematics and science, Umar Khayyam attained considerable proficiency in traditional Islamic sciences and was able to recite the Qur'an according to the seven traditional modes of recitation.

He may not have been a direct student of Ibn Sina, but Umar Khayyam was thoroughly familiar with the former's scientific and philosophical works; indeed, he was heavily influenced by Ibn Sina's philosophical thought. According to the historian al-Bayhaqi, Umar Khayyam was an Islamic philosopher in the tradition of Ibn Sina; he also found time to translate one of his works from Arabic to Persian. However, unlike Ibn Sina, Umar Khayyam did not write much although he was an able and skilful teacher who subsequently became very popular in and around Nishapur for his vast knowledge of science and philosophy. When his name and fame spread across Nishapur and Khurasan, Nizam al-Mulk, his old classmate at Nishapur College and now the Seljuk Prime Minister, invited him to Isfahan and offered him the influential post of chief scientific advisor to the Government. As an accomplished scientist who was renowned for his expertise in astronomy, he was promoted to one of the highest posts within the Seljuk civil service. He worked closely with Nizam al-Mulk and advised the incumbent Seljuk ruler, Malik Shah, on all the astronomical and scientific issues of the day. As wise rulers and renowned statesmen, both Malik Shah and Nizam al-Mulk were known for their love of learning and education. Thus it was that they founded an astronomical observatory in Nishapur to promote and facilitate advanced scientific training and research. Umar Khayyam was appointed director of this observatory, where all the leading Muslim scientists and mathematicians of the day, including Abd al-Rahman al-Hazini, pursued their scientific training and research under his supervision.

As a gifted scientist and mathematician, Umar Khayyam thrived under Seljuk patronage as did his many colleagues. One of the fruits of their research was the *jalali* calendar. Named after their Seljuk patron, Jalal al-Din Malik Shah, this calendar was more accurate than the Gregorian calendar produced in Rome in 1582 by Pope Gregory. Not surprisingly, this calendar has remained the official calendar of Iran to this day. His other important contributions were in the field of mathematics where he conducted extensive research in different branches of mathematics and became one of the most original writers on algebra since al-Khwarizmi, who is considered to be the pioneer of Arabic algebra. Although Umar Khayyam wrote around a dozen books and treatises on scientific, mathematical and philosophical topics, his most valuable work was *Risalat fi'l Barahin ala Masa'il al-Jabr wa'l Muqabalah* (Treatise on Establishing the Problems of Integration and Equation). As the title suggests, the subject of this book was similar to that of al-Khwarizmi's original work on algebra, though the scope of this book was far greater. Divided into ten different chapters, Umar Khayyam provided, in this book, a fresh and comprehensive exposition of algebra and related topics. And in so doing he demonstrated that there was an underlying metaphysical link between mathematics and geometry, as indicated by ancient Greek writers like Euclid. As a master of Euclidean geometry, he conducted a critical review of this branch of early mathematics and published his research findings in a separate treatise entitled *Risalat fi Sharh ma Ashkal min Musadarat Kitab Uqlidus* (Exposition of the Difficulties of Euclid's Elements). Nevertheless, it

is his *Risalat fi'l Barahin* which is today considered to be one of the most important mathematical treatises of the early medieval period. After completing this book, he presented a copy to Nizam al-Mulk, who publicly praised him for his efforts and encouraged him to produce more works like it. Copies of this and other important mathematical and philosophical books authored by Umar Khayyam have been preserved in manuscript form at libraries in London, Paris and Leiden.

Known in the East as a great astronomer and mathematician, Umar Khayyam became most famous in the West as a poet, however, thanks largely to his *Ruba'iyyat* (or collection of quatrains). First translated into English by the Victorian poet Edward Fitzgerald in 1859, the *Ruba'iyyat of Omar Khayyam* became an instant hit in the English-speaking world soon after its publication. In the words of Andrew Lang, who was a member of the 'Omar Khayyam Club of London' and a distinguished historian of English literature, 'The slim pamphlet of the "Rubaiyat" (1859) was a "drug in the market" till the set of Rossetti and Swinburne discovered it and talked about it. Then a wider circle of young University men made it an idol; to adore it was a sign of grace; and, in the long run, to admire Omar and the old French tale of "Aucassin et Nicolete" became a substitute for a liberal education. It was no longer necessary to have read anything else. It was Fitzgerald's fault that the saying of the Alexandrian Philistine in Theocritius, "Homer is enough for all," became "Omar is enough for all."

Born near Woodbridge, Suffolk in 1809, Edward Fitzgerald was a contemporary of Thackeray and Tennyson at Trinity College, Cambridge. In addition to being a voracious reader, he became a respected literary critic who produced translations from Aeschylus and Calderon, but it was his free rendition of Umar Khayyam's Persian quatrains which earned him widespread literary acclaim. In the process, Umar Khayyam also became the most popular and admired Muslim poet in the West. Admittedly, Fitzgerald's translation is very beautiful and eloquent, even though it is not free from error and discrepancy. Indeed, his portrayal of Umar Khayyam as a pleasure-seeking and hedonistic poet who preferred women and wine over all other things in life was nothing short of a grotesque misrepresentation of the man, who was not only a practising Muslim, but also a Sufi sympathiser. Having said that, although he had received training in traditional Islamic sciences, Umar Khayyam was not the average religious scholar in the sense that he sought to explore the meaning and purpose of Islamic rites and rituals in order to understand their 'inner' or 'spiritual' dimension. That is why, using colourful poetic language, he poked fun at people who wore the cloak of religiosity outwardly, but failed to live by the moral, ethical and spiritual demands of their faith. Umar Khayyam's social criticism, moral indignation and philosophical scepticism were therefore directed more towards the preachers – who preached but did not practice themselves – rather than towards the faith itself. Indeed, far from being a champion of rampant materialism, moral relativism and cultural hedonism, he

was steeped in Islamic morality and *tasawwuf* (or Islamic mysticism and spirituality).

By all accounts, Umar Khayyam was an outstanding mathematician, astronomer, philosopher and poet. Not surprisingly, his seminal contributions in these fields of endeavour have influenced generations of renowned Muslim, and non-Muslim, scholars, thinkers and poets including al-Ghazali, Nasir al-Din al-Tusi, Shams a-Din al-Samarqandi, al-Bayhaqi, Muhammad Baghdadi, Ulugh Beg, Girolamo Saccheri, Christoph Clavius, John Wallis, Percy Bysshe Shelley, Mark Twain, T.S. Eliot, Ezra Pound and Matthew Arnold among others. After the brutal murder of his friend and patron, Nizam al-Mulk, in 1092 by the followers of the Assassin sect, he went to Makkah to perform the sacred pilgrimage and on his return he served the new Sultan Sanjar for a period. He eventually resigned his job as a scientific advisor to the Seljuk ruler and took up his old teaching post at Nishapur College where he spent the rest of his life. Umar Khayyam died at the age of around seventy-seven and was buried in his native Nishapur.

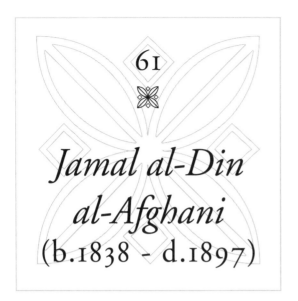

# 61

# Jamal al-Din al-Afghani
## (b.1838 - d.1897)

THE DECLINE AND disintegration of once-powerful Muslim dynasties like the Abbasids, Seljuks, Ghaznavids, Ottomans, Mughals and the Safavids paved the way for the Europeans to emerge onto the world stage after centuries of political decadence, economic depression and cultural backwardness, and flex their muscles. Led by the Portuguese, Dutch, French and the British, the leading European nations subsequently made their way into the heart of the Muslim world during the eighteenth and nineteenth centuries, and in so doing they colonised a large part of the Muslim world. The colonisation and dismemberment of the Muslim world at the hands of the European imperial powers not only represented a major blow to Islamic political unity and solidarity, but also inspired scores of influential Muslim scholars, thinkers and reformers to arise in order to reawaken the Muslim world from its slumber. Jamal al-Din al-Afghani was arguably the most charismatic and influential of them all.

Sayyid Muhammad ibn Safdar, better known as Jamal al-Din al-Afghani, was born into a noble Muslim family which traced its lineage all the way back to the Prophet of Islam, through his grandson Hussain. Despite being a high profile Muslim reformer, much of his early life is shrouded in mystery. He claimed to have been born in Asadabad in Kabul, but prominent historians like Albert Hourani have challenged this; they argue that he was born in Hamadan in Persia and was therefore of Iranian origin – even though he has become popularly known as 'al-Afghani'. Assuming that he was indeed born in Persia, his family must have migrated to Afghanistan soon after his birth, because he spent his early years in Afghanistan where his father became a respected *alim* (or Islamic scholar). Taught by his learned father, young al-Afghani studied Arabic, Persian and traditional Islamic sciences during his early years. As a precocious child who was blessed with a sharp intellect and powerful memory, it did not take him long to become thoroughly familiar with the Qu'ran, *hadith* (Prophetic traditions), *fiqh* (Islamic jurisprudence) especially *hanafi fiqh*, and other religious sciences. He was barely eighteen when he successfully completed advanced courses in Arabic, Persian, Islamic jurisprudence, and aspects of philosophy and history. Such was his eagerness to learn that he subsequently gained proficiency in aspects of medicine, mathematics, chemistry and other physical sciences.

After completing his formal education, al-Afghani bade farewell to his family and set out for

India, with a view to pursuing higher education and possibly also to go to Makkah to perform the sacred pilgrimage. On his arrival in India in 1856, he toured the country for a year and witnessed the first mutiny against British rule. This incident marked the beginning of the Indian liberation movement, and left a deep impression on young al-Afghani's mind. A year later, he left India for Makkah and successfully completed the sacred *hajj*. He then returned to Afghanistan to work in the administration of the Afghan ruler, Dost Muhammad Khan. Known for his erudition and electrifying oratory skills, he served Dost Muhammad Khan with loyalty and dedication, and even accompanied him during his military campaign to recover Herat from the Persians. Following Dost Muhammad Khan's sudden death in 1863, his son, Sher Ali Khan, succeeded him, but before he could consolidate his grip on power civil war broke out within the ruling family. During the ensuing conflict, al-Afghani fell out with some members of the royal family and he was forced to flee for his life.

Though he left Afghanistan with the intention of going to Makkah to perform another pilgrimage, he soon changed his plans and returned to India for a second time. Following the abortive mutiny of 1857, the British assumed full political and military control of India. Thus, on his arrival in India in 1869, the British initially allowed him to move around freely in the country. But, as the failed mutiny of 1857 was a disturbing and frightening experience for the British, they closely monitored the activities of everyone who was associated with the Indian liberation movement. As a loyal Muslim and a prominent scholar and political activist, the British authorities monitored al-Afghani's activities especially closely; it was not long before they came to view him as a potential troublemaker who, given the opportunity, could stir up political unrest and agitation against their rule in India. Keen to see the back of al-Afghani, the British authorities granted him a pass to board a British vessel bound for Egypt. On his arrival in Cairo, he went straight to al-Azhar University, the ancient seat of Islamic learning and scholarship, and within weeks of his arrival had gathered around him a sizeable following from the teachers and students of the university. Here he delivered regular lectures on all aspects of Islam, philosophy, history and politics. His erudition, versatility, charisma and electrifying oratory skills created a huge stir at al-Azhar, and during his short stay at Cairo, al-Afghani left a deep impression on all the scholars, teachers and students he met at al-Azhar.

From Cairo, he proceeded to Istanbul, the political capital of the Ottoman Empire, in 1870. As in Cairo, here in Istanbul, he rapidly became a popular figure, thanks to his vast erudition and regular lectures on aspects of Islam, politics and philosophy. After his name and fame spread across Istanbul, he was appointed a member of the Ottoman Educational Council. Invited to deliver regular lectures at the famous Aya Sofia (Hagia Sophia) and other mosques across Istanbul, al-Afghani's inspiring lectures moved his audiences wherever he went. Later, when he was invited to deliver a lecture at the Dar al-Funun in the presence of leading politicians, intellectuals and literary figures, Hasan Fahmi, the incumbent *shaykh al-islam* of the Ottoman State, raised objections against his rationalistic interpretation of the Islamic concept of Prophecy. In this lecture, al-Afghani argued that Prophecy was more than a spiritual gift. Prophecy had its social and political dimension too, argued al-Afghani, which if understood properly and translated into practice had the potential to transform stagnant and dormant Islamic societies into dynamic and vibrant societies. The *shaykh al-islam* not only became incensed by his socio-political interpretation of the Islamic concept of Prophecy, but also accused him of misinterpreting Islamic principles and practices in order to formulate a revolutionary brand of Islam. When Hasan Fahmi's diatribes against al-Afghani intensified, the latter was forced to leave Istanbul and return to Cairo, where he hoped to receive a more sympathetic hearing.

As expected, in Cairo he received a warm welcome from both the Egyptian authorities and intelligentsia alike. Offered a generous stipend by the Egyptian Government to teach at al-Azhar, he began to deliver regular lectures on Islamic theology, jurisprudence, philosophy and political science. His illuminating discourses on all aspects of Islam instantly won him much acclaim at the university. During this period he also gathered around him a small band of disciples, which included the influential Islamic thinker and reformer Muhammad Abduh. Moreover, having travelled extensively across the Muslim world, al-Afghani witnessed at first hand how the Muslim world had been subjugated by the foreign powers. To his dismay, he then noticed how the masses had been kept preoccupied with only 'spiritual' or 'other-worldly' activities by the traditional *ulama* (religious scholars) at the behest of the colonial powers. This prompted him to highlight and emphasise the importance of the political and social dimensions of Islam. He therefore urged the Egyptian Muslim intelligentsia to engage in political and social activism in order to liberate their land from British hegemony. His powerful and daring call for Islamic unity in the face of European colonisation and subjugation of the Muslim world not only struck a chord with his students and disciples at al-Azhar, but also inspired and galvanised the masses on the streets of Cairo.

As expected, his message of Islamic unity and solidarity soon began to ring alarm bells within the highest echelons of the Egyptian Government, wherein the British elites exercised considerable political and economic power. Accused of spreading anti-British propaganda the Egyptian ruler, Tewfiq Pasha, demanded that al-Afghani leave the country forthwith. In 1879, at the age of forty-one, he was forced to leave Egypt for India. But his eight-year stay in Egypt was an important period of his life, because during his time there he managed to successfully disseminate his progressive and revolutionary ideas across that country. After his departure, his disciples took up the cause of Islamic unity and solidarity and called on the Arabs in general, and the Egyptians in particular, to respond to the clarion call of pan-Islamism.

In India, al-Afghani settled in Hyderabad where, along with Rafat Yar Jung, he became the co-founder of the Osmania University, which became one of the first institutions of higher education in the country. During this period he also authored a treatise under the title of *Al-Radd ala al-Dahriyin* (Refutation of the Materialists). Originally written in Persian and later translated into Arabic by his disciple Muhammad Abduh, this book launched a vicious intellectual assault on the materialistic philosophy of the time (and severely criticised eminent Muslims like Sir Sayyid Ahmad Khan for seeking to strip Islam of its metaphysical dimension in order to make it compatible with Western secular and materialistic philosophies). According to W. S. Blunt, from India he went to America and stayed there for a few months before proceeding to London, where he became a good friend of Lord Salisbury. From London he moved to Paris, in 1883, and there he and Muhammad Abduh jointly published the famous journal *al-urwa al-wuthqa* (The Unbreakable Bond). Through this journal, they sought to awaken the Muslim world from its deep sleep. Both the master and disciple wrote inspiring articles to remind Muslims of their duties to God and to their fellow brethren. They urged their Muslim readers to unite under the banner of Islam and liberate the Muslim world from foreign political and military occupation. Considered to be highly inflammatory, this journal was banned by the British authorities in Egypt and India. Although the journal soon foundered, it nevertheless exerted considerable influence in many Muslim countries, especially in the Arab world.

From Paris, al-Afghani moved to Russia where he lived for four years and helped the Russian Muslims to publish the Qur'an there for the first time. He was now considered to be one of the Muslim world's most influential advocates of Islamic unity and solidarity. Later, in 1889, he met Nasir al-Din Qajar, the then Shah of Iran, in Munich and the latter persuaded al-Afghani to accompany him to Persia, where al-Afghani enjoyed the patronage of the Shah until political intrigues forced him to leave. At the invitation of the Ottoman Sultan Abd al-Hamid II, he then moved to Istanbul in 1892 where the Sultan offered him a generous monthly stipend and a furnished cottage. He spent the last five years of his life in Istanbul, although the Sultan's jealous courtiers repeatedly tried to implicate him in political intrigues. As an intellectual and a reformer, al-Afghani travelled from one end of the Muslim world to the other in order to raise the Muslims' awareness of their faith and culture, and to champion the cause of Islamic unity and solidarity. He not only had a lofty vision for the Muslim world, he also worked tirelessly to translate his vision into reality, thereby seeking to revive the *ummah* (global Islamic community) from both political and intellectual stagnation.

Indeed, as the 'father of modern pan-Islamism', al-Afghani was responsible for initiating one of the most powerful political movements of modern times. Though it is true that he did not achieve his political objectives during his lifetime, the sparks he lit later spread across the Muslim world like a raging flame, as the European colonial powers were, one by one, driven out from the Muslim world. Al-Afghani was not only a political revolutionary, he was also an outstanding intellectual and a linguist who knew more than seven languages (including Arabic, Persian, French, English and Russian). As a voracious reader of Arabic and Persian literature, he was intimately acquainted with both traditional and modern Islamic thought and scholarship. Being too occupied with political and social activism, he had no time to marry and therefore remained a confirmed bachelor all his life. Needless to say, his political and religious thoughts profoundly influenced some of the Muslim world's foremost scholars, thinkers and reformers, including Muhammad Abduh, Muhammad Rashid Rida, Sir Muhammad Iqbal, Abd al-Hamid ibn Badis and Muhammad al-Tahir ibn al-Ashur among others. The indomitable al-Afghani died at the age of fifty-nine and was laid to rest in Istanbul, Turkey. Then, on 2nd January 1945, his remains were transferred to Afghanistan and reburied at Aliabad, located on the outskirts of Kabul.

# 62

## Ibn Abd al-Wahhab
### (b.1703 - d.1792)

THE FIRST HALF of the ninth century was a defining period in Islamic intellectual history, for it was during this time that Mu'tazilism (or philosophical rationalism) gained ascendancy in the Muslim world under the patronage of Caliph Harun al-Rashid, his son al-Ma'mun and his successors Mu'tasim Billah and Wathiq. These Abbasid rulers not only became indefatigable champions of Mu'tazilism, they also enforced this creed as if it was an article of faith. But the traditionalists, led by the influential Ahmad ibn Hanbal, vehemently opposed this rationalistic creed because they considered it to be both unorthodox and heretical. That is why they not only opposed and refuted the Mu'tazilite creed, but also delineated the fundamental Islamic principles and practices in the light of the Qur'an and the Prophetic norms (*sunnah*). For more than half a century, the battle between the rationalists and traditionalists raged in and around Baghdad until Caliph Mutawakkil ala Allah ascended the Abbasid throne in 847 and restored the religious orthodoxy. Thereafter, the traditionalist approach to Islam –as espoused by Ahmad ibn Hanbal – became a symbol of Islamic orthodoxy in many parts of the Muslim world. Inspired by the ideas and thoughts of Ahmad ibn Hanbal, five centu-

ries later Ibn Taymiyyah advocated the superiority of Islamic traditionalism over all other religious methodologies, including the philosophical and mystical approaches to Islam. It was Ahmad ibn Hanbal and Ibn Taymiyyah's religious ideas and thoughts which exerted a considerable influence on Muhammad ibn Abd al-Wahhab, one of the most influential Islamic scholars and reformers of modern times.

Muhammad ibn Abd al-Wahhab was born into the tribe of Banu Sinan in the district of al-Uyayna (in the Central Arabian region of Najd). His father, Abd al-Wahhab, was a noted Islamic scholar and *qadi* (judge) who specialised in *hanbali* jurisprudence. As the son of a prominent local religious figure, young Ibn Abd al-Wahhab developed an instant affinity with the Prophetic norms and practices to which his family members were strict adherents. Educated at home by his learned father, he committed the entire Qur'an to memory when he was about ten and then pursued studies in *hadith* (Prophetic traditions) and *hanbali fiqh* (jurisprudence). Thereafter, he travelled extensively in pursuit of higher education, visiting some of the leading centres of Islamic learning and scholarship, including Makkah and Madinah. During this period he pursued advanced courses in theology, Prophetic traditions and jurisprudence under the tutelage of prominent scholars like Abdullah ibn Saif, Sulaiman al-Kurdi and Muhammad Hayat al-Sindi. As a distinguished scholar of *hanbali* jurisprudence, Abdullah ibn Saif lived in Makkah at the time and introduced Ibn Abd al-Wahhab to the religious ideas and thoughts of Ibn Taymiyyah and his disciples Ibn Qayyim al-Jawziyyah and Ibn Kathir. By contrast, both Sulaiman and al-Sindi lived in Madinah where they taught Prophetic traditions. Of Indian origin, the latter was attached to an organisation which advocated the need for reviving the Prophetic *sunnah* throughout Madinah.

From Madinah, Ibn Abd al-Wahhab moved to Basrah, where he lived for about four years, before settling in Baghdad. Here he married a relatively wealthy lady, but following her sudden death he then travelled to Kurdistan. According to some historians, he then visited parts of Persia, Syria and Egypt, while others say records taken during the time do not mention his journeys to these distant lands. In either case, Ibn Abd al-Wahhab was a precocious student who excelled in his studies. Known for his remarkable affinity to, and admiration for, the pure unadulterated principles and practices of Islam (based on a literalist interpretation of the Qur'an and the Prophetic *sunnah*), he never hid his displeasure of those who perverted the fundamental Islamic principles and practices. Thus, during his stay in Basrah, he vehemently opposed the popular culture, customs and practices of the locals. Indeed, the Shi'a population of Basrah came under attack from him because, in his opinion, the Shi'a beliefs and practices had no basis in traditional Islamic scriptural sources, namely the Qur'an and the authentic Prophetic *sunnah*. As the majority of Basrah's population was Shi'a, his criticisms sparked off a heated and controversial debate in the city. After conducting an extensive study of the Qur'an and the vast corpus of Prophetic traditions during his travels in Makkah, Madinah, parts of eastern Arabia and Basrah, he came to the conclusion that fundamental

Islamic principles and practices were becoming increasingly compromised by people's excessive reliance on mysticism, local traditions, customs and folklore. As he travelled across Arabia and the neighbouring lands, he observed, to his utter dismay, how the majority of Muslims had succumbed to the lures of *shirk* (associationism) and polytheism in their daily lives. This retrogressive move (away from authentic Islam) both shocked and alarmed the young scholar from Najd, who now decided to devote all his time and energy to the revival of authentic Islamic principles and practices as exemplified by the Prophet, his companions (*sahabah*) and their successors (*tabiun*).

After his return to Najd in around 1735, Ibn Abd al-Wahhab lived in Huraymila with his extended family. Here, too, he witnessed the same laxity in the observance of Islam as he had witnessed in eastern Arabia and Basrah during his travels there. This only confirmed his suspicion that the dilution of original, pristine Islamic principles and practices was as widespread a phenomenon as he had thought. After the death of his father in 1740, he left Huraymila and returned to his native al-Uyayna. Here he also found the locals following popular customs and practices at the expense of authentic Islamic teachings. In other words, the situation in Arabia was much worse than he had anticipated. According to the noted British Arabist Harry St. John Philby, at the time much of Arabia was under the influence of 'superstitious belief in the efficacy of charms, offerings and sacrifices, and in the powers of trees, rocks, and certain tombs to effect or hasten the gratification of normal human desires'. This, no doubt, propelled Ibn Abd al-Wahhab to launch his religious mission to arrest the degeneration of Islam and revive the authentic Islamic teachings as preserved in the Qur'an and Prophetic *sunnah*. He was thirty-seven when he formally launched his campaign to eradicate all un-Islamic beliefs, customs and practices from Arabia, the birthplace of the Prophet, and restore the pure and pristine message of Islam.

However, as soon as he began to criticise and reproach the people of Uyayna for their undue affection for mysticism, adoration of saints and the custom of visiting graves and tombs, the locals instantly turned against him. But, supported by the ruler of Uyayna, he continued to preach the message of *tawhid* (Oneness of Divinity) in the face of stiff opposition from the populace. When the opposition against him began to gather force, he had no choice but to leave town and move to al-Dar'iyah (a town situated on the outskirts of Riyadh). Muhammad ibn Saud, the ruler of the region, vowed to help and support Ibn Abd al-Wahhab in his efforts to eradicate all forms of superstitious and polytheistic practices (like saint worship and the veneration of holy men and religious shrines) from Arabian society. In so doing he hoped to rejuvenate the authentic Prophetic norms and practices which, he felt, had been corrupted due to the people's lack of Islamic knowledge, and laxity in the observance of Islam. Like Ibn Taymiyyah and Ibn Qayyim al-Jawziyyah before him, he argued that *ilm al-tawhid* (or knowledge and proper understanding of the Islamic concept of Divinity) was crucial to being a faithful Muslim, and any form of compromise or concession on this fundamental issue was tantamount to heresy. According to Ibn Abd al-Wahhab, all forms of worship, adoration and veneration must be directed to God, the One and Only, Who alone deserves to be worshipped, praised and glorified.

Like Ahmad ibn Hanbal, Ibn Taymiyyah and Ibn Qayyim al-Jawziyyah, he rejected philosophical and mystical interpretations of the Qur'an and the Prophetic teachings. Indeed, he went out of his way to develop a rigid and literalist understanding of the Qur'an and Prophetic *sunnah*. Since a literal interpretation and understanding of the Islamic concept of *tawhid* was central to his worldview and religious mission, Ibn Abd al-Wahhab devoted an entire book to the exposition of this fundamental Islamic belief. Divided into more than sixty short sections, in his *Kitab al-Tawhid* (The Book of Monotheism) he provided a comprehensive explanation of the Islamic concept of Divine Unity, based on his literalist reading of the Qur'an and authentic Prophetic

traditions. Convinced that Muslims had both compromised and deviated from pristine Islam, he urged the masses to abandon all unworthy beliefs and practices, and instead concentrate on the Qur'an and authentic *sunnah* – like the *salaf al-salih* (the pious predecessors). In addition to his *Kitab al-Tawhid*, Ibn Abd al-Wahhab authored a number of other books and treatises including *Al-Usul al-Thalatha wa Adillatuha* (The Three Principles and their Evidence) and *Khutba al-Shaykh* (Exhortations of the Shaykh), which is a collection of religious sermons. In these and other similar works, he interpreted *tawhid* in its pure and unadulterated form, and believed his understanding of this fundamental Islamic concept provided a sound basis for a modern Islamic State and society.

With this in mind, in 1744, he and Muhammad ibn Saud formed a politico-religious alliance in order to establish an Islamic State in Arabia. He actively supported Muhammad ibn Saud in his attempts to unify Arabia under his political leadership, while the latter gave him full freedom to disseminate his religious ideas and thoughts across the country. The alliance between Ibn Abd al-Wahhab and Ibn Saud provided the basis on which the Kingdom of Saudi Arabia was to be founded by Abd al-Aziz ibn Saud during the early part of the twentieth century. Thus the al-Saud – al-Shaykh pact not only played a pivotal role in the formation of Saudi Arabia as a politico-religious entity, but also defined how Islam (as a religion and way of life) was to be interpreted and practiced in that country. Indeed, with Ibn Saud's full support and backing, Ibn Abd al-Wahhab formulated a literalist interpretation of Islamic theology and jurisprudence and, being a clever political operator, he used the State apparatus to implement his interpretation of Islam across all sections of Arabian society. As a result, he became an immensely powerful religious figure in that country. As a firm believer in the Islamic concept of Divine Unity, he felt the social, political and economic spheres of human endeavour, too, must operate within the overarching principles of *tawhid* and, as such, he went out of his way to integrate the socio-political realms of the State with his *tawhid*-centred worldview. Thus the worship of saints, Sufis and veneration of tombs was not only outlawed, but the failure to conduct the social, political, legal and economic spheres of human endeavour in accordance with the Divine law (*shari'ah*) was also considered by Ibn Abd al-Wahhab to be a form of *shirk* (violation of *tawhid*). This, therefore, provided him and his followers with the religious justification for their politico-religious alliance with Muhammad ibn Saud.

However, in the realm of *fiqh*, he was against the imitation (*taqlid*) of medieval jurists (*fuqaha*) like Abu Hanifah, Malik ibn Anas, al-Shafi'i, Ahmad ibn Hanbal and others. Indeed, he considered mass and uncritical imitation of medieval jurists to be a form of blameworthy and detestable religious innovation (*bida*). Instead, he advocated the use of *ijtihad* (or independent juristic reasoning based on the Qur'an and authentic Prophetic traditions) in order to address the pressing issues of his time. As a powerful and charismatic religious reformer – and a close friend and ally of Muhammad ibn Saud and his successors – he was able to disseminate his

religious ideas and thought, throughout Arabia during his own lifetime. Even after the death of Muhammad ibn Saud in 1765, he remained a close ally of the House of Saud. This enabled him to further strengthen and consolidate his alliance with Ibn Saud's descendants; an alliance which continues to define Saudi politics and approach to Islam to this day. Over time, the Islamic revivalist movement initiated by Ibn Abd al-Wahhab became so powerful that some of the Muslim world's most prominent scholars, thinkers and reformers, like Muhammad Rashid Rida, Sayyid Ahmad Barelvi, Haji Shari'atullah of Bengal, Shah Ismail Shahid, Sir Muhammad Iqbal, Hasan al-Banna and Abul A'la Mawdudi were, one way or another, influenced by its message. Another reason why Ibn Abd al-Wahhab has been rated so highly in this book is because his teachings have profoundly influenced Islamic reform movements across the world, thanks largely to Saudi Arabia's generous funding of mosques, Islamic schools and free distribution of Islamic literature across the globe. Ibn Abd al-Wahhab died at the ripe old age of eighty-nine and was laid to rest in an unmarked grave according to his instructions.

# 63

## Rabi'a al-Adawiyyah
## (b.ca.717 - d.801)

ALTHOUGH ISLAMIC HISTORY is replete with heroic deeds performed by Muslim women, unfortunately the majority of Islamic historians have failed to acknowledge their contribution to the development of Islamic thought, culture and civilisation. Far from being on the margins of society, during the early days of Islam, Muslim women played an important role within the Muslim community founded by the Prophet in Madinah. Indeed, the first person to embrace Islam was Khadijah, the wife of the Prophet, and she stood by him steadfastly during a very difficult and challenging period in Islamic history. As an intelligent and fabulously wealthy lady, she placed all her wealth and properties at the disposal of the Prophet in order to strengthen and consolidate Islam within Makkan society. Her devotion and dedication to, and sacrifices made for, Islam were second to none. Following in Khadijah's footsteps, other distinguished women like Fatimah bint Muhammad, Umm Atiyya, Asma bint Abu Bakr, Umm Ammara, Asma bint Yazid, Hafsah bint Umar and Aishah bint Abu Bakr became important figures in the early Muslim community. They excelled in many different spheres of human endeavour; some performed heroic deeds on the battlefield; others became masters of Islamic thought and scholarship, while yet others played an active part in the socio-political affairs of the early Muslim community. The examples set by these prominent women later inspired other Muslim women to contribute and achieve as much as they did. One such remarkable woman was Rabi'a al-Adawiyyah, who is today considered to be one of the most famous and influential female spiritual figures of Islam, along with Khadijah, Aishah and Fatimah.

Rabi'a al-Adawiyyah, also known as Rabi'a al-Basri, was born in the Iraqi city of Basrah. Though very little is known about her early life, according to her biographers Farid al-Din Attar and Ibn Khallikan, she was born into a poor family belonging to the al-Atik tribe of the Qais ibn Adi clan of Basrah. This explains why the words 'al-Adawiyyah' or 'al-Qaisiyyah' are often attached to her name. Rabi'a's parents died while she was still a child. To make matters worse, famine then struck Basrah and this forced her to endure considerable personal hardship and suffering. Although it is not clear whether she had any brothers or sisters, some scholars, like Annemarie Schimmel, have argued that the name Rabi'a (fourth) suggests she may have been the fourth child of her parents. However, this view is only speculation as there is no historical evidence to prove it. But in his famous *Tadhkirah al-Awliya* (Memoirs of the Saints), Farid al-Din Attar, the celebrated biographer and poet, stated that during the famine young Rabi'a – having been displaced from her family – fell into the hands of an unscrupulous trader who sold her into slavery for six dirhams. The man who purchased her not only treated her badly, but also forced her to work round the clock without any respite. In desperation, she tried to escape from her bondage, but her attempts proved unsuccessful. Eventually, she accepted her condition and became a devout Muslim. She worked as a slave labourer during the daytime and stayed awake at night to perform supererogatory (*nafl*) prayers. The more Rabi'a prayed, the more devout she became until she began to fast during the day and spend the whole night in prayers. Her devotion and dedication to God reached such intensity that once, when her master woke up in the middle of the night, he found her in prostration, saying: 'O my Lord, You know that the desire of my heart is to obey You, and that the light of my eye is in the service of Your court. If the matter rested with me, I should not cease for one hour from Your service, but You have made me subject to a creature.' Moved by her unflinching faith and piety, her master freed her the very next morning. She then went into the desert, where she stayed with the bedouins for a period. Eventually she returned to Basrah and lived in a tiny apartment, and devoted the rest of her life to prayers, fasting and other devotional activities.

Given that Rabia's early life and her religious teachings and practices became entangled with miraculous tales and supernatural stories, even a discerning scholar and poet like Farid al-Din Attar could not help but incorporate some of them in his works. Indeed, in his *Tadhkirah al-Awliya*, he related that during her stay in the desert Rabi'a, having decided to perform the sacred *hajj* (pilgrimage), set out for Makkah. But after travelling some distance, her donkey which was carrying all her luggage, suddenly dropped dead. At this, her fellow pilgrims offered to carry her load, but

she declined, saying she only accepted God's help. When the other travellers continued their journey to Makkah, leaving her behind, she fell to the ground and cried, 'O my God, do kings deal thus with a woman, a stranger and weak? You are calling me to Your own house (the *Kabah*), but in the midst of the way You have suffered mine ass to die and You have left me alone in the desert.' As soon as she finished her supplication, the ass apparently jumped up, alive once more, and Rabi'a was able to continue her journey to Makkah. According to Attar, on another occasion, when she was travelling to Makkah for pilgrimage, halfway through her journey she apparently saw the Kabah coming towards her, whereupon she remarked, "It is the Lord of the house whom I need, what have I to do with the house? I need to meet with Him Who said, 'Whoso approaches Me by a span's length I will approach him by the length of a cubit.' The Kabah which I see has no power over me; what joy does the beauty of the Kabah bring to me?"

Farid al-Din Attar and her other biographers have ascribed these and many other miraculous and supernatural stories to her. But, frankly, these tales are no more than myth and legend; thus they have no historical value or literary veracity. Indeed, the absence of first-hand information about her life and religious teachings led to the proliferation of such mythical tales and stories. Suffice it to say that Rabi'a became fascinated by Islam from very early on in life and thereafter regularly engaged in meditation and other devotional activities. As a result, she gained profound insights into Islamic teachings and spirituality, but she always kept her feet firmly on the ground and never claimed to be special. As one of Islam's earliest mystics, she renounced all worldly comforts in favour of asceticism (*zuhd*). She also made a conscious decision not to marry and remained a confirmed spinster all her life. When Abd al-Wahid ibn Zaid, who was an eminent Islamic scholar, practising Sufi and a self-confessed ascetic of Basrah, sent her a marriage proposal, she rebuked him saying, 'O sensual one, seek another sensual like yourself.

Have you seen any sign of desire in me?' Then she recited the following couplet, 'The ways are various, the Way to the Truth is one; those who travel on the Way of Truth must keep themselves apart.' It was not long before Rabi'a's piety and asceticism won her much acclaim in and around Basrah; this also prompted many influential men like Muhammad ibn Sulaiman al-Hashimi, the ruler of Basrah, to send marriage proposals to her. Al-Hashimi even offered her a handsome dowry of a hundred thousand dinars and a generous monthly stipend of ten thousand dinars, but she shunned him saying, 'It does not please me that you should be my slave and that all you possess should be mine or that you should distract me from God for a single moment.'

According to her biographers, Farid al-Din Attar and Abd al-Rauf al-Munawi, even Hasan al-Basri, the famous Muslim theologian and mystic of Basrah, proposed to Rabi'a, but she turned him down as well saying, 'Renunciation of this world means peace, while desire for it brings sorrow. Curb your desires and control yourself and do not let others control you, but let them share your inheritance and the anxiety of the age. As for yourself, give your mind to the day of death; but as for me, God can give me all you offer and even double it. It does not please me to be distracted from Him for a single moment. So farewell.' However, all reports connecting Hasan al-Basri to Rabi'a have been dismissed by the historians as being unreliable, if not fabricated, because she was barely ten when Hasan al-Basri died in 728 at the ripe old age of eighty-six; as such, he could not have proposed to her. Nonetheless, it is true that Rabi'a led a scrupulously clean and pious lifestyle, sanctified by extreme poverty, self-denial and a refusal to marry or experience worldly pleasures and comforts in any form. Her sole objective in life was to transcend from the temporal to the highest spiritual plane through single-minded devotion and dedication to God. And in so doing she became immersed in the ocean of Divine love and gnosis. This, according to Rabi'a, was more satisfying and enduring than the transient joys and comforts of this world.

Unlike Hasan al-Basri's religious ideas and thoughts, which were invariably influenced by notions of hell-fire and eternal damnation, Rabi'a's mystical philosophy so much revolved around the concept of 'pure Divine love' that she never failed to emphasise the significance of loving God only for His sake. In her opinion, to obey God out of fear of Divine retribution – or to serve and worship Him in order to receive a handsome reward – was tantamount to selfishness. Rather, she advocated that one should love God only for His sake, without any fear of His punishment or hope of reward. This, according to Rabi'a, was 'pure Divine love' which she eloquently expressed in some of her most famous prayers. For instance, she used to say, 'O God, if I worship You for fear of Hell, burn me in Hell, and if I worship You in hope of Paradise, exclude me from Paradise. But if I worship You for Your Own sake, grudge me not Your everlasting Beauty.' On another occasion, she prayed, 'I love You with two loves – a selfish love and a Love that You are worthy of. As for the selfish love, it is that I think of You, to the exclusion of everything else. And as for the Love that You are worthy of, ah! That I no longer see any creature, but I see only You! There is no praise for me in either of these loves, but the praise in both is for You.'

Despite being illiterate, Rabi'a was a very beautiful and eloquent Arabic speaker. She used to express her feelings for God in the form of poetry and prayers – and did so in a very passionate and powerful way. When her contemporaries told her that her notion of 'pure Divine love' was very novel, she recited the following Qur'anic verses to them, 'He loves them and they love Him' (5: 59). And, 'O you, soul at peace, return to your Lord well pleased (with yourself) and well pleasing (unto Him)!' (89: 27-28) Her profound knowledge and understanding of the Qur'an and Prophetic wisdom, coupled with her illuminating exposition of Islamic values and spirituality, turned her into a powerful symbol of Islamic purity and virtue, even during her own lifetime. Indeed, when her devotional and ascetic practices became too excessive, her close friends and disciples (like Sufyan al-Thawri, Rabah al-Qais, Shaqiq al-Balkhi and Malik ibn Dinar) urged her to rest, but she responded by saying, 'I should be ashamed to ask for this world's goods from Him to Whom it belongs, and how should I seek them from those to whom it does not belong?' She also added, 'Will God forget the poor because of their poverty or remember the rich because of their riches? Since He knows my state, what have I to remind Him of? What He wills, we should also will.' Rabia's notion of 'pure Divine love', to the exclusion of all others, later became known as 'Rabia's *sidq*' (or absolute sincerity and total reliance upon God). This also became the central pillar of her religious thought and mystical philosophy which influenced and inspired generations of Sufis.

Thanks to Rabi'a's love for, and single-minded devotion to, God and Hasan al-Basri's eloquent exposition of traditional Islamic values and practices, the tide of materialism and hedonism which threatened to overwhelm the Muslim world at the time was successfully turned back; they also played a pivotal role in reviving and popularising Islamic spirituality in the form of Sufism (or Islamic mysticism). Thereafter, Sufism became a powerful spiritual methodology for those who wished to devote their entire lives to Islamic devotional practices. Inspired by both Rabi'a and Hasan al-Basri, the message of Sufism attracted hundreds and thousands of followers from across the Muslim world, many of whom, in turn, became great symbols of Islamic piety and rectitude. By virtue of her profound knowledge and understanding of Islam, Rabi'a became a major source of inspiration for Muslims during her own lifetime and even more so after her death. Living as we do at a time when anger, hatred and hostility have become so prevalent, her message of love, mercy and compassion could not be more pertinent today. Happily, many books and treatises have been written on the life and thought of this remarkable Muslim woman by some of the Muslim world's leading scholars and writers, including Farid al-Din Attar, Abd al-Rahman Jami, Ibn Khallikan and Abd al-Rahman ibn Ali ibn al-Jawzi, so there is no shortage of works on her life and thought. Likewise, in the West the prominent British poet Richard Monckton Milnes became one of the first to publish a small collection of poems under the title of *The Sayings of Rabi'a* during the nineteenth century. Thereafter, Margaret Smith's seminal biography entitled *Rabi'a, the Mystic and her Fellow Saints in Islam* was published in 1922. This book is a detailed and illuminating study of her life, thoughts and achievements. Rabi'a, the great mystical thinker and Sufi saint of Islam, died around the age of eighty-four and was buried in her native Basrah.

# 64

# Abd al-Malik ibn Marwan (b.646 - d.705)

AFTER MUAWIYAH'S DEATH in 680, his son, Yazid, ascended the Umayyad throne, but he failed to live up to his father's expectations. As a feeble and inexperienced ruler, he tried to restore peace and order across the Islamic dominion by force; however his heavy-handed tactics backfired in a spectacular fashion after the grisly murder of Hussain at the plain of Karbala. After three years of political chaos and mismanagement, Yazid was succeeded by his twenty-one year old son, Muawiyah ibn Yazid, who, unlike his father, was a sickly but peace-loving young man who abdicated within months of his accession. This led to more political chaos and uncertainty, as there was no obvious candidate to succeed him. After much political infighting and wrangling, the veteran politician Marwan ibn Hakam, who served as governor of Madinah for a long period, was sworn in as the fourth Caliph of the Umayyad dynasty. He became Caliph at a time when the political situation in the Muslim world was deteriorating rapidly, as various rival claimants to the Caliphate emerged to challenge his political authority. Thus Abdullah ibn Zubair, the son of the renowned Zubair ibn Awwam, assumed control of the entire Hijaz, while Mu'sab ibn Zubair, proclaimed himself the administrator of Iraq on behalf of his brother. By contrast, Marwan ibn Hakam, the newly appointed Umayyad Caliph, found himself in charge of only southern Syria. As an experienced politician, he understood the gravity of the situation and acted swiftly to unify the whole of Syria under his leadership. He then proceeded to Egypt and brought this important country under Umayyad control. Death intervened before he could reassert Umayyad power and authority across the rest of the Muslim world. However, he was succeeded in 685 by his son, Abd al-Malik, who went onto become one of the Umayyad dynasty's most successful rulers, along with Muawiyah ibn Abi Sufyan.

Abd al-Malik ibn Marwan ibn Hakam was born in Madinah during the early years of Caliph Uthman's reign. His father, Marwan ibn Hakam, was an influential member of the Umayyah clan. Since he was closer to Caliph Uthman by blood than Muawiyah, the Caliph appointed him his personal secretary. When Caliph Uthman was brutally murdered by a group of insurgents in 656, Abd al-Malik was still in his early teens. After completing his early education in Qur'anic sciences, Arabic literature and poetry under the watchful gaze of his learned father, he received training in political and civil administration.

When his father was appointed governor of Madinah by Muawiyah, young Abd al-Malik served as his deputy. Known for his personal piety and uprightness during his early years, he became a dedicated student of the Qur'an and *hadith* literature, but when the supporters of Abdullah ibn Zubair drove out the Umayyads from Makkah and Madinah, Abd al-Malik, who was in his mid-thirties at the time, moved with his entire family to Syria where he became his father's chief political adviser after the latter's ascension to the Umayyad throne in 684. A year later, he succeeded his father as the Umayyad Caliph in 685; he was in his early forties at the time.

Like his father, Abd al-Malik faced formidable challenges soon after becoming Caliph. Although Syria and Egypt were firmly under Umayyad control, political infighting and tribal rivalry between the Kalbi and Qaysi factions presented a major obstacle to socio-political unity and solidarity in Syria. Despite suffering defeat at the hands of the Kalbis, the Qaysi people regrouped under the leadership of Zu'far ibn al-Harith in a region not far from the Euphrates. To make matters worse, in the Hijaz the formidable Abdullah ibn Zubair had won the support of the locals, while his brother Mus'ab was busy lobbying the people of Iraq in order to win them over to their side. At the same time, Mukhtar ibn Abu Ubaid was actively looking around for a suitable candidate to challenge the Umayyads in Kufah. To add insult to injury, the Byzantines then threatened to invade the Umayyad territories at the same time. In short, Abd al-Malik could not have ascended the Umayyad throne at a more dangerous and challenging time. But, undeterred by these political challenges, he decided to confront all his opponents and reassert his political authority across the Muslim world. After signing a peace treaty with the Byzantines and agreeing to pay them an annual tribute, he reorganised and expanded his armed forces in order to crush all political and military opposition against his rule in the Hijaz, Iraq and the neighbouring territories. Under the leadership of the notorious Ubaidullah ibn Ziyad, he sent

an expeditionary force to Iraq to subdue his opponents and restore peace and security in that country. In response, Mukhtar, his rival, sent a powerful force under the command of Ibrahim ibn Malik al-Ashtar to face the Caliph's army. In the ensuing battle, Ubaidullah was killed and his army crushed by the rebels. His failure to reassert his authority in Iraq prompted Abd al-Malik to change his political and military strategy, and he decided to consolidate his position in Syria and Egypt, and patiently wait to deal with his opponents at the right moment.

For the next five years, he took no action against the rebels in Iraq where the supporters of Mukhtar regularly clashed with the supporters of Abdullah ibn Zubair, who was represented there by his brother, Mus'ab. This state of affairs persisted until Mukhtar's supporters were eventually defeated by Abdullah's forces. Now there were only two main contenders for the Caliphate, namely Abdullah in Makkah and Abd al-Malik in Damascus. Like Hussain ibn Ali, Abdullah rebelled against the Umayyads soon after the death of Muawiyah in 680, having flatly refused to acknowledge Yazid as Caliph. Although Hussain was brutally murdered by Yazid's forces at Karbala, Abdullah continued his opposition against Yazid and his successors, and in so doing established his authority across Hijaz and parts of Iraq. Unlike Abd al-Malik, however, he had no political or military training. Not surprisingly, he repeatedly failed to take advantage of Umayyad weaknesses and frailties. This only strengthened Abd al-Malik's resolve as he planned his rival's downfall. In 691, after negotiating an agreement with Zu'far ibn al-Harith and his Qaysi followers, he asked them to renounce their support for Abdullah ibn Zubair and, in return, he offered them privileged political posts and Caliphal favours; as expected, the Qaysi people agreed to his proposal.

While Abd al-Malik was busy consolidating his position in Syria by winning over his erstwhile opponents to his side, Abdullah ibn Zubair was busy fighting the *khawarij* extremists. As the *khawarij* were a stubborn lot, they severely weakened Abdullah's military power and strength. Sensing Abdullah's vulnerability, Abd al-Malik personally led a military expedition to Iraq and in the ensuing war, he not only defeated his opponents but also reasserted Umayyad authority across that country. He then dispatched a large army to Makkah under the command of the notorious Hajjaj ibn Yusuf in order to bring Abdullah to heel. Following Abdullah's defeat at the hands of the Umayyad forces in 692, Abd al-Malik reunited the Muslim world under his leadership and restored peace and security throughout his dominion. At last, he became the undisputed ruler of the Muslim world. By all accounts, this was a truly remarkable achievement, especially given that the odds were stacked firmly against him; but he made possible what once seemed a mission impossible. Not surprisingly, the majority of Islamic historians consider him to be the second founder of the Umayyad dynasty after Muawiyah himself. However, some prominent writers, like Syed Amir Ali, have accused Abd al-Malik of being a cruel and inhumane ruler, but such accusations are most unfair and unjustified considering that he always offered his opponents the chance to resolve their differences through negotiation. That is to say, he authorised military action after all other means of resolving their differences were exhausted. At the same time, it is true that two of the most notorious military generals, Ubaidullah ibn Ziyad and Hajjaj ibn Yusuf, thrived during his reign. No doubt it is their dubious reputations which, more than anything else, have helped to tarnish his image.

After restoring the political unity of the Muslim world, Abd al-Malik authorised fresh military campaigns in different parts of the world. Thanks to his vision and foresight, the Umayyad army crossed the Oxus for the first time and established their hegemony over Transoxiana. And although the Muslims first entered North Africa during the reign of Caliph Umar and had established the city of Qayrawan (located in modern Tunisia) in 670 on Muawiyah's order, subsequent political disunity within the Islamic world

severely weakened the Muslim presence in that region. Thus Caliph Abd al-Malik authorised fresh military expeditions in order to reassert Islamic authority in that part of the world. He dispatched a large army under the command of Hassan ibn al-Nu'man which, despite an initial setback, went on to capture Carthage from the Byzantines and establish Islamic rule across North Africa. In addition to this, he instigated a series of campaigns against the Hindu rulers of Kabul. While these campaigns were largely exploratory and did not lead to the annexation of any significant territories, they did pave the way for a large scale military assualt on the Indian province of Sind during the reign of his successor.

Abd al-Malik's success as a ruler did not end there. As a gifted political operator, he knew serious flaws and deficiencies existed within the Umayyad political system, so he reformed and improved both the civil and administrative systems of his Government. Having inherited a decentralised form of Government which had been created by Muawiyah, who was a very wise and skilful politician, he decided this was no longer a viable system of Government because Umayyad dominion had expanded beyond everyone's expectations. Accordingly, he changed the status quo and implemented a centralised political and administrative system of Government; this he hoped would provide a solid foundation for a stable State. The form of Government developed by Abd al-Malik proved to be more robust and effective than the model created by Muawiyah and went on to became a blueprint for political, civil and administrative governance across the Muslim world for a long time. Indeed, Abd al-Malik's influence extended far beyond the political and military spheres. He became a champion of the Arabic language and actively promoted it throughout his dominion. Decades after the Muslim conquest of Syria, Egypt and significant parts of Persia, public accounts were still kept in either Greek or Persian. Abd al-Malik changed this practice and ordered all political and administrative tasks to be performed in Arabic; this forced all his foreign officials and civil servants to learn Arabic. Then, between 696 and 698, he abolished and phased out regional coinage, thereby removing the distinction between the Sasanian dirham (silver) and Syriac, Egyptian and Palestinian dinars (gold) and replacing them with a standard Arabic coinage for the first time.

During his reign, Abd al-Malik also went out of his way to encourage the religious scholars and traditionalists to compile and standardise the Prophetic teachings in the form of books and manuscripts. And as a prolific builder, he authorised his governor, Hajjaj ibn Yusuf, to build the city of Wasit (in modern-day Iraq). In addition to this, he planned and constructed the magnificent *qubbat al-sakhra* (or the 'Dome of the Rock'). Constructed in 692 on the site of the rock (*sakhra*) from which the Prophet Muhammad ascended to heaven (*miraj*), this breathtaking Islamic edifice is today considered to be one of the world's most famous mosques along with the *masjid al-haram* (the Sacred Mosque) in Makkah and the *masjid al-nabi* (the Prophet's Mosque) in Madinah. Comprising an impressive octagonal dome, supported by four pillars with four arches over the three columns set between each pillar – and decorated with beautiful Arabic calligraphy and mosaics – this mosque is one of the Muslim world's most spectacular and breathtaking works of architecture. Renovated many times by prominent Muslim rulers throughout the ages (including by the Abbasid Caliph al-Ma'mun, the Ayyubid Sultan Salah al-Din (Saladin) and the Ottoman ruler Sulaiman the Magnificient), this stunning mosque has immortalised Abd al-Malik; his name and fame will endure as long as this Islamic architectural masterpiece continues to stand.

Caliph Abd al-Malik's highly productive reign of two decades came to an end at the age of fifty-nine; he was buried in Damascus. Along with Muawiyah, Abd al-Rahman I, Harun al-Rashid and his son al-Ma'mun, Abd al-Rahman III, Sultan Salah al-Din, Sultan Mahmud of Ghazna, Sultan Muhammad II, Sulaiman the Magnificient and Akbar the Great, he must be considered one of the Muslim world's most successful rulers. Historians often refer to him as the 'father of Kings' because he was succeeded by his four sons, al-Walid, Sulaiman, Yazid II and Hisham. The solid foundation laid by Caliph Abd al-Malik also provided his successor with the platform from which he was able to launch one of the most astonishing series of conquests ever carried out in the annals of Islamic, if not global, history.

# 65

## Al-Hallaj
## (b.858 - d.922)

THE ORIGIN OF Sufism (or the mystical dimension of Islam) is often traced back to the Qur'an and the normative practice (*sunnah*) of the Prophet by its adherents. They argue that the sacred scriptures of Islam and its Prophet provide a veritable role model for those who seek to tread the Islamic spiritual path. Thus, far from being an alien intrusion into the Muslim world, Sufism embodies the very heart and soul of Islam as a religion and way of life. The Prophet and his close companions (like Abu Bakr, Umar, Uthman and Ali) were, according to the Sufis, the initiators and first exemplifiers of Islamic spirituality in its highest form. Like the Prophet and his close companions, the early Sufis, like Hasan al-Basri, Ja'far al-Sadiq and Rabi'a al-Adawiyyah renounced worldly pleasures and engaged in devotional activities, and did so without wearing the label of Sufi. However, when the Islamic State began to expand rapidly during the second half of the seventh century and the Muslims came into contact with the wealth and treasures of Persia and Byzantium for the first time, both the masses and the ruling elites began to succumb to the lures of unbridled materialism, which grew to threaten the fabric of early Islamic societies. At this critical juncture in Islamic history, scores

of outstanding Sufi personalities like Dawud al-Ta'i, Shaqiq al-Balkhi, Habib al-Ajami, Ibrahim ibn Adham, Maruf al-Karkhi, Hasan al-Basri and Rabi'a al-Adawiyyah emerged to warn both the rulers and the people of the dangers of excessive materialism. Although these luminaries of Islam espoused a form of spirituality which was essentially traditional in its content and outlook, later on another group of influential Sufis would emerge to champion a more sophisticated and equally controversial form of Islamic spirituality. Al-Hallaj was probably one of the most prominent exponents of this strand of Sufism.

Abul Mughith Hussain ibn Mansur ibn Muhammad al-Hallaj was born at Tur near al-Bayda in the Persian province of Fars. According to one account, his ancestors were originally Zoroastrians (followers of Zoroaster, the ancient Persian prophet and sage), while according to another source, he was a descendant of Abu Ayyub al-Ansari, who was a respected companion of the Prophet. In fact, it is most likely that he had a Zoroastrian background and therefore did not have any family connection to Abu Ayyub al-Ansari. Either way, his father, Mansur, was a devout Muslim who earned his living as a wool-carder; hence the title 'al-Hallaj'. Encouraged by his father, young al-Hallaj committed the entire Qur'an to memory as a child and then pursued further education in Arabic and traditional Islamic sciences. Thereafter, he travelled to the Iraqi city of Wasit where he completed his higher education under the tutelage of its leading scholars. Founded in 702 by Hajjaj ibn Yusuf, the governor of the Umayyad ruler Abd al-Malik ibn Marwan, Wasit became a prominent centre of Islamic learning and scholarship in Iraq. Some of al-Hallaj's early teachers included Sahl ibn Abdullah al-Tustari (one of the first to formulate the Sufi theory of *nur muhammad* (or the 'Muhammadan Light') and author of an esoteric commentary on the Qur'an); Abu Talib al-Makki, the famed author of *Qut al-Qulub* (The Nourishment of Hearts), and Abu Bakr al-Shibli, who was also an influential Sufi scholar and theorist.

After completing his higher education, al-Hallaj left Wasit and moved to Basrah, which was also the home of Hasan al-Basri and Rabi'a al-Adawiyyah, and there he married the daughter of a local Sufi. As an outspoken exponent of Islamic mystical thought, he soon fell out with the local Sufis (including his own father-in-law who accused him of being careless and insensitive). From Basrah, he went to Makkah where he became renowned for his devotional and ascetic practices. After completing the sacred *hajj* (pilgrimage), he went to Baghdad which at the time was one of the Muslim world's foremost centres of Islamic learning and spirituality. Here he became a student of Abul Qasim al-Junayd al-Baghdadi (also known as al-Junayd al-Baghdadi), who was a Sufi scholar of considerable influence, and he personally taught him aspects of Islamic mystical philosophy, but al-Hallaj soon fell out with him, too. The story goes that one day he came and knocked on al-Junayd's door. When the latter asked who it was, al-Hallaj provocatively replied, '*ana al-haqq*' ('I am the Truth'). As a sober Sufi, al-Junayd reprimanded him for his blasphemous and inflammatory statement. When al-Hallaj refused to recant, al-Junayd severed his ties with him. Thereupon al-Hallaj left Baghdad and became a wandering Sufi. During his travels

in and around Khurasan he gathered around him a sizeable following and eventually went to Makkah to perform his second pilgrimage. From Makkah he went to Turkistan and from there he reportedly travelled to India and as far as the borders of China.

During his journeys he not only developed, but also passionately disseminated his mystical ideas and thoughts. According to his critics, during his stay in India he learnt the art of magic and, like Abu Yazid al-Bistami, became familiar with the Hindu mystical concepts of 'self-annihilation' and 'extinction' which, in turn, influenced his own mystical views. He returned to Baghdad when he was about fifty and a large following gathered around him. But his extragavant mystical claims and utterances soon began to alarm and offend both the sober Sufis and the orthodox religious scholars. He became such an outspoken exponent of Sufism that even the Mu'tazilites considered him to be an opportunist and charlatan. His outrageous mystical claims not only stirred up a huge religious controversy in Baghdad, but also led to him being accused of supporting and sympathising with renegade political groups like the Qarmatians. This prompted the ruling Abbasid elites to expel him from Baghdad, after which he again returned to Makkah and performed yet another pilgrimage. After completing this third pilgrimage, he returned to Baghdad completely transformed. According to his son, Ahmad, during this period he claimed to have experienced the highest form of mystical union where the distinction between 'I' and 'Thou' is removed, thus the lover and the object of his love become one (*ayn al-jam*).

While prominent Sufis like Abul Qasim al-Junayd al-Baghdadi only communicated their mystical ideas and thoughts through *isharat* (hints or indications) in order to avoid offending both the religious scholars and the ruling elites, al-Hallaj ignored the advice of his fellow Sufis and began to advocate the need for spiritual and moral reformation in Baghdad. Though his call for moral and spiritual reformation was a powerful and pertinent one as the forces of materialism and hedonism began to run amok within the Muslim world, his unpredictable political outbursts and inflammatory mystical utterances offended everyone, including the Shi'a and the Mu'tazilites. He was eventually apprehended by the Abbasid authorities and imprisoned for nine years. During his confinement he was at first treated well on account of his friendship with both the Abbasid vizier, Nasr al-Qashuri, and the mother of young Caliph al-Muqtadir, but when the religious and political controversy he had generated showed no signs of subsiding, the Abbasid elites promptly put him on trial charged with blasphemy and treason. The trial was no more than a show; thus everyone expected him to be found guilty. Mocked, vilified and branded a heretic by the orthodox religious scholars, and also shunned and excommunicated by his fellow Sufis, al-Hajjaj was sentenced to death by hanging. Were his mystical ideas and thoughts as abhorrent and unorthodox as his opponents made them out to be? Did he deserve to be executed? Was he a religious maverick, as his detractors claimed, or was he a victim of religious bigotry and political persecution, as his supporters argued?

As one of the Muslim world's most radical and controversial mystical thinkers, al-Hallaj's life and thoughts are riddled with contradictions, paradoxes and unusual insights into Islamic spirituality and gnosis. Following in the footsteps of Abu Yazid al-Bistami (who was one of the first Sufi thinkers to argue that 'self-annihilation and extinction' represented the peak of mystical experience), al-Hallaj became one of the most eloquent and bravest revealers of mystical secrets and truths. Indeed, he not only openly divulged the secrets of Sufism to the masses, but went further and expressed his mystical feelings and experiences in a way that even the uninitiated could understand. Central to al-Hallaj's mystical philosophy was the concept of love (*mahabbah*). Like Rabi'a al-Adawiyyah, he advocated the pursuit of disinterested love, that is to seek the Beloved only for His sake, rather than out of fear of eternal damnation or promise of reward. However, unlike Hasan al-Basri, Rabi'a al-Adawiyyah and

al-Junayd al-Baghdadi, all of whom unequivocally affirmed the traditional Islamic understanding of Divine Transcendence and Unity, al-Hallaj's expression of spontaneous, disinterested love proved hugely controversial because he claimed to have experienced the 'essence of union' (*ayn al-jam*), where the lover and the Beloved became one (*ittihad*); thus he blurred the crucial distinction between the Creator and His creation.

He expressed his mystical ideas and experiences in beautiful, unforced and refreshing poetic couplets. According to Ibn al-Nadim, the acclaimed bibliographer, al-Hallaj composed around forty-six books and treatises on different aspects of Islamic mysticism. However, his most famous works were his *Diwan* (collection of mystical odes) and *Kitab al-Tawasin* (The Book of Ta and Sin). The following quotations taken from his *Diwan* and *Kitab al-Tawasin* beautifully summarise the main thrust of his mystical thought:

'I do not cease swimming in the seas of love, rising with the wave, then descending; now the wave sustains me, and then I sink beneath it; love bears me away where there is no longer any shore.' (Diwan al-Hallaj): 'If ye do not recognise God, at least recognize His signs. I am that sign, I am the Creative Truth, because through the Truth I am a truth eternally. My friends and teachers are Iblis and Pharaoh. Iblis was threatened with Hell-fire, yet he did not recant. Pharaoh was drowned in the sea, yet he did not recant, for he would not acknowledge anything between him and God. And I, though I am killed and crucified, and though my hands and feet are cut off - I do not recant.' (Kitab al-Tawasin): 'I have seen my Lord with the eye of my heart, and I said: 'Who are you?' He said: 'You.' (Diwan al-Hallaj).

Taken literally, these mystical utterances and outbursts are indeed heretical and blasphemous. Not surprisingly, Baghdad's religious scholars and the ruling elites were shocked and horrified by these statements. Charged with the claim of personal apotheosis, al-Hallaj argued he was neither a heretic nor a blasphemer; rather he was an exponent of mystical experience in its highest form. Sentenced to death at the age of sixty-four for preaching 'heretical' ideas, he refused to protest even when his over-zealous persecutors dragged him to the floor like a sack of potatoes and severly tortured and flogged him, before amputating his limbs one by one. His body was then cremated and his ashes scattered in the Tigris. Indeed, according to Farid al-Din Attar, his sympathetic biographer, al-Hallaj danced to his death with joy and happiness, murmuring the words, 'All that matters for ecstatic is that the Unique should reduce him to Unity.' While his critics (such as Abu Talib al-Makki, al-Junyad al-Baghdadi, Ibn Hazm al-Andalusi, Ibn Khaldun and Ibn Taymiyyah) have argued that he was a heretic and blasphemer because he claimed self-deification, other equally renowned Islamic scholars and Sufis, like Abu Bakr al-Shibli, Abd al-Qadir al-Jilani, Abu Hamid al-Ghazali, Fakhr al-Din al-Razi, Farid al-Din Attar, Jalal al-Din Rumi and Sir Muhammad Iqbal, have exonerated him of the charge of self-deification and belief in monism.

A closer study of his mystical ideas and thoughts shows that he was far from being a blasphemer or pantheist. This view has also been endorsed,

and proved quite conclusively, by the renowned French scholar and Islamicist, Louis Massignon. In his magisterial *The Passion of al-Hallaj, Mystic and Martyr of Islam* (originally published in 1922 and translated into English in four volumes by Herbert Mason in 1982), he argued that al-Hallaj espoused a form of *wahdat al-shuhud* ('Unity of Being in perception or unity of witnesses') rather than *wahdat al-wujud* ('Unity of Being or monism'). If this view is correct, then al-Hallaj was neither a heretic nor a religious maverick; instead his unusual, spontaneous mystical flashes and utterances were both misunderstood and misinterpreted by the Sufis as well as the religious scholars of his time. By sending al-Hallaj to the gallows, argued Massignon, the Abbasid elites not only wrongly pandered to the wishes of the religious authorities, they also diverted attention away from the social, political and economic challenges and difficulties of the time, and in so doing they committed a great travesty of justice. True to form, nearly eleven centuries after his death, al-Hallaj continues to polarise the Sufis, Islamic philosophers and theologians to this day.

# 66

## Hasan al-Banna (b.1906 - d.1949)

DURING THE NINETEENTH and early twentieth centuries, a significant part of the Muslim world was colonised by prominent European powers such as France, Britain, Holland and Italy. And although Egypt has been a bastion of Islamic culture and tradition since the beginning of the seventh century, in 1882 the British invaded and colonised this important Muslim country. The ruling British elites not only maintained a tight political and military grip on Egypt, but also introduced and promoted Western education, culture and values across the country. Being loyal and proud Muslims, the Egyptians resented foreign interference in their internal affairs; indeed, the Egyptian masses considered the British attempt to liberalise and westernise their country as an open attack on their Islamic identity, culture and heritage. Faced with mass opposition and resentment, in 1922 the British were forced to grant limited autonomy to Egypt, although the Egyptian people continued to campaign for their full independence. Their campaign eventually forced the British authorities to withdraw their forces and quit Egypt. Though the British occupation of Egypt formally ended in 1936, they continued to exercise considerable political, economic and cultural influence in the country. As the main mission of the Egyptian liberation movement (led by prominent leaders like Sa'd Zaghlul) was to throw the British out of their country, they made no attempt to counter the spread of secularism and westernisation in Egypt which threatened to wreak havoc within Egyptian society at the time. The *jami'yat al-ikhwan al-muslimun* (or 'the Muslim Brotherhood') was destined to fill this moral and spiritual vacuum. Founded by Hasan al-Banna, this mass-Islamic movement attempted to arrest the spread of secularism and westernisation in Egypt by rejuvenating the Islamic ethos, morals and values across the country. And in the process, the Muslim Brotherhood became one of the twentieth century's most powerful and influential Islamic movements.

Hasan ibn Ahmad ibn Abd al-Rahman ibn Muhammad al-Banna al-Sa'ati was born in the Egyptian village of Mahmudiyyah. His father, Ahmad ibn Abd al-Rahman al-Banna, hailed from a lower-middle class Egyptian family and attended al-Azhar University, one of the Muslim world's most famous seats of Islamic learning and scholarship. He earned his living by repairing watches, and pursued research in *hadith* (Prophetic traditions) and *fiqh* (Islamic jurisprudence) during his free time. He edited and wrote several commentaries on the works of classical scholars like Ahmad ibn Hanbal and al-Shafi'i, and led prayers at his local mosque. Ahmad's personal piety and love of books (he had a large personal library of traditional Islamic literature), inspired young Hasan al-Banna to commit the entire Qur'an to memory as a child. Heavily influenced by his father, he used to say, 'Islam is my father and I have no other.' After completing his elementary education at home under the care of his learned father, he enrolled at a local Government funded Teachers' Training Centre, where he successfully completed a three-year course. He then applied to join the *dar al-uloom* (Cairo University) to pursue higher education. When he was offered a place at this institution, his family moved to Cairo where, in 1927, he passed his final examinations. Thus, at the age of twenty-one, he took up his post as a teacher at a Government school in Ismailiyyah.

During his student days at *dar al-uloom*, al-Banna observed the socio-cultural condition of his people very closely and what he saw utterly shocked and horrified him. The mass influx of western culture, values and habits into Egyptian society, he felt, had severely undermined the traditional Islamic culture and ethos. This was happening at a time when the ruling elites were busy consolidating their own political positions, while leading Egyptian intellectuals and literary figures (like Taha Hussain and Ali Abd al-Raziq) were seeking to deconstruct traditional Islam. To add insult to injury, the masses also began to succumb to the lures of modernity and westernisation, leading to a flagrant disregard for, and violation of, Islamic principles and practices across urban Egypt. When al-Banna was posted to Ismailiyyah, he was surprised to observe how the forces of modernity and westernisation had transformed that locality too. This prompted him to regularly visit the local cafes and shops to invite the locals to return to Islam. Being neither a theoretician nor an academic, he propagated the message of Islam through personal contact. Once, when he was asked why he did not write

books, he retorted, 'I write men.' True to form, he soon won the hearts and minds of the locals, thanks to his polished interpersonal skills and eloquence. And the people, in turn, came to profoundly admire and respect him for his unflinching devotion to Islam.

It was not long before al-Banna gathered around him a sizeable following in Ismailiyyah. Encouraged by his success, he formally inaugurated the *ikhwan al-muslimun* in 1928 to revive traditional Islamic principles and practices in and around Ismailiyyah. It is not clear, at this stage, whether he envisaged this organisation to be a local endeavour or the beginning of a nation-wide Islamic revivalist movement. Either way, the Brotherhood started off as a local association which sought to bring about moral and spiritual reform in Ismailiyyah by inviting the locals, both young and old, men and women, back to the original, pristine message of Islam. Al-Banna's experiment proved so successful that people from all walks of life flocked to the Brotherhood. Then again, such a response was not entirely unexpected because the people of Ismailiyyah – like their counterparts in Cairo, Alexandria and other towns and cities of Egypt – had become very angry and disillusioned with the ruling oligarchy. The rulers were keen to maintain the status quo for their own personal benefit, rather than instigate much-needed political and economic reforms in order to improve and enhance their people's lives, whether they lived in urban Cairo or in rural villages. When al-Banna's call for spiritual and moral, social and cultural, and economic and political reform struck a chord with the locals, they became his most fervent supporters, and this encouraged him to formulate the Brotherhood's religious philosophy, methodology of *da'wah* (Islamic propagation) and organisational structure.

Unlike Jamal al-Din al-Afghani and Muhammad Abduh, al-Banna was neither a political theorist/activist, nor a religious thinker. Rather he was a community activist who directly engaged with the people to bring about individual, as well as collective, reformation through preaching, exhortation and training. Just as his understanding and approach to Islam was broad and comprehensive, the organisation he founded was also inclusive and pragmatic. The Islamic concept of *tawhid* (or Divine Unity), he felt, provided the basis for a moral, spiritual, political, economic and social transformation of society for the betterment of the people. He shunned religious sectarianism and advocated the need for unity and solidarity based on a traditionalist understanding of Islamic principles and practices. Inspired by the Prophet, his companions and the early Islamic scholars, al-Banna urged his followers and supporters to engage in devotional activities during the night time and strive hard to reform their society in accordance with Islamic teachings during the daytime. Since social and cultural change cannot be brought about individually, he encouraged his followers to work collectively under the banner of the Brotherhood. Being a gradualist rather than a revolutionary, he adopted a bottom-up – as opposed to a top-down – approach to social change and reformation.

Indeed, his practical and down-to-earth approach proved hugely successful in Ismailiyyah. So much so that during his stay there he established several mosques, as well as schools for boys and girls; he also set up social welfare organisations and even created employment opportunities for the local people. Six years after its inception, the Brotherhood became one of the most powerful and active Islamic organisations in and around Ismailiyyah. During this period al-Banna also found time to marry and start his own family. Most crucially, he kept a detailed diary of his duties and daily activities. As expected, this diary (published under the title of *Mudhakkirat al-Da'wah wa'l Da'iya* (Memoirs of Propagation and Propagator) subsequently became an important source of information about his life and career. In addition to this, he wrote scores of articles on different aspects of Islam which were later published under the title of *Maqalat al-Hasan al-Banna* (Articles of Hasan al-Banna). Also, keen to encourage his followers to purify themselves both physically and spiritually, he compiled a collection of religious sayings and supplications

entitled *al-Ma'thurat*. This booklet was published and circulated widely by the members of the Brotherhood.

Al-Banna stayed in Ismailiyyah until 1933, when he was transferred to a teaching post in Cairo. By that time, the Brotherhood had expanded beyond his own expectations, and new branches began to mushroom everywhere. Eager to co-ordinate the activities of his expanding organisation, he abandoned his teaching career and became a full-time Islamic activist. As in Ismailiyyah, here now in Cairo, he noticed how the people had become angry and disillusioned with the subservient attitude of the Egyptian political and religious leaders towards the British elites. His call for Islamic unity and solidarity therefore received a favourable response from the populace, who flocked to the Brotherhood in their droves. New branches of the Brotherhood were soon established across Cairo so that by 1934 it had established its presence in no fewer than fifty suburbs of Cairo, thus attracting a mass following. At the time, al-Banna's main objective was to counter the popularity of Western culture and values in Egyptian society by calling the masses back to the original, pristine message of Islam. In so doing he hoped to bring about a moral and spiritual transformation throughout the Egyptian society. As a successful grassroots-based organisation, the Brotherhood soon spread across Egypt and won the hearts and minds of the Egyptian people (including farmers, students, teachers, doctors, engineers and lawyers). With its increasing popularity, the Brotherhood also expanded its activities in response to the people's diverse needs and requirements.

In 1938, al-Banna prepared a comprehensive programme for the Brotherhood and called for reform in all spheres of Egyptian society in the light of the Qur'an and Prophetic *sunnah*. As before, his call for educational, social, political and economic reforms went down well with the Egyptian people. Indeed, the Brotherhood's opposition to the British elites, coupled with its desire to create a fully-fledged Islamic State in Egypt, soon won it widespread support across the country and, during the period from 1939 to 1945, the Brotherhood became one of the largest and most influential Islamic organisations in Egypt. In response, al-Banna changed the Brotherhood's organisational structure so that he could co-ordinate its activities more effectively. By establishing their own mosques, schools, medical clinics, shops, community centres, women's groups, newspapers, magazines and recreational facilities (without any support or assistance from the Egypt Government), the Brotherhood effectively became a State within a State. Given its wide-ranging services and activities, the command structure of the organisation also became increasingly complex. As the Chief Guide (*murshid al-am*) of the organisation, al-Banna worked very closely with a dedicated team based at its Central Office (*maktab al-irshad*). Although the Central Office was responsible for formulating the organisation's policies and strategies, it was the members of the Executive Office (*maktab al-tanfidhi*) who were responsible for implementing its policies, procedures and guidelines at the grassroots level. Al-Banna created many other layers of command within the Brotherhood to facilitate better communication and effective delivery of its services. His extensive knowledge and understanding of Islam, coupled with his vision, foresight and organisational ability, enabled him to translate the values and principles of Islam at a practical level.

As the Brotherhood became increasingly popular in Egypt, the country's rulers, and especially the powerful British elites and their Egyptian subordinates, became very alarmed. Wrongly accused of spreading anti-State propaganda, the authorities first outlawed the Brotherhood's newspapers and journals, including the famous *al-manar* (The Lighthouse) magazine. This was followed by the imposition of Governmental restrictions and censorship on the organisation's religious activities, leading to the forced dispersal of its prominent leaders and activists from Cairo. Such measures were instigated by the Government in order to undermine the Brotherhood, its unity and organisation but, following huge public outcry, the authorities were forced to relent. Then, in 1948, the State of Israel was founded in Palestine and this prompted some members of the Brotherhood to spearhead a military campaign against the new country. A year later, the Brotherhood was outlawed by the Egyptian Government which led to widespread rioting, as well as the murder of the Egyptian police chief, allegedly by a member of the Brotherhood. In response, the Government arrested all the prominent members of the Brotherhood and curtailed its activities across the country. The ensuing crisis eventually spiralled out of control when Mahmud Fahmi al-Nuqrashi, the Egyptian Prime Minister, was assassinated, allegedly by a member of the Brotherhood.

A month later, al-Banna himself was gunned down on the streets of Cairo, allegedly by the Egyptian secret police; he was forty-three at the time. Although he was succeeded by Hasan Ismail al-Hudaybi, who was a prominent judge and Islamic scholar, the Brotherhood and its leaders continued to be harassed, persecuted and repressed by all subsequent Egyptian Governments. In spite of this, the Brotherhood remains one of the most powerful politico-religious organisations in Egypt to this day; indeed, its message and popularity has spread across the Arab world. Likewise, al-Banna's religious ideas and thoughts have influenced some of the most prominent Islamic scholars and reformers of the twentieth century, including Sayyid Qutb, the influential author of *Fi Zilal al-Qur'an* (In the Shade of the Qur'an); Taqi al-Din al-Nabhani, the founder of *hizb ut-tahrir* (the Party of Liberation), and Shaykh Ahmad Yasin, the founder of *hamas* (the popular Palestinian Islamic Resistance Movement) among others.

# 67

# Khwajah Naqshband (b.1317 - d.1389)

ALTHOUGH MUSLIMS FIRST entered Central Asia during the reign of Caliph Umar, the Islamic presence in that region was not consolidated until the time of Caliph Uthman. The Muslim conquest of Central Asia paved the way for a strongly Islamic culture and identity to emerge in that region. So much so that Central Asia produced some of the Muslim world's most influential scholars, thinkers and personalities, like al-Bukhari, al-Khwarizmi, al-Maturidi, Ibn Sina and Ulugh Beg. Amir Timur (Tamerlane), who was one of the most successful conquerors in history, was also born and raised on the cold, harsh and intimidating steppes of Central Asia. Known for his thirst for power and military conquest, this fearless military hardman nonetheless had a soft spot for *tasawwuf* (or Islamic mysticism). This is hardly surprising given the fact that Central Asia had produced some of the Muslim world's most famous and influential Sufi sages. Indeed, Sufism became part and parcel of the Central Asian religious landscape during the early days of Islam; thus prominent early Central Asian Sufis like Abu Sa'id ibn Abul Khair of Mayhana (located in present-day Turkmenistan) played a pivotal role in the development of a unique Central Asian Sufi identity. Thanks

to them, a number of indigenous Islamic mystical traditions (*tariqah*) emerged and became established in that region during the thirteenth and fourteen centuries. One such Sufi tradition was the *naqshbandiyyah tariqah*, which was championed by Kawajah Naqshband, and it is today widely considered to be one of the Muslim world's most influential Sufi traditions.

Muhammad ibn Muhammad Baha al-Din al-Bukhari, better known as Khwajah Naqshband, was born in the village of Qasr-i Hinduwan, not far from Bukhara in modern Uzbekistan in Central Asia. When he was a child, he was blessed by Muhammad Baba Sammasi, an eminent local spiritual figure, who apparently foretold that the young boy would one day become a shining star of Islamic spirituality and gnosis. After completing his early education in traditional Islamic sciences and Sufism under the tutelage of Baba Sammasi, he travelled to Bukhara to pursue higher education. During his stay in Bukhara, he married and eventually returned home after completing his formal studies. He then went to Nasaf where Sayyid Amir Kulal, a prominent scholar and spiritual successor of Baba Sammasi, lived and taught Islamic sciences and spirituality. Born in a local village, Sayyid Kulal earned his living as a potter, but had become a prominent exponent of Islamic spirituality and gnosis. Under Sayyid Kulal's guidance, Khwajah Naqshband mastered Sufi thought and practices. After the former's death, his mantle passed to his able disciple, Mawlana Arif Dikkarani, and Khwajah Naqshband served him for another few years before he went to Samarqand where he entered the service of the reigning Sultan Khalil. He served him for twelve years, until the Sultan was ousted from power in 1347. During this period of considerable socio-political uncertainty, Khwajah Naqshband had moved to Ziwartun where he received advanced training in Sufi theory and practice.

Known for his good character and personal piety, the Khwajah soon became a prominent religious figure, and the locals rated him highly for his knowledge of Islam and his spiritual qualities. His advanced training in Islamic sciences and Sufism, coupled with his remarkable ability to endure gruelling tests of hardship and self-renunciation, also won him much praise from his teachers and Sufi masters alike. Although Khwajah Naqshband led a life of renunciation, sacrifice and single-minded devotion to the ideals and practices of Islam, he knew more than anyone else that one cannot attain success in any sphere of human endeavour without a measure of Divine grace and favour. Thus, according to Khwajah Naqshband, one cannot choose to be a Sufi for, strictly speaking, a spiritual gift is granted rather than gained – although one should never despair of the mercy and grace of Divine Providence. Like all other great Sufis of the past, he fully understood and accepted this fact. Indeed, Sayyid Amir Kulal, who was one of Khwajah Naqshband's foremost teachers and spiritual guides, had travelled more than eight miles every week, on foot, to attend religious classes during his training. After twenty years of travelling back and forth, his teacher eventually told him that he had been granted the gift of Islamic spirituality and gnosis. In the same way, Sayyid Amir Kulal put Khwajah Naqshband through similar bouts of training before confirming that he, too, had been granted the gift of Islamic spirituality and gnosis.

The Khwajah was such a diligent practitioner of Islamic spirituality and self-renunciation that he even refused to accept food or gifts offered to him by his local rulers, just in case they had been obtained illegally. Once, when he was asked why he refused to keep a servant, he retorted, 'Ownership does not go with sainthood.' A strict adherent of traditional Islam, he believed in self-reliance and detested hedonistic practices; thus he defined Islamic mysticism as the path of *al-urwa al-wuthqa*, that is, an unbreakable bond between following the Qur'an and the *sunnah* (or the normative practices of the Prophet Muhammad). In other words, according to the Khwajah, the fountainhead of Islamic spirituality and gnosis was nothing other than the Qur'an and the Prophetic *sunnah*. His assertion of the supremacy of the Qur'an and the Prophetic traditions over all other sources of guidance was not only significant, it was also profoundly refreshing because, at the time, many misguided Sufis tried to dispense with these two fundamental sources of Islam in their quest for so-called ultimate spiritual experience. Likewise, Khwajah Naqshband was an uncompromising exponent of the Islamic concept of Divine Unity (*tawhid*). He also made a clear distinction between knowledge and understanding of spirituality – as opposed to feeling and experiencing spirituality. He considered the former state to be the pinnacle of *tawhid* and the latter to be the peak of *ma'rifa* (or gnosis).

According to the Khwajah's biographers, Abd al-Rahman Jami and Ali ibn Hussain Safi, his spiritual path was first unveiled to him in the form of a vision when he was a young man. In that vision he apparently saw three lamps and a throne. The three lamps represented all the Sufi luminaries of the past, while the throne was none other than the eminent Sufi Abd al-Khaliq Ghujdawani. He was informed that he had been specially blessed and that he would one day become a great Sufi and an influential disseminator of Islamic spirituality and gnosis. The following words of advice were then offered to him, 'Whatever happens, always follow the path marked out by divine command and prohibition. Keep a firm resolve and never abandon the Prophetic example and the practice of good works. Steer clear of heretical innovations, take the traditions of the blessed Muhammad Mustafa for your guide and make a profound study of all that has been recorded about God's messenger and his companions.' Although it is not possible to confirm or disprove the authenticity of this report, there is no doubt that Khwajah Naqshband believed that he was chosen by Providence to pursue and disseminate Islamic spirituality and gnosis in the light of the Qur'an and the Prophetic *sunnah*.

Following in the footsteps of his eminent predecessors such as Abd al-Khaliq Ghujdawani, the Khwajah pursued a spiritual path which was in complete harmony with traditional Islam and he shunned the company of those mystics who became embroiled in heretical or reprehensible innovations (*bida dalala*). Initiated by Khwajah Yusuf Hamadani back in the eleventh century, the *naqshbandiyyah* mystical Order (*tariqah*) evolved and spread across Central Asia under the stewardship of eminent Sufis like Abdullah Barqi, Hasan Andaqi, Ahmad Yisiwi and Abd al-Khaliq Ghujdawani before Khwajah Naqshband emerged to become one of its most influential champions. The mystical philosophy and spiritual methodology of the early *naqshbandiyyah* Sufis was summed up by Abd al-Khaliq Ghujdawani when he said, 'Learn Islamic jurisprudence (*fiqh*) and the traditions of the Prophet (*ahadith*). Do not mix with illiterate mystics…offer prayers in congregation…do not seek after fame…do not accept any office…do not be a surety for anybody…do not go to the court. Do not mix with rulers or princes…do not construct a *khanqah*… do not hear too much mystic music…do not condemn mystic music…eat only what is permitted…so far as you can, do not marry a woman who wants material comforts…laughter kills one's heart. Your heart should be full of grief, your body as if of an ailing person, your eyes wet, your actions sincere, your prayers earnest, your dress tattered, your company dervishes, your wealth poverty, your house the mosque and your friend God.'

Although the mystical thoughts and practices championed by Khwajah Yusuf Hamdani and his illustrious disciples did create considerable interest in Islam across Central Asia, the absence of a unified approach to Islamic mysticism prevented the ordinary people from harvesting the fruits from the tree of Islamic spirituality. As one of the most prominent Sufis of his generation, Khwajah Naqshband was the most able and qualified person to unify and consolidate the different strands of mysticism which then prevailed in Central Asia. And although he had extensive knowledge of Islam and was also spiritually very gifted, the Khwajah knew that the task he faced was not an easy one. Thus, after some deliberation, he initiated a mass Islamic spiritual movement which subsequently became known as the *naqshbandiyyah* Sufi Order, and in so doing he contributed to the widespread dissemination of Islam and Islamic spirituality throughout Muslim Central Asia. However, unlike, for instance, Jalal al-Din Rumi or Farid al-Din Attar, both of whom were great Sufis and prolific writers, the Khwajah did not write much; rather he became a religious-cum-spiritual reformer *par excellence*. As a devout Muslim, he was horrified to see how Islamic principles and practices were becoming increasingly sidelined in his homeland, if not across all Central Asia, and this prompted him to instigate a mass campaign to revive authentic Islamic teachings and practices, and in so doing he hoped to arrest the forces of materialism and hedonism in that part of the world.

The movement launched by the Khwajah became so popular that over time it became one of the most influential of all Sufi traditions, along with the *qadiriyyah tariqah* founded by Abd al-Qadir al-Jilani. Inspired by Khwajah Naqshband, the adherents of his Sufi tradition spread across Central Asia, and also took its message as far as the Indian subcontinent where Shaykh Ahmad Sirhindi, the renowned Muslim sage and reformer of India, became one of its foremost exponents and disseminators. Other famous Indian followers of the *naqshbandiyyah tariqah* included Emperor

Jahangir, Shah Waliullah of Delhi, Sayyid Ahmad Barelvi and Shah Ghulam Ali. In addition to this, Abd al-Rahman Jami, the prominent Persian writer and poet, was an adherent of this *tariqah* – as were the great Turkish Islamic scholar and reformer Bediuzzaman Sa'id Nursi and the Cypriot Sufi Shaykh Nazim al-Haqqani. Thanks to the latter, the *naqshbandiyyah tariqah* has today gained thousands of followers in both Europe and America. Likewise, in the Arab world, eminent scholars like Muhammad Rashid Rida and Abd al-Ghani al-Nabulusi were affiliated to this Sufi tradition, while in North Africa Amir Abd al-Qadir and Muhammad ibn Ali al-Sanusi were also influenced by the

*naqshbandiyyah tariqah*. Additionally, Imam Shamyl of Daghestan, the celebrated Caucasian warrior and freedom-fighter, was an adherent of this Sufi Order. Indeed, when Islam was being brutally suppressed across Central Asia by the Stalinist rulers of the Soviet Empire, it was the followers of this *tariqah* who kept the torch of Islam burning across that region.

Thus, it would not be an exaggeration to say that the Islamic spiritualist movement initiated by Khwajah Naqshband has few parallels in the history of Islam. He breathed his last at the age of seventy-two and was buried in his native village, where a mausoleum was later erected in his memory.

# 68

## Ibn Hazm al-Andalusi (b.994 - d.1064)

THE PERIOD FROM the eighth to the thirteenth century may have been a period of intellectual stagnation in Europe, but it was far from being this for the Muslims. Indeed, it was the Golden Age of Islamic civilisation – a time when Muslims reigned supreme politically, economically and intellectually. From Makkah and Madinah (the cradles of Islamic civilisation), to Baghdad, Damascus, Isfahan, Merv, Bukhara and Samarqand, Muslims blazed a trail which has few parallels in global history. Less than half a century after the death of the Prophet, Muslims reached North Africa and within a few more years would overwhelm the Visigothic Kingdom of Iberia. *Al-andalus* (or Islamic Spain) thus became a beacon of light for the rest of Europe. Under Islamic rule, Spain became a major centre of intellectual and literary activity; Cordova, the capital of Muslim Spain, also boasted some of the finest colleges, libraries and hospitals in Europe. When Islamic Spain reached its zenith in the tenth century, under the stewardship of Caliph Abd al-Rahman III, Cordova alone housed more than seventy public libraries, containing more than half a million books on all the sciences of the day. But following the mass expulsion of Muslims from Spain by Ferdinand and Isabella in 1492 Spain

began to lose its former glory, to the extent that in the eighteenth century there was not a single public library in Madrid. Yet, back in its heyday, Spain had produced some of Europe's most influential scholars and thinkers. One such scholar was Ibn Hazm al-Andalusi who was one of the great writers and thinkers of medieval Europe.

Abu Muhammad Ali ibn Ahmad ibn Sa'id ibn Hazm ibn Ghalib ibn Salih ibn Khalaf ibn Ma'dan ibn Sufyan ibn Yazid, known as Ibn Hazm al-Andalusi for short, was born in Cordova during the reign of Caliph Hisham II. Although Ibn Hazm traced his genealogy back to Yazid, a prominent Persian convert to Islam who lived during the early Umayyad period, according to the historian Abu Marwan ibn Hayyan, his immediate ancestors (such as his great-grandfather, Hazm) hailed from the town of Labla and were of Spanish descent. It was his grandfather, Sa'id, who first moved from Labla to Cordova where his family members became prominent scholars and politicians. It was in these roles that Ibn Hazm's father served both Caliph al-Hakam II and his successor Hisham II as an advisor. Educated at home by his learned father, Ibn Hazm studied Arabic language, grammar, Qur'anic sciences and poetry as a child. Despite suffering from an irregular heartbeat from an early age – a medical condition which continued to trouble him all his life – he never allowed his health problems to hold him back. After completing his early education, he pursued advanced training in Islamic sciences under the guidance of Cordova's leading scholars, such as the traditionist Ahmad ibn al-Jassur, historian Ibn al-Faradi and jurist Abdullah ibn Dahhun. Keen to acquire proficiency in philology, philosophy, logic, arithmetic and aspects of the natural sciences, he attended the lectures of Ibn Abd al-Warith, who was a prominent local linguist, and Ibn al-Kattani, who specialised in various scientific disciplines.

As a gifted student, Ibn Hazm was able to memorise and retain vast quantities of information. Impressed by his intellectual abilities, all his teachers predicted a bright future for the youngster. While he was still in his teens, he accompanied his father to conferences and official meetings, and thus began to mix freely with Cordova's leading scholars and politicians. Rubbing shoulders with highflying civil servants, eminent literary figures and learned scholars made him confident and ambitious, and he also became very aristocratic in his mannerisms and etiquette. Unlike Caliphs Abd al-Rahman III and al-Hakam II, the reign of Hisham II was marred by considerable political instability and social upheaval. Living during a politically unpredictable period in the history of Islamic Spain, young Ibn Hazm was forced to endure considerable personal anguish and hardship – especially after his father was humiliated and removed from his Governmental post by his political rivals following Hisham II's abdication of power in 1010. As the political situation rapidly deteriorated across Muslim Spain and ethnic conflict between the Arabs and the Berbers flared up, Ibn Hazm became actively involved in politics for the first time. In response, his opponents destroyed his family home in Balat Mughirah and he was imprisoned on more than one occasion. But, like his father, he remained loyal to the royal family and served them in the capacity of a Minister of State, a post which he held at three different oc-

casions during the reigns of Caliphs al-Murtada, al-Mustazhir and al-Mu'tadd.

During this difficult period in the history of Islamic Spain, Ibn Hazm not only fulfilled his duties as a politician and advisor to successive Caliphs, but also found time to pursue literary activities. As an extensive reader, he studied more books than probably any other scholar of his time and in so doing gained mastery of a wide range of disciplines, including speculative theology (*ilm al-kalam*), jurisprudence (*fiqh*), Prophetic traditions (*hadith*), history, comparative religion, logic and ethics. Indeed, the scope and breadth of his learning was nothing short of encyclopaedic. Despite being a busy politician and intellectual, he also found time to marry and start his own family. As it happens, Ibn Hazm's life can be divided into two parts. During the first period he worked as a high-profile politician and administrator who tried to restore peace and security across Spain in the face of escalating political conflict and ethnic tension. This was by far the most hectic and uncertain period of his life and he experienced both the highs and lows of public position. Exasperated by the never-ending cycle of violence and political rivalry, he finally turned his back on public life at the age of about forty, and entered a new phase where he focused all his time and energy on research and literary activities. He devoted the next thirty years of his life to the pursuit of knowledge, as well as writing books on a wide range of subjects including Islamic theology, jurisprudence, comparative religion, logic and ethics. This proved to be the most intellectually productive part of his life, for it was during this period that he authored some of his most influential works.

One such work was *Tawq al-Hamamah* (The Dove's Necklace). Consisting of both prose and poetry, in this book Ibn Hazm recorded his ideas and thoughts on the subject of love and lovers. Although this was not the first book to be written on the subject in Arabic (as similar works already existed in that language), his perceptive observations on the nature of love and human relationships made it an invaluable contribution to the genre. A gifted psychologist and observer of human behaviour, he produced accurate psychological profiles of Government officials, politicians and judges, as well as palace maids, by simply observing their behaviour and attitudes. According to Ibn Hazm, just as people often say one thing and do another, in the same way the lovers promise each other much but do not always deliver. In other words, his psychological observation of human behaviour revealed an inherent contradiction between language, thought and action. That is why he argued that dishonesty and mistrust between lovers could be detected by carefully observing their behaviour, because language masks people's thoughts and emotions. Having spent his early years almost exclusively among women in his father's palace, he developed a powerful understanding of female psychology, as is evident from the perceptive comments he made about women's behaviour and attitude in his *Tawq al-Hamamah*. Fascinated by human behaviour and psychology, he closely observed and recorded his views of different people, their behaviour and attitudes, and never ceased to revise and evaluate his understanding of moral theology and human psychology. He summed up his final thoughts on these subjects in his *Kitab al-Akhlaq wa'l Siyar* (The Book of Morality and Ethics). His *Tawq al-Hamamah* was first translated into English in 1953 by the distinguished British Arabist A.J. Arberry under the title of *The Ring of the Dove*, while his *Kitab al-Akhlaq wa'l Siyar* was not translated until 1990.

Ibn Hazm's other acclaimed works included *al-Ihkam fi Usul al-Ahkam* (Judgement on the Fundmental Legal Principles), *Kitab al-Muhalla* (The Book of Gems) and *Kitab al-Fasl fi'l Milal wa'l Ahwa wa'l Nihal* (The Decisive Treatise on Sects, Heterodoxies and Denominations). As an eminent jurist, in the first two books he analysed and evaluated the fundamental sources and principles of Islamic jurisprudence (*usul al-fiqh*). He argued that all human actions can be classified into one of the five following juridical categories: *fard* (compulsory), *mustahhab* (commended), *makruh* (disliked), *haram* (outlawed) and *halal* (permissible). His systematic analysis of Islamic legal philosophy and methodology enabled Ibn Hazm to develop a set of complex grammatical and linguistic tools, which, in turn, helped him to formulate the *zahiri* legal methodology. Though the *zahiri* legal concepts were first proposed by Dawud ibn Ali al-Isfahani back in the ninth century, it was Ibn Hazm who, for the first time, provided a comprehensive exposition of *zahiri* legal principles in his *al-Ihkam* and *al-Muhalla*. Like the *hanafi*, *maliki* and *shafi'i fuqaha*, he accepted the pre-eminence of the Qur'an and *sunnah* (the normative practices of the Prophet) but, unlike them, he adopted an ultra-literalist interpretation of these two fundamental sources of *shari'ah* (Islamic law). Thus he deliberately focused on the *zahiri* (or literal) – as opposed to the allegorical or mystical – interpretation of the scriptural sources. In addition, he rejected the validity of *qiyas* (analogical deduction), *istihsan* (personal welfare), *istislah* (collective welfare) and *ra'y* (rational opinion) as sources of Islamic law. However, he considered *ijma* (collective consensus) to be a valid source of law so long as it was the *ijma* of the Prophet's companions (*sahabah*), that is, the first generation of Muslims.

Perhaps Ibn Hazm's most influential work was his *Kitab al-Fasl*. Consisting of five bulky volumes in Arabic, this is a truly monumental work of scholarship and one of the first books to be written by a Muslim on comparative religion. After closely studying the ideas and thoughts of the early Muslim and non-Muslim philosophers and metaphysicians – and having also familiarised himself with the religious scriptures of Zoroastrianism, Judaism and Christianity, not to mention the Islamic theological discourses of the Mu'tazilites, Ash'arites and others – Ibn Hazm provided a systematic and critical analysis of all the prevailing Islamic and non-Islamic philosophical, theological and mystical thoughts. Indeed, in his *Kitab al-Fasl* he launched a ferocious intellectual assault on those philosophies, theologies and creeds he considered to be heretical and, in so doing, he attempted to debunk them one by one. As a theologian, Ibn Hazm only believed in revelation and sensory data; thus he considered the Word of God (*kalam Allah*) to be the most reliable and authoritative source of knowledge, along with human reason. Unlike some Muslim and non-Muslim philosophers, he emphasised the superiority of revelation over rationality; indeed, he considered both revelation and reason to be complementary rather than contradictory. To be fair to Ibn Hazm, he also advocated the need for promoting tolerance and understanding between the world's great religions; as such, he was not only a pioneer of comparative religion but also a champion of inter-faith debate and dialogue.

If Ibn Hazm was a great religious thinker, then he must also be considered one of medieval Europe's most prolific writers. The sheer quality and quantity of his works (consisting of more than four hundred books and treatises, that is, around eighty thousand pages in total) proves, if proof was required, that he was a scholar and writer of indefatigable energy. He achieved all this and more despite suffering from a catalogue of health problems, including irregular heartbeat, dry eyes and spleen abnormality. Far from being an intellectual recluse, he played an active part in politics and public affairs, and also served as a Minister of State for three different Spanish Muslim rulers. However, unlike al-Zahrawi, Ibn Tufayl and Ibn Rushd, his works were not translated into Latin and therefore his ideas and thoughts did not gain much currency in the West. By contrast, his works became popular in the Muslim world where they are rated very highly by students and scholars alike. Recently, European scholars have rediscovered the vast treasures of knowledge and wisdom he has bequeathed to posterity. Happily, many books and treatises are now available in various European languages on the life and thought of this great European Muslim writer and thinker. Thanks to Miguel Asin Palacios, his monumental *Kitab al-Fasl* is also available in Spanish. Ibn Hazm died in exile at the age of seventy and was buried in Niebla (located in the Spanish province of Seville). In recognition of his outstanding services to research and scholarship, in 1963 the Spanish authorities unveiled a life-size statue of this great Spanish Muslim thinker and writer.

# 69

## Nasir al-Din al-Tusi
## (b. 1201 - d. 1274)

THE THIRTEENTH CENTURY was one of the most destructive periods in Islamic history. As Abbasid political authority rapidly deteriorated, countless fiefdoms mushroomed across the Muslim world, dealing a lasting blow to Islamic political unity and solidarity. Increasingly seen a mere figurehead without any real political or military power, the Abbasid Caliph's apparent weakness made the Islamic East vulnerable to foreign attack; in fact, the fragility of the Caliph's position became all too clear when the Mongol hordes emerged from Asia and threatened to overwhelm the heartlands of Islam. Once a great seat of Islamic political, military and intellectual dominance, Baghdad now was a shadow of its former self. Thanks to the *bait al-hikmah* (House of Wisdom) of the early Abbasid era and the Nizamiyyah College of the Seljuk period, the Muslim world once led the world in intellectual and literary pursuits. But following the rapid decline of Islamic political power and military might during the thirteenth century, the glorious era of Islamic political, cultural and intellectual dominance seemed to be coming to an end. During this sad and tumultuous period in Islamic history, Nasir al-Din al-Tusi emerged to reinvigorate the Islamic intellectual world by founding one of Islamic history's most prominent institutions of higher education.

Abu Ja'far Muhammad ibn Muhammad ibn Hasan Nasir al-Din al-Tusi was born in Tus, in the Persian province of Khurasan. A contemporary of St Thomas Aquinas (the renowned Catholic theologian) and Albertus Magnus (also known as Albert the Great), who were two of the most influential figures of European scholastic thought, al-Tusi's father was a prominent religious scholar and jurist who ensured his son received a thorough education in Arabic, Persian and traditional Islamic sciences. Raised in a family where learning and education were considered to be a way of life, al-Tusi developed his thirst for knowledge and wisdom from an early age, so that the pursuit of knowledge became his main preoccupation in life. After completing his elementary education at home, he went to Nishapur to pursue advanced education in Islamic, philosophical and other sciences of the day. As a thriving centre of intellectual and commercial activity – and the home of the famous Nizamiyyah College where the influential al-Ghazali once lived and taught – Nishapur at the time attracted students from far and wide. Here he studied philosophy, mathematics and medicine under the guidance of prominent scholars like Farid al-Din al-Damad, a philosopher affiliated to the Peripatetic school of Ibn Sina; Kamal al-Din ibn Yunus, an eminent scientist and mathematician of the time, and Qutb al-Din al-Misri, who was a student of the illustrious Fakhr al-Din al-Razi and also an eminent authority on medical sciences in his own right.

Known to have been a gifted student, al-Tusi not only learned philosophy, mathematics, astronomy and other scientific subjects of his day, but also mastered the traditional Islamic sciences and received *ijaza* (or certification: the equivalent of a modern university degree) in *hadith* (Prophetic traditions) when he was barely twenty-one. Although he was a Shi'a scholar of the *ithna 'ashari* (Twelver) tradition, he was admired by both the Shi'a and Sunni populations of Nishapur on account of his vast learning and erudition. He was only in his early twenties when Khurasan was invaded by the Mongols and this forced him to seek sanctuary with the followers of the neo-Ismaili Assassin (*nizari*) sect. Founded by Hasan-i-Sabbah, this extremist religious sect became notorious for assassinating their opponents. Surrounded by the rough steppes of Central Asia, the followers of this group created a safe haven for themselves in Alamut. It was under the patronage of the *nizari* leader Nasir al-Din Abd al-Rahman that al-Tusi authored scores of books and treatises on philosophy, logic, ethics and mathematics. His acclaimed *Kitab al-Akhlaq-i-Nasiri* (The Book of Nasirean Ethics) was composed during this period and, as the title of the book indicates, it was dedicated to his patron, Nasir al-Din Abd al-Rahman.

Following the Mongol capture of Alamut in 1255, al-Tusi experienced considerable personal hardship and suffering. But, impressed by his vast learning and erudition, the Mongol ruler Hulagu appointed him his personal advisor. Al-Tusi was with the Mongol warlord when he launched his devastating attack on Baghdad, the seat of the Abbasid Caliphate, in 1258. The destruction of Baghdad, coupled with the manner in which the reigning Abbasid Caliph al-

Musta'sim was murdered, truly shocked and horrified the Muslim world. As Hulagu's personal advisor, he may have played some part in the carnage wrought in Baghdad, although it is not clear how significant that role was. According to some Shi'a sources, it was al-Tusi who urged the Mongols to attack Baghdad because he was eager to bring down the Sunni Abbasid Caliphate. But, according to other historians, this story has little credence because Hulagu, in their opinion, would have attacked Baghdad come what might. Therefore al-Tusi could not have instigated or prevented the attack on Baghdad because he was himself entirely reliant on the goodwill of the Mongol ruler. Being no more than a useful guide and advisor to Hulagu, his position within the Mongol political hierarchy was thus a limited one.

Nonetheless, the Mongol sack of Baghdad was a truly unprecedented event. From being once the home of some of the Muslim world's finest schools, colleges, libraries and hospitals, the Mongols turned Baghdad into rubble. As an eminent intellectual and writer, such mindless killing and wanton destruction must have shocked and horrified al-Tusi, who reportedly tried to prevent the destruction of the city's libraries and hospitals, but to no avail. His failure to save the city's libraries probably inspired al-Tusi to construct the Maraghah Observatory which later became one of the Islamic world's finest institutions of higher education and learning. Ironically, this was achieved thanks largely to the generous patronage of Hulagu himself. After the Observatory was completed in 1261, al-Tusi went out of his way to recruit some of the leading Muslim scholars and scientists of the day to this institution; they included Qutb al-Din al-Shirazi and Mu'ayyad al-Din al-Urdi, who taught and conducted research there. Also, this institution housed more than forty thousand books on all the sciences of the day; some of the books were most probably rescued from the ransacked libraries of Baghdad and Damascus.

As the director of the Observatory and a prominent astronomer, al-Tusi promoted research in

all aspects of science, philosophy, mathematics and religious studies. During this period he composed his *magnum opus*, the *Zij-i-Ilkhani* (Astronomical Catalogue of the Ilkhanid ruler) which he dedicated to Hulagu, his Mongol patron. In addition to this, he authored scores of treatises on philosophy, theology, ethics, mathematics and astronomy. In these works he not only revised and reformulated the ideas and thoughts of his predecessors, but also made considerable advances in arithmetic, trigonometry and geometry. Most significantly, in the field of astronomy he proposed a new theory of planetary motion which was different from the Ptolemaic theory, and which later inspired Qutb al-Din Shirazi, Ulugh Beg, Ibn al-Shatir and Copernicus to formulate their own theories of planetary motion. Although Copernicus is today considered to be the first person to have formulated the heliocentric theory, there is no doubt that the astronomical ideas and thoughts of al-Tusi and his successors profoundly influenced him, as Victor Roberts, a noted historian of science, has pointed out in his research paper *The Solar and Lunar Theory of Ibn al-Shatir* (1962).

Indeed, writing on spherical trigonometry, he pointed out in his *Kitab Shakl al-Qita* (The Book of the Quadrilateral) how trigonometry was an independent subject in its own right, separate from astronomy. With the publication of this book, he firmly established both planar and spherical trigonometry as distinct branches of mathematics, which later influenced prominent Muslim astronomers and mathematicians like Ghiyath al-Din Jamshid Mas'ud al-Kashi, who was a colleague of Ulugh Beg at the Timurid Observatory in Samarqand. Also, as an eloquent exponent of Peripatetic philosophy, al-Tusi wrote an extensive commentary on Ibn Sina's acclaimed philosophical treatise *al-Isharat wa'l Tanbihat* (The Remarks and Admonitions). Known as *Sharh al-Isharat wa'l Tanbihat* (Exegesis of Remarks and Admonitions), in this book, he defended Ibn Sina against the charges of heresy levelled at him by prominent scholars and thinkers like al-Ghazali and Fakhr al-Din al-Razi. If Ibn Rushd's refuta-

tion of al-Ghazali's philosophical polemic gained much acclaim in the Islamic West, then al-Tusi's defence of Ibn Sina was instrumental in the revival of Peripatetic philosophy in Persia.

In truth, he was very fond of Ibn Sina, so much so that he considered himself to be one of his students and disciples, although he was born nearly two centuries after Ibn Sina. In addition, he studied the works of other prominent thinkers like al-Ghazali, Fakhr al-Din al-Razi and Shihab al-Din Suhrawardi, and was profoundly influenced by them. Nevertheless, his *Sharh al-Isharat* is rated very highly by the Shi'a scholars; this is probably because it is an explanatory work, rather than an original philosophical treatise which attempts to espouse fresh ideas and thoughts. Not surprisingly, many commentaries have been written on this book by prominent Shi'a thinkers, like Jamal al-Din Hasan ibn Yusuf al-Hilli. As an adherent and exponent of Twelver Shi'ism, al-Tusi wrote prolifically on *ithna 'ashari* theology; indeed, he was one of the first to systematically formulate the fundamental tenets of Shi'a belief and practices. Of his theological works, *Tajrid al-Itiqadat* (The Definition of Fundamental Beliefs) is today widely considered to be the *summa theologica* of Twelver Shi'ism. This book became so popular in Persia that scores of influential Shi'a scholars and theologians, like Shams al-Din al-Bayhaqi, al-Hilli, Ala al-Din Qushji and al-Jurjani, wrote extensive commentaries on it.

However, as a religious scholar and jurist, al-Tusi believed that the masses should refrain from engaging in complex theological debates and discussions because, he believed, this could lead to doctrinal uncertainty and theological misunderstandings. Only those who were well-versed in the religious sciences were, in his view, qualified to engage in such debate. Instead, he urged the masses to fulfil their religious obligations and live their lives in accordance with the *shari'ah* (Islamic law), leaving the onus of interpreting and formulating the *shari'ah* to the religious scholars (*ulama*) and jurists (*fuqaha*). By contrast, his ethical views (which he expounded most eloquently in his *Kitab al-Akhlaq-i-Nasiri* and other treatises) are both complex and thought-provoking. Influenced by the works of Aristotle, al-Farabi, Ibn Miskawayh and Ibn al-Muqaffa on the one hand and the ideas and thoughts of ancient Persian and Indian philosophers and sages on the other, he developed a comprehensive and universalistic ethical philosophy. The purpose of his ethical philosophy was to nourish and cultivate people's moral and ethical qualities through the incessant pursuit of knowledge. This, he felt, would contribute to the development of good human character and personality. Keen to promote religious tolerance and cultural harmony, his ethical discourse sought to unite people of all religious and racial backgrounds on the basis of our common humanity. Athough his ethical thinking was not entirely original, it was nevertheless very ambitious and deserves much more recognition, especially in this day and age, than it has so far received.

Like al-Kindi, Abu Bakr al-Razi, Ibn Sina and Ibn Rushd before him, al-Tusi was a great thinker and encyclopaedist but, unlike them, his works did not gain much currency beyond the borders of Persia, perhaps because he wrote primarily in Persian. Author of more than one hundred books and treatises on almost all the sciences of his day, al-Tusi died at the age of seventy-three during the reign of Abaqa, the son and successor of Hulagu, and was buried in Kazimayn (located on the outskirts of Baghdad).

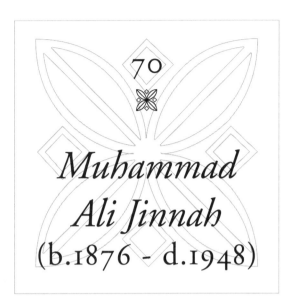

# 70

## Muhammad Ali Jinnah
## (b.1876 - d.1948)

INAUGURATED IN 1526 by Zahir al-Din Babar (Babur) and abolished by the British in 1857, the Mughal Empire was one of the foremost political dynasties to have ruled Muslim India. After more than three centuries of Mughal rule, the British arrived in India during the eighteenth century in the guise of the East India Company and began to exert its influence in that country. As Mughal political authority rapidly deteriorated, the British tightened their grip on India during the first half of the nineteenth century and assumed full military control in 1857. The establishment of British rule not only transformed the political and economic makeup of India, now its Muslim population also suddenly found themselves at the mercy of the British rulers. Being once the masters of their own destinies, they now became the subjects of a foreign power. This naturally led to widespread discontent and resentment across India, but the British imperial military apparatus suppressed all forms of dissent and rebellion. One such mass uprising took place in 1857; better known as the Indian Mutiny, it thoroughly shook the Indian consciousness and body politic, and led to the birth to the Indian liberation movement. Led initially by the Muslims and later joined by the Hindus, the purpose of this mass movement was to drive out the British from India. Under the able leadership of scores of influential Indian Muslim leaders, this movement soon gained momentum and eventually was instrumental in forcing the British to quit India. As a champion of the Indian liberation movement, a valiant fighter for the rights of Indian Muslims and the founder of Pakistan, now one of the world's most populous and powerful Muslim countries, Muhammad Ali Jinnah was undoubtedly one of the most influential Muslim political leaders of modern times.

Born in the historic Pakistani port city of Karachi, Jinnah's ancestors were originally Hindus, who hailed from the Indian province of Gujarat, but it was his grandfather who embraced Islam. His father, Jinnahbhoy Poonja, subsequently migrated from Gujarat and settled in Karachi where he became a relatively successful businessman. The modest income he generated from his business enabled him to send his young son to school, firstly in Karachi and then in Bombay (Mumbai). At the age of fifteen, while he was still at high school, Jinnah married a local girl at the behest of his parents. Thereafter, he sailed to England to study law. He arrived in London in 1892 and, although he did not like the English weather or climate, he soon settled down to his studies. Tall, slim and unusually confident, Jinnah was very intelligent; indeed, he passed all his law exams with flying colours within two years. He was then called to the Bar at the Lincoln's Inn; he was only eighteen at the time. Not known to have been a voracious reader or a studious person, Jinnah's academic achievements were nevertheless remarkable. During his stay in England he developed a passion for politics and parliamentary debates. A staunch supporter of Dadabhai Naoroji, the first Indian to be elected to the British Parliament, he assisted the latter with his election campaign. After nearly four years in England, he returned to Karachi in 1896 as a qualified barrister, only to discover that both his mother and young bride had passed away. Seeing his father struggling to make ends meet spurred the young but ambitious Jinnah to sail to Bombay to seek legal work to support his impoverished family.

For the next three years, he was forced to endure considerable personal hardship and suffering as he struggled to find suitable employment until, in 1900, he was offered the vacant post of the Presidency Magistrate of Bombay. As a result, he was able to move into a better apartment and also bring his younger sister, Fatimah, from Karachi to Bombay to pursue her further education. Jinnah's relationship with Fatimah was a very special one; his six other siblings hardly feature in his long and distinguished life, whereas Fatimah became an integral part of his life. Indeed, she not only became his foremost supporter and aide, but also stood by him like a pillar throughout his life. As a talented lawyer, Jinnah pursued his legal duties with great skill, confidence and authority. He prepared his court cases with such care and thoroughness that, after entering the courtroom, he used to move around as if the case had already been won. His confidence was disliked by his rivals, who accused him of insolence and arrogance, but Jinnah was neither arrogant nor insolent; rather he was an honest and bright lawyer who pursued his cli-

ents' cases as if they were his own. His clear and logical approach, coupled with his confident performance in court, often left his opponents spellbound. He became such a successful lawyer that his reputation soon spread in and around Bombay, which of course generated more work for him. During this period he earned around five hundred rupees a day, which was significant remuneration and allowed him to lead a comfortable lifestyle. Also, being a Muslim member of the Hindu-dominated Indian National Congress, he increasingly became involved in the political affairs of his country.

If Jinnah was a talented lawyer, then he was an equally shrewd political operator who combined his role as an advocate (working for the British elites) and his nationalistic activities with remarkable success. Keen to unite the Hindus and Muslims – and work collectively to drive out the British from India – he attended the 1906 session of the Indian National Congress in Calcutta, where he acted as secretary to Dadabhai Naoroji, who was the president of the Congress at the time. Here he was hailed as 'the best ambassador of Hindu-Muslim unity' by G. K. Gokhale, a prominent Hindu politician of the time. Jinnah's oratory skills, personal charisma and clear-thinking were also widely admired by other prominent Hindus like Sarojini Naidu, the acclaimed Indian literary figure. During this period he became a prominent defender of the rights and liberties of Indian Muslims, which made him very popular in the Muslim community. As his popularity continued to increase he was elected president of the Lucknow Muslim League in 1916, and this further increased his political standing. Under Jinnah's guidance and stewardship, the Indian National Congress and the Muslim League signed the Lucknow Pact, and India's Hindus and Muslims became united for the first time. Preoccupied with politics and his legal work, he had no time to marry again until he met young Ruttie Petit, the daughter of a successful Indian businessman. This was a classic tale of love at first sight, and they married in 1918; the atmosphere in Jinnah's Malabar Hill residence suddenly changed for the better, even if it was rather short-lived.

Hitherto Jinnah's entire political philosophy revolved around the notion of Hindu-Muslim unity and the need to liberate India from British political and military occupation. His political strategy worked well until Mahatma Gandhi left South Africa and moved to India during the 1920s. Inspired by Hindu mysticism, the latter espoused a political philosophy which was radically different from that championed by Jinnah. Couched in the language of Hinduism, Gandhi's philosophy of non-violence soon captured the imagination of his Hindu followers, even if it did not go down too well with the Muslims. As Gandhi gradually moved onto the centre stage of Indian politics under the banner of the Indian National Congress, Jinnah and the Muslim League became increasingly marginalised. To make matters worse, the ruling British elites also decided to side-step Jinnah (whom they considered to be a dangerous nationalist and a vociferous opponent of their rule) in favour of a pacifist who preached non-violence. At the same time, his personal life was devastated when his wife Ruttie suddenly died in 1929. Her death was a major blow to Jinnah, who promptly left Bombay for London where he lived with his daughter Dina and sister Fatimah. Then Liaquat Ali Khan, the future Prime Minister of Pakistan, visited him in 1934 and persuaded him to return to India to lead the Muslim League. At the time, the League was suffering from a leadership crisis following the death of prominent personalities like Hakim Ajmal Khan, Mawlana Muhammad Ali and Sir Muhammad Shafi. As a result, this powerful political body became rather impotent and ineffective. The Indian Muslims, too, were crying out for a great leader to emerge and champion their cause; Jinnah became that saviour. The Jinnah-Liaquat partnership thus became one of the most decisive alliances to be formed in modern Indian political history.

Back in India, Jinnah revitalised the Muslim League which once more became a powerful force in Indian politics. And although increasing communal tension between the Muslims and Hindus threatened to split the country, Jinnah continued to advocate the need for understanding and co-operation between the two communities. But when it became clear that the proponents of Mahasabha wanted a free and liberated India to be shaped by no other ideology than their exclusivist and increasingly fundamentalist brand of Hinduism, the Indian Muslims became alarmed; this also became a major cause of concern for Jinnah. So it was, between 1936 and 1937, that one of the major turning-points of his life took place: he exchanged several letters with Sir Muhammad Iqbal, the influential Muslim poet-philosopher of India, who urged him to take a unilateral stand and fight for the rights of the Indian Muslims. Inspired by Iqbal's visionary call for a separate homeland for the Muslims of India, Jinnah now became an indefatigable champion of Pakistan. Thus, at the age of sixty, he not only reformulated his entire political philosophy, he also completely realigned his whole outlook on life. Thereafter, the creation of a separate homeland for the Muslims of the subcontinent became his main preoccupation in life. Indeed, the decision of the Congress to declare Hindi to be the national language of a free, independent India, at the expense of other major Indian languages (such as Urdu), also prompted the Indian Muslims to demand a separate homeland for themselves. Following the passage of the Lahore Resolution in 1940 by the Indian Muslim leaders, Jinnah's quest for Pakistan moved a step closer.

After making a formal demand for the creation of a separate homeland for the Muslims of India, Jinnah travelled extensively across the country in order to mobilise support for his political project and unite the Indian Muslims under the banner of the League. During this period he eloquently expounded his vision of a new country where the Muslims of the subcontinent could live in peace and harmony. After a long and hard struggle, Jinnah's vision eventually became a reality in 1947. A year after Pakistan appeared on the world map the inspirational *quaid-i-azam* (or 'the great leader'), as he now came to be known, died at the age of seventy-two and was buried in Karachi. Though Jinnah's vision for Pakistan was both bold and powerful, death intervened before he could translate his vision into reality. A man of his word, Jinnah always meant what he said and there is no doubt that he wanted Pakistan to be a model Muslim country: independent, strong, democratic, tolerant and prosperous – all underpinned by the universal values and ethos of Islam. If Jinnah had lived for another five years, there is no doubt that he would have transformed Pakistan into a formidable political and economic power.

Unfortunately for Pakistan, his great vision remains no more than a vision as successive Pakistani leaders failed to translate his vision into reality. Pakistan may be a great military power (it is the only Muslim country to have developed nuclear weapons' capability), but its economy is in tatters. Likewise, more than forty per cent of Pakistanis are illiterate and the vast majority continue to live in abject poverty. In short, today's Pakistan is not the kind of Pakistan Jinnah had in mind; thus the brave and visionary Jinnah must be figuratively turning in his grave. Having said that, his vision for Pakistan is not dead; it is still alive and will continue to endure as long as Pakistan exists. As such, it is not beyond the realm of possibility that a Jinnah-like leader may yet emerge in the future and realise his vision. If this were to happen, then his influence and legacy would no doubt become more widely recognised around the globe.

# 71

# Fakhr al-Din al-Razi
# (b. 1149 - d. 1209)

UNDER THE PATRONAGE of Abbasid Caliph Harun al-Rashid and his son al-Ma'mun, ancient Greek scientific, philosophical and medical works were translated into Arabic for the first time during the eighth and early part of the ninth century. At the time Baghdad, the capital of the Abbasid Caliphate, became such a prominent centre of intellectual and literary activity that students and scholars from across the Muslim world flocked to the city to study and conduct research in the Islamic sciences, philosophy, medicine, mathematics and other subjects, under the guidance of its leading scholars. The intrusion of Greek philosophy into the Muslim world created a huge religious controversy between the Islamic traditionalists on the one hand, and the Neoplatonists on the other. Inspired by influential Islamic scholars like Ahmad ibn Hanbal, the traditionalists launched a blistering attack on the Neoplatonic ideas of the early Muslim philosophers – thus leading to a clash of worldviews which has continued to reverberate down the centuries. After al-Ash'ari's stinging critique of philosophical rationalism (Mu'tazilism) during the early part of the tenth century, al-Ghazali emerged in the eleventh century to defend, like his illustrious predecessor, the cause of Islamic traditional-

ism. And in so doing, he struck a powerful blow against the Neoplatonic theories of al-Kindi, Abu Bakr al-Razi, al-Farabi and Ibn Sina. His critique of Neoplatonism paved the way for the emergence of Fakhr al-Din al-Razi, who became one of the most celebrated Islamic theologians of the twelfth century. Along with al-Ash'ari and al-Ghazali, he is today considered to be one of the most influential Muslim theologians of all time.

Abu Abdullah Muhammad ibn Umar ibn Hussain, better known as Fakhr al-Din al-Razi, was born in the northern Persian city of Rayy (located close to modern Tehran) into a distinguished family of Islamic scholars and jurists. His father, Diya al-Din Umar, was widely respected across Rayy for his vast knowledge of Islam, and was also a popular *khatib* (preacher) at his local mosque, where he regularly led Friday congregational prayers (*salat al-jumu'ah*). Taught by his learned father, young al-Razi studied Arabic, Persian, the Qur'an and aspects of *hadith* (Prophetic traditions) and *fiqh* (Islamic jurisprudence) at home. After completing his early education, he pursued higher education in speculative theology (*ilm al-kalam*), philosophy (*falsafah*) and aspects of natural sciences and medicine under the tutelage of eminent scholars like Kamal al-Din

Simnani, Majd al-Din al-Jili and Muhammad al-Baghawi among others. Like his father, al-Razi was an adherent of Ash'arite theology, but in legal matters he considered himself to be a follower of *shafi'i fiqh*. He was blessed with a sharp intellect and an equally powerful memory, and was known to have been an insatiable seeker of knowledge and wisdom. Keen to learn more, he left his native Rayy and moved to Maraghah (in present-day Azerbaijan) to study the philosophical sciences of the day under the guidance of Majd al-Din al-Jili. As an eminent authority on philosophy and a tutor of Shihab al-Din al-Suhrawardi, the renowned *ishraqi* philosopher and mystic, al-Jili exercised a profound influence on al-Razi's philosophical ideas and thoughts.

He was brought up and educated at a time when Neoplatonic thought – as espoused by al-Farabi and Ibn Sina – was being increasingly subjected to scrutiny and reassessment by the traditional Muslim intelligentsia. Inspired no doubt by al-Ghazali's criticism of Neoplatonic thought, al-Razi too developed a sceptical attitude towards philosophy. He became familiar with al-Ghazali's religious ideas, philosophical thoughts and intellectual worldview through al-Jili whose own teacher, in turn, had been a student of al-Ghazali. Though al-Razi developed considerable doubts and scepticism about Neoplatonic thought, unlike al-Ghazali he adopted a more moderate approach to philosophy than one of repudiation and wholesale rejection. Indeed, by the time he had moved to Khwarizm (located in modern Uzbekistan), he was widely recognised as a master of traditional Islamic sciences, speculative theology and philosophy, in addition to being familiar with mathematics, medicine and the natural sciences. As it happens, his mastery of apeculative theology and philosophy was such that he went to Khwarizm for the sole purpose of refuting the ideas and thoughts of the Mu'tazilite rationalists who had become very active in that part of the world after being kicked out of Baghdad by the traditionalists.

Indeed, after the success of the traditionalist revolt against the Mu'tazilite creed during the middle of the ninth century, the chief exponents and supporters of this creed were demoted and banished from the highest echelons of the Abbasid administration by the traditionally-minded Caliph Mutawakkil ala Allah. The Caliph's anti-Mu'tazilite policies forced the adherents of Mu'tazilism to flee from Baghdad and regroup in and around Khwarizm. Determined to take the fight directly to the Mu'tazilites, al-Razi (who was an ambitious young theologian and philosopher) moved to that region in order to engage the prominent Mu'tazilite thinkers in philosophical and theological debate and discussion. Thanks to his polished debating skills and vast learning, he successfully repudiated and exposed the inconsistencies inherent in Mu'tazilite ideas and thought. Unable to respond to his criticism, his Mu'tazilite opponents soon wanted him out of Khwarizm. To this end, they instigated a popular revolt against al-Razi which forced him to leave the region. From Khwarizm, he proceeded to Bukhara and from there he went to Samarqand, and eventually returned to his native Rayy. But it was not long before he set out again, this time in the direction of Transoxiana, and travelled as far as the Indian territories of Punjab and Multan. His excursions in India were facilitated by the Ghurid ruler, Ghiyath al-Din, and his brother, Shihab al-Din, who were the descendants of Ala al-Din, the founder of the Ghurid Kingdom which in its heyday extended all the way from the shores of the Caspian Sea to the inner frontiers of India. The Ghurids were once the vassals of the Ghaznavids and the Seljuks, but later they carved out an independent kingdom of their own under the leadership of Ala al-Din. Impressed by the scope and breadth of al-Razi's learning, the Ghurid ruler offered him a well-paid and high-powered Governmental post, which of course alleviated his personal and financial difficulties. However, intense jealousy and incessant rivalry between the Government officials, coupled with rumours of political plots and intrigues, soon forced him to quit his job and move to Ghazna in 1185. There he lectured on traditional Islamic sciences and philosophy for a while before finally settling in Herat. Here the local ruler constructed a religious seminary for al-Razi and he began to teach Islamic sciences. When his name began to spread in and around Herat, students flocked from far and wide to listen to his illuminating lectures on the Qur'an, *hadith*, *fiqh*, *kalam* and *falsafah*.

As an outspoken exponent of Islam, al-Razi never shied away from religious or philosophical controversies; rather he became a champion of traditional Islam and never hesitated to attack those he considered to be heretical or misguided in their approach to Islamic beliefs and practices. His criticisms were robust and incisive and, more often than not, his opponents felt the impact of his intellectual onslaught. The Karramiyyah were one such group who became so incensed by his stinging critique of their beliefs and practices that they even attempted to assassinate him in 1189, but the indomitable al-Razi remained as firm as ever. Like al-Ash'ari and al-Ghazali, he was not only an outstanding intellectual, he was also an indefatigable champion of Islamic orthodoxy. And, not unlike his two illustrious predecessors, he possessed a powerful literary talent which he utilised probably better than any other scholar of his generation. Author of more than one hundred books and treatises on all the sciences of his time (including Islamic sciences, philosophy, medicine and mathematics), al-Razi was a truly gifted scholar and polymath. Although he wrote prolifically on a wide range of subjects, it was his theological and philosophical contributions which made him popular across the Muslim world. His most famous theological works include *al-Muhassal* (The Acquisition), *al-Arba'in fi Usul al-Din* (Forty Questions on Religious Principles) and *Mafatih al-Ghaib* (The Keys to the Unseen). Influenced by *imam al-haramayn* Abul Ma'ali Abd al-Malik al-Juwayni and al-Ghazali, in these and other books he provided a systematic exposition of Ash'arite theology. His *Mafatih al-Ghaib*, better known as *Tafsir al-Kabir* (The Exhaustive Commentary), is not only an outstanding Qur'anic exegesis, but also a voluminous encyclopaedia of Islamic sci-

ences. A lifelong student of the Qur'an, al-Razi thoroughly researched the *tafsir* literature before he sat down to write this monumental commentary on the Qur'an. Any learned scholar will not be able to help but appreciate the author's vast erudition and sheer breadth of learning after only a quick browse through this commentary.

Likewise, his major philosophical contributions include *al-Mabahith al-Mashriqiyyah* (Oriental Investigations), a voluminous treatise on philosophical sciences, as well as commentaries on Ibn Sina's *al-Isharat wa'l Tanbihat* (The Remarks and Admonitions) and *Uyun al-Hikmah* (The Sources of Wisdom). In these books, al-Razi critically analysed and reviewed the philosophical thoughts of the Muslim Neoplatonists from the perspective of traditional Islam. Unlike al-Ghazali, he was not an opponent of philosophical sciences; rather he was only critical of certain aspects of Neoplatonic thought. His philosophical writings therefore represented a powerful synthesis between Peripatetic (*mashsha'iyyah*) philosophy (*falsafah*) and speculative theology (*ilm al-kalam*). His successful reconciliation and harmonisation of these two strands of thought was, by any assessment, a truly remarkable achievement considering that the conflict between these two intellectual traditions had been raging in the Muslim world for many centuries – clashing most spectacularly in the philosophical and theological discourse of al-Ghazali in the eleventh century. Thus, in his *al-Matalib al-Aliya min al-Ilm al-Ilahi* (Noble Pursuits of the Science of Divinity), he developed a syncretic approach to Islamic theology by combining the methods of the *falasifah* (philosophers) with the logic of the *mutakallimun* (speculative theologians), and in so doing he developed his own theological views. This also enabled him to reconcile the thoughts of the philosophers with those of the theologians. In addition to this, al-Razi wrote prolifically on *hadith* literature, Islamic jurisprudence, comparative religion and aspects of history, mathematics and the natural sciences. As such, his *Jami al-Ulum* (The Encyclopaedia of Sciences) was a vast compendium of traditional

Islamic sciences wherein he dealt with all aspects of Islamic teachings and practices in a general, but comprehensive, manner.

Al-Razi was not only an outstanding theologian, philosopher and Islamic scholar, he was also a devout Muslim who regularly performed *nafl* (optional) prayers and observed voluntary fasts when, of course, he was not too busy reading and writing. After dedicating his entire life to the pursuit of knowledge and wisdom – and having also gained widespread recognition for his vast learning and scholarship – towards the end of his life he completely renounced the rationalistic methods of the philosophers and devoted all his time and energy to the study of the Qur'an. Nevertheless, his religious ideas and thoughts exerted considerable influence on many renowned Muslim scholars and thinkers, such as Nasir al-Din al-Tusi and his students. Indeed, his influence can even be detected in the works of such prominent modern-day Muslim scholars as Muhammad Abduh, Muhammad al-Tahir ibn al-Ashur, Abdullah Yusuf Ali and Muhammad Asad among others. But it is his *Tafsir al-Kabir*, that famous and encyclopaedic commentary on the Qur'an, which has immortalised his name. In order to acquire a thorough understanding of the Qur'an and delve deeper into the multi-layered meaning of the Divine message, all serious students and scholars of Islam will continue to consult this massive commentary for a long time to come. Al-Razi died at the age of fifty-eight and was buried in Herat (located in present-day Afghanistan).

# 72

## Abd al-Aziz ibn Saud
## (b.1880 - d.1953)

MUHAMMAD IBN SAUD, the charismatic founder of the Saudi dynasty (also known as the House of Saud), was born around 1703. After succeeding his father as the ruler of the oasis principality of Diriyyah at the age of forty, he formed an alliance with Muhammad ibn Abd al-Wahhab, the renowned Islamic scholar and reformer of Arabia, in 1744 and thereby laid the foundations of the modern Saudi State. A supporter of traditional Islam, Muhammad ibn Saud's pact with Ibn Abd al-Wahhab stipulated that Islam was to be the ideological basis of the new State, thereby providing him with the religious justification for his rule. Of the same age and having a similar understanding and approach to Islam, the two Muhammads thus joined together to create a formidable politico-religious alliance in Arabia. To further strengthen their relationship, Muhammad ibn Saud married Ibn Abd al-Wahhab's daughter in 1744 and this brought the two families even closer, as they came to share the political and religious leadership of the country. The first Saudi State was established around 1744 and it endured until it was destroyed in 1818 by the forces of Muhammad Ali Pasha, the powerful Ottoman viceroy of Egypt. Modelled on the first Saudi State, another politico-religious

order then emerged in Arabia in 1824, but incessant internal strife and political rivalry led to its disintegration in 1891. However, the credit for laying the foundations of the Kingdom of Saudi Arabia, the modern Saudi State, must go to Abd al-Aziz ibn Saud, who was undoubtedly one of the most charismatic and influential Arab leaders of modern times.

Abd al-Aziz ibn Abd al-Rahman ibn Faisal al-Saud, known as Ibn Saud for short, was born in Riyadh, the capital of modern Saudi Arabia, but he spent his early years in Kuwait. After Abd al-Rahman ibn Faisal, the father of Ibn Saud, competed with his three brothers over the right to political succession, his family became divided and this strengthened the hands of their opponents. Exasperated by his battles with his brothers, Abd al-Rahman ibn Faisal was eventually forced to leave Arabia in 1891 after Riyadh was captured by Muhammad ibn Rashid, the ruler of Najd and a political rival of the al-Saud family. During his exile in Kuwait, however, he maintained close contact with his supporters back home, hoping one day to return to his native Riyadh in triumph. Young Ibn Saud therefore grew up in Kuwait, living among the bedouins and learning the art of surviving in the dry and harsh environment of the desert. According to the custom of the day, he studied the Qur'an and aspects of religious sciences during his early years and thus became familiar with the basic principles and practices of Islam. He then received training in all aspects of desert warfare and soon became an expert in launching military raids. Tall, handsome and charismatic, Ibn Saud also became a shrewd political strategist and an accomplished military general. Indeed, having spent his early years living in the desert with the bedouins made him very tough, resilient and skilful. Moreover, his years of training in military strategy and desert warfare equipped him with much-needed skills and experience to organise and launch the military expeditions to reclaim his ancestral homeland from his rivals. From exile in Kuwait, he and his family thus waited patiently for the right moment to strike against their rivals in Arabia.

Although the British had established their political and economic influence across much of Arabia long before the twentieth century, their politico-economic hegemony of the region came under direct threat from other leading European powers (including France and Germany) at the beginning of the twentieth century. Even after Kuwait became a British protectorate in 1899, they struggled to protect their political and economic interests in the region from German and French encroachment. Keen to maintain their regional interests, during this period the British fought vigorously against their European rivals in order to keep them out of the Middle East. While the Europeans were busy competing with one another to increase their influence across the Arabian Peninsula, Ibn Saud's ancestral home remained firmly in the grip of the Rashidi rulers who at the time were actively supported by the Ottomans. Following the death of the charismatic Rashidi ruler Muhammad ibn Abdullah in 1897, Riyadh was rocked by both political upheaval and social uprisings. The situation deteriorated further as his successor, Abd al-Aziz ibn Mitaab, ruthlessly suppressed the uprising. As expected, his heavy-handed policy created much anger

and resentment leading to the locals engaging in insurgency activities against the ruling elites, which, in turn, led to more political chaos and anarchy in Arabia. Despite the volatile situation at home, the new Rashidi ruler – supported by the Ottomans – launched an unprovoked attack on Kuwait, which was still then a British protectorate, in 1900. But thanks to the British, the Rashidi ruler's attempt to annex Kuwait failed miserably. Indeed, Ibn Mitaab's attack on Kuwait backfired in a spectacular fashion, as Shaykh al-Mubarak al-Saba, the ruler of Kuwait, and Abd al-Rahman ibn Faisal, the father of Ibn Saud, now united to fight and drive out the Rashidis from Arabia. Leading a ten thousand strong force, the two men attacked the Rashidi forces with great success. During this period the twenty-two year old Ibn Saud spearheaded the attack on Riyadh, his native city.

He left Kuwait with his brother, Muhammad, along with a band of around forty determined fighters and quickly reached the outskirts of Riyadh where they camped under the cover of darkness. Accompanied by ten trustworthy supporters, he then entered Riyadh during the night and launched a surprise attack on the forces of the local governor. In the ensuing battle, the city's governor was slain by Abdullah ibn Jelawi, Ibn Saud's cousin, and they inflicted a crushing defeat on their enemy. The fall of Riyadh marked the beginning of the end for the Rashidis, as the House of Saud swiftly reasserted its authority across the country under the able stewardship of Ibn Saud and his father. The capture of Riyadh by young Ibn Saud bolstered his reputation as an able political strategist and military commander; it also won him much-deserved plaudits from both his family members and the people. Thereafter, he urged the local clerics and the people of Riyadh to pledge allegiance to his father, Abd al-Rahman ibn Faisal, as their new sovereign; the people responded to his call and pledged their allegaince to him. Later, Ibn Saud's popularity and standing with the masses prompted his father to abdicate in favour of his son, who accordingly became the King.

With Riyadh now firmly in his grip, Ibn Saud was eager to extend his rule across the rest of Arabia, but he knew that would not be an easy task given that the Rashidis were in full control in Najd. Thus, he decided to strengthen his political position and authority by entering into a series of strategic alliances through marriage. In fiercely tribal and polygamous societies, political rulers and religious scholars often extended their social ties and consolidated their political power and position in society through multiple marriages. Early twentieth century Arabia was no different in this respect, and Ibn Saud understood this better than anyone else. Thus, over the next five decades, he married more than a dozen times, fathering around forty sons and fifty daughters. Even in a society where multiple marriages were very common, his proclivity and indulgence surprised his friends and family alike. But, as a clever politician, he knew that forming alliances through multiple marriages not only helped to extend his family ties, it also strengthened his political powerbase. By the same token, he was aware that having a large family alone did not guarantee success on the battlefield. To win in the theatre of war, he had to create a strong, unified and disciplined army. Accordingly, in 1912, he established a special fighting force which came to be known as the *ikhwan* (or the 'Brotherhood'). The members of this force were loyal supporters of the House of Saud and strict adherents of Islam as interpreted by Muhammad ibn Abd al-Wahhab.

With the support of the *ikhwan* troops, Ibn Saud first conquered the wealthy region of Hasa (situated on the coast of the Persian Gulf) and then went onto smash the Rashidis of Najd in 1921. Five years later, he ousted the Hashimites from the Hijaz, thus extending his rule and authority over the holy cities of Makkah and Madinah which brought him much-needed revenue for his fledgling administration from the visiting pilgrims. After concluding his military campaigns, Ibn Saud struggled to control his over-zealous *ikhwan* troops who wanted to pursue perpetual *jihad* (military struggle) against their enemies. Not keen on pursuing endless military conquests, he swiftly disbanded the *ikhwan* and focused his full attention on improving the economic fortunes of his new kingdom. If founding the new Saudi State was a hard struggle, then ruling and administering the affairs of the State proved to be even more challenging for Ibn Saud – especially because some of the territories he conquered had no proper political or administrative structures in place at all. In response, he established a Council of Ministers to oversee the affairs of the State, and appointed close members of his family to key positions within the Government. Thus his two eldest sons, Saud and Faisal, were offered high-ranking Government posts in the province of Najd and Hijaz. Despite being heavily in debt – and unable to obtain external financial assistance – he nevertheless established a Ministry of Finance and attempted to tackle the kingdom's financial problems. During this period he also enforced the *shari'ah* (Islamic law) across the State and in due course this became the supreme law of the land.

Then, in 1930, Ibn Saud established a Ministry of Foreign Affairs and appointed his second son, Faisal, as Foreign Minister and he played a key role in establishing diplomatic relations with some of the world's leading powers, including the United States of America. Two years later, the formation of the Kingdom of Saudi Arabia was officially announced. This was followed, in the mid-1930s, by the discovery of the world's largest oil reserves beneath the barren deserts of Arabia, something which completely transformed the political and economic fortunes of Saudi Arabia and instantly catapulted the Saudi Kingdom onto the global stage. Then, by the 1940s, Saudi Arabia's diplomatic relations with the powerful industrial Western nations (especially the United States) was formalised. Keen to export the vast quantities of oil which lay beneath the Saudi deserts, Ibn Saud agreed to supply the United States with oil in order to accelerate the industrialisation of the American economy. The special US-

Saudi relationship was formalised by Ibn Saud and President Roosevelt during their meeting onboard the US naval ship USS Quincy in 1945. This relationship was further strengthened after the Second World War when the demand for oil increased phenomenally. It was also during this period that the United States became Saudi Arabia's most powerful political and economic ally. Thanks to the new petrodollars, the once backward and poverty-stricken desert kingdom suddenly became one of the world's most prosperous countries. The credit for Saudi Arabia's transformation must go to Ibn Saud, who fought single-handedly for a quarter of a century to unify the warring Arab tribes and established a State which is today considered to be one of the world's most affluent and influential countries.

Ibn Saud, the founder of the Kingdom of Saudi Arabia, eventually died at the age of seventy-three and was buried in his native Riyadh. He was succeeded by his eldest son, Saud, who ruled the kingdom for eleven years before abdicating in favour of his younger brother, Faisal. Like his father, Faisal was a wise and able ruler, but he was assassinated in 1975. Khalid, Ibn Saud's fourth son, then ascended the Saudi throne and ruled for seven years until his death in 1982. He was succeeded by Fahd who ruled the kingdom until his death in 2005. Abdullah, his half-brother, then succeeded him as King.

# 73

## Mustafa Kemal Ataturk
## (b.1881 - d.1938)

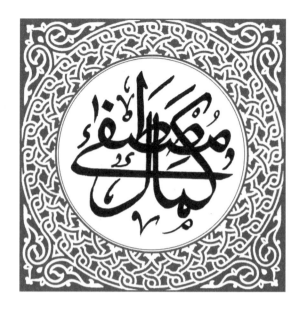

AT ITS ZENITH in the sixteenth century, the Ottoman Empire was one of the great political and military powers of the time. From the gates of Vienna in Europe to Yemen in the Arabian Peninsula, and from North Africa at one end to Persia at the other, the Ottomans reigned supreme in Europe, Asia and Africa. During this period influential Ottoman rulers like Muhammad (Fatih) II and Sulaiman the Magnificient expanded the frontiers of their empire, and promoted the arts, science and architecture throughout their dominion. And in so doing they radically transformed the fortunes of the Ottoman Empire. Once a great political, economic and cultural power, the Ottomans nevertheless began to decline irreversibly during the seventeenth century. But while the visible signs of decline and decadance became clear for all to see, the wayward Ottoman rulers underestimated the gravity of the situation which confronted them. As the Ottoman Empire declined, the leading European powers began to flex their muscles. Faced with both internal decay, and direct external threats from their European rivals, the Ottomans were no longer in a position to hold their ground; indeed, by the nineteenth century the whole empire was now on the verge of total collapse. At

this critical moment in Ottoman history, Mustafa Kemal, the founding father of modern Turkey and one of the most influential political leaders of modern times, emerged to save his motherland from total humiliation at the hands of its European rivals.

Better known by his honorific title *ataturk* (or 'father Turk'), Mustafa Kemal was born in Salonica into a lower middle class Muslim family. His father, Ali Riza, was a junior civil servant who later became a relatively successful timber merchant. During his early years Mustafa was enrolled at a Qur'anic school by his devout mother but he soon dropped out after being punished by his teacher, and instead he joined a Government-funded military school. Despite being brought up in a family where Islamic learning and education was highly valued, young Mustafa pursued a largely secular education. As a bright and confident student, he aspired to become a military officer rather than a religious instructor, as his mother wanted him to be. Following the death of his father, the burden of looking after the family fell on the shoulders of his young mother but, being deeply religious, she encouraged her son to continue his studies. At the local military preparatory school, his teacher (who was also called

Mustafa) added the word 'Kemal' to his name to distinguish the pupil from the teacher. Hereafter he became known as Mustafa Kemal. As a diligent student, he excelled at school (especially in mathematics) and graduated in 1898. He then enrolled at the War College in Istanbul at the age of eighteen.

At the War College, he worked very hard and combined his military education with nationalistic activities. He completed his studies at the age of the twenty-one and was offered a place at the elite Staff College, where some of the country's brightest and most gifted students received advanced training in military tactics and strategy. Here at the Staff College, Mustafa and his associates became increasingly concerned by the internal problems which confronted Ottoman Turkish society at the time, not to mention the external threats it faced from the encroaching European powers. Four years after completing his military training at the Staff College, he witnessed a mass uprising against the rule of Sultan Abd al-Hamid II, which culminated in the revolution of the Young Turks in 1908 under the leadership of Major Enver Pasha. Led by a group of military officers, the Young Turks advocated the need for urgent political reform – from an autocratic political system to a parliamentary system of Government – so that political power could be exercised more efficiently and effectively, taking into consideration the external challenges which confronted the Ottoman State at the time. Although the Young Turks' political aims and objectives were very pertinent and commendable, their understanding of both the internal and external challenges which confronted the Ottoman State was far too simplistic; they seriously underestimated the external threats the country faced at the time. This state of affairs angered and annoyed Mustafa who was then a member of the General Staff of the Officers' School in Salonica – so much so that he became very critical of the Young Turks' domestic and foreign policies. In truth, he felt the Young Turks were merely tinkering with the status quo rather than instigating bold and courageous political reforms in order to stop the rot. Also, their close political and economic ties with Germany filled him with anger; as a proud Turk, he wanted the Ottomans to stand on their own two feet and set their house in order by themselves, without any foreign interference.

The Sultan's and the Young Turks' failure to instigate radical reforms prompted Mustafa to espouse his own ideas and thoughts on how to save the Ottoman State from total collapse. Then, in 1911, the Italians launched a surprise military attack against the Ottoman province of Tripoli and Cyrenaica. Keen to defend his country, Mustafa took part in the campaign against the Italians, but unfavourable circumstances led to the Ottomans being forced to cede Libya to the Italians. As the Ottoman State faced serious external threats from prominent European nations, Major Enver Pasha invited the German army to come and help reorganise the Ottoman forces. Mustafa did not like this decision at all; he felt the Ottomans could do it without any foreign interference in their internal affairs. To make matters worse, in 1914 the Ottomans entered the First World War on the side of Germany. This decision shocked and horrified Mustafa. As a gifted military strategist, he considered this decision to be fundamentally flawed and predicted that it would have huge repercussions for the Ottoman State. As it transpired, immediately after the war the victorious European powers divided the Ottoman territories amongst themselves. During this critical time in Ottoman history, brave Mustafa fought vigorously to defend the Ottoman territories. After returning to Istanbul from the Arab front, he was shocked to discover how the British, Italian and French troops – after smashing all Ottoman resistance – had forced the Young Turks to flee, before they marched into the Ottoman capital.

To add insult to injury, the Allies then decided to reward the Greeks, Turkey's bitter rivals, for entering the war on their side by handing over to them the city of Smyrna (present-day Izmir). When Mustafa was informed about this decision, he could no longer contain his rage. He was not prepared to allow the Greeks, their former subjects, to exercise power and authority over an Ottoman territory. This would be nothing short of a disgrace and humiliation for the Turks. The proud Turks, he argued, could never accept such a proposition, let alone live under Greek rule. Not surprisingly, when the Greek troops landed in Smyrna, he ignored the Ottoman Government and mobilised a resistance force to fight the Greeks. Having already acquired a reputation as an able military commander and strategist in 1915, (when he successfully defended the Gallipoli Peninsula against the British, and was rightly hailed by the Ottoman military for his heroic deeds at the time), the challenge now presented by the Greeks in Smyrna was a totally different proposition altogether. But the Turks in general, and Mustafa in particular, were determined to resist the Greek occupation. An electrifying orator and great motivator of people, he toured the local towns and villages and urged the masses to join his resistance movement. According to Mustafa, the purpose of this mass movement was to preserve Ottoman territorial integrity and re-establish an independent central Government in order to reassert national sovereignty and pride. When he asked the Government in Istanbul to support his campaign, the authorities not only dismissed his suggestions, but also demanded that he return to Istanbul forthwith. He refused to do so. Instead he temporarily swapped his military uniform for civilian clothes, and organised a secret conference at his base in the Kurdish province of Sivas. Here all the delegates, who arrived under the cover of darkness, unanimously voted to form a rival Government under Mustafa's leadership.

This not only marked the beginning of the end for the puppet Government in Istanbul, it also signalled Mustafa's emergence as a champion of the Turkish liberation movement. After his election as head of a rival Government, he cut off Istanbul from the rest of the country. This instantly isolated the incumbent Government in Istanbul and forced Sultan Muhammad VI to sack his premier and order fresh elections in which Mustafa's supporters won a majority. The European powers, who had established their hegemony across the Ottoman territories, were very alarmed and they began to closely monitor events as they unfolded in Istanbul. Exasperated by the central Government's inability to restore peace and order, the British army eventually marched into Istanbul in 1920. The capital of the Ottoman State thus came under direct British military occupation. A month later, Mustafa convened the first Grand National Assembly of Turkey in Ankara, where the delegates elected him as their President. In reality, he was only a president in name, for he had no political power, money or external support. Indeed, the Allies considered him and his supporters to be no more than rebels who deserved to be captured and punished in an exemplary manner. But their failure to subdue the nationalistic fervour which now swept through Turkey eventually forced the Allies to convene an urgent meeting in Paris to agree the terms and conditions of their withdrawal from Turkey. It was during this meeting that the Greeks were given the green light to invade Smyrna. The Greek invasion of this city further strengthened Mustafa's position and authority as a political leader and military commander. If the successful defence of the Gallipoli Peninsula enhanced his military standing, then Mustafa's remarkable feat against the Greeks instantly turned him into a national hero.

At the decisive battle of Sakarya, in 1921, a force of more than two hundred thousand ill-prepared and ill-equipped Turkish forces inflicted a crushing defeat on a quarter-of-a-million-strong Greek army. Under Mustafa's able leadership, the Turks not only hammered their Greek enemies, they also forced them to flee from Smyrna – leaving all their guns and weaponry behind. Victory on the battlefield consolidated his position as the pre-eminent leader of the Turkish people. The one-time Ottoman rebel now became the saviour of the Turkish motherland. After the Turkish liberation of Smyrna from the Greeks, Mustafa demanded that the Allies withdraw from Istanbul and eastern Thrace forthwith. Thanks to his bravery and foresight, Turkey was not only saved from being dismembered by the Europeans, his actions also prevented the destruction of six hundred years of Ottoman legacy, of which the Turks are very proud today. As the leader of a free and independent Turkey, Mustafa initiated wide-ranging political, economic and cultural reforms in the country. He abolished the Ottoman Caliphate; transferred all political power to himself (the President of the Turkish Republic), and sent Abd al-Majid, the last Ottoman Caliph, into exile to Switzerland in 1924. A secular Turkish Republic thus appeared on the world map.

Influenced by the ideas and thoughts of European Enlightenment thinkers, like Voltaire and Rousseau, Mustafa wanted Turkey to be a modern, secular country like the other European nations. Unable to reconcile Turkey's historical and cultural links to Islam with his aspirations to create a modern and secular nation, he instigated wholesale political and cultural reform in order to advance his blurred and controversial vision of the future. He abolished the Turkish traditional attire, including the fez; replaced the Islamic *hijri* calendar with the Gregorian one; banned polygamy and the Islamic veil (*hijab*), and introduced the Latin script across Turkey. He also advocated equality between the sexes but failed to practise it himself. And although he was brought up and educated in a devout Muslim family, he developed an indifferent attitude towards organised religion and on more than one occasion showed his dislike of religious symbols and practices. Nevertheless, it is not possible to say categorically whether he ceased to be a Muslim, especially because he was very sympathetic towards Muslim nationalistic causes, providing, for instance, political refuge for the Sanusi Islamic leader who at the time was being pursued by the Italians. Yet, Mustafa's failure to accommodate Islam within his political and cultural framework left a huge question mark over his entire westernisation and modernisation programme in Turkey. He was of course right to carry out the necessary socio-political reforms in order to alleviate mass poverty and illiteracy in Turkey, but his indiscriminate cultural reforms

alienated his people whose attachment and loyalty to Islam he and his successors clearly underestimated – and continue to do so to this day. In other words, although Mustafa's remarkable contribution to the Turkish war of liberation is acknowledged by all, his indifferent attitude to religion and indiscriminate cultural reforms has today made him a controversial figure, both within Turkey and across the Muslim world. Yet however he is assessed today, no-one can deny that he was one of the twentieth century's most influential political leaders, particularly for his impact on the development of the modern nation-state in the Muslim world. Ataturk's model of authoritarian secularism was emulated by others like Reza Shah Pahlavi of Iran (r. 1926-1941).

So far as the future of contemporary Turkey is concerned, there is no reason why Turkey cannot be a part of modern Europe, as Mustafa wanted it to be, but Turkey must first come to terms with its own historical and cultural self. Having been an Islamic superpower for six centuries, it cannot suddenly pretend to be an integral part of a secular and humanistic Europe. Rather it needs to reconcile its political, economic and cultural debt to Islam with its future hopes and aspirations to be an integral part of the European Union. If it can achieve this balancing act, then Turkey can play an important strategic role in a constantly evolving geo-political global order. A strong, tolerant, prosperous and Islamic Turkey can also play a pivotal role in bridging the gap between the Islamic world and the West. This may not be what Mustafa wanted, but today we live in a completely different world, one that is dominated by information technology, regional politics, economic interdependence, cultural exchange, and international discourse and dialogue. Modern Turkey – founded and shaped by Mustafa – has the potential to become a major global power if it can reconcile its past with its present and thereby shape a bright future for itself. Being a heavy drinker, Mustafa Kemal Ataturk died of cirrhosis of the liver inside the Dolmababce Palace at the age of fifty-eight and was buried in Ankara, the capital of modern Turkey.

# 74

## Firdawsi of Persia
### (b.940 - d.1020)

THE PERSIAN PEOPLE have played a central role in the development of Islam as a religion, culture and civilisation. During the early days of Islam one of the close companions of the Prophet was Salman al-Farisi, who was of Persian origin. But it was after the Muslim conquest of Persia during the reign of Caliph Umar, that the Persians embraced the new faith in great numbers. Proud of their glorious past and ancient Persian language, known as *zaban-i farsi*, the people of Persia refused to abandon their culture and traditions in favour of those of their new conquerors. Thus the Persian language survived the Muslim conquest of Persia and, over time, it became the most important medium of Islamic learning and scholarship after Arabic, the language of the Qur'an and the Prophet. Indeed, the Persians have contributed more to the emergence of Islamic thought and culture than probably any other people. And this is most evident from the fact that some of the Muslim world's greatest scholars, thinkers and scientists (like Abu Hanifah, al-Tabari, al-Baladhuri, al-Bukhari, Ibn Sina, al-Biruni, al-Ghazali, al-Zamakhshari, Fakhr al-Din al-Razi and Nasir al-Din al-Tusi) were all Persians. Their vast contribution to the development of Islamic thought and culture is in

itself a testament to the greatness and versatility of the Persian mind. And more than any other people, the Persians have produced some of history's most gifted poets and literary figures. If the Arabs produced al-Mutanabbi, the Greeks produced Homer and the Indians produced the Rig-Vedic poets, then the Persians graced the Muslim world with some of its most celebrated poets, including Hafiz of Shiraz, Sana'i, Umar Khayyam, Jalal al-Din Rumi, Farid al-Din Attar and Abd al-Rahman Jami. Considered to be the *doyen* of Muslim poets, Firdawsi was not only a man of incomparable poetic genius; he was also one of the greatest epic poets of all time.

Hasan ibn Ishaq ibn Sharaf, also known as Abul Qasim Mansur Firdawsi, was born in the ancient Persian city of Tus (located in the historic province of Khurasan). Born into a well-to-do Muslim family, young Firdawsi is said to have displayed great poetic ability even as a child. It is related that his father, Ishaq, was informed in the guise of a vision that his young son would one day grow up to be a famous poet. This prompted him to make arrangements for the boy to attend his local school to receive training in Persian language, literature and the religious sciences. Thanks largely to the generous patronage of its

Samanid rulers, Tus had become a bustling centre of cultural and literary activities. Of Persian origin, the Samanids were appointed rulers of Transoxiana by the Abbasid Caliph Mu'tamid during the ninth century, but later they annexed the province of Khurasan and declared their independence from the Abbasids. In so doing they founded the Samanid dynasty, which ruled from their capital in Bukhara (located in modern Uzbekistan). The Samanids achieved their zenith under the stewardship of Nasr II, who vigorously promoted learning and scholarship across his dominion, and offered generous patronage to eminent Persian scholars and poets. Although Nasr II died when Firdawsi was still a youngster, his successors also continued to promote learning and literary activities across the Samanid Kingdom, despite the political volatility of the time. Firdawsi completed his formal education in Tus before commencing his career as a poet. As an ardent fan of ancient Persian culture and heritage, he rapidly established his reputation as a poet, thanks to his unusual ability to versify Persian mythology and history.

It was during the reign of the Samanid ruler Mansur ibn Nuh that the Turkish general Alptagin defected from the Samanid army and established an independent kingdom in Ghazna (in present-day Afghanistan). Three decades later, the increasingly powerful Ghaznavids annexed a significant part of Samanid territory and thereby secured Ghaznavid power at the expense of their Samanid rivals. During this period of considerable political uncertainty and social upheaval, Firdawsi polished his knowledge of Persian history and culture, and composed poetry which vividly described and recalled Persia's glorious past. When Sultan Mahmud, the famous Ghaznavid ruler, ascended the throne in 999, Firdawsi was about fifty-nine years old and had already started work on his poetic masterpiece, the *Shahnama* (or 'the Book of Kings'), which took him around thirty-five years to complete. Unlike the Samanids, Sultan Mahmud of Ghazna was not a Persian; in fact, he was of Turkish extraction. Yet, like the Samanids, he became a generous patron of learning and scholarship. As a learned ruler, and one who had committed the entire Qur'an to memory, the Sultan preferred the company of the wise and the educated. Also, as a fan of Persian culture and poetry, he encouraged further research and scholarship in these subjects. During his successful reign of thirty-one years, he not only transformed the political and economic fortunes of his dynasty, but also recruited some of the most influential scholars, thinkers, writers and poets of the time to his capital in Ghazna. Thus al-Biruni the famous Muslim scientist and polymath, al-Farabi a great Islamic philosopher and logician, Unsuri a prominent linguist and grammarian, and acclaimed poets like Farrukhi and Dhaqiqi all graced his court.

After Firdawsi's fame began to spread far and wide, Sultan Mahmud sent him an invitation to come to his court in Ghazna. He was, of course, delighted to receive an invitation from one of the greatest rulers of his time. Sultan Mahmud's court became a major centre of poetic activity where distinguished literary figures such as Unsuri, Farrukhi and Minuchihri lived and thrived, enjoying the generous patronage and hospitality of the Sultan, and in turn they graced Persian literature and poetry with their valuable contributions. When Firdawsi arrived at the court, he was received by the Sultan and his courtiers with respect and honour, but the other court poets resented his presence – so much so that they declined to entertain him until he first proved that he was worthy of their company. To become a member of this exclusive club of gifted poets, Firdawsi was required to produce Persian poetry of the highest quality, otherwise he would not be accepted as a member. So the court poets decided to put Firdawsi to the test. One day, while they were all sitting in the Sultan's court garden chatting with each other, Firdawsi unexpectedly appeared before them, which prompted Unsuri to ask him to provide the finishing touch to a quatrain he and his colleagues wished to compose. Firdawsi agreed to do so. Unsuri began: 'Thine eyes are clear and blue as sunlit ocean'. Asadi added, 'Their glance bewitches like a magic potion'. Farrukhi continued, 'The wounds they cause no balm can heal, nor lotion'. Firdawsi then added the finishing touch, saying: 'Deadly as those love's spear dealt out to Poshan.' His response astounded the court poets, for they did not expect Firdawsi to know the ancient Persian tale to which they were referring, but he did – and they were very impressed. They showed their appreciation by embracing Firdawsi and praising him lavishly for his great poetic ability. Thereafter, he became one of the most talented and admired poets at Sultan Mahmud's court.

In Firdawsi, the Sultan found a poet who was capable of accomplishing a task which he had in mind; namely the versification of Persia's ancient history and culture. By chance, Firdawsi had started to versify Persian history long before his arrival at the court of the Sultan. But now, encouraged by the Sultan who offered him a luxurious room in his royal palace, he decided to complete his poetic masterpiece. To keep him focused on his task, the Sultan announced that he would pay Firdawsi a gold coin for each completed couplet, in addition to a one-off payment of a thousand gold coins upon completion. Proud of his Persian culture and history, Firdawsi thus devoted all his time and energy to the composition of his monumental *Shahnama*. Consisting of around sixty thousand verses, in the *Shahnama*, he provided a detailed description of Persian manners, customs and ethics as well as military feats and heroic episodes, in addition to the religious practices and intellectual contributions of the Persian people from ancient times, up to the seventh century. The *Shahnama* drew on information compiled and preserved during the time of the Persian Emperor Chosroe I. This information was then orally transmitted from one generation to another, until Firdawsi versified it in a masterly fashion. Like the famous Indian epic *Mohabharata*, the *Shahnama* described historical events as well as mythical tales and stories. Even though the whole work revolved around the heroic deeds of Rustam and his family, Firdawsi's poetic imagination reaches its ultimate climax when he described how Rustam had inadvertently killed his son, Sohrab. In Firdawsi's own words, 'The story of Sohrab and Rustam now hear! Other tales thou hast heard: to this also give ear. A story it is to bring tears to the eyes, and wrath in the heart against Rustam will rise. If forth from this ambush should rush the fierce blast. And down in the dust the young orange should cast. Then call it just, or kind and unfair. And say we that virtue or rudeness is there?'

This tragic tale, versified so eloquently by Firdawsi, today represents the height of Persian poetry. Before Firdawsi's time, many prominent poets (like Abdullah ibn al-Muqaffa and Dhaqiqi) had versified Persia's glorious past, but their efforts were eclipsed by Firdawsi's great epic. After completing the *Shahnama*, Firdawsi visited Sultan Mahmud and gave him a copy of his poetic masterpiece. Delighted with his contribution and achievement, the Sultan offered him a camel-load of silver coins, rather than gold coins. Jealousy and political rivalry between different factions within the Sultan's court forced him to offer Firdawsi silver instead of gold, but the latter was not impressed at all. Dismayed by the Sultan's failure to keep his promise, Firdawsi left Ghazna, having poetically ridiculed his former patron and benefactor. But this was not a wise move on his part because no other ruler of the time dared to entertain him due to fear of reprisals from Sultan Mahmud. Eventually, the reigning Abbasid Caliph, moved by his plight, granted him shelter in Baghdad. Here Firdawsi composed another influential work entitled *Yusuf-i-Zulaikha* (Joseph and the Wife of Potiphar) wherein he versified the story of Prophet Yusuf as narrated in the Holy Qur'an.

Later on, Firdawsi became reconciled with Sultan Mahmud and returned to his native Tus. As a gesture of goodwill, in 1020, the Sultan sent him a camel-load of gold coins as he had originally promised, but when the camel-train carrying the money entered Tus, the Sultan's men discovered that Firdawsi's funeral procession was already underway. He died at the age of eighty and was buried in his native city. The poet Asadi, who was a contemporary of Firdawsi, was one of the first to imitate his poetic style but, as expected, he failed to produce anything comparable to the *Shahnama*. Even Matthew Arnold, the ninteenth century British writer and poet and author of *Culture and Anarchy* (1869), was deeply inspired by the grace and wonder that was, and still is, the *Shahnama*. In short, if great poets like Hafiz of Shiraz, Umar Khayyam, Sana'i, Jalal al-Din Rumi, Farid al-Din Attar and Abd al-Rahman Jami were responsible for popularising Persian poetry, then the credit for laying the foundations of Persian poetry must go to none other than Firdawsi. As the national poet of Iran and author of arguably the greatest epic poem of all time, he was undoubtedly a great genius whose contribution to Persian poetry and literature has remained unrivalled to this day.

# 75

## Mu'in al-Din Chishti
### (b.1142 - d.1236)

ALL POPULAR SUFI (or Islamic mystical) Orders, like the *qadiriyyah, naqshbandiyyah, suhrawardiyyah* and *shadhiliyyah,* trace their spiritual lineage back to the Prophet through his close companions such as Abu Bakr al-Siddiq and Ali ibn Abi Talib. However, as Abul Hasan Ali al-Hujwiri, the eleventh century Sufi scholar and theoretician pointed out in his acclaimed *Kashf al-Mahjub* (Removal of the Veil), during the early days of Islam, Sufism was a reality without the label. But after the influx of materialistic values and practices into the Islamic world, Sufism became a label without the reality. This state of affairs prompted prominent Islamic scholars and Sufis, like Abul Hasan Ali al-Hujwiri, to oppose the spread of hedonistic and materialistic values and practices which threatened to overwhelm Islamic societies at the time. It was a critical period in Islamic history, when decline in Abbasid political power and authority, coupled with the intrusion of foreign intellectual and cultural influences, began to undermine Islamic values, principles and practices. During this challenging period in Islamic history, a number of influential Sufis, like Abd al-Qadir al-Jilani, Shihab al-Din Umar al-Suhrawardi, Najm al-Din Kubra and Khwajah Yusuf Hamadani, emerged to champion Islamic

morals, ethics and spirituality. A contemporary of these luminaries was Mu'in al-Din Chishti, who became the founder of the *chishtiyyah* Sufi Order in India, which is today widely considered to be one of the subcontinent's most influential Sufi Orders.

Mu'in al-Din Muhammad ibn Hasan, also known as Aftab-i Mulk-i Hind (the 'Sun of the Kingdom of India'), was born in Sistan into a noble Muslim family. His father, Ghiyath al-Din Hasan, was a relatively successful businessman who also became renowned for his personal piety and Sufi tendencies. Keen to educate his son, he enrolled young Mu'in al-Din at his local school where he received a thorough education in Arabic, Persian and the Islamic sciences. Despite the political uncertainty and social upheaval of the times, he successfully completed his elementary and intermediate-level studies. He was barely fifteen when his father suddenly died and this forced his family to endure considerable financial hardship. Thankfully, Mu'in al-Din had inherited a share of a garden and a water mill from his father and this earned him enough income to pay for his daily expenses. To make matters worse, his beloved mother then passed away, which again forced him to experience more personal and financial hardships. Distraught and devastated by his loss, he sold his inheritance and distributed all the proceeds to the poor and the needy.

He then travelled extensively in pursuit of knowledge and wisdom. In addition to Bukhara and Samarqand, he visited many other renowned centres of Islamic learning and education, and studied under the guidance of scores of prominent scholars and Sufis. During this period he committed the entire Qur'an to memory and became a proficient exponent of traditional Islamic sciences. On his arrival in Harwan (a prominent centre of Islamic learning and scholarship located on the outskirts of Nishapur), he encountered Khwajah Uthman Harwani, who was a distinguished Islamic scholar and prominent *chishtiyyah* Sufi. Here he became a member of Khwajah Harwani's Sufi circle and spent the next two decades in his company. Under Khwajah Harwani's guidance, he mastered both the exoteric (*zahiri*) and esoteric (*batini*) dimensions of Islam, before travelling with his teacher to Makkah and Madinah to perform the sacred *hajj* (pilgrimage). After staying in Harwan for almost two decades, he left Khwajah Harwani's company and travelled to Baghdad, the capital of the Abbasid Caliphate, to receive advanced training in Islamic sciences and Sufism. During his stay in Baghdad he reportedly encountered many famous Islamic scholars and Sufis like Abd al-Qadir al-Jilani (the founder of the *qadiriyyah* Sufi Order), Shihab al-Din Umar al-Suhrawardi (the founder of the *suhrawardiyyah* Sufi Order), as well as Khwajah Yusuf Hamadani and Shaykh Abu Sa'id al-Tabrizi. Prior to this, he had also met the renowned Central Asian Sufi sage Najm al-Din Kubra, the founder of the *kubrawiyyah* Sufi Order, and studied Islamic mystical thought and practices under his tutelage for around two and a half years. Thanks to his extensive education and training in traditional Islamic sciences and spirituality, Mu'in al-Din soon established his reputation as a master of Sufism and one of its most eloquent exponents.

From Baghdad, he proceeded to Isfahan where he met another distinguished Sufi sage,

Shaykh Mahmud al-Isfahani, who admired him for his profound knowledge and understanding of Islamic sciences and spirituality. Here he also met one of his most famous disciples, Khwajah Qutb al-Din Bakhthtiyar Kaki, who originally came to Isfahan to join the company of Shaykh Mahmud al-Isfahani but, on meeting Mu'in al-Din, changed his mind and instead pledged allegiance to the latter. He was in his mid-forties when he moved from Isfahan to Ghazna (in present-day Afghanistan) accompanied by a handful of disciples he had gathered around him. Ghazna was once the thriving capital of the Ghaznavid dynasty, but it was now firmly in the grip of the Ghurid rulers who had assumed control of that region after successfully ousting the last Ghaznavid ruler in 1186. On his arrival in Ghazna, Mu'in al-Din was surprised to encounter Khwajah Uthman Harwani, his former mentor and guide. It was Khwajah Harwani who urged him to proceed to India and disseminate the message of Islam in that country. Although Muslims first entered India during the early part of the eighth century under the inspirational leadership of young Muhammad ibn al-Qasim, the majority of India's population were still Hindus, which no doubt prompted Mu'in al-Din to go to India and take the message of Islam to the idolatrous Hindus. However, according to some of Mu'in al-Din's biographers, it was the Prophet Muhammad who appeared to him in the form of a dream and urged him to proceed to India in order to propagate Islam.

Either way, he left Ghazna and reached Lahore in 1190. As a prominent centre of Islamic learning and commerce, Lahore at the time was the home of some of subcontinent's most prominent Islamic scholars and Sufis. Here Mu'in al-Din stayed for a period and visited the tomb of Abul Hasan Ali al-Hujwiri (who is better known as Data Ganj Bakhsh), and engaged in prayers and meditation for several weeks. From Lahore he moved to Multan and stayed there for about five years. During his stay in Multan he gained proficiency in Sanskrit and a number of other prominent Indian languages and dialects, and made preparations to move further into India. It was during his travels that he attracted a considerable following; indeed, his asceticism and spirituality captured the imagination of people of all faiths, thus establishing his reputation as an eminent scholar and practitioner of Islamic mysticism. After reaching Delhi with his band of followers, he settled in Ajmer (located in the Indian State of Rajasthan), which became an integral part of the Delhi sultanate in 1196. By now, he was in his mid-fifties and decided to devote the rest of his life to the propagation of Islam in the subcontinent. And although most of his biographers have attributed scores of miracles and supernatural tales to him, a close study his life, thought and achievements proves, if proof was required, that he was far from being a magician or a miracle-worker. Steeped in the traditional Islamic sciences and *tasawwuf* (Islamic mysticism), Mu'in al-Din was a humble and gracious scholar and Sufi, who was motivated by no desire other than to attain personal purity and disseminate the message of Islam in India. Thus, as a genuine practitioner of Islamic spirituality and gnosis, he did not consider himself to be special, nor did he claim to possess any form of supernatural powers, although some of his followers subsequently exaggerated his deeds, actions and achievements.

Though Mu'in al-Din was the founder of the *chishtiyyah* Sufi Order in India, he was not the originator of the *chishtiyyah tariqah* as such. That credit must go to Khwajah Ishaq Ghani Chishti, who was an outstanding exponent of Sufism and a native of Chisht (a small town located towards the east of Herat in present-day Afghanistan). He inspired his prominent disciples to go and settle in different parts of Transoxiana and Khurasan and establish *chishtiyyah* lodges (*zawiyyah*) across that region. As a result, this Sufi Order became very popular across Persia and Muslim Central Asia. However, with the passage of time, the *chishtiyyah tariqah* began to lose its former vitality and mass appeal. As with the other prominent Sufi Orders, the adherents of this *tariqah* traced their spiritual lineage back to the Prophet through Caliph Ali ibn Abi

Talib, whom they believed had communicated special knowledge to the renowned Hasan al-Basri who, in turn, conveyed this knowledge to his Sufi successors. Thus the originator of the *chishtiyyah* Order claimed to have been a recipient of special spiritual knowledge, as did many other prominent Sufis, like Abu Sa'id ibn Abul Khair of Mayhana, whom the *chishtiyyah* considered to be one of their role models. Abu Sa'id became very popular (according to others, most notorious) for his extreme ascetic practices; for instance, he used to hang himself upside down inside a well for up to forty days at a time in order to gain mystical insights and illumination. However, other prominent Sufis, like Khwajah Uthman Harwani who was a prominent disciple of Khwajah Ishaq Ghani (the founder of the *chishtiyyah* Order), disapproved of such extreme ascetic practices and urged Mu'in al-Din to follow the Prophetic *sunnah* and popularise the message of Sufism across the subcontinent.

After settling in Ajmer, Mu'in al-Din and his disciples mixed freely with the locals and engaged them in discussion and debate on religious and spiritual matters. As a fierce critic of all forms of racial and cultural segregation, he opposed the Hindu caste system and instead argued that all human beings are equal in the sight of God. "We are all children of Adam and Eve," he argued, "and both Adam and Eve were made from clay." He led a simple, austere but active life, and never failed to emphasise the need for personal purification. Likewise, he encouraged all his disciples to regularly engage in spiritual retreat and strive to move closer to the Divine proximity. His message of love, peace, compassion, equality, freedom and brotherhood struck a chord with Muslims and Hindus alike. Thanks to his efforts, thousands of non-Muslims embraced Islam, and his disciples travelled across India in order to disseminate the message of Islam. Moreover, he regularly reminded his disciples to perform the fundamental Islamic rites and rituals such as the five daily prayers (*salat*), fasting during the month of Ramadan (*siyam-i-Ramadan*) and pilgrimage to Makkah. Indeed, he was such a rigorous adherent of the Prophetic norms and practices (*sunnah*) that he married twice in his advanced age and also urged his disciples to fulfil this important Prophetic *sunnah*.

After more than forty years of preaching and propagating Islam in the subcontinent, Mu'in al-Din and his disciples had completely transformed the fortunes of Islam throughout that vast region. His great efforts and achievements earned him widespread acclaim even during his own lifetime. However, after his death he became a household name in India, Pakistan and Bangladesh. Even prominent rulers, like Sultan Qutb al-Din and Sultan Shams al-Din Iltutmish of the Slave dynasty, profoundly admired him, as did the Mughal Emperor Akbar the Great who used to travel to and from Ajmer on foot out of respect for Mu'in al-Din, the great saint of Ajmer. Likewise, Emperors Jahangir, Shah Jahan and Awrangzeb became adherents of the *chishti-yyah tariqah* and regularly went to Ajmer to pay homage to him. Mu'in al-Din died in Ajmer at the ripe old age of around ninety-seven. After his death, his mission was continued by his disciples, including Hamid al-Din Sufi and Khwajah Qutb al-Din Bakhtiyar Kaki among others. Over time, this *tariqah* spread throughout the subcontinent, thanks to prominent *chishtiyyah* Sufis like Farid al-Din Mas'ud Ganj-i Shakar (Baba Farid), Nizam al-Din Awliyah, Amir Khusraw, Abd al-Quddus Gangohi and Burhan al-Din Gharib. Even Shaykh Ahmad Sirhindi and Shah Waliul-lah were heavily influenced by the religious ideas and thoughts of Khwajah Mu'in al-Din Chishti.

# 76

## Nur al-Din Zangi
## (b.1117 - d.1174)

AFTER FOUR HUNDRED years of unrivalled political supremacy and military domination of the Middle East, the Muslims became politically disunited during the eleventh century. Hitherto the Abbasids had ruled the Islamic world without much opposition, but by the middle of the eleventh century, the Abbasid Empire had become fragmented into several fiefdoms. Thus, like the Seljuks, the Buwayhids (or Buyids) became a separate, independent political power at the time. If the political situation in the Islamic East was bad, then the situation in the Islamic West was equally gloomy. After the Umayyad rule of Islamic Spain came to an abrupt end in 1031, political chaos and anarchy became the order of the day in that part of the world. This prompted the revitalised European nations to flex their muscles and reassert their political authority in and around the Mediterranean Sea, pushing the Muslims back further into the East. Although the rise of the Seljuk dynasty did usher in a period of peace and prosperity for a time, after the death of the Seljuk ruler Malik Shah in 1092, this dynasty also began to decline rapidly. As political rivalry and social chaos spread across much of the Muslim world, the Crusaders entered the Muslim sphere of influence in 1096 and established a

Crusader Kingdom in Palestine. After capturing Jerusalem, Islam's third holiest city, the Crusaders threatened to overwhelm the entire Islamic East until Sultan Nur al-Din Zangi, the famous Saint-King of the Zangid dynasty, emerged to rally the Muslim world to confront the Crusaders for the first time.

Nur al-Din Mahmud Zangi, known as Nur al-Din Zangi for short, was born in the northern Iraqi city of Mosul. His father, Imad al-Din Zangi, was a Turkish military commander who at the time was in the service of the Seljuks. As an accomplished military commander and teacher of the Sultan's two sons, Imad al-Din led a privileged lifestyle surrounded by much wealth and luxury. Young Nur al-Din was therefore brought up and educated in his father's luxurious and secluded mansion in Mosul. Being learned, Imad al-Din ensured his son received a thorough education in Arabic and the Islamic sciences, and young Nur al-Din was known to have been very pious during his early years. In 1127, when Nur al-Din was only ten, the Seljuk ruler Sultan Mahmud II appointed Imad al-Din governor of Mosul and this prompted the latter to take pre-emptive actions to arrest the decline of Islamic political power and military might. As a gifted strategist and military commander, he could see the signs of weakness within the Seljuk administration – and across the Islamic East – and he was determined to stop the rot. Thus, soon after becoming governor, he declared his independence from the Seljuks and established a separate political entity consisting of the cities of Sinjar, Nasibin, Jazirat ibn Umar and Harran, with his political headquarters based in Mosul.

A year later, he took advantage of the chaos which prevailed in Aleppo at the time and added that city to his expanding empire. He then annexed the territories of Hamah and Hims but, to his huge disappointment, he failed to capture the historic city of Damascus. As soon as Imad al-Din began to flex his muscles, the rulers of Damascus and the Crusader Kingdom in Palestine felt threatened by his growing power, which prompted them to unite against him. Not willing to fight on two fronts simultaneously, he turned his attention towards Edessa, the capital of the oldest Crusader State in the Muslim world. The capture of this city by the Muslims under the leadership of Imad al-Din in 1144 sent a shudder through the ranks of the Crusaders, and reinvigorated the Muslims' determination to drive out the Crusaders from the Islamic East. The fall of Edessa was a truly historic event, for it marked the beginning of the end of the Crusader presence in the Muslim world, and the first major victory of Islam over its Frankish adversary. Two years after the capture of Edessa, Imad al-Din was murdered by his bodyguard in 1146. As the news of his death spread across the Zangid kingdom, chaos and confusion ensued until Nur al-Din, his second son, emerged to restore peace and order across the region.

Tall, slim, dark-skinned, bearded, and equally charming and gentle, Nur al-Din succeeded his father as the Sultan of the Zangid kingdom in 1146 at the age of twenty-nine. Like his father, Nur al-Din was a brave, intelligent and learned ruler. However, unlike his father, he was a devout Muslim whose piety and virtues turned him into a potent symbol of Islamic goodness and rectitude. As a ruler and statesman, the Sultan was determined to reunite the Muslim world under the banner of Islam and drive out the Crusaders from the Islamic East. Although the liberation of Jerusalem from the grip of its Frankish invaders was one of his foremost long-term objectives, immediately on becoming Sultan his first priority was to establish his own political authority across the Zangid Kingdom. After appointing his brother, Sayf al-Din, governor of Mosul and its surrounding territories, he moved to Aleppo to take care of that strategically important principality. On his arrival in Syria, he received news that Edessa had again fallen into the hands of the enemy. Determined not to allow Edessa to remain in the hands of the Crusaders for long, for that would have sent the wrong message and undermined Muslim morale, he organised an expeditionary force and marched to Edessa at a lightning speed. He arrived there even before the Crusaders could organise their defences properly. Seeing him marching on Edessa with a large army prompted the Crusaders to flee, leaving the city in the hands of the brave Nur al-Din. The recapture of Edessa without a fight not only won him widespread acclaim, but also helped to consolidate his position as the supreme ruler of the Zangid dynasty.

From a strategic point of view, the Sultan's political power and authority was further strengthened by the instigators of the second Crusade who, instead of taking Edessa or Aleppo, foolishly attacked Damascus whose ruler, Mu'in al-Din Unar, was the only Muslim ruler to have allied himself with the Crusader Kingdom in Palestine. However, the Crusaders' siege of Damascus backfired in a spectacular fashion when Mu'in al-Din's forces inflicted a crushing defeat on the powerful Frankish army. A year after the Franks' humiliating defeat at the Battle of Damascus, Mu'in al-Din died, leaving the door wide open for Sultan Nur al-Din to move in and further expand his empire. As expected, in 1149, the Sultan captured Antioch and five years later added Damascus to his expanding empire. As a seasoned politician, he captured both of these cities through a combination of diplomacy and limited warfare. Inspired by his desire and determination to reclaim Jerusalem from the Crusaders, Nur al-Din now became a powerful adversary of the Crusader kingdom. Soon his call for *jihad* (or armed struggle) against the Crusaders began to reverberate across the Islamic East, winning the thirty-seven year old monarch much needed support and recognition across the Muslim world. With Jerusalem now very much within his reach, his dream of liberating Islam's third holiest site from the grip of the Crusaders seemed a real possibility. But his plans were thwarted by a powerful earthquarke which struck Syria in 1157 and completely devastated the country. In the same year, he fell seriously ill. Confined to his bed for a year and a half, Ibn al-Waqqar, his personal physician, did not expect him to survive but, thanks to his tenacity and resolve, he eventually made a full recovery.

Again, as the Sultan contemplated the possibility of taking the fight to the Crusaders in Jerusalem, he received news of Byzantine military activity to the north of Syria. When he made contact with the Byzantine Emperor Manuel, the latter assured him that he had no intention of attacking Zangid territories. Even so, the presence of Byzantine forces close to his borders prevented the Sultan from launching an expedition against the Franks. Most unexpectedly, during this period, Egypt rather than Palestine became the main theatre of warfare; indeed, the Sultan's forces played a central role in reclaiming this strategically important country from the Fatimids. After Egypt became a Fatimid stronghold during the tenth century, it was ruled by a succession of Caliphs who saw themselves as rivals of the Abbasid Caliphs in Baghdad. But, by the middle of the twelfth century, the Fatimid grip on Egypt had become very precarious. So much so that from 1163 to 1169 the Fatimids clashed with the Franks and the Zangids on more than one occasion over the rich prize that was Egypt. At the insistence of his gifted general Asad al-Din Shirkuh, the uncle of the famous Salah al-Din (Saladin), Sultan Nur al-Din eventually authorised a large-scale military expedition against Egypt in order to add this country to his empire. Three determined fighters thus clashed with each other to gain control of Egypt: they were Shawar, an Egyptian Minister who seized power in Cairo in 1162 and ruled the country with an iron fist; Amalric, a Frankish ruler who was eager to annex this strategically important Muslim country, and the third was Shirkuh, the Kurdish general in the service of Sultan Nur al-Din. These three men fought each other for nearly a decade to gain control of Egypt until Shirkuh, assisted by his young nephew Salah al-Din, finally triumphed in 1169. His victory enabled Nur al-Din to add Egypt to his expanding empire. However, after Shirkuh's unexpected death, young Salah al-Din exercised power in Egypt on behalf of Sultan Nur al-Din. And although Salah al-Din remained loyal to the Sultan, in reality he came to be seen as an independent ruler in his own right.

As time passed, Sultan Nur al-Din's dream of reclaiming Jerusalem from the grip of the Crusaders began to slowly fade away. Confined to his bed as a result of an angina attack, his health was now deteriorating rapidly. When his doctors wanted to operate on him, he refused to give them permission, saying that nature should take its course. Though he was unable to liberate Islam's third holiest city from the Crusaders, the credit for unifying the Islamic East must go to Sultan Nur al-Din. More importantly, he paved the way for Salah al-Din to take the fight to the Crusaders and re-establish Islamic political authority across the region. As an unusually patriotic Muslim, he was very eager to see the flag of Islam flying high over Jerusalem and the rest of the Muslim world. By all accounts, he was a just, pious and generous ruler who possessed a truly sublime character and personality. Not surprisingly, renowned historians like Ibn al-Athir, Ibn Khallikan and Ibn al-Jawzi have lavished much praise on him, often referring to him as the 'Saint-King' of Islam.

Indeed, according to Ibn al-Athir, when the Sultan's wife once complained to him that she did not have enough money to meet their family's needs, he told her she could not have any more, for all the money and wealth kept at the *bait al-mal* (public treasury) belonged to the public. He was not prepared, he said, to cast himself into the fire by wrongfully consuming public money. Also, being very learned, he loved the company of the *ulama* (religious scholars) and shunned materialistic values and practices. He encouraged his officials to serve the public with honesty, dedication and care. He led such an exemplary lifestyle that even a bold and stubborn Salah al-Din never dared to cross his path. When Ayyub, the father of Salah al-Din, was once informed that his son wished to break his contact with Sultan Nur al-Din, he told his son in no uncertain terms that he would never tolerate any form of disobedience or disloyalty to the master of Aleppo. Ayyub's devotion to Sultan Nur al-Din may have surprised Salah al-Din, but it certainly did not surprise those who knew their

master well. Referring to Sultan Nur al-Din, the historian Ibn al-Athir wrote, 'I have studied the careers of the rulers of the past but, apart from the first four Caliphs and Umar ibn Abd al-Aziz, there has been no prince so liberal and pious, law-abiding and just (as Nur al-Din).' Sultan Nur al-Din Mahmud Zangi, the famous 'Saint-King' of Islam, passed away at the age of sixty-one and was buried in Damascus. The news of his death came like a thunderbolt from the heavens and the people of Syria crammed into the mosques to pray for his soul. The son of Zangi continues to live in our memories to this day, for he was a true *mujahid* (warrior), who devoted his entire life to the service of Islam. Is it any wonder then that today young children grow up across the Muslim world listening to stories about the virtues, heroic deeds and achievements of the son of Zangi.

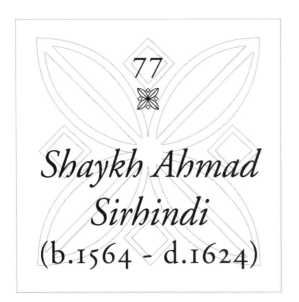

# 77

## Shaykh Ahmad Sirhindi
## (b.1564 - d.1624)

THE REIGN OF the Mughal Emperor Akbar the Great is generally considered to be the Golden Age of Muslim rule in India. After ascending the Mughal throne during the middle of the sixteenth century, he ruled India for five decades and completely transformed the fortunes of the Mughal dynasty. He not only expanded Mughal political suzerainty across the subcontinent, he also initiated far-reaching socio-cultural reforms throughout that region. In other words, as a military commander and strategist Akbar was supremely successful, but as a politician and reformer he proved to be controversial, to say the least. Not surprisingly, his cultural and religious reforms ended up as a total shambles. As a religious freethinker, he advocated a form of religious pluralism which antagonised both Muslims and Hindus. According to the Muslims, Akbar's religious synthesis, known as *din-i-ilahi* (or 'the Divine Religion'), made a complete mockery of Islamic teachings, while the orthodox Hindus considered his religious experimentation to be ill-conceived and bizzare. Thus, instead of strengthening Hindu-Muslim relations, Akbar's amateurish approach to religious dialogue and debate only served to divide the two communities further. During this critical period in the history of Muslim India, Shaykh Ahmad Sirhindi, a pioneering Sufi thinker and influential Islamic reformer, emerged to defend the cause of traditional Islam and reformulate one of the most powerful doctrines of Islamic mystical philosophy.

Also known as *mujaddid-i alf-i thani* (Renewer of the Second Millennium of Islam), Shaykh Ahmad Sirhindi was born in the town of Sirhind (located in the Indian State of Punjab) into a respected family of religious scholars and Sufi saints. His father, Shaykh Abd al-Ahad, was a prominent Islamic scholar who claimed to be a descendant of Caliph Umar through his son, Abdullah ibn Umar the famous scholar and narrator of Prophetic traditions. Brought up in a deeply religious family, young Ahmad was encouraged by his father to commit the entire Qur'an to memory before he was ten. He then pursued the standard curriculum of the day which included Arabic, Persian, literature, *fiqh* (Islamic jurisprudence), *hadith* (Prophetic traditions) and Islamic history. After completing his early education under the guidance of his learned father, he moved to Lahore and Sialkot (in present-day Pakistan), both of which at the time were prominent centres of Islamic learning in India, where he received advanced training in *tafsir* (Qur'anic exegesis), hadith, *fiqh*, logic (*mantiq*), philosophy (*falsafah*) and theology (*kalam*) under the guidance of eminent scholars like Shaykh Yaqub Sarfi, Shaykh Kamal al-Din Kashmiri and Shaykh Bahlul Badakhshani. Ahmad was a gifted student who not only possessed a highly retentive memory, but also required minimal instruction from his tutors. At the age of seventeen, he returned home after successfully completing his studies and began to teach at his local Islamic seminary.

Soon his name and fame spread throughout Sirhind on account of his vast knowledge of Islam. But subsequently he left his native town and moved to Agra, the capital of the Mughal dynasty, where he joined Emperor Akbar's circle of courtiers, only to be shocked and dismayed by the intellectual decadence and materialistic fixations of the ruling elites. When he challenged their un-Islamic ideas and practices, prominent Mughal courtiers, such as Abul Fadl and Faidi, went out of their way to make life difficult for him, thus forcing him to leave Agra and return to his native Sirhind. During this period he married and also began to study Sufism under his father's guidance. As a distinguished Sufi of the *qadiriyyah* and *chishtiyyah* lineage, his father was thoroughly familiar with the works of eminent Sufi theoreticians like Abu Bakr Muhammad ibn Ibrahim al-Kalabadhi, Shihab al-Din Umar al-Suhrawardi and Muhyi al-Din ibn al-Arabi. After his father's death in 1598, Ahmad left Sirhind to perform the sacred pilgrimage to Makkah but, on his way, he encountered the acclaimed Naqshbandi Sufi Khwajah Abd al-Baqi, better known as Khwajah Baqi Billah, who helped him to progress through all the stages of mystical experience. Thus he experienced the mystical stages of 'self-annihilation' (*fana*), 'absolute union' (*jam al-jam*), 'separation after union' (*farq ba'd al-jam*) and 'perfect station' (*maqam al-takmil*) much quicker than the Khwajah had anticipated. As a gifted scholar and Sufi, Ahmad was determined to reach the highest summit of Islamic spirituality so he could distinguish the reality of *tasawwuf* from the chaff of popular Sufism. After Khwajah Baqi Billah's death in 1603, he again returned to Sirhind where

he devoted the rest of his life to the pursuit of Islamic knowledge, wisdom and spirituality, and also became a powerful champion of traditional Islam in Muslim India.

Ahmad not only experienced all the stages (*maqamat*) of mystical experience, he also classified his experiences into three broad categories, namely the stage of 'Unity of Being or monism' (*wahdat al-wujud*); 'Unity of Being in perception or Unity of Witnesses' (*wahdat al-shuhud*) and 'Servanthood' (*ubudiyah*). According to him, the vast majority of the Sufis reached the stage of 'self-annihilation' or 'absolute union' but failed to progress to the higher stage of 'separation after union', not to mention the 'perfect station'. This, in his opinion, explained why the majority of Sufis failed to clearly distinguish the Eternal and Infinite Creator from His mortal and finite creatures. Thereafter, he undertook a thorough and systematic study of Ibn al-Arabi's doctrine of *wahdat al-wujud* (Unity of Being or monism) and refuted it in a cogent and comprehensive manner. According to Ahmad, none of God's Prophets (*anbiya Allah*) preached this doctrine, nor did any of the great Sufis of the past believe in it. The *tawhid* (Oneness of God) of the Prophets and the early mystics of Islam, he argued, stipulated that God was One, Only and Unique without any associates: that is to say, the Prophetic *tawhid* clearly distinguished the Creator (*khaliq*) from the creation (*makluq*); the former being the Eternal Lord of the entire universe, while the latter was nothing more than His creatures/servants. By contrast, Ibn al-Arabi's doctrine of *wahdat al-wujud* stipulated there was only One Being and that everything existed therein. Such a concept, argued Ahmad, had no basis whatsoever in the traditional Islamic worldview. While the *tawhid* of all the Prophets and the early mystics of Islam made a clear distinction between God and His creation – thus affirming the non-duality between the Creator and His creation – Ibn al-Arabi's *tawhid wujudi* only served to remove that important distinction by affirming the identity between the Creator and His creatures. *Tawhid wujudi*, therefore, contradicted one of the most fundamental concepts of traditional Islam and as such it must be rejected, he argued.

As an eminent Sufi thinker and theoretician, he rejected the doctrine of *wahdat al-wujud* on both theoretical as well as experiential grounds. He claimed that he had experienced 'separation after union' (*farq ba'd al-jam*), which, in itself was a higher stage of mystical experience, only revealed to a select few, where it is made clear that Being is not One; rather God is different from His creation, thus highlighting the fact that God is absolutely transcendent, while man is a mere mortal and a servant of God (*abd Allah*). The realisation that man is God's creature and servant is, according to Ahmad, the highest stage of mystical experience. He referred to this stage as *ubudiyah* (or servanthood). After clarifying the distinction between the Prophetic *tawhid* and *tawhid wujudi*, he went onto formulate his own mystical philosophy which revolved around the concept of *tawhid shuhudi*. In other words, he was of the opinion that Unity of Being, which the Sufis claimed they experienced when they reached the stage of 'absolute union' (*jam al-jam*), was merely 'Unity in perception or Unity of Witnesses' rather than 'Unity of Being or monism'. To be fair to Ibn al-Arabi, he also affirmed the distinction between God and His creatures but, according to Ahmad, this was not clear and unequivocal enough for the average Sufi, hence the controversy over the true meaning and interpretation of *tawhid wujudi*. Most interestingly, all the great *naqshbandiyyah* Sufis including Baha al-Din Naqshband, Ubaid Allah Ahrar and Abd al-Rahman Jami believed in *tawhid wujudi* but, after Ahmad's stinging critique of *tawhid wujudi*, the majority of India's *naqshbandiyyah* Sufis rejected this doctrine in favour of *tawhid shuhudi*.

His efforts to reform Islamic thought and spirituality in the light of the Prophetic norms (*sunnah*) elevated Ahmad to an exalted position in the intellectual history of Islam. And, like his great predecessors Abd al-Qadir al-Jilani and Shihab al-Din Umar al-Suhrawardi, he was a strict follower of the Prophetic *sunnah*. Indeed, he never failed to emphasise the significance of

adhering to the Prophetic methodology in one's day-to-day affairs, as well as one's spiritual practices. Both before and during his own lifetime, many practitioners and adherents of Sufism attempted to belittle, if not completely dispense with, the Prophetic *sunnah* in their quest for so-called spiritual illumination, but Ahmad insisted that adherence to the Prophetic methodology was not an option; rather it was a *sine qua non* for attaining the summit of Islamic spirituality. If he was a great scholar and perceptive Sufi thinker, then he was an equally great Islamic reformer. At the time, the Mughal Emperor Akbar the Great and his courtiers attempted to dilute the fundamental principles and practices of Islam in order to appease the Hindus. During this critical period in the history of Muslim India, Ahmad and his band of followers fought tooth and nail against the misguided Mughal ruler and his courtiers, and prevented them from stripping Islam of its doctrinal, moral and legal foundations. As a religious freethinker, Akbar regularly organised debates and discussions on different aspects of philosophy, theology and mysticism in his famed 'Hall of Religious Discussions'. Here he invited prominent Hindu, Buddhist, Jain, Zoroastrian and Christian scholars and engaged them in religious and philosophical debate. Over time, he developed – with the assistance of his chief advisors, brothers Abul Fadl and Faidi – a new religious synthesis called *din-i-ilahi*. Comprising elements of Islam, Hinduism, Buddhism, Jainism and other religions, this whole project proved to be an utter shambles, thanks largely to Ahmad and his disciples who vehemently opposed this new creed. For his opposition, he was forced to endure considerable personal hardship and suffering; he even spent a period in prison, yet he did not give up his opposition to Akbar's religious creed. This won him widespread acclaim; henceforth he became recognised as *mujjadid-i alf-i thani* (or the 'Renewer of the Second Millennium of Islam').

As a great Islamic scholar, prominent Sufi and eminent reformer, his name and fame spread across the subcontinent even during his own lifetime. He trained hundreds of disciples and sent them to different parts of India to preach Islam as well as establish *naqshbandiyyah* Sufi lodges. Soon Sufi lodges had been founded in all major Indian towns and cities including Delhi, Agra, Lahore, Allahabad, Patna, Saharanpur, Badayun and Burhanpur. His disciples even took his message beyond the borders of India and established *naqshbandiyyah* Sufi centres in Afghanistan, Iran and parts of Central Asia. As a prolific writer, he composed more than five hundred epistles on different aspects of Islam and Sufism. In these, he clarified the fundamental principles and practices of Islam, and also emphasised the virtues and importance of Islamic thought, practices

and spirituality for the benefit of scholars and lay people alike. He died at the age of sixty and was buried in his native Sirhind. After his death, his religious mission was continued by his four sons, Muhammad Sadiq, Muhammad Sa'id, Muhammad Ma'sum and Muhammad Yahya. Widely recognised as one of India's most influential Sufis and Islamic reformers, Shaykh Ahmad Sirhind's religious ideas and thoughts have influenced some of the Muslim world's most prominent Islamic thinkers and reformers including Shah Waliullah and his sons, Shah Ismail Shahid, Sayyid Ahmad Barelvi, Muhammad Ilyas, Sir Muhammad Iqbal, Abul Kalam Azad, Bediuzzaman Sa'id Nursi and Abul A'la Mawdudi among others.

# 78

# Ayatullah Khomeini
# (b.1902 - d.1989)

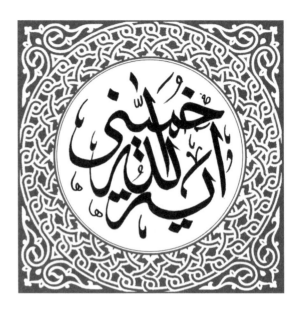

THE WORD 'IRANIAN' (meaning 'from the land of the Aryans') referred to those people who had migrated to the Iranian plateau around 1500BC and, over time, they became known as the 'Persians' until the Shah of Iran officially outlawed this term in 1935. Historically speaking, after the collapse of the ancient Persian Empire around 331, the Iranian territories were carved up by the Macedonians, Seleucids and the Parthians until the Muslims emerged from Arabia and conquered Iran in 641 during the reign of Caliph Umar. With the advent of Islam, the Iranian people embraced the religion of their conquerors and contributed immensely to the development of Islam as a religion, culture and civilisation. With the decline of the once-mighty Abbasid Empire, there then emerged many independent dynasties in the Muslim world (including the Seljuks in the eleventh century; the Mongols in the thirteenth century and the Timurids in the fourteenth century). And they ruled the Iranian people until the Safavids, a native Iranian dynasty, emerged at the beginning of the sixteenth century. They ruled for more than two hundred years before the encroaching Afghans destroyed them in 1722. Thereafter, Iran became a playground for the Turks, Russians and the British

who fought each other for control of the country until, in 1906, an independent constitutional monarchy was established in Iran which endured until the Iranian Revolution of 1979 erupted and completely transformed the political map of that part of the world. The father of this revolution was Ayatullah Khomeini, one of modern history's most influential politico-religious figures, who single-handedly brought down the Shah of Iran and established an Islamic theocracy which today plays a significant role in world politics.

Ayatullah Ruhullah al-Musavi Khomeini, known as Imam Khomeini for short, was born in Khomein, a small village in Central Iran located about two hundred miles south of Tehran, the capital of Iran. His ancestors claimed to be descendants of the Prophet, through Musa al-Kazim (the seventh Shi'a Imam). After settling in Nishapur, a town located on the outskirts of Mashhad, they migrated to India at the beginning of the eighteenth century. In India, Khomeini's immediate ancestors settled in Kintur, close to the Indian city of Lucknow, where his grandfather Sayyid Ahmad Musavi was born and raised. Later, he moved to Najaf, the famous Iraqi shrine-city, in around 1830 to pursue higher education. After completing his education, he decided not to return to India; instead he settled in Khomein, married thrice and became a successful entrepreneur. Born in 1856, Khomeini's father, Mustafa, also became a respected Shi'a cleric but he was murdered during a local dispute; Khomeini was only around five months old at the time. Raised by his mother and uncle Sayyid Murtaza Musavi, young Khomeini grew up to be a talented student and a keen sportsman. Having inherited a sizeable plot of land and few small businesses from his father, his mother was able to pay for his education and ensure the family also lived quite comfortably. After completing his early education in Arabic, Persian, Shi'ite theology, aspects of literature and poetry at his local village school, at the age of seventeen Khomeini moved to Arak where Shaykh Abd al-Karim Ha'eri-Yazdi, an eminent Shi'a scholar of the time, had founded a theological seminary, and he enrolled at this institution for further education. Here he studied Arabic grammar, literature and the religious sciences before moving to Qom, a famous centre of Shi'a learning and scholarship in Iran, along with his mentor Shaykh Ha'eri-Yazdi in 1922.

In Qom, Khomeini devoted all his time and energy to his studies, swiftly mastering the standard texts in *fiqh* (Islamic jurisprudence), *tafsir* (Quranic exegesis) *hadith* (Prophetic traditions), *ilm al-kalam* (scholastic theology) as well as logic and ethics under the tutelage of prominent Shi'a luminaries of the time including Muhammad Taqi Khonsari, Muhammad Reza Masjid Shahi, Mirza Muhammad Adib Tehrani and Abd al-Karim Ha'eri-Yazdi. Although Khomeini was a bright student of the exoteric sciences of Islam, he also became fascinated by poetry, *tasawwuf* (mysticism) and Shi'a esotericism. Accordingly, he carried out an extensive study of traditional philosophical (*hikmat*) and gnostic (*irfan*) sciences – as originally formulated by Ibn Sina, Nasir al-Din al-Tusi, *shaykh al-ishraq* Suhrawardi, Ibn al-Arabi, Qutb al-Din Shirazi, Sayyid Haidar Amuli and Mulla Sadra, and did so under the instruction of eminent teachers like Mirza Ali Akbar Yazdi, Haj Mollah Hadi Sabzevari, Mirza Javad Maliki Tabrizi and

Mirza Muhammad Ali Shahabadi. Being very fond of mystical poetry, he studied the celebrated *Mathnavi* of Jalal al-Din Rumi and the works of Hafiz of Shiraz and Umar Khayyam. Khomeini's mastery of both the exoteric and esoteric Shi'a teachings was acknowledged by his tutors who formally awarded him a diploma in traditional Islamic sciences, and he rapidly acquired a reputation as a promising young scholar and exponent of Sufism. Of all his teachers, it was Shahabadi who profoundly influenced Khomeini's ideas and thoughts on philosophy, ethics, morality and politics. Shahabadi emphasised the importance of leading a scrupulously clean, pious and austere lifestyle. Unlike the majority of the Shi'a clerics and mystics of the time, he urged his students to become intellectually and politically active. Indeed, he argued, it was the religious obligation of all Muslims, scholars and lay people alike, to oppose the anti-Islamic, oppressive and unjust policies of the Shah. His socio-political interpretation of Shi'a theology and philosophy inspired Khomeini and later provided him with the religious justification for instigating his political campaign against the Shah.

After completing his formal education in Qom, Khomeini started lecturing there while he was still in his late twenties. At the time, profound socio-political changes were taking place across Iran, and Khomeini was aware of the challenges facing the Iranian people. The rise of Reza Shah, and the founding of the Pahlavi dynasty during the 1920s, raised the hopes and aspirations of the Iranian people. Soon after gaining power, the Shah instigated wide-ranging legal and administrative reforms; he also constructed new roads and railways; established schools and colleges, and attempted to modernise Iran's towns and cities – as well as industrialise its economy – along the European lines. Following in the footsteps of Mustafa Kemal Ataturk of Turkey, the Shah was determined to Westernise Iran by force, if necessary. But his failure to reconcile modern Western secular values with the deeply entrenched Islamic culture and traditions of Iranian society was destined to create much opposition within the country. As a teacher and Shi'a cleric, Khomeini observed the events which unfolded in Iran at the time with great concern and trepidation. During this period he authored his *Kashf al-Asrar* (The Disclosure of Secrets) in which he severely criticised and lambasted the Shah for presiding over a corrupt Government and for punishing and humiliating the Shi'a luminaries. And in so doing, he formulated his views on Islam and political governance for the first time.

If Reza Shah's maltreatment of his opponents served as a wake up call for Khomeini, then it was the failure of his successor, Muhammad Reza Shah, to learn lessons from his father's mistakes which forced Khomeini to engage in political activism. Like his father, the new ruler was determined to Westernise Iran. Despite protests from the country's religious scholars, the Shah tried to change the socio-cultural values and practices of the Iranian people. But the masses – inspired by the powerful Shi'a clergy – rejected such wholesale change and reformation. This led to violent clashes between the clergy and the masses on the one hand, and the Shah's security forces on the other. Now increasingly recognised as an eminent religious figure in Qom, thanks to the popularity of his lectures on Shi'a theology, philosophy and ethics, Khomeini began to openly criticise the Shah's regime for its heavy-handed tactics and autocratic polices. As soon as he began to urge the masses to stand up against the Shah and oppose his anti-Islamic policies, Khomeini was arrested and imprisoned by the regime in 1963. But his spell in prison only helped to establish his reputation as a champion of the Iranian people. His rising popularity eventually forced the Shah to release him a year later, though soon afterwards he once again infuriated the authorities by speaking out against American interference in Iran's internal affairs. As a result, the Shah re-arrested Khomeini and in 1964 exiled him to Turkey.

He spent the next fourteen years in exile in Turkey, Iraq and France. During this period he nevertheless maintained close links with his aides and supporters back in Iran. After establishing contacts with various Iranian opposition groups in Europe and America, he openly called on the Iranian people to rise up against the Shah and his cohorts. His long stay in the Iraqi city of Najaf, a prominent centre of Shi'a religious learning and scholarship, was a critical period for Khomeini. Here he gathered around him a band of followers who supported his efforts to oust the tyrannical Shah and install an Islamic Government in Iran. The Shah, argued Khomieni, despised the clergy more than any other sector of Iranian society because they opposed his wholesale reformation of the country's educational, cultural and religious institutions, and for openly denouncing his attempts to Westernise Iranian culture and society. But Khomeini and his supporters were determined not to allow the Shah to succeed. Even the Western-educated Iranian scholars and intellectuals became embroiled in this debate; indeed, some of them argued that it would be disastrous for Iran to adopt Western secular values at the expense of its traditional Islamic culture and norms. The pro-Islamic views of intellectuals like Ali Shari'ati (the author of *On the Sociology of Islam* and *Marxism and Other Western Fallacies*); Murtaza Mutahhari (the author of *Divine Justice* and *The Rational Order of the Rights of Women in Islam*), and Jalal al-i Ahmad (the author of *Gharbzadegi* or Westoxication) also encouraged the Iranian people to join the growing Islamic movement in the country.

As the voices of Islam began to multiply, and the Shah appeared to be fighting a losing battle, Khomeini delivered a series of lectures in Najaf in 1969 in which he formulated his concept of an Islamic Government for the first time. Later published as *Vilayat -i-Faqih: Hukumat-i Islami* (The Vice-Regency of the Jurist: The Islamic State), in this book he developed a blueprint for an Islamic State in Iran. He argued that it was the duty of every Muslim, cleric or layman, to work collectively to establish an Islamic State in Iran along the lines of the seventh century Madinian prototype. He urged the religious scholars to reclaim their role as heirs of the Prophet and assume the socio-political leadership of their society. Khomeini's concept of *vilayat-i faqih* was both innovative and powerful because, in the absence of the Hidden Imam, he argued that those who possessed a sound knowledge of Islamic law and jurisprudence had no choice but to assume the political and religious leadership of the country. This, therefore, provided him with the religious justification for the rule of the clerics in the aftermath of the Iranian Revolution of 1979. Having said that, Khomeini's socio-political reading of Shi'a theology and jurisprudence was vigorously opposed by scores of influential Shi'a luminaries such as Abul Qasim al-Khoi, Muhammad Kazem Shariatmadari and Ali al-Hussaini Sistani but he simply ignored them – as did the majority of the Iranian people.

Thereafter, he published his *Jihad-i Akbar* (The Greater Struggle) in which Khomeini argued that the clerics and the masses should spiritually cleanse themselves through regular prayers and fasting which, in his opinion, was an essential pre-requisite for the attainment of success in this world and in the hereafter. It was during his time in exile that he developed his ideas and thoughts on political governance, social philosophy, Islamic morality and ethics. While he was busy working on a viable Islamic political system, the Shah's grip on power began to weaken. Indeed, as mass protest against his autocratic rule gathered pace in 1978, Khomeini, who was then living in exile in Paris, urged his supporters to continue their political campaign until the Pahlavis were ousted from power. During this momentous period in modern Iranian history, Khomeini became a powerful symbol of resistance and hope

for millions of Iranian people across the world. It was also during this period that much discussion and debate raged in Iran concerning the country's future direction. One group, led by Mehdi Bazargan the eminent leader of the Iran Freedom Movement, advocated the need for a gradualist approach to socio-political change because they wanted to establish a moderate Islamic Government in Iran. But their voices were drowned out by the supporters of Khomeini, who opted for a strict, hard-line and clergy-dominated political administration in Tehran.

Surrounded by his close associates and supporters (such as Murtaza Mutahhari, Muhammad Beheshti, Ali Akbar Hashemi-Rafsanjani, Mehdi Bazargan and Ali Khamene'i), a triumphant Khomeini returned to Tehran and proclaimed the establishment of the Islamic Republic in 1979. This marked the end of more than fifty years of Pahlavi rule, and the beginning of a new chapter in Iranian history. Khomeini ruled Iran for more than a decade and tried to address its internal, as well as external, threats and challenges with great resolve and determination. But the tussle between the proponents of moderation and Islamic liberalism on the one hand, and the advocates of traditionalism and religious literalism on the other continues to this day. And although it is not clear which of these two powerful religious factions will have the final say with regard to the future direction of their country, there is no doubt that Khomeini's legacy will play a powerful role in Iranian politics, at least for the foreseeable future. Ayatullah Khomeini died at the age of eighty-seven and was buried in the famous cemetery of Behesht-i Zahra in Tehran.

# 79

## Awrangzeb Alamgir
## (b.1618 - d.1707)

THE MUGHAL DYNASTY endured for more than three hundred years before the British assumed control of India and sent the last Mughal ruler, Bahadur Shah Zafar II, into exile in 1858. During the heyday of Mughal rule, India became one of the world's foremost political, economic and military powers. Extending from Afghanistan and Kashmir in the north, to the Deccan and beyond in the south, prominent Mughal rulers like Akbar the Great, Jahangir and Shah Jahan established an empire which became the envy of the world. The splendour and magnificence of the Mughals rivalled the glorious achievements of the Ottomans, the greatness of the Safavids and the might of the great European nations of the time. The descendants of Timur the World Conqueror ruled a vast stretch of land where people of all faiths, cultures and traditions lived and thrived, producing some of the world's most famous works of art and architecture, including the immortal Taj Mahal. And in so doing they left their indelible marks in the annals of history. The last, equally courageous and most impressive, of all the great Mughal rulers was Awrangzeb Alamgir.

Abul Muzaffar Muhammad Muhyi al-Din Awrangzeb Alamgir Badshah-i-Ghazi, known as Awrangzeb Alamgir for short, was born in Dohud in the province of Deccan during the reign of his grandfather Jahangir. His father, Shah Jahan, who was only twenty-six at the time, served as Minister of the Deccan province. Being very fond of Shah Jahan, Emperor Jahangir trained him in the arts of diplomacy and statecraft in preparation for political succession; and, as expected, Shah Jahan became an able political administrator and statesman. However, unlike Jahangir, Shah Jahan despised wine and shunned his father's hedonistic habits and practices. The real love of his life was Mumtaz Mahal (The Chosen One of the Palace), his beloved wife and consort who bore him fourteen children. As Shah Jahan's third son, Awrangzeb received the best education money could buy at the time. Moreover, since his father was more sympathetic towards Islam than his grandfather or great-grandfather, young Awrangzeb studied the Qur'an and aspects of Islamic sciences during his early years. Unlike his brothers, he excelled in Arabic, Islamic studies, literature and Persian poetry and became the first person in his family to commit the entire Qur'an to memory. By contrast, his older brother, Dara Shikuh, became a religious freethinker who, like his great-grandfather Akbar, indulged in religious experimentation, while his other brothers, Shah Shuja and Murad Bakhsh, remained religiously indifferent and aloof. But Awrangzeb became a devout Muslim who prayed five times a day and refused to engage in any form of un-Islamic activities.

He was barely ten years old when his father ascended the Mughal throne and ruled the country for three decades. During this period, Emperor Shah Jahan became very fond of Awrangzeb on account of his intellectual ability, personal piety and unusual courage and bravery. As Shah Jahan loved to watch elephant fights, one day he invited all the members of the royal family to come and watch an elephant bout; but suddenly an elephant began to run amok. Shocked and horrified by the elephant's threatening behaviour, all the members of the royal family fled the scene except the indomitable Awrangzeb who stood his ground as the wild beast came thundering towards him. When the elephant came within his reach, he threw his spear at the beast, hitting it directly on the forehead. In response, the elephant swung its trunk at him, throwing him off his horse, but he leaped up to face the raging beast again. By then, help had arrived for the fourteen year old Awrangzeb. His courage and bravery impressed Shah Jahan who offered him his weight in gold as reward for his heroism. If this incident established his reputation as a gifted and courageous young man, then he also became renowned for his mild manners, soft, gentle voice, and his sense of humility. Impressed by his son's good personal qualities and attributes, Shah Jahan appointed him commander of the Mughal army. His stint with the army proved hugely successful; indeed, his military skills and personal bravery on the battlefield soon won him the respect of the Mughal army.

Delighted with Awrangzeb's progress, Shah Jahan appointed him Minister of the Deccan province when he was only seventeen. As Shah Shuja, his other son, had failed to make progress in the Deccan, the Emperor was convinced that Awrangzeb was the only man who could restore peace and security in that important province.

True to form, he came to Deccan and soon established peace and security throughout the province using his carrot-and-stick approach. During this period he also married the daughter of a noble businessman and a year later his beautiful and talented daughter, Princess Zaib un-Nisa (who later became an acclaimed poetess and literary figure), was born. Unhappy with the pomp and pageantry of the aristocratic lifestyle, Awrangzeb soon lost interest in worldly affairs and longed to lead a simple, quiet and austere lifestyle, guided by the principles and practices of Islam. The futility of worldly power, wealth and possessions prompted him to resign as Minister and become a hermit; he was only twenty-four at the time. His decision to renounce all worldly power and possessions in favour of a life devoted entirely to meditation and asceticism earned him the anger of his father, who could not understand why the Great Mughal Emperor's son should choose to lead such a lowly lifestyle. Stripped of all worldly power and possessions, Awrangzeb was now able to see what others had failed to perceive, namely the moral degradation of aristocratic life and the degeneration of social and ethical values in society as the ruling elite presided over a corrupt and injust system which threatened to erode the very foundations of the Mughal dynasty. The rot, he felt, had to be stopped but this could only be done from within. Thus Awrangzeb decided to return to the fold of the royal family and strive to change the status quo from within. With a new sense of mission, he left his hermitage and moved to Agra where his father initially refused to pardon him for apparently disgracing the royal family's name by becoming a hermit, but eventually Shah Jahan relented and appointed him Minister of the province of Gujarat.

As a troublesome province, Gujarat at the time had become a thorn in the Mughals' side. However, on his arrival, Awrangzeb swiftly restored peace and order across that province. His achievement delighted Shah Jahan, who then decided to send an expedition to Central Asia with a view to reconquering Samarqand, the ancestral home of the great Mughals. Thus, in

1647, he ordered Awrangzeb to take charge of an expeditionary force and set out for Central Asia. A determined, resilient and motivated Awrangzeb moved swiftly towards his target, successfully conquering Balkh and Badakhshan on his way, but Samarqand proved to be a different proposition altogether. Both the ruler and the people of this historic city put up determined resistance, and the Mughals' dream of annexing Samarqand soon faded away before their eyes. Unable to break down the Uzbek fortifications, Awrangzeb was forced to pull back and return to Kabul after signing treaties with the ruler of Balkh. This was the Mughals' last effort to extend their political suzerainty through military conquest. Although Shah Jahan's military campaign against the Uzbeks, as well as the Safavids, proved disastrous for the Mughals, Awrangzeb won much acclaim for his bravery and resilience on the battlefield. Of his four sons, Shah Jahan was most impressed with Awrangzeb, on account of his superior intellect and polished military skills, than with his other sons. Nonetheless, to prevent rivalry and ill-feeling within the royal family, he made them all Ministers of their own provinces. Despite being a troublesome individual, Dara Shikuh was put in charge of Multan and Kabul. Known for his waywardness, Shah Shuja was nevertheless appointed Minister of Bengal. By contrast, Murad Bakhsh was an alcoholic who loved drink more than anything else in life but his father made him Minister of Gujarat, while the intelligent and accomplished Awrangzeb was re-appointed Chief of the Deccan province.

By putting his four sons in charge of four different provinces, Shah Jahan maintained peace and unity within the royal family until he was taken ill in 1657. The news of his illness prompted his four sons to engage in a protracted succession battle. And although it was Shah Shuja who initiated the battle for political succession, he failed to win power. After removing his brothers, one by one, from his path Awrangzeb became Emperor of the Mughal dynasty in 1658 at the age of around forty. Soon after becoming Emperor, he initiated a series of reforms which reversed the anti-Islamic policies of his predecessors and instead he established the *shari'ah* (Islamic law) in Mughal India. To Awrangzeb, India was a Muslim country even though people of other faiths and cultures lived and thrived there but, unlike his predecessors, he was not prepared to pander to the wishes and desires of the Hindus at the expense of the Muslims. He tried to treat all his citizens as fairly as he could; indeed, his acts of kindness and generosity towards the Hindus were not uncommon (for example, on more than one occasion, he donated land for the construction of Hindu temples, including the Kashi Vishwanath Temple in Varanasi).

Nevertheless, he knew that keeping both the Muslims and Hindus happy would not be an easy task. As a devout and practising Muslim, he implemented Islamic principles and practices in India, unlike his predecessors who went out of their way to appease the Hindus. Thus, in Awrangzeb, the long-suffering Indian Muslims found a true champion who not only proudly wore the badge of Islam, but also encouraged others to do the same. Contrary to what some Hindu and Western historians have written about him, Awrangzeb was far from being a racist or religious bigot; rather he was a man of sound principles who led a simple, honest and austere lifestyle. Unlike his predecessors who surrounded themselves with much wealth and luxury, he despised pomp and pageantry and lived like a hermit, sleeping on the floor, covered only with a tiger skin, and ate most frugally. Yet, strangely enough, some Hindu and Western historians have tried to malign his character and personality. But Awrangzeb's faith, devotion, good character and sincerity of purpose was beyond reproach. In fact, he cared very little about his appearance and instead wore simple, inexpensive clothes, and deliberately avoided jewellery and adornments. The restoration of peace, justice and prosperity across Mughal India was more important to him than satisfying his own personal whims and desires.

Under Awrangzeb's able stewardship, Mughal rule extended from Afghanistan in the north to the Deccan and beyond in the south, pushing the frontiers of Mughal Empire as far as Assam and Bengal, and in so doing he transformed the Mughal Empire into one of Asia's foremost political and military powers. During his long reign of fifty years, he faced many challenges (including the uprising of the Rajputs of Marwar and the Marathas of Maharashtra) but he fought and subdued them with great determination and success. As a learned ruler, he became a generous patron of learning, education and philanthropic activities, and in his spare time he used to commit the Qur'an to paper; a copy of the Qur'an written by Awrangzeb has been preserved in the *dar al-uloom* library in Deoband. Also, as a devout Muslim, he shunned all the singers and entertainers who lived at the Mughal royal court, forcing them to move to the courts of Rajasthan and Bengal instead. More importantly, during his reign, Emperor Awrangzeb established a committe of prominent Islamic scholars in order to re-examine and review aspects of Islamic law and jurisprudence in the light of the new problems and challenges which confronted the Indian Muslims at the time. In response, the scholars produced the *Fatawa-i-Alamgiri* (The Religious Edicts of Alamgir), a compendium of *hanafi* jurisprudence, which is today widely considered to be a standard work of reference on the subject.

In addition to this, Awrangzeb constructed the famous Badshahi mosque in Lahore, which is one of the Muslim world's largest and most beautiful mosques. However, unlike his father, Awrangzeb was not a prolific builder; he preferred to lead a simple and ascetic lifestyle devoted to the service of Islam and his subjects, irrespective of their faith, race or background. He set such a high standard of morals, ethics and behaviour that the title of *zinda pir* (or the 'living saint') was conferred on him by his friends and foes alike. His favourite motto was 'He is the truly great King who makes it the chief business of his life to govern his subjects with equity.'

Emperor Awrangzeb Alamgir died at the ripe old age of eighty-five and was buried at the mausoleum of Shaykh Zain al-Haq at Khuldabad (located in present-day India). He was succeeded by his sons who, unfortuantely, failed to live up to their father's high standards, and the Mughal Empire began to decline irreversibly.

# 80

## Ibn Tufayl
### (b.1101 – d.1185)

ANCIENT GREEK, Persian and Indian science and philosophy first entered the Muslim world during the eighth century and found their finest expression in the works of al-Kindi and al-Razi in the ninth century and in that of al-Farabi and *ikhwan al-safa* (The Brethren of Purity) in the tenth, culminating in the works of the great Neoplatonist Ibn Sina in the eleventh century. As the philosophical sciences gained popularity across the Muslim world and began to challenge the traditional Islamic worldview, the formidable figure of al-Ghazali emerged during the latter part of the eleventh century to launch a blistering attack on the Neoplatonic school of Ibn Sina and al-Farabi. Al-Ghazali's intellectual assault on the Neoplatonic edifice, as developed in his acclaimed *Tahafut al-Falasifah* (The Refutation of the Philosophers), struck a major blow against philosophical thought in general, and Neoplatonism in particular. As expected, his successful repudiation of philosophy elated the Ash'arites and the Hanbalites who vehemently opposed Neoplatonic thought, but it seriously undermined the progress of philosophical thinking in the Islamic world. When philosophy was in full retreat in the Islamic East, it found a warm welcome in *al-andalus* in the Islamic West. As a

result, Islamic philosophy flourished in Muslim Spain during the twelfth century, thanks largely to the efforts of great European Muslim philosophers like Ibn Bajjah (Avempace) and Ibn Rushd (Averroes). But it was in the works of Ibn Tufayl that Islamic philosophy found a refreshing, innovative and powerful expression, which subsequently exerted considerable influence on European thought and culture.

Abu Bakr Muhammad ibn Abd al-Malik ibn Muhammad ibn Tufayl, known as Abubacer in the Western world, was born at Guadix (in present-day Wadi Ash) in Islamic Granada. About a decade before his birth, Granada was annexed by the al-Moravids (*al-murabitun*), a North African dynasty which gained control of Spain in 1086, following more than half a century of political volatility and social unrest in that country. Founded by the charismatic North African Islamic leader Yusuf ibn Tashfin, the al-Moravids were, at the time, urged by the Muslim world's most prominent scholars (such as Abu Hamid al-Ghazali) to move into Islamic Spain and restore peace and security there. By the time Ibn Tufayl was born, the al-Moravids had reunited the entire country under their leadership and established much-needed peace and prosperity there. During this period of stability, young Ibn Tufayl completed his early education in Arabic, the Qur'an and traditional Islamic sciences, before pursuing mathematics, medicine, literature and philosophy. He received advanced training in these subjects at Cordova, Seville and most probably at Toledo, which at the time was one of the most renowned centres of learning and scholarship in Islamic Spain.

As a student prodigy, Ibn Tufayl excelled in both the scientific and philosophical sciences and received instant recognition for his mastery of mathematics, medicine and philosophy. During this period he also became highly versed in the philosophical discourse of Ibn Bajjah, who is widely considered to be the founding father of Andalusian philosophy. A fiercely rationalistic thinker, Ibn Bajjah attempted to revive and popularise the philosophical thought of great Muslim thinkers like al-Farabi in the Islamic West. And although Ibn Tufayl disagreed with many aspects of Ibn Bajjah's philosophy, he was nonetheless heavily influenced by the latter's ideas and thoughts. To a great extent, he is considered to be a natural successor of Ibn Bajjah, in the same way that Ibn Rushd is regarded, in turn, as his successor in the intellectual history of Islamic Spain. The philosophical sciences aside, Ibn Tufayl also excelled in medicine and surgery; indeed, he was such a popular medical practitioner that he established his own clinic, despite the deteriorating political situation in Granada.

Following the death of the al-Moravid ruler Ali ibn Yusuf in 1143, political chaos and social anarchy again returned to Islamic Spain, prompting the neighbouring Christian principalities to reorganise their forces and launch fresh incursions into the Islamic territories. Amidst the ensuing chaos there suddenly emerged another powerful Islamic dynasty in North Africa. Founded originally by Abu Abdullah Muhammad ibn Abdullah ibn Tumart, a charismatic North African Islamic reformer, the al-Mohads (*al-muwahhidun*) carved out a vast empire under the able leadership of Abd al-Mu'min, who moved swiftly to establish his rule across all the territories which were once ruled by the al-Moravids. At the time, Ibn Tufayl was in his late forties and busy practising medicine in Granada. But, after Abu Yaqub Yusuf al-Mansur ascended the al-Mohad throne, he came to hear about Ibn Tufayl's skills as a medical practitioner and arranged for him to be brought to the al-Moravid court. Educated in Arabic literature and poetry at Seville, Abu Yaqub was a wise and learned ruler who encouraged intellectual and literary pursuits at his luxurious court in Marrakesh. Indeed, he even recruited some of the best Andalusian writers, poets and philosophers to his court, and Ibn Tufayl was one such intellectual who served him as a physician, secretary and advisor. The two men became such good friends that they frequently engaged in lengthly discussions on the finer points of philosophy, theology and literature.

Like Abu Yaqub, Ibn Tufayl was also in the habit of recruiting some of the finest scholars and thinkers of the time to the court in Marrakesh. One of Ibn Tufayl's star recruits was Ibn Rushd. Born in 1126 into a distinguished family of Islamic scholars and jurists in Cordova, Ibn Rushd was an outstanding Islamic scholar blessed with a prodigious intellect. Although he was much younger than Ibn Tufayl, he became very popular throughout Cordova for his philosophical abilities. This prompted Ibn Tufayl to go out of his way to bring this rising star to the court in Marrakesh. On his arrival at the court, the al-Mohad ruler Abu Yaqub questioned the young philosopher concerning the nature of creation asking him whether he believed in the eternity of the universe. As Ibn Rushd hesitated to respond, the experienced Ibn Tufayl intervened and answered the monarch's question in a philosophically neutral way. Whether the universe was eternal or a finite creation of God was a contentious philosophical point, which was hotly debated by the Muslim philosophers and theologians alike. Considering that the al-Mohads vehemently rejected the notion of the eternity of creation – and instead championed the Ghazzalian view that the universe was a creation of God – young Ibn Rushd hesitated to answer

Abu Yaqub's question, but Ibn Tufayl's timely interjection saved the day for him. Later, the al-Mohad ruler conducted extensive philosophical discussions with Ibn Rushd and expressed his satisfaction with the young philosopher, whom he considered to be both gifted and erudite. He then rewarded him with a high-ranking Government post, working under Ibn Tufayl's supervision.

During this period Ibn Tufayl not only became Ibn Rushd's mentor and guide but, also helped him to polish his understanding of the finer points of Islamic philosophy and theology. In addition to this, he encouraged Ibn Rushd to write his famous commentaries on the works of Aristotle, which later earned him the coveted title of 'The Commentator' throughout the Western world. Unlike Ibn Bajjah, Ibn Tufayl was not a pure rationalist, nor did he subscribe to the philosophical theology of al-Ghazali, even though he was well-acquainted with both points of view. As a philosopher, Ibn Bajjah emphasised the importance of rationalism in understanding the nature of creation as well as the attainment of individual 'spiritual' fulfilment, which he claimed was attainable intellectually without the need for sensual experience. But influential Sufis like al-Ghazali disagreed with this view; they argued that spiritual fulfilment achieved through 'mystical experience' was far superior to the spirituality acquired through rational means. Ibn Tufayl was intimately acquainted with this philosophical/theological dichotomy and thus adopted a philosophical position which sought to harmonise these two conflicting views. The philosophical synthesis he formulated between the Peripatetic thought of al-Farabi and Ibn Sina on the one hand, and al-Ghazali's mystical philosophy on the other found its most profound and enduring expression in his world famous novel *Risalah Hayy ibn Yaqdhan* (The Tale of Living Son of Vigilant).

Perhaps inspired by Ibn Sina's book of the same title, in this pioneering fictional account Ibn Tufayl explained how a child born on a desert island (located in the Indian Ocean) slowly acquired new skills, improved his knowledge and gained the experience to adapt to his new environment. As he grew older and matured, his understanding of life, its meaning and purpose, increased until he was able to think and reason philosophically before going onto experience mystical union, which is the highest spiritual position attainable in conventional Sufism. Later, he came into contact with a group of people who lived on a neighbouring island and discovered that they lived by a revealed religious code, and his interaction with them enabled him to understand and appreciate the true nature and purpose of Divine revelation (*wahy*). But when he attempted to explain to the locals the full meaning and significance of Divine revelation, they showed little interest in acquiring such knowledge. Their lack of interest in such matters eventually convinced him that everyone was not necessarily the same, for the majority of people were only too happy to lead ordinary lives, while others, like himself, were very keen on pursuing philosophical matters in order to develop a better understanding of life and creation. Before leaving the island, he recommended that the people who wished to lead their lives in accordance with the laws and precepts of their religion should be allowed to do so, without being forced to engage in any form of philosophical debates or discussion. He returned to his own island, convinced that respect, tolerance and understanding were the key to survival and co-existence in this hugely diverse world.

Through the life of this fictional character, Ibn Tufayl tried to explain that the exoteric (*zahiri*) way of the ordinary believer was as valid as the esoteric (*batini*) path of the Sufis. In other words, all the believers, irrespective of whether they worshipped in the mosques, lodges or sanctuaries, were, in his opinion, seeking the One and the same Truth. Even al-Ghazali acknowledged this fact when he said that the philosophers were also seekers of truth, albeit only unintentionally. In short, Ibn Tufayl believed that in reality there was no conflict between reason and revelation; thus, in his *Risalah*, he attempted to reconcile some of the most complex and intractable philosophical, mystical and theological controversies which had been raging in the Muslim world for many centuries.

Although written in the twelfth century, this pioneering philosophical novel later inspired generations of famous Western thinkers and writers (such as Cervantes, Gracian, Chaucer, Simon Ockley and Gottfried Leibniz) who imitated his unique literary style, and did so without acknowledging their main source of inspiration. This was most certainly the case with the great French philosopher Jean-Jacques Rousseau, who was inspired to pen his *Emile* by Ibn Tufayl's *Risalah*. The same was true of John Locke whose *An Essay Concerning Human Understanding* was heavily influenced by Ibn Tufayl's philosophical ideas and thoughts. The *Risalah* was first translated into Hebrew (with an explanatory commentary) in 1349 by Moses ben Joshua of Narbonne; the Englishman Edward Pococke then published a Latin version under the title of *Philosophus Autodidactus* (or 'the self-taught philosopher') along with the original Arabic text in 1671 at Oxford.

This book was then translated into English, Dutch, Russian, Spanish, German and other Western languages. Soon it became so popular in Europe that, during the Enlightenment, it inspired Daniel Defoe to pen his famous novel *Robinson Crusoe* in 1719. In addition to the *Risalah*, Ibn Tufayl composed scores of other treatises on philosophical, astronomical and medical topics. Indeed, as an eminent astronomer, he helped his student and associate Abu Ishaq al-Bitruji (Alpetragius) to review aspects of Greek astronomy, including the writings of Ptolemy. After serving as a royal physician to Abu Yaqub Yusuf for nearly two decades, Ibn Tufayl finally retired in 1182. Ibn Rushd, his student and colleague, replaced him as physician to the al-Mohad ruler. Three years later, this great European Muslim philosopher died at the age of eighty-four and was buried in Marrakesh (in present-day Morocco).

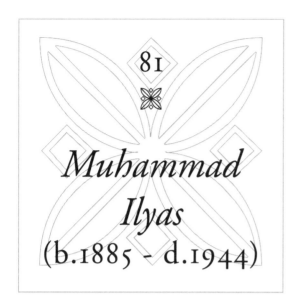

# 81

## Muhammad Ilyas
### (b.1885 - d.1944)

MUHAMMAD IBN AL-QASIM'S foray into the province of Sind at the beginning of the eighth century brought political Islam directly in contact with India. Unfortunately, his military excursion into India was brought to a sudden halt by the Umayyad Caliph Sulaiman who recalled Muhammad ibn al-Qasim to Damascus following a family dispute. And, although many Arab governors continued to rule Sind on behalf of the Umayyads and subsequently the Abbasids, it was Sultan Mahmud of Ghazna who picked up where Muhammad ibn al-Qasim left off and rapidly extended Islamic political and military rule into mainland India. As the Ghaznavids opened up India's political borders, Muslim traders and missionaries entered India *en masse* to pursue commerce and also promulgate Islam. Led by the Sufi missionaries, Muslims poured into India and began to spread the good news of Islam throughout that country. Thus influential Sufis like Abu Ali al-Sindi (who was a tutor of the renowned Persian mystic Abu Yazid al-Bistami), Abul Hasan Ali al-Hujwiri (the famed author of the Sufi classic *Kashf al-Mahjub* (Removal of the Veil), Mu'in al-Din Chishti (the founder of the *chishtiyyah* Sufi Order in India), and Shaykh Ahmad Sirhindi (the great Sufi thinker and

reformer of India) became the pioneers of the Islamic mission on the subcontinent. Thanks to the efforts of these Sufi luminaries, large numbers of Hindus embraced Islam and, as a result, the message of Islam began to spread across India. As more and more Hindus entered the fold of Islam, the need for proper Islamic education and training became ever more important. As expected, many Sufi groups filled this important gap by establishing Sufi lodges where the new converts received Islamic training and instruction. But despite the valiant efforts of the Sufis, large numbers of Hindu converts went without any formal education or training in Islamic rites and rituals. Not surprisingly, therefore, many of these converts continued to lead a Hindu lifestyle while professing to be Muslims. This state of affairs persisted in many parts of India until Muhammad Ilyas founded the *tablighi jama'at* (or Organisation for Islamic Propagation) to address their religious needs and requirements.

Muhammad Ilyas, also known as Mawlana Ilyas, was born in the town of Kandhla (located close to Delhi). His family claimed to be descendants of Shah Waliullah, the great Indian Islamic thinker and reformer, and they were steeped in traditional Islamic learning and scholarship.

Mawlana Muhammad Ismail, the father of Ilyas, was a noted Islamic scholar who was heavily influenced by Sufi ideas and thought, and he led a simple, austere lifestyle centred on devotional and missionary activities in his locality. After his father's death in 1898, young Ilyas and his brother, Muhammad Yahya, were raised by their mother, Safia. As a *hafiza* (one who had committed the entire Qur'an to memory), she ensured Ilyas also committed the whole Qur'an to memory. He then attended his local seminary to study Arabic and Islamic sciences before joining his older brother at Gangoh, a prominent centre of Islamic learning and Sufism in India, where the latter was pursuing advanced Islamic education under the tutelage of Mawlana Rashid Ahmad Gangohi, a renowned Islamic scholar and Sufi of his time. Prior to his death in 1905, Mawlana Gangohi personally initiated the twenty year old Ilyas into Sufism and during this period he completed his intermediate education and became proficient in Arabic, *tafsir* (Quranic exegesis), *hadith* (Prophetic traditions) and aspects of Sufism.

Despite suffering from poor health, Ilyas continued to pursue higher education in Islam and aspects of Sufism at Gangoh. His health problems frequently interrupted his advanced education until Mas'ud Ahmad, a local traditional physician and son of Mawlana Gangohi, diagnosed and treated him. Then, in 1908, he enrolled at the famous *dar al-uloom* (Islamic seminary) in Deoband where he completed advanced training in *tafsir* and *hadith* under *shaykh al-hind* Mawlana Mahmud ul-Hasan, and also received training in Sufism under the guidance of Mawlana Khalil Ahmad Saharanpuri. Since Mawlana Gangohi was a mentor, spiritual guide and tutor of many renowned Indian Islamic scholars (including Mawlana Ashraf Ali Thanvi and Mawlana Shah Abd al-Rahim Raipuri), Ilyas maintained close contact with these eminent scholars and personalities.

After qualifying as an Islamic scholar at the age of twenty-five, he began to teach at *mazahir ul-Islam* seminary at Saharanpur. Being the annual *hajj* (pilgrimage) season, several local teachers decided to go to Makkah to perform the sacred pilgrimage, and the newly-qualified Ilyas was offered a temporary teaching post. Two years later, he married the daughter of Mawlana Rauf al-Hasan, who was his maternal uncle, and eminent personalities like Mawlana Thanvi, Mawlana Raipuri and Mawlana Saharanpuri attended his marriage ceremony. Subsequently, in 1914, he took leave from teaching and went to Makkah to perform the sacred *hajj*, and resumed teaching on his return. In the same year his brother and mentor, Mawlana Muhammad Yahya, suddenly died. His death profoundly affected Ilyas. To make matters worse, two years later, his step-brother, Mawlana Muhammad, who at the time was in charge of the seminary founded by their father in Nizamuddin (located close to Delhi), also died from an illness. At the request of the locals, Ilyas left Kandhla and moved to Nizamuddin to take charge of this seminary. On his arrival, he found the seminary in a poor condition; indeed, lack of proper funding caused considerable hardship to all the teachers as well as the students. But, undaunted by the massive challenge he now faced, Ilyas reorganised the seminary and improved its academic performance. His new initiatives inspired the teachers and students alike, and the seminary began to thrive again.

During this period Ilyas became aware of the plight of the Muslims of Mewat, located towards the southwest of Delhi. Inspired by the great Indian Sufi sage Shaykh Nizam al-Din Awliyah and his disciples, the tribes of Mewat embraced Islam *en masse* during the fourteenth century but, deprived of proper Islamic education and training, they continued to live like Hindus while professing to be Muslims. Shocked and surprised by their political, social and economic condition, Ilyas decided to take positive action to change and improve their lives. According to his biographers, he found the Meo people's religious, moral and ethical practices to be both eclectic and confusing. Influenced by their Hindu past, the Muslims of Mewat freely partook in idol-worship, celebrated Hindu festivals and engaged in many other un-Islamic activities: to outsiders, they appeared half-Hindu and half-Muslim. To make matters worse, during the 1920s, the Meos became the target of several Hindu revivalist movements (such as the Arya Samaj) who attempted to re-convert these illiterate, tribal people to Hinduism. Since the majority of the Meo people were ignorant of Islam, the Hindus would probably not have encountered much resistance from them. Characteristically, the Meos were very brave, hardworking and courageous people; it was their lack of Islamic knowledge and education which led them into a life of crime and banditry. Shocked by the deplorable condition of these people, Ilyas began to explore ways in which he could educate the Meos about their faith, culture and traditions; this, he felt, would enable them to lead better Islamic lives and improve their existential condition.

After a period of reflection, he decided to proceed by promoting mass education, although a chronic shortage of Islamic schools in that region made his task very difficult. Undeterred by the lack of resources, he established his own religious seminary and began to train the local children in Islamic principles and practices so they could become ambassadors of Islam throughout the region. Initially he encountered some resistance from the locals, who did not want their children to attend school. Being illiterate, these people failed to understand and appreciate the importance of educating their children. But, after some persuasion, Ilyas convinced them to allow their children to attend school at least for a part of the day. Eventually, more and more locals allowed their children to attend school and, as a result, Islamic seminaries mushroomed throughout Mewat. For the first time in their history, the Meos actively encouraged their children to attend school and learn about their faith, culture and traditions. Funded partly by Ilyas and partly by local philanthropists, these schools and seminaries operated with meagre resources, but they managed to provide an adequate level of Islamic education. Later, during one of his visits to Mewat, Ilyas noticed how the Islamic education provided by his schools failed to change and

improve the local children's character, attitude and behaviour. He felt his attempts to reform Meo culture and society through the provision of free Islamic education was not achieving his aims and objectives. He therefore returned to the drawing-board and explored other possible alternatives. After due deliberation, he changed his strategy; that is to say, instead of pursuing a largely school-based educational strategy, he rolled out an informal educational programme aimed at changing people's behaviour and attitudes within their communities. In other words, he wanted to engage all the Meo people, children as well as adults, in the learning process through a mixture of school-based education and informal discussion and group work.

On his return from his second *hajj* in 1925, Ilyas recruited a number of local people and organised them into several groups. He then trained them in the fundamental principles and practices of Islam, before sending them off to their localities to preach Islam. The locals responded to the call of these Islamic workers with much interest and enthusiasm. Convinced that he had discovered a workable *tablighi* methodology, Ilyas began to organise more *jama'at* (or network of local Islamic workers) in order to carry out regular *tabligh* missions in their towns and villages. During this period he enlisted the support of all the prominent Islamic scholars of Mewat and rapidly expanded his religious activities across that region. The success of the *tablighi jama'at* enhanced his reputation as an eminent scholar and reformer of Islam. Despite being preoccupied with the supervision and expansion of *tablighi* activities, Ilyas found time to perform his third *hajj* in 1932. On his return from Makkah, he began to establish *tablighi* centres throughout Mewat, encouraging the local workers/volunteers to focus their attention on the six points or principles of *tablighi jama'at*. These were *kalima/shahadah* (the declaration of faith); *namaz/salat* (five daily prayers); *ilm-o-dhikr* (importance of seeking knowledge and engaging in meditation); *ikram-i-muslim* (the need to show respect towards fellow Muslims); *ikhlas-i-niyyat* (maintaining purity of intention and thoughts), and finally *tafrigh-i-waqt* (the necessity of volunteering for missionary activities). Learning and mastering these six points, argued Ilyas, was not an option but a *sine qua non* for all *tabligh* workers because the attainment of personal purification, spiritual elevation, and good character and personality was the key to success in *da'wah* work. In other words, according to Ilyas, to be a successful *tabligh* worker one has to exemplify true Islamic qualities and attributes.

By combining the need for personal purity with the socio-cultural reformation of society through mass volunteering and social activism, Ilyas initiated an Islamic movement which completely transformed the Mewat region. Indeed, his religious methodology proved so successful that over time the *tablighi jama'at* became one of India's most popular Islamic movements, even during his own lifetime. As an Islamic preacher and reformer, he deliberately refrained from political activism. Why? Because getting involved in politics, he felt, could distract him and his band of followers from their core objective to change, improve and strengthen people's faith, morals, character and personality. Later, accompanied by his fellow *tablighi* leaders such as Mawlana

Ihtisham ul-Hasan, Mawlana Muhammad Yusuf and Mawlana Inam ul-Hasan, Ilyas performed his fourth and last pilgrimage in 1938. Six years later, he died at the age of fifty-nine and was buried in Nizamuddin. But the Islamic movement he founded continued to prosper under the able leadership of his son, Mawlana Muhammad Yusuf (who became known to his followers as "*hazrat ji*" or 'His Excellency'). He went out of his way to tour the entire subcontinent to promote the work of *tablighi jama'at*. Thus new *tablighi* centres mushroomed in both East and West Pakistan. Subsequently, under the leadership of Mawlana Inam ul-Hasan, *tablighi jama'at* spread across the world including Southeast Asia, Africa, Europe, as well as the Americas. As a staunchly apolitical religious movement, *tablighi jama'at* has been able to operate freely both in the Muslim world and the West, unlike, for instance, the more politically active Islamic organisations like *ikhwan al-muslimun* (The Muslim Brotherhood) in the Arab world or the *jama'at-i-islami* (The Islamic Organisation) in the subcontinent. With its headquarters still based at Nizamuddin, today the *tablighi jama'at* has become one of the most influential and widely-followed Islamic movements of all time.

# 82

## Sayyid Qutb
## (b.1906 - d.1966)

AS VICEROYS OF the Ottomans, the Muhammad Ali Pasha dynasty ruled Egypt for more than half a century before the British occupied Egypt in 1882. Being proud Muslims, the Egyptians profoundly resented foreign military occupation of their country, but the nineteenth century represented a volatile period in Egyptian (and Islamic) history for two important reasons. Firstly, during this period a large part of the Muslim world was colonised by the leading European nations, who went out of their way to undermine the politico-economic infrastructure of the Muslim countries. Secondly, the influx of European culture and values into the Muslim world led to considerable socio-cultural tension and confusion. As political instability and social upheaval gripped much of the Muslim world, several powerful indigenous nationalist movements emerged to challenge the occupying forces. In Egypt, the spread of nationalist fervour during the early part of the twentieth century forced the British to grant formal independence to Egypt. Although the Egyptian nationalists (like their counterparts in many other parts of the Muslim world) fought vigorously to liberate their country, they failed to prepare for the aftermath. This proved particularly disastrous for Egypt, as rival political factions advanced competing visions for the future of the country. Some advocated a secular, European-style democratic model for Egypt; others proposed a socialist political framework, while yet others championed an Islamic approach to nation-building. According to the proponents of an Islamic political framework, both the secular and socialist models had been tried, tested and found wanting. Only an Islamic approach to nation-building was, in their opinion, most appropriate for a great Muslim nation like Egypt. One of the most influential Egyptian Islamic thinkers and ideologues of the time was Sayyid Qutb whose ideas and thoughts have exerted a profound influence on twentieth century Islam.

Sayyid Qutb Ibrahim Hussain Shadhili was born in the village of Musha, near Asyut in Upper Egypt. Although his family originally hailed from the Arabian Peninsula, it was his immediate ancestors who moved to Egypt. A devout Muslim of mystical leanings, his father earned his living as a farmer. Living under British military occupation at the time, the majority of Egyptians (whether they were wealthy businessmen, impoverished farmers, illiterate village-dwellers or high-ranking civil servants) supported *al-hizb al-watani*, an Egyptian nationalist party led by Mustafa Kamil and his associates. As a nationalist and proud Muslim, Hajj Qutb actively supported the political activities of this party, whilst working hard to provide a comfortable living for his family. He had five children, three daughters and two sons, of which Sayyid Qutb was the eldest. Keen to provide a good education for his son, Hajj Qutb ensured his son committed the entire Qur'an to memory before he was ten. Thereafter, young Qutb studied the life and times of the Prophet, his companions, and aspects of Islamic history. After completing his elementary and intermediate studies, Qutb left his native Musha and, in 1921, settled in Cairo (*al-qahira*), the capital of Egypt and a bustling centre of intellectual, cultural and literary activities.

In Cairo, he lived with his uncle and enrolled at a preparatory college in order to secure a place at *dar al-uloom* (the present-day Cairo University). Originally founded by the Egyptian Government for the purpose of training teachers for State schools, this institution offered Western-style modern education along with the more traditional disciplines. The Egyptian middle-classes were particularly eager to secure places for their children at this institution because this offered a quick route to securing a relatively well-paid Government job. Keen to pursue a career in teaching, Qutb completed his preparatory courses and secured a place at *dar al-uloom* to study for a degree in education. From 1927 to 1930, he immersed himself in his studies and became actively engaged in cultural and literary activities. He became a prolific writer and literary critic while he was still in his twenties, and regularly published articles, reviews and poems in some of Cairo's leading newspapers and journals. His incisive reviews, thoughtful articles and moving poetry soon established his reputation as a leading literary figure. Despite his traditional upbringing, Qutb's writings at the time were almost entirely modernistic and nationalistic in their tone. Nevertheless, he was not a supporter of the Western modernism and secularism which was being imported into Egypt from Europe and promoted

throughout the country by the Egyptian elite; indeed Qutb opposed such wholesale importation of Western morals and values. During this period he authored his *Ashwak* (Thorns), a love story which ends in tragedy; *Tifl min Qaryah* (Child from the Village), an autobiographical account of his early life, and *Madina al-Mashoorah* (The Bewitched City) wherein he presented a literary account of historical buildings and royal palaces. At the time, he regularly rubbed shoulders with prominent Egyptian writers and intellectuals like Taha Hussain and Abbas Mahmud al-Aqqad, and sided with Mustafa Sadiq Rafai, another great Egyptian writer, when the latter clashed with al-Aqqad. By now, Qutb was considered to be a talented writer and literary critic in his own right.

After graduating from *dar al-uloom* in 1933, he taught at local schools before joining the Ministry of Education. Keen to improve the Egyptian educational system, he drafted scores of research papers suggesting ways to reform the country's educational policies and practices, but his proposals fell on deaf ears. To add insult to injury, the Egyptian Government was only too eager to please the British elites and, as expected, this made Qutb very angry. This prompted him to openly lambast the Egyptian Government for its slavish attitude towards the British on the one hand, and its failure to reform the nation's fledgling educational system on the other. Increasingly considered to be a loose cannon by his colleagues, his superiors at the Ministry of Education were relieved when he agreed to go to America – financed by a generous Government stipend – to conduct research into American educational philosophy and methodology. However, soon after his arrival in America in 1948, he became seriously ill. Being asthmatic, the long and gruelling journey exacerbated his breathing problems, but eventually he made a full recovery and joined Wilson Teacher's College in Washington DC to learn English. He then moved to Colorado and also visited California, Chicago and San Francisco before returning home to Egypt in 1951.

Qutb's stay in America transformed his outlook on life forever. As an educated, cultured and sensitive man, Qutb felt American society had very little to offer him. He considered American values and way of life to be riddled with both moral and ethical contradictions. Behind the glitter of material wealth and luxuries, he discovered how the ugly ghosts of spiritual deprivation, moral nihilism and cultural schizophrenia reigned supreme throughout American society. He could not understand why the Egyptian elites were so keen to import such morals and values, and promote them in Egypt as products of high culture and civilisation. By sacrificing collectivism at the expense of individualism and spirituality at the expense of material prosperity, American society, he felt, had been gripped by moral relativism, social distrust and economic insecurity. Convinced that American morals and values were not the answer for a Muslim society, Qutb experienced an intellectual, as well as a cultural, transformation. If his bosses at the Ministry of Education had sent him to America to open his mind to things Western, then he returned to Egypt to become a champion of Islamic values and morality. In his *America Allati Raiyto* (America as I saw it), Qutb not only demolished the argument that American culture and values were worth emulating by the Egyptians; he also exposed the fallacies inherent in Western materialistic values and philosophies.

In 1949, while Qutb was confined to his bed in George Washington University Hospital suffering from recurring respiratory problems, he received news of Hasan al-Banna's assassination. After the murder of the Egyptian Prime Minister, Nuqrashi Pasha, allegedly by a member of *Ikhwan al-Muslimun* (The Muslim Brotherhood), al-Banna was gunned down on the streets of Cairo by the Egyptian secret service. Founded by al-Banna in 1928, the Muslim Brotherhood was a mass Islamic movement which resisted the Egyptian elite's attempts to promote Western morals and values in Egypt; instead they advocated the need for promoting and implementing Islamic morals, ethics and values throughout the country. This movement became so popular that by early 1940s, that it became too powerful and

influential for the liking of the Egyptian authorities. Thus they instigated repressive measures against its prominent leaders and activists with a view to undermining the whole organisation, but the Brotherhood continued to flourish until its founder was assassinated in 1949. On his return to Egypt in 1951, Qutb closely studied the ideas, thoughts and methodology of the Brotherhood, and a year later he formally joined the organisation. Instantly he became one of its most prominent figures, along with Hasan Ismail al-Hudaybi. The period from 1949 to 1952 was a crucial period for Qutb for a number of reasons. Firstly, his understanding of and approach to Islam radically shifted during this period. He now began to see Islam in its entirety; that is to say, it was no longer a cultural element in his worldview, but rather he began to see Islam from an ideological perspective. Secondly, convinced that Islam was much more than merely a set of do's and don'ts, he developed a conceptual approach to Islam as a religion, culture and way of life – an all-encompassing worldview. He formulated his conceptual and ideological approach to Islam in a number of books he authored at the time, including *al-Adala al-Ijtimai'yyah fi'l Islam* (Social Justice in Islam), *Ma'rakat al-Islam wa'l Ra'smaliyyah* (Conflict between Islam and Capitalism) and *al-Salam al-Alam wa'l Islam* (Islam and Global Peace). As a prolific writer and an influential Islamic thinker, Qutb knew only too well that writing books alone does not lead to change; one must also be prepared to struggle to translate one's vision into reality. This propelled him into political activism under the banner of the Muslim Brotherhood.

Having no family commitments and responsibilities – Qutb did not marry; he remained a confirmed bachelor all his life – enabled him to devote all his time and energy to writing books and treatises on Islam, and to also become an Islamic political activist on a full-time basis. The more Qutb reflected on Islamic principles and practices *vis-à-vis* Egyptian society, the more he became convinced that his country had become engulfed by *jahiliyah* (deviation from Islam) –

morally, politically, culturally and economically. He argued that *hakimiyyah* (or sovereignty) only belonged to God and that the Egyptian political and social order had to be changed to reflect that truth; thus he advocated the need for *jihad* (or individual and collective struggle) to change the status quo in favour of an Islamic socio-political order. Although the concept of *jahiliyah* and *hakimiyyah* played an important role within Qutb's ideological approach to Islam, these terms were first interpreted in a socio-political way during the 1940s by Abul A'la Mawdudi, the renowned Pakistani writer and Islamic scholar. According to some of his biographers, Qutb not only became familiar with Mawdudi's writings (after the latter's works began to appear in Arabic during the early 1950s), but he also assimilated Mawdudi's political ideas and thoughts to develop his own ideological interpretation of Islam.

As a prominent member of the Brotherhood and one of its chief ideologues, Qutb soon ran into trouble with the Egyptian authorities for advocating the need for Islamic reformation in the country. But Jamal Abd al-Nasir (who assumed power following the overthrow of King Farouk by the Free Officers) was determined to steer the country towards a secular path. However, when the Brotherhood began to oppose Nasir's secularist overtures, they were censured by the authorities. Two years later, in 1954, the Brotherhood was outlawed by Nasir's regime after an alleged attempt on his life by a member of the Brotherhood. As a result, all the prominent leaders of the Brotherhood were arrested, including Qutb. After a botched trial he was sentenced to fifteen years' incarceration, during which he authored his monumental *Fi Zilal al-Qur'an* (In the Shade of the Qur'an), a voluminous commentary on the Qur'an. Widely considered to be one of the most influential Qur'anic commentaries of the twentieth century, in this work Qutb developed an ideological interpretation of Islamic thought and worldview. Although released from prison in 1964 due to poor health, a year later he was rearrested for actively supporting and co-operating with the Brotherhood. Accused of advocating the violent overthrow of the Government, the authorities concocted evidence to prove that he was a threat to the Egyptian Government and thus deserved the death penalty. Passages were plucked out of his books, especially his *Ma'alim fi'l Tariq* (Signposts on the Road), to seal his fate. A military tribunal established by the authorities tried and sentenced him to death at the age of sixty. He walked to his death without any fear or remorse. And although it is true that Qutb advocated *jihad*, he did not preach violence, nor did he call for the overthrow of the Egyptian Government through force, even though certain radical groups in Egypt and elsewhere have since tried to justify their violent actions against their repressive regimes by misinterpreting his ideas and thoughts.

Likewise, some Western writers on Islam and Middle Eastern affairs have wrongly branded Qutb a 'philosopher of terror'. They claim that Qutb's political and ideological interpretation of Islam provided the intellectual justification for extremist groups like *al-jama'ah al-islamiyyah* and *al-Qa'ida* to perpetrate their crimes. To be fair to Qutb, this is a very sweeping generalisation which fails to take into account the full thrust and complexity of his religious thoughts and ideas. What is true, however, is that Qutb was not steeped in traditional Islamic thought and scholarship; thus his interpretation of certain aspects of Islam (for example, the concepts of *tawhid* (Divinity), *hakimiyyah* (sovereignty), *jahiliyah* (deviation from Islam) and *jihad* (personal and collective struggle) are far from being traditional. In that sense he was indeed a radical Islamic thinker and activist; however, it would be equally wrong to say that he was an advocate of religious extremism and political violence, as some Western writers have suggested.

# 83

## Yahya al-Nawawi
## (b.1233 ~ d.1277)

AFTER THE QUR'AN declared the Prophet Muhammad to be the best role model (*uswatun hasana*) for all people, the need for recording and preserving his sayings and exhortations became a major preoccupation for his companions and the early Islamic scholars. Known as the *muhaddithun* (traditionists), these scholars dominated Islamic thought and scholarship from the very outset. The historians of *hadith* literature have identified three distinct phases during which great strides were made by the traditionists in the field of *hadith*. These periods can be classified as the early, classical and pre-modern stages. The early stage comprised the Prophet's companions (*sahabah*) and their successors (*tabiun*). During this period, close companions of the Prophet (such as Abu Hurairah, Abdullah ibn Amr ibn al-As, Aishah bint Abu Bakr, Abdullah ibn Umar, Abdullah ibn Abbas and Anas ibn Malik) played a crucial role in preserving and disseminating the Prophetic *hadith*. They were supported in their efforts by their able students like Ibn Shihab al-Zuhri, Sa'id ibn Musayyib, Masruq, al-Sha'bi and Ibn Sirin among countless others, who meticulously analysed and preserved the Prophetic traditions. And in so doing they paved the way for the second stage, the classical compilers of

*hadith,* to emerge and compose their famous anthologies. *Al-Muwatta* of Malik ibn Anas, *al-Musnad* of Ahmad ibn Hanbal, *Jami al-Sahih* of both Muhammad ibn Ismail al-Bukhari and Muslim ibn al-Hajjaj, and the *Sunan* of Abu Dawud, among others, belonged to this period. These famous traditionists collected and systematically scrutinised hundreds of thousands of *hadith* before compiling their celebrated anthologies for the benefit of posterity. After the classical compilers, there emerged a number of other prominent scholars of *hadith* including Ahmad ibn Hussain al-Bayhaqi, Hussain ibn Mas'ud al-Farra al-Baghawi and Wali al-Din al-Tabrizi, but the most famous *muhaddith* of the pre-modern era was Yahya al-Nawawi who played an influential role in popularising the Prophetic traditions.

Muhyi al-Din Abu Zakariyya Yahya ibn Sharaf ibn Muri ibn Hasan ibn Hussain ibn Muhammad ibn Juma ibn Hizam al-Hizami al-Damashqi, known as Imam al-Nawawi for short, was born in the village of Nawa, near Damascus in Syria. Of Arabian descent, his ancestor Juma ibn Hizam had moved to Syria many generations earlier and settled in Nawa. Sharaf ibn Muri, the father of al-Nawawi, was well known in Nawa as a businessman who owned a retail outlet. As devout Muslims and adherents of Sufism, Sharaf and his family members led a simple and pious lifestyle. Born and raised in a staunchly Islamic environment, al-Nawawi developed an instant affinity with Islamic principles and practices. As a studious child, he successfully committed the entire Qur'an to memory before the age of twelve, much to the delight of his father and extended family. Blessed with a sharp intellect and highly retentive memory, al-Nawawi was encouraged by his father to continue his studies rather than join the family business. He initially attended the local village schools where he studied Arabic, Qur'an and aspects of Islamic sciences. He was so studious that he shunned recreational activities and instead read books. When the local children asked him to play games with them, he refused to do so, saying his studies were more important to him than anything else. His scholarly disposition and love for learning soon won him the admiration of the locals. After completing his early education, al-Nawawi's father, impressed with his son's achievements, sent him to Damascus for further education so that he could realise his full potential.

Historically speaking, Damascus became a major centre of Islamic learning and education during the early days of Islam, when some of the leading companions of the Prophet settled there in order to pursue commerce and disseminate Islamic knowledge. Then, during the Umayyad period, the city not only became the seat of the Caliphate and the dazzling capital of the Islamic world, but also became the pre-eminent centre of Islamic learning, culture and civilisation, thus attracting some of the finest scholars, thinkers and writers of the Muslim world. Although by the thirteenth century Damascus had lost much of its former glory, it nevertheless retained its position as one of the Muslim world's leading centres of learning and scholarship. At the time, some of the most renowned scholars of the Qur'an, *hadith*, *fiqh* (Islamic jurisprudence) and *tasawwuf* (mysticism) lived and taught there. Indeed, Damascus boasted no fewer than three hundred religious seminaries and colleges, where both the religious

and scientific disciplines were taught under the patronage of its rulers and prominent religious figures. In 1251, when al-Nawawi was only eighteen, he moved to Damascus and enrolled at *madrasah al-rawahiyyah* for his intermediate and advanced education. Founded and generously financed by Abul Qasim Zaki al-Din ibn Rawah, a wealthy Damascene businessman and trader, al-Nawawi first studied aspects of medicine and alchemy before switching over to traditional Islamic sciences. For two years he studied Arabic grammar, *hadith* and Islamic jurisprudence, especially *shafi'i* legal thought, under the guidance of eminent scholars like Abu Ibrahim Ishaq ibn Ahmad, Abu Muhammad Abd al-Rahman ibn Ibrahim, Abu Ishaq Ibrahim ibn Isa and Abul Abbas Ahmad ibn Salim.

His time at *madrasah al-rawahiyyah* proved to be both challenging and very fruitful. On a personal level, he pursued his studies with the utmost dedication; he slept only a few hours at night, ate most frugally, and often survived only on biscuits and water. He read intensively, until a combination of tiredness and sleeplessness would force him to take a short nap. He studied twelve subjects daily, including *hadith*, grammar, logic (*mantiq*) and jurisprudence, and he would not take a break until he had thoroughly researched and taken extensive notes on all subjects. His physical endurance, eye for detail and devotion to his studies soon won him much acclaim in both Damascus and his native Nawa. According to Shams al-Din al-Dhahabi, the author of *Tadhkirat al-Huffaz*, al-Nawawi was endowed with an unusual ability to focus on his studies, which enabled him to remain engaged in his research for prolonged periods without being distracted by worldly affairs. After completing his education at *madrasah al-rawahiyyah*, he accompanied his father to Makkah to perform the sacred pilgrimage. On his return, he resumed his studies. Like his father, al-Nawawi was influenced by Sufism (*tasawwuf*) and as such he practised asceticism (*zuhd*). But his spirituality and ascetic practices were influenced more by the *sunnah* (the normative practices of the Prophet) than any other considerations. He led a simple, austere lifestyle and showed no interest in the material possessions of this world, and even refused the offer of an annual stipend during his spell as a headteacher at *ashrafiyyah* seminary in Damascus. His main preoccupation in life was to seek and disseminate knowledge, and he carried out this task with due diligence and great determination. Despite being a prominent authority on Islamic jurisprudence, his fame spread far and wide on account of his unrivalled mastery of *hadith* literature.

Living in thirteenth century Damascus, al-Nawawi was only too aware of the challenges facing the Muslim world at the time. As the signs of Islamic political and intellectual decline became clear for all to see, the bickering Muslim rulers of the time singularly failed to resolve their differences and work collectively to stop the rot. This sorry state of affairs persisted until the Mongol hordes appeared from Asia like a thunderbolt from the heavens and destroyed Baghdad, the political capital of the Muslim world, in 1258 and threatened to overwhelm Syria and Egypt in turn. With the Mongol threat looming on the horizon, the Mamluk rulers of Syria and Egypt were forced to muster their forces and face the Mongols at the Battle of *ayn jalut* (or 'the Spring of Goliath') in 1260. By inflicting a crushing defeat on the Mongols, the Mamluks saved Syria and Egypt from the same fate that had visited Baghdad two years earlier. When the news of the Mamluk victory reached the masses, the whole of Syria erupted. At the time, al-Nawawi was living in Damascus and he too must have joined the people of Syria in their thanksgiving celebrations. Rukn al-Din Baibars, the Turkish Mamluk commander who led the charge against the Mongol forces, was later crowned the fourth Mamluk Sultan of Syria and Egypt and, as such, he became a staunch defender of the Islamic East.

Although Sultan Baibars was a gifted commander and military strategist, he was far from being a generous and sympathetic ruler; he surrounded himself with much wealth and luxury, while the poor were forced to pay for his military expeditions. On one occasion, when the Sultan was short of money, he called all the prominent scholars of Syria to a meeting and asked them to sign a decree (*fatwa*) which stipulated that it was a religious obligation for the locals to contribute to the cost of his military expeditions. As a leading scholar of Damsacus, al-Nawawi also attended this meeting but he flatly refused to sign the decree. He argued that it was unfair to impose more taxes on the poor, while the Sultan and his courtiers had surrounded themselves with so much wealth and luxury. His defiance shocked and surprised everyone who was present at the royal court. After he left, the Sultan was asked why he did not punish him; he replied that al-Nawawi's presence filled him with fear and awe.

Al-Nawawi was not only a brave scholar, but also a man of sound principles and practices. As a great scholar of Islamic jurisprudence and *hadith*, he practised what he preached and never failed to stand up for what he considered to be right, just and fair. The pressing political problems of the time aside, al-Nawawi was profoundly disturbed by the moral, ethical and spiritual decadence which threatened to overwhelm the Muslim world at the time. He therefore devoted all his time and energy to composing books and treatises on *hadith*, Islamic jurisprudence, biographical studies, grammar and *tasawwuf*. Although he composed around sixty books and treatises, his most popular and influential works include *Riyad as-Salihin* (The Garden of the Rightcous), *Al-Minhaj fi Sharh Sahih Muslim ibn al-Hajjaj* (A Commentary on *Sahih Muslim*) and *Kitab al-Arba'in* (The Book of Forty *hadith*). The *Riyad as-Salihin* is a unique and very accessible anthology of Prophetic traditions which he composed for scholars and lay people alike. Consisting of more than three hundred and fifty sections, this remarkable book contains guidance from the Qur'an and *hadith* covering all aspects of life.

After conducting a thorough study of *hadith* literature, including *al-sahih al-sittah* (or the 'six canonical collections' of al-Bukhari, Muslim, Abu Dawud, al-Tirmidhi, al-Nasa'i and Ibn Majah), he produced his anthology by drawing information from only the authentic sources. Not surprisingly, the *Riyad as-Salihin* is rated very highly by Islamic scholars and it has also been translated and published in all the prominent languages of the world. In addition to this, al-Nawawi wrote commentaries on *Sahih al-Bukhari* and *Sunan Abu Dawud*, but his commentary on *Sahih Muslim* is considered to be one of the best written on that collection of *hadith*. However, his most popular and influential work is *Kitab al-Arba'in*. Like his *Riyad as-Salihin*, this small collection of forty *hadith* has been translated into all the main languages of the world, including Persian, Urdu, Hindi, Bengali, French and English. His remarkable contributions in the field of *hadith* literature aside, al-Nawawi was one of the most respected exponents of *shafi'i* jurisprudence along with al-Rafi'i, Ibn Hajar al-Asqalani and al-Ramli. Through his countless books on Prophetic traditions, jurisprudence and Islamic spirituality, he attempted to revive and popularise the Prophetic norms and practices at a time when the Muslim world was becoming increasingly detached from its Islamic roots.

Al-Nawawi lived in Damascus for more than twenty-five years and he studied, taught and authored all his books during this period. Most interestingly, despite being a strict adherent of the Prophetic *sunnah*, he refused to marry and instead remained a confirmed bachelor all his life. In 1277, he returned all the books he had borrowed from his friends and colleagues, and left Damascus for Jerusalem where he performed prayers at the *masjid al-aqsa* (or farthest mosque) and visited the tomb of Prophet Abraham (*Ibrahim*) in Hebron, before returning home to Nawa. Soon after his arrival, he passed away at the age of forty-four; his father was still alive at the time of his death. He was buried in Nawa where a tomb was later erected as a tribute to his memory; also the anthologies of *hadith* he composed continue to be read and studied by millions of people across the globe to this day.

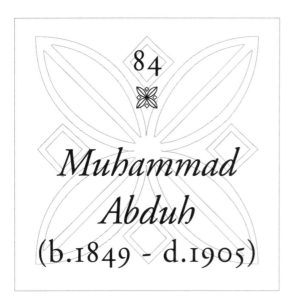

# 84

## Muhammad Abduh
## (b.1849 - d.1905)

THE NINETEENTH CENTURY was one of the most politically traumatic and intellectually degenerative periods in the annals of Islam. Historically speaking, as and when the Muslim world succumbed to the lures of materialism, or went through a period of intellectual stagnation, influential religious reformers or political leaders emerged to warn the masses and call them back to the original, pristine message of Islam. Thus during the Umayyad period, Hasan al-Basri and Umar ibn Abd al-Aziz emerged to warn the masses of the dangers of unbridled power, greed and hedonism. Ahmad ibn Hanbal and his successors did the same during the Abbasid period. Later, as intellectual confusion and moral decadence began to rear their ugly heads in the eleventh century, towering figures like al-Ghazali and Ibn Hazm al-Andalusi appeared to defend traditional Islam. Amidst the chaos wrought by the Mongols in the thirteenth century, Ibn Taymiyyah and al-Nawawi attempted to revive the Prophetic norms, practices and methodology (*minhaj al-sunnah*). Likewise, in the sixteenth century, Shaykh Ahmad Sirhindi, the influential Indian Muslim reformer, and Muhammad ibn Pir Ali (better known as Imam Birgivi), the renowned Turkish Islamic scholar and Sufi sage, emerged

to champion Islamic moral, ethical and spiritual teachings for the benefit of their people. The rise of Muhammad ibn Abd al-Wahhab in Arabia and the pan-Islamist reformer and activist Jamal al-Din al-Afghani, in the eighteenth and nineteenth centuries respectively, proved that Islam was capable of renewing itself in times of crises. It also paved the way for Muhammad Abduh, an eminent disciple of al-Afghani and the 'father of Islamic modernism' to emerge and become one of the most influential Islamic thinkers and reformers of the nineteenth century.

Born in a village in northern Egypt close to the Nile, Abduh's father was a relatively well-off trader of some standing in his locality. Brought up in the traditional ambience of the Nile Delta, young Abduh showed signs of unusual intellectual ability from an early age. Keen to educate and support him, his family sent him to his local village *maktab* (or religious school) where he committed the entire Qur'an to memory, which won him much praise from his teachers. Impressed by his rapid progress, Abduh's family then enrolled him at the noted Ahmadi mosque-cum-seminary in Tanta at the age of thirteen. Here he received further education in Arabic language, grammar, literature and traditional

Islamic sciences. Thanks to his ability to retain and assimilate vast quantities of information, he successfully completed his further and intermediate education. During his time at this institute, Abduh developed keen interest in the speculative sciences, including philosophy and mysticism. He then enrolled at al-Azhar University in Cairo to pursue higher education in Arabic literature, logic, philosophy and mysticism. Originally founded by the Fatimids in the tenth century, al-Azhar is not only one of the world's oldest institutions of higher education, it is also one of the Muslim world's most famous seats of Islamic learning and scholarship. Abduh excelled in his studies, passing his final examinations with flying colours at the age of twenty-six. On account of his great talent and intellectual ability, the university authorities asked him to stay on and teach the undergraduate students. For the next two years he lectured at al-Azhar and became a popular figure due to his great learning and refreshing approach to Islam.

It was during his tenure as a lecturer at al-Azhar that Abduh first met Jamal al-Din al-Afghani, the famous Muslim thinker and pan-Islamist politician of the nineteenth century. He found al-Afghani to be an inspirational intellectual, captivating lecturer and highly motivated political activist who formulated a new and original pan-Islamist political ideology in order to unify the Muslim world under the banner of Islam. Since a large part of the Muslim world was suffering under European colonial rule at the time, Abduh was convinced that al-Afghani's rallying call for Islamic unity and solidarity was the only way the Muslims could liberate their lands from foreign occupation. Though al-Afghani's message of Islamic unity and solidarity never went down well with the colonial rulers (whether in India, Egypt or for that matter in Ottoman Turkey), here at al-Azhar his call for Islamic political unity won him a large following. Alarmed by al-Afghani's ideological interpretation of Islam, the British, who exercised real political power in Egypt at the time, expelled him from the country in 1879. Before being thrown out, he had managed to

plant the seeds of pan-Islamism in the intellectual circles of Cairo; Abduh would continue to oversee the development of pan-Islamism in that country.

Following al-Afghani's expulsion from Egypt, Abduh returned to his native village, presumably to allow the dust of the political storm which raged in Cairo to settle, before he returned again to the capital to take up the post of editor of *al-waqa'i al-misriyyah* (The Egyptian Gazette, a Government publication). In this Gazette, he published scores of articles, calling for Islamic unity and the need for social, political and religious reform in Egypt. But the voices of nationalism became louder by the day after the formal British military occupation of Egypt in 1882, and it was during this period that Abduh fell out with the British authorities for supporting the nationalists, and he was forced to live in exile for about six years. But from his safe haven in Lebanon he continued his opposition to the British. He also found time to establish a modern Islamic school to train students in both traditional Islamic sciences and modern philosophical thought. Despite being brought up in a traditional environment – and having also received a thorough education in traditional Islamic sciences –Abduh had a modern mindset; he was also very eager to explore the political and intellectual problems which confronted the Islamic world at the time. He found the Egyptian educational system far too didactic, cumbersome and uninspiring. Moreover, he felt the absence of political unity, social progress and intellectual creativity in Egypt and the rest of the Muslim world had undermined the people's confidence, self-belief and collective will to face the social, political, economic and intellectual challenges posed by Western modernity and secularism.

Convinced that the traditional methods of teaching the Islamic sciences did not promote intellectual creativity and fresh thinking, which was the cornerstone of modern Western educational philosophy, he began to rethink his entire approach to Islam. The answers to the challenges of Western modernity were unlikely to come from the bastion of Islamic traditionalism, for the champions of traditionalism were, in his opinion, determined to cling to their outmoded religious methodologies. Likewise, an entirely modernistic approach to Islam was not the answer either, because he felt this could lead to a rapid dilution of quintessential Islam. Combining the traditional methods of teaching Islamic sciences with a modern approach was the only viable alternative, argued Abduh. This would enable Islamic institutions to produce a new generation of Islamic scholars, intellectuals and reformers who could tackle the challenges which confronted the Muslim world at the time. A few years later, Abduh left Beirut for Paris where he joined forces with al-Afghani, his former mentor and guide, to bring about political change and reform in the Muslim world.

Shocked by the plight and predicament of the Muslim *ummah* (global community), the master and disciple worked tirelessly to reform Islamic thought and reawaken the Muslim world from its deep slumber. In Paris, they established an institute for socio-political reform in the Muslim world and published their famous journal *al-urwa al-wuthqa* (The Unbreakable Bond) – a phrase which appears twice in the Qur'an and refers to those people who place their absolute trust in Divine power and judgement. Through this journal, Abduh and his mentor launched a blistering intellectual assault on the European colonial powers, especially the British who at the time exercised power in India and Egypt, and these countries soon became the main focus of their political agitation. Their call for the masses to rise against the colonial powers and liberate their lands from Western domination, instantly turned Abduh and al-Afghani into heroic figures in many parts of the Muslim world. And although al-Afghani was a powerful thinker who possessed an encyclopaedic mind, unfortunately he exhausted much of his physical and intellectual energy in uncoordinated socio-political activism.

By contrast, Abduh sought to explore and rethink the entire Islamic intellectual framework in order to devise a new educational methodology which would be relevant for his time. In so doing he hoped to combat the forces of Westernisation and secularism which threatened to overwhelm the Muslim world. Abduh and al-Afghani's political ideas and religious thoughts – formulated most eloquently in *al-urwa al-wuthqa* – struck a chord with the masses in many parts of the Muslim world. In response, the British authorities in Egypt imposed a ban on their journal, but it was regularly smuggled into the country where it acquired a large following. After publishing only eighteen issues, the journal became defunct due to lack of funding, censorship and political restrictions. Yet, within a relatively short period, it had created a huge political stir in the Muslim world.

After the demise of *al-urwa al-wuthqa* in 1884, Abduh left Paris and returned to Beirut where he gathered around him a number of talented young intellectuals and activists, including Muhammad Rashid Rida who became one of his most able and trusted disciples. Abduh then lost contact with al-Afghani and the political situation in his native Egypt began to improve, so the British authorities allowed him to return to Cairo in 1888. Now considered to be an eminent Islamic thinker and jurist, he was appointed a judge (*qadi*). Over the next decade, he changed and re-formulated his views on many aspects of Islam and worked tirelessly to develop a balanced approach to Islamic thought and jurisprudence in the light of his existential condition. He wrote scores of articles, treatises and a partial commentary on the Qur'an. He always expressed his views on Islam and Islamic jurisprudence in a clear and forthright manner. His most famous book was *Risalat al-Tawhid* (A Treatise on Divine Unity) in which he developed a fresh and challenging exposition of Islamic philosophy and theology in the light of Western modernity. According to Abduh, although reason and revelation are two distinct sources of knowledge, they are not contradictory; rather they are two complementary sources of knowledge. As such, both reason and revelation are necessary for developing a comprehensive and authentic interpretation of Islamic philosophical, theological, ethical and legal thought. Much confusion and chaos, he argued, had become set in the Muslim mind and morals due to the Islamic scholar's failure to relate the fundamental principles of Islam to their existential realities. In other words, Abduh was of the opinion that the universal principles of Islam are timeless and unchangeable, but our existential condition constantly changes and evolves; thus the principles of Islam must always underpin our personal as well as collective actions.

His reformist (or modernist) approach to Islamic thought and jurisprudence enabled him to refute the practice of *taqlid* (uncritical imitation of tradition). Instead he argued in favour of *ijtihad* (exercising individual scholarly judgement or discretion). Influenced by the 'critical jurisprudence' of Abu Ishaq Ibrahim al-Shatibi, the renowned Andalusian Islamic jurist and thinker, Abduh believed it was the Muslim failure to exercise *ijtihad* on a continuous basis which helped to create the unfavourable circumstances in which the Muslim world found itself at the time. Blind or uncritical imitation of tradition not only undermined the Muslim's self-belief and confidence, it also curtailed all forms of creativity and fresh thinking among the Muslim scholars and intellectuals. In order to reinvigorate the Muslim mind and regenerate Islamic societies, he, like al-Shatibi, called for a return to the original sources of Islam, namely the Qur'an and the authentic Prophetic *sunnah*. A fresh approach to, and understanding of, the two fundamental scriptural sources of Islam would, he felt, enable the Muslims to break out of the cycle of intellectual poverty, social degeneration and political subjugation, and usher in a new era of peace, progress and development across the Muslim world.

After working as a judge for about a decade, in 1899 Abduh was appointed Grand Mufti of Egypt, which was the highest judicial post in the country; he also became a member of the Egyptian Legislative Council. During his period as Grand Mufti, he carried out much-needed reform of the judicial system and sponsored the publication of the renowned journal *al-manar* (The Lighthouse), which was founded by his disciple Muhammad Rashid Rida back in 1898. Six years after becoming the Grand Mufti, Abduh died at the age of fifty-four and was buried in Cairo. However, his religious ideas and thoughts continued to be championed for another three decades by Rashid Rida, who also authored a comprehensive biography of Abduh under the title of *Tarikh al-Ustadh al-Imam Muhammad Abduh*. His efforts to reconcile the timeless values and principles of Islam with the new challenges and realities of his time earned Abduh much praise from his admirers as well as criticism from many religious conservatives. However, as the 'father of Islamic modernism', his reformist ideas and thoughts have influenced generations of Islamic scholars, thinkers and reformers across the Muslim world, especially in Egypt and Indonesia.

# 85

## Sir Muhammad Iqbal
## (b.1877 - d.1938)

DURING THE LATE nineteenth and early twentieth century, India produced some of the most influential Muslim leaders, thinkers and writers of the modern period. Not willing to live under British rule, the Indian Muslims spearheaded the Indian liberation movement. Thus influential Muslim leaders like Mawlana Muhammad Ali Jauhar of the *khilafat* fame; AKM Fazlul Haq, better known as *sher-i bangla* (or the 'tiger of Bengal'), and Muhammad Ali Jinnah, who became known as *quaid-i-azam* (or the 'great leader') rallied the Muslim masses and urged them to liberate their country from foreign occupation. And in so doing they left their indelible marks in the annals of modern history. Celebrated Indian Muslim scholars and writers of the time included Allama Shibli Numani, the famous author of *Sirat un-Nabi* (Biography of the Prophet); Sayyid Amir Ali, the renowned jurist and popular author of *The Spirit of Islam*; Abdullah Yusuf Ali, the celebrated translator and interpreter of the Qur'an into English, and last but not least, Mawlana Abul Kalam Azad, the towering Islamic intellectual and author of *Tarjuman al-Qur'an* (a commentary on the Qur'an). Sir Muhammad Iqbal, the hugely influential Muslim thinker and poet-philosopher of

the subcontinent, belonged to this generation of outstanding Indian Muslims. His original poetic output, coupled with his invaluable contribution to Islamic thought and philosophy, has today made him a household name especially in Iran and the subcontinent.

Muhammad Iqbal's date of birth is hotly contested by the historians. Some say he was born in 1873; others say he was born in 1877, while according to others he was born in 1876. However, the majority of his biographers say he was born in 1877. His ancestors were Hindu Brahmins who originally hailed from Kashmir and embraced Islam during the seventeenth century. Later, they left the Kashmir valley and settled in Sialkot in the Punjab, located between the historic citadel of Lahore and Kashmir. Iqbal was born in Sialkot into a lower-middle class Muslim family. A tailor by profession, his father, Nur Muhammad, was an illiterate Sufi who owned a small business. The modest income he generated from his business enabled him to lead a simple but comfortable lifestyle. Young Iqbal grew up under the watchful gaze of his devout father, who enrolled him at his local *maktab* (religious school) where he received elementary education in Persian, Arabic, Urdu and aspects of Islamic sciences under the tutelage of Sayyid Mir Hasan. As an expert in Islamic sciences and classical Persian and Urdu literature, Mir Hasan encouraged Iqbal to learn Persian and Urdu poetry; thus he read and learnt to compose poetry while he was still in his teens. Iqbal was a bright student whose poetic imagination and ability impressed Mir Hasan, who encouraged him to enrol at the Scotch Mission School in Sialkot where he took his matriculation examination in 1893.

When he was sixteen, Iqbal joined the Scotch Mission College (the present-day Murray College) and successfully completed his intermediate studies. During this period he married the daughter of a local physician and she bore him three children, two daughters and a son. At the age of about nineteen, he moved to Lahore and enrolled at the Government College. Here he studied Arabic, English literature and philosophy under the guidance of Sir Thomas Arnold, a distinguished British Orientalist and author of *The Preaching of Islam* (1896), who encouraged him to pursue higher education. As a prominent scholar and historian of Islam, Sir Thomas was a lecturer at Aligarh's Muhammadan Anglo-Oriental College where he collaborated closely with Allama Shibli Numani before moving to Lahore; he was also well-known for his fair and sympathetic views about Islam. Inspired by Sir Thomas's love of learning and scholarship, Iqbal hoped to pursue higher education in Europe in order to widen his intellectual horizons by acquiring first-hand knowledge of modern Western philosophy and sciences. After graduating with honours in Arabic and English literature, and also obtaining a master's degree in philosophy, he became a lecturer in Arabic at the Oriental College in Lahore; he was only twenty-three at the time.

During this period he established his reputation as a gifted poet who could compose elegant and moving verses in Urdu, which he regularly recited in front of large audiences in *musha'irahs* (or poetic symposiums). Distinguished Urdu poets of the time included Nawab Mirza Khan Dagh and Mirza Arshad, who rated Iqbal very highly and encouraged him to compose more

poetry. He duly obliged by writing scores of poems on romantic, nationalistic, mystical and emotional themes including *Nala-i-Yatim* (The Orphan's Cry), *Gul-i-Pashmurdah* (The Withered Rose), *Tarana-i-Milli* (National Anthem), *Naya Shiwala* (The New Altar) and *Taswir-i-Dard* (Picture of Grief), which instantly won him recognition throughout Lahore. During this period he failed a law exam and was unable to secure a civil service job due to medical reasons, but he did not despair and continued to teach at some of Lahore's leading institutions of higher education, including the Government and Islamia Colleges. Following Sir Thomas Arnold's departure from Lahore for London in 1904, Iqbal followed suit and moved to England in 1905.

He arrived in England at the age of twenty-eight and joined Trinity College, Cambridge, where he attended James Ward and J.E. McTaggart's lectures on philosophy, and closely collaborated with distinguished British Orientalists like Edward G. Browne and Reynold A. Nicholson. After obtaining a degree in philosophy, he moved to Munich University in Germany where he pursued continental philosophy and wrote a doctoral thesis on the development of metaphysics in Persia. Thereafter, he returned to England where he was called to the Bar at London's Lincoln's Inn and qualified as a barrister. Iqbal's stay in Europe was an academically very successful period for him; it was also one of the most intellectually and spiritually defining moments of his life. In Europe, he closely studied European philosophy and thought, and observed Western culture and civilisation at first-hand, but what he saw both shocked and surprised him. Full of life and vitality, he found the European people friendly, hardworking and studious. Thanks to their eagerness to study and explore the wonders of creation, a culture of learning and inquisitiveness emerged in Europe which enabled the Europeans to make great strides in philosophy, science and technology. By contrast, the Muslim world (which was once the pioneer of science, philosophy, culture and civilisation) now seemed to him to have become stuck in the past. The vigour and vitality of European civilisation compared with the sterile and decadent condition of Islamic thought and culture was bound to shock and alarm a proud Muslim like Iqbal, who now began to explore his own faith, its meaning and purpose in the modern world.

Iqbal had left India in 1905 as a young scholar, poet and nationalist, but his stay in Europe radically transformed his view of Islam and its place and role in history. Living in an increasingly Western-dominated political, economic, educational and cultural landscape, he began to see his faith in a different light. Detached from the romanticism of the past, the nationalism of his own time and the materialistic philosophies of the West, he explored European thought and culture and the challenges which confronted the Muslim world then, in the light of the timeless values and principles of Islam. The results of his intellectual inquiry and evaluation again shocked and disturbed him: if Western civilisation had made great progress in the fields of science and technology, it did so at the expense of moral and spiritual advancement. This, in his opinion, did not constitute progress or advancement; it was similar to building a castle on shifting sand; a disaster waiting to happen. As for the Islamic world, although the Muslims were in possession of the final Divine revelation, he felt the Muslims had become obsessed with the form rather the spirit of the Divine scripture; and this contributed to the gradual ossification of the Muslim mind, thought, culture and civilisation. This prompted him to explore ways in which he could revitalise the Muslim mind and thought, and expose the dangers inherent in scientific and cultural progress which lacked the moral and spiritual dimension of humanity. After leaving London in 1908, he returned home to India at the age of thirty-one and began to explore the problems and predicaments of modern civilisation in the light of Islamic values and principles. Like Malik ben Nabi, the eminent Algerian social scientist and Islamic thinker, and Sayyid Qutb, the Egyptian Islamic ideologue, Iqbal went to the West in search of knowledge and wisdom but returned home a committed Muslim, having discovered how fragile the foundations of modern Western civilisation were, and tried to reawaken his fellow Muslims from their slumber. As a gifted poet and philosopher, Iqbal expounded his ideas and thoughts in his elegant and powerful poetry, which he wrote in both Urdu and Persian. He analysed and critiqued modern philosophy and science through the philosophical lens of Islam, and attempted to reinvigorate Muslim thought and culture by creating a synthesis between Islamic and modern Western thought, culture and values.

The period from 1908 to 1936 was the most intellectually productive period of his life. As a qualified lawyer he could have earned a lucrative salary and led a luxurious lifestyle, but instead he chose to teach philosophy at the Government College in Lahore and practice law on a part-time basis. This enabled him to earn enough to live comfortably and devote all his spare time and energy to developing his ideas and thoughts on how to reconstruct Islamic thought and reinvigorate Muslim societies in the face of Western political, intellectual and cultural domination of the Islamic world. Iqbal expounded his religious ideas and philosophical thoughts in scores of books of poetry published over more than thirty years. Thus, the *Shikwa* (Complaint) and *Jawab-i-Shikwa* (Response to Complaint) appeared in 1911; they were followed by *Asrar-i-Khudi* (The Secrets of the Self) in 1915. Three years later, his *Ramuz-i-Bekhudi* (The Mysteries of Selflessness) was published; likewise, *Payam-i-Mashriq* (Message of the East) appeared in 1923, while *Bang-i-Dara* (The Call of the Caravan Bell) followed a year later. Thereafter, *Zabur-i-Ajam* (The Persian Psalms) appeared in 1927; this was followed by *Javid Namah* (The Song of Eternity) in 1932, while *Bal-i-Jibril* (Gabriel's Wing), *Zarbi-i-Kalim* (The Stick of Moses) and *Armughan-i-Hijaz* (Gift of the Hijaz) were published in 1935, 1936 and 1938, respectively.

Heavily influenced by the religious ideas and thoughts of al-Ghazali, the great Islamic iconoclast of the eleventh century, and Jalal al-Din

Rumi, the renowned thirteenth century Sufi poet and thinker, as well as the philosophical ideas of several European thinkers like Henri Bergson, Friedrich Nietzsche and J.E. McTaggart, Iqbal developed a powerful and dynamic philosophy which called on the Muslims to rise up and boldly face the challenges posed by Western modernity, secularism and nationalism. Couched in poetic language and a degree of philosophical sophistication, his message was as simple as it was effective: he urged the Muslims to take their destiny in their own hands by freeing themselves from European colonial rule, and to rediscover the creativity and dynamism that is inherent in the meaning and message of Islam. Iqbal made this point most eloquently in a series of lectures he delivered between 1928 and 1929 at the universities of Madras, Hyderabad and Mysore. Later published as *The Reconstruction of Religious Thought in Islam*, in these lectures, he attempted to reformulate Islamic thought in the light of modern Western scientific and philosophical thought, and did so without completely breaking away from the traditional Islamic worldview. The lack of intellectual creativity, philosophical sophistication and cultural vitality in the Muslim world had contributed, he felt, to the gradual decline of Islamic culture and civilisation. He therefore urged the Muslims to engage in a continuous process of *ijtihad* (or exercise of individual judgement) in order to reinvigorate Islamic thought and culture.

If Iqbal was an outstanding Islamic thinker, then he was also one of the greatest Urdu poets since Mir Taqi Mir and Mirza Asadullah Khan Ghalib. Far from being an intellectual recluse, he urged Muslims to become activists and lead a vibrant life underpinned by Islamic morals and values. He practised what he preached and became actively involved in Indian politics. He served as a member of Punjab Legislative Council, was knighted in 1922 and became the president of All-India Muslim League in 1930, thus occupying a prominent position in Indian public life. It was during his tenure as president of the Muslim League that he developed the idea of creating a separate homeland for the Muslims of India. Later, in 1947, Muhammad Ali Jinnah pursued and realised his vision in the form of the Islamic Republic of Pakistan. Iqbal did not live long enough to witness this momentous event; he died of illness at the age of sixty-one and was buried next to the famous Badshahi mosque in Lahore. As the national poet of Pakistan and an influential Islamic thinker, Iqbal's poetry and message continues to inspire Muslims to this day; he is especially popular in Pakistan, Iran, India and Bangladesh.

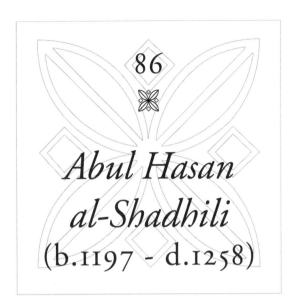

# 86

## Abul Hasan al-Shadhili (b.1197 - d.1258)

ACCORDING TO A famous Prophetic tradition (*hadith*), at the turn of every century there will emerge a *mujaddid* (or religious regenerator) who will call the Muslims back to the original, pristine message of Islam. Renowned Muslim rulers, reformers and personalities like Umar ibn Abd al-Aziz, Abu Hanifah, Malik ibn Anas, al-Shafi'i, Ahmad ibn Hanbal, al-Ghazali, Ibn Taymiyyah, Shaykh Ahmad Sirhindi and Shah Waliullah were considered to be religious regenerators of their time. But eminent Sufi sages like Hasan al-Basri, Abd al-Qadir al-Jilani, Jalal al-Din Rumi, Khwajah Naqshband, Shihab al-Din Umar al-Suhrawardi, Mu'in al-Din Chishti and Najm al-Din Kubra (who contributed immensely to the preservation and dissemination of Islam as a religion and a way of life) were not considered to be *mujaddid* as readily as the former. Yet, had it not been for the valiant efforts of these great spiritual figures of Islam, the forces of materialism and hedonism would have overwhelmed the Muslim world a long time ago. Of the numerous Sufi Orders (*tariqah*) which emerged in the Muslim world over the last fourteen centuries, the *qadiriyyah*, *naqshbandiyyah* and the *chishti-yyah* are considered to be the most popular and prominent. However, the Sufi Order founded by

Abul Hasan al-Shadhili, the great North African Sufi scholar and sage, also played a pivotal role in the preservation of Islamic thought and practices in North Africa, as well as the dissemination of Islam across Europe and America.

Abul Hasan Ali ibn Abdullah al-Shadhili, known as Imam Shadhili for short, was born in the district of Ghumara, located close to modern Ceuta in Morocco. His family members were devout Muslims and adherents of *maliki* jurisprudence, and traced their lineage back to the Prophet through his grandson, Hasan ibn Ali. Brought up and educated in an Islamic environment, young Shadhili absorbed Islamic knowledge and wisdom from his family members before he went on to pursue further and higher education under the guidance of luminaries such as Muhammad Abu Abdullah ibn Harazin. Living during the relatively peaceful rule of the al-Mohads (this dynasty was founded in the middle of the twelfth century by Abu Abdullah Muhammad ibn Abdullah ibn Tumart, a prominent North African Islamic reformer of the time), Shadhili became a devout student of Islam from an early age. He was such a talented student that he gained recognition throughout his locality for his vast knowledge of Islamic sciences while he was still in his early twenties.

His knowledge of Islamic jurisprudence, especially *maliki* legal thought, was so exceptional that he regularly participated in legal discussions and debates with other prominent local scholars. Despite being a bright student and a skilled debater, he became bored with dry legalistic debate and argumentation, and longed for personal fulfilment and inner peace. Thus began his quest for a spiritual teacher who could guide him in the ways of Islamic spirituality (*tasawwuf*) and gnosis (*ma'rifa*). His quest for a genuine spiritual teacher and guide eventually brought him into contact with the renowned Moroccan Sufi luminary Shaykh Abd al-Salam ibn Mashish of Fez, who at the time was based at his *zawiyyah* (Sufi lodge) in Jabal al-Alam where he was engaged in spiritual retreat with his small band of disciples. When Shadhili approached Shaykh Mashish, the latter reportedly told him to go away and return after performing a full bath. When he returned after the ritual cleansing, he was told to go back and purify himself again. Shadhili did as he was told and returned once more. For the third time, Shaykh Mashish told him to go away and purify himself thoroughly. This time Shadhili understood what the master was hinting at; thus he told him that he had indeed thoroughly cleansed himself of his previous habits and practices. The first cleansing act apparently referred to the physical purification of the body; the second represented the rejection of all forms of unsavoury deeds and actions, and the third referred to the cleansing of the heart, mind and soul. After going through this cleansing process, the master invited Shadhili into his company and trained him in the methods of Islamic mysticism and gnosis. His time with Shaykh Mashish represented a major turning point in Shadhili's life, for it was during this period that he mastered the rigorous methods of Sufism and began to experience Islamic spirituality in its highest form. As the first part of his life (namely that of an exoteric scholar who kept himself preoccupied with scholarly discussions and legal argumentation) came to an end, a new and fresh chapter began, one where the pursuit of spiritual illumination,

inner peace and contentment became his main priority in life.

After completing his training with Shaykh Mashish, Shadhili left his native Morocco and moved to a town called Shadhila in Tunisia; henceforth he became known as Imam Shadhili. During his stay in Tunisia he engaged in spiritual retreat for long periods and gathered around him a small band of followers who helped him to establish a *zawiyyah* in 1228. It was during one of his retreats here that he claimed to have been blessed with a vision wherein he was instructed to go out and call the locals back to the original, pristine message of Islam. In response, he trained his disciples in Islamic sciences and spirituality, and then sent them to the local towns and villages to propagate Islam. This movement later became known as *tariqah al-shadhiliyyah* (or the *shadhiliyyah* Sufi Order). The locals responded to his call with much enthusiasm and became adherents of the *shadhiliyyah* Order. Islamic spirituality – as championed by Shadhili – thus spread across Tunisia, Morocco and many other parts of North Africa during his own lifetime. Indeed, the message of this *tariqah* became so popular that even the local ruler and his family became staunch followers of this Sufi brotherhood. Later, during his visit to the Islamic East to perform the sacred pilgrimage to Makkah, Shadhili came into contact with the Ayyubid ruler, Sultan al-Aziz, the second son of the famous Salah al-Din Ayyubi (Saladin), who, impressed by Shadhili's spiritual accomplishments, offered him one of the great towers overlooking the historic Egyptian city of Alexandria so he could establish a *zawiyyah* there. He accepted the Sultan's gift and returned to Tunisia with a view to revisiting Egypt at a later date.

In 1244, at the age of forty-seven, Shadhili claimed to have been blessed with another vision wherein he was instructed to leave Tunisia and go to Egypt to propagate Islam there. Accompanied by his family, friends and disciples, he left North Africa and moved to Alexandria where he established a *shadhiliyyah zawiyyah* inside the multi-floored tower which had been given to him by the Ayyubid Sultan many years earlier. Another possible explanation for his move from Tunisia to Egypt could be that the *shadhiliyyah* Order had by then become a permanent part of the North African landscape, and he decided to proceed to Egypt in order to extend its influence and establish a permanent base there. Either way, on his arrival in Egypt, Shadhili received a warm welcome from the Egyptian people in general and the religious scholars, Government officials and other Sufi groups in particular. Thus, luminaries like al-Izz al-Din ibn Abd al-Salam, who was a great authority on Islam, Shaykh al-Mundhiri, the eminent *shafi'i* jurist, and Abul Fath al-Wasiti, a prominent *rifa'iyyah* Sufi thinker and sage, supported his efforts to revive Islamic teachings and spirituality.

Trained in both the exoteric (*zahiri*) and esoteric (*batini*) dimensions of Islam, Shadhili developed an harmonious synthesis between the practical and spiritual teachings of Islam, and in so doing he won the hearts and minds of the Egyptian people. As an expert in traditional Islamic sciences, especially in *fiqh* (Islamic jurisprudence) and *hadith* (Prophetic traditions), he constantly emphasised the importance of adhering to the Prophetic norms and practices in the pursuit of mystical illumination. Adherence to the Prophetic *sunnah*, he argued, was a *sine qua non* for success on the mystical path. In this respect, his understanding and interpretation of Sufism was no different from that of other great Sufis like Abd al-Qadir al-Jilani, Khwajah Naqshband and Mu'in al-Din Chishti. To prove that there was no contradiction between the Prophetic way (*minhaj al-sunnah*) and the ways of *tasawwuf*, he took part in the Battle of al-Mansura, where the Muslims fought against the Crusaders led by St. Louis of France. He insisted on taking part in the battle, despite being blind, and thereby proved that one does not have to become a hermit to be a Sufi. On the contrary, he argued, it was possible to lead a normal, ordinary life, as did the Prophet Muhammad, and yet attain the summit of Islamic spirituality and gnosis.

The age of Shadhili was indeed one of the most significant periods in the annals of Sufism. It was during this period that scores of influential Sufis emerged in different parts of the Muslim world; they kept the flame of Islam burning across the Islamic world, and did so in the face of overwhelming political, social and cultural challenges which confronted the Muslims at the time. Some of these great luminaries included Mu'in al-Din Chishti, Shihab al-Din Umar al-Suhrawardi and Jalal al-Din Rumi in the East and Abu Madyan Shu'aib al-Maghrebi, Muhyi al-Din ibn al-Arabi, Abd al-Salam ibn Mashish and Abd al-Haq ibn Sabin in the Islamic West. These influential Sufis inspired the Muslim masses to reject the forces of materialism and self-indulgance which threatened to overwhelm Islamic societies both in the East and the West. At the same time, the Muslim world faced a serious political and military threat from the Mongol hordes. As it transpired, the Mongols soon overran the fragile defence put up by the Muslims and marched into Baghdad, the capital of the Abbasid Caliphate, in 1258 and reduced the great city to rubble. Shadhili received the news of the fall of Baghdad while he was on his way to Makkah to perform his last pilgrimage. As a proud Muslim, he must have been shocked and horrified by this tragedy. But, deep down, he probably knew that it was none other than the Muslims who had brought this disaster on themselves by creating unnecessary political disunity and division within the *ummah* (global Muslim community) by championing tribal factionalism and materialistic values and practices at the expense of Islamic unity and solidarity.

Unlike, for example, Jalal al-Din Rumi or Ibn al-Arabi, Shadhili did not write any books or treatises. Instead, he preferred to expound the meaning and message of Islam and Islamic spirituality through regular lectures, which he delivered from the mosque he founded in Egypt. He also trained hundreds of disciples who spread throughout North Africa and Egypt and began to popularise his teachings. The main focus of his teachings was the attainment of inner purification and spiritual illumination through the incessant practice of *dhikr,* or invocation of Divine Names and Attributes (*al-asma wa'l sifat*). Unlike Abu Sa'id ibn Abul Khair of Mayhana (who practised an extreme form of asceticism (*zuhd*)), Shadhili refrained from such practices; instead he practised and preached a balanced and moderate form of asceticism which sought to uplift and elevate the spirit, without harming the flesh. After Shadhili's death at the age of sixty-one, collections of his invocations, or litanies (*adkhar*), were published by his prominent disciples (such as Abul Abbas al-Mursi) and later became the bedrock of *sha-dhiliyyah* teachings. These collections included *Hizb al-Bahr* (Invocation of the Sea), *Hizb al-Nasr* (Invocation of Help) and *Hizb al-Barr* (Invocation of the Earth). Later on, Ahmad ibn Muhammad ibn Ata'Allah al-Iskandari, who was one of al-Mursi's successors, authored scores of mystical treatises including *Kitab al-Hikam* (The Book of Aphorisms), wherein he systematically delineated the fundamental tenets of this *tariqah* for the benefit of posterity.

Subsequently, the teachings of this Sufi Order flourished across North Africa (especially in Morocco) under the guidance of eminent North African Sufis like Shaykh Muhammad ibn Sulaiman al-Juzuli, Shaykh Abdullah al-Ghazwani and Sharif Mawlay al-Arabi al-Darqawi. Thanks to the efforts of Shaykh Abd al-Rahman Illish, Shaykh Ahmad al-Alawi and Shaykh Muhammad al-Hashimi, the teachings of this Sufi Order have also spread across Europe and America. Distinguished European Sufis like Rene Guenon (Abd al-Wahid Yahya), Frithjof Schuon (Isa Nur al-Din Ahmad al-Shadhili al-Darqawi al-Alawi al-Maryami), Titus (Ibrahim) Burckhardt and Martin Lings (Abu Bakr Siraj al-Din) were profoundly influenced by *shadhiliyyah* teachings and practices. Buried in the village of Humaithra on the coast of the Red Sea, Imam Shadhili's enduring message of Islamic morality, ethics, spirituality and gnosis continues to influence millions of Muslims across North Africa, Egypt, Sudan, Turkey, Iran, parts of East Africa and the Balkans to this day.

# 87

## Shah Waliullah
## (b.1703 - d.1762)

AS THE SIGNS of Islamic political, economic and intellectual decline became all too clear for everyone to see during the early years of the eighteenth century, the once-great dynastic powers like the Ottomans, Safavids and the Mughals faced challenges at home and external threats from foreign powers. Their failure to address the mounting political, economic and intellectual crises which confronted them at the time undermined their political authority at home and made them increasingly vulnerable to the ambitious European colonial powers. Caught between a rock and a hard place, the Muslim rulers of the time struggled to maintain their grip on power. Amidst the prevailing chaos and confusion, however, there emerged a number of remarkable Muslim scholars and reformers who dedicated their lives to the revival of authentic Islamic teachings and practices, and fought valiantly to rejuvenate Islamic culture and society. Though these scholars and reformers were not in a position to organise large armies and instigate military action against the encroaching foreign powers, they nevertheless managed to defend and champion Islamic values and principles at a critical point in Muslim history. One such remarkable intellectual and reformer was Shah

Waliullah, who emerged to champion Islamic thought, culture and practices at a time when Muslim India was passing through one of the most difficult periods in its history.

Qutb al-Din Ahmad ibn Abd al-Rahim, better known as Shah Waliullah Dihlawi, was born in the Indian district of Muzaffarnagar into a prominent Muslim family of religious scholars and Sufi luminaries. His father, Shah Abd al-Rahim, was a notable Islamic scholar and exponent of Sufism who traced his ancestry back to the Prophet through one of his grandsons, and also considered famous Indian Sufis such as Shaykh Ahmad Sirhindi, Khwajah Baqi Billah and Abd al-Haqq Muhaddith Dihlawi to be his spiritual progenitors. As a respected scholar of Islamic sciences, especially that of *hanafi* jurisprudence, Shah Abd al-Rahim helped to compile the *Fatawa-i-Alamgiri* (Religious Edicts of Alamgir), a famous compendium of *hanafi* jurisprudence, at the request of the great Mughal Emperor Awrangzeb Alamgir. Widely respected for their family's services to Islam and unflinching support for the Mughals, Shah Abd al-Rahim's father, Shah Wajih al-Din Ghazi, had served as a commander in the Mughal army and was awarded the title of *ghazi* (or warrior) by

Emperor Awrangzeb on account of his exceptional bravery and loyalty.

Shah Waliullah spent his early years in Muzaffarnagar and then moved to Delhi with his father, where the latter had established *madrasah-i-rahimiyyah*, a religious seminary, in which he taught Islamic sciences. Shah Waliullah therefore grew up in Delhi under the care of his father and committed the entire Qur'an to memory by the age of seven. He then studied Arabic, Persian and traditional Islamic sciences including *tafsir* (Qur'anic exegesis), *hadith* (Prophetic traditions), *fiqh* (jurisprudence) and *mantiq* (logic) at *madrasah-i-rahimiyyah*. After completing his undergraduate studies at fifteen, he married but unfortunately his wife died a few years later. During this period his father introduced him to Sufism and he received initiation into the *chishtiyyah*, *naqshbandiyyah* and *qadiriyyah* Orders before resuming his higher education in Islamic sciences. In 1719, when Shah Waliullah was only sixteen, his father died and suddenly the full operational responsibilities of *madrasah-i-rahimiyyah* fell on his shoulders. However, he proved to be a competent young man who not only managed the administrative affairs of the seminary, but also started teaching there.

For the next decade he remained preoccupied with the administration of the seminary, and in his spare time he pursued advanced studies and research into the Islamic sciences, philosophy, mysticism, logic, history, aspects of traditional medicine and mathematics. During this period he read widely and expanded his intellectual horizons so he could think in a multi-disciplinary way. Convinced that he had attained intellectual maturity, he then went to Makkah to perform the sacred pilgrimage; he was only twenty-eight at the time. After completing the *hajj*, he stayed in Makkah and Madinah for over a year and engaged in further study and research in the Islamic sciences, especially in *hadith* and *fiqh* under the tutelage of such prominent scholars as Abu Tahir Muhammad ibn Ibrahim al-Kurdi and Muhammad Wafd Allah al-Maghrebi, who taught him *hadith* and aspects of *fiqh*. Shah Waliullah

then received initiation into the *shadhiliyyah* Sufi Order, which was widely followed in Egypt and other Arab countries at the time, and he closely observed the social, political, economic and spiritual condition of the Muslims in Arabia. Though he did not meet his contemporary, Muhammad ibn Abd al-Wahhab the famous Arabian Islamic reformer, his stay in Arabia enriched his knowledge of Islam and enabled him to experience and analyse the condition of Muslims in the heartland of Islam at first hand.

As a perceptive thinker and gifted intellectual, Shah Waliullah preferred to analyse and evaluate issues, whether they were religious or otherwise, in a systematic and multi-disciplinary way. He was also in the habit of relating things to their contingencies, rather than analysing things in isolation from the wider picture. What he saw during his sojourn in Arabia confirmed his suspicion that the problems which confronted the Muslims in India were not unique; the Muslims of Arabia, as well as other Islamic nations, also suffered from the same predicament, namely the Muslim preoccupation and obsession with the form of Islam at the expense of its substance. He felt the failure of the Muslim scholars and intellectuals to address the new challenges which confronted Islamic societies – both theoretically and practically – helped to create this sorry state of affairs. Convinced that the problems which Muslims faced at the time could not be addressed without reformulating Islamic thought in a systematic and holistic way (focusing on both the material and spiritual spheres of life), Shah Waliullah hoped to develop a fresh and integrated understanding of Islamic traditions in the light of his existential condition. Not surprisingly, on his return to India he witnessed the same socio-political commotion as he had seen in Arabia. Indeed, after the death of Awrangzeb (the last of the great Mughal rulers) in 1707, the Mughal dynasty began to decline rapidly as a result of incessant political rivalry and infighting within the royal family. The decline of Mughal power and authority encouraged many dissident groups like the Marathas, Rajputs, Jats and the Sikhs to become active and carry out politically subversive activities in order to overthrow the Mughals.

As one Mughal ruler after another tried but failed to reassert their authority across the empire, their grip on India became increasingly precarious. Though Shah Waliullah was not a royalist in spirit, he nevertheless had no desire to see Mughal rule in India come to an end, not least because the Mughals were Muslims and his own ancestors had once served the Mughals with great distinction. But, as a talented scholar and thinker, he could clearly see what others failed to perceive, namely that the Mughal dynasty was now in deep trouble. There was very little he could do to stop the rot other than directly engage with the masses and encourage them to partake in educational, social and religious activities across the country. Despite the political uncertainty and social upheaval of the time, he inspired the Muslims to renew their faith and strengthen their commitment to Islam by leading an Islamic lifestyle. As an intellectual rather than a politician, Shah Waliullah devoted the next three decades of his life to writing and researching on all aspects of Islam, and in so doing he developed a powerful and compelling Islamic intellectual response to the challenges of his time. He lived at a time of profound political, social, economic, cultural and intellectual crises in Mughal India, when the encroaching Europeans began to exert influence on the affairs of the nation, while the reigning Mughal rulers struggled to restore peace and order across the vast empire.

After centuries of Mughal rule, the Indian Muslims now felt threatened by the Hindus from within India, and the European colonial powers from outside. As a multi-disciplinary thinker, Shah Waliullah tackled these complex and overlapping social, political, economic, cultural, philosophical and religious issues in more than forty books which he authored in both Arabic and Persian. Just as Shaykh Ahmad Sirhindi claimed to be the *mujaddid* (religious regenerator) of his age, so Shah Waliullah considered himself to be the *mujaddid* of the eighteenth century. After returning from his trip to Arabia,

his main priority was to return to the original scriptural sources of Islam and analyse them in the context of eighteenth century Mughal India. He approached his task with great determination and resolve, writing prolifically on a wide range of Islamic disciplines, and in so doing provided Islamic answers to some of the most burning issues of his time. Some of his well-known books include *Tafhimat al-Ilahiyyah* (The Divine Explanations), *Lamahat* (Flashes), *Sata'at* (Illuminations), *Shifa al-Qulub* (Curing the Hearts), *Budur al-Bazighah* (Full Rising Moons), *Izalat al-Khafa an Khilafat al-Khulafa* (Removal of Ambiguity about the Early Caliphate) and *Hujjat Allah al-Balighah* (God's Conclusive Argument). In these and many other books, he presented a systematic analysis of historical, philosophical, theological and mystical thought, and thereby hoped to harmonise the different strands of Islamic thought to create a unified worldview.

Thus, for instance, he systematically examined Shaykh Ahmad Sirhindi's mystical concept of *wahdat al-shuhud* ('unity of Being in perception, or unity of witnesses') *vis-à-vis* Ibn al-Arabi's doctrine of *wahdat al-wujud* ('unity of Being, or monism'), and in so doing he showed how – behind the form of the language – there existed a neutral ground where these seemingly conflicting theories of mystical experience actually converged. Indeed, he argued that there existed a common thread across all branches of knowledge which unified the core structures of human thought, even if the scholars of the past either failed to notice this generic truth, or completely overlooked it in their quest for the specific – as opposed to the full picture. This innovative approach to Islamic thought enabled Shah Waliullah to reconcile some of the most complex and controversial theories which prevailed within Islamic philosophical, theological and mystical circles at the time. In addition to philosophy, theology and mysticism, he conducted extensive research in Islamic jurisprudence, history, political affairs, cultural development, social morality and ethics. His *Izalat al-Khafa an Khilafat al-Khulafa* is a refreshing study of early Islamic social, political and cultural history; likewise, his commentaries on *al-Muwatta* of Malik ibn Anas in both Arabic and Persian provided a detailed exposition of Islamic religious beliefs, morals and ethical teachings, while his treatises on Qur'anic sciences are today considered to be some of the best works ever composed by an Indian Muslim in the field of Qur'anic thought and scholarship.

Shah Waliullah was convinced that Islam provided a comprehensive *modus vivendi* which integrated all aspects of human life (including the spiritual, psychological and biological nature of human relationships), without overlooking the political, economic, cultural and aesthetic dimensions. The integrated concept of life envisaged by Islam had not only become completely eroded in Muslim India in both theory and practice, but to Shah Waliullah, Indian Muslims had lost touch with the original, pristine sources of Islam. That is why he translated the Qur'an into Persian, despite the opposition of the conservative *ulama* (religious scholars), so as to make the Qur'an more accessible to the masses. In addition to this, in his *Hujjat Allah al-Balighah*, which is perhaps his most famous book, he developed an holistic and integrated view of life for the benefit of the Indian Muslims. He emphasised the role and importance of *ijtihad* (exercise of individual judgement) in Islamic jurisprudence and argued that through the exercise of *ijtihad* the timeless teachings of Islam (as preserved in the Qur'an and authentic *hadith*) could be applied in all times and conditions. As an indomitable champion of Islamic learning and education, Shah Waliullah supported the view that the Qur'an should be translated into other languages; thus his pioneering Persian translation of the Qur'an later inspired his talented son, Shah Rafi al-Din, to produce an Urdu translation for the first time in the history of India. This way he and his son made the Qur'an accessible to millions of people throughout the subcontinent, Muslims and non-Muslims alike.

At a time when the Indian Muslims became surrounded by nothing but doom and gloom, Shah Waliullah's refreshing and enlightening books lifted their hearts and spirits. His reformist ideas and encyclopaedic knowledge of Islam, coupled with his analytical approach to Islamic principles and practices, influenced generations of prominent Islamic scholars, thinkers and reformers across the subcontinent and elsewhere, including Muhammad Murtada al-Zabidi, Sir Sayyid Ahmad Khan, Sayyid Ahmad Barelvi, Shah Ismail Shahid, Sir Muhammad Iqbal, Muhammad al-Ghazali, Ubaidullah Sindhi, Abul Kalam Azad, Abul A'la Mawdudi and Abul Hasan Ali Nadwi. Also, for a long time, his famous *Hujjat Allah al-Balighah* was used as a standard textbook at al-Azhar University, one of the Muslim world's most famous seats of Islamic learning and scholarship. Shah Waliullah died at the age of fifty-nine and was buried in Meruli, a suburb of Delhi, in India.

# 88

# Shamyl of Daghestan (b.1796 - d.1871)

THE DEMISE OF the Soviet Union during the early 1990s heralded a new era in the history of Muslim Central Asia. Historically speaking, the people of this region began to embrace Islam during the Caliphate of Uthman in the middle of the seventh century and, as a result, this region became a flourishing centre of Islamic learning, culture and civilisation. Also, during the heyday of Islamic rule, prominent Central Asian cities like Bukhara, Samarqand and Tashkent became thriving centres of business and cultural exchange, positioned astride the ancient Silk Road. Thus Central Asia became a melting pot of different cultures, races and traditions, although the Caucasus later became embroiled in political unrest and turmoil. Tough, talented and unusually brave, the people of this region not only survived the horrors of Mongol invasion in the thirteenth century, they also resisted the formidable Russian and Soviet military machines for more than a century. Being fiercely independent-minded, they resented Soviet encroachment; indeed their desire to preserve their Islamic faith, culture and traditions inspired them to resist the imposition of Soviet Marxist-Communist ideology throughout the region. But, following the disintegration of Soviet Union in the 1990s,

the Central Asian Muslim countries finally gained their independence, although the battle for the hearts and minds of the Caucasian people continues to this day. The man who inspired the Caucasian Muslims to rise up and liberate their homeland from Russian domination, and revive their Islamic culture and heritage was none other than the legendary Muslim warrior and freedom fighter, Shamyl of Daghestan.

Born in the village of Gimiri in North-eastern Daghestan into a noble Muslim family, Shamyl's real name was Ali, but he later became known as Imam Shamyl, for it was a popular local custom to change the names of the newborn to protect them from evil spirits. As a youngster, Shamyl studied Arabic language, literature, aspects of Islamic sciences and Sufism under the guidance of Mulla Jamal al-Din, a local teacher and Sufi guide. He also became highly skilled in one-to-one combat and warfare. It was the custom of the Caucasian people to provide basic Islamic education to their young ones before they received training in archery, horse-riding and the use of a dagger. Brought up and trained in the ancient Caucasian tradition of chivalry and heroism, young Shamyl showed signs of intelligence and physical ability from the outset. After being badly beaten up and bruised by a group of local boys, he received training in self-defence and became an accomplished athlete and fighter. Known for his religiosity and devotion to Sufi teachings from an early age, he preferred to perform prayers and engage in other devotional activities at his local mosque, rather than play games or take part in recreational activities. Gripped by all sorts of superstitious beliefs and practices, the people of Daghestan hardly ventured outside their homes after dark, but brave Shamyl had no time for such imaginary fears and he regularly went out at night, perhaps to prove to his people that there were no devils lurking out there under the cover of darkness.

Like the majority of Daghestanis, he was brave, stoic and a committed Muslim but, unlike them, he was not superstitious or fatalistic. His unflinching faith in the power and majesty of God left no room for fear of men or evil spirits. In that sense, Shamyl was a true believer who attained a far superior understanding of Islam than most of his countrymen, who had come under the spell of a mystic-cum-superstitious brand of Islam. While he was in his twenties he became very fond of elegant Sufi robes, which had to be either black or white in colour, and he grew a long, flowing beard in imitation of the Prophet of Islam. At the same time, his extraordinary acts of valour and chivalry earned him something of a reputation in his locality. He was not only a fast runner, but he could also leap over seven-foot high walls and cut down his opponents from their horses with ease. As the *naqshbandiyyah* Sufi *tariqah* was one of Central Asia's most widely followed Sufi Orders, Shamyl became an adherent and exponent of this *tariqah*. Also known to have been a gentle and compassionate young man, he was keen to change and reform his society in the light of the authentic teachings of Islam as promulgated by great Sufis like Khwajah Naqshband and his disciples. However, given the widespread ignorance and stubbornness of his people – and the incessant inter-tribal rivalry and infighting which prevailed in the Caucasus at the time, especially in Daghestan – he knew it would not be an easy

task to change and reform his society. But he did not lose heart; he presevered and worked hard to improve his people's existential condition.

Aware of his predecessors' attempts to eradicate superstitious beliefs and practices from their society, and unify Daghestan and the neighbouring States in order to face the challenges which confronted their people, Shamyl knew it was the petty religious-cum-political differences within his society which represented the main obstacle to unity and solidarity. Unless such differences were surmounted or put aside, he felt it would not be possible to unify and organise his people to put up a united front against their external enemies. And although historically the battle for the hearts and minds of the people of Daghestan and the neighbouring States was first initiated by the Naqshabandi Sufi Mulla Muhammad of Yarghi long before Shamyl's time, his mission was later championed by the *ghazi* (or warrior) Muhammad ibn Ismail of Gimiri (who was also known as Ghazi Mulla) and his successor Hamzah Beg (who became the second *imam,* or spiritual leader, of Daghestan and Chechnya). But it was Shamyl who was destined to bring about wide-ranging social and religious reform in and around Daghestan, and in so doing unite his people under his leadership to fight against Russian encroachment. While he was still in his early thirties, Shamyl had gathered around him a small band of followers who recognised him as their religious leader and spiritual guide, and together they travelled across Daghestan and Chechnya in order to educate their people and unite them under the banner of Islam. Shamyl and his disciples received a favourable reception from the locals, who soon began to learn more about Islam.

This way, Shamyl and his disciples began to exercise considerable influence on their people. And although it is true that the Caucasian people were Muslims who regularly attended mosques, sent their children to their village *maktab* (religious school) and were heavily influenced by the *naqshbandiyyah* Sufi *tariqah*, they nevertheless continued to lead their daily lives in accordance with local tribal customs and traditions, which often contradicted fundamental Islamic principles and practices. Shamyl and his small band of followers tried to eradicate such contradictions and discrepancies by implementing the *shari'ah* (Islamic law). Despite being a strict adherent of the *naqshbandiyyah* Sufism (which was well known for its ascetic ways and practices), Shamyl married more than once and had an extended family of his own. Indeed, his understanding of Sufism was a balanced one, where the quest for spirituality and the requirements of the *shari'ah* blended harmoniously – with both being inter-linked and inter-dependent within the panorama of the Islamic universe. In other words, according to Shamyl, both the law (*shari'ah*) and the principle (Sufism) were indispensable for leading a balanced Islamic life, even if circumstances beyond his control often forced him to spend most of his time waging war against Russian aggression, rather than leading a normal, ordinary life at home with his family.

As early as 1801, the Russians had conquered Georgia and made their way towards the mountainous region of Daghestan and Chechnya in order to add these territories to their expanding empire. But as soon as Shamyl and his disciples succeeded in unifying the warring tribes of the Caucasus under the banner of Islam, the Tsar became alarmed, for he considered this to be a major obstacle to his imperialist designs. From past experience, the Russians knew that the Caucasian people were great warriors who came to the battlefield, wearing their Sufi robes, to die rather than live under foreign occupation. If capturing Georgia had been straightforward, then the Russians knew that subduing the brave and valiant Muslims of Daghestan and Chechnya would be a different proposition altogether. To make matters worse, the mountainous terrain, dense forests and the cold, freezing climate of Daghestan and Chechnya would present serious hindrances to the mighty Russian military machine. Since the Muslims knew the terrain well, and could potentially keep the Russians engaged in a prolonged and expensive military campaign with no end in sight, the Tsar's forces advanced with much care and caution. By ditching their policy of containment, the Russians effectively declared war against the Muslims of Chechnya and Daghestan. In response, Shamyl and his people united to fight their enemy and defend their motherland. In the ensuing battle, the Tsar's vastly superior forces bulldozed village after village, until there was hardly anything left standing in Chechnya. Though the brave but ill-equipped and hopelessly outnumbered Muslims of Chechnya fought valiantly, they were easily defeated by the Tsar's superior army. In the end, Ghazi Mulla, the then *imam* of Chechnya and Daghestan, and Shamyl only narrowly escaped the massacre in Chechnya and moved to Daghestan in order to reorganise their forces and continue their resistance against the Russian army.

After Ghazi Mulla died fighting in 1832, Hamzah Beg succeeded him as *imam* of Chechnya and Daghestan. Two years later he was assassinated, and Shamyl succeeded him as the political and spiritual leader of the Caucasus. Unlike his predecessors, he implemented the *shari'ah* throughout Daghestan and inspired his people to continue resisting Russian aggression. As a brave and accomplished warrior (*mujahid*), Shamyl personally spearheaded the battle against the Russian army. Furthermore, during the *hajj* (pilgrimage) season in Makkah in 1828, he met Amir Abd al-Qadir of Algeria and returned home convinced that he was not fighting a lonely battle; rather he was engaged in a global battle against imperialism, for Muslims in other parts of the world were also busy fighting foreign occupation at the time. This strengthened his resolve as he urged his people to continue their armed struggle against Russian attacks. For the next quarter of a century (that is, from 1834 to 1859), the brave people of Chechnya and Daghestan fought against the mighty Russian war machine under Shamyl's inspirational leadership. During this period, they not only fought, frustrated and demoralised one of the world's most formidable military forces, but also kept more than three hundred and fifty thousand Russian troops trapped in the Caucasus.

And although Shamyl knew he was fighting a losing battle because resisting such a large Russian force indefinitely would be a mission impossible, the fact that they held back such a powerful army for as long as they did was in itself a colossal achievement. If the international community had responded to his appeal for help and support, then the situation might have been rather different. As it transpired nothing more than sympathy and moral support was forthcoming, which meant the brave people of the Caucasus had no alternative but to continue their struggle against the Russian army on their own; this effectively sealed the fate of Chechan resistance for the time being. To save his beleaguered people from total annihilation, Shamyl reluctantly agreed to sign a peace treaty with the Tsar, which temporarily brought Chechen resistance to an end. But Shamyl's heroic struggle against the Tsar not only won

him international recognition, he also became famous in the Muslim world and across Europe as the 'lion of Daghestan'.

He sacrificed everything (including losing members of his own family and relatives) in his battle against Russian aggression. He eventually died in exile at the age of seventy-five and was buried in Madinah (in present-day Saudi Arabia). But the *jihad* (military struggle) he launched against Russian imperialism continues to this day; his bravery and acts of chivalry and heroism have become major sources of inspiration for the people of Chechnya as they continue to fight for their freedom from Russian occupation. Of all the great Muslim freedom fighters of the nineteenth century (such as Amir Abd al-Qadir of Algeria, al-Sanusi of Libya and Sayyid Ahmad Barelvi of India), there is no doubt that it is Shamyl's influence and legacy which has proved to be the most powerful and enduring.

# 89
## Abul A'la Mawdudi
## (b.1903 - d.1979)

IF THE NINETEENTH century was the age of European domination of the Muslim world, then the twentieth century must be considered the period when the Muslims finally woke from sleep and began to liberate their lands from foreign occupation. At the height of European colonisation, Muslim leaders and the people channelled all their energy in one direction, namely the liberation of their countries from European colonial rule. But following the departure of the British, French, Italians and the other European colonial powers from the Muslim world, a powerful and pertinent debate took place in all the Muslim countries concerning their political and constitutional futures. The secular, liberal Muslim political elites favoured a Western-style political and constitutional arrangement. Others, on the other hand, argued that a socialist model of political governance and economic management was more suitable option, while the Islamists championed the need for a political framework based on their understanding and interpretation of Islamic principles. After decades, if not centuries, of European politico-economic hegemony, the debate concerning the future direction of Muslim countries raged across the Islamic world, providing a perfect opportunity for Muslims to

develop a system of political governance and economic management based on Islamic principles and practices. One Islamic scholar and activist contributed more to this debate than probably any other Muslim thinker or reformer of his generation; he was Abul A'la Mawdudi of Pakistan.

Sayyid Abul A'la Mawdudi, better known as Mawlana Mawdudi, was born in the town of Awrangzabad in the Indian State of Hyderabad (located in present-day Andhra Pradesh). His father, Sayyid Ahmad Hasan, was a lawyer by profession, who claimed to be a descendant of the Prophet through a chain of Indian Sufi luminaries (including Khwajah Qutb al-Din Mawdud, who was affiliated to the prominent *chishtiyyah* Sufi Order). Born and brought up in a family where learning, personal piety and devotion to Sufism was valued and respected, young Mawdudi received his early education at home from his father. When he reached school age, he enrolled at *madrasah al-fawqaniyyah*, a local seminary, to pursue traditional religious education. Although Sayyid Ahmad Hasan himself had received a largely Western education at the Muhammadan Anglo-Oriental College (present-day Aligarh Muslim University), founded by Sir

Sayyid Ahmad Khan back in 1877, and qualified as a lawyer, he encouraged his young son to become an *alim* (traditional Islamic scholar). As a bright and gifted student, Mawdudi successfully completed his studies at *madrasah al-fawqani-yyah* before joining the *dar al-uloom*, an Islamic college, in Hyderabad for further education in Urdu, Arabic and traditional Islamic sciences. But his further education was interrupted at the age of seventeen when his father suddenly died in 1920. Sayyid Ahmad Hasan's mystical tendencies, coupled with his ascetic ways, contributed to his family's economic difficulties, and after his father's death, Mawdudi was forced to abandon his studies and work to earn a living.

According to Mawdudi's biographers, he acquired a powerful command of Urdu and Arabic and became sufficiently familiar with traditional Islamic sciences to pursue his own study and research. At the same time, he began to write articles and essays on different aspects of Islam with unusual clarity and vision. His knowledge of current affairs – and his awareness and understanding of the problems which confronted the Indian Muslims at the time – enabled him to secure the editorship of a local Muslim newspaper. He then became editor of the more prominent *al-Jam'iyat,* the official publication of Jam'iat-i Ulama-i Hind a national Islamic umbrella organisation which represented the Indian Muslims at the time. His stint as editor of these publications enabled Mawdudi to polish his writing skills, earn a decent income and also acquire a better understanding of Indian politics and public affairs. During this period he also composed scores of articles wherein he delineated the Islamic concept of *jihad* (or struggle) so as to clarify prevailing misconceptions about this important Islamic obligation. These articles were later collected and published under the title of *al-Jihad fi'l Islam* (War and Peace in Islam) in 1930.

Following his resignation as editor of *al-Jam'iyat* in 1928, Mawdudi left Delhi and moved to Hyderabad where he continued his literary activities, writing and translating books from both Arabic and Persian into Urdu under the supervision of eminent Islamic scholars like Abd al-Majid Daryabadi and Sayyid Manazir Ahsan Gilani. During this period he also composed his *Risalat-i Diniyat* (Towards Understanding Islam), a small but popular treatise on fundamental Islamic beliefs and practices. By the time Mawdudi had completed this book in 1932, his understanding of, and approach to, Islam had shifted considerably. As a journalist and editor of *al-Jam'iyat*, he was clean-shaven and wore Western clothes, but now he grew a beard and adopted a revivalist approach to Islam. Convinced that the Indian Muslims were facing considerable political challenges from the British elites as well as the Hindus masses, he responded to the ever-changing socio-political situation by promoting Islamic knowledge and raising awareness of Indian political affairs. With this in mind, he took charge of *Tarjuman al-Qur'an* (Interpretation of the Qur'an) in 1932. This was a monthly Islamic journal which was originally founded and published by an independent Muslim scholar in Hyderabad. Through this journal (which only had a couple of hundred subscribers at first, but later acquired a much wider readership), Mawdudi established himself as a prominent exponent of Islam in India. As a prolific writer, he contributed most of the articles in the journal and his concise, pertinent and refreshing approach to Islamic political, legal and social issues instantly won him much praise from other renowned Indian Islamic scholars and thinkers like Sir Muhammad Iqbal, Sayyid Sulaiman Nadwi, Mufti Muhammad Kifayatullah and Sayyid Manazir Ahsan Gilani. This convinced Mawdudi that his intellectual efforts were having the desired effect and thus he continued to champion the cause of the Indian Muslims and write prolifically.

Mawdudi continued to publish the *Tarjuman* from Hyderabad until 1937, when Sir Muhammad Iqbal invited him to move to Pathankot (located in East Punjab, India) and help him to establish an Islamic research centre there. After his move to Pathankot in 1938, he continued to edit and publish the *Tarjuman* and also began work on the proposed research centre. With the help and assistance of some of India's prominent Islamic scholars, he eventually established the centre and began to supervise its activities, and in his spare time he continued to write prolifically on all aspects of Islam. However, over time he felt that conducting research and writing books alone was unlikely to lead to political reform and social change. Rather a combination of socio-political activism, underpinned by the enduring values and principles of Islam, was more likely to bring about such change. With the active support of a number of leading Indian Islamic scholars, in 1941 he formally launched the *jama'at-i-islami* (The Islamic Organisation), an Islamic political party, in order to reform Indian politics, culture and society in the light of Islam. As an Islamic scholar and writer, Mawdudi's monthly articles in the *Tarjuman*, coupled with his books and treatises, soon captured the imagination of both the traditional Islamic scholars as well as the modern, educated Indian Muslims. However, as the founder and chief (*amir*) of *jama'at-i-islami*, he was still a marginal political figure; but this situation changed radically following the formation of Pakistan as an independent country in 1947. Along with his close friends and supporters, Mawdudi left India in favour of Pakistan and tried to establish an Islamic political, economic and cultural order there.

Although the *Tarjuman* became the chief vehicle for the exposition and dissemination of his politico-religious ideas and thoughts, it was the formation of *jama'at-i-islami* in 1941 – and his subsequent migration to Pakistan in 1947 – which provided the ideal opportunity for him to engage in politics on a full-time basis for the first time. Prior to his arrival in Pakistan, Mawdudi was known primarily as an Islamic scholar and writer, and his *jama'at-i-islami* was viewed as yet another religious organisation, but after his move to Pakistan he became an active politician and the *jama'at-i-islami* also became known as a political party which actively campaigned for an Islamic constitution, as well as the need to implement the *shari'ah* (Islamic law) in that country. During this period Mawdudi wrote prolifically on

Islamic political, legal and constitutional matters, hoping to influence both the politicians and the masses in the devising and implementation of a system of political governance, economic policies and legal framework which was compatible with Islamic principles and values. Unlike his eminent contemporary, Abul Hasan Ali Nadwi of India (also known as Ali Mian), Mawdudi did not believe in the pursuit of intellectual activity minus socio-political activism.

Indeed, influenced by the reformist ideas and thoughts of prominent Islamic thinkers like Ibn Taymiyyah, Shaykh Ahmad Sirhindi, Shah Waliullah and Sir Muhammad Iqbal, Mawdudi combined theology with politics, spirituality with social activism and philosophy with the need for cultural renewal. And although his political activism landed him in prison on more than one occasion, he remained as firm and steadfast as ever. Islam in its broadest sense, argued Mawdudi, was an all-inclusive religion and ideology, and thus there was no room for the compartmentalisation of politics from Islam, economics from justice, and freedom from responsibility. Rather, he considered Islamic teachings to be holistic and all-encompassing, covering all aspects of human life in a structurally inter-connected and inter-dependent way – emanating from one Divinely-inspired source, namely the Qur'an, and the authentic *sunnah* (normative practice of the Prophet); thus, he believed, there was no room for the depoliticisation of Islam. Accordingly, Mawdudi and his *jama'at-i-islami* fully embraced socio-political activism; indeed, they believed this to be one of the most effective ways to bring about political change and social reform in Muslim societies, especially at a time when the rulers deliberately chose to sideline or undermine Islamic principles concerning political governance, economic management, educational policy, social justice, law and order, and cultural development and social morality.

As an Islamic ideologue and author, Mawdudi wrote more than one hundred books and treatises on all aspects of Islam, and his exposition of Islam as a religion and complete way of life was always clear and comprehensive. Some of his most important books and treatises were the *Khutbat* (Collection of Lectures), *Tafhimat* (Elucidations), *Tajdid-o Ihya-i-Din* (A History of Islamic Revivalist Movements), *al-Jihad fi'l Islam* (War and Peace in Islam), *Risalat-i Diniyat* (Towards Understanding Islam), *Sud* (Usury), *Purdah* (The Veil), *Rasa'il-o-Masa'il* (Questions and Answers), *Tanqihat* (Explications), *Islam ka Nizam-i Hayat* (The Islamic Way of Life) and *Islam ka Nazariya-i Siyasi* (The Islamic Political Theory). However, it is his *Tafhim al-Qur'an* (Towards Understanding the Qur'an), a voluminous Urdu translation and commentary on the Qur'an, which is today considered to be his most influential work. In this vast and unusual commentary, he tried to explain the *raison d'etre* of the Qur'anic revelation in a clear and logical way. As a politician and activist, Mawdudi not only tried to highlight the fundamental teachings of the Qur'an for the benefit of scholars as well as lay-people, but also went out of his way to explain how one could translate the message of the Qur'an into one's daily life. Mawdudi was not interested in intellectual discussion or debate for its own sake; rather he was motivated by the desire to reform Muslim societies in the image of the Divine message, and in so doing he hoped to improve people's quality of life.

However, according to Mawdudi's critics (such as Abul Hasan Ali Nadwi), he emphasised the socio-political dimension of Islam at the expense of its moral and spiritual dimension. That is to say, his critics have argued that his books read more like manuals for socio-political action, rather than works of Islamic wisdom and spirituality. In the final analysis, however, Mawdudi was more successful as a writer and Islamic ideologue than he was as a politician and activist. But the *jama'at-i-islami* party which he founded and led for more than three decades continues to operate in Pakistan, India, Bangladesh and Sri Lanka to this day. Though the party has not been as successful as Mawdudi and his associates had anticipated, its influence is still quite considerable in the subcontinent. By contrast, Mawdudi's writings have been translated and published in all the major languages of the world and he is today considered to be one of the most widely-read Muslim authors of modern times. He died in hospital in Buffalo (New York) at the age of seventy-five and was buried in front of his house in Lahore. Prior to his death, Mawdudi received the prestigious King Faisal International Award for his services to Islam. Likewise, his religious ideas and thoughts have influenced scores of prominent modern Muslim scholars and thinkers including Sayyid Qutb, Muhammad al-Ghazali, Abul Hasan Ali Nadwi, Muhammad Manzur Numani, Amin Ahsan Islahi, Ghulam Azam, Israr Ahmad, Wahiduddin Khan and Khurshid Ahmad among others.

# 90

## Shihab al-Din Suhrawardi
## (b.1154 - d.1191)

AS THE FATHER of Islamic philosophy, the career of Abu Yusuf Yaqub ibn Ishaq al-Kindi (Alkindus) flourished in the ninth century during the reign of Abbasid Caliphs al-Ma'mun, Mu'tasim and Wathiq. Thanks to his profound knowledge and understanding of traditional Islamic sciences and ancient Greek thought, he played a pivotal role in the development of Islamic philosophical thought and discourse which later became known as Peripatetic (*mashsha'iyyah*) philosophy. After al-Kindi, scores of renowned Muslim philosophers, like Abu Bakr al-Razi, al-Farabi and Ibn Sina, emerged in the Islamic East and they conducted a detailed study of the Islamic sources *vis-à-vis* the ancient Greek philosophical heritage, and in so doing they tried to create a synthesis between the supposedly irreconcilable Islamic scriptural sources and Hellenistic thought. As *mashsha'iyyah* philosophy gradually captured the imagination the of Muslim intelligentsia in many parts of the Islamic East, the towering figure of al-Ghazali emerged in the eleventh century to launch a blistering intellectual assault on the Peripatetic thought of al-Razi, al-Farabi and Ibn Sina. Following al-Ghazali's stinging critique of Peripatetism, philosophy rapidly declined in the Islamic East, even if prominent Muslim phi-

losophers like Ibn Bajjah (Avempace), Ibn Tufayl (Abubacer) and Ibn Rushd (Averroes) later revived the Peripatetic tradition in the Islamic West. At a time when the Islamic East turned its back on Peripatetic philosophy – and the Islamic West openly embraced what the East had rejected – Shihab al-Din Suhrawardi emerged to develop a powerful synthesis between Peripatetic philosophy and mysticism.

Shihab al-Din Yahya ibn Habash Suhrawardi, also known as *shaykh al-ishraq* (Master of Illumination), was born in Suhraward in Northwestern Persia. He received his early education in Arabic, Persian and traditional Islamic sciences in his locality. As a gifted student, he completed his elementary and intermediate studies while he was still in his early teens. He then developed a keen interest in philosophical sciences and mysticism. Eager to pursue higher education in Islamic philosophical sciences, he left his native Suhraward and moved to Maraghah to study under the guidance of Majd al-Din al-Jili, a notable Persian scholar and thinker, who was teaching and conducting research at an institute there. He completed his advanced education in the religious sciences, philosophy and mysticism while he was still in his early twenties. He then left Maraghah and proceeded to the historic Persian city of Isfahan where he conducted research in logic and philosophical sciences under the tutelage of such eminent scholars as Fakhr al-Din al-Mardini and Zahir al-Din al-Farisi, who introduced him to the writings of the famous logician, Umar ibn Sahlan al-Sawi. He travelled extensively during this period and visited Anatolia and other prominent Islamic cities and provinces, before finally settling in Aleppo. Suhrawardi lived during one of the most politically turbulent periods in Islamic history, when the Crusaders emerged from Europe and threatened to overwhelm the Islamic East. Thankfully, their advance was first checked by the Zangids, before the heroic figure of Salah al-Din Ayyubi, better known in the West as Saladin, defeated the Franks and recaptured Jerusalem (al-quds), the third sacred city of Islam, from the Crusaders.

Born in 1138 in northern Iraq, Salah al-Din became a prominent Zangid military commander during the reign of Sultan Nur al-Din Mahmud. However, during the final years of Nur al-Din's reign, he achieved political eminence as the administrator of Fatimid Egypt. But after the Sultan's death in 1174, Salah al-Din consolidated his powerbase in Egypt and then went on to annex Syria, Iraq, Western Arabia and parts of North Africa, including Tunisia. As a result, he carved out a vast empire which extended from Yemen in the south, to Tunisia in the west; thus he successfully united the Islamic East under his able leadership, with a view to confronting the Frankish Crusaders once and for all. Suhrawardi may have been motivated to move to Aleppo in the hope of attracting the attention of the Ayyubid rulers who were known for their patronage of learning and artistic pursuits. As a versatile young intellectual, it did not take long for him to establish his reputation in Aleppo as an erudite scholar. However, according to some historians it was the governor of Aleppo, Malik al-Zahir Ghazi, Sultan Salah al-Din's young son, who summoned Suhrawardi to his court and offered him a lucrative Government post. Either way, as soon as they met they became good friends and regularly engaged in intellectual debate and discussion on all aspects of religious sciences, philosophy and mysticism. Young Malik al-Zahir Ghazi was so impressed with Suhrawardi's learning that he began to study aspects of philosophy and Islamic mysticism under his guidance.

Although he became a prolific writer in both Arabic and Persian while he was still in his early twenties, Suhrawardi actually authored most of his influential books and treatises in Arabic, and did so after his arrival in Aleppo in 1183. These include *al-Talwihat* (The Intimations), *al-Muqawamat* (The Apposites), *al-Mashari wa'l Mutarahat* (The Roads and Refuges) and *Hikmat al-Ishraq* (The Philosophy of Illumination). He began work on the latter, which is his most influential philosophical work, during his sojourns in Anatolia and Syria while he was in his late twenties, and completed it in Aleppo. In addition to these books, he composed scores of other shorter books and treatises on both doctrinal and esoteric matters, including *Hayakil al-Nur* (The Luminous Bodies), *al-Lamahat* (The Glimpses) and *Bustan al-Qulub* (The Garden of the Hearts). However, it was his four philosophical works which subsequently exerted immense influence on Muslim philosophers and mystics, especially in Persia. Like Ibn Sina, he analysed Peripatetic philosophy in a new and original way, but he did not agree with everything the former wrote. Indeed, he rejected aspects of Ibn Sina's philosophical ideas and thoughts, and refined some of his other ideas. Having thoroughly assimilated the philosophical and mystical thoughts of the early Muslim thinkers, Suhrawardi was not only in a position to analyse and evaluate their ideas and thoughts, but also to develop a fresh and alternative understanding of the Islamic scriptural sources in the light of his own investigations.

Suhrawardi may have written commentaries on Ibn Sina's *al-Isharat wa'l Tanbihat* (The Remarks and Admonitions) and portions of the Qur'an and *hadith* (Prophetic traditions), but he was more than just a commentator. In fact, he was an original thinker who mastered Islamic sciences, Peripatetic philosophy, Sufi thought and ancient

Zoroastrian wisdom, in addition to concepts and information from many other sources – and in so doing he developed a powerful synthesis between mystical philosophy and the Neoplatonic thought of the early Muslim philosophers (even though al-Ghazali had already attacked them for supposedly compromising fundamental Islamic principles in their eagerness to harmonise Greek philosophy with the Islamic tradition.). The synthesis created by Suhrawardi became known as the 'philosophy of illumination' (or *hikmat al-ishraq*). The proponents of 'illuminationism' considered this to be a distinct and comprehensive system of thought because it transcended the philosophical and epistemological contradictions inherent in the Peripatetic thought of Ibn Sina and his like, while at the same time reinforcing the illuminationist dimension of philosophy and mysticism within the broader nexus of the Islamic worldview. In other words, by harmonising Peripatetism (*mashsha'iyyah*), Oriental philosophy (*hikmat al-mashriqiyyah*) and speculative theology (*ilm al-kalam*) with Islamic mysticism (*tasawwuf*), Suhrawardi created a new philosophical-cum-mystical synthesis which he delineated in his major philosophical works, especially his *Hikmat al-Ishraq* (The Philosophy of Illumination).

Suhrawardi's 'philosophy of illumination' was the outcome of a long and ambitious intellectual project. He began by investigating all the major intellectual trends which prevailed in the Islamic world at the time. He then identified and examined the epistemological foundation of the Islamic worldview, and in so doing he came to the conclusion that human reason (or rationalism) had its own limits; thus he argued that Truth cannot be discovered through rational effort alone. By the same token, he felt the mystical approach was not in itself sufficient for attaining the Truth – and the whole Truth. Instead, he proposed a new methodology which combined elements of rationality, experiental wisdom and intellectual intuition which, he argued, was more likely to lead to a deeper and comprehensive understanding of the Truth as such. By adopting a multi-disciplinary approach to Islamic thought and worldview, Suhrawardi attempted to bring the different strands of thought which prevailed within the Islamic world at the time under one philosophical banner, namely the 'philosophy of illumination'. This way he was not only able to demonstrate that the conflict between Neoplatonism, speculative theology, mysticism and aspects of ancient Persian thought and wisdom was not as deep-rooted as previously thought, but he also pointed out how the core elements of these traditions had much in common; thus they were, in his opinion, far from being outside the intellectual tradition of Islam.

Heavily influenced by the philosophical thought of Ibn Sina, Suhrawardi became an ardent Neoplatonist during his early years. But, after reportedly seeing Aristotle in a vision, he became aware of the weaknesses that were inherent in Neoplatonic thought and this prompted him to seek a philosophical alternative to it. After many years of intensive study and research, he finally discovered the 'philosophy of illumination' which he considered to be a far superior system of thought than Peripatetic philosophy. However, when his new and innovative philosophical-cum-mystical ideas became known to his opponents (especially those based at Malik Zahir Ghazi's court in Aleppo), they accused him of corrupting the young governor by introducing him to un-Islamic ideas and practices. Since Sultan Salah al-Din Ayyubi and his family members were strict Sunni Muslims, the charge of promoting a heterodoxical creed (consisting of elements of Zoroastrianism, Neoplatonic thought and Shi'a theology and mysticism) was bound to offend the senior courtiers at Aleppo. As a result, Suhrawardi's opponents pressured Malik Zahir Ghazi to put him on trial for promoting heretical beliefs and practices, but the young governor flatly refused to do so. Indeed, Malik Zahir Ghazi's refusal to give into the courtiers' demands prompted them to send a petition directly to Sultan Salah al-Din. This petition – formulated by the eminent judge and jurist al-Fadil – stated that Suhrawardi espoused heretical theological and philosophical views which were similar to those of the Ismailis, and urged Sultan Salah al-Din to order his son to execute Suhrawardi. Sultan Salah al-Din agreed with the petition and ordered his son to put Suhrawardi to death.

In normal circumstances, the Sultan would probably have investigated this matter further before sentencing Suhrawardi to death, but at the time he was facing an imminent attack from the Crusaders and therefore decided not to upset the senior courtiers in Aleppo by refusing to comply with their demand. The master of the 'philosophy of illumination' (*shaykh al-ishraq*) was sentenced to death at the age of thirty-seven. However, within such a short life span, he managed to author a large collection of books and treatises on a wide range of topics. In addition, he founded a new school of philosophical-cum-mystical thought which is today influential in Iran, parts of Iraq, India and Pakistan, especially within the Shi'a intellectual circles. Not surprisingly, Suhrawardi's religious, philosophical and mystical ideas have influenced many prominent Shi'a thinkers like Shams al-Din Muhammad al-Shahrazuri, Sa'd ibn Mansur ibn Kammunah, Qutb al-Din al-Shirazi, Qiyas al-Din Mansur Dashtaki, Jalal al-Din Dawwani, Nizam al-Din Harawi, Sadr al-Din al-Shirazi (better known as Mulla Sadra) and Shihab al-Din Kumijani. Since his works were not translated into Western languages until relatively recently, his ideas and thoughts did not gain much currency in the West although this situation is now changing, thanks to the efforts of scholars like Henry Corbin, Seyyed Hossein Nasr, John Walbridge, Hossein Ziai and Mehdi Aminrazavi.

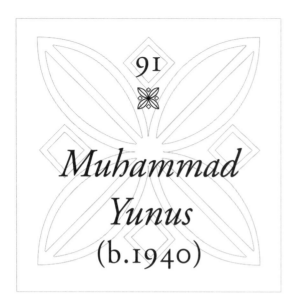

# 91

# Muhammad
# Yunus
# (b.1940)

WHEN THE EARLY Muslim traders and merchants first arrived in the coastal regions of India in the seventh century, they were welcomed with open arms by the locals. Though these pioneering Muslims came primarily to conduct business, over time they married and settled in some of the most remote coastal towns and villages of India, Ceylon, Sumatra and Maldives. When Ibn Battutah, the celebrated fourteenth century Muslim globetrotter, visited those areas he was surprised to find thriving indigenous Muslim communities in all the major coastal regions of India, Ceylon and Sumatra. One of the most prominent seaports of the subcontinent at the time was Chittagong (in present-day Bangladesh) where Muslim traders came regularly from as far away as Yemen to conduct trade and business. This city not only became a commercial hub for the early Muslim traders, it also became a prominent centre of Islamic spirituality (Sufism). As the home of one of Bangladesh's largest seaports, Chittagong has remained a thriving centre of trade and commerce to this day. Muhammad Yunus, one of the most radical economists of contemporary times and arguably the single most influential banker of the twentieth century, hailed from this age-old centre of commerce and spirituality.

Born and brought up in a lower middle-class Muslim family, young Yunus attended his local schools where he studied Bengali language, literature, mathematics and aspects of science. He grew up during a politically volatile and culturally confusing time in the history of the subcontinent. The Second World War had started in 1939 and the British - who still maintained their grip on India - had joined the fight against the Nazis in Europe. As an integral part of British India, East Bengal also faced an imminent military invasion from the Japanese who were, at the time, making rapid progress in the East. To make matters worse, the people of East Bengal were, at the same time, passing through a period of considerable socio-cultural conflict and confusion. What did it actually mean to be a Bengali Muslim? Should the people of India remain loyal to the Crown during a difficult period in British history, or should they rebel? What would happen to the Indian Muslims if the British decided to quit? Could the Hindus and Muslims live side-by-side in a free and independent India? Yunus spent his early childhood in the heart of Chittagong's commercial district at a time when the people of India and, especially its large Muslim minority, were asking themselves such politically pertinent and culturally relevant questions.

As it transpired, the British had no choice but to quit India in 1947 after agreeing to Muhammad Ali Jinnah's demand for a separate homeland for the Muslims of India; Yunus was only seven at the time. The Muslims of East Bengal, which later became known as East Pakistan, were obviously delighted with the outcome, although Yunus was too young to understand and appreciate the signficance of this historic event. As a talented student, he excelled in his studies and completed his further education at Chittagong College before proceeding to Dhaka University for higher studies. After graduating from Dhaka University in 1961, he lectured on economics at Chittagong College until 1965 when he won a Fulbright scholarship to read economics in the United States. He left his native East Pakistan and moved to the United States to pursue research in economics at Vanderbilt University in Tennessee. In 1972 he returned to a new country – now named Bangladesh – with a doctorate in economics. As a Bengali nationalist, Yunus was happy to see Bangladesh appear on the world map. And as an economist, he was keen to help his new country re-organise its crumbling economic infrastructure but, according to Yunus, the country's leaders were not very keen to utilise his skills. On a personal level, his relationship with his Russian wife, who bore him a daughter, also deteriorated until she finally left him and returned to the United States. Following a brief stint at the planning commission, he became a professor and head of the department of economics at the University of Chittagong in 1972.

While he was busy teaching economics, Yunus observed, to his utter dismay, the harrowing impact of abject poverty on those who lived in the villages adjacent to the university campus. He could not understand why the locals did not make better use of their agricultural land, which remained uncultivated season after season. The villagers' failure to make better use of fertile and cultivatable land did not make economic sense to Yunus. Although he was not an agriculturalist,

he was very keen to find out why the locals did not grow crops, fruits and vegetables which they could consume and also sell in the local markets. From 1972 to 1976, he explored different ways in which he could improve the economic condition of the local villagers. As a result he established small farming and irrigation projects to improve the use of the local agricultural land. While working on these projects, he discovered that the wealthier farmers tended to dominate their poorer counterparts. Moreover, making the local villagers completely dependent on their land did not seem to him to be a good idea either, especially given the fact that he had yet to identify the underlying causes of their economic backwardness. Although the main purpose of these projects was to help the poor to become self-reliant and independent, Yunus's failure to address the root causes of poverty made him rethink his research methodology and objectives. During his study and research, and also drawing on his practical experience of devising and delivering small agricultural projects, Yunus came up with the idea of lending small amounts of money to the very poor in order to encourage them to set up small businesses. The borrower was required to repay the sum, plus a nominal amount of interest, over a period of time out of the profits generated from the business. Pioneered by Yunus in 1976, this method of lending small sums of money to some of the world's poorest people became known as the 'system of micro-credit'. Since the conventional financial system refused to give loans to people who had no fixed assets, he felt the poor and the destitute could never obtain loans from the banks because they had no valuables or collateral. So the question of where the poor could go to obtain small loans needed to be resolved.

In his attempts to obtain bank loans for the poor, Yunus discovered that conventional banks operated on a principle which automatically excluded the very poor from receiving any form of credit. This prompted him to set up the Grameen ('village') Bank experiment in 1977 in order to provide credit to the poor, especially to the women, in rural areas of Bangladesh. By giving out such loans he hoped to encourage women to set up small-scale businesses and self-help ventures, and in so doing enable them to stand on their own two feet and gradually improve their socio-economic condition. In theory, the concept of micro-credit seemed to be a commendable one, but it was not clear whether it would actually work in practice. In Yunus's own words, "At first I did not know if I was right. I had no idea what I was getting into...learning as I went along, learning empirically from experience. Our work became a struggle to show that the financial untouchables are actually touchable, even huggable. To my amazement and surprise the repayment of loans by people who borrow without collateral is much better than those whose borrowings are secured by enormous assets. Indeed, more than 98 percent of our loans are repaid, because the poor know this is the only opportunity they have to break out of poverty."

When in 1979 he was granted a two-year break from teaching at Chittagong University, he replicated the Grameen Bank scheme in a deprived part of Tangail, which is located on the outskirts of Dhaka, the capital of Bangladesh. When the experiment proved a success, Yunus and his colleagues deployed the micro-credit self-help programme in other areas of Tangail. From then on, the Grameen Bank gradually expanded across rural Bangladesh so that today it provides help to millions of poor and needy people across Bangladesh through its micro-credit self-help schemes. But, one may ask, what is so unique and special about the Grameen Bank? First and foremost, the Grameen Bank is nothing like a conventional bank; indeed, it has no resemblance whatsoever to a conventional bank. A conventional bank's basic operating principle is, 'The more you have, the more you get.' and conversely, 'If you don't have it, you don't get it.' In other words, the conventional banks have designated the poor and needy people to be 'not credit-worthy', that is to say, 'we can't touch you'. Therefore, wittingly or unwittingly, the conventional banks have created a kind of financial apartheid, argues Yunus in his inspirational autobiography, *Banker to the Poor*. However, the Grameen Bank has turned this basic banking principle on its head, because it does not operate on the premise of collateral. That means the very poor and needy who have no land or assets of their own can obtain micro-credit loans from the Grameen Bank to set up small businesses or self-help initiatives in order to improve their socio-economic condition and boost their morale, confidence and self-esteem.

The system of micro-credit pioneered by Yunus back in the 1970s has not only proved to be a great success in rural Bangladesh; the concept has since been successfully replicated in more than sixty countries around the world including the United States, United Kingdom, Canada, France, Australia, Malaysia, China, Norway and Finland. In addition to this, the system of micro-credit has been hailed by some of the world's most powerful leaders and global financial institutions (including the World Bank and the International Monetary Fund (IMF)) as an important tool in the fight against abject poverty and deprivation. Though Yunus studied conventional economics in a conventional way, his understanding of economics is surprisingly unconventional; rather, it is very radical indeed. In his acceptance speech for the World Food Prize, awarded to him in 1994, he stated, "Brilliant theories of economics do not take into account issues of poverty and hunger. They tend to imply that these problems will be solved when the march of economic prosperity will sweep through the nations. Economists spend all their talents detailing the processes of development and prosperity, but none on the processes of poverty and hunger. I feel very strongly that if the world recognizes poverty alleviation as an important and serious agenda, we can create a world that we can be proud of, rather than feel ashamed of, as we do now."

Yunus's radical approach to economics in general and poverty alleviation in particular was initially dismissed as being simplistic and unworkable by his critics at the World Bank and other global financial institutions but, by turning the Grameen Bank into a successful venture, he proved all his detractors wrong. A quick browse through the Grameen Bank's Balance Sheet shows how far it has come since its inception. In July 2005, total loans disbursed by the Grameen Bank topped $5 billion. The bank crossed the first billion dollar mark in March 1995, about eighteen years after it was formally inaugurated in 1976 by lending $27 to forty-two people. Since then the Grameen Bank has expanded so rapidly that today it disburses more rural loans each year than all other Bangladeshi banks put together. It has also established thousands of branches across rural Bangladesh, serving around 5 million borrowers on their doorsteps, in more than forty thousand villages. And with a workforce of more than twenty thousand, the bank collects millions of dollars in weekly repayment instalments. By all accounts, this is a truly great achievement. As a self-help programme, the Grameen Bank seeks to improve the socio-economic condition of the poor and needy people in Bangladesh; but as a system of micro-credit, it seeks to tackle poverty and deprivation across the world. According to Yunus, poverty is an example of a cancer which humans have created and foisted upon their fellow humans. It is so widespread because political oppression, economic inequality and social injustice are rife in many parts of the world. Moroever, the way international trade and business is conducted plays a major role in the proliferation of poverty and deprivation in the Third World. For this reason, Yunus's pioneering effort to tackle abject poverty through micro-credit schemes deserves more support and recognition from both politicians and the world's leading financial institutions than it has received so far. However, one of the reasons why

Yunus's micro-credit scheme has not been as popular and successful in the Muslim world as it ought to be is because it is an interest (or usury) based scheme. Since interest-based transactions have been outlawed by the Holy Qur'an, many Muslims have understandably refused to support such a scheme.

Neverthless, poverty – both relative and absolute – can only be eradicated when the world's most powerful leaders and financial institutions make poverty eradication their first priority. And this will not happen until the world's prominent leaders are prepared to tackle the root causes of global inequality and injustice by addressing the imbalances and disparities which clearly exist in international trade between the wealthy Western nations and the poor Third World countries. In other words, according to Yunus, poverty will not be completely eradicated until the restrictive practices which sustain the structures of global economic inequality and injustice are first dismantled. Thus, he is realistic enough to acknowledge that micro-credit alone cannot, and will not, be able to tackle the cancer of global poverty and deprivation, but he is hopeful that it will encourage the world's leaders and global financial institutions to make poverty alleviation their main priority. Nevertheless, it would not be an exaggeration to say that by pioneering the concept of micro-credit, Yunus has made a significant contribution to the global fight against absolute poverty and deprivation. In recognition of his outstanding achievements, he has been awarded scores of prestigious international prizes and awards, including the Noble Peace Prize in 2006. Muhammad Yunus lives in Dhaka, Bangladesh with his wife and daughter.

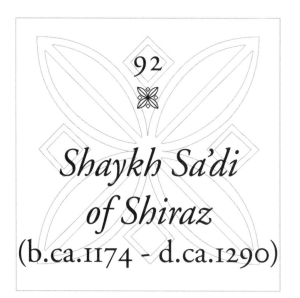

# 92

## Shaykh Sa'di of Shiraz
### (b.ca.1174 – d.ca.1290)

THE WORDS 'ETHICS' and 'morality' are often used interchangeably even though they do not mean the same thing. Derived from the Greek *ethikos*, ethics means 'ethos and character'. The words 'custom' and 'usage' also fall within the wider definition of ethics. By contrast, the word 'morality' comes from its Greek root *moralis*, which refers to the nature of a human action rather than the character of the actor. While ancient Greek moral philosophers like Plato and Aristotle had developed detailed theories of morality, the nature of the relationship between the 'actor' and his 'action' remained both ambigious and contentious within their ethical framework. After Muslims came into contact with the ancient Greek philosophical and scientific heritage during the eighth and ninth century, influential Muslim philosophers like al-Kindi and al-Farabi formulated new ethical theories in the light of the Islamic worldview. The works of these early Muslim thinkers laid the foundations for a new science which became known as *ilm al-akhlaq* (or the 'science of ethics'). In their quest to define the 'common good', the Muslims adopted a different approach to ethics and morality. Thus some, like al-Farabi, Ibn Bajjah and Ibn Tufayl, adopted a philosophical approach to ethics; others, like

al-Ghazali and Fakhr al-Din al-Razi, pursued a theological approach, while yet others (Ibn Taymiyyah and Ibn Qayyim al-Jawziyyah, for instance) adopted a more religious-cum-scriptural approach to ethics. However, it was Shaykh Sa'di of Shiraz who became one of the most influential exponents of practical ethics; indeed, he not only clearly defined the 'common good', he also played a pivotal role in popularising Islamic morality and ethics.

Shaykh Muslih al-Din Sa'di, known as Shaykh Sa'di for short, was born in the Persian city of Shiraz into a middle-class Muslim family. His father, Abdullah, was a civil servant by profession and served the then rulers of Shiraz. When Sa'di was still an infant, his father died and this forced his family to experience considerable financial hardship. The poverty and destitution experienced by Sa'di during his childhood remained fixed in his mind and was later recalled most vividly in his writings. In desperation, he and his mother sought refuge with an Arab chieftain who understood their pain and showed sympathy. Normally, when people face such economic hardship, they seek to alleviate their situation by seeking suitable employment, but Sa'di's mother encouraged her son to continue his studies. Being very studious, young Sa'di used to bury himself in his books rather than go out to play games or have fun with his peers. His devotion to his studies impressed his teachers and this also prompted a local wealthy patron to volunteer to pay for his education. At school he followed the standard curriculum of the day and excelled in his studies; thus his teachers encouraged him to pursue higher education. Some of the leading centres of Islamic learning and education at the time were in Baghdad, Damascus, Basrah, Nishapur, Hira and Isfahan. Accordingly, he proceeded to Baghdad for his higher education and there he composed scores of essays and poems on both religious and moral themes; he was around twenty-one at the time. He dedicated these essays to his teacher, Shaykh Shams al-Din, who was a professor of literature at the famous Nizamiyyah College in Baghdad. Impressed by the young writer's erudition and literary ability, the venerable Shaykh agreed to fund his advanced education at Nizamiyyah out of his own pocket.

An insatiable seeker of knowledge, Sa'di studied a wide range of subjects including traditional Islamic sciences, philosophy, logic, history, geography, science and *tasawwuf* (mysticism) at Nizamiyyah College under the tutelage of eminent professors like Hafiz Abd al-Rahman ibn Ali ibn al-Jawzi and Farah ibn al-Jawahir. As the capital of the Abbasid Caliphate, Baghdad at the time was home to some of the Muslim world's leading scholars and thinkers, who willingly imparted knowledge and wisdom to those who were eager to learn. Sa'di thus moved freely in and out of the religious circles of all the prominent scholars of Baghdad and drank deep from the fountain of Islamic knowledge. During his stay in Baghdad, he also encountered the celebrated Sufi sage Shihab al-Din Umar al-Suhrawardi, the founder of the *suhrawardiyyah* Sufi Order, who initiated him into his *tariqah*. According to some of his biographers, he also met Abd al-Qadir al-Jilani, the famous founder of the *qadiriyyah* Sufi Order, but this view is clearly erroneous because Abd al-Qadir had died in 1166, almost a decade

before Sa'di was born. Nevertheless, having completed his higher education and mastered several languages in addition to Arabic and Persian (which was his mother tongue), Sa'di eventually returned home to Shiraz. Here, he discovered to his dismay, how the socio-political situation had become very volatile and unpredictable.

Indeed, while Sa'di was still in Baghdad, his former patron Atabek Sa'd ibn Zangi had been ousted from power by his arch-rival Sultan Ghiyath al-Din Isfahani, the Khwarizmshah, and the latter was very suspicious of those who allied themselves with the son of Zangi. To make matters worse, the Mongols were threatening to wreak havoc throughout that region. This prompted Sa'di to leave Shiraz and travel in pursuit of knowledge. For the next three decades (that is, from 1226 to 1256), he travelled extensively across the Muslim world and explored the lifestyle, culture, tradition and habits of Muslims and non-Muslims alike. During his travels, he visited Arabia in order to perform the sacred pilgrimage (*hajj*) and then proceeded to Syria, Egypt and North Africa. In Tripoli, he was captured by the Franks and forced into hard labour, but he was rescued by a well-wisher who married his daughter to him. However, the marriage did not last long because Sa'di found the girl too intemperate and aggressive for his liking. From North Africa, he travelled to Turkistan, Afghanistan and India where he met the Hindus for the first time. In India, he visited Punjab, Somnath, Gujarat and Delhi and later, he vividly recorded his experiences of these countries in the form of poetry. From there he travelled to Yemen and Abyssinia (present-day Ethiopia) before proceeding to Makkah to perform yet another pilgrimage. In all, he performed more than a dozen pilgrimages and freely interacted with people of all races and cultural backgrounds, which enabled him to gain an unrivalled insight into human nature, its frailities and shortcomings, as well as its positive aspects. His advanced training in Islamic theological, philosophical and mystical sciences, coupled with his three decades of travel across the Muslim world, not only broadened Sa'di's intellectual horizon but also enriched his awareness and understanding of the diversity which is so characteristic of the human family. Indeed, his observations and admiration of the vast tapestry which constitutes our humanity inspired him to formulate and champion a universalistic ethic which belonged neither to the East, nor to the West. Rooted in the timeless axis of Divine wisdom, his global ethic was all about the 'common good'; the common good of all humanity rather than that of a specific group or nation.

After returning to his native Shiraz in 1256 at the age of eighty-one, he authored most of his books, treatises and poetry. Considered to be a remarkable example of late blooming, Sa'di completed two of his most famous works, namely the *Bustan* (The Fruit Garden) and *Gulistan* (The Rose Garden) after his eightieth birthday. The former was finished in 1257, while the latter was completed in 1258. These years were also some of the most traumatic periods in the annals of Islam. While Sa'di was busy writing about the enduring values and principles which are common to all people, highlighting the importance of truth, honesty, wisdom and toleration in fostering healthy human relationships, the Mongol hordes emerged from Asia and marched into Baghdad. The Mongol attack on Baghdad was so devastating that it shocked and horrified Muslims and non-Muslims alike. Although Sa'di made no specific reference to the Mongol sack of Baghdad in his works, as a devout Muslim and practising Sufi, he must have been devastated by the brutal nature of Mongol assault on the seat of the Abbasid Caliphate. When the Mongol advance was eventually halted in 1260 by the Mamluks of Egypt, the entire Muslim world breathed a sigh of relief. Amidst the prevailing socio-political chaos, an increasingly frail Sa'di came to enjoy the patronage of Atabek Abu Bakr ibn Sa'd, the son and successor of his former patron, Atabek Sa'd ibn Zangi. He admired this young ruler so much that he dedicated his *Bustan* to him, saying that as long as the sun and the moon continue to rise in the skies, the name of Abu Bakr ibn Sa'd would be fondly remembered by the readers of his *Bustan*.

Comprising more than four thousand couplets, the *Bustan* is today considered to be one of the most widely-read works of Persian poetry. Before Sa'di, Persia had produced some of the most influential and gifted poets of the Muslim world, including Abul Majd Majdud Sana'i, Umar Khayyam and Farid al-Din Attar but, with the publication of the *Bustan*, he established his reputation as one of the most polished and ethical poets of the Muslim world. Although steeped in Islamic theology, jurisprudence and mysticism, Sa'di's poetry transcended religious formalism to capture the essence of universal Prophetic wisdom. That is why theological and dogmatic debates and discussion never interested him; his understanding of Islam was primarily a moral and ethical one – underpinned by the universal Qur'anic principles and Prophetic wisdom. Inspired by the timeless teachings of Islam, Sa'di's moral philosophy combined religious principles, practical ethics and spirituality to create a comprehensive moral code of behaviour in society. This moral code was a universal one where the kings, queens, rulers, saints, philosophers, theologians as well as lay people had their roles and responsibilities assigned to them. It was not a code in a legal sense; rather it was a humane, tolerant and all-inclusive code of behaviour – and its foremost objective was the promotion of the 'common good' of all people. In his *Bustan*, Sa'di spoke a universal language – which transcended formal speech – by addressing the human heart, which he considered to be the mirror of universal truth. That is to say, his moral philosophy sought to connect mankind to Divinity at a practical level, without compromising the sacredness of the latter or undermining the humanity of the former. The *Bustan* therefore presents a powerful and compelling exposition of universal moral and ethical teachings, underpinned by the timeless wisdom of the Qur'an and Prophetic wisdom, without in anyway overlooking their practical dimensions.

In comparison, Sadi's *Gulistan* is primarily a lyrical work which consists of interesting, witty and instructive anecdotes, stories and tales which seek to inspire the reader to lead a normal and, equally, moral life inspired by the timeless wisdom of Islam. An optimist by nature and a gifted communicator, he analysed human relationships and behaviour through personal observation and he rejoiced when people exemplified good behaviour and etiquette but, at the same time, he refused to condemn those who fell short of his high moral and ethical standards. He persevered with such people, knowing only too well that we all have our own share of mistakes and misdemeanours; therefore he preferred to drop hints and make suggestions to those who fell short of his high ethical standards. Indeed, he operated like a universal friend who informed people of what they needed to know – and in a language they could all understand – without offending anyone. He was wise and entertaining, and never dull or boring. A reader of the *Gulistan* cannot help but smile, reflect and ponder, and do so without having to stretch themselves either physically or intellectually. If his wit was refreshing and his eloquence breathtaking, then his understanding of human nature and behavioural psychology was precise. Yet, strangely enough, Saʿdi claimed to have composed his *Gulistan* in a hurry, with information left over from the *Bustan*.

In short, in his *Bustan* and *Gulistan*, Saʿdi managed to capture the very essence of Islamic moral and ethical teachings, and in so doing he helped to popularise the moral and ethical code of Islam as never before. As an Islamic scholar and moralist, he is still very popular in Persia and the subcontinent. But, as a writer and poet, he is considered to be one of the most polished and gifted Muslim poets of all time. So much so that an Iranian is not generally considered to be literate until he learns to quote Saʿdi by heart. Originally written in Persian, Saʿdi's *Gulistan* and *Bustan* have also been translated into all the prominent languages of the world including English, Arabic, Hindi, Urdu, French, German, Bengali, Russian, Turkish and even Latin. Unfortunately, his exact age at the time of his death is not known. Some say he died at the advanced age of one hundred and sixteen, while others suggest he died at the age of ninty-nine. Either way, he was laid to rest in his native Shiraz. But his powerful and enduring poetry and moral teachings have continued to influence scholars, writers, poets and lay people alike, both in the East and the West, up to the present time. Indeed, the following couplet from his *Gulistan* (which has also been inscribed on the Hall of the United Nations) beautifully summarises his entire moral and ethical philosophy: 'The humanity are the limbs of one frame, as in Creation their origin is the same. If fate causes one of the limbs to sting, others too will cry in suffering.' (The Book of Adab-i-Shabat or 'Manners of Companionship').

# 93

## Sir Sayyid Ahmad Khan
## (b.1817 - d.1898)

THE ASIAN SUBCONTINENT has produced some of the Muslim world's most influential rulers, thinkers and reformers. Thus, famous Mughal rulers like Akbar the Great, Shah Jahan and Awrangzeb feature in this book on account of their enduring political and cultural contributions. Likewise, influential Muslim thinkers, reformers and politicians of the subcontinent like Shaykh Ahmad Sirhindi, Shah Waliullah, Sir Muhammad Iqbal, Mawlana Muhammad Ilyas, Muhammad Ali Jinnah, Abul A'la Mawdudi and Muhammad Yunus appear in this book by virtue of their wide-ranging contribution to Islamic thought, political leadership, cultural reformation or economic development. These remarkable and gifted individuals were pioneers in their chosen fields of endeavour. Their skill, courage and dedication – as political leaders, religious thinkers and socio-economic reformers – have rightly earned them a special place in the annals of the subcontinent. Sir Sayyid Ahmad Khan, an illustrious Indian Muslim educationalist and reformer, also belongs to this select group of inspirational subcontinental Muslims.

Sayyid Ahmad Khan, also known simply as Sir Sayyid, was born in Delhi, the capital of India, during the reign of the Mughal Emperor

Akbar Shah II. His ancestors originally hailed from Arabia and settled in Herat before moving to Delhi during the sixteenth century. As loyal Muslims, his family members became fervent supporters of the Mughal ruler Akbar the Great and his successors, and the Mughals, in turn, rewarded them handsomely for their unflinching support and loyalty. One of those who attained a pre-eminent position was Khwajah Farid al-Din Khan, the maternal grandfather of Ahmad Khan, who not only served the Mughals in his capacity as a Minister of State, but also developed a good working relationship with the British, who wielded considerable political and economic power in India at the time. While Ahmad Khan was a child his devout father, Sayyid Muhammad Muttaqi Khan, embraced Sufism (Islamic mysticism); thus he retreated from worldly affairs and became an ascetic (*zahid*). Young Ahmad was therefore raised by his aristocratic maternal grandfather, who ensured he received a thorough education in Arabic, Persian, Urdu and traditional Islamic sciences before pursuing mathematics and traditional medicine. During his early years, Ahmad became very fond of Persian poetry and studied the *Bustan* and *Gulistan* of Shaykh Sa'di and the *Diwan* of Hafiz of Shiraz with great interest and enthusiasm. But, after the successive deaths of his older brother and father, his whole outlook on life changed. He grew a beard and became a practising Muslim. At the same time, he was forced to look for a job to earn his livelihood. Thus, at the age of nineteen, he secured a job as a record-keeper at the courts in Delhi. Being hardworking and meticulous, he was swiftly promoted to the post of *munsif* (or subordinate judge) by the British authorities; thus he earned a monthly salary of one hundred rupees which was paid to him by the East India Company.

During this period Ahmad became a prolific writer who devoted all his spare time to research and writing. However, his essays and writings failed to capture the imagination of the populace until, in 1846, he published his *Athar al-Sanadid* (Traces of the Great), which was an historical survey of Delhi's monuments. This book established his reputation as a writer and scholar. Then, in 1855, he edited and re-published the famous sixteenth century historical work *Ain-i-Akbari*, which was originally compiled by Emperor Akbar's favourite courtier, Abul Fadl. Although this book received much acclaim, Mirza Asadullah Khan Ghalib (a great Urdu poet and a contemporary of Ahmad), wrote a critical review of the book and did not rate it highly. According to Ghalib, it was inappropriate to focus on past glories at a time when the existential condition of Indian Muslims was deteriorating rapidly, especially in the face of British political and military onslaught. Instead, he urged Ahmad to focus more on the socio-political challenges which confronted the Indian Muslims at the time. Following the horrific events of 1857 known as the Indian Mutiny, which led to the mass slaughter of Muslims at the hands of the British army as well as the expulsion of the last Mughal ruler, Bahadur Shah Zafar II, from India, more than three centuries of Mughal rule came to an abrupt end. A year later, Queen Victoria was proclaimed Empress of India. These events prompted Ahmad to take stock of the new socio-political situation in India and fight for the rights of the Indian Muslims. Indeed, dismayed by the political upheavals of the time, he initially decided to leave India and settle in Egypt, but soon he changed his mind and instead decided to work with his fellow Muslims to improve their social, political, economic and cultural conditions. As a deep thinker and persuasive interlocutor, Ahmad knew the political situation in India had changed irreversibly and as such it was in the interest of the Indian Muslims to proactively engage with the new rulers of their country so as to protect their interests. In the circumstances, he felt opposing the British would be both futile and suicidal for the future of Indian Muslims; thus he decided to co-operate with the British authorities.

Being a shrewd politican, he had no desire to see the Indian Muslims become second-class citizens in their own country. He therefore declared his loyalty to the Crown and this, of course, endeared him to the ruling British elites. In fact, he played a central role in improving the Indian Muslims' relationship with the British authorities who, in turn, hailed him as one of their most 'loyal Mohammedans'. Thereafter, the British rulers regularly sought his advice on all important matters relating to the Indian Muslims. So, for instance, when he analysed and identified the root cause of the 1857 rebellion in his report entitled *Asbab-i-Baghawat-i-Hind* (The Causes of the Indian Mutiny), the British elites accepted his criticism of the British army and the way in which the rebellion had been handled. Many of his recommendations for change were accepted and implemented by the ruling elite, in order to facilitate better communication between the rulers and the ruled. Thanks to Ahmad's co-operation with the Raj and close contact with its leading figures, his attitude towards the British, their culture and way of life began to change for the better. The more he interacted with his British friends and acquaintances, the more educated, cultured and loyal he found them to be. In comparison, the majority of his fellow countrymen were too busy fighting each other and engaging in both tribal rivalry and religious hairsplitting.

However, as a devout Muslim and a patriotic Indian, he was determined to improve the social, cultural and educational conditions of his countrymen (especially those of the Indian Muslims), and he was prepared to harness the salient features of British culture and education for this purpose. Convinced that a thorough reformation of Indian Muslim society was the key to improving the Indian Muslims' existential condition, he became a powerful voice for educational and cultural reform across the country. He argued that there was no contradiction between modern science and Islamic teachings. He also urged the Indian Muslims to study the Qur'an and the life of the Prophet Muhammad in a unified and holistic way. The Indian Muslims, he felt, had nothing to fear from modern Western science and educational philosophy; rather, the pursuit of science and education was the key to understanding Islam and its role in the modern world. Moreover, he urged the Indian Muslims to remain loyal to the Crown and strive hard to improve their socio-economic situation by educating themselves and engaging in business and trade. To prove that he was not only a preacher but also a man of action, in 1864 the British authorities helped him to establish a scientific society in Ghazipur in order to translate high quality, modern Western philosophical and scientific literature into Urdu, so as to make the treasures of modern scientific knowledge and scholarship accessible to the Indian Muslims.

Following his move to Aligarh, and subsequent visit to England during 1869 and 1870, he conducted a detailed study of the British educational system and its methodology. As a result, he developed the idea of establishing a college where the traditional Islamic sciences would be taught in parallel with modern scientific and literary subjects. During his stay in England, he became profoundly impressed by the scientific and technological achievements of the Western world and he hoped that his college would inspire the Indian Muslims to revive the Islamic intellectual and cultural heritage. While in England he also found time to author his *Essays on the Life of Muhammad,* wherein he refuted the charges levelled against the Prophet of Islam by his European detractors (such as Sir William Muir). As a proud Indian Muslim, he was not prepared to let the Orientalists have a field day against the venerable Prophet. The publication of this book also proved that he was not a blind imitator of all things Western. On the contrary, he showed himself to be a very intelligent and discerning champion of Islam and its Prophet. After his return from England, he enlisted the help of several prominent British officials, including Lord Northbrook and Lord Lytton, and together they laid the foundations of the Muhammadan Anglo-Oriental College (MAO) in 1877. Patronised by the British authorities and supported by a group of eminent Indian Muslims (such as Altaf Hussain Hali, Nawab Muhsin al-Mulk and Mawlvi Chiragh Ali), this college offered degree courses in science, arts, law and Islamic sciences. Prominent British academics like Theodore Beck, Theodore Morison, Sir Thomas W. Arnold as well as celebrated Islamic scholars like Allamah Shibli Numani were recruited to teach at this college. Now known as Aligarh Muslim University, this famous institution of higher education has produced generations of renowned Indian Muslim scholars, thinkers and leaders, including Mawlvi Abdul Haq, Ziauddin Ahmad, Muhammad Ali Jauhar, Liaquat Ali Khan and Zakir Hussain among others.

Ahmad's efforts to change and reform the social, cultural and educational condition of the Indian Muslims initially received a lukewarm response from his countrymen. But after he had developed a fresh interpretation of Islamic scriptural sources in the light of modern Western scientific and philosophical thought, the conservative *ulama* (religious scholars) became a thorn in his side. Since the Indian *ulama* thought he was seeking to dilute and undermine the fundamental principles and practices of Islam under the guise of modernisation and progress, they branded him a religious innovator. However, this charge was only partially justified; although his desire to improve and enhance the existential condition of the Indian Muslims was both genuine and sincere, the *ulama* were right to question his reformist approach to Islam. Heavily influenced by nineteenth century European philosophical and scientific thought, Ahmad attempted to reconcile religion and science, as if Islam and scientific thought were somehow incompatible. Since he considered nature to be a creation of God and the Qur'an as His final revelation, he argued that the modern sciences (*ulum al-jadid*) and the Divine revelation (*wahy*) were complementary rather than contradictory. To prove his point, he interpreted the Qur'an and the Prophetic traditions (*hadith*) from a philosophical-cum-scientific perspective. And in so doing he explained away all the miraculous events mentioned in the Qur'an (for example, he considered the story about the elephants in *Surat al-Fil* to be either a natural phenomenon, or the manifestation of human energy, rather than an act of Divine miracle.). Given his ultra-rationalistic approach to the Qur'an, it is not surprising that the *ulama* severely criticised him for his neo-Mu'tazilite approach to the Islamic scriptural sources. However, the *ulama*'s opposition to his socio-cultural reforms (including the need to study and explore modern Western scientific thought and methodology) was unjustified. In other words, Ahmad was right to urge the *ulama* to face reality and provide Islamic answers to the challenges posed by Western modernity. In fact, even Jamal al-Din al-Afghani – who was very critical of Ahmad for his rationalistic approach to the Qur'an and political loyalty to the Crown – was of the opinion that Muslims had to change and reform their social, cultural and educational conditions if they were to liberate their lands from foreign occupation and revive their Islamic heritage.

A pioneer of Urdu prose, Ahmad not only became a prolific writer on religious, educational and cultural topics, but also founded a number of important educational institutions. Moreover, he published two periodicals, namely *Aligarh Institute Gazette* and *Tahdhib al-Akhlaq* (The Muslim Social Reformer), wherein he published scores of articles on all the pressing issues of his day. Most of his essays and articles were later collected and published in sixteen volumes by Muhammad Ismail Panipati under the title of *Maqalat-i Sir Sayyid* (Articles of Sir Sayyid). During the 1860s he also wrote a commentary on the Bible, while his incomplete Qur'anic exegesis was later published in seven volumes. In short, Ahmad's wide-ranging political, social, cultural and educational activities won him widespread acclaim from his fellow countrymen, Muslims and Hindus alike. In recognition of his outstanding services to his people, he was knighted by the British Government in 1888. His religious ideas and thoughts, coupled with his educational contribution in the form of Aligarh Muslim University, have continued to exert a considerable influence on the Muslims of the subcontinent to this day. Additionally, his reformist ideas have influenced scores of renowned Muslim scholars, thinkers and writers like Altaf Hussain Hali, Nazir Ahmad, Shibli Numani, Sir Muhammad Iqbal, the Ali Brothers, Sayyid Sulaiman Nadwi, Abul Kalam Azad, and Ghulam Ahmad Parvez. He died at the age of eighty-one and was buried in Aligarh. Hali, who was a celebrated Urdu poet and a fervent supporter of Ahmad, later wrote a voluminous biography of this great Muslim scholar and reformer under the title of *Hayat-i-Javid* (The Life of Sir Sayyid Ahmad Khan).

# 94

## The Mahdi of Sudan
### (b.1844 - d.1885)

SUDAN IS AN enormous African country; it borders eight other countries, is about half the size of Europe, and links the Arab world with the continent of Africa. Its topography includes deserts, savannah and forests; the River Nile and its tributaries have also been a key feature in Sudan's politico-economic development, making it an attractive target for foreign colonial powers. Due to its geo-strategic importance, the forces of Muhammad Ali Pasha, the Ottoman viceroy of Egypt, established their politico-economic hegemony over Sudan during the 1870s. Divided into two large regions, namely the north and south, the former region is inhabited primarily by Arabic speaking Muslims, and Khartoum, the capital of Sudan, is located in this part of the country. By contrast, southern Sudan is inhabited mainly by tribal people, some of whom are either converts to Christianity or Islam, while the majority are pagans who speak Sudanic languages and observe traditional African customs and traditions. However, as a strategically important country, Sudan became the centre of a global power struggle between the Ottomans, the Egyptians and the British during the nineteenth century as they fought each other to establish their politico-economic control in that country.

Amidst the prevailing political chaos and socio-economic uncertainty, the towering figure of the Mahdi emerged to free Sudan from the grip of the imperial powers and return that country to its people.

Muhammad Ahmad ibn Abdullah, better known as the Mahdi of Sudan, was born on Labab Island, located in the province of Dongola in northern Sudan. His family claimed to be the descendants of the Prophet through his grandson Hasan, the eldest son of Caliph Ali. His father, Abdullah Fahl, was a successful businessman who earned his living building and supplying wooden boats to local merchants, traders and fishermen. When Muhammad Ahmad was only five, his family was forced to leave Dongola due to an acute shortage of timber in that province and they settled in Karari, located close to Omdurman and Khartoum, where timber was readily available at the time. Following in the footsteps of their father, Muhammad Ahmad's brothers also became carpenters and they provided much needed support for their father to meet the growing demand for timber boats in that locality. Since both his parents were practising Muslims, Muhammad Ahmad grew up in a religious atmosphere. Keen to provide a sound religious education for his son, Abdullah Fahl enrolled him at his local village school. But, after his father's death, his oldest brother assumed responsibility for the entire family and he encouraged Muhammad Ahmad to continue his studies. As a gifted student, he not only learned Arabic but also committed the entire Qur'an to memory before he was ten. Impressed by his educational achievements, both his teachers and brothers encouraged him to continue his education. For the next seven years, he pursued further and higher education in Islamic sciences, including *kalam* (theology), *tafsir* (Qur'anic exegesis), *fiqh* (Islamic jurisprudence) and *hadith* (Prophetic traditions) under the tutelage of eminent scholars like Sharaf al-Din Abu al-Sadiq.

During this period Muhammad Ahmad became thoroughly familiar with the writings of classical Islamic scholars like Muhammad ibn Ismail al-Bukhari, Ahmad ibn Hanbal and al-Shafi'i, in addition to the theological and juridical works of Ibn Taymiyyah and his prominent students (such as Ibn Qayyim al-Jawziyyah and Ibn Kathir), as well as the mystical writings of popular Sufis like Ibn al-Arabi, Ahmad ibn Idris and Muhammad Ali al-Sanusi. His literalist theological and juridical training, along with a thorough familiarisation with Islamic mystical thought and philosophy, later helped him to create a powerful synthesis between Islamic law and spirituality in order to develop a balanced Islamic character and society. After completing his formal studies at the age of seventeen, he was initiated into the *sammaniyyah* Sufi Order by its influential exponent, Shaykh Muhammad Sharif Nur al-Da'im. Since it was commonly accepted by the Sufis that one could not pursue the mystical path and make spiritual progress without the aid of a competent guide, Muhammad Ahmad joined the *sammaniyyah tariqah*. As the renowned Persian Sufi Abu Yazid al-Bistami (who is also known as Bayazid Bistami) once remarked, 'One who has no guide has taken *shaytan* (Satan) as his guide.' Muhammad Ahmad agreed with this view and became a loyal follower of Shaykh al-Da'im who guided him along the mystical path for around

five years until he attained the rank of a Shaykh himself; he was only twenty-two at the time.

Unlike the majority of the Sufis of his time, Muhammad Ahmad's understanding of mysticism combined both spirituality and socio-political activism. That is to say, his early training in Islamic theology, jurisprudence and mysticism encouraged him to lead an austere and ascetic lifestyle but, at the same time, following in the footsteps of the Prophet, he married and set up his own family. He was only twenty-four when he built a new mosque and Sufi *zawiyyah* (lodge) in order to disseminate Islamic moral, ethical and spiritual teachings. Likewise, he encouraged his people to seek Islamic knowledge and wisdom within Sudan, rather than go abroad to study at prominent Islamic institutions like al-Azhar University. As a bright student, he could have gone to al-Azhar if he wanted, but Muhammad Ahmad decided to stay in Sudan and help revive Islamic principles and practices in that country. When his family left Karari in 1870 and moved to Aba Island in search of timber so they could continue their boat-making business, Muhammad Ahmad followed suit. Here he married for the second time and his fame began to spread throughout the island on account of his vast knowledge and understanding of Islam. He then established a Sufi lodge and gathered around him a small band of followers. By coincidence, Shaykh al-Da'im his former teacher and spiritual guide, also moved to an adjacent town and he apparently became jealous of his former pupil's popularity with the locals. Soon the two men clashed and Muhammad Ahmad was formally expelled from the *sammaniyyah* Order by Shaykh al-Da'im himself. Infuriated by the latter's snub, Muhammad Ahmad went and pledged allegiance to Shaykh Quraishi Wad al-Zain, who was a master of another branch of *sammaniyyah* Sufi Order, and strengthened his ties with the latter by marrying his daughter. Following Shaykh Quraishi's death in 1878, Muhammad Ahmad succeeded him as the leader of this Sufi branch and his reputation began to spread across the wider region.

As a religious leader and spiritual guide, his main priority was to promote Islamic education and improve the socio-economic condition of his people. Since Sudan was an Ottoman-Egyptian colony at the time, the country's colonial rulers not only failed to exercise proper political leadership, they also did not seem to have any plans to improve the Sudanese people's socio-economic condition. The ruling elite's failure to tackle the people's socio-economic problems and difficulties eventually led to widespread resentment across the country. Prompted by the colonialists' indifference to the plight of the people, he began to preach a new form of religious activism which emphasised the importance of personal purification and rectitude, along with the need for social morality, collective responsibility and political activism across Sudan. While Muhammad Ahmad was busy formulating his new religious-cum-political ideology – underpinned by Islamic principles and practices – a man named Abdullahi ibn Muhammad Adam (who hailed from the province of Kordofan) came to visit him in 1880. The two men instantly became close friends and resolved to work together for the political, economic and spiritual betterment of their people. Even before Abdullahi's arrival, Muhammad Ahmad told some of his close disciples that he was the long-awaited Mahdi (or the 'centenarian renewer of faith') whom the East Africans expected to arrive during the thirteenth century of Islam and help them to liberate their land from foreign occupation. After his arrival, Abdullahi convinced Muhammad Ahmad that he was indeed that 'renewer of faith' long expected by his countrymen. Urged on by Abdullahi, he then announced that he had been blessed with a series of visions wherein he was informed that he *was* the expected Mahdi. He reinforced his claim to Mahdihood by reinterpreting the Prophetic traditions (*hadith*) concerning the emergence of Imam Mahdi towards the end of time.

As the self-proclaimed saviour of his people, he now began to tour Sudan (especially the province of Kordafan and the Nubian mountain regions) in order to propagate Islam and establish his authority as the spiritual and political leader of his people. His call for political unity and a return to the original, pristine teachings of Islam went down well with the masses. Having endured decades of political oppression and economic hardship under foreign rule, the Sudanese people gave him a warm reception. As his followers began to increase rapidly, Muhammad Ahmad lambasted the oppressive policies of the colonial rulers. It was not long before his religious-cum-political opposition against the colonialists won him widespread support in Sudan; indeed, soon a mass anti-colonial movement began to take shape. And although he was not a politician, Muhammad Ahmad's authority as a leader of his people transcended such categorisation. As it was, the religious-cum-political strategy he pursued in Sudan was very similar to that championed by the Prophet Muhammad back in seventh century Arabia. Like the Prophet, he asked his followers to pledge loyalty (*bay'ah*) to him; he also performed a migration (*hijrah*) from Aba Island to Jabal Qadir in the same way the Prophet migrated from Makkah to Madinah, and finally he named his supporters *al-ansar* (the helpers) just as the Prophet had. Being intimately acquainted with the life and teachings of the Prophet (*sirah*), Muhammad Ahmad pursued a reformist methodology which he believed was Divinely-inspired, like the mission of the Prophet Muhammad.

However, when he and his disciples began to intensify their religious-cum-political activities, the Khartoum-based Ottoman-Egyptian rulers became very alarmed. They tried to pacify Muhammad Ahmad's followers (known as the *mahdiyyah*) by agreeing to some of their demands, but he denounced them in no uncertain terms. After some deliberation, the authorities in Khartoum decided to launch a military action against the *mahdiyyah*. Thus, in 1882, two successive military expeditions were sent by the Egyptian forces against the *mahdiyyah* in which the latter inflicted a crushing defeat on the Egyptian army. The unexpected success of the *mahdiyyah* won Muhammad Ahmad widespread recognition throughout Sudan, and more and more people responded to his call for national religious and political unity and solidarity. Encouraged by their success, the *mahdiyyah* then advanced towards central Kordafan where they received a warm reception from the locals and laid siege to the town of al-Ubayyid (El-Obeid). After capturing the town in 1883, Muhammad Ahmad became the undisputed ruler of Kordofan and its neighbouring territories.

As a charismatic leader and an electrifying orator, he inspired his followers to pursue *jihad* (military struggle) against their enemies; he promised to lead them all the way to Makkah and Madinah, two of Islam's most sacred cities, via Cairo. Muhammad Ahmad and his *mahdiyyah* became so powerful that they eventually captured Khartoum in 1885 after inflicting a crushing defeat on the forces of Charles Gordon, a British military general, who died fighting on the battlefield. Although General Gordon's defeat at the hands of the Sudanese revolutionary army created a huge political storm in Britain at the time, Muhammad Ahmad and his forces went on to reunite the whole country under his leadership. However, six months after establishing himself in Omdurman, which became the new capital of Sudan, he suddenly died of fever at the age of forty-one. Within a short period of time, he not only managed to unite his people under the banner of Islam, he also forced out the combined might of the Ottoman, Egyptian and the British

armies from his country. After abolishing the tribal customs and traditions which prevailed in the Sudan at the time, he promulgated the *shari'ah* (Islamic law) across the country and in so doing he initiated a process of Islamisation and Arabisation which subsequently spread across all Sudan and East Africa.

Though the *mahdiyyah* State established by Muhammad Ahmad was destroyed by an Anglo-Egyptian army barely fourteen years after its inception, his influence and legacy continues to play a powerful role in Sudanese politics to this day. And although his claim to have been the Mahdi was rightly dismissed by the orthodox Muslims, his contribution to the Islamic revival and resurgence in the Sudan and East Africa was nothing short of remarkable. For this reason, he deserves to be recognised as one of the most influential Islamic warriors (*mujahid*) of modern times. Regarded as the 'father of modern Sudan', Muhammad Ahmad's legacy later inspired his son, Sir Sayyid Abd al-Rahman al-Mahdi, to establish the *ummah* party (a national Sudanese political and religious party) in 1945. Currently led by his grandson, Sayyid Sadiq al-Mahdi, this party continues to exert considerable political influence in Sudan to this day. Internationally, however, Muhammad Ahmad's heroic struggle against the colonial powers turned him into a powerful symbol of pride and prestige among Black nationalists across Africa, Europe and the United States.

# 95

## Al-Mutanabbi
## (b.915 - d.968)

LIKE ARAMAIC AND Hebrew, Arabic is a Semitic language. However, unlike the other Semitic languages, Arabic is today a global language. As the *lingua franca* of the Arab world, Arabic is the official language of almost all the Middle Eastern and North African countries. As the language of the Qur'an and the linguistic medium of the Islamic civilisation, Arabic – like Greek and Latin – exerted a profound influence on the medieval world to the extent that it became the foremost language of science, philosophy, arts, culture and scholarly discourse during the heyday of Islamic civilisation. And although the Abbasid era is generally considered to be the Golden Age of Islamic science, philosophy and literature, it was during the reign of Harun al-Rashid and his son, al-Ma'mun, that Baghdad became the world's foremost centre of philosophical, scientific and literary activities. Once the language of the desert nomads, Arabic soon became the bedrock of the Islamic civilisation – extending as it did from Spain in the West, to the Indus valley in the East. At the time, the Arabs developed an impressive intellectual and literary culture which was very rich in both content and quality. Indeed, from pre-Islamic poetry to the Qur'an, and from the prose literature of Ibn al-Muqaffa, al-Jahiz and

Ibn Qutaiba to the splendours of medieval Arabic poetry, the Arabs soon became the messengers of knowledge, wisdom and literature. Arabic poetry – otherwise known as *diwan al-Arab* (register of the Arabs) – also reached its zenith during this period. Widely considered to be the greatest of all Arabic poets, al-Mutanabbi lived and thrived during this Golden Age of Arabic literature and poetry.

Abul Tayyib Ahmad ibn Hussain al-Jufi, better known as al-Mutanabbi (the 'would-be prophet'), was born in the southern Iraqi city of Kufah. Originally from Yemen, his ancestors later moved to Kufah where they became prominent members of the Arab tribe of al-Kindah. Young Mutanabbi showed signs of intelligence and unusual linguistic ability from an early age. Born and brought up in a lower-middle class Muslim family, he experienced considerable social and economic hardship as a child, but such unfavourable circumstances did not deter him from his studies. Indeed, while he was still a youngster, his family was forced to leave their home and stay for about two years on the outskirts of Samawa due to the Qarmatian insurrection. A faction of the Shi'a Ismaili (Sevener) sect, the Qarmatians emerged in the Iraqi city of Wasit during the latter part of the ninth century. From Wasit they spread across eastern Arabia before establishing their presence in parts of Syria, Iraq and Khurasan. Politically speaking, they vehemently opposed the Abbasids, but ideologically they were heavily influenced by a system of thought which incorporated elements of Gnosticism, Mazdakism and Shi'ism. At the beginning, the Qarmatians managed to instigate much socio-political havoc across Iraq, eastern Arabia and Syria but eventually they lost their momentum and declined in influence.

Hounded out by the Qarmatians, al-Mutanabbi and his family lived in the safer region of Samawa where he polished his command of Arabic among the bedouins, who were renowned for their mastery of the language in its purest form. When he was about twelve, his family returned to Kufah where he began to compose poetry. His lack of formal education was however compensated for by his natural poetic skills and ability. Nonetheless, al-Mutanabbi was a voracious reader of Arabic poetry and he became thoroughly familiar with the works of his illustrious predecessors like Hasan ibn Hani (better known as Abu Nuwas), Habib ibn Aws (also known as Abu Tammam), and Walid ibn Ubayd al-Buhturi. These celebrated Arabic poets lived and thrived in and around Baghdad during the early Abbasid period. Their poetic genius and literary ability endeared them to the ruling Abbasid elites who lavished money and gifts on them; some even attained positions of power and authority. For instance, Abu Nuwas was a celebrated poet who composed more than fifteen hundred poems on a wide range of subjects and, at the same time, he was a close companion of the Abbasid Caliph Harun al-Rashid. Likewise, Abu Tammam and al-Buhturi were famous court panegyrists who enjoyed Caliphal patronage and they were also known to have been very prosperous and wealthy individuals. Al-Mutanabbi not only read the works of these celebrated poets; he hoped to emulate them and become famous and wealthy himself.

He began his poetic career in Kufah where he became popular after composing his early poems. Impressed with his poetic skills and ability, the local ruler became his first patron and benefactor. This paved the way for al-Mutanabbi to reach the summit of Arabic poetry, although his road to success was far from being a smooth one, and was fraught with considerable personal difficulties and hardship. After leaving Kufah, he moved to Baghdad in 928. Here he experienced more personal and financial hardships; indeed, the local people's failure to understand and appreciate his poetry made him very bitter and despondent. Lack of response from the locals forced him to leave Baghdad and go to Syria, where he stayed for about two years. Here he earned his livelihood working as a freelance singer and entertainer. Hired by local Government officials to perform on special occasions, he earned just about enough to live comfortably. However, as an ambitious poet and performer he was not happy with such a lowly position, and was determined to rise to the peak of his chosen career. But his failure to attain instant success had a profoundly negative psychological impact on him. He could not understand why the masses failed to rate his poetry as highly as he did. This made him so unhappy, depressed and angry that he not only stopped working as a freelance singer and entertainer, but also became actively involved with the Qarmatians who at the time were engaged in a bitter political and military campaign against the Abbasids. Inspired by the religious eclecticism and communistic philosophy of the Qarmatians, coupled with his lack of personal success and recognition, al-Mutanabbi began to sympathise with the plight of this religious sect. Like the latter, he was a passionate activist and a pessimistic thinker whose philosophy of life was gloomier than even the Qarmatians. Perhaps it was the similarities between his pessimistic view of life and the messianic philosophy of the Qarmatians which prompted him to join this group and champion their politico-religious cause. However, according to some of his biographers, it was the plight of the Qarmatians which profoundly moved him and so he decided to support them. Either way, he eventually became a fully-fledged member of this group.

Later, when the Syrian authorities arrested a group of Qarmatians and threw them into prison, al-Mutanabbi happened to be one of them. During his two-year internment, he continued to refine his poetic skills and, soon after his release from captivity, he resumed his career as a freelance singer and entertainer. Thereafter, he travelled extensively via Damascus, Antioch and Aleppo, and entertained the masses with his songs and poetry. As a result, his reputation began to spread throughout Syria. This marked the beginning of his rise as a poet and performer. In fact, it was Badr al-Kashani, the incumbent governor of Damascus, who recognised al-Mutanabbi's poetic talent and recruited him into his court, where he soon established himself as an eminent court panegyrist at the age of twenty-nine. Here he composed elegant verses in praise of the governor, who rewarded him with both money and gifts. This, of course, made the other courtiers very jealous of him, so much so that he became the main target of their innuendoes and intrigues and was eventually forced to flee for his life, seeking refuge with the desert nomads on the outskirts of Damascus. But soon his fame reached the Hamadanid ruler Sayf al-Dawlah, who recruited him to his famous court in Aleppo.

The Hamdanid dynasty was established during the early part of the tenth century by Abu al-Haji Abdullah and their rule extended all the way from northern Iraq and Syria, to Armenia in the north. Of nomadic Arab extraction, the Hamdanid rulers, including Sayf al-Dawlah (who ruled for more than two decades), became very generous patrons of learning, art and architecture throughout their dominion. Under the patronage of Sayf al-Dawlah, al-Mutanabbi's poetic talent finally began to flourish like never before. He stayed with the Hamdanid ruler for nearly a decade and during this period he regularly accompanied him on his military campaigns. Since al-Mutanabbi considered Sayf to be a brave and noble Muslim warrior who was at the time busy defending the Islamic world from its enemies, he never grew tired of praising and glorifying him. Once, while

Sayf was locked in a vicious but hopeless battle against the Byzantines, al-Mutanabbi composed scores of inspiring poems in praise of Sayf, which pleased the latter so much that thereafter he regularly called on him to sing verses to inspire his forces during military expeditions. As a master of the Arabic language, he composed poetry for all occasions and to suit all tastes. His way with words, emotional spontaneity and, especially, his ability to capture the mood of the moment has remained unrivalled in the history of Arabic poetry. For instance, refering to his patron Sayf al-Dawlah, he once wrote:

'Whither do you intend, great prince? We are the herbs of the hills, and you are the clouds; we are the ones time has been miserly towards respecting you, and the days cheated of your presence.'

'Whether at war or at peace, you aim at the heights, whether you tarry or haste. Would that we were your steeds when you ride forth, and your tents when you alight!

Every day you load up fresh, and journey to glory, there to dwell; and when souls are mighty, the bodies are weared in their quest.'

'Even so the moons rise over us, and even so the great seas are unquiet; and our wont is comely patience, were it with anything but your absence that we tried. Every life you do not grace is death; every sun that you are not is darkness.'

In addition to traditional themes, al-Mutanabbi composed philosophical verses and love poetry. And although it is true that outstanding classical Arabic poets like Zuhayl ibn Abi Sulma, Tirimmah ibn Hakim, Bashshar ibn Burd, Abu Nuwas and Abu Tammam laid the foundations of early Arabic poetry, it was in the works of al-Mutanabbi that Arabic poetry reached its peak and greatest glory. If Bashshar ibn Burd was the father of Abbasid poetry and Ibn al-Muqaffa the pioneer of Abbasid prose, then al-Mutanabbi must be considered one of the most influential and gifted court panegyrists of all time. An outstanding poetic genius as he was, al-Mutanabbi was equally volatile and unpredictable; he liked his intellectual independence but frequently changed allegiance. Yet his ability to champion goodness, boast about his self-importance, mock and deride his opponents, while simultaneously displaying acts of generosity and kindness has continued to entertain and bemuse millions of fans of classical Arabic poetry up to the present time. As a Muslim and proud Arab, he was very fond of the history and symbolism of pre-Islamic Arabia, its culture and heritage. In his opinion there was no contradiction between his Islamic faith and ancient Arabian culture and heritage. Not surprisingly, his poetry reflected nationalistic, philosophical, mystical, romantic as well as cultural themes. Like Abu Nuwas, he was a wise and cosmopolitan poet who lived his life to its full, experiencing its ups and downs, joys and sorrows in equal measure.

After a decade at Sayf al-Dawlah's court in Aleppo, al-Mutanabbi moved to Egypt for a period, before returning to his native Kufah. From Kufah he went to Baghdad and eventually settled in the Persian city of Shiraz, where he graced the court of the Buwayhid (or Buyid) ruler Adud al-Dawlah for a long time. Here he composed a large collection of poetry in praise of the incumbent ruler, who rewarded him handsomely for his poetic output. Ambushed by a group of desert bandits, al-Mutanabbi died at the age of fifty-three while he was on his way to Baghdad. But his poetry was of such a high quality that famous classical Arabic poets like Abul Ala al-Ma'arri and Abd al-Malik ibn Muhammad al-Tha'alibi were profoundly influenced by his works. Indeed, even some of the leading modern Arabic poets and literary figures like Badr Shakir al-Sayyab, Taha Hussain, Nizar Qabbani and Ali Ahmad Sa'id (who is better known as Adunis) have acknowledged their debt to al-Mutanabbi. In other words, his adventurous life, eclectic thought and inspirational poetry has continued to influence Arabic thought, culture and heritage to this day.

# 96

## Uthman Dan Fodio
### (b.1754 ~ d.1817)

ISLAM BECAME AN integral part of Africa as early as the seventh century. After the Muslim conquest of parts of North Africa during the Caliphates of Umar and Uthman, Islamic rule was reasserted throughout that region during the reign of Muawiyah, thus permanently establishing an Islamic presence in North Africa and the region which the early Muslim historians referred to as *bilad al-Sudan* (the land of Sudan) in East Africa. Prior to the arrival of Islam on the other side of the continent, the West Africans were animists who worshipped animals and other natural objects, and led a largely tribal lifestyle. But after the Islamic expansion, Muslim missionaries and traders moved into West Africa and won the locals over to Islam, so that today more than half of Africa's Muslim population happen to live in West Africa where Islam continues to play an influential role in all sectors of the society. Needless to say, some of Africa's most powerful and enduring Islamic revivalist movements also emerged in West Africa. Inspired by the locals' desire to reassert Islamic morals and values in their societies, these movements played a pivotal role in addressing the challenges which confronted the West African Muslims at the time. Led by influential leaders like Sheku Hamada

in Mansina and al-Hajj Umar in the Bambara States of Nyoro and Segu, it was, however, the nineteenth century *jihad* movement of Shaykh Uthman Dan Fodio in Hausaland which became a great source of inspiration for the West African Muslims.

Uthman ibn Muhammad ibn Uthman ibn Salih, known as Uthman (or Usuman) Dan Fodio for short, was born in the town of Maratta in the Hausa State of Gobir. During his childhood his family left Maratta and settled in Degel, a village which is located close to present-day Sokoto. Young Uthman grew up under the care of his parents who ensured that he received a thorough education. As a noted Islamic scholar and a man of letters, Muhammad Fodio, Uthman's father, encouraged his son to continue the family tradition by specialising in traditional Islamic sciences. Brought up in a strongly Islamic environment, Uthman learned Arabic and memorised the whole Qur'an before he was ten. His ability to assimilate Islamic knowledge and wisdom with ease prompted his father to encourage him to undertake advanced training in traditional Islamic sciences. He began by attending the lectures of prominent local scholars like Shaykh Uthman Binduri, Shaykh Muhammad Sambo and Shaykh

Jibril ibn Umar, who influenced him the most. A strict adherent of the Prophetic norms and traditions (*sunnah*), Uthman became a close disciple of Shaykh Jibril who taught him Arabic literature, *tafsir* (Qur'anic exegesis), *hadith* (Prophetic traditions), *fiqh* (Islamic jurisprudence), *sirah* (life of the Prophet) and *tasawwuf* (Islamic mysticism). Of medium height, light complexion and slim build, Uthman led a simple and austere lifestyle. He was also a charismatic and gifted intellectual who earned his living working as a rope twister, and in his spare time he read widely and wrote poetry in praise of the Prophet. Thanks to his vast learning and spiritual ability, he soon attracted a sizeable following and established his reputation as an up-and-coming religious scholar and leader of his people.

During this period Uthman began to observe his people's existential condition and what he saw did not please him in the least. He thought the people had not only drifted away from the pure and pristine teachings of Islam, as preserved in the Qur'an and Prophetic *sunnah*, but that they had also fallen under the spell of ignorance and superstition (*jahiliyah*). Rather than compete with one another in the pursuit of things good and wholesome, they engaged in blameworthy and detestable activities. And in the process, some became actively involved in practices which clearly contradicted fundamental Islamic principles, and did so without even realising that that was the case; this state of affairs prevailed in and around Degel while Uthman was a youngster. To add insult to injury, as religious innovation (*bida*) and pseudo-mystical activities proliferated, the local ruling elites were busy accumulating wealth and property at the expense of the poor and needy. The religious scholars, who were supposed to be the custodians of faith, knowledge and wisdom, had also succumbed to worldly pleasures and luxuries. By failing to address the challenges which confronted their society and provide Islamic answers to the problems of their time, they had effectively abdicated their role as the champions of truth, justice and fair play. When the reality of the situation confronting his people became all too clear for Uthman to see, he was shocked and appalled. Indeed, the plight of the ordinary people – who were forced to endure untold personal suffering and hardship – moved him so much that he decided to do something to change the status quo.

While still in his early twenties, Uthman became a prolific writer and speaker. He wrote scores of articles and poems on Islamic topics and delivered public lectures on aspects of Islamic beliefs and social practices. He was keen to correct his people's misconceptions about the fundamental principles and practices of Islam, and also offer guidance to them in their socio-cultural affairs. As a gifted scholar, Uthman was not only aware of the burning issues of his time, he was also eager to tackle those issues head-on. The people of Degel responded very positively to his call for educational and socio-cultural reform. Accordingly, he gathered around him a group of young men who subsequently became his devout followers and together they began the task of reforming their society in the image of Islam. His younger brother, Abdullahi ibn Muhammad, who became a prolific writer and esteemed scholar in his own right, soon joined him in his efforts to change and reform their society. When the reform movement initiated by Uthman became very popular with the locals, the official *ulama* (who were in the pay of the ruling elites) tried to undermine his credentials as a religious scholar and leader. But he never wavered in his efforts to promote goodness and discourage blameworthy activities (*al amr bi'l ma'ruf wa nahy an'il munkar*). This, according to Uthman, was the mission of all the Divinely-inspired Prophets and since the *ulama* were the *warith* (inheritors) of the Prophets, their main task should be to promote goodness and eradicate evil from all sectors of society. However, he felt the *ulama* of his community had abandoned this noble duty by currying favour with the local ruling elites. Although this state of affairs shocked and dismayed him, he was very determined to expand his *da'wah* (Islamic missionary) activities despite the opposition of the local *ulama* and Hausa rulers.

During this period he wrote prolifically, authoring more than fifty books and treatises on a wide range of Islamic topics including beliefs and concepts, moral and ethical teachings, and Islamic spirituality and guidelines for his followers. In addition, he fully explained Islamic rules and regulations pertaining to women, and defined their role in society. His unusually progressive attitude towards women's education, their role and responsibility in society earned him the wrath of the official Hausa *ulama,* who vehemently opposed his liberalist stance on this issue. Undeterred by their opposition and criticism, Uthman encouraged the Hausa women to pursue education and engage in literary activities. The women of his own household led the way in this respect, thus his daughter, Nana Asma'u, became one of the most prominent literary figures of her generation. As an inspirational leader and a practical thinker, Uthman's balanced understanding and interpretation of Islamic principles and practices not only won over the people of Degel, but soon his reputation spread throughout Hausaland. This prompted the King of Gobir to approach him with gifts of money and expensive presents in order to win him over to his side but Uthman told him in no uncertain terms that he was not interested in the wealth or material possessions of this world. His prime objective, he said, was to revive the message of Islam and eradicate political oppression, social inequality and economic injustice from Hausaland.

As the Islamic movement continued to expand rapidly, Uthman's followers began to oppose the oppressive policies of the local rulers. Not surprisingly, the Hausa rulers felt threatened by the growing Islamic movement. This forced them to take action against Uthman's followers, who were now routinely harassed and obstructed by the Government officials. When the situation became unbearable, in 1804 Uthman ordered his close disciples to migrate (*hijrah*) to Gudu, a town located on the northern outskirts of Gobir but, here too, they were harassed by the local Hausa rulers who decided to drive them out of that area. This prompted Uthman's disciples to

pledge allegiance to him as their *imam* (religious leader) and *amir al-mu'minin* ('commander of the believers'), and in so doing they instigated a mass campaign against all forms of injustice and oppression. Determined to wipe out this small Muslim community before they could properly organise themselves, the Hausa rulers decided to attack them first. This left Uthman and his followers with no option but to fight back. As news of the declaration of the *jihad* (struggle for Islam) began to spread, Uthman's supporters and sympathisers throughout Hausaland revolted against their cruel and oppressive rulers. An all-out military conflict soon ensued in which his forces inflicted a crushing defeat on their enemies and in the process they captured Gobir (the most powerful State in Hausaland) in 1808, thus securing a great victory for Islam. During this period of warfare and conflict, he lost some of his most trusted and capable disciples on the battlefield and their tragic loss was deeply felt soon after victory was secured. His followers had gained control of a vast stretch of land which they were suddenly expected to govern, and do so without their most able and experienced leaders. This proved a massive challenge for Uthman because he considered himself to be a religious scholar rather than a politician, yet circumstances forced him to assume both political and religious leadership. After five years of internecine warfare, the entire political, civil and administrative systems of Government in Hausaland lay in ruins, as did the local economy. He might have won the war, but now his greatest challenge was to win the peace. This task, he knew, would not be an easy one but, assisted by his brother Abdullahi and his son Muhammad Bello, he formed a consultative (*shura*) council consisting of some of the leading members of the new Muslim community, and together they tried to reconstruct the political, economic and educational infrastructure throughout Hausaland.

After founding Sokoto, the new capital of Hausaland, Uthman placed his brother Abdullahi and son Muhammad in charge of administering the new Muslim State, and they reported directly to him. He then implemented the *shari'ah* (Islamic law) across the land and gradually the political and economic situation in Hausaland began to improve. During this period he continued to write prolifically, focusing on the problems and challenges which confronted the new Muslim State he had founded, and as a result he developed political guidelines, socio-economic policies and religious instructions for the civil servants, administrators and Ministers who were entrusted with the task of serving the public. Uthman spent the last years of his life in Sifawa, situated on the outskirts of Sokoto, where he eventually died at the age of sixty-three, without nominating a successor. However, his son Muhammad Bello, who was an eminent scholar and accomplished military commander, succeeded his father as *amir* (leader) of the Sokoto Caliphate. Although the Caliphate founded by Uthman endured until the beginning of the twentieth century, the impact of his reformist ideas, thoughts, military campaigns (*jihad*), as well as the legacy of the Sokoto Caliphate, continues to influence the religious practices of the West African Muslims to this day (especially in northern Nigeria).

In total, Uthman wrote more than one hundred books and treatises on all aspects of Islam and in so doing he became a powerful champion of Islamic learning and scholarship across West Africa. His younger brother Abdullahi and son Muhammad followed in his footsteps and authored more than eighty books each. Despite being a *maliki* jurist (*faqih*) and a Sufi of the *qadiriyyah* Order, he found time to read and study the works of other *madhahib* (schools of Islamic law) and also considered the adherents of the *tijaniyah* Sufi Order to be his own followers. In short, Uthman was a great Islamic scholar, thinker and one of the most influential Muslim reformers of the nineteenth century.

# 97

## *Mulla Sadra* (b.1571 - d.1641)

THE ENCOUNTER BETWEEN Islam and ancient Greek, Syriac and Persian thought and culture first took place during the mid-seventh century, after the Muslim conquest of Egypt, Syria and Iraq. As a result, *falsafah* (or Islamic philosophy) emerged as a distinct intellectual tradition in the Muslim world, although it was not until the early part of the ninth century that Muslim philosophers like al-Kindi began to write widely on Islamic philosophy. Their writings subsequently inspired other great philosophers like Abu Bakr al-Razi, al-Farabi and Ibn Sina to produce their own philosophical works. Islamic philosophy thus continued to flourish in the Islamic East, until Islamic iconoclasts like al-Ghazali and Fakhr al-Din al-Razi emerged in the eleventh and twelfth centuries to launch a blistering intellectual attack against the *falasifah* (Muslim philosophers). In this battle of ideas, the traditionalists emerged victorious, which marked the beginning of the end of philosophical thought in much of the Islamic East. However, in parts of Persia and Muslim India, Islamic philosophy continued to thrive thanks largely to the efforts of influential Shi'a philosophers and thinkers like Qutb al-Din al-Shirazi (who lived in the thirteenth century) and Baha al-Din al-

Amili and Mir Damad (both of whom lived in the sixteenth century). But it was in the works of Mulla Sadra that Islamic philosophy found a new, fresh impetus and a degree of intellectual rigor and sophistication.

Sadr al-Din Muhammad ibn Ibrahim al-Qawami al-Shirazi, better known as Mulla Sadra, was born in the Iranian city of Shiraz into a notable Persian family. His father, Ibrahim, worked as a senior civil servant for the local ruler and attained a position of political eminence. As the only boy in the family, Mulla Sadra was brought up in a comfortable environment surrounded by much wealth and luxury. Although he began his early education at home, Mulla Sadra was known to have been very studious and a voracious reader of books. His sharp intellect, coupled with his highly retentive memory, enabled him to learn and retain a large quantity of information with relative ease. Impressed by his intellectual abilities, his family enrolled him at his local school for a thorough education in Persian, Arabic, Islamic sciences, literature and philosophy. It was not long before he successfully completed his elementary education. If Shiraz was a prominent centre of Islamic learning, then Isfahan (which was the capital of Persia and the commercial heart of the country at the time) was an equally famous centre of learning and scholarship. This prompted Mulla Sadra to leave his native Shiraz and move to Isfahan where he pursued advanced training in both the religious and philosophical sciences, under the guidance of eminent scholars and thinkers like Shaykh Baha al-Din al-Amili and Shaykh Mir Muhammad Baqir Damad, better known as Mir Damad.

As a highly respected authority on Islamic sciences, Baha al-Din became the *shaykh al-Islam* (supreme religious authority) of Safavid Persia, in addition to being a noted mathematician, alchemist and Sufi (Islamic mystic). Mir Damad, on the other hand, was one of the most influential philosophers and jurists of his generation, and was thoroughly familiar with the philosophical thoughts of the early Muslim thinkers and also excelled in Shi'a jurisprudence. Mulla Sadra studied Islamic theological, philosophical and mystical thought under the tutelage of these eminent scholars, before joining the class of Shaykh Mir Findiriski, who was a renowned Sufi and one of his contemporaries. The latter taught him both Peripatetic (*mashsha'iyah*) philosophy and traditional theosophy (*hikmah*), in addition to aspects of Sufi thought and practices. After completing his advanced education while he was still in his mid-twenties, Mulla Sadra became very enthusiastic about mysticism, which infuriated the conservative *ulama* (religious scholars) in Isfahan who accused him of espousing un-Islamic ideas and thoughts. When the hostility of the religious scholars became unbearable, he was forced to leave Isfahan and return to Shiraz. But here, too, he became embroiled in religious controversy because he chose to defend certain mystical-cum-gnostic doctrines which the *ulama* considered to be heretical and blameworthy from a traditional Shi'a perspective. Happily, on this occasion, his influential father came to his rescue and protected him from his opponents.

The Shi'a scholars' reaction against his 'unorthodox' interpretation of mysticism eventually convinced him to leave Shiraz and settle in Kahak, a remote village located on the outskirts of Qom, one of Iran's most famous centres of Shi'a religious learning and scholarship. During his long stay in Kahak, he led a simple and ascetic lifestyle, and devoted much of his time to meditation, spiritual retreat and intellectual activities. Being competent in both the religious (*ulum al-din*) and philosophical sciences (*ulum al-aqliyyah*), Mulla Sadra analysed and re-evaluated the religious, philosophical and mystical ideas and thoughts of his predecessors (especially the Illuminationist philosophy of Shihab al-Din Suhrawardi and the beliefs of Mir Damad and the School of Isfahan) in order to shed new light on Islamic philosophical and metaphysical thought. His retreat at Kahak not only enabled him to re-examine the ideas and thoughts of his predecessors, but he also developed his own religious, philosophical and metaphysical ideas during this period. Reminiscent of al-Ghazali's spiritual experience and awakening, he recalled how his mind became infused with the Divine 'intuitive truths' during his retreat. This, he said, revitalised his body and spirit, and sharpened his intellect so much that he no longer felt depressed or despondent about anything, for the Divine light (*nur*) which entered his being henceforth illuminated his path.

After almost a decade in Kahak, Mulla Sadra returned to Shiraz, where he began to lecture on religious sciences and write books and treatises on metaphysics, philosophy, mysticism and Shi'a theology. When his name spread throughout Shiraz on account of his vast learning and scholarship, the ruling Safavid elites offered him lucrative Government jobs but he politely turned them down. The Safavids came to power in Persia at the beginning of the sixteenth century and being *ithna 'ashari* (or Twelver) Shi'as, they made this the official religion of Persia. Under Safavid patronage, Shi'a religious learning and scholarship began to flourish across Persia. Mulla Sadra lived during the heyday of Safavid rule; a time when the ruling elite competed with each other to build schools and colleges throughout Persia, and in so doing they created a culture of education across the land. After his name reached the corridors of power, the Safavid ruler Shah Abbas II reportedly ordered the governor of Fars to build a religious seminary in Shiraz where Mulla Sadra could teach and train a new generation of Shi'a religious scholars and thinkers. Despite his busy teaching schedule, he found time to author many books and treatises including *Kitab al-Mabda wa'l Ma'ad* (The Book of Origin and Return), *al-Shawahid al-Rububiyyah* (The Divine Witnesses), *al-Hikmat al-Arshiyyah* (The Wisdom of the Throne), *al-Masha'ir* (The Apprehensions) and *Kasr Asnam al-Jahiliyyah* (Demolishing the Idol of Ignorance), not to mention scores of commentaries on the works of Ibn Sina and Suhrawardi.

Although Mulla Sadra wrote about fifty books and treatises in total, his most famous and influential work was *al-Hikmat al-Muta'aliyyah fi'l Asfar al-Arba'ah* (The Transcendental Wisdom Regarding the Four Journeys). In this book he provided a comprehensive but, equally, fresh and integrated exposition of Islamic philosophical and metaphysical thought. According to him, philosophy and prophecy are like two sides of the same coin being, as they are, repositories of the same heavenly truth. Just as revelatory and mystical approaches to Reality can provide a sound expression of the Truth, in the same way, he argued, a philosophical approach to Reality can also shed fresh light on the Truth. In Mulla Sadra's opinion, there was no contradiction between revelation (*wahy*), reason (*aql*) and gnosis (*irfan*); on the contrary, he argued that they were all complementary sources of knowledge which help to create a clear, correct and comprehensive understanding of the Truth. To prove this point, he traced the history of religion and philosophy from his own time – through the Muslim philosophers, Shi'a Imams and Sufis – all the way back to the ancient Greek philosophers who, he claimed, had received inspiration from Abraham who, in turn, received the Truth directly from Adam. By developing such an unusual interpretation of philosophical history, he was able to argue that revelation (*wahy*), philosophy (*hikmat*) and gnosis (*irfan*) had originated from one and the same source; thus they had to be complemen-

tary rather than contradictory. This paved the way for him to create a synthesis between Greek philosophy, the gnostic wisdom of the Sufis and the Peripatetic thought of the *falasifah,* with Shi'a theology. It is this synthesis which became known as *hikmat al-muta'aliyyah* (or the 'transcendental wisdom').

As an unusually industrious scholar and thinker, Mulla Sadra painstakingly surveyed the intellectual history of Islam before undertaking a thorough study of the Greek philosophical tradition. Thereafter, he presented his findings in his *Asfar al-Arba'ah*. Heavily influenced by the Peripatetic thought of Ibn Sina; the Illuminationist (*ishraqi*) philosophy of Suhrawardi; the Sufi cosmology of Ibn al-Arabi as well as Shi'a theology, Mulla Sadra accepted Neoplatonic emanationism, but rejected Aristotelian philosophy. He also adopted Ibn al-Arabi's concept of *nur muhammadiyyah* (or the 'Muhammadan Light') but vehemently opposed Ibn Sina's notion of the eternity of the world. Furthermore, he accepted that the Prophet Muhammad was the 'Seal of the Prophets' (*khatm al-anbiya*) but, at the same time, he stated that the true meaning of the revelation would not become clear until after the advent of the *mahdi*, the final Shi'a Imam. In so doing he not only reconciled philosophical and gnostic thought with Shi'a theology, he also developed a fresh and integrated Islamic worldview. In other words, through his metaphysical philosophy (*hikmat al-muta'aliyyah*), Mulla Sadra attempted to harmonise philosophy, gnosticism and theology in order to answer some of the most fundamental questions concerning God, His Nature and Attributes, the meaning of life, the purpose of creation and the nature of resurrection – all surveyed through the lenses of revelation, reason, intuition and experience – thus being, as it were, the final summing up of a whole philosophy. Whether one agrees with all his ideas or not, one cannot fail to admire his sincerity of purpose, vast erudition and considerable analytical skills and ability.

Despite being a full-time teacher and a prolific writer, Mulla Sadra found time to train scores of influential scholars who also became prominent exponents of philosophy, mysticism and theology in Persia. His most famous students included thinkers like Muhammad ibn Murtada (who is better known as Mulla Fayd Kashani) and Abd al-Razzaq al-Lahiji – both of whom were married to his daughters. In addition to this, Mulla Sadra performed the sacred *hajj* (pilgrimage to Makkah) seven times and died in Basrah at the age of seventy while he was on his way home from completing his seventh pilgrimage. Today, he is considered to be one of the great Islamic philosophers of all time on account of his original contributions in the field of Islamic philosophy. However, other than in Iran and parts of Iraq and India, his ideas and thoughts are not widely known in the Muslim world. Moreover, his works were not translated into Western languages until relatively recently; as such, his religious, philosophical and mystical thoughts have not received much exposure in the West either. By contrast, in Iran some of the country's most eminent scholars and thinkers like Mulla Hadi Sabziwari, Mulla Ali Nuri, Mulla Ali Mudarris, Sayyid Abul Hasan Qazwini, Sayyid Muhammad Kazim Assar, Sayyid Muhammad Hussain Tabataba'i and Mehdi Ha'iri Yazdi have acknowledged their profound debt to Mulla Sadra. Thanks to some contemporary scholars like Max Horten, Henry Corbin, Fazlur Rahman and Seyyed Hossein Nasr, his works are now being increasingly disseminated across Europe and America.

# 98
## Malcolm X
## (b.1925 - d.1965)

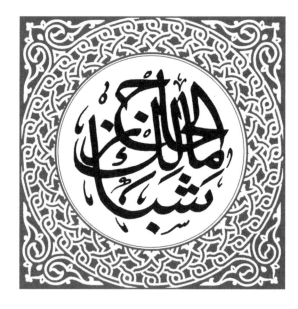

IT IS A well-known fact that the African people did not go to North America of their own volition; they were taken there by force. But what is not so well known is that the enslavement of black Africans (in the British colonies of North America) began as early as the 1640s and this state of affairs persisted until Abraham Lincoln, the sixteenth President of the United States, formally abolished slavery (in the Northern States) by signing the Emancipation Proclamation in 1863. The Southern States, however, resisted such measures until the tide of history overwhelmed them. The ratification of the fourteenth Amendment granted American citizenship to all former slaves and, two years later, the passage of the fifteenth Amendment gave them the right to vote. The offer of constitutional rights to the African-Americans represented a fundamental shift in America's attitude towards its black population, even if this did not make much difference to their social, political and economic conditions at the time. Later, when millions of African-Americans began to move to the North in search of a better life, its white population, fearing increasing competition for jobs and housing, rose up against the black migrant workers. The Depression years of 1930s only helped to exacerbate racial strife and

tension across America, which led to widespread rioting and racial violence between the whites and blacks in both the Northern and Southern States. Inspired by Marcus Garvey, a black nationalist movement then swept America, paving the way for the Civil Rights Movement to emerge during the 1940s. Malcolm X, one of the most charismatic and influential African-American leaders of the twentieth century, rose to prominence during this period and left his indelible marks in the annals of modern history.

Born Malcolm Little in Omaha in the State of Nebraska, Malcolm X was the son of a Baptist Minister. His father, Reverend Earl Little, and his mother, Louise, were active members of Marcus Garvey's Universal Negro Improvement Association (UNIA). Despite being on the receiving end of white racism and violence, his parents worked hard to improve their socio-economic condition until the Ku Klux Klan (a white supremacist group) forced his family to leave Omaha and settle in Lansing, Michigan; Malcolm was only a youngster at the time. Here the family struggled to overcome their socio-economic difficulties; no doubt their situation was exacerbated by Earl Little's drinking habits and waywardness, which often created tensions within his family, but Louise remained loyal to her husband. When Malcolm was six his father died, and this again forced his family to experience more difficulties. The challenge of raising nine children on her own proved too stressful for his mother who subsequently had a mental breakdown and was confined to a psychiatric institution. Like his brothers and sisters, Malcolm was brought up in foster homes before he enrolled at Mason Junior High school in Lansing, where he completed the eighth grade. At school, his white teacher urged him to become a carpenter since becoming a lawyer, in his opinion, was an unrealistic aspiration for a black boy. Malcolm quit formal education in disgust. From Lansing he travelled to Boston where he was surprised to discover how the black working-classes had become content with the very little wealth and money they had accumulated. He felt that the ideals which had inspired generations of black nationalists and freedom fighters had all but been forgotten by the black working-classes who at the time lived in the suburbs of Boston and New York. Happy with their share of material benefits and comforts, he thought these people were no longer willing to fight for the cause of Black Nationalism like the previous generations. This state of affairs troubled young Malcolm, even though he was not in a position to do anything about it at the time.

During this period he visited Boston and New York regularly, as the urban black working-class neighbourhoods (such as Boston's Roxbury and New York's Harlem) became his favourite hideouts. Sucked into the murky world of drugs, prostitution and crime, he soon became a seasoned street hustler and the leader of a gang of thieves, and thereby established his reputation as a fearsome leader of the local criminal fraternity. The one time 'Detroit Red' – a nickname given to him for the reddish colour of his hair – was eventually arrested, he was found guilty of armed robbery. Imprisoned for six years, he soon experienced a life-changing transformation. After years of criminal activity, he now began to think about his life, its meaning and purpose, and also began

to ask questions about the higher things of life. Keen to explore these issues, he read books on history, philosophy, culture and religion. During this time he became a something of a hermit and read voraciously with the result that his eyesight became strained and he began to wear glasses. Reading widely enabled Malcolm to explore and understand the true nature and complexities of human life, culture and civilisation. So it was that, whilst still in prison, his brother introduced him to the teachings of Elijah Muhammad and the Nation of Islam.

Inspired by Fard Muhammad, Elijah (who was the son of a Baptist preacher from Georgia) established the Nation of Islam, a religious-cum-black-nationalist movement, during the 1930s. Over time it became a hugely controversial, but powerful, force within the African-American community. According to Elijah, the white people were devils who were created by black scientists, and Fard Muhammad was the incarnation of God. Though his racialistic interpretation of Islam was dismissed by mainstream Muslims, Malcolm found the tone and confidence of his message irresistible. As a religious and nationalistic movement, the Nation of Islam was a highly-organised and disciplined organisation which championed the rights of poor and disenfranchised black people. Having experienced much racism and hardship at the hands of the white supremacists, in the Nation of Islam he found a socio-religious movement which was not afraid to speak up for the rights of black people. Indeed, the Nation of Islam was not only a champion of Black Nationalism; it also advocated a form of black supremacy over the whites. This proved most attractive to Malcolm who became very fond of Elijah and the Nation of Islam while still in prison.

As expected, on his release from prison in 1952, Malcolm became an active member of the Nation. Furthermore, his determination to recruit more disenfranchised blacks to the Nation met with instant success. As an eloquent orator and great motivator of people, he took the message of the Nation directly to the people and of course his success won him much-needed recognition and acclaim from the Nation's hierarchy, including Elijah himself. His hard work, coupled with his indefatigable energy and commitment to his task, soon saw him rise from being an obscure assistant Minister of the Nation's Detroit Temple Number One, to its national spokesman within a short period. Most interestingly, when Malcolm first joined the Nation in the early 1950s, it had no more than several thousand followers but under his able leadership the Nation of Islam became a powerful mass-movement with more than a hundred thousand loyal followers. He regularly visited the black ghetto areas of Detroit, Boston and New York and urged the poor and disenfranchised black people to join the Nation and fight for their rights and liberty. The locals responded to his call very positively, so that by the 1960s the Nation of Islam had more than forty temples in various cities. Moreover, it owned several local radio stations which, in turn, enabled them to reach yet more people.

Thanks to Malcolm's sharp intellect, electrifying oratory skills and charismatic personality, the Nation of Islam's image of being a fringe fundamentalist group soon changed for good. Also, when his high-profile attacks on the root causes of economic inequality, social deprivation, political powerlessness and cultural ghettoisation of the African-Americans struck a chord with the masses, his popularity hit an all-time high. His 'tell it as you see it' approach soon turned him into a cult figure within the black communities. By the same token, his frank and outspoken attack on the ruling classes began to anger the Establishment. It was not long before the right-wing American press began to brand him 'the angriest black man in America'. According to his critics, Malcolm was a racist who preached a concocted, confused message of racial supremacy, religious hatred and cultural separatism. Undeterred by such criticism, he continued to champion the cause of the poor and dispossessed black people. Unlike Martin Luther King Jr. (whom he considered to be a 'chump, not a champ'), Malcolm became a voice for millions of voiceless African-Americans

who had been enduring economic hardship and social deprivation for many generations in the ghettos of Detroit, Boston, New York, Chicago, Philadelphia, Cleveland and Indianapolis. By contrast, the Civil Rights Movement led by Martin Luther King Jr., hardly made any difference to the lives of the poor and disadvantaged African-Americans of the South, but Malcolm's call for black liberation, economic self-help and political empowerment instantly captured the imagination of his fellow black Americans in the North. Indeed, under his stewardship, the Nation of Islam became a very powerful and influential voice for America's black proletariat.

As Malcolm's popularity continued to rise, Elijah Muhammad became concerned by the increasing politicisation of the Nation of Islam. Since he considered himself to be a religious leader rather than a politician, he was not too keen to get involved in politics and public affairs. And although Malcolm's loyalty to Elijah was absolute, the latter's apolitical stance on many important issues of the day dismayed him. A furious and uncompromising Malcolm was itching to go out and openly advocate the need for black resistance, if that was what was required to achieve real liberation and freedom for the African-American people. However, his fusion of religious fervour with political activism horrified a laidback Elijah, who now began to see him more as a liability than an asset. Soon afterwards, when a newsreporter asked Malcolm for his response to the assassination of John F. Kennedy on November 22, 1963, he replied, '[I] never foresaw that the chickens would come home to roost so soon. Being an old farm boy myself, chickens coming home to roost never did make me sad. They've always made me glad.' This comment was the final straw which broke the camel's back: Elijah considered this to be a provocative and insensitive comment and banned him from speaking in public. During this period Malclom became aware of Elijah's mismanagement of the Nation's finances, as well as his amoral sexual practices (such as his involvement in extra-marital affairs), which of course shocked and horrified him. This prompted

Malcolm to leave the Nation of Islam in 1964. Although this was by no means an easy decision for him, the moral and financial corruption which prevailed under Elijah's leadership left him with no other choice. After leaving the Nation, he and his supporters inaugurated two separate organisations, namely the Muslim Mosque, Inc., and the Organisation of Afro-American Unity (OAAU). The former was essentially a religious institution, while the latter became the political wing of the Muslim Mosque.

Thereafter, Malcolm travelled across Africa and the Middle East, and also performed the sacred *hajj* (pilgrimage to Makkah) where he experienced yet another life-changing transformation. For the first time, he came into contact with mainstream Muslims and his experience of the universal brotherhood of man championed by Islam captured his imagination. In response, he openly renounced Elijah's distorted and racialistic interpretation of Islam and became an orthodox Muslim; from then on he became known by his new Muslim name, al-Hajj Malik al-Shabazz. From Makkah, he wrote scores of letters wherein he explained the reasons why he had had a change of heart and clearly spelled out his new thoughts and ideas on race relations, human rights, cultural co-existence and socio-political issues. On his return to America, he began to champion mainstream Islam and advocated the need for both racial and cultural tolerance and understanding across all sectors of American society. Furthermore, he developed an internationalist approach to human rights and Third World politics, and became an advocate of social equality, economic justice, political independence and freedom for the world's poor and dispossessed people – especially his fellow African-Americans. Unfortunately, he did not live long enough to develop his thoughts on these issues in a rigorous and systematic way, as he fell prey to an assassin's bullet on February 21 1965, three months short of his fortieth birthday (although according to another source, he was assassinated on his fortieth birthday).

As a result, three Nation of Islam loyalists were arrested and found guilty of his murder, although it is not clear whether the Central Intelligence Agency (CIA) or the Federal Bureau of Investigation (FBI) had played a role in his assassination. According to some of his biographers, the CIA and FBI did play a part in his murder, even though this view has not been proved conclusively. Thankfully, just before his death, Malcolm had completed his autobiography with the assistance of Alex Haley. Published immediately after his death, *The Autobiography of Malcolm X*, provided a detailed and vivid account of his life and thoughts in his unique and inimitable style.

In the final analysis, Malcolm X was a truly revolutionary leader who became an undisputed champion of America's poor and disadvantaged black people, and did so by the sheer force of his extraordinary character and personality. Today, he is not only considered to be one of the founding fathers of the anti-racist movement; in my opinion, he was also one of the most influential Muslim leaders of the twentieth century.

# 99

## Sa'id Nursi
## (b.1877 - d.1960)

THE DECLINE OF Ottoman political power and authority in the face of a European assault on its territories in both Europe and the Middle East, coupled with the rise of the Young Turks within the Ottoman State, propelled Mustafa Kemal (who was an ambitious Turkish military commander) to rise to the challenge of defending mainland Turkey from European encroachment. After six hundred years of Ottoman rule, Mustafa Kemal sent the last Ottoman Caliph, Abd al-Majid, into exile in Switzerland and inaugurated the Turkish Republic in 1924. Hailed as the saviour of Turkey, the honorific title of *ataturk* (or 'Father Turk') was later conferred on Mustafa Kemal for his personal heroism and military accomplishments. As the founder and undisputed leader of modern Turkey, he went out of his way to reform the political, educational and cultural institutions and practices of the Turkish people. Inspired by European Enlightenment thoughts and values, he attempted to change and reform Turkish culture and society in the light of modern European secular values and ethos. By distancing Turkey from its historical, cultural and linguistic links to the Islamic East, he hoped to make Turkey an integral part of modern Europe. Turkey, he

argued, belonged to Europe and thus he tried to thoroughly modernise and secularise Turkey, although the majority of his people did not share his vision of the future. When the true colour of his socio-cultural reforms became clear for all to see, an influential Turkish Muslim thinker and reformer emerged to challenge Mustafa Kemal's secular crusade. This great Islamic scholar and reformer was none other than Sa'id Nursi.

Bediuzzaman Sa'id Nursi was born in the village of Nurs, in the eastern Turkish province of Bitlis. Of Kurdish origin, his parents were devout Muslims who led a simple and pious lifestyle. Sa'id began his education at home and learned the basics of Islam from his devout mother who inspired him to take a keen interest in religious matters. He became attracted to Sufism (Islamic mysticism) during his early years and the life and teachings of the famous Abd al-Qadir al-Jilani, the influential founder of the *qadiriyyah* Sufi Order, fascinated him the most. Indeed, his spiritual link and attachment to Shaykh al-Jilani grew stronger by the day, as he claimed to have been guided by this venerable Sufi Shaykh during some of the most testing and turbulent periods of his life. Encouraged by his elder brother, Abdullah, he enrolled at his village school when he was around nine. Blessed with a precocious memory and a sharp intellect, he committed the entire Qur'an to memory with ease. His intellectual superiority over his fellow students, he later recalled, filled him with much pride and confidence. He relished religious debate and discussion, and his arrogant display of intellectual superiority often landed him in trouble.

However, after obtaining a diploma in Islamic sciences at the age of fourteen, he considered abandoning formal education for good. Thereafter, however, he claimed to have been visited by the Prophet Muhammad in the form of a dream and this prompted him to resume his studies. He mastered traditional Islamic sciences under the guidance of prominent teachers like Shaykh Mehmed Celali and Shaykh Mehmed Emin Efendi. After qualifying as an Islamic scholar, he moved to nearby Siirt where Shaykh Fetullah Efendi, a notable local scholar, bestowed the title of *bediuzzaman* (the 'Wonder of the Age') on him, on account of his vast learning and erudition. When his popularity spread across Siirt, the local clergy reportedly became very jealous of him. Forced to leave Siirt, he then travelled to Bitlis, Sirvan, Tillo and Mardin where he encountered similar opposition from local scholars on account of his great learning and unrivalled debating skills. During his travels, he enhanced his reputation as a gifted scholar, skilled debater and accomplished athlete and warrior. Thanks to his unusual physical strength and endurance, he was able to run rings around his enemies, and flee from danger on more than one occasion. At the time when Sa'id was busy pursuing his studies, the Ottoman State was passing through a period of considerable political uncertainty and cultural confusion. Once a great Islamic superpower, the Ottoman State now faced imminent political and economic collapse in the face of Russian – and subsequently Anglo-French – assault on its territories. Although Sultan Abd al-Hamid II tried to stop the rot, his efforts proved futile as mass discontent continued to spread across the country. This gave rise to the 'Young Turk' movement which, in turn, led to the removal of

the Sultan from the Ottoman throne. The revolution of 1908 may have brought much-needed relief to the masses, but the Young Turks also failed to consolidate their grip on power.

Amidst the prevailing chaos, Mustafa Kemal emerged to save his country from European encroachment. The victory of 1922 confirmed his position as the founder and undisputed ruler of the new Turkish republic. During this period of considerable political uncertainty, social upheaval and economic hardship, Sa'id openly supported the reformists because he wanted his people's socio-economic condition to change for the better. Even so, he opposed the Young Turks' efforts to reconcile Islamic political theory with European constitutionalism; furthermore, he considered their attempts to compartmentalise education into three separate categories, namely religious (Islamic), mystical (Sufi) and secular (modern), to be both flawed and inconsistent from an Islamic perspective. Since his approach to Islam was a universal and holistic one, he felt the division of knowledge into such watertight compartments was un-Islamic, unwarranted and counter-productive.

Indeed, after mastering the traditional Islamic sciences, he had pursued advanced training in philosophy, mysticism, history, aspects of mathematics and the physical sciences. His exposure to modern sciences opened his mind to the dangers that were inherent in modern Western secular ideas and thought. This prompted him not only to oppose the compartmentalisation of the Turkish educational system, but also to urge the country's political and religious leaders to reform Turkey's traditional religious educational curriculum so a new generation of Islamic scholars could be trained-up to counter the challenges posed by modern Western atheistic philosophies and ideologies. During this period he became actively involved in the socio-political affairs of the State, and even participated in the war against the Russians on the Caucasian front. Captured by the Russians, he spent two years as a prisoner of war in Russia. He managed to escape in 1918 and returned to Istanbul, via

Vienna. Here he paid homage to Abu Ayyub al-Ansari, the famous companion of the Prophet, who lies buried on the outskirts of the city. His spiritual retreat near the tomb of Abu Ayyub profoundly changed his outlook on life. He then carried out a detailed study of the Qur'an, the *Futuh al-Ghaib* (Disclosure of the Unseen) of Abd al-Qadir al-Jilani and the *Maktubat* (Epistles) of Imam Rabbani Shaykh Ahmad Sirhindi. As a result, he claimed to have attained the height of Islamic spirituality, as 'Old Sa'id' became transformed into 'New Sa'id'. Hereafter, the Qur'an became his main source of guidance and spiritual illumination. Given his track record as a soldier who had fought valiantly against the Russians in defence of the Turkish motherland, together with his mastery of Islam and aspects of modern sciences, it was clear that he could not be dismissed as a religious zealot. Rather he became a widely admired religious scholar and in 1923 Mustafa Kemal personally invited him to Ankara, the capital of the new Turkish republic, in order to officially recognise his contribution to the Turkish War of Independence.

But, on his arrival in Ankara, Sa'id was shocked and dismayed by the culture of decadence which had gripped the capital during Ataturk's tenure. Devoid of tact, humility and gratitude, Mustafa Kemal and his subordinates actively promoted a programme of Westernisation, which he felt was utterly inconsistent with the history, culture and ethos of the Turkish people and their faith. From Ankara, he retreated to Van where he engaged in meditation and spiritual exercises. His short visit to Ankara had confirmed his worst fears; the new Turkish rulers were no better than their predecessors. In fact, he considered Mustafa Kemal's eagerness to de-Islamicise Turkish society by introducing Western-style reforms both alarming and dangerous. By abolishing the Caliphate; banning the traditional Turkish attire; replacing the *hijri* calendar with the Georgian one, and by overhauling the Turkish traditional educational system in favour of a secular Western model, Mustafa Kemal hoped to thoroughly undermine all major symbols of Turkey's Islamic past, but

the *ulama* (Islamic scholars) and the Sufis led a rebellion against his reforms. He responded by brutally suppressing his opponents. Sa'id became embroiled in this conflict even though he did not play a direct role in the insurrection. However, as the Turkish authorities became suspicious of all the prominent religious scholars and Sufis, he was forced to flee to Western Anatolia. Here he spent the next twenty-five years living in exile, travelling from Burdur to Isparta, and from there to Barla, Kastamonu and Afyon. During this period he found time to teach and train hundreds of students who later became prominent members of the *nurculuk* (or the 'Nur Movement') founded by Sa'id in order to preserve Turkey's glorious Islamic history, culture and heritage.

Even in exile, the Turkish authorities did not leave him alone; they continuously harassed, intimidated and persecuted him and his close associates. Later, arrested and charged with 'crimes' (such as writing seditious books, and aiding and abetting political opposition against the ruling junta, among other things), he was brought before the courts on more than one occasion, but he cogently refuted all the charges levelled against him. During this period he authored his *Risale-i Nur* (The Epistle of Light), a monumental commentary on the Qur'an of more than six thousand pages. Although this work has no resemblance to a traditional *tafsir*, it is nevertheless considered to be one of the most influential Qur'anic commentaries of the twentieth century, along with Sayyid Qutb's *Fi Zilal al-Qur'an* (In the Shade of the Qur'an) and Abul A'la Mawdudi's *Tafhim al-Qur'an* (Towards Understanding the Qur'an). In his book, he provided a systematic exposition of fundamental Islamic beliefs and concepts, and did so in a logical, rational and scientific way. He felt such an approach to the Divine revelation was much-needed in Turkey at the time, as Western secular ideas began to gain the upper hand in that country. Since Sa'id considered Western philosophy to be purely rationalistic, and modern science to be entirely atheistic, he deliberately pursued a logical, rational and scientific approach to the Qur'an in order to protect the Turkish people from the menace of Western atheistic thoughts and ideologies. If Mustafa Kemal and his successors were eager to champion secular ideas and thoughts under the guise of modernism and progress, then Sa'id was determined to prove that the Qur'an was far from being out-moded and retrogressive.

On the contrary, the treasures of Islamic thought, culture and spirituality were, in his opinion, far superior to Western thought and culture because the Islamic worldview, unlike the Western worldview, was based on an holistic understanding of the whole of creation – one where man and nature are considered to be co-workers (thus seeking to exemplify the highest expression of heavenly wisdom, beauty and power) rather than as competing adversaries. As expected, his intellectual assault on the Kemalist secular idol

made him an open target for the ruling junta who felt he was seeking to undo their entire programme of Westernisation and secularisation in Turkey. However, their harsh treatment of Sa'id only helped to strengthen his cause and his popularity began to spread throughout Turkey. By the time of his death at the age of eighty-three, he had tens of thousands of followers across the country. Likewise, his *nurculuk* movement became a powerful force in Turkish society. Not surprisingly, his religious ideas and thoughts, as preserved in his monumental *Risale-i Nur*, have become hugely popular in Turkey today. Also, eminent Islamic scholars and thinkers like Fethullah Gulen, Muhammad Sa'id Ramadan al-Buti, Necmettin Erbakan and Harun Yahya have been deeply influenced by his religious thinking and Qur'anic scholarship.

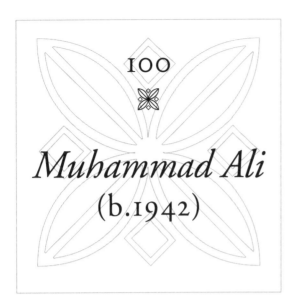

# 100

# *Muhammad Ali*
# (b.1942)

IF THE ISLAMIC contribution to philosophy, mathematics, science, arts and achitecture is not widely known in the Muslim world and the West, then the Muslim contribution to international sports has received even less recognition. This is most unfortunate given the fact that some of history's most famous and influential sportsmen have been Muslims. Thus, internationally acclaimed sportsmen like the French footballing legend Zinedine Zidane; the American basketball superstar Karim Abd al-Jabbar; the Pakistani cricketing star Imran Khan and the celebrated North African athlete and long-distance runner Nuredine Mousalli were all Muslims. Their contribution to the world of competitive sports was both unique and unprecedented. On an equal footing with these remarkable sporting stars, Muhammad Ali, the legendary American boxer and philanthropist became, during his career, the undisputed king of the ring. Widely considered to be the most famous sportsman of all time, and one of the most influential boxers in history, he is arguably one of the two most famous people alive, along with Nelson Mandela the former South African President and legendary freedom-fighter.

Muhammad Ali was born Cassius Marcellus Clay Jr., in Louisville, Kentucky into a working-class African-American family. His father, Cassius, Sr., and mother, Odessa, were a hardworking couple who, like any other parents, tried to provide the best for their children. Young Ali inherited both the sweet, bubbly and steadfast qualities of his mother and the fast-talking, creative qualities and attributes of his artistic father. Ali and his brother Rudy grew up in the happy but conservative environment of Western Louisville, which at the time was a predominantly black area. Since the white areas of the city were strictly 'no-go' areas for its black population, the Clay family's movements were restricted to the city's black areas. Like many other parts of America, the racial segregation of Louisville was symptomatic of the wider racial and cultural segregation which plagued American culture and society at the time. As a youngster, Ali was known to have been both shy and reserved but thanks to Rudy, his younger brother, and Joe Elsby Martin, a local police officer, he soon became interested in sports. According to Ali, when he was about twelve, his father bought him a new bike for Christmas, but it was stolen from him by thieves. This prompted a disconsolate Ali to go to Joe Martin to make a complaint. Joe compiled a police report and asked Ali to join him at his Columbia Boxing Gym.

A tall, slim and shy Ali went to the gym and put on his boxing gloves for the first time. His agility, athleticism and frightening speed impressed Joe Martin, who asked him to attend his gym on a regular basis. Keen to improve his boxing skills, he began to take additional lessons with his brother Rudy, who trained him by hurling stones at him, to improve his reflexes, and which he learnt to evade with ease. If Joe Martin introduced Ali to boxing, then Fred Stoner became his first serious boxing instructor. As a respected black boxer himself, Stoner taught Ali the art of boxing in a rigorous and systematic way. Indeed, he considered Ali to be highly-gifted and encouraged him to develop his stamina, technique and speed, something all aspiring professional boxers had to master at the outset. Young Ali's ability to move with ease, dance around the ring and deliver crushing blows to his opponents with frightening speed soon convinced Stoner that he was a great boxing talent who could reach the heights of sporting stardom. Ali confirmed Stoner's prediction when he was barely sixteen by winning the Louisville Golden Gloves lightweight tournament. Whilst still at high school, he progressed to the quarter-finals of the regional boxing championship in Chicago. Then, after graduating from Louisville's Central High school at the age of eighteen, he won the National Golden Gloves tournament and also the Amateur Athletic Union competition. His achievements at both local and national level included a further six title fights, which established his reputation as an emerging star.

Thanks to his success, Ali was chosen to represent his country at the Olympics in Rome in 1960, where he won a Gold Medal and of course this made him instantly famous. Aware of his achievements, good looks and electrifying personality, he was also in the habit of bragging about his boxing ability and greatness even when he was a youngster. And no one (includ-

ing his parents, trainers and fans) ever doubted his physical ability, boxing talent and way with words. Those who knew the eighteen year old Ali described him as inspiring, energetic and sophisticated. After returning home from Rome with an Olympic Gold Medal, a group of white millionaire businessmen came together and formed the Louisville Sponsoring Group, a business consortium which sponsored and promoted his fights. He signed a lucrative contract with this consortium and began his professional boxing career at the age of eighteen. Sponsored by the company, he fought his first professional bout in 1960 and scored a sixth round victory. His emergence as a professional boxer created considerable interest in the sport; also, his flamboyant style, self-confidence, ingenuity and arrogance turned him into an overnight celebrity. Keen to show the world that he was not a one-time wonder, he then approached Angelo Dundee, a renowned boxing trainer, to join his team and supervise his training needs and requirements. The two men soon became good friends and Ali flourished under Dundee's tutelage.

During this period he trained hard, mastered his footwork and became a polished boxer. His physical power, coupled with his lightning speed, agile movement and quick-thinking made him a formidable boxer who, in 1962, thoroughly mesmerised and out-fought Archie Moore. The press and the American public were bowled over by the quick-witted, boastful and ferocious Ali, who was increasingly considered to be one of the most entertaining boxing sensations of his generation. In reality, however, Ali had barely started his professional boxing career. Nevertheless, his convincing victory over Moore paved the way for him to challenge Sonny Liston, the then-reigning heavyweight champion of the world. Ali, the challenger, entered the ring with Liston in 1964. Chanting 'Float like a butterfly, sting like a bee', he demolished the feared and revered Liston. By combining his unconventional boxing skills with his colossal punching power, Ali stunned the American public by becoming the heavyweight champion of the world. Prior to the bout Liston predicted, 'I might hurt that boy bad', and every American believed him (including the press, the public and the pundits), but a confident and arrogant Ali, then only twenty-two, proved them all wrong. After soundly beating the world heavyweight boxing champion, he emerged to proclaim, 'I am the greatest!'

The year 1964 represented an important period in American history. It marked the beginning of a decade of student protests under the banner of the Free Speech Movement. In the same year, the American army was given the green-light to attack Vietnam, while the white supremacists affiliated to the Ku Klux Klan began to terrorise prominent Civil Rights activists in Mississippi (which led to the ratification of the Civil Rights Act) and, of course, the Beatles took America by storm. But it was Ali's historic victory over Liston in 1964 which represented a milestone in the history of global sporting achievements. Even before the dust of his victory over Liston could settle, he announced his conversion to the Nation of Islam. This represented another bombshell so far as the mainstream American press and public were concerned. No one expected Ali to outsmart Liston, but he proved his critics wrong and then, to add insult to injury, he announced his conversion to an organisation which was widely considered to be a racist, black-separatist movement. As expected, soon after his conversion to the Nation of Islam, Ali's career and public image took a battering from the American press. He felt mainstream America had failed to understand him, not least because his conversion to Elijah Muhammad's Nation of Islam was far from being a moment of madness. Taught and mentored by none other than Malcolm X (al-Hajj Malik al-Shabazz), he closely studied the Nation's religious thoughts and methodology for more than a year before formally becoming a member.

In fact, his change of religion was a real change of heart and conviction, rather than a publicity stunt. Encouraged by Malcolm X and Elijah Muhammad, he then changed his name to Muhammad Ali, for he no longer wished to be known by his 'slave name'. Like him, tens of thousands of other African-Americans found true freedom, liberation and self-respect in the fold of the Nation of Islam. During this period Ali married for the first time and continued to box, allowing his fists to do all the talking inside the ring. He not only retained his heavyweight championship title by defeating Liston for the second time in 1965, but also successfully defended the title another six times in 1966, with five knockouts. A year later, another public outcry broke out when Ali refused to sign up for military duties in Vietnam. As a conscientious objector, he responded to his critics in rhyme, 'Keep asking me, no matter how long. On the war in Vietnam, I sing this song. I ain't got no quarrel with the Viet Cong.' Found guilty of draft evasion by an all-white jury, he was fined ten thousand dollars and sentenced to five years in prison. Although freed on appeal, his boxing licence was suspended, and he was also stripped of his World Boxing Association (WBA) title. At a time when his promising boxing career appeared to be in ruins, an indomitable Ali remained as firm as ever. During this period he married for the second time, and three years later the Supreme Court quashed his conviction for draft evasion. He responded by returning to the boxing ring with a bang, winning two successive bouts before losing against Joe Frazier. But he regained his title in 1974 and successfully defended it against Frazier a year later in the 'Thrilla in Manilla'. Ali's autobiography entitled '*The Greatest - My Own Story*', which he co-authored with Richard Durham, appeared in 1975.

Two years later, Ali married for the third time and in the following year fought one of his most memorable bouts against George Foreman in the famous 'Rumble in the Jungle' in Zaire, which earned him five million dollars. He then lost against Leon Spinks, but regained his title for the third time and in so doing he became the only man to have won the world heavyweight championship three times. After two more fights – one against Larry Holmes in 1980 and the other against Trevor Burbick in 1981 – Ali finally retired from boxing in 1981 at the age of forty-one, having fought a total of sixty-one bouts. A few years later, he told the New York Times Magazine that he was suffering from Parkinson's syndrome, probably as a result of repeated blows to the head. As a result, he developed speech problems even though his mental faculties were not affected. Ali made more than fifty million dollars from boxing, and gave away a substantial amount to fund charitable activities. In other words, after his retirement from boxing, he became one of America's most prolific philantrophists and charity workers.

Moreover, as a sporting legend and a distinguished statesman, he went to Lebanon in 1985 and Iraq in 1990 to secure the release of hostages from those countries. In 1991, Thomas Hauser published his popular biography of Ali under the title of '*Muhammad Ali: His Life and Times*' and eight years later Robert Cassidy's definitive study

'*Muhammad Ali: The Greatest of All Time*' was published. However, one of the most memorable sporting images of recent times was that of an ailing Ali carrying the Olympic torch in Atlanta in 1996. The public story of this great sportsman culminated in the release of Micheal Mann's Hollywood film-blockbuster '*Ali*' in 2001, starring Hollywood superstar, Will Smith. Furthermore, Ali was honoured by the Kings of Saudi Arabia and Morocco for his services to Islam. Recently, the Muhammad Ali Centre for the Advancement of Humanity, which consists of a museum and resource centre, was unveiled in Ali's hometown of Louisville, Kentucky in recognition of his outstanding sporting achievements and charitable activities. The Ali Centre intends to 'preserve and share the legacy and ideals of Muhammad Ali' for the benefit of posterity. Ali lives in Michigan with Lonnie Williams, his fourth wife.

# Conclusion

LIKE MANY OTHER great world religions, Islam created a dazzling global culture and civilisation which endured for more than a thousand years, yet today the majority of the world's Muslims do not know much about Islam's theological, philosophical, scientific, mathematical, cultural and architectural contribution to world civilisation. Despite being a religion of learning and scholarship, it is true that today a significant proportion of the world's Muslims cannot even read or write, let alone pursue advanced study and research. If the Prophet Muhammad came to visit us, I wonder what he would say. It would not be an exaggeration to say that he would probably not recognise most of his followers. Why? Because more than half of the world's Muslims are illiterate and ignorant. Yet, more than fourteen hundred years ago, the Prophet had unequivocally told all his followers that seeking knowledge was not an option; it was an obligatory duty upon all Muslims, men and women alike. If Islam is a religion, culture and civilisation of the book (*kitab*) and pen (*qalam*), then the lives and careers of the early Muslims, as opposed to today's Muslims, is the living proof of this fact.

Although brought up and educated in England, I began to study the history of many civili-

sations from an early age. Over time, the library became my second home. There I read widely on Islam, history, philosophy, comparative religion, English literature and the modern social sciences. At the time, most of the books I read on Islamic thought, history and culture were those written by modern Muslim scholars like Shibli Numani, Sayyid Amir Ali, Sir Muhammad Iqbal, Bediuzzaman Sa'id Nursi, Abdullah Yusuf Ali, Sayyid Qutb, Muhammad Marmaduke Pickthall, Ali Shari'ati, Abul A'la Mawdudi, Muhammad Asad, Fazlur Rahman, Muhammad Hamidullah, Ismail al-Faruqi, Abul Hasan Ali Nadwi, Martin Lings, Masudul Hasan, Muhammad Hussain Haykal and Seyyed Hossein Nasr among others. Thereafter, I read the works of some renowned non-Muslim scholars and historians such as Louis Massignon, Henry Corbin, Hamiliton A.R. Gibb, Alfred Guillaume, Reynold A. Nicholson, A.J. Arberry, John B.Glubb, Maxime Rodinson, Philip K. Hitti, Albert H. Hourani, William M. Watt, Bernard Lewis and Kenneth Cragg. But it was Ibn Khaldun's pioneering *Muqaddimah fi'l Tarikh* (Introduction to History) which really captured my imagination. A work of great scholarship, it was most inspiring to learn that a Muslim had written this book as long ago as the fourteenth century. Was Ibn Khaldun a one-off, or were there many others like him? If so, who were they? Where were they born? What were their ideas, thoughts and achievements? And why are they not so widely-known today?

In vain I searched for a good quality book on the lives, thoughts and achievements of the Muslim world's most influential people. So I began to explore Islamic thought, history, culture and civilisation myself. And in the process, I discovered so many remarkable and outstanding Muslims that I decided to write this book. Here my main aim was to briefly introduce the lives, thoughts and achievements of one hundred of the most influential Muslims of all time. In other words, I have tried to explore Islamic thought, history, culture and civilisation through the lives of one hundred most influential Muslim rulers and conquerors, religious scholars and philosophers, writers and literary figures, scientists and explorers, military generals and freedom fighters, reformers and educationalists. And in so doing I hoped to develop a new and exciting approach to the study of more

than fourteen centuries of Islamic history and culture. Whether I have succeeded in my task, is for you, dear reader, to decide. But please remember: these are only my chosen one hundred. Some of you will agree with my selection; others no doubt will disagree, but either way I hope you enjoyed reading this book. During my study and research I gathered a considerable amount of information and data which could not be incorporated into this book, so it is my intention to publish a sequel to this volume, wherein some of the people not included here will feature.

As I say farewell to you, dear reader, I humbly ask you to pray for my well-being, as I will pray for your good health and well-being, too. And to Him is our final return. 'There is no moving creature on earth but its sustenance depends on God: He knows the time and place of its definite abode and its temporary deposit: all is in a clear record. He it is Who created the heavens and the earth in six days – and His Throne was over the water – that He might try you, which of you is best in conduct.' (Holy Qur'an, *Surat Hud*: 6-7).

# Chronology of Islamic History*

| DATES | EVENTS |
|---|---|
| **555 CE** (Common Era) | **Birth of Khadijah bint Khuwailid.** |
| **570** | **Birth of Muhammad.** Persians expel Byzantines from Yemen. Muhammad's father Abdullah dies. |
| **573** | **Birth of Abu Bakr al-Siddiq.** |
| 575 | Muhammad's mother Amina dies. Abd al-Muttalib dies. |
| **576** | **Birth of Uthman ibn Affan.** |
| **579** | **Birth of Bilal ibn Rabah.** |
| 580 | The Quraysh begin a five year war with the rival tribe of Hawazin. |
| **581ca.** | **Birth of Umar ibn al-Khattab.** |
| **584** | **Birth of Khalid ibn al-Walid.** |
| 589 | Chosroes II ascends the Persian throne. |
| 595 | Muhammad marries Khadijah. |
| **601ca.** | **Birth of Abu Hurairah.** **Birth of Ali ibn Abi Talib.** |
| **605ca.** | **Birth of Muawiyah ibn Abi Sufyan.** |
| **607** | **Birth of Fatimah bint Muhammad.** |
| 608 | Rebuilding of the Ka'bah. |
| **610ca.** | **Birth of Aishah bint Abu Bakr.** Muhammad becomes Prophet. Heraclius becomes Emperor of Byzantium. |
| 612 | Muhammad begins preaching in Makkah. |
| 614 | Damascus falls to the Persians. |
| 615 | Persians capture Jerusalem. |

---

\* This is not an exhaustive chronology of Islamic history nor is it meant to be one. Rather, the purpose of this simple and hopefully useful chronology is to enable the readers to place all the influential people covered in this book within the matrix of more than fourteen centuries of Islamic history. The names and dates of birth and death of the one hundred people covered in this book have been highlighted to facilitate quick referencing. All the entries have been kept short and simple, and all complicated historical information has been omitted where it was possible to do so. Along with the Gregorian dates, the Hijri (or Islamic) dates have also been provided to assist lay readers and scholars alike.

| | |
|---|---|
| 617 | Muslims migrate to Abyssinia. |
| 619 | Death of Abu Talib.<br>**Death of Khadijah bint Khuwailid.**<br>Muhammad marries Sawdah. |
| 620 | Prophet's heavenly journey takes place. |
| **622/1 AH**<br>**(After Hijrah)** | **Prophet's migration to Madinah**<br>**(hijrah).**<br>The first mosque is built in Quba.<br>Heraclius defeats Chosroes II. |
| 623/2 | The 'Constitution of Madinah' is formulated. |
| 624/3 | The change of Qibla takes place.<br>Muslims gain victory at the Battle of Badr.<br>Muhammad marries Hafsah, daughter of Umar ibn al-Khattab. |
| **625/4** | **Birth of Hussain ibn Ali.**<br>The Battle of Uhud takes place. |
| 627/6 | The Battle of the Trench is won by Muslims.<br>Persians are beaten at the Battle of Nineveh. |
| 628/7 | The first Hajj delegation leaves for Makkah.<br>Quraysh sign the Treaty of Hudaibiyyah.<br>Death of Chosroes II of Persia. |
| 629/8 | Muslims go to Makkah for pilgrimage.<br>Bilal becomes the first *Mu'adhdhin*.<br>Zayd ibn Haritha killed at the Battle of Muta. |
| 630/9 | 360 idols stored in the Ka'bah are destroyed.<br>The Battle of Hunayn takes place. |
| 631/10 | The 'Year of Delegations'. |
| **632/11** | **The Prophet dies; Abu Bakr succeeds**<br>**him.**<br>**Death of Fatimah bint Muhammad.** |
| 633/12 | Harb al-Ridda or 'War against the Apostates' launched by Caliph Abu Bakr. |

| | |
|---|---|
| **634/13** | **Death of Abu Bakr; Umar succeeds**<br>**him.** |
| 637/16 | The Islamic Calendar is formalised by Umar. |
| 638/17 | Muslims occupy historic city of Jerusalem. |
| **640/19** | **Birth of Musa ibn Nusayr.** |
| **641/20** | **Death of Bilal ibn Rabah.** |
| **642/22** | **Birth of Hasan al-Basri.**<br>The Battle of Nehawand.<br>**Death of Khalid ibn al-Walid.** |
| **644/24** | **Death of Caliph Umar; Uthman**<br>**succeeds him.** |
| **646/26** | **Birth of Abd al-Malik ibn Marwan.** |
| 648/28 | Muslims launch assault against Cyprus. |
| **650ca./30** | **Birth of Tariq ibn Ziyad.**<br>The Qur'an is standardised.<br>Yazdegird III is murdered. |
| 651/31 | The Prophet's ring is lost. |
| 653/33 | Muslim control of Armenia is consolidated. |
| **656/36** | **Death of Uthman; Ali becomes**<br>**Caliph.**<br>The Battle of Jamal.<br>Struggle over succession leads to political split. |
| 657/37 | The Battle of Siffin. |
| **661/41** | **Ali is murdered; Hasan becomes**<br>**Caliph.**<br>Muawiyah establishes Umayyad rule. |
| 663/43 | Muslims launch raids against Sicily. |
| 670/50 | Uqba ibn Nafi occupies Northwest Africa. |
| **677/58** | **Death of Aishah bint Abu Bakr.** |
| **679/59** | **Death of Abu Hurairah.** |

| | | | |
|---|---|---|---|
| 680/61 | **Birth of Umar ibn Abd al-Aziz.** **Death of Muawiyah; Yazid succeeds him.** The Battle of Karbala and the beginning of the second *fitna*. Umayyads gain control of Makkah/Madinah. **Civil War; Hussain is martyred at Karbala during this period.** | 719/101 | **Death of Umar ibn Abd al-Aziz.** |
| 683/64 | Death of Yazid I; Muawiyyah II succeeds him. Ibn al-Zubayr proclaims himself Caliph. | 720/102 | Muslims occupy Sardinia. Yazid ibn Muhallah declares *jihad* against the Umayyads and dies fighting them. |
| 685/66 | Abd al-Malik promotes the use of Arabic. | 724/106 | Yazid II is succeeded by his brother Hisham. |
| 691/72 | The Dome of the Rock is completed. | 728/110 | **Death of Tariq ibn Ziyad.** **Death of Hasan al-Basri, the great theologian and Sufi sage of the Umayyad period.** |
| 692/73 | Hajjaj ibn Yusuf recaptures Makkah. | 729/111 | **Birth of Abd al-Rahman I.** |
| 693/74 | Abd al-Malik issues the first Islamic currency. | 731/113 | Death of Muhammad al-Baqir; his son Ja'far al-Sadiq becomes sixth Shi'a Imam |
| **694/75** | **Birth of Muhammad ibn al-Qasim.** | 732/114 | The Battle of Tours. |
| 697/78 | High taxation causes unrest in Egypt. | **738/121** | **Birth of Jabir ibn Hayyan.** |
| **700/80-81** | **Birth of Abu Hanifah.** **Birth of Ja'far al-Sadiq.** | 740/123 | Zayd ibn Ali is killed by Umayyads. |
| **704/85** | **Birth of Ibn Ishaq.** | 743/126 | Death of Caliph Hisham. |
| **705/86** | **Death of Abd al-Malik; Walid succeeds him.** | 744/127 | Death of al-Walid II; succeeded by Yazid III. |
| **711/93** | **Birth of Malik ibn Anas.** Muslims march into Europe. | 744-750/127-133 | The third Civil War leads to the defeat of the Umayyads at the hands of the Abbasids. Constantine V captures Syria. Abbasid leader Ibrahim al-Abbas is captured. Abul Abbas al-Saffah is declared Caliph. Marwan II killed by Abbasid agents. |
| 712/94 | Musa ibn Nusayr crosses into al-Andalus. | 751/134 | Chinese craftsmen captured; use of papyrus introduced. |
| 714/96 | Death of Hajjaj and Ali Zain al-Abideen. | 754/137 | Death of Abul Abbas al-Saffah; Abu Ja'far al-Mansur becomes Caliph. |
| **715/97** | Al-Walid is succeeded by Sulaiman as Caliph. **Death of Muhammad ibn al-Qasim.** | 756/139 | Islamic Kingdom established in Spain by Umayyad prince Abd al-Rahman I. Caliph al-Mansur orders the execution of Ibn al-Muqaffa, the famous poet. |
| **716/98** | **Death of Musa ibn Nusayr.** | | |
| **717ca./99** | **Birth of Rabi'a al-Adawiyyah.** Umar II succeeds Sulaiman as Caliph. | | |

| | |
|---|---|
| 758/141 | Al-Mansur builds the city of Baghdad. |
| 762/145 | Baghdad becomes Abbasid capital. 'Muhammad the Pure Soul' leads rebellion. |
| **765/148** | **Death of Ja'far al-Sadiq.** |
| **766/149** | **Birth of Harun al-Rashid.** |
| **767/150** | **Birth of al-Shafi'i. Death of Abu Hanifah, founder of Hanafi school of legal thought Death of Ibn Ishaq.** |
| **780/163** | **Birth of Ahmad ibn Hanbal. Birth of al-Khawrizmi.** |
| 785/169 | Death of Caliph al-Mahdi; al-Hadi succeeds him as Caliph. |
| **786/170** | **Birth of Abdullah al-Ma'mun.** Death of Abbasid Caliph al-Hadi. |
| **786-809/170-194** | Harun al-Rashid becomes Caliph and initiates Golden Age of Abbasid Caliphate. **Death of Abd al-Rahman I.** Death of al-Khalil ibn Ahmad, a prominent scholar of Basrah. **Death of Malik ibn Anas. Birth of al-Kindi. Death of Rabi'a al-Adawiyyah. Death of Caliph Harun al-Rashid. Birth of al-Bukhari.** |
| **813/198** | Abbasid Caliph al-Amin is murdered; al-Ma'mun is appointed new Caliph. Use of Arabic numerals becomes widespread. **Death of Jabir ibn Hayyan.** |
| **817/202** | **Birth of Muslim ibn al-Hajjaj** Ali al-Rida becomes eighth Shi'a Imam. |
| 818/203 | Death of Ali al-Rida; al-Taqi al Jawad becomes ninth Shi'a Imam. |
| **820/205** | **Al-Shafi'i dies in Cairo.** |
| 823/207 | Al-Waqidi (compiler of the Prophet's military campaigns) dies. |
| 830/215 | Caliph al-Ma'mun renames Bayt al-Hikmah (House of Wisdom), Dar al-Hikmah (Abode of Wisdom) and expands its activities. |
| **833/218** | **Death of Abdullah al-Ma'mun.** |
| 836/222 | Abbasid capital transferred from Baghdad to Samarra. |
| **838/223** | **Birth of al-Tabari.** |
| **841/226** | **Birth of Abu Bakr al-Razi.** |
| 842/228 | Abbasid Caliph Mu'tasim is succeeded by his son, Wathiq. Michael III appointed new Byzantine Emperor. |
| **846/232** | **Death of al-Khwarizmi, the father of Algebra.** |
| 847/233 | Death of Wathiq; al-Mutawakkil becomes new Abbasid Caliph. |
| **855/241** | **Death of Ahmad ibn Hanbal, founder of the Hanbali School of legal thought.** |
| 857/243 | Death of Harith al-Muhasibi, a prominent early Sufi thinker and practitioner. |
| **858/244** | **Birth of al-Hallaj.** |
| 862/248 | Death of Abbasid Caliph al-Muntasir; al-Mustain succeeds him. |
| 866/252 | Al-Mu'tazz is proclaimed new Caliph after al-Mustain is overthrown. |
| 868/254 | Death of Ali Al-Hadi; his son Hasan al-Askari becomes eleventh Shi'a Imam. |
| 869/256 | Black Africans brought to Basrah to work in the plantations. |
| **870/257** | **Birth of al-Farabi. Death of al-Bukhari.** Death of Caliph Muhtadi; he is succeeded by Mu'tamid, a son of Caliph Mutawakkil. |

| | | | | |
|---|---|---|---|---|
| **873/260** | Birth of Abul Hasan al-Ash'ari. Death of al-Kindi. Death of Hunayn ibn Ishaq, the Nestorian Christian physician and translator. | | 910/298 | Al-Junayd al-Baghdadi, a prominent 'sober' Sufi master, dies in Baghdad. |
| 874/261 | Twelfth Shi'a Imam goes into hiding; end of direct rule of Shi'a Imams. Death of Abu Yazid al-Bistami, a prominent Sufi master. | | **915/303** | **Birth of al-Mutanabbi.** |
| | | | 921/309 | The Fatimids capture Morroccan province of Fez. |
| **875/262** | **Death of Muslim ibn al-Hajjaj.** | | **922/310** | **Al-Hallaj is crucified in Baghdad for alleged heresy and blasphemy.** |
| 877/264 | Construction of the famous Ibn Tulun mosque in Cairo begins. | | **923/311** | **Death of al-Tabari, the great historian and commentator of the Qur'an.** |
| 883/270 | Ahmad ibn Tulun, founder of the Tulunid kingdom, dies in Cairo; he is succeeded by his son. | | **925/313** | Al-Munis, a Turkish general, becomes *de facto* ruler of Baghdad, to the dismay of Caliph al-Muqtadir. **Death of Abu Bakr al-Razi.** |
| **890/277** | **Birth of Abd al-Rahman III of Islamic Spain.** | | 929/317 | Abd al-Rahman III becomes Caliph in Islamic Spain. |
| 892/279 | Death of Abbasid Caliph Mu'tamid; Mu'tadid succeeds him. Death of al-Tirmidhi and al-Baladhuri, two prominent Muslim scholars. | | 930/318 | Qaramatians attack Makkah and escape with the 'Black Stone'. |
| 893/280 | Rise of the Ismaili Shi'as to prominence under Fatimid leadership. | | 932/320 | Al-Munis murders al-Muqtadir and al-Qadir is made new Caliph. |
| **895/282ca.** | **Birth of Abul Hasan al-Mas'udi.** | | 933/321 | Al-Munis himself is executed. |
| 897/284 | Death of al-Yaqubi, a famous Muslim geographer and historian. | | 934/323 | Caliph al-Qadir is captured and blinded by Ibn Muqla, a former Abbasid vizier. Al-Radi succeeds al-Qadir as Caliph. |
| 898/285 | Yahya ibn al-Hussain al-Rassi, the Imam of the Zaydi Shi'as establishes himself in Yemen. | | 935/324 | Death of Ibn Mujahid, a celebrated Arabic linguist and grammarian. |
| 900/287 | Abu Bakr al-Razi identifies diagnosis for 'smallpox' at Baghdad hospital. | | **936/ 325** | **Birth of Abul Qasim al-Zahrawi.** Execution of Ibn Muqla; he is replaced as vizier by Ibn Raiq. |
| 902/290 | Abbasid Caliph al-Muktafi succeeds al-Mu'tadid. | | **940/329** | **Birth of Firdawsi of Persia.** Caliph al-Radi succeeded by his brother al-Muttaqi. |
| 908/296 | Death of al-Muktafi; al-Muqtadir succeeds his brother as Caliph. | | **941/328** | **Death of Abul Hasan al-Ash'ari, founder of the Ash'arite school of Islamic theology.** |
| 909/297 | Fatimids oust their rivals the Rustamids from Western Algeria. | | 944/333 | Al-Muttaqi is blinded and succeeded by al-Mustakfi as Abbasid Caliph. |

| | |
|---|---|
| **950/339** | **Death of al-Farabi, the famous Islamic philosopher and writer.** |
| 951/340 | The Qarmatians return the 'Black Stone' to the Kabah in Makkah. |
| 953/342 | Al-Muizz becomes Fatimid Caliph. |
| **957/346** | **Death of Abul Hasan al-Mas'udi, the famous Muslim historian and traveller.** |
| **961/350** | **Death of Abd al-Rahman III; he is succeeded by al-Hakam II in al-Andalus.** |
| **965/354** | **Birth of Ibn al-Haytham.** **Death of al-Mutanabbi.** |
| **967/357** | **Birth of Mahmud of Ghazna.** Adud al-Dawlah challenges Izz al-Dawlah and takes power. Death of Muizz al-Dawlah; Izz al-Dawlah Bakhtiyar succeeds him. |
| 969/359 | Fatimid commander Jawhar conquers Egypt. |
| 970/360 | Adud al-Dawlah commissions a great hospital in Baghdad. |
| 972/362 | Construction of al-Azhar mosque begins. |
| **973/363** | **Birth of al-Biruni.** Fatimids gain control of Makkah and Madinah. |
| 977/367 | Adud al-Dawlah defeats his cousin Bakhtiyar at Ahwaz. |
| 978/368 | Fatimids capture Damascus. |
| **980/370** | **Birth of Ibn Sina.** |
| 983/373 | Death of Adud al-Dawlah; Samsan al-Dawlah succeeds him. |
| 987/377 | Sharaf al-Dawlah triumphs over Samsan al-Dawlah. |
| 990/380 | Abul Qasim al-Zahrawi completes his *Tasrif*, a famous medical encyclopaedia. |
| **994/384** | **Birth of Ibn Hazm al-Andalusi.** |
| 998/388 | Sebuktekin is succeeded by his son Mahmud as ruler of Ghazna. |
| 1005/396 | Fatimids build the Dar al-Hikmah (House of Wisdom). |
| 1009/400 | Fatimids damage the Church of the Holy Sepulchre during uprising. |
| 1012/403 | Baha al-Dawlah succeeded by Sultan al-Dawlah. |
| **1013/404** | **Death Abul Qasim al-Zahrawi.** |
| 1015/406 | Fatimids seize Aleppo. |
| **1020/411** | **Birth of Nizam ul-Mulk.** **Death of Firdawsi in Tus.** |
| **1030/421** | **Death of Sultan Mahmud; he is succeeded by Mas'ud.** |
| 1031/423 | Al-Qaim succeeds al-Qadir as Caliph. Umayyad rule in Andalus comes to an end. |
| **1037/429** | Seljuk Turks capture Nishapur from the Ghaznavids. **Death of Ibn Sina.** |
| **1039/431** | **Death of Ibn al-Haytham.** |
| **1048/440** | **Birth of Umar Khayyam.** Al-Malik al-Rahim becomes the last Buwayhid (Buyid) ruler. |
| **1051/443** | **Death of al-Biruni.** |
| 1055/447 | Tughrul Beg enters Baghdad and becomes Sultan. |
| **1058/450** | Tughrul Beg's half-brother is executed. **Birth of Abu Hamid al-Ghazali.** |
| 1059/451 | The Seljuks sign a fifty year peace treaty with the Ghaznavids. |
| 1060/452 | The Normans launch their first attack against Sicily. |
| 1063/455 | Death of Tughrul Beg; he is succeeded by Alp Arsalan |

| | | | |
|---|---|---|---|
| 1064/457 | **Death of Ibn Hazm al-Andalusi, the great jurist and theologian of Islamic Spain.** | 1111/505 | **Death of Abu Hamid al-Ghazali.** |
| 1065/458 | Nizam al-Mulk founds Nizamiyyah College in Baghdad. In Egypt a seven year famine begins. | 1117/511 | **Birth of Nur al-Din Zangi.** |
| | | 1121/515 | Death of al-Malik al-Afdal. |
| 1071/464 | Battle of Manzikert; Turkish nomads defeat Byzantine emperor. | 1126/520 | **Birth of Ibn Rushd.** |
| 1072/465 | Alp Arsalan is murdered; Malik Shah succeeds. | 1130/525 | Death of Ibn Tumart; succeeded by Abd al-Mu'min. |
| 1073/466 | The Seljuk general Atzis captures Jerusalem from the Fatimids. | 1131/526 | **Death of Umar al-Khayyam, the famous poet, astronomer and mathematician.** |
| 1075/468 | Death of Caliph al-Qaim; he is succeeded by al-Muqtadir. | 1138/533 | **Birth of Salah al-Din Ayyubi.** |
| 1077/470 | **Birth of Abd al-Qadir al-Jilani.** | 1142/537 | **Birth of Mu'in al-Din Chishti.** |
| 1085/478 | Alfonso VI, King of Leon-Castile, captures Toledo. | 1143/538 | First translation of Quran into Latin by Peter the Venerable. |
| 1091/484 | Death of Malik Shah. | 1149/544 | **Birth of Fakhr al-Din al-Razi.** |
| **1092/485** | **Death of Nizam al-Mulk.** | 1154/549 | Almohads seize Granada. **Birth of Shihab al-Din Suhrawardi.** |
| 1094/487 | Mahmud succeeds Malik Shah as Sultan. Al-Mustazir succeeds al-Muqtadi as Caliph. Death of al-Jawali in Egypt; succeeded by al-Malik al-Afdal. | 1164/560 | Hasan declares himself Ismaili Imam. |
| | | 1165/561 | **Birth of Ibn al-Arabi.** Works of Islamic philosophy and sciences translated into Latin in Toledo. |
| 1095/488 | Pope Urban II calls for Crusade against Islam at Council of Clermont. Death of Mahmud; he is succeeded by his uncle Tutush. | 1166/562 | **Death of Abd al-Qadir al-Jilani.** |
| | | 1171/567 | Egypt conquered by Salah al-Din; Fatimid rule ends and Sunni rule restored. |
| 1099/493 | Jerusalem captured by Crusaders and Latin Kingdom is established. | 1174/570 | **Birth of Shaykh Sa'di of Shiraz. Death of Nur al-Din Zangi.** |
| **1101/495** | **Birth of Ibn Tufayl.** | 1180/576 | Al-Nasir becomes Caliph in Baghdad. |
| 1105/499 | Al-Ghazali completes Ihya Ulum al-Din (The Revivification of Religious Sciences) on his return to Baghdad. Death of Yusuf ibn Tashfin, leader of Almoravids. | 1185/581 | **Death of Ibn Tufayl.** |
| | | 1187/583 | Battle of Hittin; Salah al-Din recovers Jerusalem for Islam. |
| | | 1190/586 | Frederick I Barbarossa drowns in Cilicia. |
| 1108/502 | Alfonso VI of Leon is defeated by the Almoravids. | 1191/587 | **Death of Shihab al-Din Suhrawardi.** |

| | |
|---|---|
| 1192/588 | Richard I taken prisoner by Leopold of Austria. |
| **1193/589** | **Death of Salah al-Din Ayyubi.** |
| 1194/591 | Death of Tughrul III. |
| **1197/594** | **Birth of Abul Hasan al-Shadhili.** |
| **1198/595** | **Death of Ibn Rushd.** |
| **1201/598** | **Birth of Nasir al-Din al-Tusi.** |
| 1202/599 | Fourth Crusade authorised by Pope Innocent III. |
| 1203/600 | Muhammad of Ghur completes conquest of northern India. |
| 1206/603 | Muhammad of Ghur is murdered. |
| **1207/604** | **Birth of Jalal al-Din Rumi.** |
| **1209/606** | **Death of Fakhr al-Din al-Razi.** |
| 1210/607 | Jalal al-Din claims to be Shi'a Imam. Muhammad Khwarazmshah occupies Transoxiana. Death of Sultan Aibak. |
| 1212/609 | Alfonso VIII of Castile defeats Spanish Muslims. |
| 1218/615 | Genghis Khan destroys the Qarakhitai Empire. Pope Innocent III sanctions fifth Crusade. |
| 1219/616 | Francis of Assisi attempts to convert Muslims to Christianity. |
| 1220/617 | Death of Shah Muhammad of Khwarizm. |
| 1221/618 | Tolui Khan destroys Herat. |
| 1225/622 | Death of al-Nasir, the Abbasid Caliph. |
| 1227/625 | Death of Genghis Khan. |
| 1228/626 | Frederick II leads sixth Crusade. |
| 1229/627 | Malik al-Kamil crowns himself King of Jerusalem. |
| **1233/631** | **Birth of Yahya al-Nawawi.** |
| **1236/634** | **Death of Mu'in al-Din Chishti.** |
| 1238/636 | James I of Aragon captures Valencia. |
| **1240/638** | **Death of Ibn al-Arabi.** |
| 1248/646 | Louis II of France launches seventh Crusade. |
| 1250/648 | The seventh Crusade ends in humiliation. |
| 1256/654 | Hulagu storms the fortress of Alamut, killing Rukn al-Din. |
| **1258/656** | Mongols sack Baghdad; end of Abbasid Caliphate. **Death of Abul Hasan al-Shadhili.** |
| 1259/658 | Death of Mongke Khan. |
| 1260/659 | Mamluks defeat Mongols at Ayn Jalut. |
| **1263/662** | **Birth of Ibn Taymiyyah in Harran.** |
| 1265/664 | Death of Hulagu Khan; he is succeeded by his son Abaqa. |
| 1266/665 | Death of Sultan Mahmud; Balban seizes power. |
| 1270/669 | Louis IX dies after proclaiming eighth Crusade. |
| **1273/672** | **Death of Jalal al-Din Rumi, the world famous Persian mystical poet.** |
| **1274/673** | **Death of Nasir al-Din al-Tusi.** |
| **1277/676** | **Death of Yahya al-Nawawi.** |
| 1281/680 | The Mamluks inflict a crushing defeat on the Mongols at Hims. |
| 1282/681 | Death of Abaqa; he is succeeded by Teguder. |
| 1284/683 | Arghun executes his uncle Teguder. |
| **1290/689** | **Death of Shaykh Sa'di of Shiraz.** |

| | |
|---|---|
| 1292/692 | Marco Polo mentions Islamic presence in Sumatra. |
| 1295-1304/694-704 | Ghazan becomes the first Mongol Khan to convert to Islam |
| **1304/704** | **Birth of Ibn Battutah.** Death of Ghazan; he is succeeded by Oljeitu. |
| 1316/716 | Death of Oljeitu; he is succeeded by Abu Sa'id. |
| **1318/718** | **Birth of Khwajah Naqshband.** |
| 1320/720 | The Khaljis are overthrown by Tughlaqs in India. |
| 1321/721 | Death of Dante Alighieri, the famous Italian poet who was inspired by Islamic philosophy. |
| 1325/726 | Death of Sultan Ghiyas al-Din Tughlaq. |
| 1326/727 | The Ottomans capture Bursa. Death of Uthman, the founder of the Ottoman dynasty; he is succeeded by Orhan. |
| 1327/728 | Abu Sa'id overthrows Chopan. |
| **1328/729** | **Death of Ibn Taymiyyah in a prison in Damascus.** |
| **1332/733** | **Birth of Ibn Khaldun.** |
| 1335/736 | Death of Abu Sa'id. |
| **1336/737** | **Birth of Timur the Conqueror.** |
| 1341/742 | Six years of civil disturbance begins within Byzantium. |
| 1347/748 | John VI Cantacuzenus restores order within Byzantium. Shah Mirza inaugurates a new dynasty in India. |
| 1354/755 | The Ottomans capture Ankara. |
| 1362/764 | Death of Orhan; Murad I succeeds him. |
| 1366/768 | Pope Urban V announces a fresh Crusade against the Ottomans. |
| 1370/772 | Timur (or Tamerlane) continues his conquests. |
| **1378/780** | **Death of Ibn Battutah.** |
| **1389/792** | At the Battle of Kosovo, the Ottomans defeat the Serbs. Death of Sultan Murad; he is succeeded by Bayazid I. **Death of Khwajah Naqshband.** |
| 1402/805 | Ibn Khaldun meets Timur the Conqueror. |
| 1403/806 | Sultan Bayazid I commits suicide. |
| **1405/808** | **Death of Timur the Conqueror.** |
| **1406/809** | **Death of Ibn Khaldun.** |
| 1413/816 | Tughlaq dynasty is overthrown and replaced by the Sayyid dynasty in India. |
| 1421/824 | Sultan Muhammad I is succeeded by his son Murad II as ruler of the Ottoman Empire. |
| 1423/827 | Murad II kills his brother Mustafa. |
| **1429/833** | **Birth of Sultan Muhammad II.** |
| 1430/834 | Murad II expels the Venetians from Salonika. |
| 1447/851 | Death of Shah Rukh; he is succeeded by his son Ulugh Beg. |
| 1449/853 | Death of Ulugh Beg and his brother Abd al-Aziz. |
| 1451/855 | The Lodis displace the Sayyids as rulers of Delhi. Death of Murad II; he is succeeded by Muhammad II 'the Conqueror'. |
| 1453/857 | Ottomans capture Constantinople (Istanbul). Death of Constantine IX of Byzantium. |
| 1462/867 | Ottomans capture Wallachia. |

| | |
|---|---|
| 1469/874 | Death of Abu Sa'id; he is succeeded by Hussain Bayqara. |
| 1475/880 | The first coffee house opens in Istanbul. |
| 1478/883 | Islamic conquest of Majapait Kingdom in Java. |
| 1479/884 | Treaty of Constantinople concluded. |
| **1481/886** | **Death of Muhammad II; he is succeeded by Bayazid II.** |
| **1489/895** | **Birth of Sinan, the Ottoman architect.** |
| 1492/898 | Granada, the last Spanish Muslim kingdom, falls to Ferdinand and Isabella. Christopher Columbus 'discovers' America. |
| **1494/900** | **Birth of Sulaiman the Magnificent.** |
| 1502/908 | Ferdinand and Isabella outlaw Islam in Spain. |
| 1503/909 | Ottomans gain control of Greece. |
| 1508/914 | Shah Ismail establishes his rule over Iraq. |
| 1512/918 | Death of Bayazid II; he is succeeded by his son Salim I. |
| 1514/920 | At the Battle of Chaldiran, the Ottomans defeat the Safavids. |
| 1517/923 | Ottomans gain control of Egypt, Syria, Makkah and Madinah. |
| 1520/927 | Death of Selim I; Sulaiman succeeds him. |
| 1520-1566/927-974 | The reign of Sulaiman the Magnificent; the Ottoman Empire reaches its zenith. |
| 1524/331 | Shah Ismail is succeeded by his son Tahmasp I. |
| 1526/933 | The Battle of Mohacs. Death of King Louis II of France. Battle of Panipat and establishment of Mughal rule in the subcontinent. |

| | |
|---|---|
| 1529/936 | The Ottoman siege of Vienna. |
| 1530/937 | Babar is succeeded by his son Humayun. Paginus Brixiensis prints the first Qur'an in Rome. |
| 1534/941 | The Ottomans occupy Baghdad. |
| 1539/946 | Death of Guru Nanak, the founder of Sikhism. |
| 1540/947 | Humayun is overthrown by Sher Shah. |
| **1542/949** | **Birth of Akbar the Great.** |
| 1545/952 | Sultan Sulaiman I and Ferdinand of Austria sign treaty. Sher Shah is succeeded by son Islam Shah. |
| 1555/963 | The Ottomans and Safavids conclude peace treaty at Amasya. |
| 1556/964 | Akbar consolidates Mughal rule in India. The Sulaimaniyyah complex in Istanbul is completed by Sinan. |
| **1564/972** | **Birth of Shaykh Ahmad Sirhindi.** |
| 1566/974 | Death of Sulaiman I; Salim II succeeds him. The Mughals reign supreme in India. |
| **1571/979** | **Birth of Mulla Sadra.** The Battle of Lepanto; the Europeans block Ottomans from the Mediterranean. |
| 1574/982 | Death of Salim II; his son Murad II succeeds him as Ottoman ruler. |
| 1576/984 | Death of Tahmasp I ; Shah Ismail II succeeds him as ruler of the Persian Safavid dynasty. |
| 1578/986 | Death of Shah Ismail; Muhammad Khudabanda succeeds him. The Battle of the Three Kings takes place in Morocco. |
| 1583/991 | The British negotiate the first trade treaty with the Ottomans. |

| | | | |
|---|---|---|---|
| **1588/997** | Muhammad Khudabanda is deposed; Shah Abbas becomes Safavid ruler. **Death of Sinan.** Under Shah Abbas, the Safavids reach their zenith. | 1647/1057 | A. du Ryer translates the Qu'ran into French. Ibrahim is replaced by Muhammad IV. |
| **1592/1001** | **Birth of Shah Jahan.** | 1658/1069 | Awrangzeb succeeds his father Shah Jahan. |
| 1595/1004 | Murad III is succeeded by Muhammad III. | 1664/1073 | Awrangzeb instigates reforms and bans *suttee*. |
| 1600/1009 | The East India Company is founded in London by Royal charter. | **1666/1077** | **Death of Shah Jahan.** Death of Shah Abbas II; succeeded by his son Safi I. |
| 1603/1012 | Death of Sultan Muhammad III; he is succeeded by his son Ahmad I. | 1674/1085 | East India Company begins to operate from Mumbai (Bombay). |
| **1605/1014** | **Death of Akbar the Great; his son Jahangir succeeds him as Mughal ruler.** | 1682/1093 | The Ottoman and Austrian Empires slide into war. |
| 1608/1017 | Jahangir grants trading rights to the British. | 1686/1098 | East India Company begins to operate from Calicut. |
| 1617/1026 | Ahmad I is succeeded by Mustafa I. | 1687/1099 | Sultan Muhammad IV succeeded by Sulaiman II |
| **1618/1028** | **Birth of Awrangzeb Alamgir.** Mustafa I is replaced by his brother Uthman II. | 1691/1103 | Sultan Sulaiman II is succeeded by his brother Ahmad II. |
| 1622/1032 | Death of Uthman; Mustafa I is restored to the throne. | 1694/1106 | Shah Safi II is succeeded by his son Shah Hussain. |
| 1623/1033 | Mustafa I hands over power to Murad IV. | 1695/1107 | Ahmad II is succeeded by Mustafa II as Ottoman ruler. |
| **1624/1034** | **Death of Shaykh Ahmad Sirhindi.** | **1703/1115** | **Birth of Ibn Abd al-Wahhab. Birth of Shah Waliullah.** Mustafa II is succeeded by Ahmad III. |
| 1627/1037 | Jahangir is succeeded by son Shah Jahan. | **1707/1119** | **Death of Awrangzeb.** |
| 1629/1039 | Death of Shah Abbas of Persia. | 1716/1129 | East India Company exempted from tax by the Mughals. |
| 1639/1049 | With the Treaty of Qasr Shirin, the borders of Iraq and Iran are established. | 1722/1135 | The Afghans capture Isfahan; Safavid rule in Iran comes to an end. |
| 1640/1050 | Sultan Murad IV is succeeded by Ibrahim. | 1729/1142 | Nadir Shah overthrows Shah Ashraf. |
| **1641/1051** | **Death of Mulla Sadra.** | 1730/1143 | Ahmad III is overthrown by Mahmud I. |
| 1642/1052 | Death of Shah Safi; succeeded by son Shah Abbas II. | 1734/1147 | George Sale translates the Qur'an into English. |

| | |
|---|---|
| 1744/1157 | Ibn Abd al-Wahhab is expelled from Makkah. |
| 1745/1158 | Beginning of 'Wahhabi' movement in Arabia |
| 1747/1160 | Death of the Afghan ruler Nadir Shah. |
| **1754/1168** | **Birth of Uthman Dan Fodio.** |
| 1761/1172 | The second Battle of Panipat. |
| **1762/1173** | **Death of Shah Waliullah of Delhi.** |
| 1774/1188 | Treaty of Kuckuk Kaynarja as the Russians seize Black Sea from the Ottomans. |
| 1789/1204 | Salim III ascends Ottoman throne. |
| 1789-1807/ 1204-1222 | Al-Sanusi of Libya establishes an Islamic State. |
| 1792/1207 | Ottomans carry out reform. **Death of Ibn Abd al-Wahhab of Arabia.** |
| **1796/1211** | **Birth of Shamyl of Daghestan.** |
| 1798/1213 | The French occupy Egypt under Napoleon as Muhammad Ali Pasha comes to power. |
| 1808/1223 | Death of Mustafa IV; Mahmud II is proclaimed Ottoman ruler. |
| 1812/1227 | Muhammad Ali Pasha massacres 480 leaders in Cairo at a banquet. |
| **1817/1232** | **Birth of Sir Sayyid Ahmad Khan. Death of Uthman Dan Fodio.** |
| 1830/1246 | French invade Algeria and Amir Abd al-Qadir leads resistance movement. |
| 1836/1252 | Death of Ahmad ibn Idris, the Sufi reformer. |
| **1838/1254** | **Birth of Jamal al-Din al-Afghani.** |
| 1839/1255 | Mahmud II is succeeded by son Abd al-Majid as Ottoman ruler. |
| **1844/1260** | **Birth of Muhammad Ahmad, the Mahdi of Sudan and founder of the Islamic State.** |
| **1849/1266** | **Birth of Muhammad Abduh, the father of Islamic modernism.** Death of Muhammad Ali Pasha; he is succeeded by Abbas Hilmi I. |
| 1854/1271 | Death of Abbas Hilmi I; he is succeeded by Muhammad Sa'id Pasha. |
| 1858/1275 | Beginning of British rule in India. |
| 1862/1279 | Ma Ba leads resistance against the French in Senegal. |
| 1863/1280 | Sa'id Pasha is succeeded by Ismail Pasha in Egypt. |
| **1871/1288** | **Death of Shamyl of Daghestan.** |
| **1876/1293** | **Birth of Muhammad Ali Jinnah, founder of Pakistan** |
| 1876/1293 | Murad V ascends Ottoman throne; Abd al-Hamid II replaces Murad V. |
| **1877/1294** | **Birth of Sir Muhammad Iqbal. Birth of Sa'id Nursi of Turkey.** |
| **1880/1298** | **Birth of Abd al-Aziz ibn Saud, founder of modern Saudi Arabia.** |
| **1881/1299** | **Birth of Mustafa Kemal Ataturk, founder of the Turkish Republic.** |
| **1885/1303** | **Birth of Muhammad Ilyas, founder of the Tabligi Jama'at movement.** |
| 1889/1307 | Sultan Abd al-Hamid II officially abolishes slavery. |
| 1896/1314 | Death of Nasir al-Din Shah. |
| **1897/1315** | The first Zionist Organisation is founded in Switzerland. **Death of Jamal al-Din al-Afghani.** |
| **1898/1316** | The British defeat Mahdist State of Sudan; Muhammad Rashid Rida begins publication of *al-Manar* journal in Egypt. **Death Sir Sayyid Ahmad Khan.** |

| | |
|---|---|
| **1902/1312** | **Birth of Ayatullah Khomeini, founder of Islamic Republic of Iran.** |
| **1903/1313** | **Birth of Abul A'la Mawdudi, founder of Jama'at-i-Islami movement in the subcontinent.** |
| **1905/1323** | **Death of Muhammad Abduh.** |
| **1906/1324** | **Birth of Hasan al-Banna, founder of the Muslim Brotherhood in Egypt. Birth of Sayyid Qutb, the influential Egyptian Islamic ideologue.** |
| 1908/1326 | Young Turk Revolution takes place in Ottoman Turkey. |
| 1909/1327 | Muhammad V replaces Abd al-Hamid II as Ottoman ruler. |
| 1911/1329 | African slave trade ended. |
| 1913/1332 | The first Balkan War comes to an end. |
| 1917/1336 | The British support Balfour Declaration. Death of Muhammad V; he is succeeded by Muhammad VI. |
| 1919-1924/ 1338-1342 | The creation of the secular Turkish Republic marks the end of Ottoman rule. |
| **1919-1925/ 1338-1343** | Khilafat Movement in India supports the Ottoman Caliphate. **Birth of Malcolm X.** King Abdullah is expelled from Saudi Arabia. |
| 1928/1347 | Hasan al-Banna establishes Muslim Brotherhood in Egypt. |
| 1930/1349 | Iraq becomes independent under King Faisal I. |
| 1931/1350 | Elijah Muhammad becomes leader of the Nation of Islam. |
| 1936/1355 | Persia is officially renamed Iran by the Shah. |
| **1938/1357** | **Death of Sir Muhammad Iqbal. Death of Mustafa Kemal Ataturk** |

| | |
|---|---|
| **1940/1359** | **Birth of Muhammad Yunus.** |
| 1941/1360 | Abul A'la Mawdudi establishes Jama'at-i- Islami in India. |
| **1942/1361** | **Birth of Muhammad Ali, the legendary American boxer.** |
| **1944/1364** | **Death of Muhammad Ilyas.** |
| 1945/1365 | Abd al-Rahman Azzam founds the Arab League. The first meeting of the United Nations General Assembly takes place. |
| 1947/1367 | Pakistan is established as an independent homeland for the Muslims of India. |
| **1948/1368** | State of Israel founded in Palestine. **Death of Muhammad Ali Jinnah.** |
| **1949/1369** | First Arab-Israeli War ends. TransJordan becomes known as Jordan. **Hasan al-Banna is assassinated in Cairo.** |
| 1951/1371 | Idris ibn al-Mahdi becomes King of newly created Libya. |
| 1952/1372 | Jamal Abd al-Nasir gains power in Egypt as King Farouk is forced into exile. Turkey becomes a member of NATO. Prince Husain becomes King of Jordan. |
| **1953/1373** | **Death of King Abd al-Aziz ibn Saud.** |
| 1956/1376 | Pakistan becomes an Islamic Republic. |
| 1957/1377 | King Muhammad V becomes ruler of independent Morocco. |
| 1958/1378 | General Ayub Khan gains power in Pakistan. |
| **1960/1380** | Organisation of Oil Producing Countries (OPEC) is founded in Baghdad. **Death of Sa'id Nursi of Turkey.** |
| 1961/1381 | Al-Azhar University is brought under Government control by Nasir. |

| | |
|---|---|
| 1964/1384 | The Palestine Liberation Organisation (PLO) is founded by Yasser Arafat. Muhammad Ali joins the Nation of Islam. |
| **1965/1385** | The Egyptian authorities crackdown on the Muslim Brotherhood in Egypt. **Malcolm X is assassinated just before his fortieth birthday.** |
| **1966/1386** | **Sayyid Qutb is sentenced to death by Nasir's Government.** |
| 1967/1387 | Arab/Israeli War. |
| 1969/1389 | Muammar al-Qadhafi gains power in Libya and King Faisal of Saudi Arabia calls for war against Israel after al-Aqsa mosque is burnt. Organisation of the Islamic Conference (OIC) is founded. |
| 1970/1390 | Death of Nasir; Anwar Sadat succeeds him. Islamist Party for National Order is founded in Turkey. Zulfikhar Ali Bhutto gains power in Pakistan. |
| 1971/1391 | ABIM (Malaysian League of Muslim Youth) is founded. Gulf States of Bahrain & Qatar gain independence from Britain. East Pakistan breaks away and becomes Bangladesh. |
| 1973/1393 | Second Arab/Israeli War. The Islamic Development Bank is founded in Jeddah. |
| 1974/1394 | Yasser Arafat addresses UN and calls for a Palestinian State. |
| 1975/1395 | Civil War takes place in Lebanon. |
| 1976/1396 | Wallace Muhammad succeeds his father Elijah Muhammad as head of Nation of Islam. |
| 1977/1398 | General Zia ul-Haq begins Islamisation of Pakistan. |
| 1978/1399 | Camp David Peace Accord signed. |

| | |
|---|---|
| **1979/1400** | Ayatullah Khomeini establishes Islamic Republic in Iran. The Soviet Union invades Afghanistan. **Death of Abul A'la Mawdudi** |
| 1980/1401 | Hizbullah (The Party of God) is founded in Lebanon. |
| 1981/1402 | Anwar Sadat is assassinated; he is succeeded by Husni Mubarak. Ronald Reagan becomes US President. |
| 1982/1403 | Israel invades Lebanon for the second time and massacres take place in Sabra and Shatila. |
| 1987/1408 | First Intifada takes place in Palestine. Shaykh Ahmad Yassin establishes HAMAS, the Palestinian Resistance Movement. |
| 1988/1409 | Benazir Bhutto becomes first female head of a Muslim country. raq-Iran War comes to an end. Death of Zia ul-Haq of Pakistan. Salman Rushdie's *The Satanic Verses* leads to worldwide protest against the book. |
| **1989/1410** | **Death of Ayatullah Khomeini; he is succeeded by Ayatullah Ali Khameinei.** Omar Hasan al-Bashir gains power in Sudan and Soviet Union is defeated in Afghanistan. |
| 1990/1411 | Nawaz Sharif gains power in Pakistan. Death of Abdullah Azzam, a prominent leader of *jihad* against the Soviets in Afghanistan. |
| 1990-1992/ 1411-1413 | First Gulf War. FIS (Islamic Salvation Front) wins election in Algeria. The demise of USSR. Civil War erupts in Yugoslavia. |
| 1993/1414 | Benazir Bhutto returns to power in Pakistan. |
| 1995/1416 | Necmettin Erbakan becomes Turkey's first Islamist Prime Minister. Death of Yitzhak Rabin. |

| | | | |
|---|---|---|---|
| 1996/1417 | Sheikh Umar Abd al-Rahman is sentenced to life imprisonment in the US for plotting terror attacks. | 2002/1423 | US and British invade Iraq to depose Saddam Hussein. |
| 1997/1418 | Muhammad Khatami becomes president of Iran. | 2004/1425 | Al-Qa'ida bombs trains in Madrid. |
| 1998/1419 | US embassies in Kenya and Tanzania are bombed. | 2005/1426 | Al-Qa'ida inspired bombings take place in London. Yasser Arafat dies in Paris. Tony Blair re-elected British Prime Minister. |
| 1999/1420 | General Pervez Musharraf ousts Nawaz Sharif from power in Pakistan. Abdullah II succeeds his father as King of Jordan. Abdurrahman Wahid becomes president of Indonesia. | 2006/1427 | Israel invades Lebanon for the third time. Saddam Hussain, President of Iraq, hanged by American and British backed Iraqi Government. |
| 2000/1421 | Second Intifada breaks out in Palestine. Slobodan Milosevic put on trial for war crimes. | 2007/1428 | Palestinians form unity Government after months of violence between Fatah and Hamas. Military-backed Caretaker Government in power in Bangladesh after months of political uncertainty and upheaval. Iran vows to continue with nuclear programme. |
| 2001/1422 | US Postal Service issues stamp to celebrate Muslim festival of Eid. Al-Qaida attacks World Trade Centre in New York. Ariel Sharon becomes Prime Minister of Israel. Khatami re-elected president of Iran. US attacks Afghanistan for harbouring Osama bin Ladin. Pakistan becomes first Muslim nuclear power. | | |

# Select Bibliography*

Abbasi, S.M.M., *Daughters of the Holy Prophet*, New Delhi: International Islamic Publishers, 1987.

Abbot, N., *Aishah the Beloved of Mohammed*, New York: Arno Press, 1973.

Abdel Haleem. M.A.S., *The Qur'an: A New Translation*, Oxford: Oxford University, Press, 2004.

Abu Dawud, *Sunan*, 3 vols, translated by A. Hasan, Lahore: Muhammad Ashraf, 1984.

Abu Laylah. M., *In Pursuit of Virtue*, London: Ta Ha Publishers, 1990.

Abu Zahra. M., *The Four Imams: Their Lives, Works and their Schools of Thought*, London: Dar al-Taqwa, 2001.

*Advice for the Muslim*, published by Hakikat Kitabevi, Istanbul, Turkey, 1993.

Addas, C., *Quest for the Red Sulphur: The Life of Ibn Arabi*, Cambridge: The Islamic Text Society, 1993.

Adams, C.C., *Islam and Modernism in Egypt: A Study of the Modern Reform Movement Inaugurated by Muhammad Abduh*, London: Oxford University, Press, 1933.

Ahmad, A., *Islamic Modernism in India and Pakistan* 1857-1964, Oxford: Oxford, University Press, 1967.

Ahmad, J., *Hundred Great Muslims*, Lahore: Ferozsons Ltd, 1984.

Ahmad, F., *Hussain the Great Martyr*, Lahore: Muhammad Ashraf, 1984.

_____: *Mohy-ud-Din Alamgir Aurangzeb*, Lahore: Muhammad Ashraf, 1976.

Ahmad, K. & Ansari, Z.I. (ed.), *Islamic Perspectives: Studies in Honour of Sayyid Abul Ala Mawdudi*, Leicester: The Islamic Foundation, 1980.

Ahmad, N., *Muslim Contribution to Geography*, Lahore: Muhammad Ashraf, 1972.

Ahmed, A.S., *Discovering Islam: Making Sense of Muslim History and Society*, London: Routledge, 1988.

_____: *Islam Today: A Short Introduction to the Muslim World*, London: I.B.Tauris, 2001.

_____: *Jinnah, Pakistan and Islamic Identity: The Search for Saladin*, London: Routledge, 1997.

---

\* The readers can trace most of the information contained in this book in the sources listed below. And although the vast majority of the titles listed here are in English (including English translations of original Arabic works), some items are in Bengali and Arabic. I have incorporated names of authors, translators, publishers as well as dates of publication to enable the readers to locate these books with ease. Where a publisher did not include the date of publication, I have indicated this by 'no date'.

Ahmed, L., *Women and Gender in Islam; Historical Roots of a Modern Debate*, New Haven: Yale University Press, 1992.

Ahmed, M.B. et al. (eds.), *Muslim Contributions to World Civilisation*, Richmond: IIIT& AMSS, 2005.

Ahmed, N., *Forty Great Men and Women in Islam*, New Delhi: Adam Publishers, 1990.

Akgun, K., *Bedee-u-Zaman Said Noorsi of Turkey*, Ankara: Ihlas Nur Nesriyat, no date.

Akram, A.I., *The Muslim Conquest of Egypt and North Africa*, Lahore: Ferozsons, 1977.

_____: *Sword of Allah, Khalid bin al-Walid: A Biographical Study of the Greatest Military General in History*, Birmingham: Maktabah Publishers, 2004.

Alam, Z., *Education in Early Islamic Period*, New Delhi: Markazi Maktaba Islami, 1991.

Allen, R., *An Introduction to Arabic Literature*, Cambridge: Cambridge University, Press, 2000.

Ali, A.Y., *The Meaning of the Holy Qur'an: New Edition with Revised Translation, Commentary and Index*, Maryland: Amana Publications, 2001.

Ali, M.M., *The Early Caliphate*, Lahore: Ahmadiyya Anjuman Isha'at Islam, 1983.

_____: *The Religion of Islam*, Lahore: Ahmadiyya Anjuman Isha'at Islam, 1973.

Ali, S.A., *A History of the Saracens*, New Delhi: Kitab Bhavan, 1994.

_____: *The Spirit of Islam*, New Delhi: Kutub Khana, no date.

Ali. M. S. et al. (ed.), *Muslim Contribution to Science and Technology*, Dhaka: Islamic Foundation, 1996.

al-Alwani, T.J., *Ijtihad*, Virginia: IIIT, 1993.

_____: *Adab al-Ikhtilaf*, translated as 'The Ethics of Disagreement in Islam', Virginia: IIIT, 1993.

Aminrazavi, M., *Suhrawardi and the School of Illumination*, Surrey: Curzon, 1996.

_____: *The Wine of Wisdom: The Life, Poetry and Philosophy of Omar Khayyam*, Oxford: Oneworld, 2005.

Ansari, M.A.H., *Sufism and Shari'ah: A Study of Shaykh Ahmad Sirhindi's Effort to Reform Sufism*, Leicester: The Islamic Foundation, 1986.

Appleyard, B., *Understanding the Present: Science and the Soul of Modern Man*, London: Pan Books Ltd, 1992.

Arberry, A.J., *Revelation and Reason in Islam*, London: Allen & Unwin, 1957.

_____: *The Islamic Art of Persia*, New Delhi: Goodword Books, 2001.

_____: *Aspects of Islamic Civilisation: As Depicted in the Original Texts*, London: Allen & Unwin, 1964.

_____: *Sufism: An Account of the Mystics of Islam*, London: Allen & Unwin, 1969.

Archer, N.P. (ed.), *The Sufi Mystery*, London: Octagon Press, 1988.

Armstrong, K., *A History of God*, London: Mandarin, 1994.

_____: *Islam: A Short History*, London: Phoenix Press, 2001.

_____: *The Battle for God: Fundamentalism in Judaism, Christianity and Islam*, London: HarperCollins, 2001.

_____: *Holy War: The Crusades and their Impact on Today's World*, London: Papermac, 1992.

Arnold, T.W., *The Preaching of Islam*, Lahore: Muhammad Ashraf, 1979.

_____: *The Caliphate*, New Delhi: Adam Publishers, 1988.

_____: *The Islamic Art and Architecture*, New Delhi: Goodword Books, 2001.

Arsalan, A.S., *Our Decline and Its Causes*, Lahore: Muhammad Ashraf, 1990.

Asad, M., *The Message of the Qur'an*, Gibraltar: Dar al-Andalus, 1980.

_____: *The Road to Mecca*, Tangier: Dar al-Andalus, 1974.

_____: *This Law of Ours and Other Essays*, Gibraltar: Dar al-Andalus, 1987.

al-Askari, A.M., *Abdullah ibn Saba and Other Myths*, vol 1, Tehran: Group of Muslim Brothers, 1978.

Attar, F., *Tadhkirat al-Awliyah*, translated as 'Muslim Saints and Mystics', by A.J. Arberry, London: Routledge and Keegan Paul, 1976.

Ayoub, M.M., *The Crisis of Muslim History: Religion and Politics in Early Islam*, Oxford: Oneworld Publications, 2005.

_____: *The Qur'an and Its Interpreters*, 2 vols, Albany: State University of New York Press, 1992.

Azad, A.K., *Tarjuman al-Qur'an*, 2 vols, Lahore: Sind Sagar Academy, 1976.

Azami, M.M., *Studies in Hadith Methodology and Literature*, Indianapolis: American Trust Publications, 1977.

_____: *Studies in Early Hadith Literature: with a Critical Edition of some Early Texts*, Indianapolis: American Trust Publications, 1978.

_____: *On Schacht's Origins of Muhammadan Jurisprudence*, Cambridge: The Islamic Text Society, 1993.

_____: *The History of the Qur'anic Text from Revelation to Compilation*, Leicester: UK Islamic Academy, 2003.

Azimabadi, B., *Great Personalities in Islam*, New Delhi: Adam Publishers, 1998.

Azzam, A.R., *The Eternal Message of Muhammad*, London: Quartet Books, 1984.

Bakhash, S., *The Reign of the Ayatollahs*, London: Unwin, 1986.

Bakar, O., *Classification of Knowledge in Islam*, Cambridge: Islamic Text Society, 1998.

_____: *The History and Philosophy of Islamic Science*, Cambridge: Islamic Text Society, 1999.

Baldock, J., *The Essence of Sufism*, Hertfordshire: Eagle Editions Ltd, 2004.

al-Banna, H., *Memoirs of Hasan al-Banna*, translated by N.M.Shaikh, Karachi: International Islamic Publishers, 1982.

Barber, N., *Lords of the Golden Horn: The Sultans, their Harems and the Fall of the Ottoman Empire*, London: Macmillan, 1973.

Bashier, Z., *Hijra: Story and Significance*, Leicester: Islamic Foundation, 1983.

Baz, A. bin, *Arab Nationalism: An Analysis in the Light of Qur'an and Sunnah*, Karachi: International Islamic Publishers, 1985.

Beg, M.A.J., *Brief Lives of the Companions of Prophet Muhammad*, Cambridge: 21st Century Publications, 2003.

_____: *Essays on the Origins of Islamic Civilisation*, Cambridge: MAJ Beg, 2006.

_____: *Social Mobility in Islamic Civilisation*, Cambridge: MAJ Beg, 2006.

_____: *Islamic and Western Concepts of Civilisation*, Cambridge: MAJ Beg, 2006.

_____: *Wisdom of Islamic Civilisation*, Cambridge: MAJ Beg, 2006.

_____: (ed.) *Historic Cities of Asia*, Kuala Lumpur: MAJ Beg, 1985.

_____: *The Reign of Muawiyah: A Critical Survey*, Islamic Culture, pp.83-107, 1977.

Bennett, C., *Victorian Images of Islam*, London: Grey Seal Books, 1992.

Berger, P.L., *Facing up to Modernity*, New York: Penguin, 1979.

Berinstain, V., *Mughal India: Splendours of the Peacock Throne*, London: Thames & Hudson, 1998.

Birgivi, Imam, *al-Tariqah al-Muhammadiyyah*, translated as 'The Path of Muhammad' by Shaykh T. al-Halveti, Indiana: World Wisdom, 2005.

Blanch, L., *The Sabres of Paradise: Conquest and Vengeance in the Caucasus*, London: I.B. Tauris, 2004.

Bloom, J. & Blair, S., *Islam: Empire of Faith*, London: BBC Worldwide Ltd, 2001.

Blunt, W., *Splendours of Islam*, London: Angus & Robertson, 1976.

Bolitho, H., *Jinnah: Creator of Pakistan*, London: John Murray, 1960.

Bonney, R., *Jihad: From Qur'an to bin Ladin*, Basingstoke: Palgrave Macmillan, 2004.

Bosworth, C.E., *New Islamic Dynasties*, Edinburgh: Edinburgh University Press, 2004.

al-Bukhari, *Sahih al-Bukhari*, Arabic text with English translation by M.M. Khan, 9 vols, New Delhi: Kitab Bhavan, 1987.

Bullock, A. & Trombley, S. (ed.), *The New Fontana Dictionary of Modern Thought*, London: HarperCollins, 1999.

Burckhardt, T., *Introduction to Sufism*, London: Thorsons, 1995.

_____: *Mirror of the Intellect*, Cambridge: Quinta Essentia, 1987.

Burke, J., *Al-Qaeda: The True Story of Radical Islam*, London: Penguin, 2004.

Burns, K., *Eastern Philosophy*, London: Arcturus Publishing, 2004.

Braudel, F., *A History of Civilisations*, London: Allen Lane, 1994.

Brockleman, C., *History of the Islamic Peoples*, London: Routledge and Keegan Paul, 1948.

Browne, E.G., *Arabian Medicine*, Lahore: Kazi Publications, no date.

Brunner, R., *Islamic Ecumenism in the 20th Century: The Azhar and Shi'ism between Rapprochement and Restraint*, Leiden: Brill, 2004.

Cain, P.J. & Hopkins, A.G., *British Imperialism: Innovation and Expansion 1688-1914*, Harlow: Longman Group, 1993.

Canning, J. (ed.), *100 Great Kings, Queens and Rulers of the World*, London: McDonald & Co., 1979.

Castleden, R., *People Who Changed the World*, London: Time Warner Books, 2005.

el-Cheikh, N.M., *Byzantium Viewed by the Arabs*, Cambridge: Harvard University Press, 2004.

Chowdhry, S.R., *al-Hajjaj ibn Yusuf*, New Delhi: Kutub Khana, 1979.

Clark, K., *Civilisation: A Personal View*, London: Book Club Associates, 1972.

Clot, A., *Suleiman the Magnificient*, London: Saqi Books, 2005.

Collins, R., *The Arab Conquest of Spain 710-797*, Oxford: Basil Blackwell, 1989.

Collins, L. and Lapierre, D., *Freedom at Midnight: The Epic Drama of India's Struggle for Independence*, London: HarperCollins, 1997.

Cook, M., *Commanding Right and Forbidding Wrong in Islamic Thought*, Cambridge: Cambridge University Press, 2000.

Cook, S.B., *Colonial Encounters in the Age of High Imperialism*, New York: HarperCollins, 1996.

Cooper, J. et al. (ed.), *Islam and Modernity*, London: I.B. Tauris, 1998.

Cowan, J.M., *A Dictionary of Modern Written Arabic*, Beirut: Libraire Du Liban, 1980.

Cragg, G., *The Church and the Age of Reason 1648-1789*, London: Penguin Books, 1990.

Cragg, K., *Counsels in Contemporary Islam*, Edinburgh: Edinburgh University Press, 1965.

_____: *The Mind of the Qur'an*, London: Allen & Unwin, 1973.

al-Daffa, A.A., *The Muslim Contribution to Mathematics*, London: Croom Helm, 1977.

Daftary, F., *The Ismailis: Their History and Doctrines*, Cambridge: Cambridge University Press, 1990.

Daniel, N., *Islam and the West: The Making of an Image*, Oxford: Oneworld Publications, 1993.

Davidson, B., *Africa in History*, London: Phoenix Press, 2001.

Dawisha, A., *Arab Nationalism in the Twentieth Century*, New Jersey: Princeton University Press, 2003.

Dawson, R. (ed.), *The Legacy of China*, London: Oxford University Press, 1964.

De Bruijn, J.T.P., *Persian Sufi Poetry: An Introduction to the Mystical Use of Classical Poems*, Surrey: Curzon Press, 1997.

Delgoda, S.T., *History of India*, Gloucester: Windrush Press, 1997.

Descartes, R., *Key Philosophical Writings*, Hertfordshire: Wordsworth Edition, 1997.

Dio, A.R.I., *Shari'ah: The Islamic Law*, London: Ta Ha Publishers, 1984.

Dyson, M.E., *Making Malcolm: The Myth and Meaning of Malcolm X*, New York: Oxford University Press, 1995.

Ehrlich, E., *Nil Desperandum: A Dictionary of Latin Tags and Phrases*, London: Guild Publishing, 1987.

Enayat, H., *Modern Islamic Political Thought*, Kuala Lumpur: Islamic Book Trust, 2001.

Esack, F., *The Qur'an: A User's Guide*, Oxford: Oneworld Publications, 2005.

Esin, E., *Mecca the Blessed, Madinah the Radiant*, Novara: Paul Elek Productions, 1963.

Esposito, J.L. (ed.), *The Oxford Dictionary of Islam*, New York: Oxford University Press, 2003.

_____: (ed.), *The Oxford History of Islam*, New York: Oxford University Press, 1999.

_____: (ed.), *The Voices of Resurgent Islam*, New York: Oxford University Press, 1983.

_____: (ed.), *Islam in Asia: Religion, Politics & Society*, New York: Oxford University Press, 1987.

_____: *The Oxford Encyclopaedia of the Modern Islamic World*, 4 vols, Oxford: Oxford University Press, 1995.

Esposito, J.L. and Tamimi A. (eds.), *Islam and Secularism in the Middle East*, London: C. Hurst & Co, 2000.

Essien-Udom, E.U., *Black Nationalism*, Chicago: University of Chicago Press, 1962.

Fakhry, M., *Islamic Philosophy, Theology and Mysticism*, Oxford: Oneworld Publications, 2000.

_____: *A History of Islamic Philosophy*, New York: Columbia University Press, 1970.

Faivre, A. and Needleman, J. (eds.), *Modern Esoteric Spirituality*, London: SCM Press, 1993.

Faruqi, B.A., *The Mujjaddid's Conception of Tawhid*, Lahore: Muhammad Ashraf, 1979.

al-Faruqi, I.R., *Al-Tawhid: Its Implications for Thought and Life*, Virgina: IIIT, 1992.

_____: *The Cultural Atlas of Islam*, New York: Macmillan, 1986.

_____: *Islam and Other Faiths*, edited by A. Siddiqui, Leicester: The Islamic Foundation, 1998.

Finley, M.I., *The Use and Abuse of History*, London: Pimlico, 2000.

Findley, C.V., *The Turks in World History*, New York: Oxford University Press, 2005.

Fisher, H.A.L., *A History of Europe*, London: Edward Arnold & Co., 1949.

Fitzgerald, E., *The Rubaiyat of Omar Khayyam*, New York: Dover Publications, 1990.

Frazer, J., *The Golden Bough: A Study in Magic and Religion*, Hertfordshire: Wordsworth Editions, 1993.

Frye, R.N., *The Golden Age of Persia*, London: Phoenix Press, 2000.

Fukuyama, F., *The End of History and the Last Man*, London: Penguin Books, 1992.

Gandhi, R., *Understanding the Muslim Mind*, London: Penguin, 1987.

Gauhar, A. (ed.), *The Challenge of Islam*, London: Islamic Council of Europe, 1978.

Gatje, H., *The Qur'an and its Exegesis: Selected Texts with Classical and Modern Muslim Interpretations*, Oxford: Oneworld, 1996.

Ghadanfar, M.A., *Great Women of Islam*, Riyadh: Darussalam, 2001.

Ghaffar, S.H.A., *Criticism of Hadith among Muslims with Reference to Sunan Ibn Maja*, London: Ta Ha Publishers, 1986.

al-Ghazali, *Kimiyat-i-Sa'adat*, translated as 'The Alchemy of Happiness' by Claud Field, London: Octagon Press, 1983.

_____: *Munqidh min al-Dalal*, translated as 'The Confessions of al-Ghazali' by Claud Field, New Delhi: Kitab Bhavan, 1992.

_____: *Tahafut al-Falasifah*, translated by S.A. Kamali, Lahore: Pakistan Philosophical Congress, 1958.

_____: *Mishkat al-Anwar*, translated by W.H.T. Gairdner, New Delhi: Islamic Book Service, 1997.

_____: *Ihya Uloom al-Din*, translated as 'The Revival of Religious Learning' by Fazlul Karim, 4 vols, Lahore: Muhammad Ashraf, 2000.

al-Ghazali, M., *Al-Tafsir al-Mawdu'i li-Suwar al-Qur'an al-Karim*, translated as 'Journey through the Qur'an', London: Dar al-Taqwa, 1998.

al-Ghazali, M., *The Socio-Political Thought of Shah Waliallah*, New Delhi: Adam Publishers, 2004.

Gibb, H.A.R. and Kramers, J.H. (eds.), *Shorter Encyclopaedia of Islam*, London: Luzac & Co., 1961.

_____: *The Travels of Ibn Battutah* (an Abridged Edition), New Delhi: Goodword Books, 2001.

_____: *The Travels of Ibn Battutah, AD* 1325-1352. 5 vols, London: Hakluyt Society; Syndics of the Cambridge University Press, 1956.

al-Gilani, *Futuh al-Ghaib*, translated by M.A. Ahmad, Lahore: Muhammad Ashraf, 1996.

Glasse, C., *The Concise Encyclopaedia of Islam*, London: Stacey International, 1989.

Glubb, J.B., *The Great Arab Conquests*, London: Hodder & Stoughton, 1963.

_____: *A Short History of the Arab Peoples*, London: Quartet Books, 1978.

Goodwin, J., *Lords of the Horizons*, London: Vintage, 1999.

Goff, R. et al. (ed.), *The Twentieth Century: A Brief Global History*, New York: McGraw-Hill, 1998.

Goswami, K., *Kazi Nazrul Islam: A Biography*, Dhaka: Nazrul Institute, 1996.

Haddad, G.F., *Sunna Notes: Studies in Hadith and Doctrine*, UK: Aqsa Publications, 2005.

Haeri, S.F., *Living Islam: East & West*, Dorset: Element Books, 1989.

Hahn, L. E. et al. (ed.), *The Philosophy of Seyyed Hossein Nasr*, Illinois: Open Court Publishing, 2001.

Haig, W., *Comparative Tables of Islamic and Christian Dates*, New Delhi: Kitab Bhavan, 1981.

al-Hajjaj, M.I., *Jami al-Sahih*, translated as 'Sahih Muslim' by A.H.Siddiqi, 4 vols, Lahore: Muhammad Ashraf, 1996.

Haley, A., *The Autobiography of Malcolm X*, London: Penguin, 1968.

Hamid, A.W., *Companions of the Prophet*, 3 vols, London: MELS, 1985.

Hamidullah, M., *Le Prophete de'l Islam: Sa Vie et Son Oouvre*, translated as 'The Life and Work of the Prophet of Islam', New Delhi: Adam Publishers, 2004.

_____: *The Emergence of Islam*, New Delhi: Adam Publishers, 1995.

_____: *The Battlefields of the Prophet Muhammad*, New Delhi: Kitab Bhavan, 1992.

_____: *The First Written Constitution in the World*, Lahore: Muhammad Ashraf, 1981.

_____: *Muhammad Rasulullah: A Concise Survey of the Life and Work of the Founder of Islam*, Luton: Apex Books Concern, 1974.

_____: *Sahifah Hammam ibn Munabbih*, Hyderabad: Habib & Co., 1961.

_____: *The Muslim Conduct of State*, Lahore: Muhammad Ashraf, 1987.

Haque, A., *Muslim Heroes of the World*, London: Ta Ha Publishers, 1990.

Harrison, P., *Pantheism: Understanding Divinity in Nature and the Universe*, Dorset: Element Books, 1999.

Hart, M., *The 100: A Ranking of the Most Influential Persons in History*, London: Simon & Schuster, 1993.

Harvey, L.P., *Islamic Spain, 1250 to 1500*, Chicago: Chicago University Press, 1990.

_____: *Muslims in Spain, 1500 to 1614*, Chicago: Chicago University Press, 2005.

Hasan, M., *History of Islam*, 2 vols, Lahore: Islamic Publications Ltd, 1992.

_____: *Siddiq-i-Akbar: Hazrat Abu Bakr*, Lahore: Ferozsons Ltd, no date.

al-Hassani, S.T.S. (ed.), *1001 Inventions: Muslim Heritage in Our World*, Manchester: FSTC, 2006.

Hattstein, M. and Delius, P. (ed.), *Islam: Art and Architecture*, Konigswinter: Konemann, 2004.

Hauser, T., *Muhammad Ali: His Life and Times*, New York: Simon and Schuster, 1991.

al-Haqqani, S.N., *The Divine Kingdom*, London: Al-Haqqani Trust, 1993.

Haykal, M.H., *Hayat Muhammad,* translated as 'The Life of Muhammad' by I.R. al-Faruqi, Indiana: The North American Islamic Trust, 1976.

Hiskett, M., *The Sword of Truth*, Illinois: NUP, 1994.

Hitti, P.K., *History of the Arabs: From the Earliest Times to the Present*, Basingstoke: Palgrave Macmillan, 2002.

Hodgson, M.G.S., *The Venture of Islam: Conscience and History in a World Civilisation*, 3 vols, Chicago: Chicago University Press, 1974.

Holt, P.M. et al. (ed.), *The Cambridge History of Islam*, 4 vols, Cambridge: Cambridge University Press, 1970.

Hourani, A., *Arabic Thought in the Liberal Age: 1798-1939*, Cambridge: Cambridge University Press, 1983.

_____: *A History of the Arab Peoples*, London: Faber & Faber, 1991.

Huff, T.E., *The Rise of Early Modern Science: Islam, China and the West*, Cambridge: Cambridge University Press, 1993.

Hughes, T.P., *Dictionary of Islam*, New Delhi: Cosmos Publications, 1978.

Hussain, M.H. and Kamali, A.H., *The Nature of the Islamic State: A Critical Study of Muslim Political Thought*, Karachi: National Book Foundation, 1977.

al-Hujwiri, *Kashf al-Mahjub*, Karachi: Darul Ishaat, 1990.

Ibn Hajar, *Bulugh al-Maram*, Riyadh: Darussalam, 1996.

Ibn Ishaq, M., *Sirat Rasul Allah*, translated as 'The Life of Muhammad' by A. Guillaume, Karachi: Oxford University Press, 1990.

Ibn Khaldun, *The Muqaddimah: An Introduction to History*, translated by F. Rosenthal, 3 vols, New Jersey: Princeton University Press, 1980.

Ibn Rushd, *Bidayat al-Mujtahid*, translated as 'The Distinguished Jurist's Primer' by Imran Nyazee and MA Rauf, Reading: Garnet, 1994.

Ibn Taymiyyah, *Muslims under Non-Muslim Rule*, texts translated and annotated by Y. Michot, Oxford: Interface Publications, 2006.

_____: *Al-Hisbah fi'l Islam*, translated as 'Public Duties in Islam' by Muthar Holland, Leicester: Islamic Foundation, 1983.

_____: *Al-Furqan Bayna Awliyah al-Rahman wa Awliyah ash Shaytan*, Beirut: Maktab al-Islami, 1977.

_____: *A Muslim Theologian's Response to Christianity: Ibn Taymiyya's al-Jawab al-Sahih*, edited and translated by T.F. Michel, New York: Caravan Books, 1984.

Ibn Shaddad, *Al-Nawadir al-Sultaniyya wa'l Mahasin al-Yusufiyyah*, translated as 'The Rare and Excellent History of Saladin' by D.S. Richards, Aldershot: Ashgate, 2002.

Ibn al-Naqib al-Misri, *Umdat al-Salik*, translated as 'The Reliance of the Traveller' by N.H.M. Keller, Evanston: Sunna Books, 1991.

Ibrahim, D., *The Islamization of Central Asia*, Leicester: The Islamic Foundation, 1993.

Imamuddin, S.M., *Arabic Writing and Arab Libraries*, London: Ta Ha Publishers, 1983.

Iqbal, A., *Culture of Islam*, Lahore: Institute of Islamic Culture, 1974.

_____: *Life and Work of Muhammad Jalal-ud-Din Rumi*, New Delhi: Kitab Bhavan, 1999.

Iqbal, M., *The Reconstruction of Religious Thought in Islam*, Lahore: Muhammad Ashraf, 1982.

Irwin, R., *The Alhambra*, London: Profile Books, 2004.

_____: *For Lust of Knowing: The Orientalists and their Enemies*, London: Penguin, 2006.

al-Isfahani, H.A., *Akhlaq al-Nabi*, Dhaka: The Islamic Foundation, 1998.

Islahi, A.A., *Islamic Law: Concept and Codification*, Lahore: Islamic Publications, 1979.

*Islam: Source and Purpose of Knowledge*, edited and published by International Institute of Islamic Thought, Herndon, Virginia, USA, 1988.

Izetbegovic, A.A., *Islam between East and West*, Indiana: American Trust Publications, 1999.

Jalbani, G.N., *Teachings of Shah Waliyullah of Delhi*, New Delhi: Islamic Book Service, 1998.

Jameelah, M., *Islam in Theory and Practice*, New Delhi: Taj Company, 1983.

Jones, L. (ed.), *Encyclopaedia of Religion*, 14 vols, New York: Thomson Gale, 2005.

Kamali, M.H., *Principles of Islamic Jurisprudence*, Cambridge: Islamic Text Society, 1991.

_____: *A Textbook of Hadith Studies: Authenticity, Compilation, Classification and Criticism of Hadith*, Leicester: The Islamic Foundation, 2005.

Kanda, K.C., *Masterpieces of Urdu Ghazals*, New Delhi: Sterling Publisher, 1994.

Karim, M.F., *Al-Hadis: Translation and Commentary of Mishkat ul-Masabih*, 4 vols, Lahore: The Book House, no date.

Keay, J., *Sowing the Wind: The Mismanagement of the Middle East 1900-1960*, London: John Murray, 2004.

Kennedy, H., *The Prophet and the Age of the Caliphates*, Harlow: Pearson Education Ltd, 1986.

_____: *The Courts of the Caliphs: The Rise and Fall of Islam's Greatest Dynasty*, London: Weidenfeld & Nicolson, 2004.

Kepel, G., *The Roots of Radical Islam*, London: Saqi, 2005.

Khalidi, T., *Arabic Historical Thought in the Classical Period*, Cambridge: Cambridge University Press, 1994.

Khan, A.M., *Elements of Islamic Philosophy*, Lahore: Muhammad Ashraf, 1992.

Khan, Q., *The Political Thought of Ibn Taymiyah*, New Delhi: Adam Publishers, 1988.

Khan, M.A., *The Pious Caliphs*, Kuwait: Islamic Book Publishers, 1987.

Khan, S.A., *Essays on the Life of Muhammad*, Lahore: Premier Book House, 1968.

Khan, M.A.R., *Muslim Contribution to Science and Culture*, Lahore: Muhammad Ashraf, 1973.

Khan, M.W., *Tabligh Movement*, New Delhi: Maktaba al-Risala, 1986.

Khandhlawi, M.Y., *Hayat-us Sahabah*, 3 vols, New Delhi: Idarat Isha'at-i-Diniyat, 1989.

Khomeini, A., *Islam and Revolution*, Berkeley: Mizan Press, 1981.

Kiernan, V.G., *Poems from Iqbal*, Oxford: Oxford University Press, 1999.

Koestler, A., *The Sleepwalkers: A History of Man's Changing Vision of the Universe*, London: Arkana, 1989.

Koya, P.K., *Hadith and Sunnah: Ideals and Realities*, Lahore: National Book Service, no date.

Kunt, M. and Woodhead, C. (ed.), *Suleman the Magnificent and His Age*, Harlow: Longman Group, 1995.

Lane, E.W., *Arabic-English Lexicon*, Cambridge: Islamic Text Society, 1984.

Lane-Poole, S., *The Muslims in Spain*, New Delhi: Goodword Books, no date.

Law, J. (ed.), 1000 *Great Lives*, Bath: Parragon, 1999.

Lemon, M.C., *Philosophy of History*, London: Routledge, 2003.

Lewis, B., *The Arabs in History*, London: Hutchinsons University Library, 1956.

_____: *The Middle East: 2000 Years of History from the Rise of Christianity to the Present Day*, London: Phoenix Press, 2000.

_____: (ed.) *The World of Islam*, London: Thames & Hudson, 1976.

Lewis, B. and Holt, P.M., *Historians of the Middle East*, Oxford: Oxford University Press, 1962.

Lincoln, C.E., *The Black Muslims in America*, New Jersey: Africa World Press, 1994.

Lings, M., *Muhammad: His Life Based on the Earliest Sources*, Lahore: Suhail Academy, 1987.

_____: *A Sufi Saint of the Twentieth Century*, Cambridge: Islamic Text Society, 1993.

_____: *What is Sufism?* London: Unwin Paperbacks, 1981.

Lombard, M., *The Golden Age of Islam*, Oxford: North Holding Publishing, 1975.

Lunde, P. and Wintle, J., *A Dictionary of Arabic and Islamic Proverbs*, Oxon: Routledge & Kegan Paul, 1984.

Maalouf, A., *The Crusades through Arab Eyes*, London: Al-Saqi Books, 1984.

Madelung, W., *The Succession to Muhammad: A Study of the Early Caliphate*, Cambridge: Cambridge University Press, 1997.

Magowan, R., *Fabled Cities of Central Asia: Samarkand, Bukhara and Khiva*, London: Cassell Publishers, 1989.

Mahdi, M., *Ibn Khaldun's Philosophy of History*, London: Allen & Unwin, 1957.

Majumdar, R.C. et al., *An Advanced History of India*, vol.1, Lahore: Aziz Publishers, 1980.

Makdisi, G., *The Rise of Humanism in Classical Islam and the Christian West: With Special Reference to Scholasticism*, Edinburgh: Edinburgh University Press, 1990.

Malik, Imam, *Al-Muwatta*, translated by M. Rahimuddin, Lahore: Ashraf Press, 1985.

Mansfield, P., *The Arabs*, London: Allen Lane, 1976.

Mango, A., *Ataturk*, London: John Murray, 1999.

Marenbon, J. (ed.), *Routledge History of Philosophy*, vol. 3, London: Routledge, 1998.

Marozzi, J., *Tamerlane, Sword of Islam, Conqueror of the World*, London: HarperCollins, 2004.

Martin, R.C. (ed.), *Encyclopaedia of Islam and the Muslim World*, 2 vols, New York: Thomson Gale, 2004.

Martin, R.C. and Woodward, M.R., *Defenders of Reason in Islam: Mu'tazilism from Medieval School to Modern Symbol*, Oxford: Oneworld, 1997.

al-Mas'udi, *Muruj al-Dhahab wa Ma'adin al-Jawhar*, translated as 'The Meadows of Gold' by P. Lunde & C. Stone, London: Keegan Paul International, 1989.

Matar, N., *Islam in Britain: 1558-1685*, Cambridge: Cambridge University Press, 1998.

Mawdudi, S.A.A., *Tafhim al-Qur'an*, translated as 'The Meaning of the Qur'an', 6 vols, Delhi: Board of Islamic Publications, 1973.

_____: *Jajdid-o-Ihya-i-Din*, translated as 'A Short History of the Revivalist Movement in Islam', Lahore: Islamic Publications, 1986.

_____: *Islam ka Nizam Zindigi*, translated as 'The Islamic Way of Life', Leicester: The Islamic Foundation, 1986.

_____: *Islamic Law and Constitution*, Lahore: Islamic Publications, 1986.

Mazrui, A.A., *Cultural Forces in World Politics*, London: James Currey, 1990.

Menocal, M.R., *The Ornament of the World: How Muslims, Jews, and Christians Created a Culture of Tolerance in Medieval Spain*, New York: Back Bay Books, 2002.

Mirza, M.R. et al. (ed.), *Muslim Contribution to Science*, Lahore: Kazi Publications, 1986.

Moazzam, A., *Jamal al-Din al-Afghani: A Muslim Intellectual*, New Delhi: Concept Publishing, 1984.

Mohyuddin, A., *Ali the Superman*, Lahore: Muhammad Ashraf, 1980.

Mousalli, A.S., *Radical Islamic Fundamentalism: The Ideological and Political Discourse of Sayyid Qutb*, Beirut: American University of Beirut Press, 1992.

Moin, B., *Khomeini: Life of the Ayatollah*, London: I.B. Tauris, 1999.

Momen, M., *An Introduction to Shi'ite Islam*, New Haven: Yale University Press, 1985.

Mooney, B., *Shaping History: 100 Great Leaders from Antiquity to the Present*, London: Arcturus Publishing, 2004.

Mottahedeh, R., *The Mantle of the Prophet: Religion and Politics in Iran*, Harmondsworth: Penguin Books, 1985.

al-Mubarakpuri, S.R., *Ar-Raheeq al-Makhtum*, Riyadh: Darussalam, 1996.

Muhammad, E., *Message to the Blackman in America*, Philadelphia: House of Knowledge Publications, 1965.

al-Mujahid, S., *Allama Iqbal*, London: UK Islamic Mission, 1986.

Muzaffar, A., *The Language of Political Islam: India 1200-1800*, London: C. Hurst &Co, 2004.

an-Nabahani, T., *The Islamic State*, London: Al-Khilafah Publications, no date.

Nadvi, S.S., *Hazrat Aishah Siddiqa: Her Life and Works*, Kuwait: Islamic Book Publishers, 1986.

_____: *Heroic Deeds of Muslim Women*, New Delhi: Adam Publishers, 1985.

Nadvi, S.M., *A Geographical History of the Qur'an*, Lahore: Muhammad Ashraf, 1974.

Nadvi, S.M., *The Ideal Caliphs of Islam*, Lahore: Idara-e-Islamiat, 1996.

Nadwi, A.H.A., *Asr-e Hazir Men Din Ki Tafhim Aur Tashrih*, translated as 'Appreciation and Interpretation of Religion in the Modern Age', Lucknow: Academy of Islamic Research & Publications, 1982.

_____: *The Glory of Iqbal*, Lucknow: Academy of Islamic Research and Publications, 1979.

_____: *Islam and the Earliest Muslims: Two Conflicting Portraits*, Lucknow: Academy of Islamic Research and Publications, 1985.

_____: *Life and Mission of Maulana Muhammad Ilyas*, Bombay: Taj Publishers, 1983.

_____: *Saviours of Islamic Spirit*, 4 vols, Karachi: Darul Isha'at, 1994.

Nadwi, S.M., *Muslim Thought and its Sources*, Lahore: Muhammad Ashraf, 1992.

Nadwi, A.S., *Umar bin Abdul Aziz*, Lahore: Institute of Islamic Culture, 1978.

Nadwi, S.S., *Khutabat-i-Madras*, Lucknow: Academy of Islamic Research and Publications, 1981.

Nasr, S.H. and Leaman, O. (ed.), *History of Islamic Philosophy*, 2 vols, Qum: Ansariyan Publications, 2001.

Nasr, S.H. (ed.), *Islamic Spirituality*, 2 vols, London: SCM Press, 1989.

_____: *Science and Civilisation in Islam*, Cambridge: Islamic Text Society, 1987.

_____: *An Introduction to Islamic Cosmological Doctrines*, London: Thames and Hudson, 1978.

_____: *Islamic Science: An Illustrated Study*, London: World of Islam Festival Publishing Company, 1976.

_____: *Three Muslim Sages*, Cambridge: Harvard University Press, 1964.

_____: *Knowledge and the Sacred*, Albany: State University of New York Press, 1989.

_____: *Islamic Philosophy from its Origins to the Present: Philosophy in the Land of the Prophecy*, Albany: State University of New York, 2006.

Nasr, S.V.R., *Mawdudi and the Making of Islamic Revivalism*, New York: Oxford University Press, 1996.

_____: *The Shi'a Revival: How Conflicts within Islam Will Shape the Future*, New York: Norton & Company, 2006.

Nasir, S.M., *Islam: Its Concepts and History*, New Delhi: Kitab Bhavan, 1984.

al-Nawawi, *Riyadh us-Saliheen*, 2 vols, Riyadh: Darussalam, 1998.

_____: *Arba'in al-Nawawi*, Arabic text with English translation by E. Ibrahim & D.Johnson-Davies, Beirut: The Holy Koran Publishing House, 1976.

Newby, P.H., *Saladin in His Time*, New York: Dorset Press, 1992.

Newman, A., *Safavid Iran*, London: I.B.Tauris, 2005.

Nicholson, R.A., *The Mystics of Islam*, London: Arkana, 1989.

Nicolle, D., *Historical Atlas of the Islamic World*, London: Mercury Books, 2004.

Nicoll, F., *The Mahdi of Sudan and the Death of General Gordon*, Gloucester: Sutton Publishing, 2004.

an-Nisaburi, *Asbab al-Nuzul*, Karachi: Darul Isha'at, 2005.

No'mani, M.M., *Ma'ariful Hadith*, 4 vols, Karachi: Darul Ishaat, 2002.

North, J., *The Fontana History of Astronomy and Cosmology*, London: Fontana Press, 1994.

Numani, S., *Al-Faruq*, translated as 'Life of Umar the Great' by Maulana Zafar Ali Khan, 2 vols, Lahore: Muhammad Ashraf, 1975.

_____: *Sirat-i-Numan*, translated as 'Imam Abu Hanifa: Life and Works' by M. Hadi Hussain, Bombay: Taj Publishers, 1991.

Numani, S. and Nadvi, S.S., *Sirat-un-Nabi*, 7 vols, Karachi: Darul Ishaat, 2003.

Nursi, B.S., *The Words*, translated by Sukran Vahide, Istanbul: Sozler Publications, 1992.

_____: *The Letters*, translated and published by Truestar, London, 1994.

O'Hear, A., *After Progress: Finding the Old Way Forward*, London: Bloomsbury, 1999.

O'Leary, D.L., *How Greek Science Passed to the Arabs*, New Delhi: Goodword Books, 2001.

Oliphant, J., *Victorian Novelists*, London: Blackie & Son Ltd, 1899.

Ormerod, P., *The Death of Economics*, London: Faber & Faber, 1995.

O'Shea, S., *Sea of Faith: Islam and Christianity in the Mediterranean World*, London: Profile Books, 2006.

Passmore, J., *A Hundred Year of Philosophy*, London: Penguin, 1994.

Payne, R., *The Crusades: A History*, London: Robert Hale Ltd, 1994.

Philips, A.A.B., *The Evolution of Fiqh*, Riyadh: Tawheed Publications, 1990.

\_\_\_\_\_: *Tafseer Soorah al-Hujuraat*, Riyadh: Tawheed Publications, 1990.

Pickthall, M.M., *The Cultural Side of Islam*, Lahore: Muhammad Ashraf, 1979.

Pryce-Jones, D., *The Closed Circle: An Interpretation of the Arabs*, London: Paladin, 1990.

Qadir, C.A., *Philosophy and Science in the Islamic World*, London: Routledge, 1990.

Qazi, M.A., *Bilal in Hadith*, Lahore: Kazi Publications, 1976.

Quick, A.H., *Deeper Roots*, London: Ta Ha Publishers, 1998.

Qureshi, S.A., *Letters of the Holy Prophet*, New Delhi: Noor Publishing House, 1986.

Qutb, S., *Ma'alim fi'l Tariq*, translated as 'Milestones', New Delhi: Naushaba Publications, 1991.

\_\_\_\_\_: *Fi Zilal al-Qur'an*, translated as 'In the Shade of the Qur'an', by A. Salahi and A.A. Shamis, vols 1-11 and 18, Leicester: The Islamic Foundation, 1999 – on-going.

\_\_\_\_\_: *Hadha al-Deen*, Delhi: Markazi Maktaba Islami, 1974.

Qutb, M., *Islam and Modern Materialistic Thought*, Delhi: Hindustan Publications, 1985.

Rahim, M.A. et al., *Islam in Bangladesh through the Ages*, Dhaka: Islamic Foundation, 1995.

Rahman, F., *Revival and Reform in Islam*, Oxford: Oneworld Publishers, 2000.

\_\_\_\_\_: *The Philosophy of Mulla Sadra*, Albany: State University of New York Press, 1975

\_\_\_\_\_: *Islam*, Chicago: Chicago University Press, 1979.

\_\_\_\_\_: *Islamic Methodology in History*, Karachi: CIIR, 1965.

Rahman, M.N., *Tadhkirat al-Awliyah*, vols 1-5, Dhaka: Imdadiyyah Library, 1989.

Rahman, M. and Rahman, G., *Geography of the Muslim World*, Chicago: Iqra, 1997.

Rahnema, A., *An Islamic Utopian: A Political Biography of Ali Shari'ati*, London: I.B.Tauris, 2000.

\_\_\_\_\_: *Pioneers of the Islamic Revival*, London: Zed Books, 2005.

Read, J., *The Moors in Spain and Portugal*, London: Faber & Faber, 1974.

Redhead, B. (ed.), *Plato to NATO: Studies in Political Thought*, London: Penguin, 1995.

Riches, W.T.M., *The Civil Rights Movement: Struggle and Resistance*, Basingstoke: Macmillan Press, 1997.

Robinson, F. (ed.), *Cambridge Illustrated History of the Islamic World*, Cambridge: Cambridge University Press, 1996.

Robinson, N., *Discovering the Qur'an: A Contemporary Approach to a Veiled Text*, London: SCM Press, 1996.

Rodenbeck, M., *Cairo: The City Victorious*, London: Picador, 1998.

Rogers, J.A., *World's Great Men of Color*, vol.1, New York: Collier Books, 1972.

Rosenthal, E., *Political Thought in Medieval Islam*, Cambridge: Cambridge University Press, 1958.

Rosenthal, F., *The Classical Heritage in Islam*, London: Routledge & Keegan Paul, 1975.

Rumi, J., *The Mathnawi of Jalaluddin Rumi*, 3 vols translated by R.A. Nicholson, Lahore: Islamic Book Service, 1989.

Russell, B., *A History of Western Philosophy*, London: Unwin Paperbacks, 1979.

Ruthven, M., *A Fury for God: The Islamist Attack on America*, London: Granta, 2002.

\_\_\_\_\_: *Islam in the World*, London: Granta, 2006.

Sabiq, S., *Fiqh us-Sunnah*, 5 vols, translated by M.S. Dabas and J.M. Zarabozo, Indiana: American Trust Publications, 1991.

Sa'di, *Bustan*, New Delhi: Kitab Bhavan, 2000.

Said, E.W., *Orientalism: Western Conceptions of the Orient*, London: Penguin, 1995.

_____: *Power, Politics and Culture*, London: Bloomsbury, 2005.

Salik, S.A., *The Saint of Jilan*, New Delhi: Kutub Khana Ishayatul Islam, 1978.

al-Sadiq, I.J., *The Lantern of the Path*, Dorset: Elements Books, 1989.

as-Saduq, S., *Itiqadatu'l Imamiyyah*, Tehran: WOFIS, 1982.

Sankari, J., *Fadlallah: The Making of a Radical Shi'ite Leader*, London: Saqi Books, 2005.

Sardar, Z., *Desperately Seeking Paradise: Journeys of a Sceptical Muslim*, London: Granta Books, 2004.

_____: *Islamic Futures: The Shape of Ideas to Come*, London: Mansell, 1985.

Sarton, G., *Introduction to the History of Science*, 3 vols, Baltimore: Williams & Wilkins, 1927.

Schacht, J. and Bosworth, C.E. (ed.), *The Legacy of Islam*, Oxford: Clarendon Press, 1974.

Schuon, F., *The Transcendent Unity of Religions*, Illinois: The Theosophical Publishing House, 1993.

_____: *Understanding Islam*, London: Allen & Unwin, 1965.

Segal, R., *Islam's Black Slaves: A History of Africa's Other Slave Diaspora*, London: Atlantic Books, 2001.

Shaban, M.A., *Islamic History: A New Interpretation*, 2 vols, Cambridge: Cambridge University Press, 1971.

al-Shafi'i, *al-Risalah*, translated by Majid Khadduri, Cambridge: The Islamic Text Society, 1987.

Shah, I., *Thinkers of the East*, London: Penguin, 1974.

Shah, T. (ed.), *The Middle East Bedside Book*, London: Octagon Press, 1991.

Shah-Kazemi, R., *Justice and Remembrance: Introducing the Spirituality of Imam Ali*, London: I.B. Tauris, 2006.

Sharif, M.M. (ed.), *A History of Muslim Philosophy*, 2 vols, Delhi: Adam Publishers, 2001.

Shari'ati, A., *On the Sociology of Islam*, Berkeley: Mizan Press, 1979.

_____: *Marxism and Other Western Fallacies: An Islamic Critique*, Berkeley: Mizan Press, 1980.

Sheikh, M.S., *Islamic Philosophy*, London: Octagon Press, 1982.

Sherif, M.A., *Searching for Solace: A Biography of Abdullah Yusuf Ali*, Malaysia: Islamic Book Trust, 1994.

Sherwani, H.K., *Muslim Colonies in France, North Italy and Switzerland*, Lahore: Muhammad Ashraf, 1964.

Shushud, H., *Masters of Wisdom of Central Asia*, Moorcote: Coombe Springs Press, 1983.

Shushtery, A.M.A., *Outlines of Islamic Culture*, Lahore: Muhammad Ashraf, 1976.

Siddiqi, A.H., *Decisive Battles of Islam*, Kuwait: Islamic Book Publishers, 1986.

Siddiqi, A.H., *The Islamic Concept of History*, Lahore: Kazi Publications, 1981.

Siddiqi, M., *The Qur'anic Concept of History*, Islamabad: Islamic Research Institute, 1984.

_____: *Modern Reformist Thought in the Muslim World*, Delhi: Adam Publishers, 1993.

Siddiqi, M.I., *al-Asharah al-Mubashsharah*, New Delhi: Idara Isha'at-i-Diniyat, 1990.

Siddiqi, M.R. et al., *Iqbal as a Thinker*, Lahore: Muhammad Ashraf, 1991.

Siddiqi, M.S., *The Blessed Women of Islam*, New Delhi: Taj Company, 1983.

Siddiqi, M.Z., *Hadith Literature: Its Origin, Development and Special Features*, Cambridge: Islamic Text Society, 1993.

Sieny, M.E., *Heroes of Islam*, Riyadh: Darussalam, 2000.

Smith, M., *Rabia the Mystic and Her Fellow Saints in Islam*, Cambridge: Press Syndicate, 1984.

[ 433 ]

Smith, J.Z., *The HarperCollins Dictionary of Religion*, London: HarperSanFrancisco, 1996.

Smith, W.C., *Islam in Modern History*, New Jersey: Princeton University Press, 1977.

Sohail, M., *Administrative and Cultural History of Islam*, New Delhi: Adam Publishers, 2002.

Sowell, K.R., *The Arab World: An Illustrated History*, New York: Hippocrene Books, 2004.

Stierlin, H., *Islamic Art and Architecture: From Isfahan to Taj Mahal*, London: Thames and Hudson, 2002.

Sulaiman, I., *A Revolution in History: The Jihad of Uthman Dan Fodio*, London: Mansell Publishing, 1986.

Surty, M.I.H.I., *A Course in the Science of Reciting the Qur'an*, Leicester: The Islamic Foundation, 2000.

Suvorova, A., *Muslim Saints of South Asia: The Eleventh to Fifteenth Centuries*, London: Routledge, 2004.

al-Suyuti, *Tarikh al-Khulafa*, Beirut: Mu'assasat Izz al-Din, 1992.

al-Tabari, *Tarikh al-Rusul wa'l Muluk*, translated as 'The History of al-Tabari', 38 vols, edited by Y. Yarshater, Albany: State University of New York Press, 1985-2000.

al-Tabrizi, *Mishkat al-Masabih*, Arabic text with English translation by A.H. Siddiqi, 2 vols, Delhi: Kitab Bhavan, 1990.

Taha, A.D., *The Muslim Conquest and Settlement of North Africa and Spain*, London: Routledge, 1989.

Taji-Farouki, S. (ed.), *Modern Muslim Intellectuals and the Qur'an*, Oxford: Oxford University Press, 2004.

Tarnas, R., *The Passion of the Western Mind: Understanding the Ideas that have Shaped Our World*, London: Pimlico, 1996.

Thomson, A., *Blood on the Cross: Islam in Spain in the Light of Christian Persecution Through the Ages*, London: Ta Ha Publishers, 1989.

al-Tirmidhi, *Shamail-i-Tirmidhi*, New Delhi: Kitab Bhavan, 1997.

de Tocqueville, A., *Democracy in America*, Hertfordshire: Wordsworth Edition, 1998.

Toynbee, A.J., *A Study of History*, London: Oxford University Press, 1972.

_____: *Civilisation on Trial*, London: Oxford University Press, 1948.

_____: *The World and the West*, London: BBC Reith Lectures, 1954.

Trimingham, S., *The Sufi Orders in Islam*, Oxford: Oxford University Press, 1971.

Troll, C.W., *Sayyid Ahmad Khan: A Reinterpretation of Muslim Theology*, New Delhi: Vikas Publishing, 1978.

al-Umari, A.D., *Madinan Society at the Time of the Prophet*, 2 vols, Virginia: IIIT, 1991.

Umaruddin, M., *The Ethical Philosophy of Al-Ghazali*, New Delhi: Adam Publishers, 1996.

Usmani, S.A., *Tafseer-i-Usmani*, translated from Urdu by M.A. Ahmad, 3 vols, Lahore: Aalameen Publications, 1993.

Vahide, S., *Bediuzzaman Said Nursi*, Istanbul: Sozler Publications, 1992.

Vesey, G. and Foulkes, P., *Unwin Hyman Dictionary of Philosophy*, Leicester: Bookmart, 1999.

Waliullah, S., *Sufism and the Islamic Tradition: The Lamahat and Sata'at of Shah Waliullah of Delhi*, translated by G.N. Jalbani, London: Octagon Press, 1980.

_____: *Hujjat Allah al-Balighah*, Dhaka: Rashid Book House, 1992.

Walker, C.J., *Islam and the West: A Dissonant Harmony of Civilisations*, Gloucester: Sutton Publishing, 2005.

Wallace-Murphy, T., *What Islam did for us: Understanding Islam's Contribution to Western Civilisation*, London: Watkins Publishing, 2006.

Warren, J., *History and the Historians*, Oxon: Bookpoint Ltd, 2004.

Watt, W.M., *The Formative Period of Islamic Thought*, Oxford: Oneworld Publications, 1998.

_____: *The Influence of Islam on Medieval Europe*, Edinburgh: Edinburgh University Press, 1972.

_____: *A Great Muslim Mystic*, Studia Missionalia, vol 35, pp.161-78, 1986.

_____: *Women in Early Islam*, Studia Missionalia, vol 40, pp. 161-73, 1991.

Webster, J., *Andalus*, London: Transworld Publishers, 2004.

al-Wahhab, M.I.A., *Kitab al-Tawhid*, Kuwait: IIFSO, 1979.

Williams, R., *Keywords: A vocabulary of culture and society*, London: Fontana Press, 1988.

Wintle, J., *History of Islam*, London: Rough Guides, 2003.

Wynbranbt, J., *A Brief History of Saudi Arabia*, New York: Checkmark Books, 2004.

al-Yunini, *Dhayl Mir'at al-Zaman*, 2 vols, translated as 'Early Mamluk Syrian Historiography' by L. Guo, Leiden: E.J. Brill, 1998.

Yunus, M. and Jolis, A., *Banker to the Poor*, London: Aurum Press, 1999.

Yusuf, A.R.I., *Fiqh al-Imam*, California: White Thread Press, 2004.

Zakariyyah, M.M., *Al-Iti'daal fi Maraatibur Rijaal*, Lenasia: Darul Uloom Zakariyyah, 1994.

_____: *Faza'il-i-A'mal*, Dewsbury: Anjuman-i-Islahul Muslimeen, no date.

# Index of Names and Places

# Index of Ideas
# and Concepts

Scholars, Muslim  54, 56, 69, 70, 73, 75, 80, 87, 89-90, 94, 111, 119, 121-2, 139, 142, 148-9, 160, 180, 181, 183, 184, 189, 200, 204, 227, 239, 267, 319, 321, 348, 374

Sciences: alchemy  75, 148, 188, 189, 190, 196, 333; biology 111, 140, 188; botany 154; chemistry 77, 112, 140, 141, 189, 197, 244; cosmology 166, 178, 189, 197, 233; ecology 231; empiricism 69, 189; evolution 56, 140; geology 77, 140, 141, 228, 229; information technology 295; methodology 189, 198, 205; natural history 228, 231; natural sciences 228, 273, 284; oceanography 231; optics 112-14, 141, 205, 206; pharmacology 141; physical sciences 139, 196, 244; physics 77, 100, 102, 112, 113, 140, 141, 166, 188, 205, 206; technology 341 (*see also* Astronomy, Medicine)

Scientists  75, 77, 112, 125, 176, 230, 233

Second World War  291, 364

Sects: Ash'arism  61, 67, 105, 274, 285, 320; Assassins (Nizaris) 107, 120, 241, 243, 277; Ithna ashari (or Twelver) Shi'as 102, 150, 277-8, 389; Khawarij 11, 13, 35, 36, 58, 88, 117, 257; Modernists 336, 339; Mu'tazilism 58, 59, 60, 61, 66, 80, 105, 148, 162, 203, 228, 248, 261, 262, 274, 284, 285; Neo-Ismaili 107, 120, 277; Neo-Mu'tazilite 375; Qarmatians 261, 380-1; Shi'ism 10-11, 13, 57-8, 71, 88, 102, 150, 249, 262, 277, 278, 313-15, 363, 380-1, 388-90; Sunnis 11, 102, 108, 142, 150, 277, 362

Secularisation  399

Shari'ah  54, 67, 70-2, 79, 85, 89, 121, 142, 144, 164, 186, 251, 274, 278, 290, 318, 319, 354, 358, 379, 387

Shaytan  4, 377 (*see also* Iblis)

Silver  188, 190

Slavery  3, 47, 49, 132, 253, 392

Social activism  327, 338, 358

Social sciences  141, 180; Sociology 85

Successors of the Prophet (Tabi'un)  182, 230, 249, 332

Sufi Orders: Chishtiyyah  203, 300, 302-3, 324, 344, 349, 356; Kubrawiyyah 301; Naqshbandiyyah 17, 203, 268, 270, 300, 309-10, 344, 349, 353; Qadiriyyah 98, 203, 270, 300-1, 309, 344, 349, 369, 387, 396; Sammaniyyah 377; Shadhiliyyah 345; Tijaniyah 387

Sufi Thought: Esoteric (batini)  67, 84, 97, 189, 197, 237, 301, 322, 346; Exoteric (zahiri) 97, 237, 301, 322, 346; Fana 309; Farq ba'd al-jam 309, 310; Gnosis (ma'rifah) 96, 121, 237, 254, 262, 268, 269, 302, 313, 345, 347, 390; Illuminationism 362, 389; Love (mahabbah) 262; Self-annihilation (fana) 261-2, 309; ubudiyah (servanthood) 309-10; unveiling (kashf) 237; wahdat al-shuhud 239, 263, 309, 350; wahdat al-wujud (monism) 239, 263, 309, 310, 350; zuhd (asceticism) 88, 120, 202, 253, 261, 302, 317, 333, 347

Sufism (Islamic Mysticism)  11, 17, 66-9, 82, 95, 96-7, 105, 106, 120, 121, 122, 137, 147, 148, 149, 175, 188-9, 200, 201, 202, 203, 236-8, 243, 249, 250, 254-5, 260, 266, 268-70, 300-2, 308-9, 310, 311, 313, 322, 324-5, 330, 333, 344-5, 346, 349, 352-4, 360, 362, 370, 372, 389, 390, 396, 398; experience 309, 322; guides and saints 95, 119, 121, 150, 203, 237, 250, 251, 269, 345, 348, 356, 377; insight and illumination 237, 302, 310, 398; lodge (zawiyyah) 62, 67, 302, 311, 324, 345, 377; music 121, 122; path 346, 377; retreat 97, 189, 237, 302, 345, 389, 398; whirling dervishes 122

Sunnah  4, 8, 38, 50, 54, 56, 66, 70, 72, 86, 87, 88, 97, 103, 250, 303, 333

Superstitions  189, 353

Tayammum  24

Theology (ilm al-kalam)  55, 59, 60, 61, 66, 67, 71, 75, 82, 89, 100, 104, 105, 111, 113, 120, 122, 165, 166, 189, 197, 199, 237, 246, 249, 250, 309-10, 321, 322, 286, 313, 370; causality 114; metaphysics 38, 41, 52, 56, 73, 79, 83-4, 87, 89, 96, 100, 102-3, 105, 156-7, 164, 190, 197, 230, 236-8; theologians (mutakallimun) 58, 68, 286

Theosophy (hikmah)  389

Tolerance  138, 142, 144, 146, 174, 219, 275, 395

Torture  47, 81

Traditional Islam  202, 288, 308

Traditionalism  (*see* Orthodoxy)

Turkish Republic  295, 396, 397

Turks  108, 168, 294, 312

Umayyads  37, 78, 90-3, 115, 118, 123, 127-8, 130, 136, 149, 151, 164, 183, 188, 200, 202, 212, 221, 222, 232, 236, 256-8, 324, 333, 336; Umayyads of Spain 154

Ummah  6, 12, 62, 92, 247, 338, 346

Universe  47, 95, 96, 122, 204, 321

Uzbeks  227, 318

viziers  125, 130, 136

Wanderjahren  229

Warfare  131-2, 161, 169, 171, 193, 306, 352, 354, 386

Western world  77, 101, 153, 163, 176, 196, 240, 320, 322;

Wine  225, 243, 316

Women  3, 4, 22-4, 26, 28, 44, 45, 93, 154, 234, 239, 243, 252, 365, 386; education 386

World Bank  366

Yemenite tribes  128, 129

Young Turk movement  293, 396-7